Silver Burdett Ginn

Mathematics

THE PATH TO MATH SUCCESS!

Silver Burdett Ginn

Parsippany, NJ • Needham, MA

Atlanta, GA • Deerfield, IL • Irving, TX • Santa Clara, CA

Program Authors

Francis (Skip) Fennell, Ph.D.
Professor of Education and Chair, Education Department
Western Maryland College
Westminster, Maryland

Joan Ferrini-Mundy, Ph.D.
Professor of Mathematics
University of New Hampshire
Durham, New Hampshire

Herbert P. Ginsburg, Ph.D.
Professor of Psychology and Mathematics Education
Teachers College, Columbia University
New York, New York

Carole Greenes, Ed.D.
Professor of Mathematics Education and Associate Dean, School of Education
Boston University
Boston, Massachusetts

Stuart J. Murphy
Visual Learning Specialist
Evanston, Illinois

William Tate, Ph.D.
Associate Professor of Mathematics Education
University of Wisconsin-Madison
Madison, Wisconsin

10 9 8 7 6 5 4 VH 07 06 05 04 03 02 01 99 98

Grade Level Authors

Mary Behr Altieri, M.S.
Mathematics Teacher
1993 Presidential Awardee
Lakeland Central School District
Shrub Oak, New York

Jennie Bennett, Ed.D.
Instructional Mathematics Supervisor
Houston Independent School District
Houston, Texas

Charles Calhoun, Ph.D.
Associate Professor of Elementary Education Mathematics
University of Alabama at Birmingham
Birmingham, Alabama

Lucille Croom, Ph.D.
Professor of Mathematics
Hunter College of the City University of New York
New York, New York

Robert A. Laing, Ph.D.
Professor of Mathematics Education
Western Michigan University
Kalamazoo, Michigan

Kay B. Sammons, M.S.
Supervisor of Elementary Mathematics
Howard County Public Schools
Ellicott City, Maryland

Marian Small, Ed.D.
Professor of Mathematics Education
University of New Brunswick
Fredericton, New Brunswick, Canada

Contributing Authors

Stephen Krulik, Ed.D.
Professor of Mathematics Education
Temple University
Philadelphia, Pennsylvania

Donna J. Long
Mathematics/Title 1 Coordinator
Metropolitan School District of Wayne Township
Indianapolis, Indiana

Jesse A. Rudnick, Ed.D.
Professor Emeritus of Mathematics Education
Temple University
Philadelphia, Pennsylvania

Clementine Sherman
Director, USI Math and Science
Dade County Public Schools
Miami, Florida

Bruce R. Vogeli, Ph.D.
Clifford Brewster Upton Professor of Mathematics
Teachers College, Columbia University
New York, New York

Silver Burdett Ginn
A Division of Simon & Schuster
299 Jefferson Road, P.O. Box 480
Parsippany, NJ 07054-0480

Contents

Chapter 1 Place Value and Money

Chapter 2 Addition and Subtraction

Chapter 3 Addition and Subtraction With Greater Numbers

Chapter Resources

Chapter 4 Time and Measurement

Chapter Resources

Chapter 5 Multiplication Concepts

Chapter 6 Multiplication Facts

Chapter 7 Using Data and Probability

Chapter 10 Geometry

Chapter 11 Fractions and Decimals

Chapter 12 Multiplying and Dividing Greater Numbers

Chapter 1

Place Value and Money

Chapter Theme: COLLECTIONS

Career Spotlight Meet Mel Fisher, a diver and treasure hunter. He has spent many years searching for sunken ships and their treasures. He finds jewelry, coins, and all sorts of great things. He displays many of his coins in his own museum.

Collectors keep track of how many of each kind of coin they have.

30 + 3 = 33 silver coins

Chapter Project

Design a Coin

Suppose that you have been asked to design a new coin.

- What will your coin look like? Make some drawings. Show what might be on the coin. Will you put an animal on it? a person? a pattern?
- Decide which ideas will work best on your coin. Remember that a coin has two sides, so you will need two different pictures.

Using Algebra

Even It Out

You can use patterns to find out if a number is even or odd!

Learning About It

How do you know if a number is even or odd?

Work with your group to find out.

Word Bank

even
odd

Step 1 Use a hundreds chart like the one shown.

Step 2 Use counters to show each number from 1 to 10. Put the counters into pairs whenever you can.

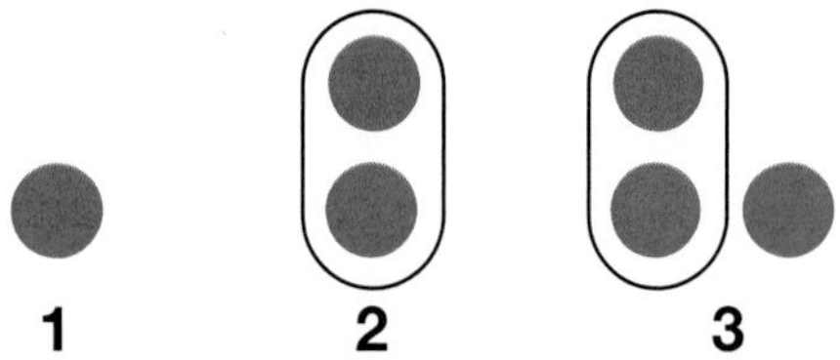

What You Need

For each group:
hundreds chart
counters
blue crayons
red crayons

- Which numbers have no counter left over? Circle those numbers on your chart in blue.
- Which numbers have a counter left over? Circle those numbers on your chart in red.

1	2	3	4	5	6	7	8	9	10
11	12	13	14	15	16	17	18	19	20
21	22	23	24	25	26	27	28	29	30
31	32	33	34	35	36	37	38	39	40
41	42	43	44	45	46	47	48	49	50
51	52	53	54	55	56	57	58	59	60
61	62	63	64	65	66	67	68	69	70
71	72	73	74	75	76	77	78	79	80
81	82	83	84	85	86	87	88	89	90
91	92	93	94	95	96	97	98	99	100

All numbers that make pairs and have no counters left over are **even.**

All numbers that make pairs but have 1 counter left over are **odd.**

Step 3 Use counters to show each number from 11 to 20. On your chart, circle even numbers in blue and odd numbers in red.

Step 4 What pattern do you see on the chart? Use the pattern to complete the chart. Circle even numbers in blue and odd numbers in red.

- Look at the even numbers. Which digits are in the ones place?

- Look at the odd numbers. Which digits are in the ones place?

Think and Discuss Use your chart to skip count aloud by 3s. Describe the pattern you see in the even and odd numbers you say.

Practice

Use the hundreds chart. Write the missing numbers in each pattern.

1. 1, 3, 5, ■, ■, 11, ■

2. 0, 2, ■, 6, ■, ■, 12

3. 93, ■, 73, 63, ■, ■, 33

4. ■, 10, ■, 30, 40, ■, 60

5. 21, 24, 27, ■, ■, ■

6. 95, 90, 85, ■, ■, ■

7. Which numbers between 60 and 74 are odd?

8. Skip count by 10s. Start at 32. Press [3] [2] [+] [1] [0] [=]. Continue pressing [=] five times. Which digit changes each time? Why?

Get in Line

Sometimes numbers are used to show the order of objects or people.

Learning About It

Many people like to collect things as a hobby. These students are in line to share their collections with the class.

Anna is third in line. Chris is fifth in line. The numbers *third* and *fifth* are ordinal numbers.

Word Bank

ordinal numbers

▶ **Ordinal numbers** are used to tell the order or position of something.

Here are the first twenty-one ordinal numbers.

1st first	2nd second	3rd third	4th fourth	5th fifth	6th sixth	7th seventh
8th eighth	9th ninth	10th tenth	11th eleventh	12th twelfth	13th thirteenth	14th fourteenth
15th fifteenth	16th sixteenth	17th seventeenth	18th eighteenth	19th nineteenth	20th twentieth	21st twenty-first

Think and Discuss Suppose you got in line behind the last student in the picture. What ordinal number would name your position in line?

Try It Out

Write the word name for each ordinal number.

1. 3rd **2.** 21st **3.** 9th **4.** 14th **5.** 11th

6. 1st **7.** 18th **8.** 25th **9.** 7th **10.** 68th

Use the picture of the children in line to answer these questions.

11. What position in line is David?

12. If you are the last person in a line, how many people are behind you?

13. Five people are in line behind Chris. What ordinal number tells the position of the last person?

14. **Analyze** If Joe gets in line in front of Mitsu, what position would Mitsu be in?

www.sbgmath.com

Practice

Write the word name for each ordinal number.

15. 2nd **16.** 12th **17.** 16th **18.** 4th **19.** 20th

20. 8th **21.** 13th **22.** 5th **23.** 46th **24.** 99th

Problem Solving

Use the list at the right for Problems 25–34.

Name the collection in each position.

25. 3rd **26.** 15th **27.** 9th

28. 4th **29.** 6th **30.** 16th

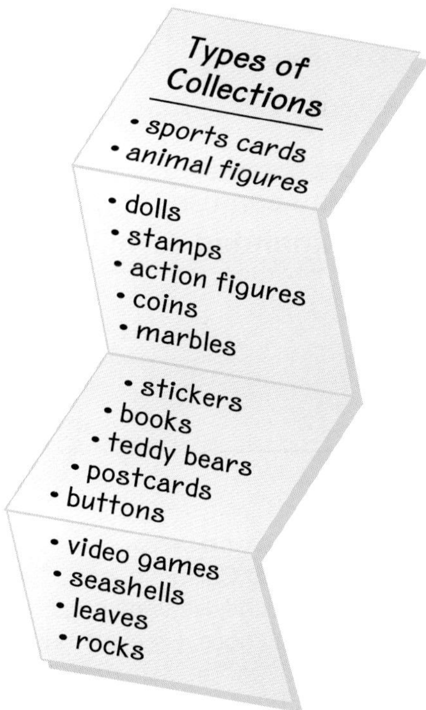

In which position is each type of collection?

31. teddy bears **32.** stickers

33. sports cards **34.** marbles

Review and Remember

Add or subtract.

35. 1 + 0 **36.** 3 + 4 **37.** 2 − 2 **38.** 1 + 3 **39.** 0 + 4

40. 7 − 2 **41.** 9 − 1 **42.** 4 + 4 **43.** 5 − 3 **44.** 6 − 4

For Extra Practice, see Set A, page 36.

Name That Number

You can show and describe numbers in many different ways.

Learning About It

James Fujita has an amazing collection—of bugs. He has been collecting them since he was in first grade. Among his many insects, James has 26 butterflies.

You can show the number 26 in different ways.

THERE'S ALWAYS A WAY!

- You can use **place-value blocks.**

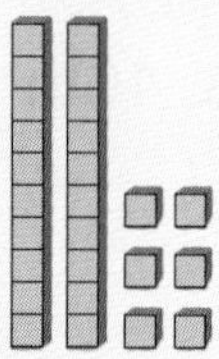

2 tens 6 ones

- You can use a **place-value chart.**

tens	ones
2	6

- You can use **expanded form.**

20 + 6

- You can use **standard form.**

26

- You can use **words.**

twenty-six

Kid Connection ➤
James Fujita, of California, has hundreds of bugs. He finds bugs everywhere he goes. He even found a new kind of cricket. James gives some of his bugs to museums and zoos. He brought two of his largest bugs to a TV talk show. They became the stars of the show.

Connecting Ideas

You can also show three-digit numbers in a different way.

Here are some ways to show the number 348.

THERE'S ALWAYS A WAY!

- You can use **place-value blocks**.

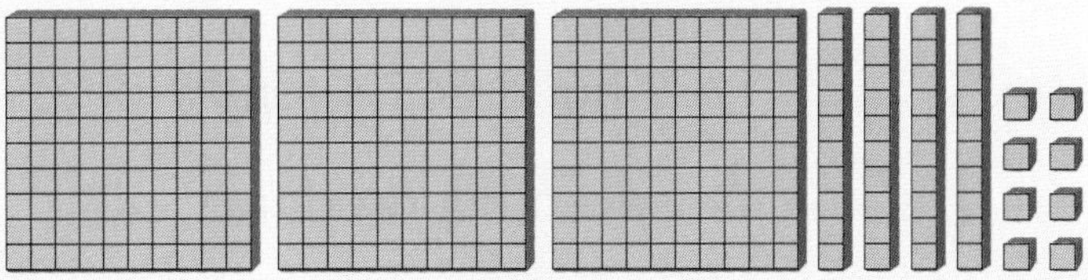

3 hundreds 4 tens 8 ones

- You can use a **place-value chart**.

hundreds	tens	ones
3	4	8

- You can use **expanded form**.

300 + 40 + 8

- You can use **standard form**.

348

- You can use **words**.

three hundred forty-eight

Another Example

Here are some ways to show the number 108.

- **place-value blocks**

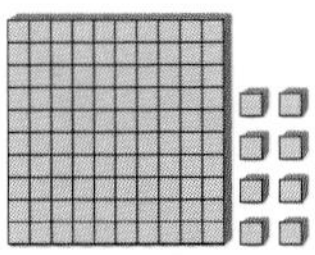

1 hundred 8 ones

- **place-value chart**

hundreds	tens	ones
1	0	8

- **expanded form**

100 + 8

- **standard form**

108

- **words**

one hundred eight

Think and Discuss Look at the place-value chart for the example above. What does the digit 0 mean?

Try It Out

Write each number in standard form.

1. 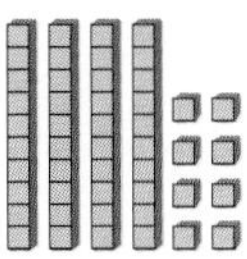

2. 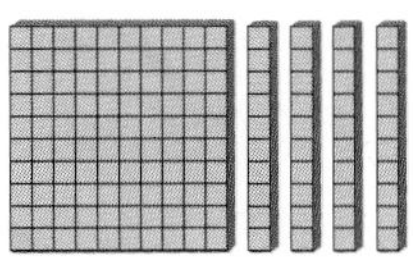

3. 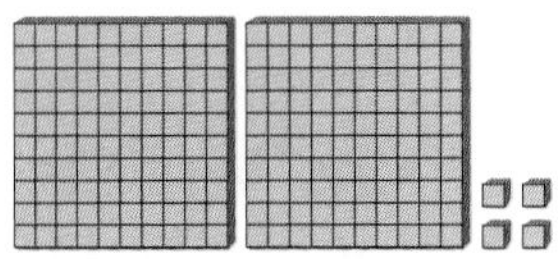

4. 300 + 60 + 8

5. 500 + 30

6. 400 + 60 + 5

7. 6 hundreds 7 ones

8. forty-seven

9. six hundred two

Practice

Write each number in standard form.

10. 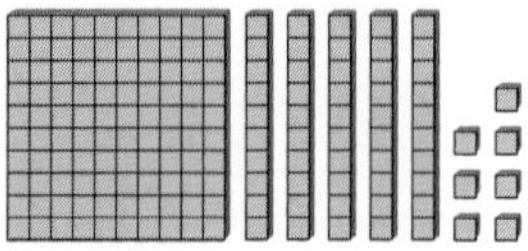

11. 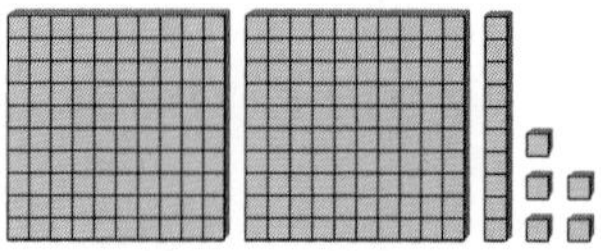

12. 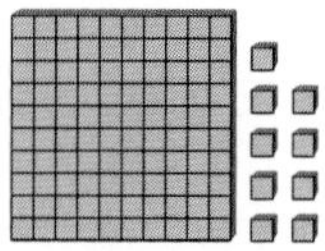

13. 100 + 60 + 4

14. 300 + 5

15. 900 + 20 + 9

16. one hundred twenty-nine

17. 2 hundreds 4 tens 2 ones

18. 7 hundreds 7 tens

19. seven hundred five

20. five hundred nineteen

21. 9 hundreds 7 ones

How many hundreds, tens, and ones blocks would you need to show each of these numbers? Use the fewest number of blocks possible.

22. 341

23. 30

24. 829

25. 704

26. 48

27. 507

28. 600

29. 396

Using Algebra **Complete each pattern.**

30. 486, 586, 686, ■, ■, ■

31. 799, 699, 599, ■, ■, ■

32. 68, 168, 268, ■, ■, ■

33. 574, 474, 374, ■, ■, ■

34. 335, 330, 325, ■, ■, ■

35. 216, 226, 236, ■, ■, ■

Problem Solving

36. James has 100 beetles in one tray and 30 spiders in another tray. He put 1 walking stick next to the 2 trays. How many bugs are there in all?

37. Suppose you had a collection of two hundred fifty-four bugs. Write the number that shows how many that is.

Science Connection
Walking sticks look like real sticks. Their shape and color helps to hide them from enemies when on a branch.

38. Using Algebra What missing number would you write to make this sentence true?

800 + ■ + 3 = 863

39. **Analyze** Suppose a number has the same number of hundreds, tens, and ones. If the sum of the digits is 6, what is the number?

40. **Analyze** Suppose you had 50 ones cubes and 3 tens blocks. How could you use them to show the number 48?

Project Link

Think about what your coin will look like.

- Will it be a circle, like most coins? Or will it be a different shape?
- Will it be the same size as some coin that you already know about? Or will it be a new size?

Review and Remember

Add or subtract.

41. 7 + 6	**42.** 15 − 8	**43.** 13 − 8	**44.** 6 − 6
45. 6 − 3	**46.** 18 − 9	**47.** 8 + 5	**48.** 10 + 10
49. 6 + 3 + 2	**50.** 5 + 1 + 4	**51.** 7 + 5 + 2	**52.** 8 + 1 + 9

Time for Technology

Using a Calculator

Showing Numbers

To show the number nine hundred three on a calculator, press [9] [0] [3].

Show each of the numbers below on a calculator. Write the keys you pushed. Then write the number in standard form.

1. forty-seven	**2.** six hundreds four ones	**3.** fifty
4. two hundred fifteen	**5.** seventy-four	**6.** eight hundreds

For Extra Practice, see Set B, page 36.

Close Enough

You can round numbers when you do not need an exact number.

Iroquois corn husk doll

Seminole palmetto and patchwork dolls

Plains rag doll

Learning About It

Many people collect dolls. Three kinds of Native American dolls are shown at the right. Suppose you had 22 patchwork dolls, 25 corn husk dolls, and 28 rag dolls. You could say that you have about 20 patchwork dolls, about 30 corn husk dolls, and about 30 rag dolls.

The word *about* means that the numbers are not exact. The numbers have been **rounded** to the nearest 10.

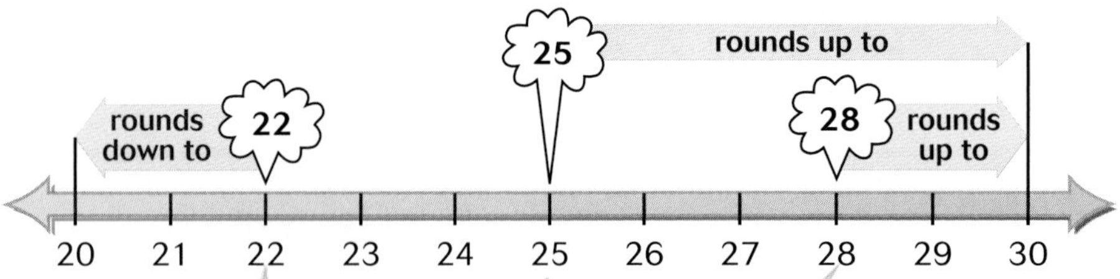

22 is closer to 20 than to 30.
22 rounds down to 20.

28 is closer to 30 than to 20.
28 rounds up to 30.

25 is halfway between 20 and 30.
If a number is halfway between 2 tens, you round up.
25 rounds up to 30.

More Examples

You can round money to the nearest ten cents.

A. 84¢ rounds down to 80¢. **B.** 86¢ rounds up to 90¢.

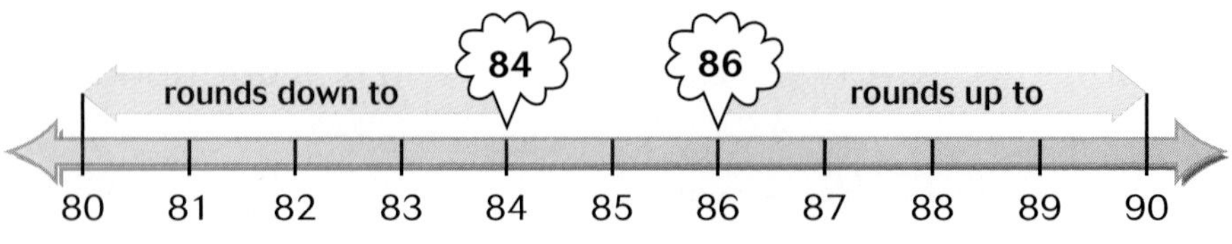

Connecting Ideas

You can use what you learned about rounding two-digit numbers to round three-digit numbers.

This is how you would round 215, 250, and 275 to the nearest hundred.

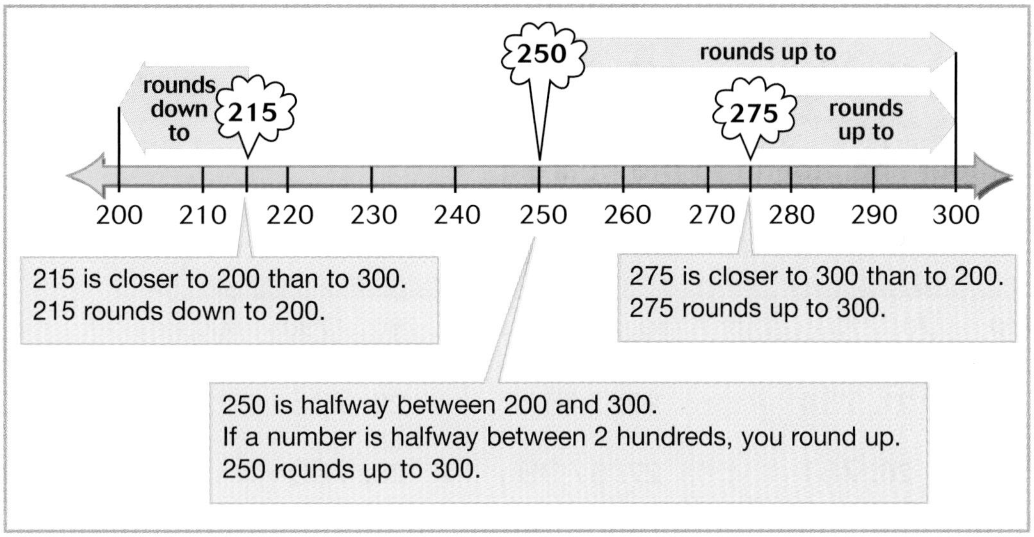

More Examples

You can round money to the nearest dollar.

A. \$5.49 rounds down to \$5.00. **B.** \$5.74 rounds up to \$6.00.

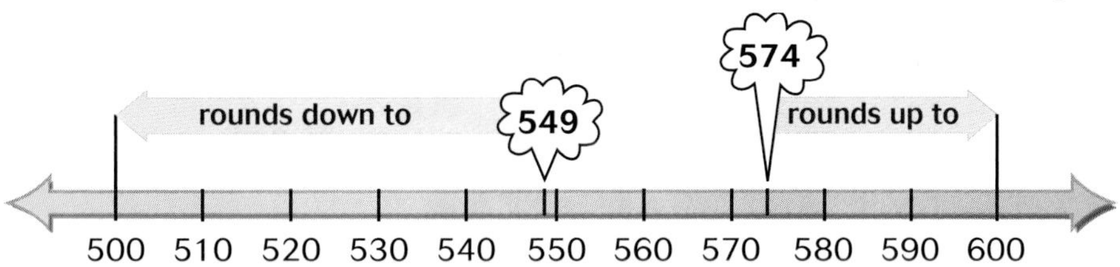

Think and Discuss Explain how you would round the number 958 to the nearest hundred.

Try It Out

What number is halfway between these numbers?

1. 20 and 30 **2.** 60 and 70 **3.** 10 and 20

4. 80 and 90 **5.** 200 and 300 **6.** 400 and 500

7. 600 and 700 **8.** 800 and 900 **9.** 100 and 200

▲ Hopi kachina doll

Use the number line. Round to the nearest ten or ten cents.

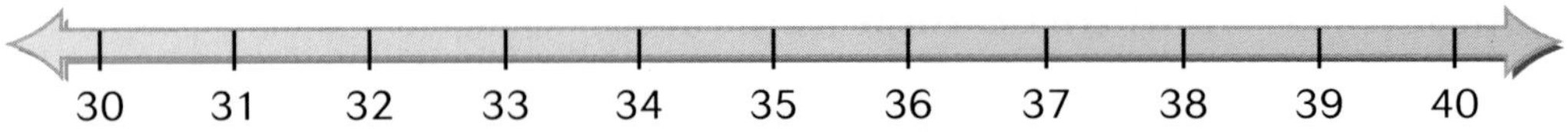

10. 36 **11.** 31¢ **12.** 35 **13.** 39¢ **14.** 32

15. 33¢ **16.** 38 **17.** 37¢ **18.** 31 **19.** 40

Use the number line. Round to the nearest hundred or dollar.

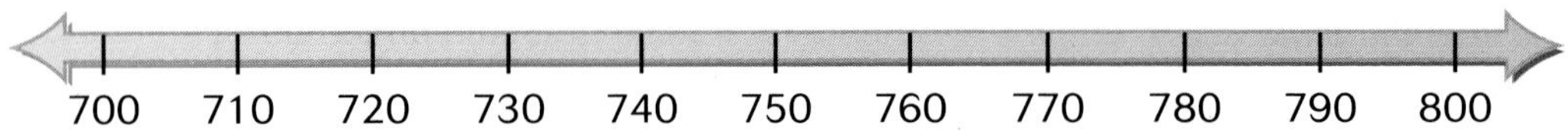

20. 719 **21.** 754 **22.** 748 **23.** 726 **24.** $7.76

25. $7.03 **26.** 781 **27.** $7.99 **28.** 760 **29.** $7.30

Practice

Use the numbers at the right to answer Exercises 30–33.

30. Which numbers round to 80?

31. Which numbers round to 90?

32. Which numbers round to 800?

33. Which numbers round to 700?

Round to the nearest ten or ten cents.

34. 55 **35.** 87 **36.** 34 **37.** 49¢ **38.** 22

39. 56¢ **40.** 16 **41.** 93¢ **42.** 45¢ **43.** 76¢

Round to the nearest hundred or dollar.

44. $7.49 **45.** 571 **46.** 360 **47.** 852 **48.** 442

49. $1.30 **50.** $4.18 **51.** $9.78 **52.** 323 **53.** $2.60

Problem Solving

54. A museum has 32 storytelling dolls in a special display case. About how many dolls are in the case?

55. Suppose 5 corn husk dolls, 7 rag dolls, and 10 storytelling dolls are on display. How many dolls are on display?

56. **Analyze** A number has the digits 3, 4, and 6. When you round the number to the nearest hundred, you get 500. What is the number?

▲ Cochiti Pueblo storytelling doll

Review and Remember

Add or subtract.

57. 4 + 7 **58.** 15 − 6 **59.** 6 + 9 **60.** 3 + 8 **61.** 12 − 7

62. 18 − 9 **63.** 5 + 7 **64.** 8 + 6 **65.** 16 − 8 **66.** 14 − 7

Critical Thinking Corner

Number Sense

Rounding Up and Rounding Down

This number line shows the numbers that round to 600.

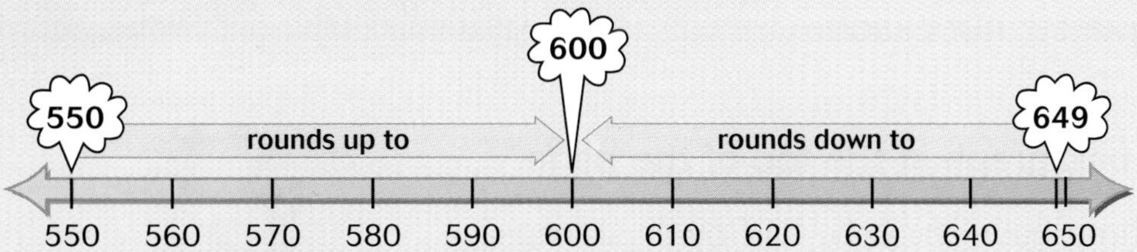

- 550 is the least whole number that rounds up to 600.
- 649 is the greatest whole number that rounds down to 600.

What are the least and the greatest whole numbers that round to each number?

1. 700 **2.** 500 **3.** 900 **4.** 400

Developing Skills for Problem Solving

First read for understanding and then focus on whether the numbers are exact numbers or estimates.

READ FOR UNDERSTANDING

Emma has more than 500 stamps in her stamp collection. She has almost 40 flower stamps. She also has 22 bird stamps and 12 stamps from foreign countries. Her bird stamps cost $0.32 each.

1. How many stamps does Emma have?
2. How many flower stamps does she have?
3. How many stamps from foreign countries does she have?

THINK AND DISCUSS

MATH FOCUS

Exact Numbers or Estimates
Estimates are not exact numbers. Words like *more than*, *almost*, and *about* can tell you that numbers are estimated, not exact.

Reread the paragraph at the top of the page.

4. Does Emma have exactly 40 flower stamps? If not, does she have more or fewer? How can you tell?

5. Does Emma have exactly 12 stamps from foreign countries? If not, does she have more or fewer? How can you tell?

6. When might the number 30 stand for an exact amount? When might it be an estimate?

Show What You Learned

Answer each question. Give a reason for your choice.

Ed's aunt gave him almost 300 stamps. His grandfather gave him 50 airplane stamps and 30 dog stamps. His uncle gave him about 100 stamps of famous people.

1. Which word helps you know that 300 stamps is an estimate?
   - **a.** gave
   - **b.** stamps
   - **c.** almost

2. Which word helps you know that 100 stamps is an estimate?
   - **a.** gave
   - **b.** about
   - **c.** stamps

3. Which sentence tells how many airplane stamps Ed received from his grandfather?
   - **a.** Ed received exactly 50 airplane stamps.
   - **b.** Ed received almost 50 airplane stamps.
   - **c.** Ed received less than 50 airplane stamps.

Use the ad at the right to answer Problems 4–7.

4. There are 4 numbers in the ad. How many of the numbers are estimates?
   - **a.** two of the numbers
   - **b.** three of the numbers
   - **c.** all of the numbers

5. How much would 4 stamps cost altogether?
   - **a.** less than 40¢
   - **b.** more than 40¢
   - **c.** exactly 40¢

6. Which of the following could be the number of stamps available?
   - **a.** 700 stamps
   - **b.** 697 stamps
   - **c.** 720 stamps

7. **Explain** How do you know which numbers in the ad are estimates and which numbers are exact?

Checkpoint

Understanding Numbers to 999

Use a word from the list to complete each sentence.

Word List
even
odd
ordinal
round

1. __?__ numbers are used to show the order or position of something.
2. Numbers that end with the digit 1, 3, 5, 7, or 9 are __?__ numbers.
3. When an exact number is not needed, you can __?__ a number to the nearest ten or hundred.
4. Numbers that end with the digit 0, 2, 4, 6, or 8 are __?__ numbers.

Using Algebra **Write the numbers that come next in each pattern.** (pages 2–3)

5. 25, 30, 35, ■, ■ **6.** 21, 18, 15, ■, ■

7. 30, 26, 22, ■, ■ **8.** 41, 43, 45, ■, ■

Write the word name for each ordinal number. (pages 4–5)

9. 7th **10.** 2nd **11.** 3rd **12.** 11th **13.** 72nd

Write each number in standard form. (pages 6–9)

14. six hundred ten **15.** 400 + 50 + 9

16. 8 hundreds 7 tens **17.** 1 hundred 3 tens 5 ones

18. 300 + 6 **19.** 800 + 40 + 3

20. five hundred sixty-two **21.** two hundred sixteen

Round to the underlined digit. (pages 10–13)

22. $\underline{6}2$ **23.** $\underline{3}7$ **24.** $\underline{1}5$ **25.** $\underline{4}6$ **26.** $\underline{8}1$

27. $\underline{8}85$ **28.** $\underline{6}10$ **29.** $\underline{5}15$ **30.** $\underline{3}24$ **31.** $\underline{1}45$

32. $\underline{4}71$ **33.** $\underline{6}3$ **34.** $\underline{7}09$ **35.** $\underline{2}7$ **36.** $\underline{9}33$

Problem Solving

37. Sally is 16th in a line of 20 people. How many people are ahead of her? How many people are behind her?

38. Suppose you want to buy a doll for $7.85 to add to your collection. About how many dollars would you need?

39. A collection of key chains totals eight hundred ninety-six. Write the number in standard form.

40. If a display has 36 beetles, about how many beetles are there?

What do you think?

Many people always round up when estimating how much something will cost. Why do you think that might be a good idea?

Journal Idea Create two or three number patterns. Then challenge a classmate to add three numbers to each of your patterns.

Critical Thinking Corner

Using Algebra **Logical Thinking**

What's the Order?

Fran, Mike, Jeff, and Tia are waiting in line.
Tia is standing between Fran and Mike.
Jeff is the last person in line.
Fran is not first in line.

List the order in which the four friends are standing in line. Draw a picture like the one shown to help you.

Count Them Out

This activity will help you understand the number 1,000.

A stack of 1,000 pennies is about 5 feet high.

Learning About It

Do you collect pennies or other coins? What do you think 1,000 pennies would look like? Do this activity to find out.

Your class needs to be divided into ten groups. You can use beans to stand for the pennies.

Work with your group.

Step 1 Count 10 beans. Put them into a paper cup. Then put 10 beans into each of 9 more cups.

Step 2 Pour the beans from all 10 cups into a plastic bag. How many beans are in the bag?

What You Need

For each group:
100 beans
10 cups
1 plastic bag
various-sized containers

Step 3 Place your plastic bag of beans with the bags of all the other groups.

- How many bags are there?
- How many beans are in each bag?
- How many beans are there altogether?

Step 4 Choose a container that you think will hold all the beans. Empty each bag of beans into it. Is the container big enough to hold all 1,000 beans?

Think and Discuss Do 1,000 beans look like you thought they would? Do they look like more beans or fewer beans?

Practice

1. How many plastic bags of beans did your class fill? How many hundreds are there in a thousand?
2. How many cups did your class fill with beans? How many tens are there in a thousand?
3. How many beans did your class count? How many ones are there in a thousand?
4. **Describe** How would you describe 1,000 to a younger student who has no idea what 1,000 means? Share your ideas with other groups.

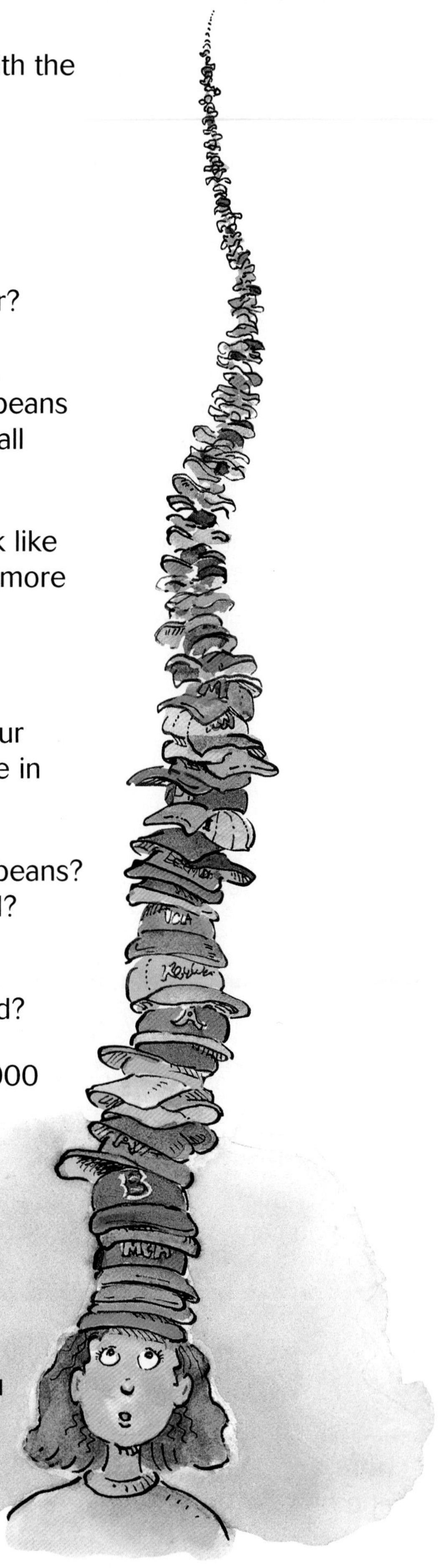

What do you think 1,000 hats would look like? Would you need a larger container to hold 1,000 hats or 1,000 beans?

Lots of Labels

You know about place value of three-digit numbers. You can use what you know to write larger numbers.

Learning About It

Sometimes even labels from cans are worth collecting. Some schools collect labels to get computer equipment.

Suppose a school needs 2,345 soup labels to get a tape recorder. In what ways can you show this number?

THERE'S ALWAYS A WAY!

- You can use **place-value blocks**.

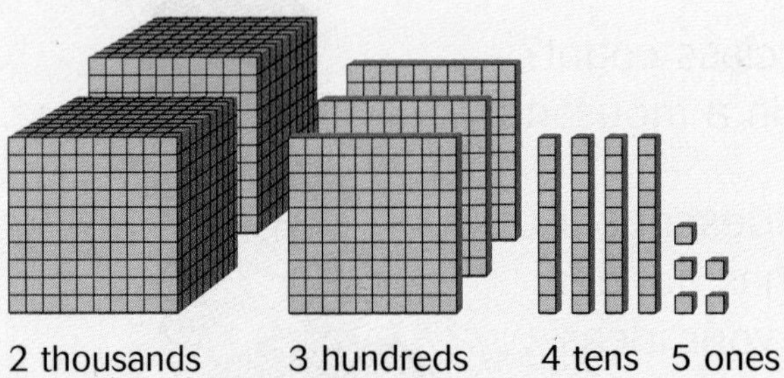

- You can use a **place-value chart**.

thousands	hundreds	tens	ones
2,	**3**	**4**	**5**

A comma is used to separate thousands from hundreds.

- You can use **expanded form**. 2,000 + 300 + 40 + 5
- You can use **standard form**. 2,345
- You can use **words**. two thousand, three hundred forty-five

Think and Discuss How could you show 1,340 using only hundreds and tens blocks?

Try It Out

Write each number in standard form.

1. 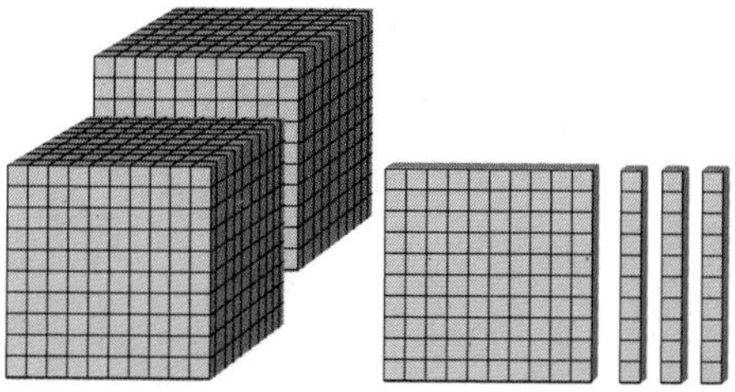

2,130

2. 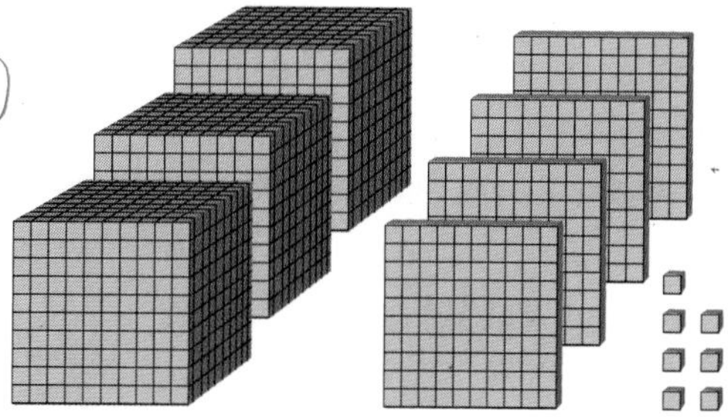

3,407

Practice

Write each number in standard form.

3. 2,000 + 100 + 50 + 2 **4.** 4,000 + 600 + 20 + 5

5. 8,000 + 500 + 70 + 7 **6.** five thousand, forty

7. 4 thousands 9 hundreds 8 tens 3 ones **8.** three thousand, seven hundred twenty

Write each number in expanded form and in words.

9. 3,324 **10.** 6,048 **11.** 1,746 **12.** 9,400

13. 2,946 **14.** 4,806 **15.** 2,164 **16.** 3,266

Problem Solving

17. A school collected 1,351 labels in a month. Suppose 2,000 more can labels were needed to get a computer. How many labels altogether would have to be collected?

18. **Analyze** Use the digits 5, 0, 9, and 2. Write the greatest possible four-digit number. Write the least possible four-digit number.

Review and Remember

Write the total amount.

19. 4 dimes, 2 nickels **20.** 1 quarter, 1 nickel, 3 dimes, 3 pennies

21. 2 quarters, 8 pennies **22.** 4 dimes, 5 nickels, 11 pennies

For Extra Practice, see Set D, page 37.

Rock and Roll

You can use place value to compare and order larger numbers.

Learning About It

Do you ever pick up rocks and carry them home? If you do, you have a rock collection. Wyatt has collected 345 rocks. Teresa Ann has 397 rocks. Who has more rocks?

Use the place-value chart to compare 345 and 397.

The hundreds digits are the same.

The tens digits are different. 4 tens < 9 tens

hundreds	tens	ones
3	4	5
3	9	7

< means "is less than."
> means "is greater than."
The arrow points to the lesser number.

So 345 < 397 or 397 > 345.

Teresa Ann has more rocks than Wyatt has.

Another Example

Compare 1,136 and 1,167.

The thousands digits are the same.

The hundreds digits are the same.

thousands	hundreds	tens	ones
1,	1	3	6
1,	1	6	7

The tens digits are different. 3 tens < 6 tens

So 1,136 < 1,167 or 1,167 > 1,136.

Connecting Ideas

You have been using place-value charts to compare numbers. Now you can use them to help you put three or more numbers in order.

Here's how to put the numbers 468, 460, and 574 in order from greatest to least.

Step 1 Compare the hundreds.

hundreds	tens	ones
4	6	8
4	6	0
5	7	4

5 hundreds > 4 hundreds

So 574 is the greatest number.

Step 2 Compare the tens for 468 and 460.

hundreds	tens	ones
4	6	8
4	6	0
5	7	4

The tens for 468 and 460 are the same.

Step 3 Compare the ones for 468 and 460.

hundreds	tens	ones
4	6	8
4	6	0
5	7	4

The ones are different.
8 ones > 0 ones
So 468 > 460.

The order of the numbers from greatest to least is:
574 468 460

Another Example

Order these numbers from least to greatest.
5,364 536 5,464

Step 1 Compare the thousands.

thousands	hundreds	tens	ones
5,	3	6	4
	5	3	6
5,	4	6	4

0 thousands < 5 thousands

So 536 is the least number.

Step 2 Compare the hundreds for 5,364 and 5,464.

thousands	hundreds	tens	ones
5,	3	6	4
	5	3	6
5,	4	6	4

3 hundreds < 4 hundreds

So 5,364 < 5,464.

The order of the numbers from least to greatest is:
536 5,364 5,464

Think and Discuss Suppose there are 3 four-digit numbers that have the same digit in the thousands, tens, and ones places. Which digit would you use to compare and order the numbers?

Try It Out

Write each number sentence, using the symbol for the underlined words.

1. 2,386 is greater than 2,178 **2.** 789 is less than 798

Compare the numbers. Write them in order from greatest to least. Use a place-value chart if you wish.

3. 258 209 352 **4.** 617 754 654 **5.** 1,008 1,096 999

Practice

Write >, <, or = for each ●.
Use a place-value chart if you wish.

6. 366 ● 336 **7.** 251 ● 251 **8.** 482 ● 487

9. 672 ● 678 **10.** 7,091 ● 8,541 **11.** 8,245 ● 8,240

12. 1,467 ● 1,567 **13.** 4,923 ● 4,823 **14.** 6,954 ● 6,945

Write the numbers in order from least to greatest.

15. 448 232 238 **16.** 642 602 649

17. 784 748 782 **18.** 3,012 3,168 3,199

19. 4,002 4,200 4,020 **20.** 6,475 6,745 6,457

Use the numbers at the right to answer Exercises 21–24.

21. Which number is between 645 and 650?

22. Which number is less than 645?

23. Which numbers are more than 3,257?

24. Which number is between 5,834 and 5,839?

Problem Solving

25. **Science Connection** Suppose one collection of rocks has 264 granite rocks. Another collection has 255 sandstone rocks. A third collection has 268 quartz rocks. Which collection is the largest? Which is the smallest?

26. Some kinds of rocks can be carved. Suppose you have 129 carved jade pieces. A friend has collected 187 carved quartz pieces. Who has more pieces?

27. **Create Your Own** Pick any four digits. Write the greatest number you can with your digits. Write the least number. Then write a number that comes between the other numbers.

Fine Arts Connection
Jade has been used in Chinese carvings for hundreds of years. The sculpture in the picture was carved from one piece of jade.

Using Algebra

Review and Remember

Write the next four numbers in each pattern.

28. 20, 22, 24, ■, ■, ■, ■

29. 15, 20, 25, ■, ■, ■, ■

30. 30, 33, 36, ■, ■, ■, ■

31. 40, 44, 48, ■, ■, ■, ■

Project Link

Take the last step in planning your coin. Decide how much it will be worth. Choose any value in dollars or cents that you want.

Now put all your ideas on paper. Make a drawing of your coin. Don't forget to draw both sides of the coin. Remember to put its value on your coin.

For Extra Practice, see Set E, page 37.

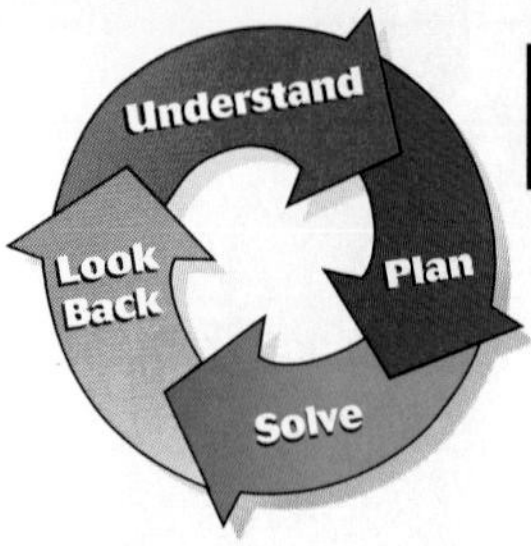

Problem Solving
Use Logical Reasoning

Sometimes you can use logical reasoning to solve problems.

Sam and Leah are arranging four model cars. Leah puts the red car in front of the blue car. Sam puts the yellow car between the blue car and the red car. Leah puts the purple car next to the red car but not next to the yellow car. What is the order of the cars?

UNDERSTAND

What do you need to find?

You need to find how Sam and Leah are arranging the four model cars.

PLAN

How can you solve the problem?

You can use **logical reasoning** to help you organize the facts. As you read each sentence of the problem, start listing the order of the cars. Adjust your list each time you find new information.

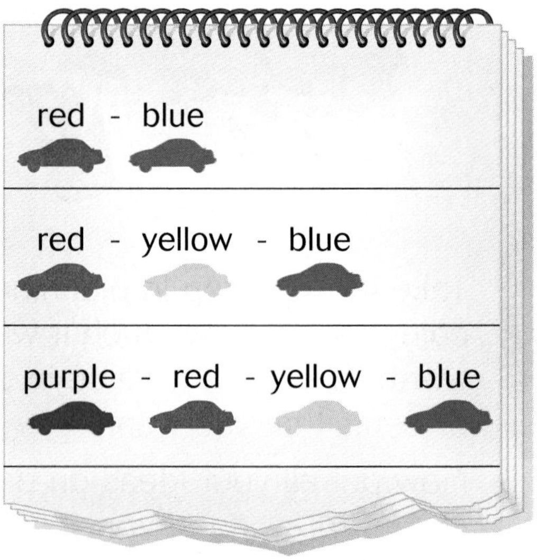

SOLVE

The order of the cars is purple, red, yellow, and blue.

LOOK BACK

Compare your answer with the facts in the problem. Does your answer match the facts?

Using the Strategy

Use logical reasoning to solve each problem.

1. Julie has 4 glass horses on a shelf. The black horse is between the brown horse and the silver horse. The brown horse is fourth. The other horse is red. What is the color of the third horse?

2. Mary is thinking of an even number that uses the digits 0, 1, 2, and 3. The number is greater than 2,000 but less than 3,000. There is a 3 in the tens place. What is the number?

3. Aaron gave Melinda a hint about the number of trucks in his collection. He said, "It is an odd number less than 20 and greater than 10. The sum of the digits is 6." How many trucks are in Aaron's collection?

4. Kent is looking at a picture of himself and his family. His mom and dad are on each end. Kent's brother is next to Kent and to the left of his dad. Kent's sister is to the right of his mom. Who is in the middle of the picture?

Mixed Strategy Review

Try these or other strategies you have learned.

THERE'S ALWAYS A WAY!

- *Write a Number Sentence*
- *Use Logical Reasoning*
- *Find a Pattern*
- *Draw a Picture*

5. Jeff's class is arranging fall leaves around the edge of a bulletin board in this order: brown, green, red, yellow. If the class continues the pattern, what color will the 16th leaf be?

6. Josh is thinking of a number between 25 and 60. There is a 4 in the ones place. The sum of the digits is 9. What is the number?

7. You have 11 toy boats. Eight of them are red. If you want 15 red boats, how many more red boats do you need?

Mounds of Marbles

You can use what you know about place value to write five-digit and six-digit numbers.

Learning About It

How many marbles do you think fit into a backpack? This backpack holds 13,783 marbles. Here are some ways to show this number.

THERE'S ALWAYS A WAY!

- Use a **place-value chart**.

ten thousands	thousands	hundreds	tens	ones
1	3,	7	8	3

- Use **expanded form**. 10,000 + 3,000 + 700 + 80 + 3
- Use **standard form**. 13,783
- Use **words**. thirteen thousand, seven hundred eighty-three

Another Example

Here are some ways to show the number 180,401.

- Use a **place-value chart**.

hundred thousands	ten thousands	thousands	hundreds	tens	ones
1	8	0,	4	0	1

- Use **expanded form**. 100,000 + 80,000 + 400 + 1
- Use **standard form**. 180,401
- Use **words**. one hundred eighty thousand, four hundred one

Think and Discuss Suppose you could put 100 more marbles in the backpack. How many marbles would be in the backpack then?

Try It Out

Write each number in standard form.

1. 200,000 + 30,000 + 6,000 + 400 + 50 + 9
2. four hundred thirty thousand, two hundred six
3. 9 hundred thousands 2 ten thousands 4 hundreds 3 ones

Practice

Write the value of the underlined digit.

4. $866{,}\underline{5}04$	**5.** $11{,}06\underline{5}$	**6.** $\underline{5}92{,}124$	**7.** $7\underline{5}7{,}492$	**8.** $34{,}6\underline{5}2$
9. $\underline{6}32{,}191$	**10.** $124{,}\underline{8}30$	**11.** $42\underline{7}{,}931$	**12.** $\underline{2}3{,}507$	**13.** $889{,}41\underline{6}$
14. $\underline{2}5{,}422$	**15.** $19{,}0\underline{9}7$	**16.** $651{,}\underline{4}64$	**17.** $\underline{3}48{,}770$	**18.** $21{,}0\underline{8}0$

Write each number in expanded form.

19. 824,034	**20.** 199,349	**21.** 55,312
22. 890,760	**23.** 34,871	**24.** 1,003
25. 612,459	**26.** 888,888	**27.** 9,640

Problem Solving

28. A store has 100,000 blue marbles, 30,000 red marbles, and 800 green marbles. How many marbles does the store have?

29. Suppose a museum has a collection of 354,000 clay marbles. If another 10,000 marbles are brought to the museum, how many marbles will be in the collection?

Kid Connection
A secret spin on her shooter marble helped Amanda Burn, from Tennessee, win the national marbles championship.

Using Algebra

Review and Remember

Write the next two numbers in each pattern.

30. 997, 998, 999, ■, ■
31. 176, 175, 174, ■, ■
32. 322, 321, 320, ■, ■
33. 470, 480, 490, ■, ■

Dinosaur Shopping

Coins and bills are worth different amounts.

Learning About It

Suppose you had the money shown. Could you buy this toy for your dinosaur collection?

When you count money, start with the bill of greatest value. End with the coin of least value.

How much money is there?
Could you buy the toy?

Another Example

Use play money to count. How much do you have?

Think and Discuss What is the least number of bills and coins needed to make $5.33?

What You Need

For each student:
play bills and coins

Math Note

Use a dollar sign and decimal point to write money.
$1.28 $0.63

Try It Out

Write each amount. Use play money if you wish.

1. 

2. 

Practice

Write each amount. Tell whether it is enough money to buy the dinosaur on page 30.

3. 

4. 

5. 

6. 

www.sbgmath.com

Problem Solving

7. Describe two ways to show 50¢.

8. Describe three ways to show 60¢.

9. **Analyze** Suppose you have six coins worth 50¢. If four of the coins are dimes, what are the other two coins?

10. **Explain** Suppose you have four coins worth 50¢. Is one of the coins a quarter? Explain how you know.

Review and Remember

Add or subtract.

11. $8 + 9$ **12.** $16 - 8$ **13.** $11 - 6$ **14.** $7 + 7$ **15.** $18 - 9$

16. $5 + 8$ **17.** $13 - 8$ **18.** $12 - 5$ **19.** $9 + 6$ **20.** $4 + 8$

For Extra Practice, see Set G, page 38.

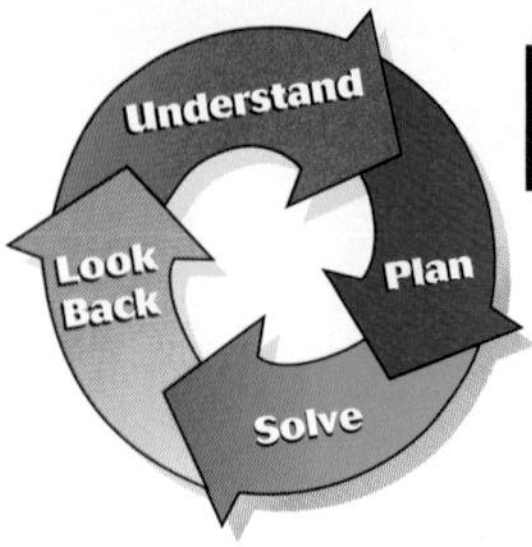

Problem Solving
Using Money

Knowing how to make change can help you solve problems.

Shaun spent \$3.68 on insect stickers. He paid with a \$5 bill and got 97¢ change. Did Shaun get the correct change?

UNDERSTAND

What do you need to find?

You need to find whether 97¢ is the correct change.

PLAN

How can you solve the problem?

You can **act it out** to see if the correct change is 97¢.

SOLVE

Start with the cost of the stickers and use play money to count up to \$5. The money you add to count up to \$5 will be the correct change.

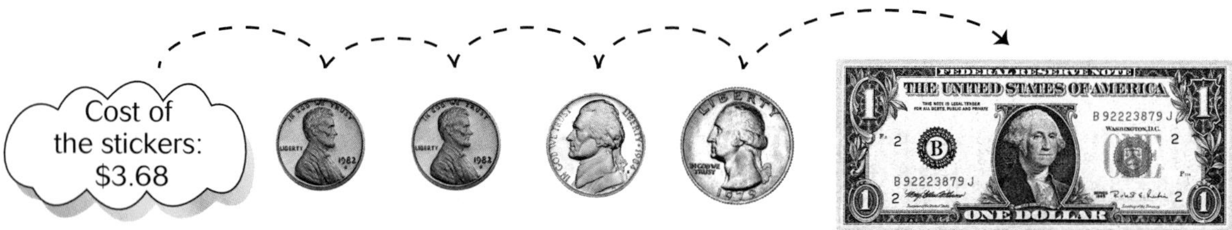

\$3.68 → \$3.69 → \$3.70 → \$3.75 → \$4.00 → \$5.00

The correct change is \$1.32.

Shaun did not get the correct change.

LOOK BACK

How could you subtract to find the correct change?

Show What You Learned

Use what you know about money to solve these problems.

1. Cam buys Safari Fun animal stickers that cost $3.31. She gives the clerk $5.00. Cam's change includes 4 pennies, 2 quarters, 1 dollar bill, and 2 other coins. What are the other 2 coins Cam receives?

2. Kit spends $2.46 on lion stickers. Brian buys a hippo sticker for $0.99 and zebra stickers for $1.45. They each pay with three $1 bills. Who gets more change? How much more?

3. Barb buys Safari Fun animal stickers for $5.79. She pays with a $10 bill. List one combination of coins and bills that Barb could get as change.

4. **Explain** Dan buys a sticker album for $6.59 and tiger stickers for $1.69. Will he get enough change from a $10 bill to lend his friend one dollar?

5. Suppose you spend $1.36 on a panda sticker and $1.10 on a tiger sticker. You give the clerk $2.50. What is your change?

6. **Create Your Own** Write a problem about making change. Give your problem to a classmate to solve.

Suppose 3 friends buy the sticker packages listed below. The chart shows how much money they each give the clerk and the cost of the stickers.

Name of Friend	Sticker Package	Amount of Money Given	Cost of Sticker Package	Change
Bill	Package A	$1.00	$0.72	
Sue	Package B	$5.00	$4.33	
Cindy	Package C	$10.00	$8.97	

7. Copy the chart. Then complete it to show the change that each person should receive.

8. What's the total amount of money that the 3 friends gave the clerk? How much money in all did they spend on stickers?

Checkpoint

Understanding Numbers to 999,999

Write each number in standard form. (pages 20–21, 28–29)

1. seven thousand, nine hundred eighty-five

2. 4 thousands 8 hundreds 2 tens 5 ones

3. 400,000 + 20,000 + 300 + 5

4. five hundred nineteen thousand, eighty-two

Write the value of the digit 7 in each number. (pages 20–21, 28–29)

5. 2,307 **6.** 5,790 **7.** 8,378 **8.** 7,023

9. 83,709 **10.** 30,007 **11.** 570,020 **12.** 987,002

Compare. Write >, <, or = for each ●. (pages 22–25)

13. 34 ● 43 **14.** 57 ● 60 **15.** 235 ● 237

16. 7,503 ● 7,511 **17.** 3,823 ● 3,799 **18.** 2,802 ● 2,799

Write the numbers in order from least to greatest. (pages 22–25)

19. 26 14 28 **20.** 19 37 2 **21.** 4,223 4,232 4,242

22. 305 289 351 **23.** 703 699 694 **24.** 3,580 3,780 3,680

Write each amount. (pages 30–31)

25.

26.

Problem Solving

27. Risa has 1,249 stamps in her stamp collection. Miguel has 1,439 stamps in his collection. Who has more stamps?

28. Wayne has 2 quarters, 3 dimes, 3 nickels, and 3 pennies. A super pack of baseball cards costs $1.00. Does he have enough money to buy the cards?

29. Rodney has a ten-dollar bill, 2 five-dollar bills, and 8 one-dollar bills. He wants to use as few bills as he can to pay for a sticker album that costs $17.98. How should he pay?

30. Using Algebra I am a number less than 800 and greater than 500. I have a 4 in the tens place. My ones digit is less than 3 but greater than 0. All of my digits are even numbers. What number am I?

What do you think?
When you count coins, why is it usually better to start with the coin that has the greatest value?

Journal Idea How does knowing place value help you understand the difference between 20 and 200?

Project Wrap-Up

A Class Collection

When all the coins have been designed, put them together in a class coin collection.

- Put the coins in order from the least valuable to the most valuable. How much is the most valuable coin worth? the least valuable coin?
- Compare the coins and talk about their designs. Which ones do you think would make the best real coins? Why?

Extra Practice

Set A (pages 4–5)

Write the word name for each ordinal number.

1. 5th **2.** 22nd **3.** 19th **4.** 17th **5.** 13th

6. 8th **7.** 21st **8.** 45th **9.** 7th **10.** 82nd

11. Suppose you are in line at the post office to buy stamps for your collection. You are the eighteenth person in line. How many people are in front of you?

12. Mindy was the tenth person in line to buy stamps. She let Ben get in front of her. What was Mindy's new position in line?

Set B (pages 6–9)

Write each number in standard form.

1. 500 + 40 + 7 **2.** five hundred ninety **3.** 3 hundreds 7 tens 2 ones

4. 600 + 30 **5.** four hundred two **6.** 5 hundreds 2 ones

7. 400 + 20 **8.** one hundred fourteen **9.** 2 hundreds 8 tens

10. The stamps you are buying come in sheets of 100. Suppose you needed 275 stamps to fill your stamp album. How many sheets should you buy?

Set C (pages 10–13)

Round to the nearest ten or ten cents.

1. 37 **2.** 83 **3.** 54¢ **4.** 85¢ **5.** 19

6. 29 **7.** 25¢ **8.** 61¢ **9.** 82 **10.** 86¢

Round to the nearest hundred or dollar.

11. \$1.85 **12.** 119 **13.** 904 **14.** \$5.63 **15.** \$8.09

16. 412 **17.** 787 **18.** 549 **19.** 550 **20.** \$6.98

Extra Practice

Set D (pages 20–21)

Write each number in standard form.

1. six thousand, fourteen

2. nine thousand, two hundred eighty-seven

3. 7 thousands 2 tens 3 ones

4. 5 thousands 3 hundreds 5 tens 4 ones

5. 9,000 + 500 + 3

6. 2,000 + 800 + 90 + 7

7. 3,000 + 400 + 9

8. 4,000 + 40 + 4

Write each number in expanded form.

9. 7,009 **10.** 6,200 **11.** 7,030 **12.** 2,902

13. There are 2,386 baseball cards in your collection. Your friend has 200 more cards. How many cards does your friend have?

14. Jasper has four thousand, two hundred three cards in his collection. Write this number in standard form.

Set E (pages 22–25)

Write >, <, or = for each ●.

1. 57 ● 74

2. 182 ● 179

3. 107 ● 170

4. 1,354 ● 1,354

5. 2,000 ● 2,010

6. 9,035 ● 9,029

7. 2,396 ● 2,936

8. 6,540 ● 6,504

9. 6,624 ● 6,624

Write the numbers in order from least to greatest.

10. 28 37 54

11. 391 395 380

12. 539 832 604

13. 2,005 2,050 2,500

14. 3,842 3,482 3,284

15. 6,500 6,050 6,005

16. Sharon has 373 dolls. She has cases to hold 337 dolls. Does she have enough cases to hold all her dolls?

17. Can 2,386 people attend a doll collector's show in a gym that holds 2,025 people?

Extra Practice

Set F (pages 28–29)

Write each number in standard form.

1. eight hundred thousand, four hundred

2. 700,000 + 7,000 + 3

3. four hundred six thousand, nine hundred twenty-three

4. 600,000 + 50,000, + 5,000 + 9

5. 5 hundred thousands 8 ten thousands 5 thousands 8 tens 3 ones

6. 7 hundred thousands 8 tens

Write each number in expanded form.

7. 587,030	**8.** 602,357	**9.** 823,005	**10.** 422,208
11. 261,911	**12.** 400,345	**13.** 116,000	**14.** 943,829

Set G (pages 30–31)

Write each amount.

1.

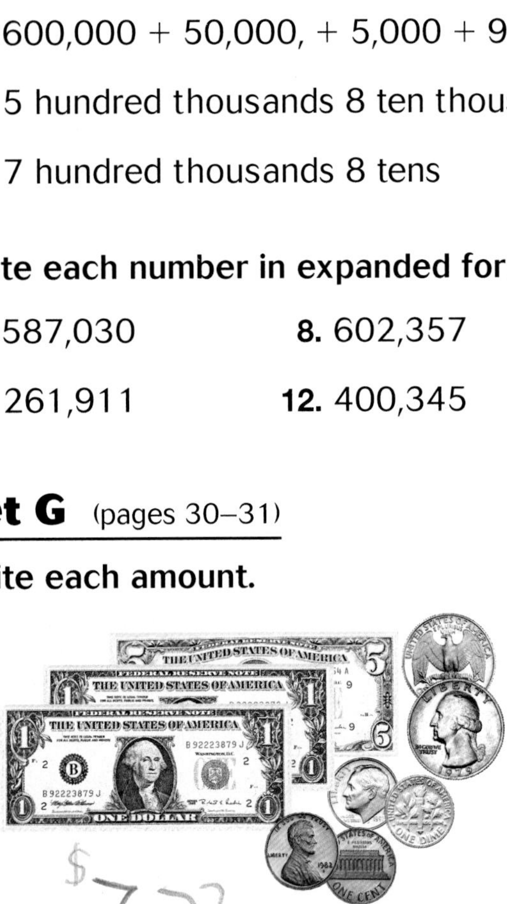

$7.72

2.

3.

4.

Chapter Test

Write the word name for each ordinal number.

1. 41st **2.** 5th **3.** 12th **4.** 63rd **5.** 19th

Write each number. Then put the numbers in order from greatest to least.

6. eight thousand, forty

7. 1,000 + 70 + 9

8. four hundred, two thousand, eighty-five

9. 200,000 + 10,000 + 8,000 + 500 + 70 + 8

Round to the nearest ten or ten cents.

10. 83 **11.** 75¢ **12.** 67 **13.** 33¢ **14.** 38 **15.** 98¢

Round to the nearest hundred or dollar.

16. 249 **17.** $2.53 **18.** 870 **19.** $1.99 **20.** 351 **21.** $4.50

Write each amount.

22.

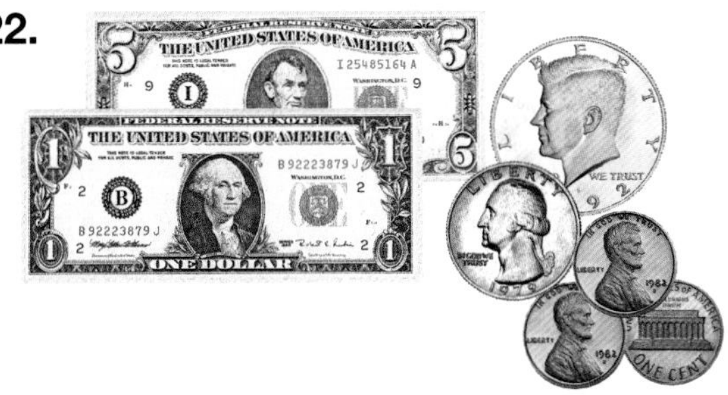

23.

Solve.

24. Roy has 2 five-dollar bills, 4 one-dollar bills, 3 quarters, and 3 nickels. Does he have more or less than $14.89?

25. Johanna bought a pack of stickers for $3.23. She paid with a five-dollar bill. How much change should she get back?

Self-Check

Look back at Exercises 10–21. Did you write dollar signs and cents signs when they were needed?

Performance Assessment

Show What You Know About Numbers

What You Need

base-ten blocks

1. Use the numbers 206, 126, and 260 for Questions 1a–1c.

   a. Show each number with base-ten blocks.

   b. Write the numbers in order from least to greatest.

   c. Round the greatest number to the nearest hundred. Write the rounded number. Then show it with base-ten blocks.

2. Complete the story below by writing a number for each blank. Choose from the numbers at the right. Use each number only once. Reread your story to make sure it makes sense.

   a. Max is in third grade. He has gone to school since he was _?_ years old. There are _?_ students in Max's class. The other third-grade class is smaller. It has only _?_ students. There are a total of _?_ students in the school.

   One day Max brings his collection of pennies to class. He has more than _?_ pennies, so the collection is very heavy! One penny is from the year _?_. After he shows the pennies to his class, it is time for lunch. Max spends _?_ on milk, soup, and a sandwich. His lunch costs less than his lunch box, which cost _?_.

Self-Check

For Question 1b, did you remember to start in the hundreds place to compare the numbers?

For Question 2a, did you use each number once?

Extension

Babylonian Numbers

Social Studies Connection
Babylon was an ancient city that existed about 5,000 years ago.

Ancient number systems are different from our number system. About 5,000 years ago the Babylonians used wedge-shaped symbols instead of numbers. The chart shows what their number system looked like.

BABYLONIAN NUMBER SYSTEM

1	2	3	4	5	6	7	8	9	10	11	12	13	20
▼	▼▼	▼▼▼	▼▼▼ ▼	▼▼▼ ▼▼	▼▼▼ ▼▼▼	▼▼▼ ▼▼▼ ▼	▼▼▼ ▼▼▼ ▼▼	▼▼▼ ▼▼▼ ▼▼▼	◀	◀▼	◀▼▼	◀▼▼ ▼	◀◀

Use the chart to answer these questions.

1. Look at the symbols for 1 and 10. How are they the same? How are they different?

2. Look at the symbols for 12. What does each symbol stand for? What would 14 look like?

3. Look at the symbols for 20. What does each symbol stand for? What would 30 look like?

Look at these Babylonian numbers. Write each number using our number system.

4. ◀▼▼▼▼▼

5. ◀◀◀▼▼▼▼▼▼

6. ◀◀◀◀▼

7. ▼▼▼▼▼▼

8. ◀◀◀◀◀▼▼▼

9. ◀◀◀◀◀▼▼▼▼

10. **Create Your Own** Write a number less than 60 using Babylonian symbols. Then give your number to a classmate to write in our number system.

Detail above: Painting by Maurice Bardin, 1936; Oriental Institute, University of Chicago

Chapter 2

Addition and Subtraction

Chapter Theme: ANIMALS

Career Spotlight Meet Dana Brenfleck. She works for the Arizona–Sonora Desert Museum. She teaches people about the many kinds of birds found in the desert. The birds in the photograph are called Harris hawks.

At many nature museums and zoos, workers keep track of the number of animals.

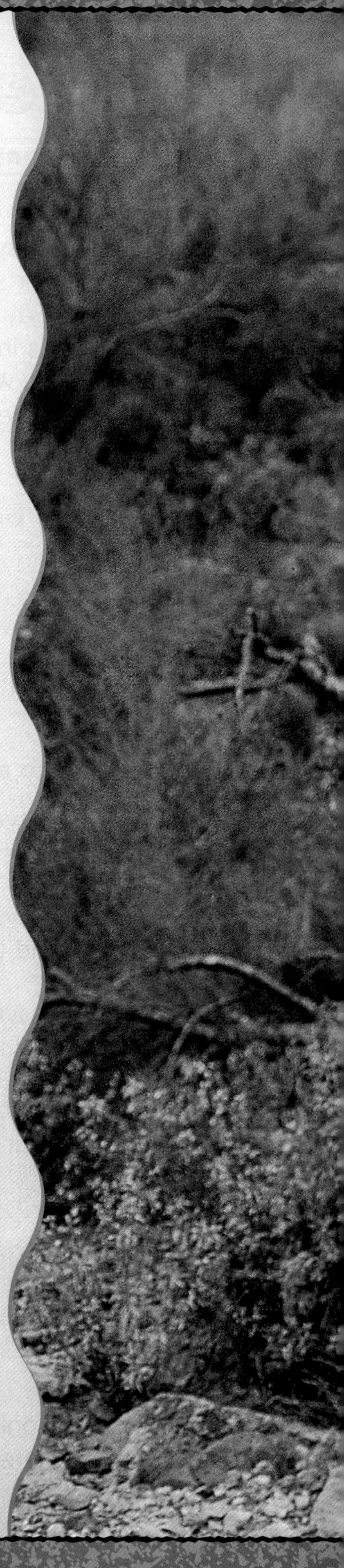

Chapter Project

Create an Animal Poster

A desert is one kind of *habitat.* A habitat is a place where a certain kind of animal or plant is normally found.

In this project, you will make a poster that shows a habitat. You will show some of the animals that live there.

- Decide what habitat you want to show. You might choose a desert, a rain forest, the Arctic, or an ocean.
- Make lists of plants and of animals that live in the habitat you chose. How many are on each list? How many plants and animals are there in all?

A Real Plus

There are different strategies you can use to add.

Learning About It

There are 7 skunks hunting for insects. Then 2 more skunks join them. To find how many skunks there are in all, you can add.

To add 1, 2, or 3, you can **count on.**

7 + 2 = ■

Start with 7.
Count 2 more.

You end at 9. So 7 + 2 = 9.
There are 9 skunks in all.

Suppose 5 skunks joined the 7 skunks.
How many skunks would there be?

To add numbers greater than 3, sometimes you can **make a ten**.

7 + 5 = ■

Make a ten. Then add the rest.

7 + 5 = ■

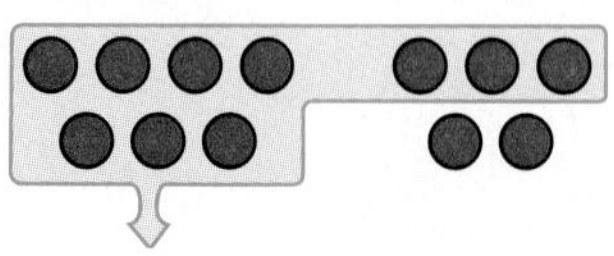

10 + 2 = 12 So 7 + 5 = 12.

There would be 12 skunks.

More Examples

Count on to find these sums.

A. 6 + 3 = 9

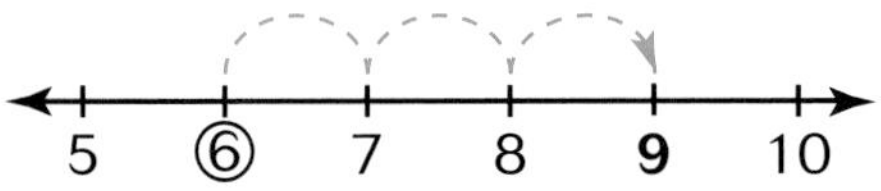

B. 9 + 2 = 11

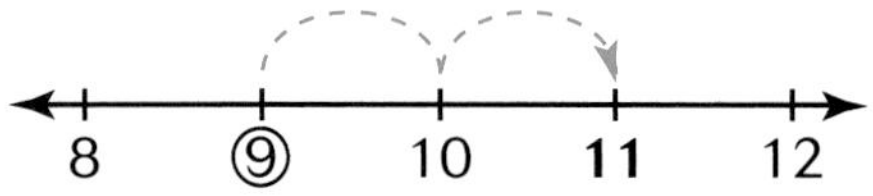

Make a ten to find these sums.

C. 9 + 5 = 14

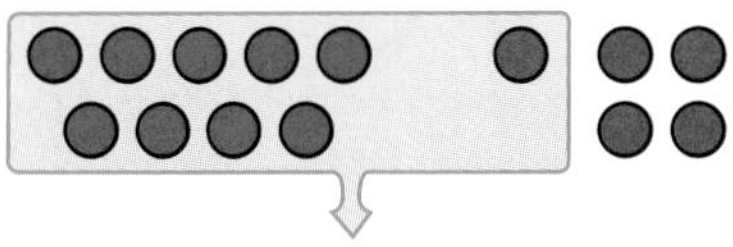

10 + 4 = 14

D. 8 + 3 = 11

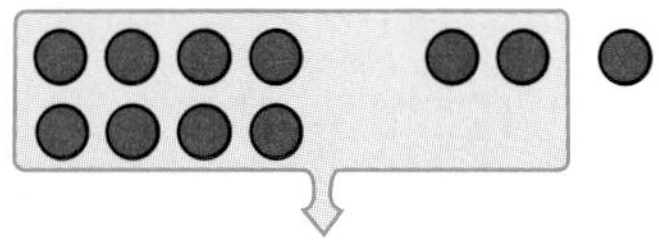

10 + 1 = 11

Connecting Ideas

So far you have learned strategies for counting on and for making a ten. When numbers are close to each other, you can use doubles to add them.

Suppose 8 skunks joined 7 skunks.
How many skunks would there be?

7 + 8 = ■

You can use the **doubles** 7 + 7.

7 + 7 = 14
7 + 8 is one more.
So 7 + 8 = 15.

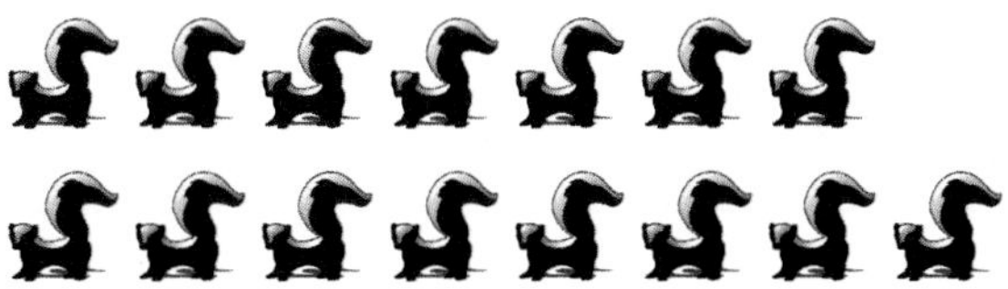

Or you can use the doubles 8 + 8.

8 + 8 = 16
7 + 8 is one less.
So 7 + 8 = 15.

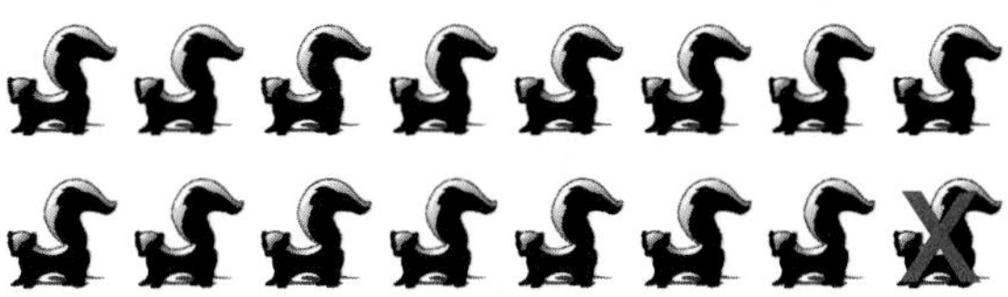

There would be 15 skunks.

Think and Discuss Explain how you could use doubles to find the sum of 4 + 5.

Try It Out

Count on to find these sums.

1. 9 + 1 2. 9 + 3 3. 5 + 2 4. 8 + 2 5. 7 + 3

Make a ten to find these sums.

6. 5 + 8 7. 4 + 7 8. 9 + 6 9. 9 + 7 10. 4 + 8

Use doubles to find these sums.

11. 6 + 7 12. 9 + 8 13. 3 + 4 14. 5 + 6 15. 8 + 7

Practice

Add.

16. 2 + 2	17. 4 + 2	18. 5 + 1	19. 3 + 1	20. 3 + 3	21. 3 + 7
22. 4 + 1	23. 6 + 4	24. 8 + 6	25. 8 + 0	26. 1 + 9	27. 5 + 9
28. 5 + 3	29. 2 + 4	30. 8 + 9	31. 6 + 5	32. 8 + 8	33. 3 + 8
34. 1 + 6	35. 5 + 5	36. 2 + 7	37. 5 + 0	38. 8 + 5	39. 7 + 9

Using Algebra

Compare. Write >, <, or = for each ●.

40. 2 + 6 ● 6 + 3 41. 8 + 0 ● 9 + 0

42. 8 + 5 ● 0 + 5 43. 7 + 4 ● 9 + 2

44. 6 + 1 ● 1 + 2 45. 3 + 0 ● 7 + 0

Science Connection Animals have ways to protect themselves from other animals. A skunk protects itself with a spray. The spray has a very unpleasant smell.

Problem Solving

46. Jasmin saw 5 chipmunks by a tree and 2 more on a log. How many did she see in all?

47. Fred counted 4 squirrels and 9 rabbits. How many animals did Fred count?

48. **Science Connection** Some skunks can spray as far as 15 feet. Suppose a skunk is 9 feet from a rabbit. The rabbit moves back 7 more feet. Could the spray reach the rabbit? Explain your answer.

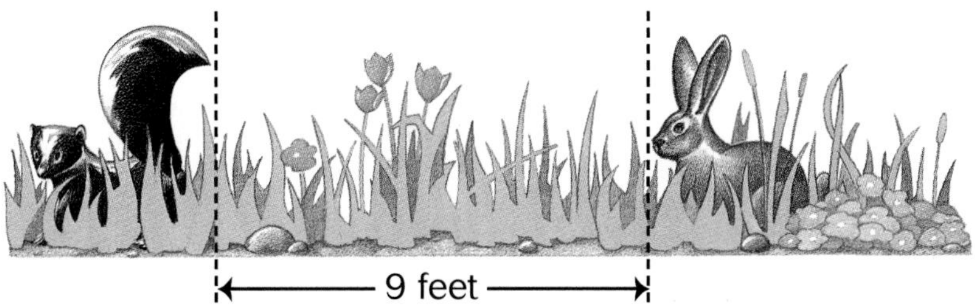

Review and Remember

Compare. Write >, <, or = for each.

49. 12 ● 8
50. 25 ● 41
51. 126 ● 83
52. 345 ● 345
53. 1,746 ● 1,764
54. 4,965 ● 3,285

Time for Technology

Using CD-ROM

Names for Ten

Use manipulatives to show different names for 10.

- Link a connecting cubes space to a number space.
- Click 1 blue cube and 9 red cubes. Click in the number space, then =.
- Show different names for 10. Use other colors.

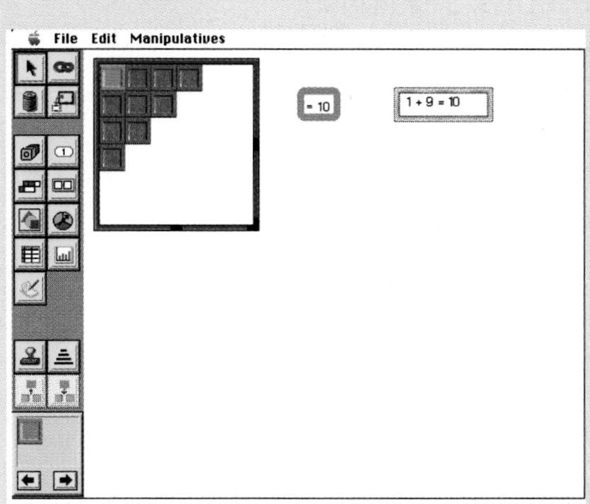

Using Algebra

Facts About Facts

There are special rules that can help you remember your addition facts.

Word Bank

addends
sum

Learning About It

Amanda is buying goldfish. She buys 3 lionhead goldfish and 4 fantail goldfish. How many goldfish does she buy in all?

3	+	4	=	7
↑ addend		↑ addend		↑ sum

4	+	3	=	7
↑ addend		↑ addend		↑ sum

She buys 7 goldfish.

▶ Changing the order of the **addends** does not change the **sum.**

Kyle buys 5 fantail goldfish and 0 lionhead goldfish. How many goldfish does he buy?

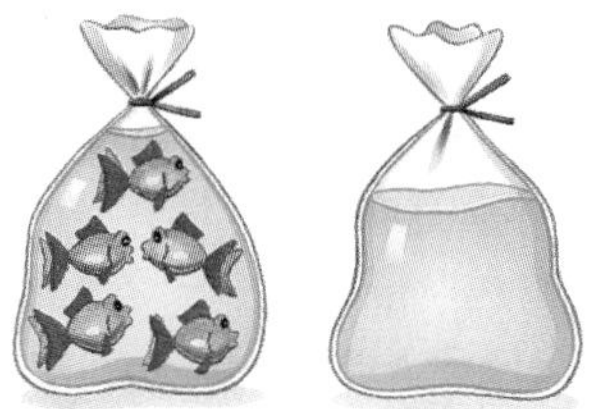

He buys 5 goldfish.

$5 + 0 = 5$

▶ When you add 0 to a number, the sum is that number.

Think and Discuss How does knowing $5 + 2 = 7$ help you find $2 + 5$?

Try It Out

Find each sum.

1. $2 + 3$
$3 + 2$

2. $8 + 1$
$1 + 8$

3. $0 + 7$
$7 + 0$

4. $6 + 2$
$2 + 6$

Practice

Find each sum.

5. 7 + 1
6. 1 + 7
7. 9 + 4
8. 4 + 9
9. 7 + 5
10. 5 + 7
11. 0 + 6
12. 4 + 3
13. 9 + 0
14. 3 + 5
15. 6 + 1
16. 6 + 6
17. 5 + 8
18. 9 + 9
19. 5 + 4
20. 7 + 6
21. 6 + 9
22. 8 + 4

Follow each rule to complete each table.

Rule: Add 2

	Input	Output
	5	7
	7	9
23.	0	
24.	9	

Rule: Add 8

	Input	Output
	2	10
25.	8	
26.	1	
27.	5	

Problem Solving

28. Amanda visited a goldfish pond. She saw 8 tiger head goldfish, 4 bubble eye goldfish, and 3 frogs. How many goldfish did she see?

29. Chun's family has different colored goldfish in their goldfish pond. They have 9 red, 8 black, and 6 white goldfish. How many red and white goldfish do they have?

30. **Analyze** The sum of two numbers is 13. One number is 1 more than 5. What are the numbers?

Social Studies Connection
For years Chinese people have used goldfish ponds to make their gardens more beautiful.

Review and Remember

Write the next four numbers in each pattern.

31. 100, 90, 80, ■, ■, ■, ■
32. 48, 46, 44, ■, ■, ■, ■
33. 150, 250, 350, ■, ■, ■, ■
34. 125, 130, 135, ■, ■, ■, ■

For Extra Practice, see Set B, page 72.

Using Algebra

Bird Watching

If you have more than two numbers, you can add them in any order you like!

Learning About It

How many birds are there in all?

3 + 4 + 6 = ■

$$\begin{array}{r} 3 \\ 4 \\ +\ 6 \\ \hline \end{array}$$

There are many ways to find the sum of three numbers.

THERE'S ALWAYS A WAY!

You can add down.

$$\begin{array}{r} 3 \\ 4 \\ +\ 6 \\ \hline \end{array} \quad \begin{array}{r} 7 \\ +\ 6 \\ \hline 13 \end{array}$$

You can add up.

$$\begin{array}{r} 3 \\ 4 \\ +\ 6 \\ \hline \end{array} \quad \begin{array}{r} 3 \\ +10 \\ \hline 13 \end{array}$$

You can add in any order.

$$\begin{array}{r} 3 \\ 4 \\ +\ 6 \\ \hline \end{array} \quad \begin{array}{r} 9 \\ +\ 4 \\ \hline 13 \end{array}$$

There are 13 birds in all.

▶ The way you group addends does not change the sum.

Think and Discuss Which of the ways above do you think is the easiest way to add? Why?

Try It Out

Find each sum.

1. $\begin{array}{r} 2 \\ 8 \\ +\ 3 \\ \hline \end{array}$ **2.** $\begin{array}{r} 4 \\ 6 \\ +\ 1 \\ \hline \end{array}$ **3.** $\begin{array}{r} 5 \\ 0 \\ +\ 7 \\ \hline \end{array}$ **4.** $\begin{array}{r} 9 \\ 2 \\ +\ 2 \\ \hline \end{array}$ **5.** $\begin{array}{r} 2 \\ 8 \\ 5 \\ +\ 6 \\ \hline \end{array}$ **6.** $\begin{array}{r} 4 \\ 2 \\ 5 \\ +\ 1 \\ \hline \end{array}$

Social Studies Connection
These birds all live along the southern coast of Florida.

Practice

Find each sum.

7.	8.	9.	10.	11.	12.
3	5	1	7	6	2
5	1	6	3	9	7
+ 8	+ 3	+ 4	+ 9	+ 5	+ 4

13.	14.	15.	16.	17.	18.
2	4	2	3	1	8
2	5	6	8	4	5
0	2	1	4	2	6
+ 6	+ 5	+ 3	+ 2	+ 2	+ 9

19. 5 + 3 + 6 **20.** 2 + 9 + 1 **21.** 4 + 3 + 1

22. 7 + 2 + 5 **23.** 3 + 6 + 8 **24.** 6 + 3 + 4

Problem Solving

25. A toad caught 5 grasshoppers, 3 mosquitoes, and 8 flies with its sticky tongue. How many insects did it catch altogether?

26. At the zoo, Kim saw 2 sea turtles, 4 alligators, and 6 snakes. She drew a picture of each animal. How many animals did she draw?

Review and Remember

Write the numbers in order from least to greatest.

27. 37 24 98 **28.** 247 553 197 **29.** 2,637 9,314 3,000

Write the value of the underlined digit.

30. 40,$\underline{2}$46 **31.** $\underline{5}$24,187 **32.** 1$\underline{4}$7,296 **33.** 2$\underline{9}$,780 **34.** $\underline{3}$7,904

For Extra Practice, see Set C, page 72.

Developing Skills for Problem Solving

First read for understanding and then focus on whether to add or subtract to solve problems.

◀ Shetland Pony

READ FOR UNDERSTANDING

Jenny visited a horse farm. In the barn she saw 2 Arabian horses and 8 Morgan horses Out in the field, she saw 7 Shetland ponies and 3 Welsh ponies.

1. What kinds of horses did Jenny see?
2. How many of each kind of horse did she see?
3. Did Jenny see more Arabian horses or Morgan horses?

◀ Morgan Horse

THINK AND DISCUSS

MATH FOCUS

Choose the Operation Adding and subtracting are operations you sometimes use to solve problems. To find out how many of something there are altogether, you add. To find how many more of one thing you have than another, you subtract.

◀ Welsh Pony

Reread the paragraph at the top of the page.

4. Which operation would you use to find how many ponies Jenny saw? Explain why.
5. How many more Morgan horses than Arabian horses did Jenny see? Did you add or subtract? Explain why.
6. Explain how you know whether to add or subtract.

▼ Arabian Horse

Show What You Learned

Answer each question. Give a reason for your choice.

Jenny learned that the height of a horse is measured in hands. A Shetland pony is 8 hands high. A Welsh pony is 12 hands high.

This Welsh pony is 12 hands high. A hand is equal to 4 inches. That means this pony is 48 inches or 4 feet high.

1. How tall is a Shetland pony?
   - **a.** 8 hands
   - **b.** 8 feet
   - **c.** 8 inches

2. Which of the ponies is taller, the Shetland pony or the Welsh pony?
   - **a.** Shetland pony
   - **b.** Welsh pony
   - **c.** neither

3. How would you find how much taller the Welsh pony is than the Shetland pony?
   - **a.** Add 8 and 12.
   - **b.** Subtract 8 from 12.
   - **c.** Subtract 12 from 8.

There are 2 groups of people riding horseback on trails near the horse farm. One group of 9 people is riding on the blue trail. The other group of 4 people is riding on the red trail. Suppose the two groups join each other. How many people are riding together?

4. What do you need to know?
   - **a.** the number in both groups
   - **b.** the number on the blue trail
   - **c.** how many more there are in one group than in the other

5. What number sentence could you use to find the answer?
   - **a.** $9 - 4 = \blacksquare$
   - **b.** $9 > 4$
   - **c.** $9 + 4 = \blacksquare$

6. **Explain** Suppose you want to know how many more people rode on the blue trail than on the red trail. Would you add or subtract? Explain how you know.

Checkpoint

Addition

Add. (pages 44–49, 50-51)

1. $\begin{array}{r} 3 \\ +\ 4 \\ \hline \end{array}$ **2.** $\begin{array}{r} 5 \\ +\ 1 \\ \hline \end{array}$ **3.** $\begin{array}{r} 1 \\ +\ 0 \\ \hline \end{array}$ **4.** $\begin{array}{r} 4 \\ +\ 2 \\ \hline \end{array}$ **5.** $\begin{array}{r} 2 \\ +\ 6 \\ \hline \end{array}$ **6.** $\begin{array}{r} 8 \\ +\ 6 \\ \hline \end{array}$

7. $\begin{array}{r} 2 \\ +\ 5 \\ \hline \end{array}$ **8.** $\begin{array}{r} 0 \\ +\ 9 \\ \hline \end{array}$ **9.** $\begin{array}{r} 3 \\ +\ 9 \\ \hline \end{array}$ **10.** $\begin{array}{r} 2 \\ +\ 7 \\ \hline \end{array}$ **11.** $\begin{array}{r} 1 \\ +\ 8 \\ \hline \end{array}$ **12.** $\begin{array}{r} 5 \\ +\ 5 \\ \hline \end{array}$

13. $\begin{array}{r} 2 \\ 3 \\ +\ 1 \\ \hline \end{array}$ **14.** $\begin{array}{r} 3 \\ 0 \\ +\ 3 \\ \hline \end{array}$ **15.** $\begin{array}{r} 4 \\ 4 \\ +\ 5 \\ \hline \end{array}$ **16.** $\begin{array}{r} 6 \\ 4 \\ +\ 2 \\ \hline \end{array}$ **17.** $\begin{array}{r} 9 \\ 5 \\ +\ 1 \\ \hline \end{array}$ **18.** $\begin{array}{r} 2 \\ 8 \\ +\ 4 \\ \hline \end{array}$

19. $4 + 7 + 3$ **20.** $6 + 3 + 8$ **21.** $5 + 3 + 5$

22. $5 + 0 + 3 + 2$ **23.** $4 + 3 + 8 + 4$ **24.** $7 + 9 + 1 + 1$

Using Algebra **Compare. Write $>$, $<$, or $=$ for each ●.** (pages 44–49)

25. $3 + 8$ ● $6 + 2$ **26.** $4 + 0$ ● $5 + 0$

27. $5 + 3$ ● $1 + 7$ **28.** $4 + 9$ ● $6 + 6$

29. $7 + 6$ ● $9 + 5$ **30.** $2 + 4$ ● $0 + 7$

Use the first fact to help you complete the second.
(pages 48–49)

31. $6 + 1 = 7$
$1 + 6 =$ ■

32. $3 + 2 = 5$
$2 + 3 =$ ■

33. $0 + 2 = 2$
$2 + 0 =$ ■

34. $5 + 4 = 9$
$4 + 5 =$ ■

35. $5 + 8 = 13$
$8 + 5 =$ ■

36. $8 + 7 = 15$
$7 + 8 =$ ■

37. $7 + 3 = 10$
$3 + 7 =$ ■

38. $0 + 6 = 6$
$6 + 0 =$ ■

39. $8 + 9 = 17$
$9 + 8 =$ ■

Problem Solving

40. Corell likes to paint pictures of lions. She has painted 8 pictures so far. If she paints 3 more pictures, how many will she have?

41. Bill has 3 fish and 4 turtles. Kate has 2 cats and 6 rabbits. Who has more pets?

42. Mrs. Simon spent $4 on dog treats, $3 on a dog brush, and $9 on rabbit food for her pets. How much money did she spend for her dog?

43. Carissa's family has 5 cows, 3 goats, and 6 horses in their barn. How many animals are in their barn in all?

44. **Generalize** If you add two even numbers, will the sum be even or odd?

45. **Analyze** Robert added two numbers and got a sum of 14. What two numbers might he have added?

What do you think?

Does changing the order in which you add numbers change their sum?

Journal Idea Suppose you needed to add 6 + 3 + 4. Show how you would find the sum.

Critical Thinking Corner

Using Algebra **Logical Thinking**

Magic Squares

The box at the right is a Magic Square.

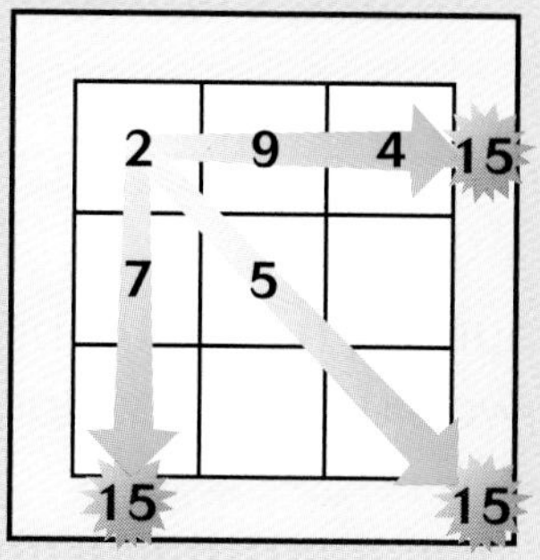

Copy the square. Then fill in the missing boxes so that each row, column, and diagonal has the same sum. Then see if you can make your own Magic Square.

Take It Away!

There are different strategies you can use to subtract.

Learning About It

Iguanas can lose parts of their tails. There are 7 sections on this iguana's tail. If 3 sections break off, how many sections are left?

To subtract 1, 2, or 3, you can **count back**.

7 − 3 = ■

Start at 7. Count back 3 numbers.

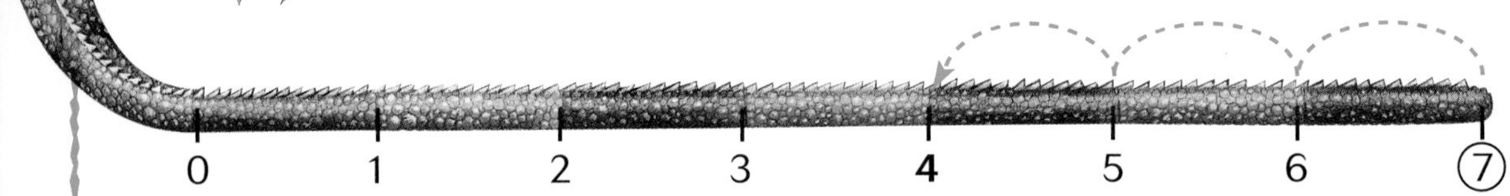

You end at 4. So 7 − 3 = 4.
There are 4 sections left.

Suppose 5 sections of the tail broke off. How many sections would be left? To subtract numbers that are close to each other, you can **count up**.

7 − 5 = ■

Start at 5. Count up to 7.

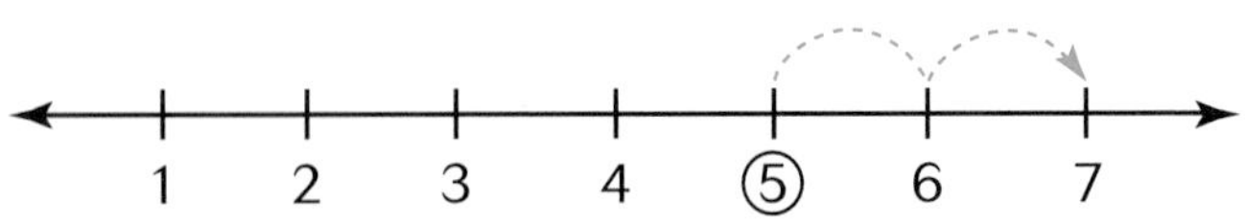

You counted up 2 numbers. So 7 − 5 = 2.
There would be 2 sections left.

Think and Discuss Is it easier to count back or count up to find 9 − 8? Explain why.

Science Connection
Iguanas are lizards that live in many places throughout the world. If a piece of an iguana's tail breaks off, it will often grow back.

Try It Out

Find each difference.

1. $\begin{array}{r} 10 \\ -\ 8 \\ \hline \end{array}$	**2.** $\begin{array}{r} 9 \\ -\ 3 \\ \hline \end{array}$	**3.** $\begin{array}{r} 7 \\ -\ 1 \\ \hline \end{array}$	**4.** $\begin{array}{r} 17 \\ -\ 2 \\ \hline \end{array}$	**5.** $\begin{array}{r} 15 \\ -\ 1 \\ \hline \end{array}$	**6.** $\begin{array}{r} 11 \\ -\ 3 \\ \hline \end{array}$

7. $5 - 5$ **8.** $6 - 2$ **9.** $8 - 1$ **10.** $14 - 2$

Practice

Subtract.

11. $\begin{array}{r} 1 \\ -\ 1 \\ \hline \end{array}$	**12.** $\begin{array}{r} 9 \\ -\ 1 \\ \hline \end{array}$	**13.** $\begin{array}{r} 11 \\ -\ 9 \\ \hline \end{array}$	**14.** $\begin{array}{r} 5 \\ -\ 3 \\ \hline \end{array}$	**15.** $\begin{array}{r} 10 \\ -\ 2 \\ \hline \end{array}$	**16.** $\begin{array}{r} 18 \\ -\ 9 \\ \hline \end{array}$
17. $\begin{array}{r} 8 \\ -\ 6 \\ \hline \end{array}$	**18.** $\begin{array}{r} 5 \\ -\ 4 \\ \hline \end{array}$	**19.** $\begin{array}{r} 13 \\ -\ 5 \\ \hline \end{array}$	**20.** $\begin{array}{r} 12 \\ -\ 7 \\ \hline \end{array}$	**21.** $\begin{array}{r} 8 \\ -\ 8 \\ \hline \end{array}$	**22.** $\begin{array}{r} 10 \\ -\ 9 \\ \hline \end{array}$

23. $2 - 2$ **24.** $6 - 1$ **25.** $4 - 3$ **26.** $10 - 7$

27. $8 - 4$ **28.** $9 - 8$ **29.** $5 - 2$ **30.** $8 - 3$

Problem Solving

31. Marc rode his bike 9 blocks to the zoo. Eve rode her bike 7 blocks to the zoo. George rode his bike 5 blocks to the zoo. How many more blocks did Marc ride than Eve?

32. Yesterday Jan put 9 rocks in her lizard's terrarium. Today she put in 2 more rocks. How many rocks are in the terrarium?

Review and Remember

Find each sum or difference.

33. $11 - 6$ **34.** $9 + 7$

35. $8 + 4$ **36.** $13 - 9$

37. $12 - 5$ **38.** $6 + 3 + 4$

Project Link

Pick two animals to put on your habitat poster.

- Collect some pictures of each animal. You can cut out pictures from magazines, or you can draw them yourself.
- Count how many pictures of each animal you have.

For Extra Practice, see Set D, page 73.

Take Ten!

Sometimes you can use a ten-frame to help you subtract.

Learning About It

There are 13 penguins on the ice.
Eight of them jump into the water.
How many penguins are still on the ice?

13 − 8 = ▪

Think of 13 as 10 + 3.

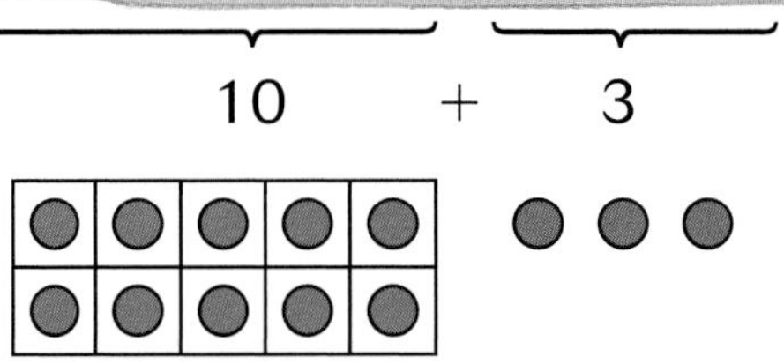

You can use a ten-frame to solve the problem.

Take away 8.

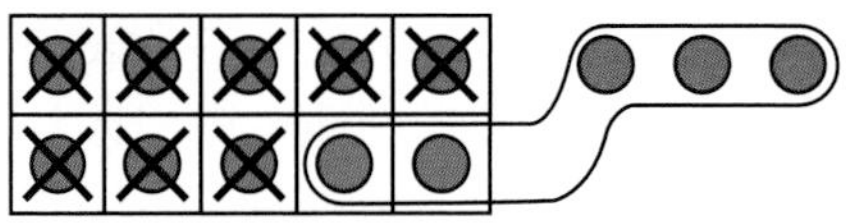

There are 5 left.
So 13 − 8 = 5.

Five penguins are still on the ice.

Think and Discuss Could you use a ten-frame to help you find 9 − 5? Why or why not?

Try It Out

Look at each ten-frame. Then find each difference.

1. 15 − 9

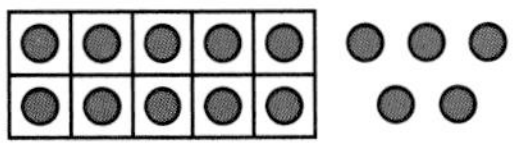

2. 12 − 8

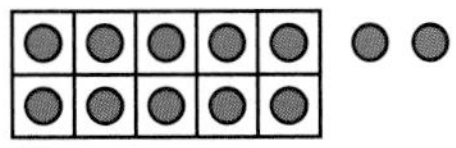

3. 14 − 6

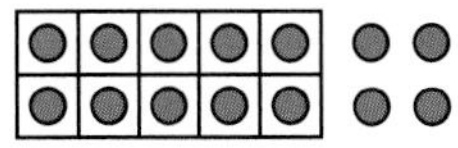

4. 18 − 9 **5.** 13 − 6 **6.** 11 − 7

7. **Explain** Draw a picture to show how you could use a ten-frame to find 16 − 9.

Practice

Subtract.

8. $\begin{array}{r} 13 \\ -\ 4 \\ \hline \end{array}$ **9.** $\begin{array}{r} 12 \\ -\ 6 \\ \hline \end{array}$ **10.** $\begin{array}{r} 8 \\ -\ 6 \\ \hline \end{array}$ **11.** $\begin{array}{r} 14 \\ -\ 7 \\ \hline \end{array}$ **12.** $\begin{array}{r} 15 \\ -\ 6 \\ \hline \end{array}$ **13.** $\begin{array}{r} 8 \\ -\ 2 \\ \hline \end{array}$

14. $\begin{array}{r} 15 \\ -\ 7 \\ \hline \end{array}$ **15.** $\begin{array}{r} 12 \\ -\ 3 \\ \hline \end{array}$ **16.** $\begin{array}{r} 14 \\ -\ 8 \\ \hline \end{array}$ **17.** $\begin{array}{r} 16 \\ -\ 8 \\ \hline \end{array}$ **18.** $\begin{array}{r} 11 \\ -\ 5 \\ \hline \end{array}$ **19.** $\begin{array}{r} 17 \\ -\ 9 \\ \hline \end{array}$

20. 10 − 6 **21.** 12 − 7 **22.** 14 − 5 **23.** 15 − 8

24. 17 − 8 **25.** 11 − 8 **26.** 13 − 7 **27.** 14 − 9

Problem Solving

28. Science Connection A king penguin must weigh 16 pounds to have enough stored fat for the winter. Suppose a penguin chick weighs 7 pounds. How many pounds must it gain to be ready for the winter?

29. There are 15 ducks in a pond. Suppose 4 ducks join them and 3 ducks fly away. How many ducks are in the pond?

▲ King penguin and chick

Review and Remember

Write the numbers in order from least to greatest.

30. 5 8 4 **31.** 67 45 31 **32.** 19 103 50

33. 95 17 58 **34.** 236 623 326 **35.** 428 691 694

For Extra Practice, see Set E, page 73.

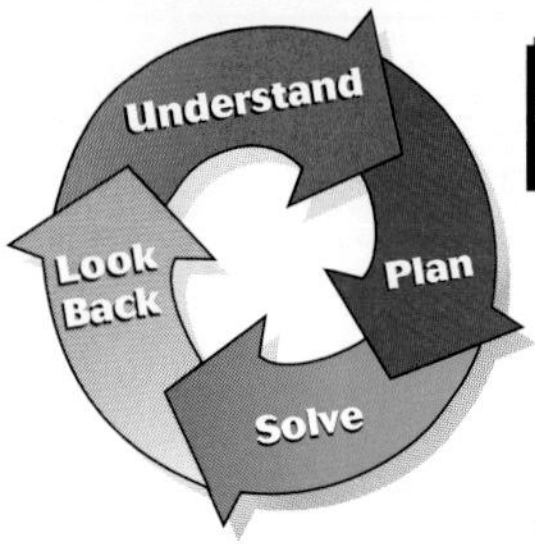

Problem Solving
Act It Out

Sometimes acting out a problem will help you solve it.

Billy, Millie, and Tillie are seals. They like to play catch. First their trainer tosses the ball to Billy. Then Billy tosses it to Millie. Millie tosses it to Tillie. Tillie tosses it back to Billy. And around it goes again and again. If Billy catches the ball first, which seal makes the twelfth catch?

UNDERSTAND

What do you need to know?

You need to know that the ball is tossed from Billy to Millie to Tillie and then back to Billy.

PLAN

How can you solve the problem?

One strategy you could use is to **act it out**. Three students can pretend to be the seals. Use the facts in the problem to follow the order of the tosses.

SOLVE

Toss a ball from person to person. Using ordinal numbers, count the order of the catches.

Tillie makes the twelfth catch.

LOOK BACK

How did acting it out help you solve the problem? What is another strategy you could use?

Using the Strategy

Use the act it out strategy to solve each problem.

1. In the picture at right, there are five seals in a line. The first seal barks 2 times. The second seal barks 4 times. The other seals each bark 2 more times than the seal before. How many times did the last seal bark?

2. Millie has 4 fish. Billy has 4 more fish than Millie. Tillie has 1 less fish than Billy. How many fish does Billy have? How many fish does Tillie have?

3. There are 8 dolphins in the big pool and no dolphins in the little pool. Two of the dolphins swim to the little pool. Later 1 dolphin swims from the little pool to the big pool. Then 1 more dolphin swims from the little pool to the big pool. How many dolphins are in each pool now?

Mixed Strategy Review

Try these or other strategies you have learned.

THERE'S ALWAYS A WAY!

- *Find a Pattern*
- *Draw a Picture*
- *Act It Out*
- *Make a List*

4. A bus that has no passengers picks up 4 people at its first stop. At its second stop, 3 people get on and 2 people get off. At its third stop, 5 people get on and 1 person gets off. At its fourth stop, no one gets on but 2 people get off. How many passengers are on the bus now?

5. Find the next three numbers in this pattern:
4, 9, 14, 19, 24, 29, ?, ?, ?

6. List all the ways you can make 25¢ using dimes, nickels, and quarters. You do not need to use all 3 types of coins.

Using Algebra

What's Missing?

You can use addition to help solve subtraction facts.

Learning About It

There are 14 prairie dogs in this family. Five of them are above ground. The rest are underground. How many are underground?

Word Bank

missing addend
difference

14 − 5 = ■

Think: 5 + ■ = 14
5 + 9 = 14 (9: missing addend)

So 14 − 5 = 9 (9: difference)

There are 9 prairie dogs underground.

Think and Discuss How does knowing 8 + 2 = 10 help you find 10 − 2?

Try It Out

Use the addition fact to find each subtraction fact.

1. 2 + ■ = 10
10 − 2 = ■
10 − 8 = ■

2. 5 + ■ = 12
12 − 5 = ■
12 − 7 = ■

3. ■ + 6 = 15
15 − 6 = ■
15 − 9 = ■

Practice

Use the addition fact to find each difference.

4. $4 + ■ = 13$	**5.** $8 + ■ = 11$	**6.** $■ + 7 = 13$
$13 - 4 = ■$	$11 - 8 = ■$	$13 - 7 = ■$
$13 - 9 = ■$	$11 - 3 = ■$	$13 - 6 = ■$

Think addition to help you find each difference.

7. $2 - 1$	**8.** $3 - 2$	**9.** $10 - 1$	**10.** $9 - 4$	**11.** $7 - 7$	**12.** $6 - 4$
13. $9 - 9$	**14.** $15 - 7$	**15.** $14 - 9$	**16.** $16 - 8$	**17.** $11 - 6$	**18.** $12 - 4$
19. $10 - 7$	**20.** $16 - 9$	**21.** $8 - 5$	**22.** $18 - 9$	**23.** $9 - 5$	**24.** $12 - 6$

Problem Solving

25. There are 9 adult prairie dogs and 8 baby prairie dogs at the city zoo. How many prairie dogs are at the zoo?

26. A prairie dog has 8 toes on its front feet. It has 10 toes on its back feet. How many more toes does it have on its back feet?

27. There are 12 prairie dogs in a field. Four guard their tunnels while the rest play. How many prairie dogs are playing?

28. There are two groups of prairie dogs standing in a field. There are 11 prairie dogs in one group. There are 9 prairie dogs in the other group. How many more prairie dogs are in the larger group?

Science Connection
Prairie dogs live in the grasslands of North America. They dig large underground homes called burrows.

www.sbgmath.com

Review and Remember

Add or subtract.

29. $4 + 9$	**30.** $9 - 1$	**31.** $8 - 3$	**32.** $5 + 6$	**33.** $7 + 6$
34. $12 - 3$	**35.** $14 - 7$	**36.** $10 - 4$	**37.** $18 - 9$	**38.** $8 + 5$

For Extra Practice, see Set F, page 74.

Time for a Checkup

You can use addition to check subtraction.

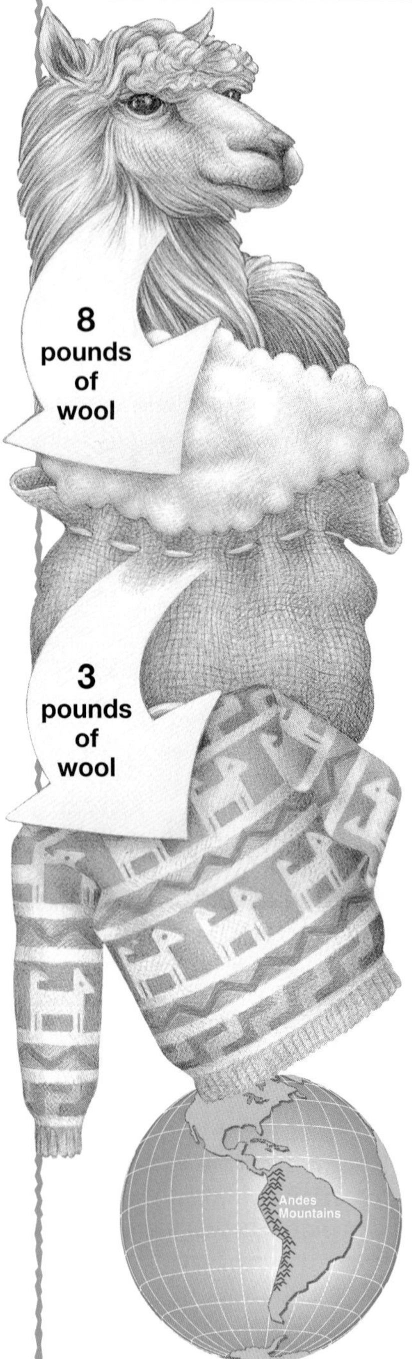

▲ The alpaca is related to the camel. It lives in the Andes Mountains in South America. Alpacas are very good at climbing steep hills and mountains.

Learning About It

Pedro and his father have sheared 8 pounds of wool from an alpaca. So far 3 pounds of wool have been used to make a sweater. How many pounds of wool are left?

$8 - 3 = ■$
$8 - 3 = 5$

Five pounds of wool are left.

Addition and subtraction are opposite operations, so you can use addition to check subtraction.

$$\begin{array}{r} 8 \\ -\ 3 \\ \hline 5 \end{array} \quad \text{same} \quad \begin{array}{r} 5 \\ +\ 3 \\ \hline 8 \end{array}$$

Since $5 + 3 = 8$, you know that $8 - 3 = 5$.

More Examples

A. $$\begin{array}{r} 6 \\ -\ 2 \\ \hline 4 \end{array} \quad \text{same} \quad \begin{array}{r} 4 \\ +\ 2 \\ \hline 6 \end{array}$$

B. $$\begin{array}{r} 15 \\ -\ 9 \\ \hline 6 \end{array} \quad \text{same} \quad \begin{array}{r} 6 \\ +\ 9 \\ \hline 15 \end{array}$$

Think and Discuss What addition sentence could you use to check that $13 - 6 = 7$?

Try It Out

Write an addition sentence to check each subtraction sentence.

1. $12 - 8 = 4$
■ + ■ = 12

2. $14 - 9 = 5$
■ + ■ = 14

3. $10 - 3 = 7$
■ + ■ = 10

Practice

Subtract. Use addition to check your answer.

4. $9 - 2$ **5.** $6 - 5$ **6.** $6 - 3$ **7.** $8 - 0$ **8.** $10 - 6$ **9.** $11 - 7$

10. $15 - 6$ **11.** $17 - 9$ **12.** $12 - 3$ **13.** $8 - 6$ **14.** $4 - 2$ **15.** $7 - 3$

Problem Solving

16. Luisa sheared 9 pounds of wool from one alpaca and 8 pounds of wool from another. How many pounds did she shear in all?

17. Social Studies Connection Many Latin American clothes and blankets are made from alpaca wool. Often the wool is dyed different colors. Suppose a weaver makes 9 blankets to sell at the market. If 5 are sold, how many are left?

Review and Remember

Write the value of the underlined digit.

18. $6\underline{4}2$ **19.** $35\underline{9}$ **20.** $2,\underline{4}10$ **21.** $\underline{9},005$ **22.** $\underline{1}4,028$

Project Link

Now make your poster. Draw a picture of your habitat on heavy paper. Paste your animal pictures onto it.

Then answer these questions.

- How many of each animal are on your poster?
- How many animals do you have altogether on your poster?
- What kind of animal do you have the most pictures of?
- How many more pictures of that animal do you have than of the other animals?

A Family of Facts

You can use counters to discover addition and subtraction facts that are related.

Word Bank

fact family

Learning About It

Work with your partner.

What You Need

For each pair:
18 two-color counters

Step 1 Use counters to show how the rabbits are grouped.

Write two addition sentences to show how many rabbits there are in all. Write two subtraction sentences to show how you could separate the rabbits into the two groups.

What number sentences did you write?

▶ When addition and subtraction sentences all use the same numbers, they make a **fact family.**

5, 3, and 8 make a fact family.

5 + 3 = 8	**8 − 5 = 3**
3 + 5 = 8	**8 − 3 = 5**

Step 2 Use 8 counters. Show the fact family that uses the numbers 6, 2, and 8. Then write the addition and subtraction sentences for the fact family.

Step 3 Now make other fact families, using only 8 counters. Write the addition and subtraction sentences for each fact family.

Think and Discuss Look at all the fact families you wrote. Do they all have 2 addition and 2 subtraction sentences? Why or why not?

Practice

1. Can 5, 8, and 12 make a fact family? Explain why or why not.

2. How does knowing the addition facts in a fact family help you find the subtraction facts?

3. Ricky used 9, 9, and 18 to make a fact family. How many addition and subtraction sentences can he make?

4. Which of the pictures below could be used to show the fact family for 2, 3, and 5?

a. 

b. 

c. 

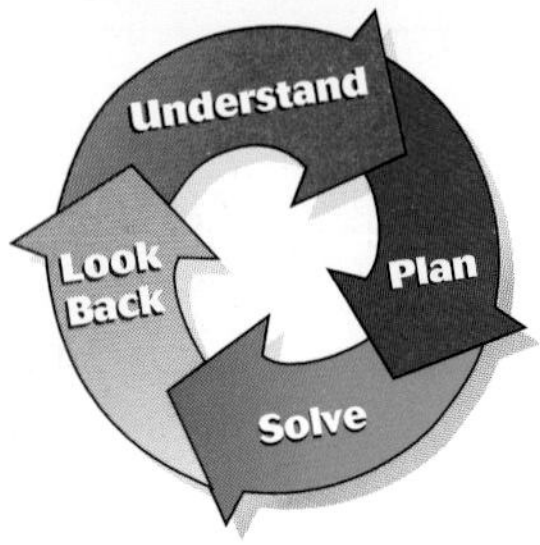

Problem Solving
Using Data From a Graph

Using data from a bar graph can help you solve problems.

The bar graph at the right shows the number of animals Lucy's class saw on their trip to the zoo. How many more turtles than lizards did the class see?

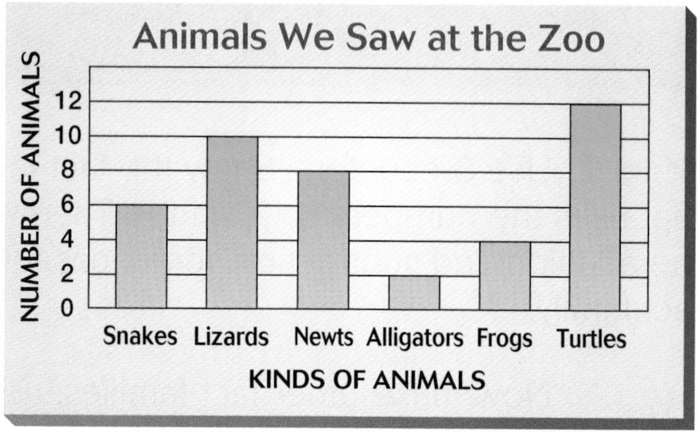

UNDERSTAND

What do you need to know?

You need to know that you can use the numbers on the side of the graph and the height of the bars to tell how many of each kind of animal the class saw.

PLAN

How can you solve the problem?

You can use the bar graph to compare how many turtles and how many lizards the class saw.

Science Connection

The five animals shown on these pages all have backbones. The newt and the frog are amphibians, which have smooth, wet skin. The three other animals are reptiles. A reptile's body is dry and is covered with scales or plates.

SOLVE

The class saw 12 turtles and 10 lizards.

12 − 10 = 2 turtles

The class saw 2 more turtles than lizards.

LOOK BACK

How many turtles and lizards did the class see altogether?

▲ Red-bellied turtle

Show What You Learned

Use the graph on page 68 to help you solve these problems.

Alpine newt

1. Which kind of animal did the class see the least on their trip to the zoo?

2. Which kind of animal did the class see the most?

3. How many lizards and snakes did the class see altogether?

4. How many more lizards than snakes did the class see?

5. How many turtles and frogs did the class see altogether?

6. How many more turtles than frogs did the class see?

7. List the animals the class saw in order from the least animals seen to the most animals seen.

8. What is the total number of animals the class saw on their trip to the zoo?

9. **Analyze** Sarah said she saw two large snakes, a green sea turtle and a painted turtle. Can you tell for certain if this is true by looking at the graph? Tell why or why not.

10. **Analyze** Henry said he saw a bullfrog, a grass frog, a toad frog, and a red-eyed tree frog. Look at the graph. Could this be true? Tell why or why not.

11. **Explain** Which animals did the class see more of: frogs and newts or turtles and snakes? Explain how you know.

12. **Create Your Own** Write a problem using the information in the bar graph. Then give your problem to a classmate to solve.

Harlequin flying tree frog

Boa constrictor

American alligator

Checkpoint

Subtraction

Subtract. (pages 56–59)

1. $\begin{array}{r} 4 \\ -\ 2 \\ \hline \end{array}$	**2.** $\begin{array}{r} 3 \\ -\ 0 \\ \hline \end{array}$	**3.** $\begin{array}{r} 6 \\ -\ 4 \\ \hline \end{array}$	**4.** $\begin{array}{r} 10 \\ -\ 5 \\ \hline \end{array}$	**5.** $\begin{array}{r} 9 \\ -\ 6 \\ \hline \end{array}$
6. $\begin{array}{r} 9 \\ -\ 1 \\ \hline \end{array}$	**7.** $\begin{array}{r} 5 \\ -\ 4 \\ \hline \end{array}$	**8.** $\begin{array}{r} 8 \\ -\ 8 \\ \hline \end{array}$	**9.** $\begin{array}{r} 12 \\ -\ 6 \\ \hline \end{array}$	**10.** $\begin{array}{r} 13 \\ -\ 8 \\ \hline \end{array}$
11. $\begin{array}{r} 14 \\ -\ 7 \\ \hline \end{array}$	**12.** $\begin{array}{r} 7 \\ -\ 6 \\ \hline \end{array}$	**13.** $\begin{array}{r} 11 \\ -\ 4 \\ \hline \end{array}$	**14.** $\begin{array}{r} 18 \\ -\ 9 \\ \hline \end{array}$	**15.** $\begin{array}{r} 16 \\ -\ 9 \\ \hline \end{array}$
16. $\begin{array}{r} 9 \\ -\ 7 \\ \hline \end{array}$	**17.** $\begin{array}{r} 13 \\ -\ 5 \\ \hline \end{array}$	**18.** $\begin{array}{r} 10 \\ -\ 3 \\ \hline \end{array}$	**19.** $\begin{array}{r} 15 \\ -\ 7 \\ \hline \end{array}$	**20.** $\begin{array}{r} 17 \\ -\ 9 \\ \hline \end{array}$

Using Algebra **Find the missing number.** (pages 62–63)

21. 3 + ■ = 7	**22.** ■ + 4 = 10	**23.** 3 + ■ = 9
24. 8 + ■ = 12	**25.** ■ + 2 = 10	**26.** 9 + ■ = 14
27. ■ + 9 = 11	**28.** 6 + ■ = 12	**29.** ■ + 4 = 11

Subtract. Use addition to check your answer.
(pages 64–65)

30. 7 − 1 = ■ 6 + 1 = ■	**31.** 5 − 5 = ■ 0 + 5 = ■	**32.** 13 − 7 = ■ 6 + 7 = ■
33. 9 − 4 = ■ 5 + 4 = ■	**34.** 8 − 5 = ■ 3 + 5 = ■	**35.** 12 − 9 = ■ 3 + 9 = ■

Write the fact family for each group of numbers.
(pages 66–67)

36. 2, 3, 5	**37.** 1, 4, 5	**38.** 6, 7, 13
39. 4, 8, 12	**40.** 7, 1, 8	**41.** 2, 9, 11

Problem Solving

42. Ronnie needs to buy a dog leash. The extra-long leash can unwind to 12 feet. The long leash can unwind to 9 feet. How much longer is the extra-long leash?

43. There are 14 monkeys playing in a tree. If 8 jump out, how many monkeys are left in the tree?

44. Tony has \$5. Erika has \$1. Angelo has \$3. How much more do they need to buy a \$10 birthday gift for a friend?

45. **Analyze** Andy is making a collage. He has pictures of 3 cats, 9 dogs, and 4 ducks. How many more pictures of dogs does Andy have than of cats and ducks together?

What do you think?
Does changing the order in which you subtract numbers change the answer?

Journal Idea Write a word problem that uses the numbers 12, 3, and 9.

Project Wrap-Up

Home Sweet Home

Display all the posters. Then meet with students who chose the same habitat that you did.

- Count and add to find the total number of animals on your group's posters.
- Compare your number of animals with another group's number. Subtract to find out how many more or fewer animals your habitat has.

Extra Practice

Set A (pages 44–47)

Add.

1. $7 + 3$ **2.** $6 + 7$ **3.** $4 + 9$ **4.** $2 + 8$ **5.** $8 + 3$ **6.** $6 + 2$

7. Jill has 4 black cats and Susan has 2 gray cats and 1 dog. How many cats do they have in all?

8. One squirrel gathered 8 acorns. Another squirrel gathered 5 acorns. How many acorns did they gather altogether?

Set B (pages 48–49)

Add.

1. $9 + 0$ **2.** $0 + 4$ **3.** $2 + 0$ **4.** $1 + 0$ **5.** $7 + 0$ **6.** $0 + 7$

7. $5 + 9$
$9 + 5$

8. $9 + 7$
$7 + 9$

9. $6 + 4$
$4 + 6$

10. $3 + 5$
$5 + 3$

Set C (pages 50–51)

Add.

1. $3 + 8 + 6$ **2.** $6 + 4 + 1$ **3.** $4 + 4 + 4$ **4.** $9 + 8 + 1$ **5.** $9 + 0 + 6$ **6.** $7 + 3 + 0$

7. $4 + 5 + 2$ **8.** $6 + 3 + 5$ **9.** $9 + 3 + 4$

10. $7 + 2 + 4$ **11.** $5 + 5 + 1$ **12.** $9 + 1 + 8$

13. Bart has 3 bird cages. One holds 4 birds, another holds 1 bird, and the third holds 9 birds. How many birds can Bart's cages hold?

14. Beatriz has a collection of stuffed animals. She has 3 bears, 1 dolphin, and 2 dogs. How many stuffed animals does she have?

Extra Practice

Set D (pages 56–57)

Subtract.

1. $8 - 1$ **2.** $6 - 3$ **3.** $12 - 8$ **4.** $7 - 6$ **5.** $9 - 9$ **6.** $11 - 9$

7. $12 - 3$ **8.** $9 - 7$ **9.** $7 - 2$ **10.** $10 - 6$ **11.** $11 - 5$ **12.** $14 - 6$

13. 9 − 1 **14.** 8 − 6 **15.** 11 − 8 **16.** 13 − 5

17. Science Connection A skink is a kind of lizard. Suppose a skink has a body 5 inches long and a tail 6 inches long. How much longer is its tail than its body?

18. Erik counted 12 cows, 6 horses, 4 sheep, and 5 calves. How many more cows did he count than calves?

Set E (pages 58-59)

Subtract.

1. $15 - 8$ **2.** $12 - 7$ **3.** $16 - 7$ **4.** $14 - 9$ **5.** $13 - 9$ **6.** $12 - 4$

7. $10 - 7$ **8.** $11 - 4$ **9.** $9 - 5$ **10.** $16 - 9$ **11.** $10 - 1$ **12.** $17 - 8$

13. 12 − 9 **14.** 15 − 6 **15.** 18 − 9 **16.** 13 − 8

17. Penguins huddle close together to keep warm in very cold weather. There are 12 penguins in one group and 5 penguins in another group. How many more penguins are in the first group?

18. Andy counts 11 geese flying in the sky. He sees 7 of the geese land in a pond. The rest of the geese land on a grassy hill. How many geese are on the grassy hill?

Extra Practice

Set F (pages 62–63)

Use the addition fact to find each difference.

1. 6 + 3 = ■
9 − 6 = ■
9 − 3 = ■

2. 8 + 6 = ■
14 − 6 = ■
14 − 8 = ■

3. 7 + 8 = ■
15 − 8 = ■
15 − 7 = ■

4. 6 + 9 = ■
15 − 6 = ■
15 − 9 = ■

5. 4 + 7 = ■
11 − 7 = ■
11 − 4 = ■

6. 5 + 9 = ■
14 − 5 = ■
14 − 9 = ■

7. A zoo tour bus can hold 10 people. If 7 people are already on the bus, how many more people can get on?

8. Serena left a bag of 15 dog biscuits on the floor. Her dog found the bag and ate 7 biscuits. How many biscuits are left?

Set G (pages 64–65)

Subtract. Use addition to check your answers.

1. $\begin{array}{r} 10 \\ -\ 8 \\ \hline \end{array}$ **2.** $\begin{array}{r} 7 \\ -\ 5 \\ \hline \end{array}$ **3.** $\begin{array}{r} 12 \\ -\ 6 \\ \hline \end{array}$ **4.** $\begin{array}{r} 15 \\ -\ 7 \\ \hline \end{array}$ **5.** $\begin{array}{r} 11 \\ -\ 2 \\ \hline \end{array}$ **6.** $\begin{array}{r} 11 \\ -\ 3 \\ \hline \end{array}$

7. $\begin{array}{r} 6 \\ -\ 6 \\ \hline \end{array}$ **8.** $\begin{array}{r} 10 \\ -\ 3 \\ \hline \end{array}$ **9.** $\begin{array}{r} 8 \\ -\ 4 \\ \hline \end{array}$ **10.** $\begin{array}{r} 8 \\ -\ 0 \\ \hline \end{array}$ **11.** $\begin{array}{r} 14 \\ -\ 5 \\ \hline \end{array}$ **12.** $\begin{array}{r} 16 \\ -\ 8 \\ \hline \end{array}$

13. 13 − 4 **14.** 3 − 1 **15.** 9 − 4 **16.** 14 − 7

17. 5 − 0 **18.** 15 − 9 **19.** 11 − 6 **20.** 17 − 9

21. 10 − 4 **22.** 7 − 7 **23.** 16 − 5 **24.** 10 − 7

25. Felicia bought 3 lion posters and 2 dolphin posters. Marta bought 6 zebra posters. How many more posters did Marta buy than Felicia?

26. One week Anita's horse ate 9 carrots and 7 apples. How many more carrots than apples did her horse eat?

Chapter Test

Add.

1. $\begin{array}{r} 4 \\ +\ 3 \\ \hline \end{array}$ **2.** $\begin{array}{r} 2 \\ +\ 9 \\ \hline \end{array}$ **3.** $\begin{array}{r} 7 \\ +\ 7 \\ \hline \end{array}$ **4.** $\begin{array}{r} 5 \\ +\ 0 \\ \hline \end{array}$ **5.** $\begin{array}{r} 9 \\ +\ 4 \\ \hline \end{array}$

6. $5 + 5 + 4$ **7.** $3 + 5 + 2$ **8.** $9 + 6 + 1$

Subtract.

9. $\begin{array}{r} 8 \\ -\ 3 \\ \hline \end{array}$ **10.** $\begin{array}{r} 12 \\ -\ 5 \\ \hline \end{array}$ **11.** $\begin{array}{r} 13 \\ -\ 7 \\ \hline \end{array}$ **12.** $\begin{array}{r} 6 \\ -\ 5 \\ \hline \end{array}$ **13.** $\begin{array}{r} 15 \\ -\ 9 \\ \hline \end{array}$

14. $16 - 8$ **15.** $12 - 3$ **16.** $14 - 5$

Find each missing addend.

17. $7 + ■ = 13$ **18.** $2 + ■ = 8$ **19.** $4 + ■ = 4$ **20.** $8 + ■ = 12$

Write a fact family for each group of numbers.

21. 2, 7, 9 **22.** 6, 8, 14 **23.** 3, 1, 4

Solve.

24. A pet store has 8 puppies, 6 rabbits, and 4 kittens. How many puppies and kittens are there in all?

25. Tom is walking his neighbors' dogs. He picks up 5 dogs. Then he picks up 2 more dogs. He takes 3 dogs home. Then he picks up 1 more dog. How many dogs does Tom have now?

Self-Check Look back at Exercises 21–23. Did you write all four facts in each fact family?

Performance Assessment

Show What You Know About Addition and Subtraction

What You Need

18 two-color counters
paper bag

1. Put 18 two-color counters in a bag. Shake some of the counters out on a table. How many yellow counters are showing? How many red counters are showing?

   a. Write as many addition sentences as you can to show how many red and yellow counters there are.

   b. Write subtraction sentences to show how many counters are left if you take away all of the red counters or all of the yellow counters.

   c. Put the counters back in the bag and repeat the activity two more times.

2. Bella wants to buy a toy for each of her 2 brothers. She has $17. Use the chart to answer the questions below. Use counters, pictures, numbers, or words to show your work.

   a. What could Bella buy for each brother? How much would she spend on the toys?

   b. Suppose Bella wanted to buy something for herself, too. What could she buy? How much money would she spend on all the toys she buys?

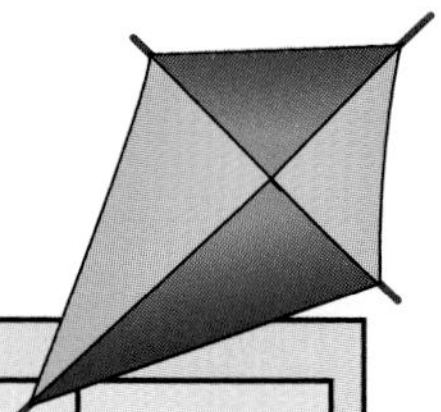

Toy	Price
Race car	$5
Kite	$8
Rubber ball	$1
Action doll	$4
Lizard robot	$6
Water squirter	$7

Self-Check

For Question 1a, did you write two addition sentences?

For Question 2a, did you add the prices of the toys correctly?

Using Algebra

Extension

Track It Down!

These animals have made puzzles with their tracks. Can you figure out what number each track stands for?

1. 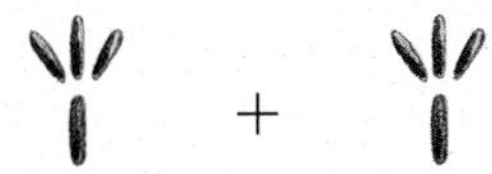 = 4

2. 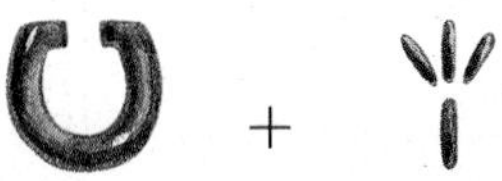 = 5

3. 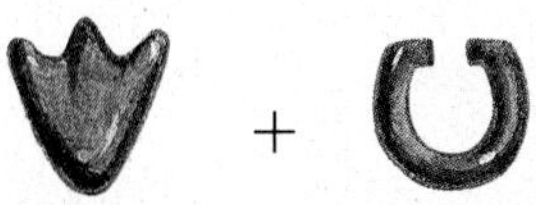 = 9

4. 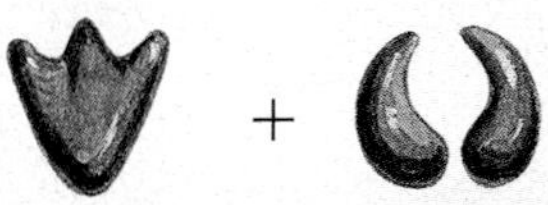 = 11

5. 

6. What is the sum of these tracks?

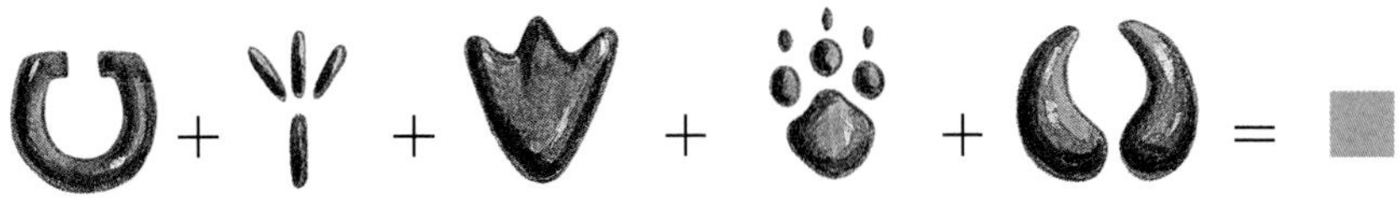

Chapter 3

Addition and Subtraction With Greater Numbers

Chapter Theme: TRAVEL

Career Spotlight Meet Keith Jardin, a wilderness guide. He teaches people to safely paddle on rafts as he guides trips along America's rivers.

Guides can use addition and subtraction to keep track of how many riders they have. Look at the example below.

Reserved

$$\begin{array}{r} 664 \\ 1{,}295 \\ +\ 1{,}725 \\ \hline 3{,}684 \end{array}$$

Cancelled

412

Actual Riders

$$\begin{array}{r} 3{,}684 \\ -\ 412 \\ \hline 3{,}272 \end{array}$$

Chapter Project

Keep a Travel Log

In this chapter, a Math Mobile will take you on trips to exciting places. You can invent a Math Mobile of your own. And you can make a Travel Log, to keep track of

- the places you will go.
- the number of miles you travel.
- the number of people who go with you.

As you work on your Travel Log, you'll have a chance to show what you are learning about addition and subtraction.

Pro-tec
Pro-tec
OARS
Pro-tec
OARS

Get a Head Start

Sometimes you can solve problems in your head.

Learning About It

Your class is going on a trip in the Math Mobile! There are 20 seats upstairs and 30 seats downstairs. How many seats are on the Math Mobile?

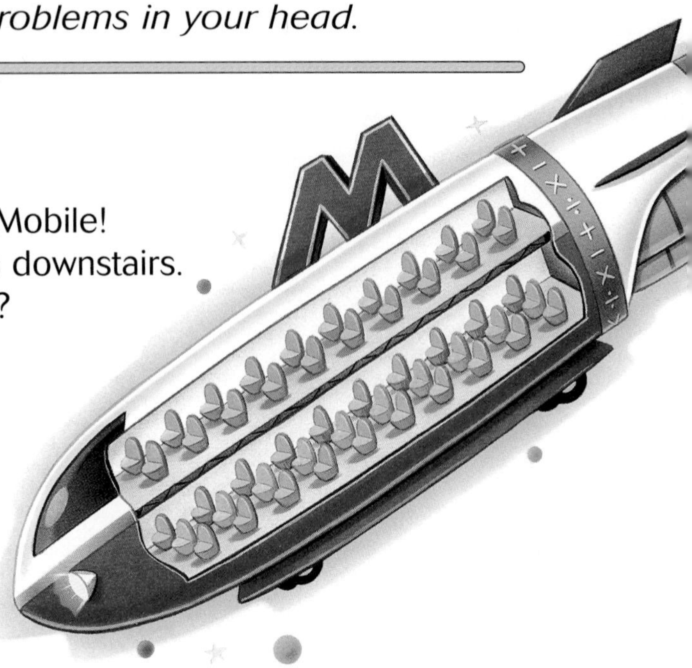

20 + 30 = ■

You can use mental math to find the sum. Use addition facts you know.

Think: $\begin{array}{r} 2 \\ +\ 3 \\ \hline 5 \end{array}$ So $\begin{array}{r} 2\text{ tens} \\ +\ 3\text{ tens} \\ \hline 5\text{ tens} \end{array}$ So $\begin{array}{r} 20 \\ +\ 30 \\ \hline 50 \end{array}$

There are 50 seats on the Math Mobile.

If 40 seats on the Math Mobile are blue and the rest are green, how many seats are green?

50 − 40 = ■

You can use mental math to find the difference. Use subtraction facts you know.

Think: $\begin{array}{r} 5 \\ -\ 4 \\ \hline 1 \end{array}$ So $\begin{array}{r} 5\text{ tens} \\ -\ 4\text{ tens} \\ \hline 1\text{ ten} \end{array}$ So $\begin{array}{r} 50 \\ -\ 40 \\ \hline 10 \end{array}$

There are 10 green seats.

More Examples

A. $\begin{array}{r} 500 \\ +\ 300 \\ \hline 800 \end{array}$ **B.** $\begin{array}{r} 900 \\ -\ 200 \\ \hline 700 \end{array}$ **C.** $\begin{array}{r} 3{,}000 \\ +\ 4{,}000 \\ \hline 7{,}000 \end{array}$ **D.** $\begin{array}{r} 8{,}000 \\ -\ 7{,}000 \\ \hline 1{,}000 \end{array}$

Think and Discuss Use 7 + 3 = 10 and mental math to find 70 + 30. Explain your thinking.

Try It Out

Use mental math to find each sum.

1. 4 + 2   **2.** 40 + 20   **3.** 400 + 200   **4.** 4,000 + 2,000

Practice

Find each sum or difference.

5. 60 + 50   **6.** 80 − 20   **7.** 100 + 700   **8.** 700 − 500   **9.** 6,000 − 2,000

10. 500 + 0   **11.** 700 + 600   **12.** 120 − 80   **13.** 900 − 600   **14.** 9,000 + 8,000

15. 600 + 400   **16.** 700 − 200   **17.** 900 + 400   **18.** 8,000 + 1,000   **19.** 5,000 − 3,000

Using Algebra **Complete each pattern.**

20. 20, 30, 40, ■, ■, ■

21. 2, 12, 22, ■, ■, ■

22. 103, 203, 303, ■, ■, ■

23. 80, 70, ■, ■, 40, ■

24. 540, ■, ■, 240, ■, 40

25. 215, ■, ■, ■, 615, 715

Problem Solving

26. Each television on the Math Mobile has 200 regular channels and 400 cable channels. How many channels are there in all?

27. Mega computers on the Math Mobile have 900 games. Mini computers only have 700 games. How many more games are there on the Mega computer?

Review and Remember

Round each number to the nearest ten.

28. 59   **29.** 31   **30.** 65   **31.** 87

For Extra Practice, see Set A, page 118.

That's About It

Rounding can help you estimate greater sums.

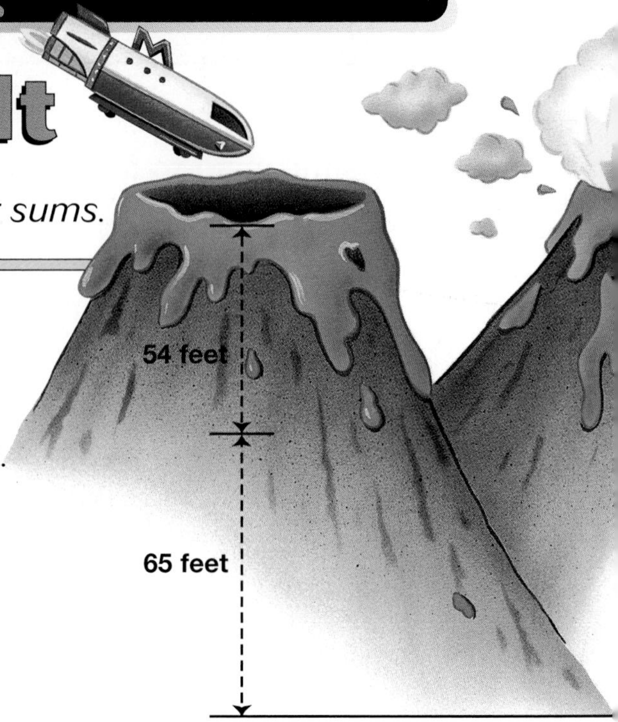

Learning About It

The Math Mobile's first stop is inside a volcano! The Math Mobile goes down 54 feet. Then it goes down 65 feet more. About how many feet does it go down in all?

Since you want to know *about* how many feet, you do not need an exact answer. You can round to **estimate** the sum.

Round to the nearest ten.

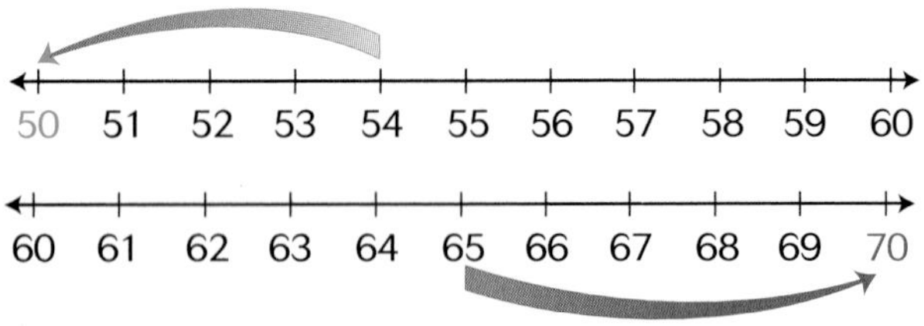

Add the rounded numbers.

54	rounds to	50
+ 65	rounds to	+ 70
		120

The Math Mobile goes down *about* 120 feet.

You can estimate the sum of three-digit numbers the same way.

Estimate 450 + 326.

Round to the nearest hundred.

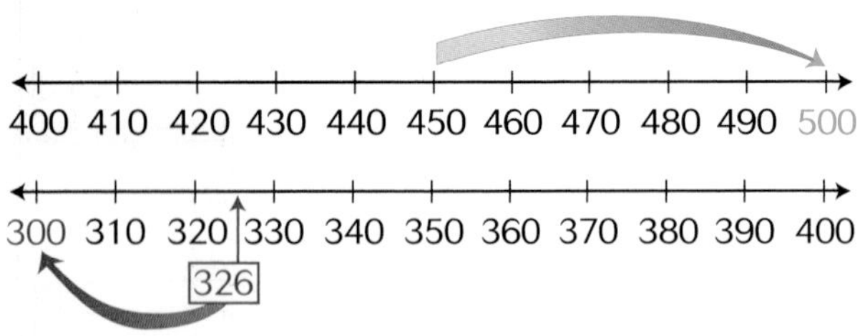

Add the rounded numbers.

450	rounds to	500
+ 326	rounds to	+ 300
		800

450 + 326 is *about* 800.

Think and Discuss Would you round \$3.54 up to \$4.00 or down to \$3.00? Explain how you know.

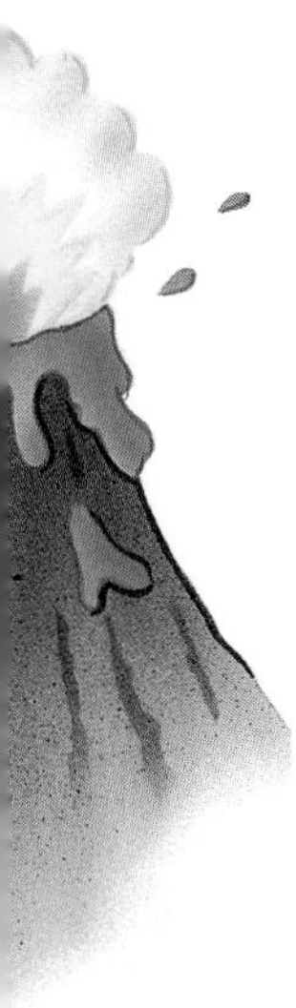

Try It Out

Estimate by rounding to the nearest ten.

1. 62 + 38 **2.** 45 + 72 **3.** 96 + 28 **4.** 74 + 76

5. 29 + 53 **6.** 58 + 17 **7.** 40 + 68 **8.** 21 + 93

Estimate by rounding to the nearest hundred or dollar.

9. 421 + 683 **10.** \$9.85 + \$3.12 **11.** 513 + 891 **12.** \$4.95 + \$7.86

Practice

Estimate by rounding to the nearest ten.

13. 57 + 36 **14.** 24 + 37 **15.** 51 + 65 **16.** 98 + 21 **17.** 33 + 22

Estimate by rounding to the nearest hundred or dollar.

18. 186 + 321 **19.** 495 + 384 **20.** \$2.06 + 9.18 **21.** 715 + 850 **22.** 521 + 649

23. \$4.81 + 2.53 **24.** 690 + 280 **25.** 718 + 531 **26.** \$9.27 + 4.63 **27.** 361 + 417

Problem Solving

28. The volcano was hot! The Math Mobile made 425 ice cubes. Then it made 861 ice cubes. About how many ice cubes did it make?

29. Andy found 2 lava rocks near the volcano. Together they weighed 100 pounds. One rock weighed 40 pounds. How much did the other rock weigh?

Social Studies Connection
Kilauea is a volcano in Hawaii. Visitors can see lava flow from it!

Using Algebra

Review and Remember

Complete each pattern.

30. 4, 5, 6, ■, ■, ■

31. 6, 8, ■, ■, ■,16

32. 420 ■, ■, 720, ■ , 920

33. 135, 140, ■, ■,155, ■

For Extra Practice, see Set B, page 118.

Developing Skills for Problem Solving

First read for understanding and then focus on whether you need an exact answer or an estimate.

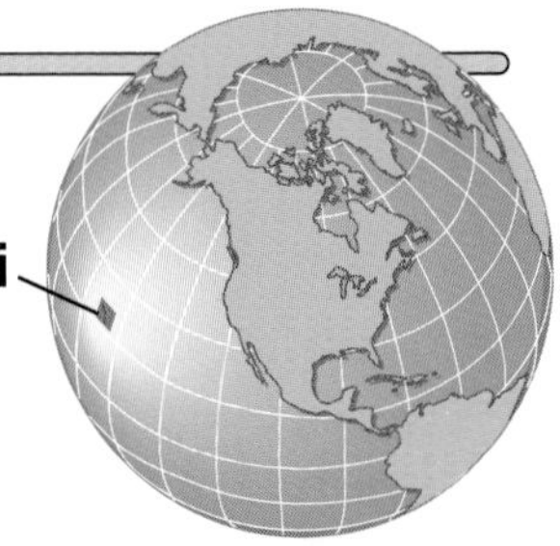

Read for Understanding

The Math Mobile has landed in Hawaii, a state known for its friendly people and tasty pineapples. Suppose a restaurant there needs 100 pineapples for a party. The restaurant only has the 2 crates of pineapples shown.

1. How many pineapples does the restaurant need?
2. How many pineapples are in each crate?

▲ **Social Studies Connection**
Hawaii is a group of islands. It became the fiftieth state in 1959. Almost all the pineapples grown in the United States come from Hawaii.

Think and Discuss

MATH FOCUS

Deciding When to Estimate
Sometimes all you need to solve a problem is an estimate. If the question asks "about how many" or "are there enough", often you just need to find an estimate.

Reread the paragraph at the top of the page.

3. Would you estimate or find an exact answer to find *about* how many pineapples the restaurant has?
4. Does the restaurant have enough pineapples for the party? Can you estimate to solve the problem? Why or why not?
5. Why is it sometimes helpful to be able to estimate instead of finding an exact answer?

Show What You Learned

Answer each question. Give a reason for your choice.

Alani wants to make 4 flower necklaces, called leis. She uses 48 flowers for each lei.

1. How many leis is Alani making?
   a. 48
   b. 4
   c. 220

2. Which of the following is true?
   a. 100 flowers is enough for 2 leis.
   b. 100 flowers is enough for 3 leis.
   c. 100 flowers is enough for 4 leis.

3. Which number sentence should you use to estimate how many flowers Alani needs for 4 leis?
   a. 48 + 48 + 48 + 48 = ■
   b. 50 + 50 + 50 + 50 = ■
   c. 48 + 4 = ■

4. Which number sentence should you use to find *exactly* how many flowers Alani needs for 4 leis?
   a. 48 + 48 + 48 + 48 = ■
   b. 50 + 50 + 50 + 50 = ■
   c. 48 + 4 = ■

Nick hiked 2 miles alongside a waterfall. It took him 124 minutes to hike up and 105 minutes to hike down. About how long did Nick hike?

5. What are you asked to find?
   a. the exact time it took to hike up and down
   b. about how long it took to hike up and down
   c. how much longer it took to hike up than to hike down

6. Which do you need to know?
   a. the distance of the hike
   b. the name of the waterfall
   c. the number of minutes it took Nick to hike up the waterfall

7. **Explain** Do you need to find an exact answer or an estimate to solve the problem?

Lots of Blocks

You can use base-ten blocks to add numbers.

Learning About It

Work with your group.

Use base-ten blocks to add 356 + 67.

What You Need

For each group:
base-ten blocks

Step 1 Show 356 and 67 with hundreds, tens, and ones blocks.

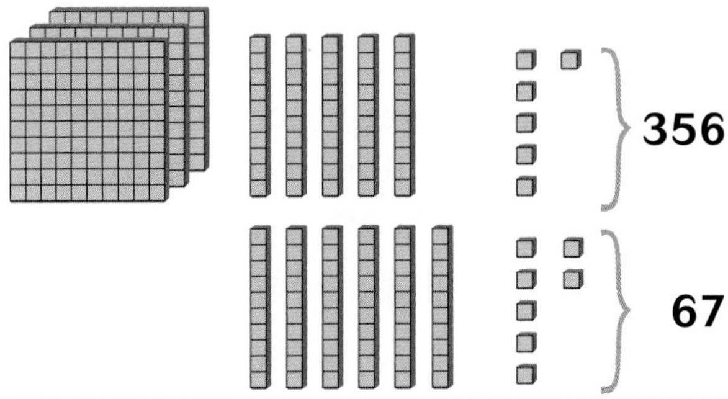

Step 2 Look at the ones. Regroup 10 ones as 1 ten.

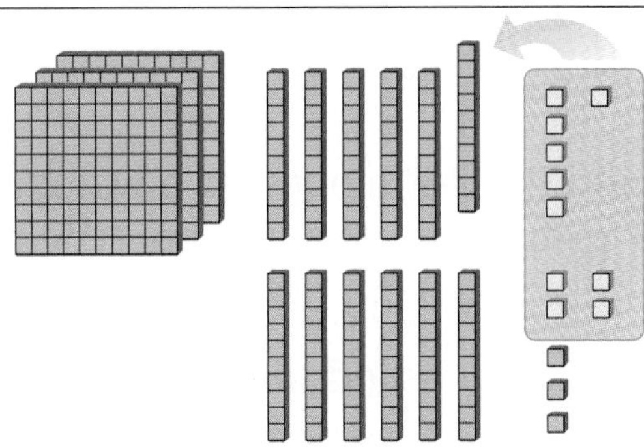

Step 3 Look at the tens. Regroup 10 tens as 1 hundred.

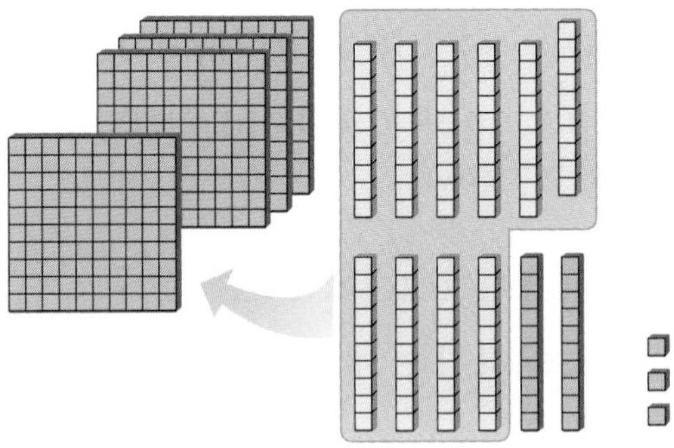

Step 4 Look at the hundreds. There are not enough hundreds to regroup.

Count the blocks you have. What is the sum of 356 + 67?

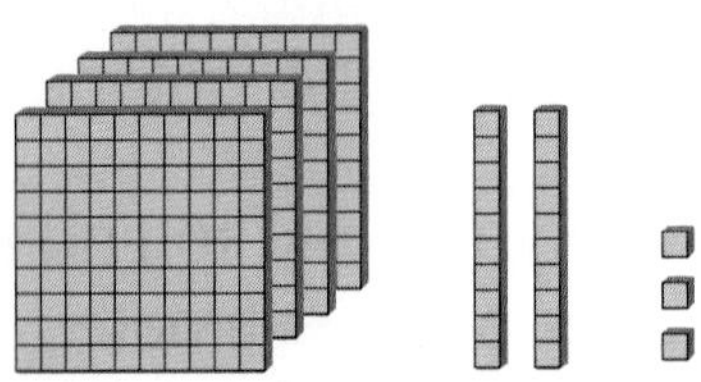

Step 5 Record your work in a chart like this.

Addition Sentence	Did I regroup 10 ones for 1 ten?	Did I regroup 10 tens for 1 hundred?	Did I regroup 10 hundreds for 1 thousand?
356 + 67 = 423	yes	yes	no

Step 6 Repeat Steps 1 to 5 four or more times. Take turns picking different numbers each time. Regroup when you can.

Think and Discuss How can you know just by looking at an exercise whether or not you need to regroup?

Practice

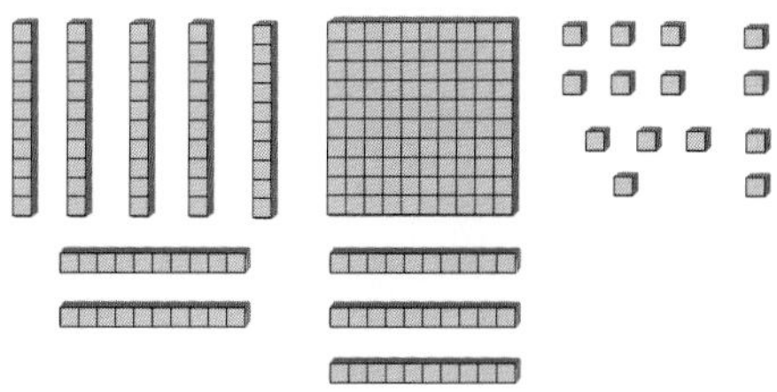

1. Ann and Sal's blocks looked like this after they put them together. What regrouping can they do?

2. Manolo looked at the problem 347 + 158. He said he needs to regroup 10 tens for 1 hundred. Is he right? Explain your answer.

3. Karen and Teri showed the numbers 621 and 238 with blocks. Will they need to regroup when they add their numbers together? Explain your answer.

Step by Step

Use what you know about regrouping to help you add two- and three-digit numbers.

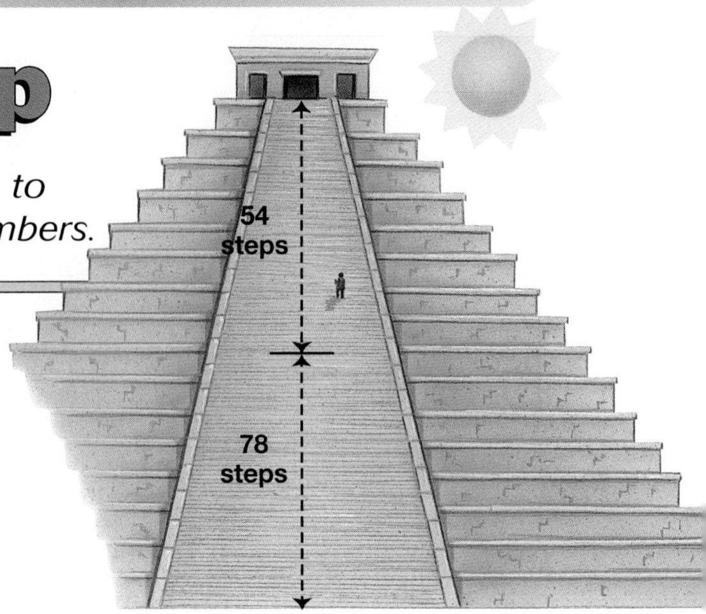

Learning About It

OLÉ! The Math Mobile is at a Maya pyramid. You climb 78 steps and stop. Then you climb 54 steps to get to the top. How many steps did you climb?

78 + 54 = ■

Social Studies Connection
The Maya people lived hundreds of years ago in Mexico, Guatemala, and Honduras. They built stone pyramids that are still standing today.

Estimate first.

$$\begin{array}{r} 78 \\ +\ 54 \\ \hline \end{array} \quad \text{rounds to} \quad \begin{array}{r} 80 \\ +\ 50 \\ \hline 130 \end{array}$$

Then add to find the exact answer.

Step 1
Add ones.
8 + 4 = 12 ones
Regroup 12 ones as 1 ten 2 ones.

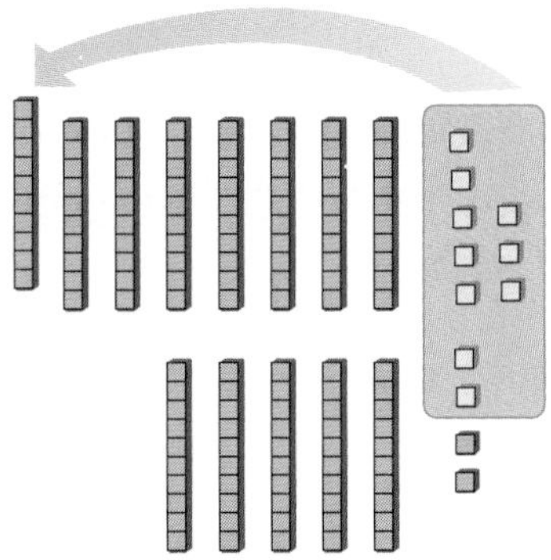

$$\begin{array}{r} {}^{1}\ \ \\ 78 \\ +\ 54 \\ \hline 2 \end{array}$$

12 ones

Step 2
Add tens.
1 + 7 + 5 = 13 tens
Regroup 13 tens as 1 hundred 3 tens.

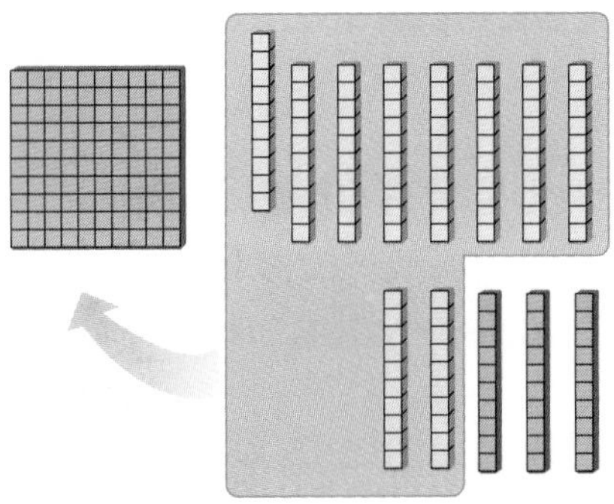

$$\begin{array}{r} {}^{1}\ \ \\ 78 \\ +\ 54 \\ \hline 132 \end{array}$$

13 tens

You climbed 132 steps in all.

Look at the estimate of 130. Is 132 a reasonable answer?

Connecting Ideas

Adding three-digit numbers is like adding two-digit numbers, only now you can regroup hundreds.

Find the sum of 564 + 551.

Step 1

Add ones.

4 + 1 = 5 ones

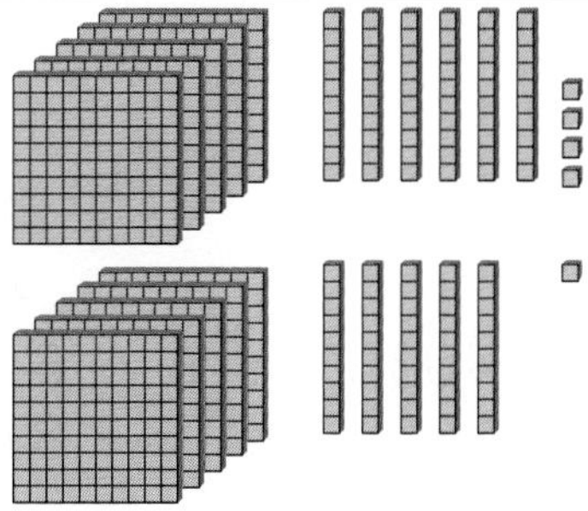

```
  564
+ 551
-----
    5
```

Step 2

Add tens.

6 + 5 = 11 tens

Regroup 11 tens as
1 hundred 1 ten.

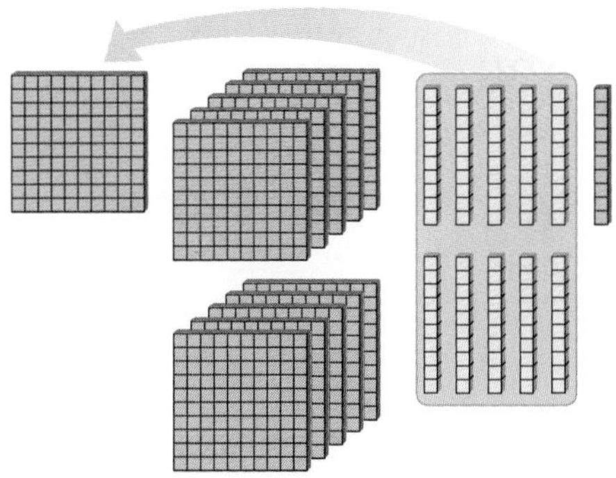

```
   1
  564
+ 551    11 tens
-----
   15
```

Step 3

Add hundreds.

1 + 5 + 5 = 11 hundreds

Regroup 11 hundreds as
1 thousand 1 hundred.

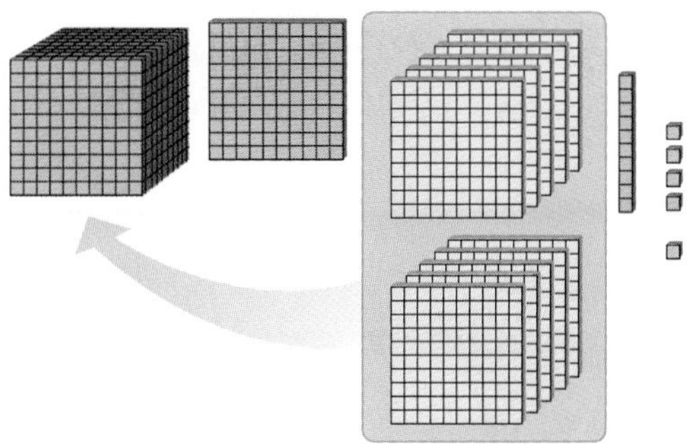

```
   1
   564
 + 551    11 hundreds
 -----
 1,115
```

The sum of 564 + 551 is 1,115.

More Examples

```
        1
A.  $ 5.49
    + 2.13
    ------
    $ 7.62   12 pennies = 1 dime 2 pennies
```

```
        1
B.  $ 5.92
    + 3.47
    ------
    $ 9.39   13 dimes = 1 dollar 3 dimes
```

Think and Discuss How can the sum of 2 three-digit numbers be a four-digit number?

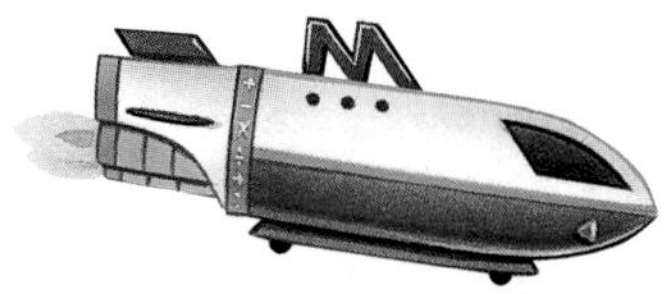

Try It Out

Estimate first. Then add.

1. $14 + 93$ **2.** $842 + 193$ **3.** $204 + 735$ **4.** $32 + 88$ **5.** $647 + 965$

Practice

Find each sum.

6. $29 + 32$ **7.** $403 + 256$ **8.** $64 + 87$ **9.** $312 + 98$ **10.** $486 + 975$

11. $52 + 98$ **12.** $563 + 139$ **13.** $212 + 500$ **14.** $47 + 6$ **15.** $\$7.18 + 3.90$

16. $\$6.84 + 2.71$ **17.** $70 + 46$ **18.** $\$4.08 + 7.65$ **19.** $95 + 87$ **20.** $374 + 992$

Using Mental Math **Use the first exercise to help you answer the second.**

21. $462 + 375 = 837$
$462 + 475 = ■$

22. $289 + 706 = 995$
$286 + 706 = ■$

23. $537 + 246 = 783$
$537 + 146 = ■$

With a partner, decide where you would like your Math Mobile to go. Write some facts like these.

- My Math Mobile will go to 34 different places.
- It will travel 32,640 miles.
- It will carry 1,722 people.
- Wild River Canyon is 689 miles away from here.
- At least 45,000 people visit the canyon each year.

Gather facts about your trip.

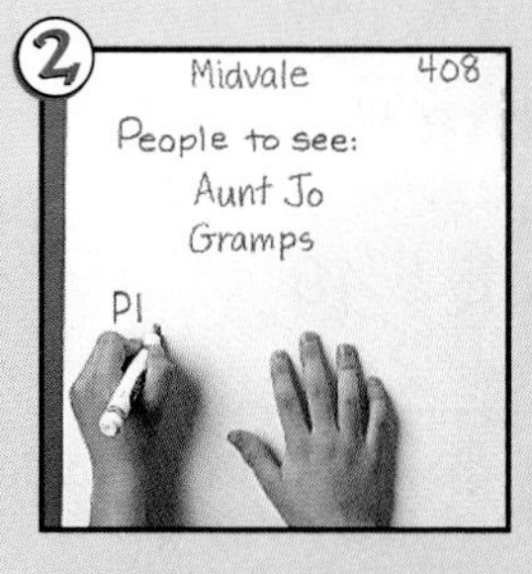

Begin to make your Travel Log.

Problem Solving

24. Lina helps her mother make pottery. One week, Lina makes 12 bowls and her mother makes 17 bowls. They sell 27 of them. How many bowls are left?

25. A large bowl costs \$63 and a small bowl costs \$49. How much would 2 small bowls cost?

26. Handmade necklaces cost \$16. Is \$30 enough money to buy 2 necklaces?

27. Toni, Meg, and Jim are waiting in the line to buy souvenirs. Toni is behind Meg and Jim. Jim is in front of Meg. Who is first in line?

Social Studies Connection Traditional Maya pottery is still made today in Chiapas and other Mexican states.

Review and Remember

What time does each clock show?

28. 

29. 

30. 

31. 

Time for Technology

Using CD-ROM

Use base-ten blocks to show 234 + 678 = ■.

- Click [1000] to open a base-ten workspace. Link it to two number spaces [1].
- Show 234 with base-ten blocks. Add 678 blocks.
- Click trade up until regrouping is no longer possible.

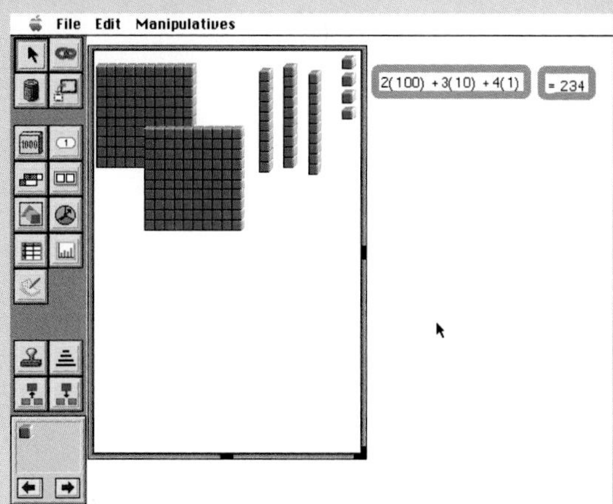

For Extra Practice, see Set C, page 118.

Floating Along

You can regroup ones, tens, hundreds, and thousands to add four-digit numbers.

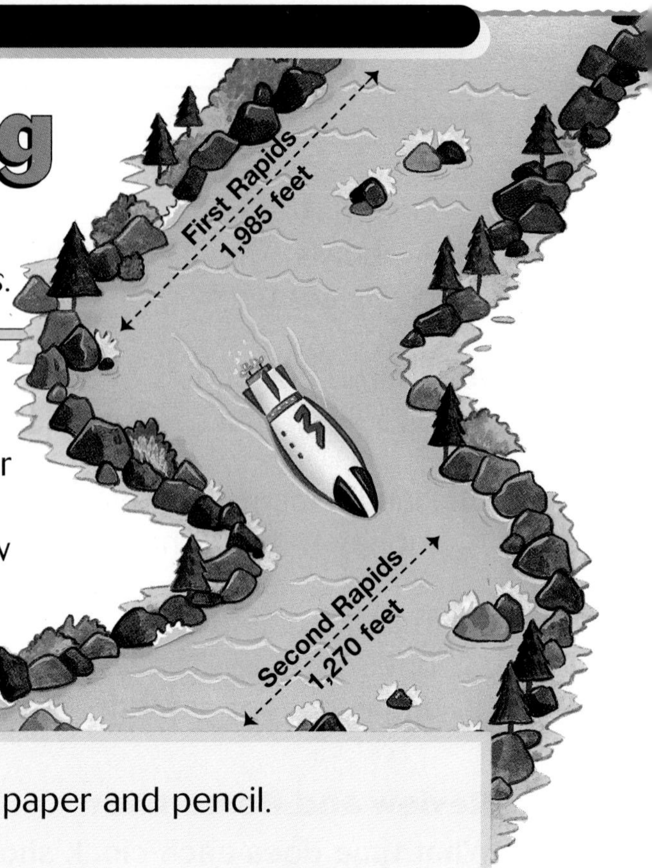

Learning About It

Splash! The Math Mobile lands in some river rapids. The first rapids are 1,985 feet long. The second rapids are 1,270 feet long. How long are the rapids altogether?

1,985 + 1,270 = ■

THERE'S ALWAYS A WAY!

- **One way** to find the sum is to use paper and pencil.

Step 1 Add ones.	**Step 2** Add tens. Regroup 15 tens as 1 hundred 5 tens.	**Step 3** Add hundreds. Regroup 12 hundreds as 1 thousand 2 hundreds.	**Step 4** Add thousands.
$\begin{array}{r} 1{,}985 \\ +\ 1{,}270 \\ \hline 5 \end{array}$	$\begin{array}{r} \scriptstyle 1 \\ 1{,}985 \\ +\ 1{,}270 \\ \hline 55 \end{array}$	$\begin{array}{r} \scriptstyle 1\ 1 \\ 1{,}985 \\ +\ 1{,}270 \\ \hline 255 \end{array}$	$\begin{array}{r} \scriptstyle 1\ 1 \\ 1{,}985 \\ +\ 1{,}270 \\ \hline 3{,}255 \end{array}$

- **Another way** is to use a calculator.

Press: 1 9 8 5 + 1 2 7 0 = Display: 3255

The rapids are 3,255 feet long altogether.

More Examples

A. $\begin{array}{r} \scriptstyle 1 \\ \$\ 23.96 \\ +\ 45.62 \\ \hline \$\ 69.58 \end{array}$

B. $\begin{array}{r} \scriptstyle 1\ 1 \\ \$\ 39.64 \\ +\ 28.71 \\ \hline \$\ 68.35 \end{array}$

Think and Discuss Why should you always estimate before using a calculator to solve a problem?

Try It Out

Find each sum.

1. 4,836 + 3,053
2. 6,394 + 5,735
3. $4.08 + 2.96
4. 5,241 + 6,593
5. 6,498 + 3,795

Practice

Choose a Method **Use paper and pencil or a calculator to find each sum. Tell which method you used.**

6. 1,316 + 4,802
7. 2,614 + 7,210
8. 5,469 + 3,275
9. 6,378 + 7,225
10. 5,062 + 8,761
11. 3,025 + 4,365
12. $62.24 + 16.40
13. 6,387 + 5,984
14. 8,627 + 499
15. $86.20 + 3.49
16. 4,329 + 8,990
17. 2,536 + 4,718
18. $68.21 + 47.14
19. 1,473 + 914
20. $23.65 + 58.77

Problem Solving

21. One month, 3,642 people went rafting. The next month 4,396 people went rafting. How many people went rafting in the two months?

22. A small life vest costs $34.99, a medium life vest costs $50.99, and a large life vest costs $63.95. How much would it cost to buy both a medium and a large life vest?

23. **Analyze** A number is less than 3,425 + 8,630 and greater than 7,614 + 4,429. What could the number be?

www.sbgmath.com

Review and Remember

Add or subtract.

24. 7 + 6
25. 12 − 8
26. 15 − 6
27. 9 + 8

For Extra Practice, see Set D, page 119.

Line Up!

Use what you know about adding two numbers to add three or four numbers.

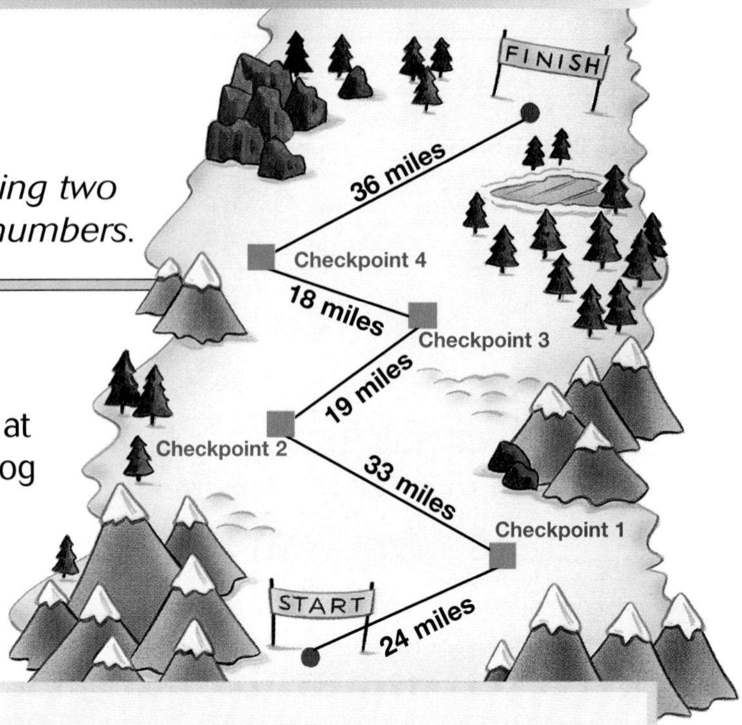

Learning About It

Brrr! The Math Mobile has landed at a sled-dog race. Kipanik and his dog team are in the race. How far is it from Start to Checkpoint 3?

24 + 33 + 19 = ▪

THERE'S ALWAYS A WAY!

- **One way** to find the sum is to use paper and pencil.

Step 1 Add ones. Regroup 16 ones as 1 ten 6 ones.	Step 2 Add tens. There are 7 tens in all.	Step 3 Check by adding up.
$\begin{array}{r} {}^{1} \\ 24 \\ 33 \\ +\ 19 \\ \hline 6 \end{array}$ 16 ones	$\begin{array}{r} {}^{1} \\ 24 \\ 33 \\ +\ 19 \\ \hline 76 \end{array}$ 7 tens	$\begin{array}{r} {}^{1} \\ 24 \\ 33 \\ +\ 19 \\ \hline 76 \end{array}$

- **Another way** to find the sum is to use a calculator.

Press: 2 4 + 3 3 + 1 9 = Display: 76

It is 76 miles from Start to Checkpoint 3.

More Examples

A.
$$\begin{array}{r} {}^{1} \\ 524 \\ 203 \\ +\ 691 \\ \hline 1{,}418 \end{array}$$

B.
$$\begin{array}{r} {}^{1} \\ 2{,}431 \\ 6{,}350 \\ +\ 4{,}912 \\ \hline 13{,}693 \end{array}$$

Think and Discuss What are the most ones you could regroup as tens when you add three numbers? Explain how you know.

Try It Out

Add. Check each answer by adding up.

1.	**2.**	**3.**	**4.**	**5.**
64	311	712	6,012	8,341
21	926	260	294	2,965
+ 38	+ 475	+ 49	+ 658	+ 3,477

Practice

Choose a Method **Use paper and pencil or a calculator to find each sum. Tell which method you used.**

6.	**7.**	**8.**	**9.**	**10.**
58	35	627	437	2,600
62	46	480	652	354
+ 19	+ 99	+ 71	+ 801	+ 896

11.	**12.**	**13.**	**14.**	**15.**
427	\$7.34	\$18.51	9,462	42
614	2.50	22.45	5,021	36
+ 182	+ 3.69	+ 96.83	+ 4,934	15
				+ 98

16. 51 + 84 + 23 **17.** 60 + 71 + 84 **18.** 200 + 400 + 850

Problem Solving

19. Suppose a sled-dog team travels 13 miles in one hour, 11 miles the next hour, and 12 miles the hour after that. How many miles does the sled-dog team travel?

20. **Create Your Own** Write a problem about a sled-dog race. Use the numbers from the map on page 94. Have a friend solve your problem.

Review and Remember

Add.

21.	**22.**	**23.**	**24.**
2	3	9	7
6	2	2	4
+ 1	+ 4	+ 4	+ 3

Social Studies Connection
The Iditarod is a sled-dog race that is held every year in Alaska. The race is over 1,000 miles and can last more than 20 days.

www.sbgmath.com

For Extra Practice, see Set E, page 119.

Checkpoint

Adding Numbers

Estimate by rounding to the nearest ten. (pages 82–83)

1. 50 + 32
2. 86 + 29
3. 63 + 74
4. 81 + 35
5. 43 + 17

Estimate by rounding to the nearest hundred or dollar. (pages 82–83)

6. 361 + 225
7. \$8.51 + 6.43
8. 193 + 674
9. \$9.20 + 4.81
10. 405 + 739

Add. (pages 80–81, 88–95)

11. 60 + 40
12. 53 + 47
13. 63 + 29
14. 88 + 13
15. 700 + 600
16. 674 + 452
17. 436 + 240
18. 153 + 65
19. \$3.51 + 4.29
20. 6,505 + 133
21. \$22.17 + 44.93
22. 3,509 + 8,799
23. 921 + 540
24. 1,177 + 386
25. 4,000 + 3,000
26. 41 + 36 + 84
27. 25 + 39 + 43
28. 405 + 276 + 340

Using Algebra **Compare. Use >, <, or = for each ●.** (pages 80–81, 88–95)

29. 25 + 78 ● 100
30. 260 ● 101 + 17
31. 805 ● 612 + 58
32. 98 + 112 ● 210
33. 40 + 25 ● 40 + 26
34. 62 + 15 ● 15 + 65
35. 3,146 + 200 ● 3,500
36. 1,803 ● 1,650 + 145

Problem Solving

37. The Math Mobile game room has 43 puzzles and 68 games. How many games and puzzles are there?

38. The Math Mobile has 3 staircases. One has 11 steps, another has 12 steps, and another has 15 steps. How many steps are there?

39. The music library on the Math Mobile has 548 tapes, 1,283 CDs, and 8 very, very old records. How many more tapes than records are there?

40. Analyze For trips to cold places, the Math Mobile has a supply of mittens. There are 34 pairs of blue mittens and 87 pairs of green mittens. How many mittens are on the Math Mobile?

Journal Idea Why is it important to line up digits correctly when adding numbers with two or more digits?

What do you think?

Is adding two-digit numbers always easier than adding four-digit numbers? Why or why not?

Critical Thinking Corner

Using Algebra **Number Sense**

Missing Numbers

Find each missing number.

1.	2.	3.	4.
5 4	3 7 ■	■ 7 8	4 8 ■
+ 3 ■	+ 2 ■ 3	+ 2 7 ■	+ ■ ■ 5
■ 3	■ 6 3	6 ■ 4	■, 4 8 1

5.	6.	7.	8.
2 ■ 6	8 2 ■	6, ■ 4 1	■, 4 8 ■
+ 3 5 4	+ 1 ■ 3	+ ■ 2 8 ■	+ 7, ■ ■ 6
■ 9 ■	■, ■ 1 7	9, 6 ■ 8	■ 4, 8 4 3

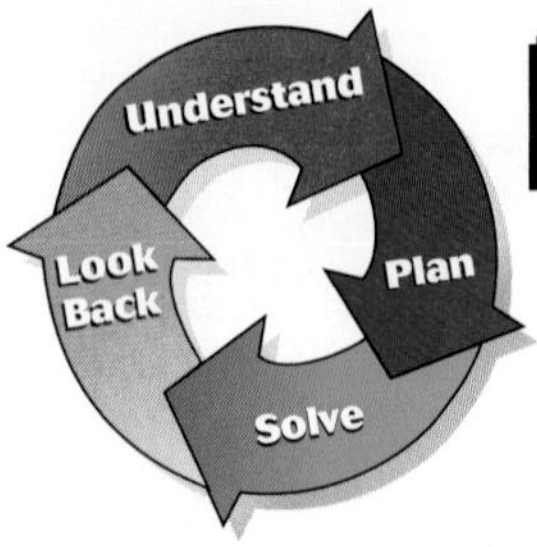

Problem Solving
Make a Table

You can make a table to help you solve a problem.

Start digging! It's 1848 and the Math Mobile has landed near a California gold mine. On the first day you find 3 gold nuggets. Each day after that you find twice as many nuggets as you found the day before. If this pattern continues, how many gold nuggets will you find on the fifth day?

▲ **Social Studies Connection** These men are panning and digging for gold. In the 1800s many people traveled to parts of the American West to find gold.

Understand

What do you need to know?

You need to know that you find 3 gold nuggets on the first day. Then you need to know that you always find twice as many nuggets as you found the day before.

Plan

How can you solve the problem?

You can **make a table** like the one at the right.

Day	Number of Gold Nuggets Found
First	3
Second	6
Third	12
Fourth	24
Fifth	48

Solve

List the number of gold nuggets you find each day. Remember to double the number each day.

You find 48 gold nuggets on the fifth day.

Look Back

Explain another strategy you could use to solve this problem.

Using the Strategy

Try making a table to solve Problems 1–3.

1. In 1848, many people traveled west on wagons hoping to find gold. Suppose each wagon was pulled by 4 oxen. How many oxen would be needed to pull 5 wagons? 8 wagons? 10 wagons?

2. Suppose 4 wagons are packed and ready to travel west. If there are 13 oxen, are there enough oxen to pull all the wagons? Why or why not?

3. **Explain** Eight wagons are on the trail. Two wagons have stopped to give their oxen water. How many oxen still need to get water?

A wagon train on the Oregon Trail

Mixed Strategy Review

Try these or other strategies you have learned.

THERE'S ALWAYS A WAY!

- *Act It Out*
- *Make a Table*
- *Use Logical Reasoning*
- *Write a Number Sentence*

4. Four children are standing in line to ride a pony. Joshua is behind Mary. Sue is between Mary and Cal. Cal is in the front. In what order are the children standing?

5. One gold nugget is worth $24. Another is worth $38, and a third is worth $29. How much are the gold nuggets worth altogether?

6. One gold nugget is worth more than $37 but less than $40. If the amount is an odd number, how much is the gold nugget worth?

Gold nuggets that have been cleaned after they were found

Dinosaur Differences

Rounding can help you estimate differences.

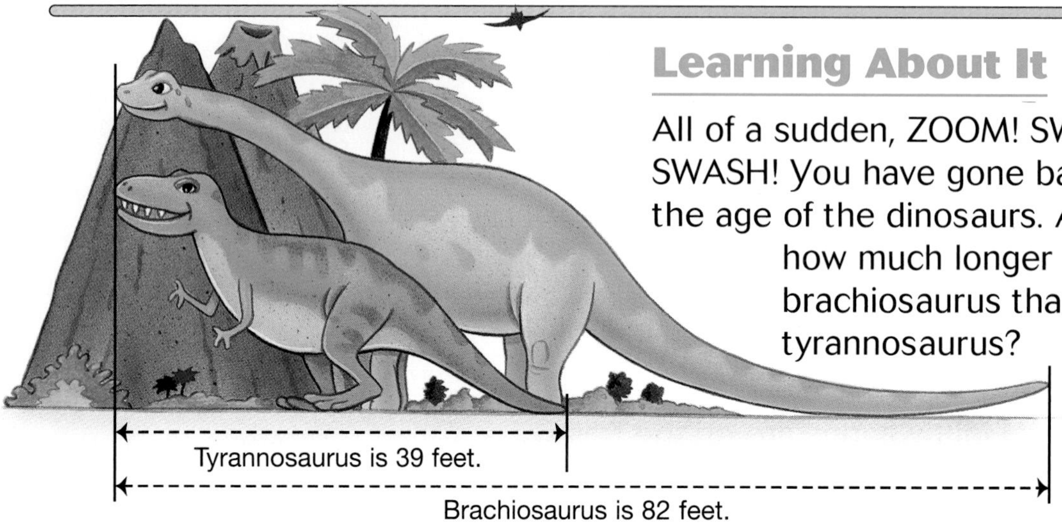

Learning About It

All of a sudden, ZOOM! SWISH! SWASH! You have gone back to the age of the dinosaurs. About how much longer is the brachiosaurus than the tyrannosaurus?

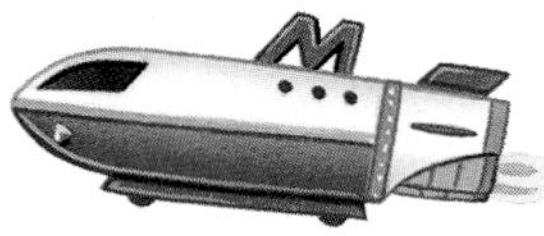

Since you want to know *about* how much longer, you do not need an exact answer.
You can round to **estimate** the difference.

Round to the nearest ten.

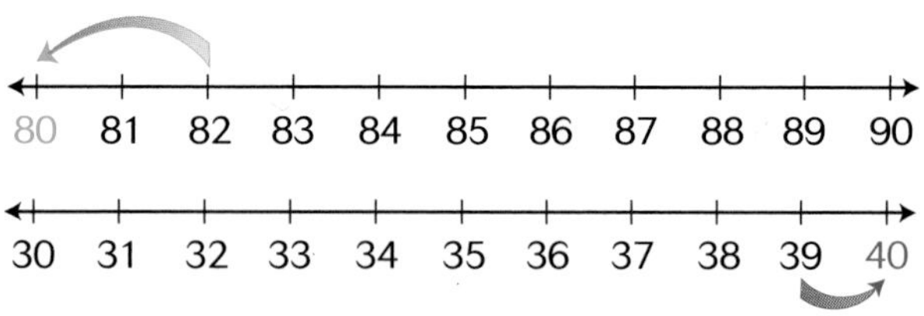

Then subtract the rounded numbers.

82	rounds to	80
− 39	rounds to	− 40
		40

The brachiosaurus is about 40 feet longer.

Estimate the differences of three-digit numbers the same way.

Estimate 750 − 467.

Round to the nearest hundred.

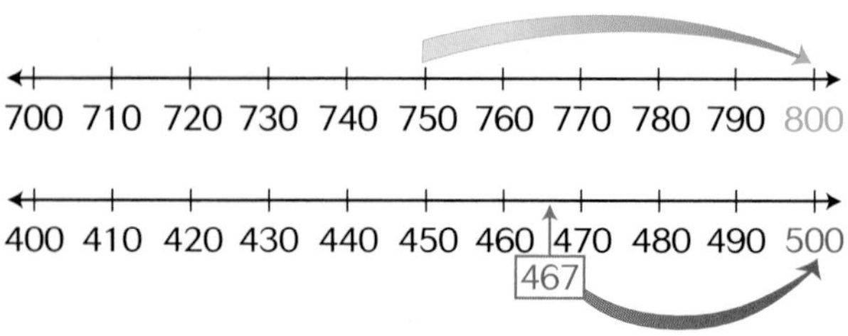

Then subtract the rounded numbers.

750	rounds to	800
− 467	rounds to	− 500
		300

750 − 467 is *about* 300.

Think and Discuss How would you estimate $1.33 − $0.72?

Try It Out

Estimate by rounding to the nearest ten.

1. 53 − 12	**2.** 68 − 39	**3.** 89 − 22	**4.** 72 − 49	**5.** 33 − 14

Estimate by rounding to the nearest hundred or dollar.

6. 325 − 114	**7.** 967 − 654	**8.** $7.14 − 2.86	**9.** 510 − 312	**10.** $5.96 − 4.89

Practice

Estimate by rounding to the greatest place value.

11. 94 − 76	**12.** 79 − 62	**13.** 85 − 25	**14.** 87 − 36	**15.** 64 − 36
16. 51 − 12	**17.** $8.81 − 2.53	**18.** 620 − 416	**19.** $7.32 − 5.41	**20.** $6.50 − 2.75
21. $5.24 − 2.95	**22.** $4.52 − 3.51	**23.** 647 − 236	**24.** 816 − 297	**25.** 995 − 730

Problem Solving

26. A protoceratops weighed 908 pounds. A dryosaurus weighed 172 pounds. About how much more did the protoceratops weigh?

27. A paleontologist has already put together 464 dinosaur bones. She has 368 bones left. How many bones are there altogether?

Science Connection
Scientists who study dinosaur bones are called paleontologists. They put dinosaur bones together to show what dinosaurs looked like.

Using Algebra

Review and Remember

Compare. Write >, <, or = for each ●.

28. 3 + 4 ● 4 + 3

29. 9 − 5 ● 6 − 3

30. 1 − 1 ● 4 − 4

31. 1 + 9 ● 5 + 6

For Extra Practice, see Set F, page 119.

Disappearing Blocks

Use base-ten blocks to subtract greater numbers.

Learning About It

Work with your group.

Use base-ten blocks to subtract 412 − 35.

What You Need

For each group:
base-ten blocks

Step 1 Show 412 with hundreds, tens, and ones blocks.

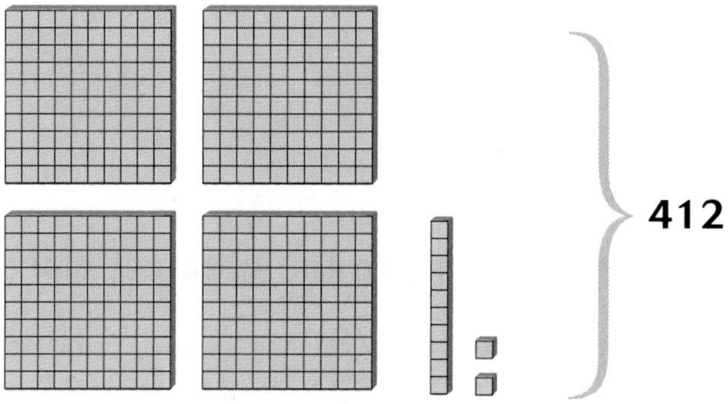

Step 2 Look at the ones. Try to take 5 ones away. You need more ones, so regroup 1 ten as 10 ones. Then take the 5 ones away.

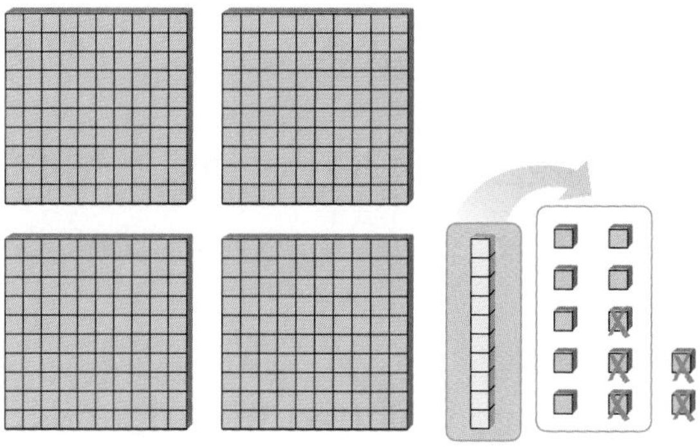

Step 3 Look at the tens. Try to take 3 tens away. You need more tens, so regroup 1 hundred as 10 tens. Then take the 3 tens away.

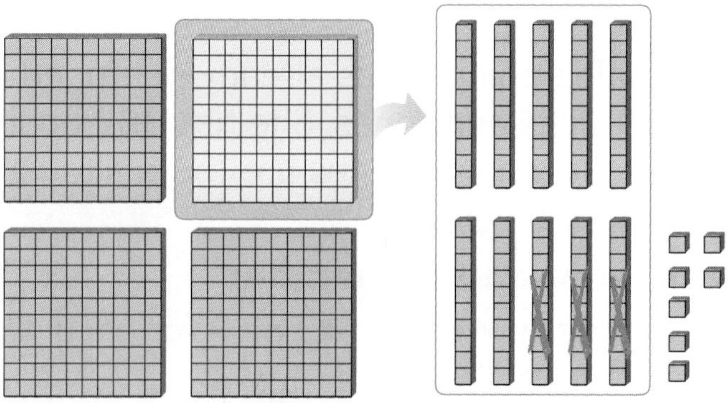

Count the blocks you have left. What is 412 − 35?

Step 4 Record your work in a chart like this. Notice when you need to regroup.

Subtraction Sentence	Did I need to regroup a ten as 10 ones?	Did I need to regroup a hundred as 10 tens?
412 − 35 = 377	yes	yes

Step 5 Repeat Steps 1 to 4 five or more times. Take turns picking different numbers each time.

Think and Discuss Think of a subtraction exercise where you need to regroup. Explain how you decided what numbers to use in your exercise.

Practice

1. In which of the exercises at the right do you regroup a ten as 10 ones?

2. In which of these exercises would you regroup a hundred as 10 tens?

a. $642 - 351$ b. $45 - 28$ c. $593 - 234$

3. *Using Algebra* Fill the boxes at the right with the digits 1, 3, 7, 4, 0, and 8. Write two problems that you can solve without regrouping.

□□□ − □□□

Blasting Off

Use what you know about regrouping to help you subtract two- and three-digit numbers.

Learning About It

You're headed for the moon! It will take 62 hours to get there. If 39 hours have gone by, how many more hours are left?

62 − 39 = ■

Estimate first.

62	rounds to	60
− 39	rounds to	− 40
		20

Then subtract to find the exact difference.

www.sbgmath.com

Step 1

Since 2 < 9, regroup 1 ten as 10 ones.

Then subtract the ones.

12 − 9 = 3 ones

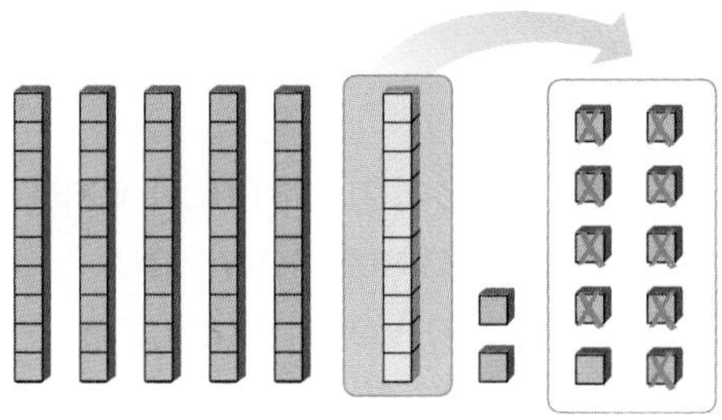

$$\begin{array}{r} {}^{5\,12} \\ \not{6}\not{2} \\ -\ 39 \\ \hline 3 \end{array}$$

Step 2

Subtract the tens.

5 − 3 = 2 tens

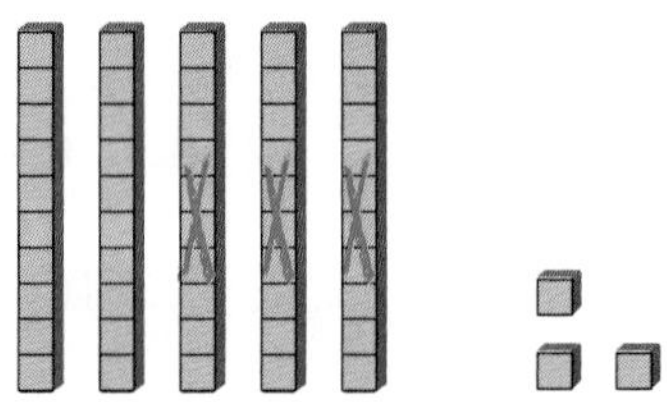

$$\begin{array}{r} {}^{5\,12} \\ \not{6}\not{2} \\ -\ 39 \\ \hline 23 \end{array}$$

There are 23 more hours left.

Look at the estimate of 20. Is 23 a reasonable answer?

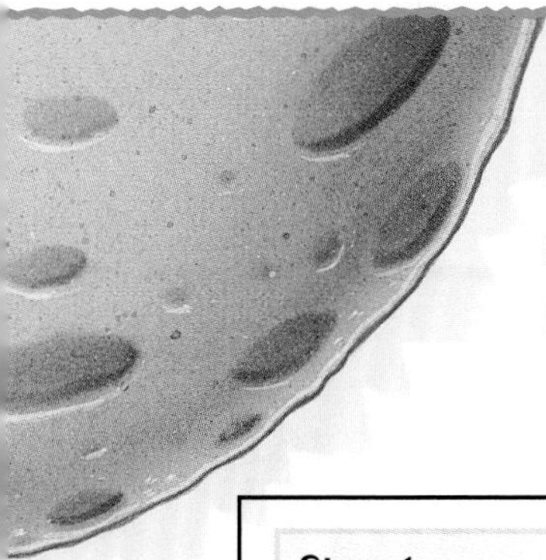

Connecting Ideas

Subtracting three-digit numbers is like subtracting two-digit numbers, only now you may need to regroup a hundred.

Find the difference of 217 − 186.

Step 1

Subtract ones.

7 − 6 = 1 one

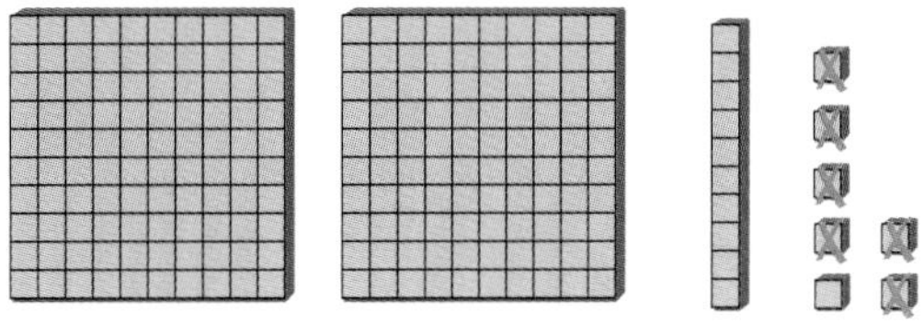

$$\begin{array}{r} 217 \\ -\ 186 \\ \hline 1 \end{array}$$

Step 2

Since 1 < 8, regroup 1 hundred as 10 tens.

Then subtract the tens.

11 − 8 = 3 tens

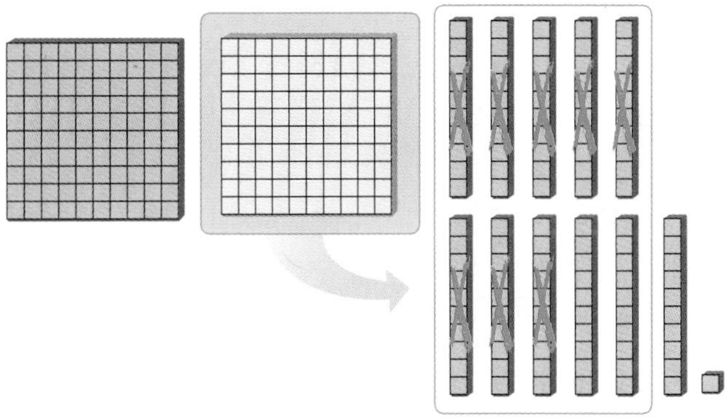

$$\begin{array}{r} {\scriptstyle 1\ 11} \\ \not{2}\not{1}7 \\ -\ 186 \\ \hline 31 \end{array}$$

Step 3

Subtract hundreds.

1 − 1 = 0 hundreds

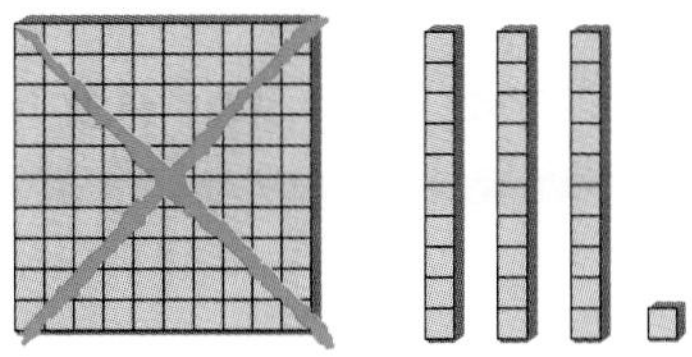

$$\begin{array}{r} {\scriptstyle 1\ 11} \\ \not{2}\not{1}7 \\ -\ 186 \\ \hline 31 \end{array}$$

The difference of 217 − 186 is 31.

More Examples

A.

$$\begin{array}{r} {\scriptstyle 7\ 14} \\ \$7.\not{8}\not{4} \\ -\ 2.36 \\ \hline \$5.48 \end{array}$$

4 pennies < 6 pennies
Trade 1 dime for 10 pennies.

B.

$$\begin{array}{r} {\scriptstyle 4\ 14} \\ \$9.\not{5}\not{4} \\ -\ 3.28 \\ \hline \$6.26 \end{array}$$

4 pennies < 8 pennies
Trade 1 dime for 10 pennies.

Think and Discuss Do you need to trade a dollar to subtract $6.15 − $3.82? Explain your answer.

Try It Out

Subtract.

1. 43 − 11	**2.** 283 − 135	**3.** 67 − 28	**4.** 924 − 367	**5.** 836 − 162

Practice

Find each difference.

6. 986 − 342	**7.** 63 − 28	**8.** 359 − 126	**9.** 70 − 34	**10.** 481 − 236
11. 624 − 257	**12.** 75 − 59	**13.** 541 − 260	**14.** 82 − 34	**15.** 674 − 359
16. 700 − 250	**17.** 57 − 24	**18.** $4.12 − 1.69	**19.** 80 − 33	**20.** 295 − 124
21. 813 − 266	**22.** 72 − 61	**23.** $9.08 − 8.23	**24.** 64 − 29	**25.** 827 − 409

Using Algebra **Compare. Use >, <, or = for each ●.**

26. 82 − 13 ● 60

27. 54 − 19 ● 54 − 17

28. 654 − 312 ● 342

29. 270 ● 961 − 849

30. 583 − 24 ● 483 − 24

31. 91 − 64 ● 412 − 250

Estimate first. Then use a calculator to find each difference.

32. 579 − 387

33. 600 − 254

34. 851 − 399

35. 782 − 64

36. 415 − 87

37. 800 − 253

38. 415 − 209

39. 974 − 382

40. 625 − 119

41. 643 − 539

42. 891 − 587

43. 761 − 58

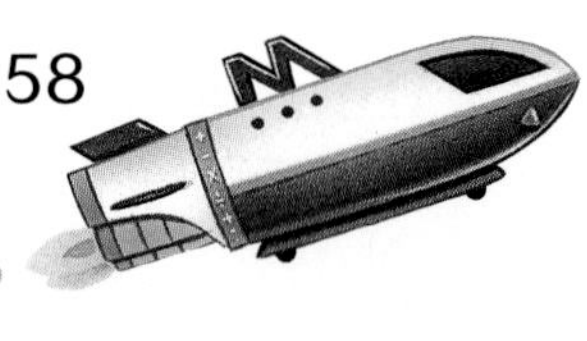

Problem Solving

You weigh less on the moon than on Earth! Look at the scale. How much more does each person weigh on Earth than on the moon?

44. Mrs. Kay **45.** Ali **46.** Joey

47. Analyze There are about 27 days between full moons. Paulo sees a full moon. After 43 days he looks at the moon and wonders when it will be full again. How many days will he have to wait?

Using Algebra

Review and Remember

Find each missing number.

48. 3 + ■ = 7 **49.** 10 − ■ = 7 **50.** ■ + 6 = 12 **51.** 8 + ■ = 14

52. 6 + ■ = 15 **53.** ■ − 9 = 9 **54.** ■ − 2 = 8 **55.** 17 − ■ = 9

56. ■ + 6 = 13 **57.** 6 + ■ = 11 **58.** 9 + ■ = 12 **59.** 8 − ■ = 0

Critical Thinking Corner

Number Sense

Front-End Estimation

Front-end estimation is a quick way to estimate!

- Look at the front digit of each number.
- Use zeros for all the other digits.
- Then add or subtract.

```
 76 ⟶   70
−45 ⟶ − 40
        30
```

76 − 45 is *about* 30.

Use the front digits to estimate each sum or difference.

1. 89 − 68 **2.** 51 + 22 **3.** 62 − 41 **4.** 843 + 619 **5.** 562 − 159

For Extra Practice, see Set G, page 120.

Under the Sea

Use regrouping to subtract greater numbers.

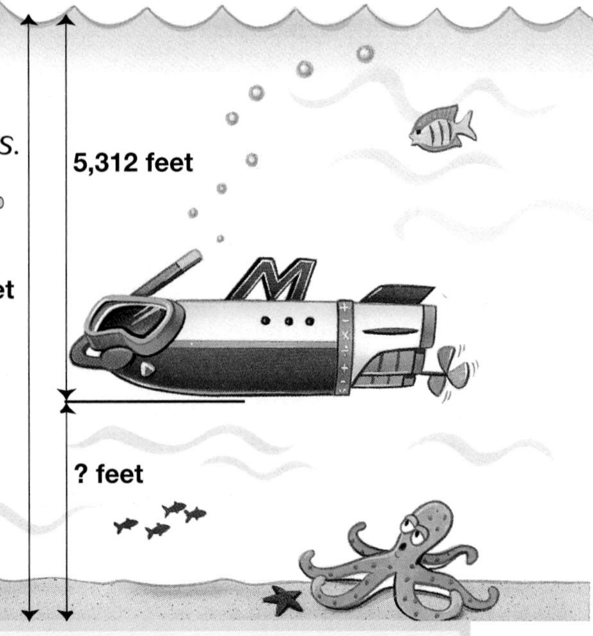

Learning About It

The Math Mobile is in the Caribbean Sea. The sea floor is 8,264 feet below the surface. The Math Mobile stops 5,312 feet down. How far is it from the sea floor?

8,264 − 5,312 = ■

THERE'S ALWAYS A WAY!

- **One way** to find the difference is to use paper and pencil.

Step 1 Subtract ones.	**Step 2** Subtract tens.	**Step 3** Subtract hundreds. Regroup 1 thousand as 10 hundreds.	**Step 4** Subtract thousands.
8,264 − 5,312 = 2	8,264 − 5,312 = 52	(7 12) 8,264 − 5,312 = 952	(7 12) 8,264 − 5,312 = 2,952

- **Another way** is to use a calculator.

Press: 8 2 6 4 − 5 3 1 2 = Display: 2952

The Math Mobile is 2,952 feet from the sea floor.

More Examples

A. Subtract.

```
    8 12
  $4,928
  −  374
  $4,554
```

Use addition to check.

```
  $4,554
  +  374
  $4,928
```

B. Subtract.

```
     11 12
   4  1  2 16
    5,236
  − 1,459
    3,777
```

Use addition to check.

```
    3,777
  + 1,459
    5,236
```

Think and Discuss How could you check that 8,264 − 5,312 = 2,952?

Try It Out

Subtract. Use addition to check your answer.

1. 4,687 − 1,346

2. 9,247 − 3,162

3. 7,342 − 2,658

4. $8,163 − 2,418

5. 6,431 − 5,928

Practice

Choose a Method Use paper and pencil or a calculator to subtract. Tell which method you used.

6. 5,329 − 3,107

7. 8,284 − 4,196

8. 9,318 − 6,403

9. 7,213 − 5,894

10. 7,318 − 6,093

11. 3,162 − 2,428

12. 4,293 −3,160

13. 6,308 − 1,127

14. $7,450 − 2,814

15. 5,214 − 3,699

16. $6,574 − $2,248

17. 3,641 − 2,195

18. 6,918 − 2,534

19. 9,218 − 1,463

20. 7,400 − 365

21. 4,289 − 4,160

Problem Solving

22. A fisherman caught 486 pounds of snapper and 1,199 pounds of tuna in a month. How many pounds of fish did he catch?

23. The Math Mobile thermometer says the water at the surface is 74 degrees Fahrenheit and the water way below is 39 degrees Fahrenheit. How much warmer is the water at the surface?

24. Using Algebra What numbers could fill the boxes?

3,■35
− ■2■
2,414

Social Studies Connection
People on many Caribbean islands depend on fish as a source of food.

Review and Remember

What is the value of the digit 2 in each number?

25. 12

26. 25,647

27. 29

28. 217

29. 12,465

For Extra Practice, see Set H, page 120.

Zeroing In

Sometimes when you subtract, you need to subtract across zeros.

▲ **Social Studies Connection**
Mammoth Cave National Park in Kentucky is the largest cave system in the world.

Learning About It

Who turned out the lights? The Math Mobile is underground. You are in Mammoth Cave! Suppose there are 300 passages you can explore. If your class explores 124 passages, how many passages are left to explore?

300 − 124 = ■

Step 1	Step 2	Step 3	Step 4
0 ones < 4 ones, so you need more ones to subtract. There are no tens, so regroup 1 hundred as 10 tens. Then regroup 1 ten as 10 ones.	Subtract ones.	Subtract tens.	Subtract hundreds.
300 − 124 (regrouped: 2 9 10)	300 − 124 = 6	300 − 124 = 76	300 − 124 = 176

There are 176 passages left to explore.

More Examples

A. 1,603 − 275 = 1,328 (regrouped: 5 9 13)

3 ones < 5 ones
There are no tens, so regroup 1 hundred as 10 tens.
Then regroup 1 ten as 10 ones.

B. \$2,004 − 1,521 = \$483 (regrouped: 1 9 10 4)

0 tens < 2 tens
There are no hundreds, so regroup 1 thousand as 10 hundreds. Then regroup 1 hundred as 10 tens.

Think and Discuss To find 6,000 − 8, would you use paper and pencil or mental math? Explain why.

Try It Out

Find each difference.

1. $600 - 348$	**2.** $8{,}000 - 4{,}291$	**3.** $5{,}000 - 241$
4. $703 - 659$	**5.** $\$4{,}000 - 2{,}360$	**6.** $8{,}200 - 6{,}143$

Project Link

When your Travel Log is finished, discuss your facts and numbers with a partner. Then write addition and subtraction problems for your Log.

Practice

Subtract.

7. $900 - 349$	**8.** $4{,}000 - 2{,}056$	**9.** $200 - 58$
10. $6{,}020 - 4{,}340$	**11.** $\$25.00 - 12.65$	**12.** $502 - 279$

Using Mental Math **Use mental math to find each difference.**

13. 500 − 80

14. 7,000 − 160

15. \$9.00 − \$1.50

16. \$40.00 − \$4.99

Problem Solving

17. The Math Mobile has 200 kneepads to help you crawl through passages. The 28 children in your class each used 2 kneepads. How many are left?

18. Suppose you bring 105 meals to eat as you explore the cave. If 27 meals are left at the end of the trip, how many meals were eaten?

Social Studies Connection
Stephen Bishop was the first modern-day explorer of Mammoth Cave. He began exploring the cave in 1838.

Review and Remember

Find each answer.

19. $7 + 6$	**20.** $9 - 9$	**21.** $14 - 8$	**22.** $6 + 9$	**23.** $12 - 7$	**24.** $7 + 8$

For Extra Practice, see Set I, page 120.

Do It Your Way!

There are many ways to add or to subtract.

Learning About It

You're back home. Luckily you have videotapes and photos of the trip. You can use mental math to find how many minutes long the videotapes are altogether.

360 + 210 = ■

Using Mental Math

Start with 360.
Think: 210 is the same as 200 + 10.
Add: 360 + 200 = 560
560 + 10 = 570

The videotapes are 570 minutes long.

You can use paper and pencil or a calculator to find how many photos there are altogether.

2,496 + 456 = ■

Using Paper and Pencil

Step 1 Add ones.	**Step 2** Add tens.	**Step 3** Add hundreds.	**Step 4** Add thousands.
$\begin{array}{r} {}^{1} \\ 2,496 \\ +\ 456 \\ \hline 2 \end{array}$	$\begin{array}{r} {}^{1\,1} \\ 2,496 \\ +\ 456 \\ \hline 52 \end{array}$	$\begin{array}{r} {}^{1\,1} \\ 2,496 \\ +\ 456 \\ \hline 952 \end{array}$	$\begin{array}{r} {}^{1\,1} \\ 2,496 \\ +\ 456 \\ \hline 2,952 \end{array}$

Using a Calculator

Press: 2 4 9 6 + 4 5 6 = Display: 2952

There are 2,952 photos altogether.

Think and Discuss Explain how you would find 3,250 + 4,000.

Try It Out

Would you use mental math, paper and pencil, or a calculator to find each answer? Explain why.

1. 28 + 10 **2.** 239 + 651 **3.** 600 − 200 **4.** 8,400 − 2,957

5. 9,219 + 8,465 **6.** 300 + 800 **7.** 12 + 8 **8.** 162 − 14

Practice

Choose a Method **Use mental math, paper and pencil, or a calculator to add or subtract. Tell which method you chose.**

9. 70 + 60 **10.** 580 − 291 **11.** 60 − 40 **12.** 600 + 250 **13.** 842 − 367

14. 561 − 294 **15.** 400 − 20 **16.** 3,000 − 400 **17.** 900 + 300 **18.** 75 − 25

19. 8,000 − 1,000 **20.** 7,214 − 4,695 **21.** 5,000 − 2,500 **22.** 520 + 98 **23.** 7,342 + 6,584

Problem Solving

24. After the trip you decide to find out more about volcanoes on CD-ROM. One CD has 254 pictures. Another has 398 pictures. How many pictures are there in all?

25. On the Internet you find out that 4,329 students have taken trips in the Math Mobile! Of these students, 2,794 are from the United States. How many students are from other countries?

Review and Remember

Write the numbers in order from least to greatest.

26. 50 24 42 **27.** 78 76 71 **28.** 632 575 236

29. 303 780 117 **30.** 158 218 185 **31.** 2,480 1,999 9,080

For Extra Practice, see Set J, page 120.

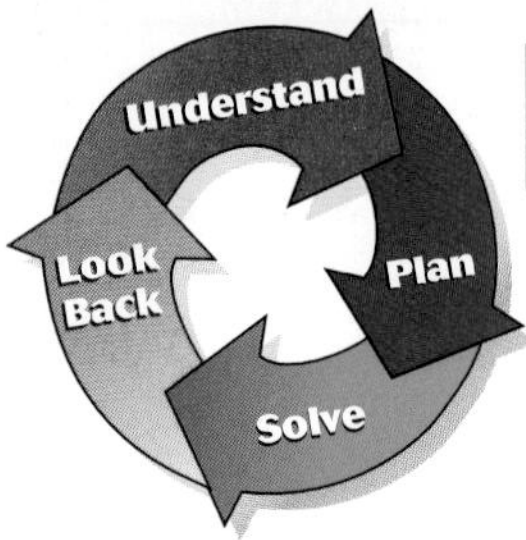

Problem Solving
Using Money

You can add and subtract money to solve problems.

It's time to go shopping! The Math Mobile has taken you to a shopping mall in the future. Look at the prices on the sign. How much money do you save if you buy the river raft while it is on sale?

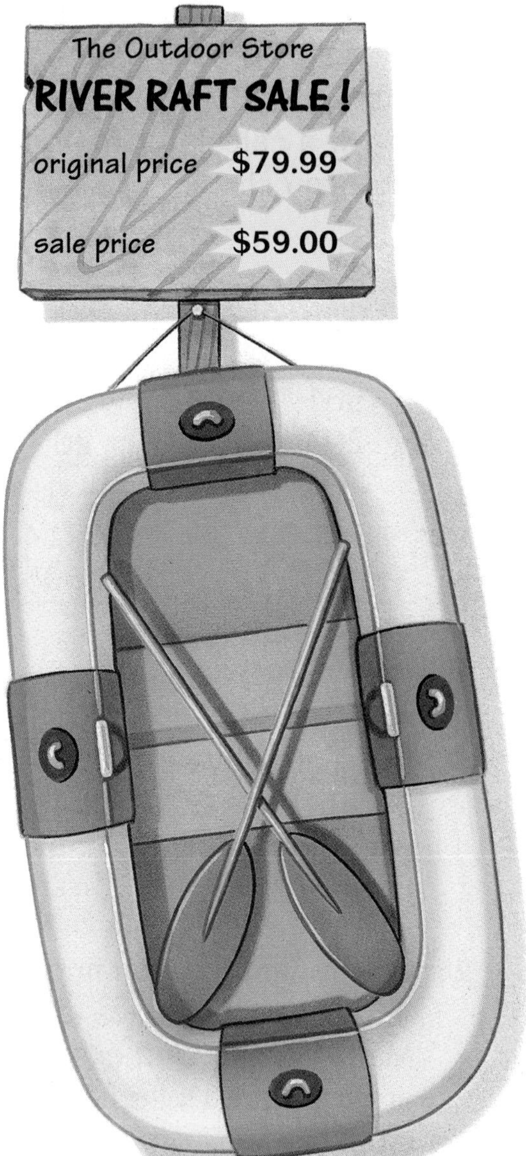

UNDERSTAND

What do you need to find?

You need to find the difference between the original price and the sale price, since that is the money you save.

PLAN

How can you solve the problem?

You can subtract the sale price from the original price to find how much money you save.

SOLVE

$$\begin{array}{r l} \$79.99 & \leftarrow \text{original price} \\ -\ 59.00 & \leftarrow \text{sale price} \\ \hline \$20.99 & \leftarrow \text{savings} \end{array}$$

You save $20.99 if you buy the raft on sale.

LOOK BACK

How can you use addition to check your answer?

Show What You Learned

Use the information below to answer each question.

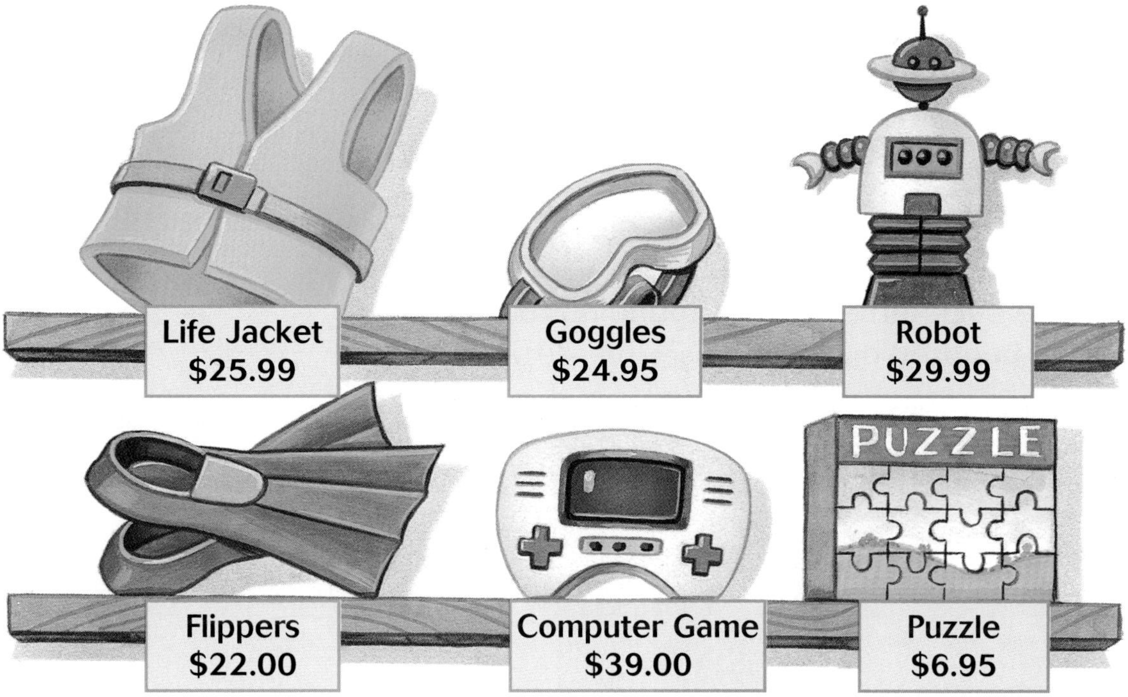

1. How much money would you spend if you bought goggles and a pair of flippers?

2. How much money would you spend if you bought a robot and 2 puzzles?

3. **Using Estimation** How many puzzles can you buy with $25?

4. **Using Estimation** How many toy robots can you buy with $50?

5. You buy both the toy robot and the computer game. About how much money do you spend?

6. How much more will it cost to buy a computer game than to buy a toy robot?

7. You buy both the life jacket and the flippers. If you give the cashier $50, how much change should you get back?

8. You have $15 and your friend has $19. Together, do you have enough money to buy the computer game? Explain.

9. **Analyze** You bought the flippers and one other item pictured above. Together the items cost $46.95. What was the other item that you bought?

10. **Create Your Own** Write a word problem that can be solved by using information from the picture above. Give it to a classmate to solve.

Checkpoint

Subtracting Numbers

Estimate each difference by rounding to the nearest ten. (pages 100–101)

1. $92 - 74$ **2.** $56 - 48$ **3.** $78 - 22$ **4.** $61 - 28$ **5.** $93 - 49$

Estimate each difference by rounding to the nearest hundred or dollar. (pages 100–101)

6. $807 - 296$ **7.** $434 - 177$ **8.** \$7.98 − 2.79 **9.** $750 - 610$ **10.** \$9.72 − 1.15

11. $579 - 365$ **12.** \$4.68 − 1.51 **13.** $812 - 327$ **14.** \$9.04 − 2.91 **15.** $618 - 194$

Subtract. (pages 104–113)

16. $46 - 35$ **17.** $64 - 31$ **18.** $74 - 69$ **19.** $58 - 29$

20. \$6.08 − 4.59 **21.** $317 - 108$ **22.** \$6.15 − 4.28 **23.** $817 - 645$

24. 2,211 − 1,788 **25.** \$25.01 − 10.75 **26.** 3,002 − 1,999 **27.** 8,000 − 7

28. \$54.96 − \$31.34 **29.** 5,831 − 2,205

30. 6,073 − 3,174 **31.** 7,021 − 5,833

Using Algebra

Mixed Practice

Compare. Use >, <, or = for each ●.

32. 86 − 26 ● 55 **33.** 83 − 33 ● 475 − 425

34. 912 − 412 ● 850 − 350 **35.** 810 − 212 ● 810 − 210

36. 4,936 − 2,102 ● 2,834 **37.** 6,008 − 2,216 ● 5,432 − 1,234

Problem Solving

38. The Math Mobile visited a city for two days. On Monday, 2,324 people toured the ship. On Tuesday, 2,499 people toured it. How many people toured the ship in all?

39. Everyone who toured the Math Mobile was given a free lunch. How many more lunches were given on Tuesday than Monday?

40. On Tuesday morning, the Math Mobile's radar showed that a storm was 107 miles from the city. That afternoon the storm was 79 miles away. How many miles had the storm moved?

What do you think?

Would you use mental math or paper and pencil to find 487 − 407? Explain your choice.

Journal Idea

Write a word problem about the Math Mobile that can be solved by using addition or subtraction. Then see if a classmate can solve it.

Project Wrap-Up

A Travel Talk

With your partner, show your finished Travel Log.

Share your addition and subtraction problems with the class. Challenge your classmates to solve each problem by adding or subtracting.

Now you have shared your world travels!

Extra Practice

Set A (pages 80–81)

Find each sum or difference.

1. $50 + 70$
2. $90 - 30$
3. $300 + 800$
4. $8{,}000 - 4{,}000$
5. $6{,}000 + 9{,}000$

6. The first 100 children to sign up for soccer were given a $3 coupon for sports equipment. The next 200 children were given a $1 coupon. How many coupons were given out?

7. Last week, 580 children signed up for softball. Two hundred of the children have received their team shirts. How many children still need to receive their shirts?

Set B (pages 82–83)

Estimate by rounding to the nearest ten.

1. $37 + 54$
2. $83 + 29$
3. $45 + 34$
4. $44 + 34$
5. $16 + 28$

Estimate by rounding to the nearest hundred or dollar.

6. $263 + 358$
7. $\$9.73 + 2.53$
8. $\$8.03 + 4.48$
9. $595 + 405$
10. $812 + 279$

Set C (pages 88–91)

Estimate first. Then add.

1. $57 + 63$
2. $49 + 58$
3. $\$4.35 + 7.80$
4. $478 + 807$
5. $\$3.13 + 7.29$

6. Lauren has 119 U.S. stamps and 187 Canadian stamps in her collection. How many stamps does she have?

7. Lee collects posters. He bought a large poster for $6.95 and a small poster for $3.29. How much money did he spend?

Extra Practice

Set D (pages 92–93)

Find each sum.

1. $\begin{array}{r} 1,790 \\ +\ 2,304 \\ \hline \end{array}$
2. $\begin{array}{r} 3,448 \\ +\ 7,348 \\ \hline \end{array}$
3. $\begin{array}{r} \$35.98 \\ +\ \ 14.29 \\ \hline \end{array}$
4. $\begin{array}{r} 6,393 \\ +\ 3,744 \\ \hline \end{array}$
5. $\begin{array}{r} \$38.25 \\ +\ \ 11.75 \\ \hline \end{array}$

6. Rebecca spent $29.50 for tickets to a game and $10.50 for food. Janet spent $24.00 for tickets and $12.65 for food. Who spent more?

7. There are 2,350 seats in the lower part of a stadium. There are 1,890 seats in the upper part of the stadium. How many seats are there in the stadium?

Set E (pages 94–95)

Find each sum.

1. $\begin{array}{r} 23 \\ 27 \\ +\ 94 \\ \hline \end{array}$
2. $\begin{array}{r} 305 \\ 479 \\ +\ 813 \\ \hline \end{array}$
3. $\begin{array}{r} 3,045 \\ 1,989 \\ +\ 7,053 \\ \hline \end{array}$
4. $\begin{array}{r} 6,234 \\ 8,975 \\ +\ 3,437 \\ \hline \end{array}$
5. $\begin{array}{r} \$82.13 \\ 15.89 \\ +\ 19.08 \\ \hline \end{array}$

6. Students at Smith School want to collect 1,000 soup labels. The first grade saved 246 labels. The second grade saved 338 labels. The third grade saved 340 labels. Did the students reach their goal?

7. Ray, Bob, and Phil sold plants to raise money for their school band. Ray sold 27 plants. Bob sold 38 plants, and Phil sold 63 plants. How many plants did the three boys sell?

Set F (pages 100–101)

Estimate by rounding to the greatest place value.

1. $\begin{array}{r} 58 \\ -\ 29 \\ \hline \end{array}$
2. $\begin{array}{r} 74 \\ -\ 53 \\ \hline \end{array}$
3. $\begin{array}{r} 36 \\ -\ 25 \\ \hline \end{array}$
4. $\begin{array}{r} 48 \\ -\ 29 \\ \hline \end{array}$
5. $\begin{array}{r} 62 \\ -\ 45 \\ \hline \end{array}$
6. $\begin{array}{r} 536 \\ -\ 215 \\ \hline \end{array}$
7. $\begin{array}{r} 812 \\ -\ 388 \\ \hline \end{array}$
8. $\begin{array}{r} 627 \\ -\ 289 \\ \hline \end{array}$
9. $\begin{array}{r} 587 \\ -\ 293 \\ \hline \end{array}$
10. $\begin{array}{r} 882 \\ -\ 617 \\ \hline \end{array}$

Extra Practice

Set G (pages 104–107)

Find each difference.

1. $\begin{array}{r} 57 \\ -\ 24 \\ \hline \end{array}$
2. $\begin{array}{r} 83 \\ -\ 21 \\ \hline \end{array}$
3. $\begin{array}{r} 690 \\ -\ 354 \\ \hline \end{array}$
4. $\begin{array}{r} \$6.29 \\ -\ 2.98 \\ \hline \end{array}$
5. $\begin{array}{r} 912 \\ -\ 235 \\ \hline \end{array}$

6. Jill paid $9.99 for a cassette tape. Sarah bought the same tape on sale for $8.29. How much money did Sarah save?

7. Music Mania sold 112 CDs in January and 170 CDs in February. How many more CDs did they sell in February?

Set H (pages 108–109)

Subtract.

1. $\begin{array}{r} 2,584 \\ -\ 1,063 \\ \hline \end{array}$
2. $\begin{array}{r} 5,480 \\ -\ 1,705 \\ \hline \end{array}$
3. $\begin{array}{r} \$32.55 \\ -\ 15.97 \\ \hline \end{array}$
4. $\begin{array}{r} 8,827 \\ -\ 6,987 \\ \hline \end{array}$
5. $\begin{array}{r} \$17.84 \\ -\ 12.19 \\ \hline \end{array}$

Set I (pages 110–111)

Find each difference.

1. $\begin{array}{r} 507 \\ -\ 238 \\ \hline \end{array}$
2. $\begin{array}{r} \$36.00 \\ -\ 19.25 \\ \hline \end{array}$
3. $\begin{array}{r} \$60.00 \\ -\ 8.59 \\ \hline \end{array}$
4. $\begin{array}{r} 7,000 \\ -\ 1,327 \\ \hline \end{array}$
5. $\begin{array}{r} 5,000 \\ -\ 1,450 \\ \hline \end{array}$

6. Randy bought party decorations for $2.89. He gave the cashier $5.00. How much change did he get?

7. Bev has 300 balloons for a party. Sixty-five of them are red. How many balloons are not red?

Set J (pages 112–113)

Choose a Method **Use mental math, paper and pencil, or a calculator to add or subtract. Tell which method you chose.**

1. $\begin{array}{r} 800 \\ +\ 600 \\ \hline \end{array}$
2. $\begin{array}{r} 956 \\ -\ 253 \\ \hline \end{array}$
3. $\begin{array}{r} 7,000 \\ +\ 6,000 \\ \hline \end{array}$
4. $\begin{array}{r} 9,035 \\ -\ 5,035 \\ \hline \end{array}$
5. $\begin{array}{r} 7,350 \\ -\ 1,728 \\ \hline \end{array}$

Chapter Test

Estimate by rounding to the greatest place value.

1. $\begin{array}{r} 45 \\ +\ 39 \\ \hline \end{array}$ **2.** $\begin{array}{r} 74 \\ -\ 62 \\ \hline \end{array}$ **3.** $\begin{array}{r} 282 \\ +\ 724 \\ \hline \end{array}$ **4.** $\begin{array}{r} 782 \\ -\ 275 \\ \hline \end{array}$ **5.** $\begin{array}{r} \$8.50 \\ +\ 7.49 \\ \hline \end{array}$

Find each sum.

6. $\begin{array}{r} 541 \\ +\ 306 \\ \hline \end{array}$ **7.** $\begin{array}{r} 26 \\ +\ 78 \\ \hline \end{array}$ **8.** $\begin{array}{r} \$3.05 \\ +\ 6.48 \\ \hline \end{array}$ **9.** $\begin{array}{r} 7{,}356 \\ +\ 4{,}732 \\ \hline \end{array}$ **10.** $\begin{array}{r} \$81.33 \\ +\ 15.69 \\ \hline \end{array}$

11. 24 + 36 + 98

12. 300 + 200 + 720

13. 14 + 22 + 63

14. \$5.15 + \$2.08 + \$1.35

Find each difference.

15. $\begin{array}{r} 48 \\ -\ 29 \\ \hline \end{array}$ **16.** $\begin{array}{r} 80 \\ -\ 44 \\ \hline \end{array}$ **17.** $\begin{array}{r} \$4.39 \\ -\ 2.47 \\ \hline \end{array}$ **18.** $\begin{array}{r} 6{,}202 \\ -\ 5{,}347 \\ \hline \end{array}$ **19.** $\begin{array}{r} \$30.00 \\ -\ 25.98 \\ \hline \end{array}$

20. 563 − 473

21. 5,682 − 4,391

22. 89 − 17

23. \$38.06 − \$13.47

Solve.

24. One week the Math Mobile made a tour of some special places. It visited 624 places in New York, 470 places in Illinois, and 336 places in Nevada. How many places did it visit in all three states?

25. Students traveled to Paris, France, in the Math Mobile. They found that the Eiffel Tower is 984 feet tall. The Washington Monument in Washington, D.C., is 555 feet tall. How much taller is the Eiffel Tower?

Self-Check

Look back at Exercises 15 to 23. Use addition to check that your answers are correct.

Performance Assessment

Show What You Know About Addition and Subtraction

What You Need

play money:
2 quarters
5 dimes
8 nickels
35 pennies

1. Use play money to answer Questions 1a and 1b.

   a. Show 30¢ in as many ways as you can. Make a chart like the one below to show your work.

Quarters	Dimes	Nickels	Pennies	Total

   b. How can you make 30¢ with the fewest number of coins? with the greatest number of coins?

2. This chart shows the time it takes the Math Mobile to travel from the United States to different countries.

Country	Travel Time
France	67 minutes
Colombia	80 minutes
Kenya	156 minutes
Australia	208 minutes

   a. Pick a country to visit. How many minutes would it take the Math Mobile to travel there and back?

   b. Pick two other countries to visit. Which country would it take longer to travel to? How many more minutes would it take to travel there than to the other country?

   c. Suppose you visited each country and returned to the United States after each visit. How much time would you spend traveling?

Self-Check

For Question 1a, did you check that each combination of coins has a sum of 30¢?

For Question 2c, did you make sure you included minutes both *to* and *from* each country?

Extension

Palindromes!

Palindromes are words or numbers that read the same forward and backward. Can you find 9 palindromes in this picture?

You can make any number into a palindrome.

Suppose you want to make 14 into a palindrome.

Step 1	Start with the number 14.	14
Step 2	Reverse the digits.	+ 41
Step 3	Add.	55

55 is a palindrome.

Sometimes you have to repeat the steps. Suppose you want to make 58 into a palindrome.

Step 1	Start with the number 58.	58
Step 2	Reverse the digits.	+ 85
Step 3	Add.	143
Step 4	Reverse the digits.	+ 341
Step 5	Add.	484

484 is a palindrome.

Now, you try it! Use the steps to make palindromes from these numbers.

1. 47 **2.** 423 **3.** 73 **4.** 528 **5.** 18 **6.** 62 **7.** 85

Cumulative Review

Preparing for Tests

Choose the correct letter for each answer.

1. $\begin{array}{r} 5 \\ 6 \\ 3 \\ +\ 4 \\ \hline \end{array}$

A. 18
B. 19
C. 17
D. 11
E. none of these

2. $8 + \blacksquare = 15$

A. 15
B. 8
C. 7
D. 5
E. none of these

3. $\begin{array}{r} 7{,}000 \\ +\ 9{,}000 \\ \hline \end{array}$

A. 1,600
B. 1,500
C. 14,000
D. 16,000
E. none of these

4. $\begin{array}{r} 11 \\ -\ 8 \\ \hline \end{array}$

A. 9
B. 17
C. 7
D. 5
E. none of these

5. $\begin{array}{r} 85 \\ +\ 39 \\ \hline \end{array}$

A. 124
B. 56
C. 66
D. 57
E. none of these

6. $\begin{array}{r} 17 \\ -\ 9 \\ \hline \end{array}$

A. 6
B. 9
C. 8
D. 7
E. none of these

7. $\begin{array}{r} \$2.79 \\ +\ 9.27 \\ \hline \end{array}$

A. $12.96
B. $12.06
C. $11.06
D. $11.96
E. none of these

8. $\begin{array}{r} \$8.05 \\ -\ 3.75 \\ \hline \end{array}$

A. $5.30
B. $5.70
C. $4.30
D. $11.80
E. none of these

9. $\begin{array}{r} 3{,}247 \\ +\ 9{,}783 \\ \hline \end{array}$

A. 13,300
B. 13,020
C. 12,030
D. 12,020
E. none of these

10. $\begin{array}{r} \$50.00 \\ -\ 18.89 \\ \hline \end{array}$

A. $41.11
B. $42.21
C. $32.21
D. $31.11
E. none of these

11. $\begin{array}{r} 583 \\ 865 \\ +\ 622 \\ \hline \end{array}$

A. 2,170
B. 2,070
C. 2,060
D. 1,960
E. none of these

12. $284 - 135$

A. 149
B. 351
C. 419
D. 151
E. none of these

13. Which of these symbols goes in the ●?

2,750 − 2,250 ● 500

A. >
B. <
C. =
D. > or <

14. What is the value of the underlined digit $2\underline{8}7{,}406$?

A. 8
B. 800
C. 800,000
D. 80,000

15. What is the value of a one dollar bill, 2 quarters, 2 dimes, a nickel, and 3 pennies?

A. $1.78
B. $1.73
C. $1.58
D. $0.78

16. If you were between the thirty-ninth and forty-first person in a line, what would your position be?

A. 37th
B. 40th
C. 41st
D. 38th

17. Bill has 1 quarter, 2 dimes, and 3 pennies. What coins does he need to make 79¢?

A. 1 dime, 1 nickel, and 1 penny
B. 1 quarter and 1 penny
C. 2 dimes, 2 nickels, and 1 penny
D. 2 nickels and 1 penny

This table shows the number of baseball cards owned by members of a baseball trading card club. Study the table. Then answer Questions 18 to 20.

Spring City Baseball Trading Card Club

Member	Cards Owned
Jean	1,085
Vicki	850
Sean	1,805
Mark	1,580
Rob	580

18. Who owns the least number of cards?

A. Vicki
B. Sean
C. Mark
D. Rob

19. Which members own more than 1,200 cards?

A. Jean and Sean
B. Vicki and Rob
C. Sean and Mark
D. Mark and Rob

20. Who owns more cards than Jean?

A. Sean and Mark
B. Sean and Rob
C. Vicki and Rob
D. Vicki and Sean

Chapter 4 Time and Measurement

Chapter Theme: SPORTS and FITNESS

Career Spotlight Meet Peggy Chee-Romero, who teaches math at Santa Fe Indian School in New Mexico. She coaches track, too. With her help, students learn to sprint, long jump, and run cross-country!

Track coaches keep track of how their athletes are doing. To do this, they use time and measurement.

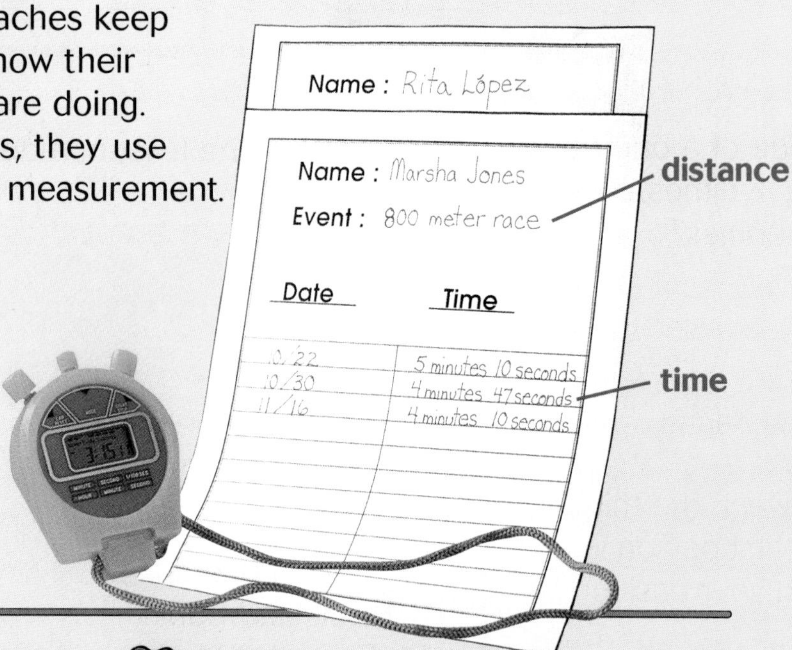

Chapter Project

Run a Relay Race

Plan and hold a relay race. In a relay race, each team member runs only a part of the whole distance.

- To form teams, write your name on a slip of paper. Then fold the slip. Put it in a bag with your classmates' names.
- Pull four names at a time out of the bag to pick teams.

The next step is to meet with your relay-race team. Work together to choose a good name for your team!

Right on Time!

You can tell time to the hour, quarter hour, and half hour.

Learning About It

The community center has sports activities after school. Look at the schedule. Here's how the times look on a clock.

Schedule

Lesson	Time
Soccer	4:00
Tennis	4:15
Karate	4:30
Volleyball	4:45

Soccer

- 4:00
- four o'clock

Tennis

- 4:15
- four-fifteen
- quarter past four
- fifteen minutes after four

Karate

- 4:30
- four-thirty
- half past four
- thirty minutes after four

Volleyball

- 4:45
- four forty-five
- quarter to five
- forty-five minutes after four

The short hand, or hour hand, on a clock shows hours. It takes 60 minutes, or 1 hour, for the hour hand to move from one number to the next number.

The long hand, or minute hand, shows minutes. It takes 5 minutes for the minute hand to move from one number to the next number.

A day has 24 hours. The hours from 12 midnight to 12 noon are A.M. The hours from 12 noon until 12 midnight are P.M.

60 minutes (min) = 1 hour (h)
30 minutes = 1 half hour
15 minutes = 1 quarter hour

Think and Discuss Where is the hour hand when the clock shows half past five?

Try It Out

Write the correct time.

1. 

2. 

3. 

4. 

Choose the time when each activity is more likely to happen.

5. going to school
a. 8 A.M. **b.** 8 P.M.

6. going to sleep
a. 9 A.M. **b.** 9 P.M.

7. eating dinner
a. 6 A.M. **b.** 6 P.M.

Practice

Write each time in two ways using words.

8. 

9. 

10. 

11. 

Write each time using numbers.

12. quarter to ten
13. thirty minutes after two
14. seven-fifteen
15. eight-forty
16. three forty-five
17. twelve-fifty

Problem Solving

18. Suppose you arrive at soccer practice at 4:15. Practice starts at 4:00. Are you early or late?

19. The soccer game begins at 11:45. Is this time closer to 11:00 or 12:00?

20. Soccer practice ends at quarter to six. Write this time in numbers.

Social Studies Connection
In 1753, an African American named Benjamin Banneker built a clock entirely of wood. The clock kept perfect time for over 50 years.

Review and Remember

Add or subtract.

21. 14 + 32
22. 243 − 115
23. 64 − 47
24. 437 + 287

For Extra Practice, see Set A, page 166.

Every Minute Counts

You can use a clock to tell time to the minute.

Learning About It

The swim team started warm-up laps at 3 o'clock. They finished at five minutes after three. How does this look on a clock?

Start at 12. Count 5 minutes. Read this time as 3:05.

Kickboard practice started at 4 o'clock. It ended at seventeen minutes after four. How does this look on a clock?

Start at 12. Count 15 minutes by 5s. Then count 2 minutes more. Read this time as 4:17.

Think and Discuss How long does it take the minute hand to move once around the clock? How long does it take the hour hand to move once around the clock?

Try It Out

Write each time using numbers.

1. 

2. 

3. 

4. 

Practice

Write each time in two ways.

5. 

6. 

7. 

8. 

9. 

10. 

11. 

12. 

13. one forty-three **14.** three forty-six **15.** five minutes to six

16. eleven-fourteen **17.** nine-eleven **18.** seven twenty-one

Problem Solving

19. It is 6 minutes after 10 in the morning. Write the time in numbers. Use P.M. or A.M. to show the time of day.

20. A sundial tells time by using a shadow made by sunlight shining on a stick. Why couldn't you use a sundial all the time?

Social Studies Connection
The ancient Egyptians used sundials to keep track of time.

21. Find the number of minutes in 1 day. First press [6][0] for the number of minutes in 1 hour. Then press [×][2][4] to multiply the minutes by 24 hours. What does the display show? How could you find the number of minutes in 2 days?

Review and Remember

Round to the greatest place value.

22. 33 **23.** 48 **24.** $1.49 **25.** 53 **26.** $6.89

27. 861 **28.** 28 **29.** $9.12 **30.** 656 **31.** $3.59

For Extra Practice, see Set B, page 166.

As Time Goes By

A clock can help you find out how much time has passed.

Learning About It

Little League baseball is popular all over the world. Suppose a game in Chinese Taipei starts at 2:00. It lasts two hours and forty-five minutes. When does it end?

Start at 2:00.

Count ahead 2 hours to 4:00.

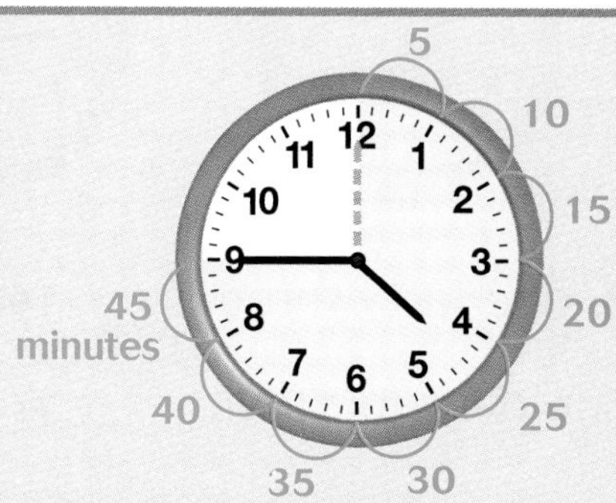

Then count ahead 45 minutes. The time is 4:45.

The game ends at 4:45.

The first inning of a game started at 11:05. If it ended at 11:27, how long did the inning last?

Start at 11:05.
Count by 5s to 11:25.
Then count 2 more minutes.
The total time counted is 22 minutes.

The inning lasted 22 minutes.

Kid Connection This Little League team from Chinese Taipei won the 1996 World Series Championship.

Think and Discuss You want to be at a game at 3:30. It takes 20 minutes to get there. When should you leave?

Try It Out

Write the time each clock will show in 5 minutes.

1. 
2. 
3. 
4. 

5. Look at Exercises 1 and 2. How much time has passed from the first clock to the second clock?

Practice

Write the time each clock will show in 20 minutes.

6. 
7. 
8. 
9. 

Look at each pair of times. Write how much time has passed.

10. Start 10:50 P.M.
End 11:50 P.M.

11. Start 6:17 A.M.
End 6:20 A.M.

12. Start 7:35 A.M.
End 8:00 A.M.

Problem Solving

13. A ball game begins at 10:00 A.M. It lasts 2 hours and 30 minutes. When does it end?

14. **Analyze** The swimming pool is open from 9:00 A.M. to 11:30 A.M and from 1:00 P.M. to 5:00 P.M. each day. How long is the pool open each day?

Review and Remember

Choose a Method **Use paper and pencil or mental math to solve. Name your method.**

15. 7 + 4 + 8 + 2

16. 246 + 110

17. 49 − 38

18. 77 − 22

19. 18 + 9 + 3

20. 66 − 4

Project Link

Get ready for the team relay race.

- Practice with your team.
- Keep track of the time it takes each runner to run the same distance.

Keep practicing!

Developing Skills for Problem Solving

In this lesson you'll first read for understanding and then focus on whether numbers are exact numbers or estimates.

READ FOR UNDERSTANDING

In an exciting soccer game yesterday the Eagles beat the Hornets 8 goals to 5. Over 120 fans watched the game, which lasted about 90 minutes. After the game, Coach Ramos and 4 parents treated the winning team to ice cream.

1. How many goals did the Eagles score?
2. How long did the game last?
3. Who treated the players to ice cream?

THINK AND DISCUSS

MATH FOCUS

Exact Numbers or Estimates Estimates are not exact numbers. Words like *about*, *over*, *less than*, and *almost* can tell you that numbers are estimated, not exact.

Reread the paragraph at the top of the page.

4. Can you tell exactly how many fans there were? Why or why not?
5. How many people treated the winning team to ice cream? Is your answer an exact number or an estimate? Explain how you know.
6. When could a number like 30 be used to show an exact amount? When could it be used to show an estimated amount?

Show What You Learned

Answer each question. Give a reason for your choice.

Cara played in a soccer game for almost 15 minutes. Her team scored 2 goals in that time. Then a rainstorm stopped the game for over 30 minutes. About 25 fans left the game during the storm. Two of them returned when the rain stopped.

1. How long was the game stopped by rain?
   a. Exactly 30 minutes
   b. Less than 30 minutes
   c. More than 30 minutes

2. Which of these numbers is *not* an estimate?
   a. 15 minutes
   b. 2 goals
   c. 30 minutes

3. Which of these words tells you that 25 fans is an estimate?
   a. game
   b. about
   c. left

One Eagles game that was played during a light rain, lasted for over 50 minutes. About 40 people watched the game. Only 8 people had umbrellas. The Eagles won 2 to 1.

4. How many people might have watched the game?
   a. 42 people
   b. 20 people
   c. 73 people

5. How many people at the game had umbrellas?
   a. 8 people
   b. More than 8 people
   c. Fewer than 8 people

6. **Explain** Is it correct to say that the Eagles played for almost 50 minutes? Why or why not?

It's a Date

A calendar helps you know the date.

7 days = 1 week
12 months = 1 year
365 days = 1 year

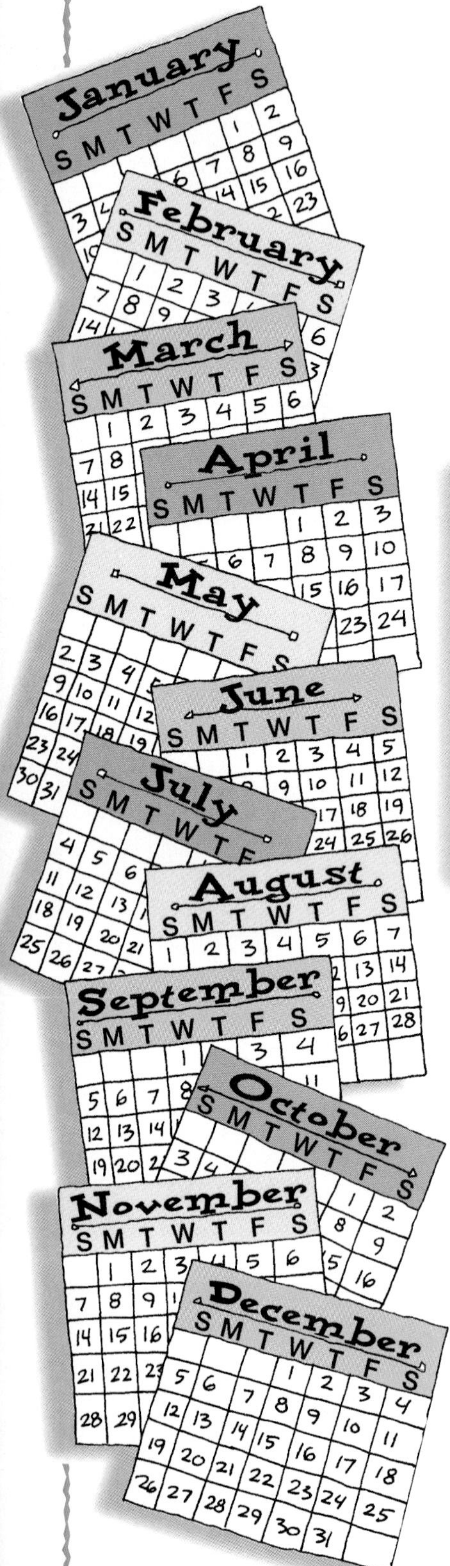

Learning About It

A **calendar** shows the days, weeks, and months of the year in order. Look at the calendar below. A karate class starts on Saturday, June 12.

You can write that date in two ways.

June 12, 1999 (month, day, year)   6/12/99 (month, day, year)

June

Sunday	Monday	Tuesday	Wednesday	Thursday	Friday	Saturday
		1	2	3	4	5
6	7	8	9	10	11	12 Karate Class
13	14 Flag Day	15	16	17	18	19
20 Father's Day	21	22	23	24	25	26
27	28	29	30			

Now look at the months of the year at the left. June is the 6th month of the year. What is the 10th month?

Think and Discuss What is today's date? What day of the week is it?

Try It Out

Use the calendar pages for Exercises 1–6. Write the name of the month.

1. 9th month **2.** 1st month **3.** 12th month

Write the day of the week.

4. June 22 **5.** June 16 **6.** June 25

Practice

Use the calendar below for Exercises 7–11.

▲ Every fourth year is called a **leap year**. A leap year has 366 days. The extra day in a leap year is February 29.

7. What is honored throughout the month of February?

8. What holiday do we celebrate on February 21? What day of the week is that?

9. What is the date of the fourth Monday?

10. What is the date of the bowling party?

11. On what day is the basketball game?

Name the month that is 4 months before each month.

12. May **13.** December **14.** July **15.** February

16. April **17.** September **18.** October **19.** March

Problem Solving

20. If today is Saturday, August 3, what will be the date in two weeks?

21. **Analyze** What will the date be exactly 1 year after January 1, 1999?

22. A basketball game will be held on October 12. Today is October 2. In how many days will the game be played?

23. **Create Your Own** Make up two questions about the calendar above. Ask a classmate to answer them.

www.sbgmath.com

Using Algebra

Review and Remember

Write the missing numbers in each pattern.

24. 383, 483, 583, ■, 783, ■

25. 625, 525, 425, ■, 225, ■

26. 49, 149, 249, ■, ■, ■

27. 382, 482, ■, ■, 782, ■

28. 921, 821, 721, ■, ■, 421

29. 704, 604, ■, ■, ■, 204

For Extra Practice, see Set D, page 166.

Checkpoint

Time

Complete. Use words from the list.

Word List
calendar
minutes
hours

1. There are 60 __?__ in 1 hour.
2. A __?__ shows the months of a year.
3. There are 24 __?__ in a day.

Write each time using numbers. (pages 128–131)

4. 

5. 

6. 

7. 

8. three twenty-four **9.** twelve-thirty **10.** six minutes to two

Write the time each clock will show in 5 minutes. (pages 132–133)

11. 

12. 

13. 

14. 

Write how much time has passed. (pages 132–133)

15. 5:30 P.M. to 7:00 P.M. **16.** 10:25 A.M. to 11:15 A.M.

Use the calendar at the right. (pages 136–137)

17. What date is the karate class?

18. What is the date of the third Friday?

19. What holiday is on November 25?

20. What is the date 2 weeks from November 8?

21. On what day of the week is November 1?

November

Sunday	Monday	Tuesday	Wednesday	Thursday	Friday	Saturday
	1	2	3	4	5	6
7	8	9	10	11	12	13
14 Football Game	15	16	17	18	19	20
21	22	23	24	25 Thanksgiving	26	27 Karate Class
28	29	30				

Problem Solving

22. Suppose you get to a roller skating rink at 4:30 P.M. You leave at 6:00 P.M. How long were you at the rink?

23. A school team played softball from 12:45 P.M. until 1:30 P.M. Is that more or less time than 1 hour?

24. Suppose you go to the playground at 15 minutes after 2 in the afternoon. Write the time in numbers.

25. The school field day is May 18. Today is May 5. How many days are there until the field day?

Journal Idea Write a few sentences telling what you usually do in school at these times: 9:30 A.M., 11:30 A.M., 2 P.M.

What do you think?

How much time do you spend in school each day?

How much time do you spend in school each week?

Critical Thinking Corner

Number Sense

Time Estimation

Seconds are a very short period of time. There are 60 seconds in a minute. Estimate whether it will take *seconds, minutes,* or *hours* to complete each of these activities. Explain your answer.

1. 

2. 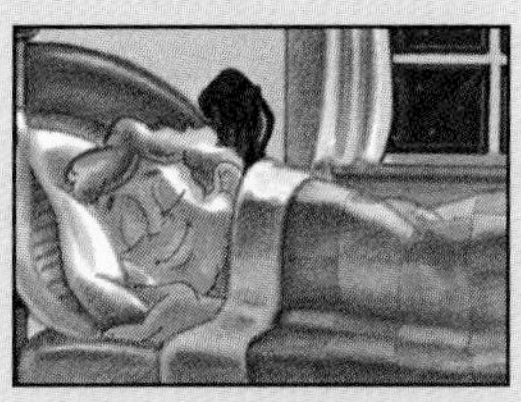

3. 

4. 

5. 

6. 

Inch by Inch

You can measure length and distance using different units of measurement.

Learning About It

Olympic gymnasts tumble and jump on a bar called a balance beam. How can you find the width of the beam?

You can use paper clips to measure the width of the beam below. Estimate how many clips you can put end to end on the line. Then check.

You can also use a ruler to measure the width of the beam in inches. An **inch** is a unit used to measure length or distance.

Word Bank

inch (in.)
foot (ft)
yard (yd)
mile (mi)

What You Need

For each student:
- *paper clips*
- *ruler*
- *yardstick or string*

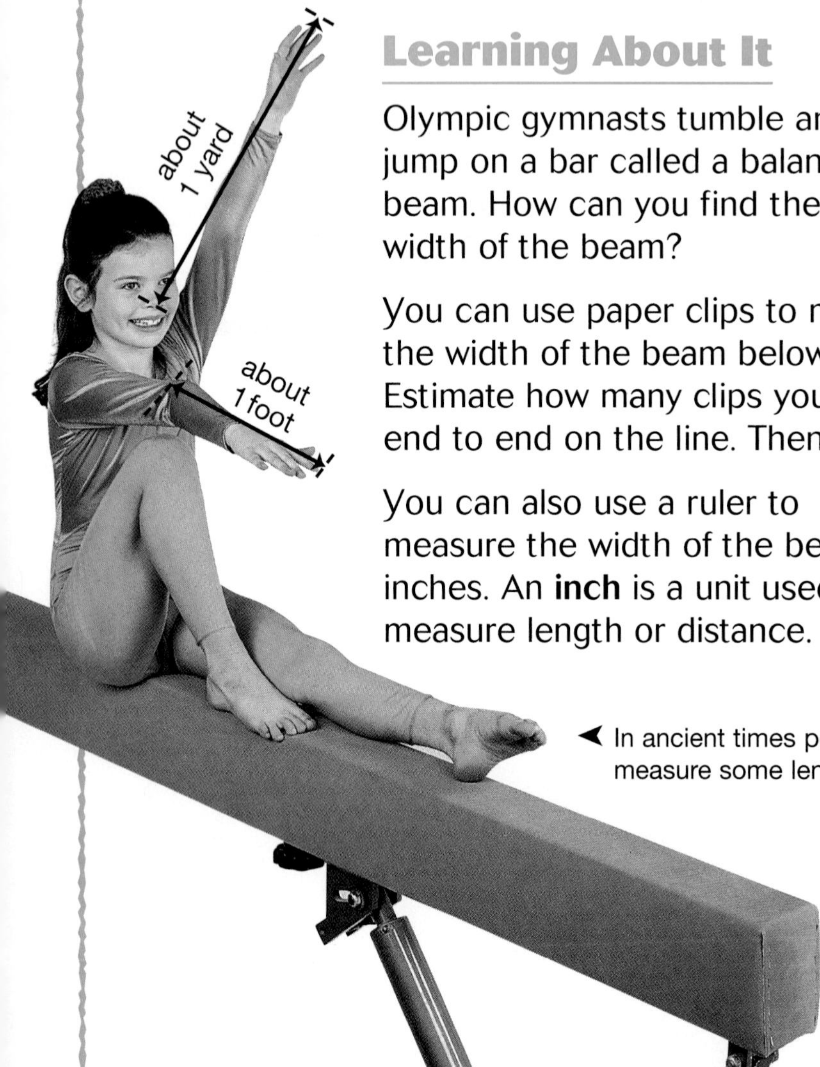

In ancient times people used their arms and hands to measure some lengths. What problems might that cause?

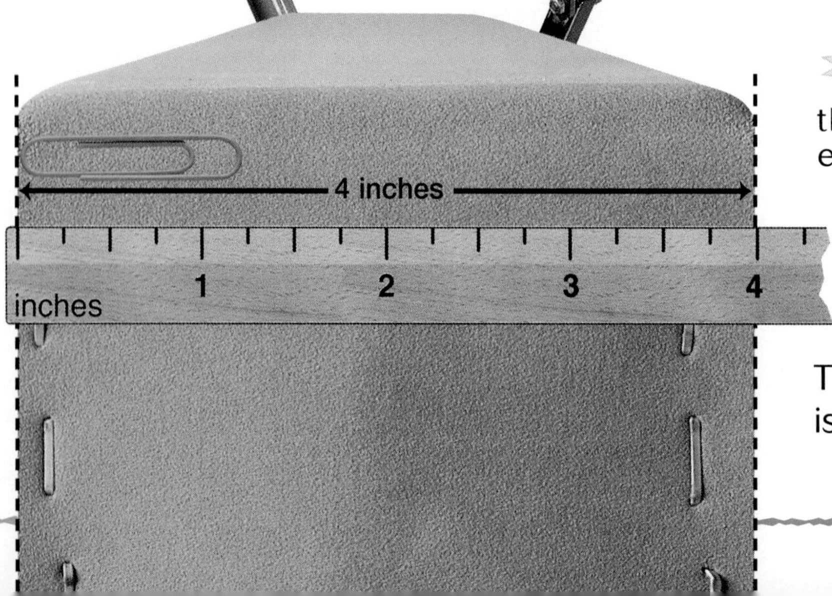

Hint Line up the first mark on the ruler with the left end of the line.

The balance beam is 4 inches wide.

More Examples

Some things are not an exact number of inches long. You can measure them using the $\frac{1}{2}$-inch mark and the $\frac{1}{4}$-inch mark on the ruler.

A.

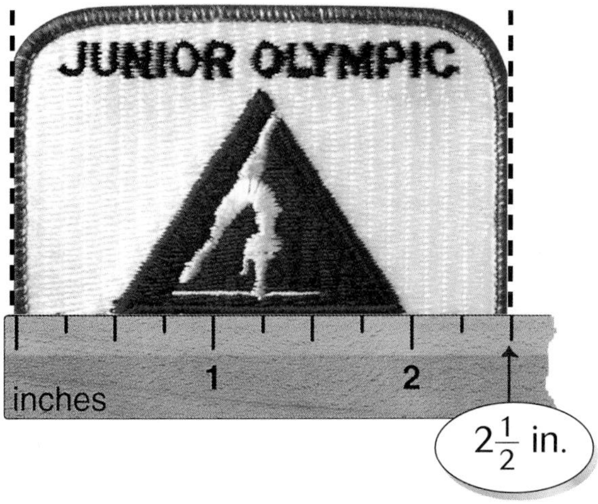

B.

Connecting Ideas

Inches are used to measure short lengths. Feet, yards, and miles are units used to measure longer lengths.

Look at the picture of the girl on the balance beam on page 140. On many people, the distance from the elbow to the end of the fingers is about 1 **foot.** The distance from the nose to the end of the fingers is about 1 **yard**. The distance a person can walk in 20 minutes is about 1 **mile.**

12 in. = 1 ft
1 yd = 3 ft
1 yd = 36 in.
1 mi = 1,760 yd
1 mi = 5,280 ft

- Find 3 objects that you think are each about 1 foot long.
- Find 3 objects that you think are each about 1 yard long.
- Check your estimates by measuring each object with a ruler or yardstick.

Think and Discuss How do you decide whether it's best to measure an object using inches, feet, yards, or miles?

Try It Out

Using Estimation **Estimate the length of each object to the nearest inch. Check your estimate with a ruler.**

1. 

?

2. 

?

What unit would you use to measure each item? Write *inch, foot, yard,* or *mile.*

3. length of a finger

4. width of your classroom

5. height of a door

6. length of the Mississippi River

Practice

Estimate and measure to the nearest $\frac{1}{2}$ inch.

7. 

?

8. 

?

Estimate and measure to the nearest $\frac{1}{4}$ inch.

9. 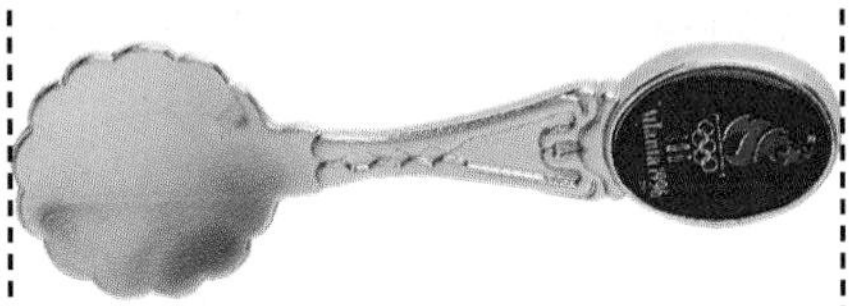

?

10. 

?

Use an inch ruler. Draw each length.

11. 4 in.

12. 6 in.

13. $3\frac{1}{2}$ in.

14. $4\frac{1}{4}$ in.

15. $2\frac{3}{4}$ in.

Choose the best unit.

16. The length of a shoe: 10 inches or 10 feet

17. The distance between two towns: 6 inches or 6 miles

18. The height of a balance beam: 4 feet or 4 miles

19. The length of a room: 14 inches or 14 feet

Complete.

20. 12 in. = __?__ ft

21. 3 ft = __?__ yd

22. 36 in. = __?__ ft

23. 5,280 ft = __?__ mi

24. 36 in. = __?__ yd

25. 2 yd = __?__ ft

26. 1 yd = __?__ in.

27. 1,760 yd = __?__ mi

28. 2 ft = __?__ in.

Problem Solving

29. The Tumblers Club made a banner that measures 10 feet long. About how many yards long is the banner?

30. The distance from school to a practice field is 1,240 yards. Is that less than, more than, or the same as a mile?

31. Suppose it takes 40 minutes by car to go from your house to a gymnastics class. Would the distance be measured in miles or in yards?

32. Zoë estimates a balance beam is about 17 feet long. Hy estimates it's about 18 feet long. The balance beam measures 16 feet. Whose estimate is closer?

Review and Remember

Using Mental Math **Find each sum or difference.**

33. 60 + 30

34. 70 − 40

35. 90 − 10

36. 20 + 70

37. 35 + 20

38. 100 + 25

39. 42 − 20

40. 200 − 50

41. 45 − 30

42. 350 − 75

43. 30 + 25

44. 100 − 95

Project Link

As a class, decide where you will hold your race. Will it be indoors or outdoors?

- Work together to decide the distance each runner will run.
- Measure the distance on your race course and mark both ends.

For Extra Practice, see Set E, page 167.

Pour Some More

You can use different units to measure how much a container holds.

Learning About It

The amount of liquid a container holds is called its **capacity.**

Units used to measure capacity include **cups, pints, quarts,** and **gallons.**

Suppose you want to take 4 cups of water to a track meet. What size container will you take?

Work with your group to find out.

Word Bank

capacity
cup (c)
pint (pt)
quart (qt)
gallon (gal)

What You Need

For each group:
measuring cup
pint, quart, and gallon containers
water
marker
tape

Step 1 Collect empty pint, quart, and gallon containers. Label each container.

Step 2 Estimate how many cups of water you think each container will hold. Record your estimates on a chart like the one shown.

Size of container	Estimate of cups it holds	Actual cups it holds	Actual pints it holds	Actual quarts it holds	Actual gallons it holds
Cup	1	1	0	0	0
Pint				0	0
Quart					0
Gallon					

Step 3 Use a measuring cup to fill a pint container. How many cups of water are needed to fill a pint? Record your results in your chart.

Step 4 Now find out how many cups are needed to fill a quart container. Then do the same for a gallon container. Record your results in your chart.

Step 5 Repeat the activity. This time find out how many pints, quarts, or gallons each container can hold. Record what you find.

Think and Discuss Do containers need to have the same shape to hold the same amount? Explain why or why not.

Practice

Choose the best estimate for each container.

1. 

1 c or 1 gal

2. 

1 c or 1 qt

3. 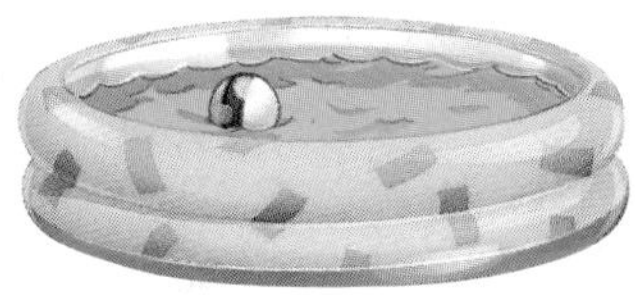

50 c or 50 gal

4. 

2 pt or 2 gal

5. 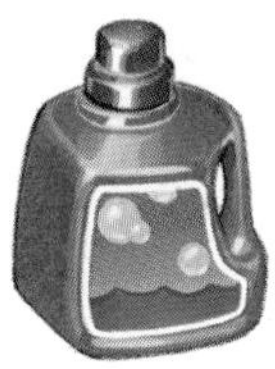

1 c or 1 gal

6. 

35 qt or 35 gal

7. How many cups are there in 1 quart? in 1 gallon?

8. How many pints are there in 1 gallon?

9. **Health and Fitness Connection** You need to drink about 8 cups of water a day to help you stay healthy. How many quarts is that?

10. **Analyze** Suppose you want to take 10 cups of water to a track meet. What is the least number of quart containers you should take?

Bouncing Ounces

You can use customary units to estimate and measure weight.

Word Bank
ounce (oz)
pound (lb)

Learning About It

Ounces and **pounds** are units used to measure weight.

A football weighs about 1 pound.

A tennis ball weighs about 2 ounces.

16 ounces = 1 pound

- Find 3 objects that you think weigh about 1 pound each.
- Find 3 objects that you think weigh about 1 ounce each.
- Check your estimates by weighing each object.

What You Need

For each class:
a balance scale
1-ounce weight (or 10 pennies)
1-pound weight (or 160 pennies)

Think and Discuss Which unit would you use to weigh small objects? large objects? Explain why.

Try It Out

Choose a unit to measure each item. Write *ounces* or *pounds*.

1. swimsuit **2.** jump rope **3.** bicycle **4.** baseball cap

5. golf ball **6.** bowling ball **7.** rowboat **8.** swimming goggles

Choose the best estimate.

9.

2 lb or 2 oz

10.

1 lb or 1 oz

11.

8 lb or 8 oz

12.

3 oz or 3 lb

Practice

Use the chart for Exercises 13–16.

Ball	Weight
basketball	about 21 oz
soccer ball	about 17 oz
tennis ball	about 2 oz
child's bowling ball	about 6 lb

13. Which ball is the lightest? the heaviest?

14. Which ball weighs about 1 pound?

15. About how heavy is a basketball in pounds and ounces?

16. About how heavy is a soccer ball in pounds and ounces?

Write the weight that is more.

17. 13 oz or 1 lb

18. 2 lb or 35 oz

19. 2 lb or 18 oz

20. 3 lb or 50 oz

Problem Solving

Use the chart above for Problems 21 and 22.

21. **Explain** Suppose you put five basketballs in a bag. Would the bag weigh more than 5 pounds? How do you know?

22. **Analyze** Suppose you have a plastic bag of tennis balls that weighs 1 pound. About how many tennis balls are in the bag?

23. A badminton racket weighs about 4 ounces. A tennis racket weighs about 12 ounces. How much heavier is the tennis racket?

24. Patty's baseball bat weighs 1 pound 14 ounces. Her baseball glove weighs 12 ounces. How much heavier is the baseball bat?

Review and Remember

Write the amount.

25.

26.

27.

28.

For Extra Practice, see Set F, page 167.

Fun in the Sun

You can use a thermometer to estimate and measure temperature.

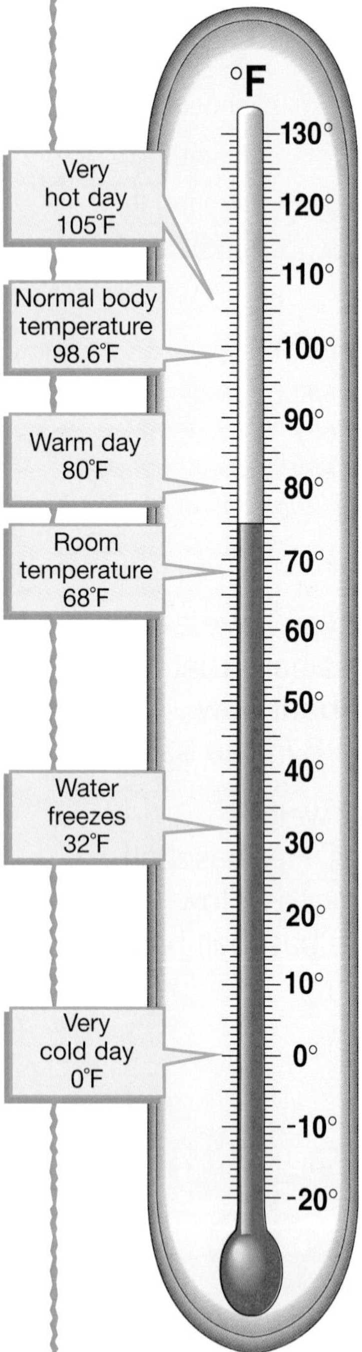

Read: seventy-five degrees Fahrenheit
Write: 75°F

Learning About It

To measure temperature, you can use **degrees Fahrenheit** (°F).

- The thermometer shows 75°F.
- Water boils at 212°F.
- Water freezes at 32°F.

Estimate the temperature for each of the activities shown. Use the thermometer to help you.

Think and Discuss What kind of clothing would you wear if the temperature was 10°F? What if it was 89°F?

Try It Out

Write each temperature. Describe the temperature as *hot, cold, warm,* or *cool*.

1.
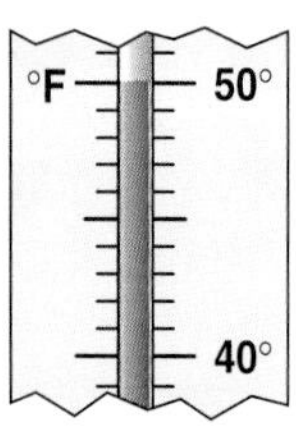

2.
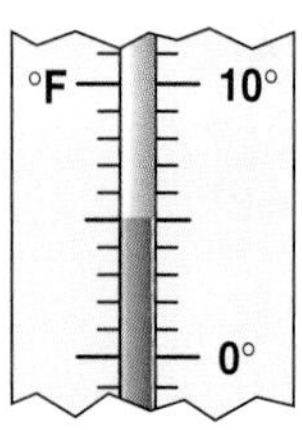

3.
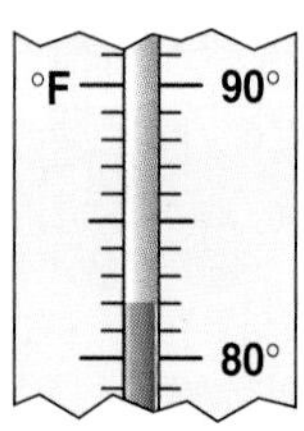

4.
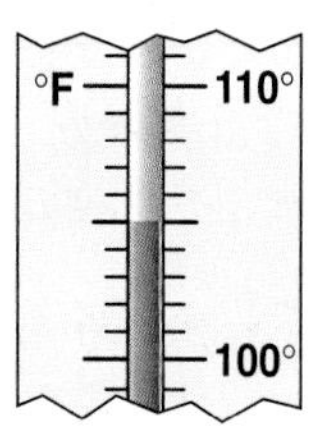

Which temperature is colder?

5. 20°F or 30°F **6.** 60°F or 56°F **7.** 15°F or 5°F

Practice

Write each temperature. Describe the temperature as *hot, cold, warm,* or *cool.*

8. 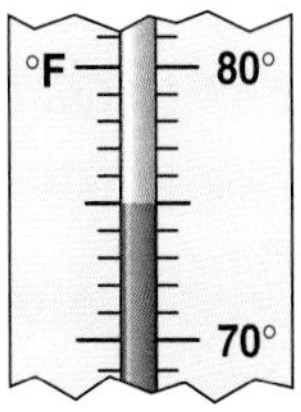

9. 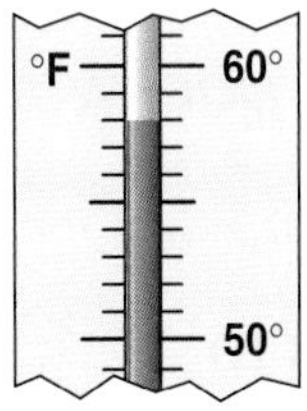

10. 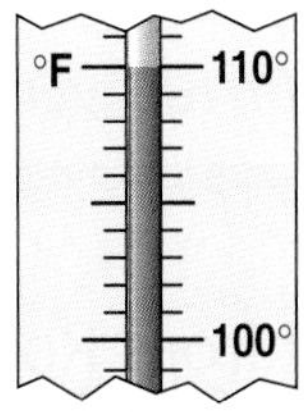

11. 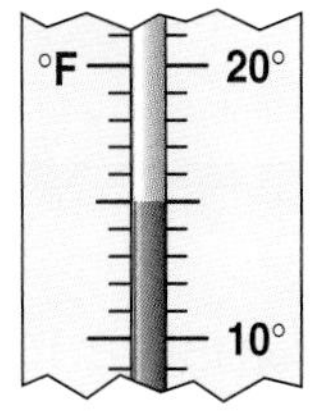

Problem Solving

12. The temperature is 92°F in Miami and 41°F in Seattle. In which city would you rather swim outdoors?

13. Suppose the temperature in your home freezer is 30°F. Can you make ice? Explain why or why not.

14. Analyze The temperature in the morning is 72°F. By noon it has risen 6°. Then it drops 10°. What is the final temperature?

15. Create Your Own Write a problem about a day with three temperature changes. Give your problem to a classmate to solve.

Review and Remember

Add or subtract.

16. 39 + 52 **17.** 190 − 76 **18.** 1,284 + 4,315 **19.** 127 + 465

20. 31 − 12 **21.** 36 + 93 **22.** 1,740 − 246 **23.** 654 − 439

Time for Technology

Surf the Net

Check Out the Weather

You can use the internet to find information about weather in other parts of the world.

Explore one of these sites.

www.weather.com **www.usatoday.com** **www.intellicast.com**

Share your findings with the class.

For Extra Practice, see Set G, page 167.

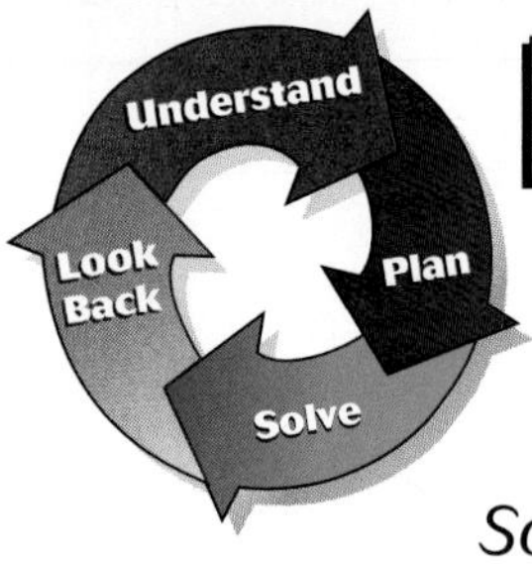

Problem Solving
Work Backwards

Sometimes you can work backwards to solve a problem.

Leah and Dan hiked from Roaring Rapids to Tall Falls. It took 1 hour and 5 minutes to hike from Roaring Rapids to Big Rock. Then it took 25 minutes to get from Big Rock to Tall Falls. They arrived at Tall Falls at 2:45 P.M. At what time did they leave Roaring Rapids?

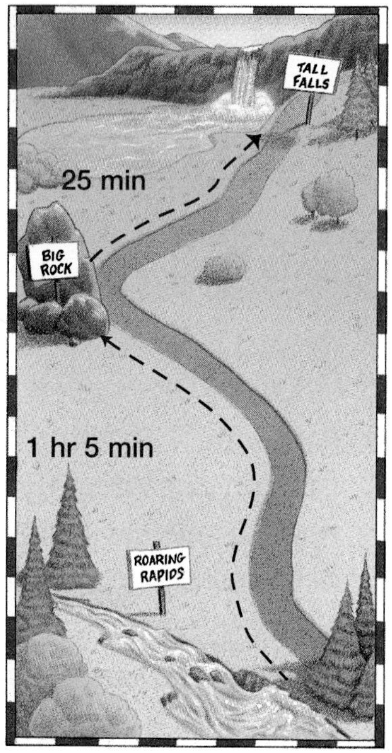

UNDERSTAND

What do you need to find?

You need to find what the time was when the hikers left Roaring Rapids.

PLAN

How can you solve the problem?

You can **work backwards** from the time the hikers reached Tall Falls. Subtract the time it took to hike from Big Rock to Tall Falls. Then subtract the time it took to hike from Roaring Rapids to Big Rock.

SOLVE

Start at 2:45.	Subtract 25 minutes.	Subtract 1 hour and 5 minutes.
This is the time the hikers reached Tall Falls.	This is the time it took to get from Big Rock to Tall Falls.	This is the time it took to get from Roaring Rapids to Big Rock.

Leah and Dan left Roaring Rapids at 1:15 P.M.

LOOK BACK

How can you check if your answer is reasonable?

Using the Strategy

Work backwards to solve each problem.

1. One day when Dan was hiking, he stopped every 2 hours to rest. When he stopped for the fourth time, it was 4:00 P.M. When did Dan start his hike?

2. Leah goes on a hike every other month. She went on her fourth hike in October. In what month did Leah go on her first hike?

3. Beth got $16 change when she bought a hiking map for $2.50 and a bottle of water for $1.50. How much money did she give the salesperson?

4. The temperature at Roaring Rapids was 2° higher than the temperature at Big Rock. At Big Rock the temperature was 6° higher than at Tall Falls. The temperature at Tall Falls was 72° Fahrenheit. What was the temperature at Roaring Rapids?

Mixed Strategy Review

Try these or other strategies you have learned.

THERE'S ALWAYS A WAY!

- *Guess and Check*
- *Act It Out*
- *Draw a Picture*
- *Write a Number Sentence*

5. A bag of mixed nuts and raisins costs $1.25. How many bags can you buy with $5.00?

6. A folded map is 4 inches long. How many folded maps can fit end to end in a box 1 foot long?

7. Walt drank 2 cups of water during the first hour of his hike. If his water bottle holds 8 cups, how many cups of water does he have left?

8. Bob, Joan, and Pat are hiking on a trail in the woods. Joan is in front of Bob. Pat is between Joan and Bob. Who is first in line? Who is last in line?

Off by a Centimeter!

You can use metric units to estimate and measure length.

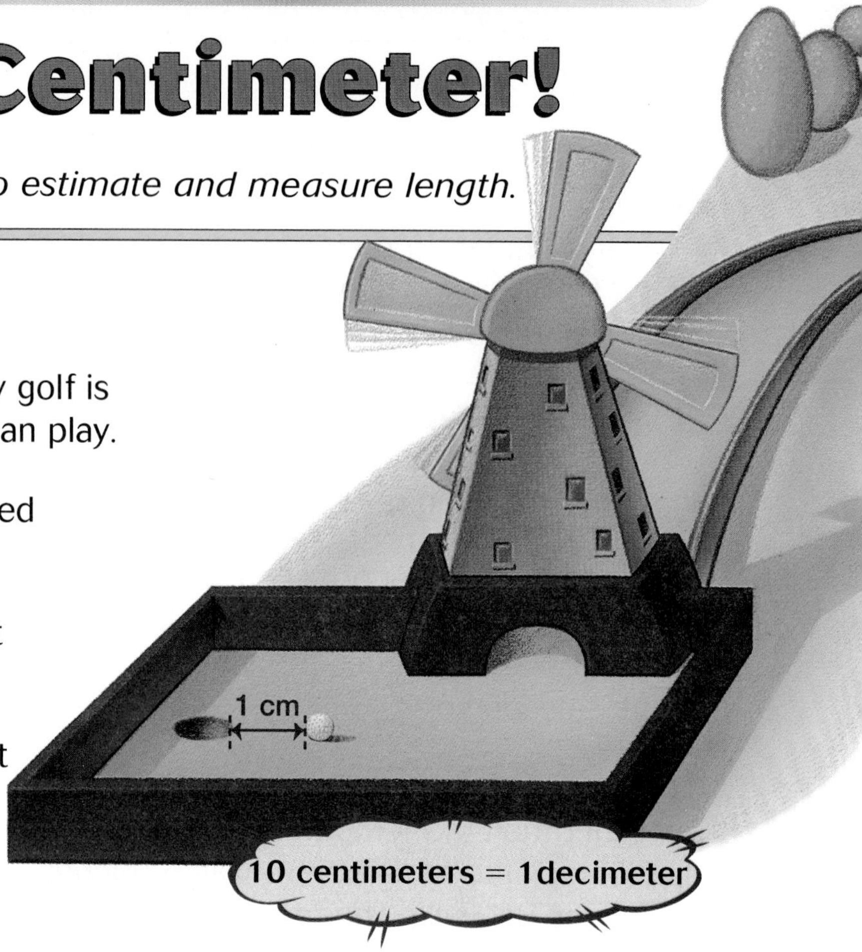

Learning About It

At the Family Fun Park, goofy golf is one of many games people can play.

Tom hit the golf ball. It stopped 1 centimeter from the hole.

A **centimeter** is a metric unit used to measure length.

When Chris hit the golf ball, it stopped 10 centimeters, or 1 **decimeter**, from the hole. That distance would look like this.

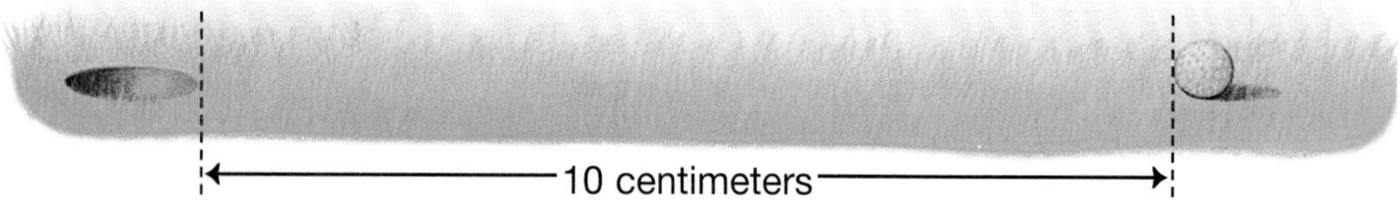

More Examples

Some objects may not be an exact number of centimeters in length. You can measure them to the nearest centimeter.

Look at these golf tees.

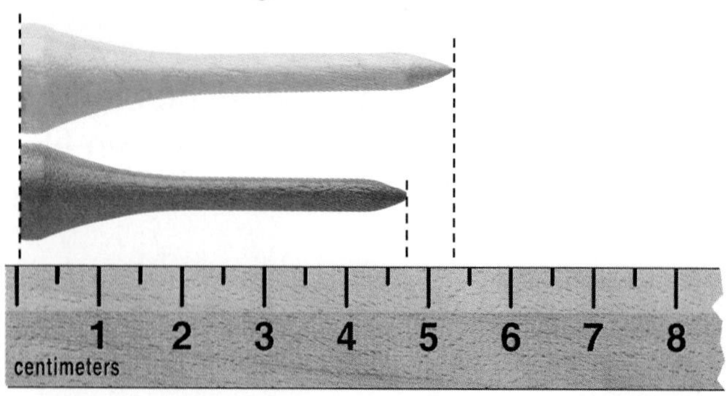

To the nearest centimeter, each golf tee measures 5 centimeters.

Word Bank

centimeter (cm)
decimeter (dm)
meter (m)
kilometer (km)

What You Need

For each student:
centimeter ruler
meterstick

1 m = 100 cm
1 m = 10 dm
1 km = 1,000 m

Connecting Ideas

Centimeters and decimeters are used to measure short lengths. Meters and kilometers are used to measure longer lengths.

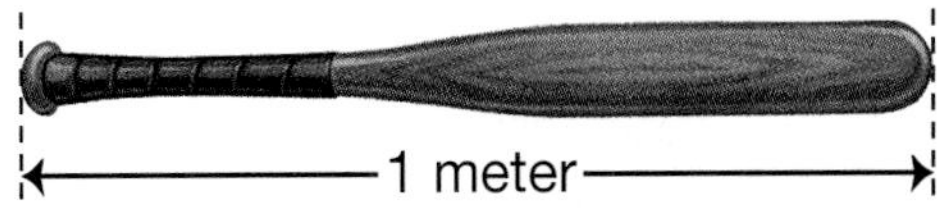

At the Fun Park you can hit baseballs in batting cages. The length of each baseball bat is about 1 **meter**.

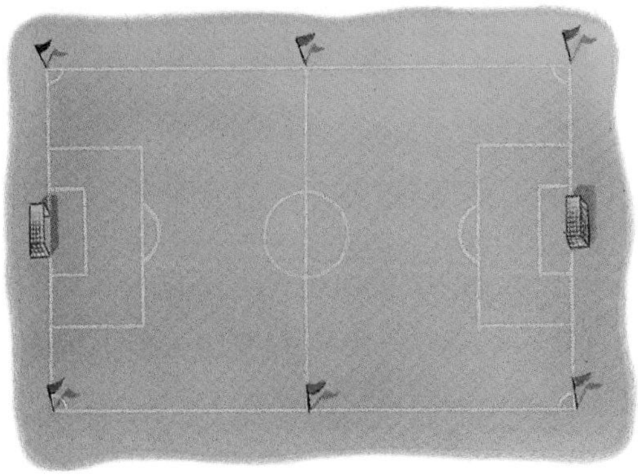

▲ The length of 11 soccer fields end to end is about 1 kilometer.

There is a soccer field at the Fun Park. The length of 11 soccer fields is about 1 **kilometer**.

- Find three things that you think are each about 1 meter long.
- Use a meterstick or a centimeter ruler to check your estimates.
- Name three things you think you could measure in kilometers.

Think and Discuss Would you use a strip of paper 1 cm, 1 m, or 1 km long to measure your height? Explain your choice.

Try It Out

Write the best estimate.

1.

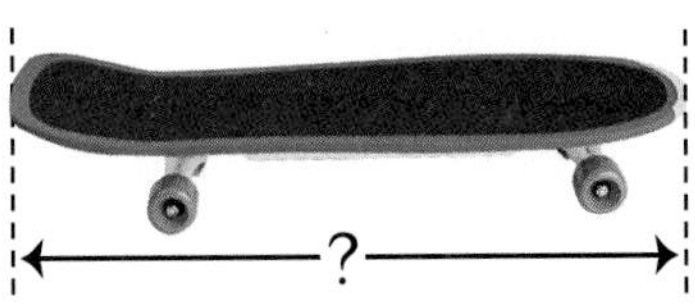

70 cm or 7 cm

2.

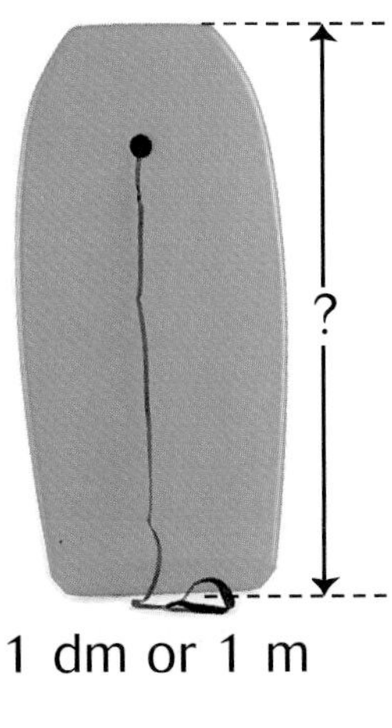

1 dm or 1 m

3.

30 cm or 30 km

Practice

Estimate and measure to the nearest centimeter.

4.

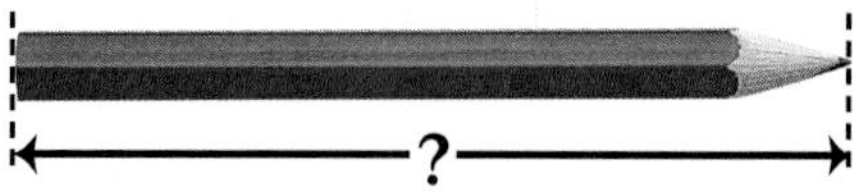

5.

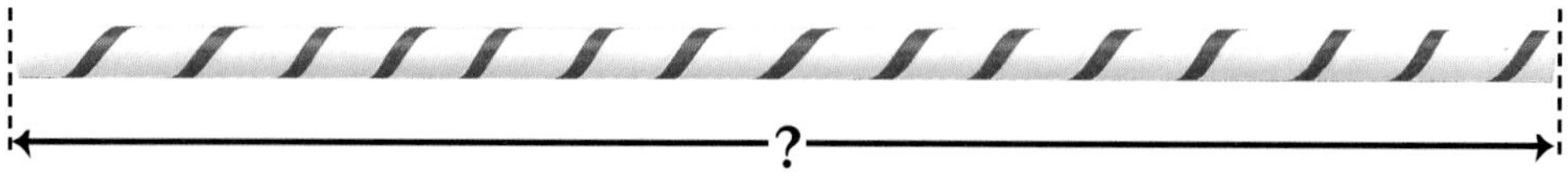

6.

What unit would you use to measure each item? Write *centimeter, decimeter, meter,* or *kilometer.*

7. length of your foot

8. length of a fingernail

9. distance between cities

10. length of your classroom

Complete. Use the information on pages 152–153 to help you.

11. 100 cm = __?__ m

12. 1 km = __?__ m

13. 10 cm = __?__ dm

14. 2,000 m = __?__ km

15. 3 m = __?__ cm

16. 400 cm = __?__ m

The map shows the route of a park path. Use the map for Exercises 17–19.

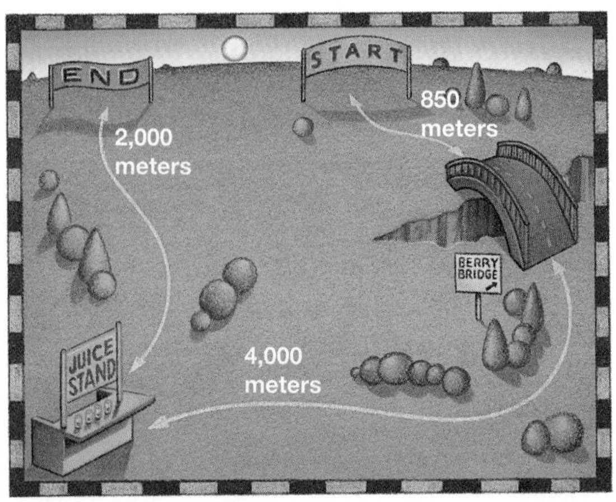

17. Is the distance from Start to Berry Bridge more or less than 1 kilometer?

18. How many kilometers is the distance from Berry Bridge to the juice stand?

19. Is the distance from the juice stand to the end of the path less than, more than, or the same as the distance from Start to Berry Bridge?

Problem Solving

20. Members of a bicycle club rode 5 kilometers around a path before stopping to rest. Did they ride more or less than 1,000 meters?

21. A runner ran in an 800-meter race. Did she run more or less than a kilometer?

22. A shoelace measures 3 decimeters. How many centimeters long is it?

23. **Explain** One person estimated a bench to be 75 cm wide. Another person estimated it to be 55 cm wide. The actual width is 60 cm. Which estimate is closer to the actual measurement?

Project Link

In a relay race, each runner hands a baton on to the next runner. Use rolled newspapers and masking tape to make a baton for your team.

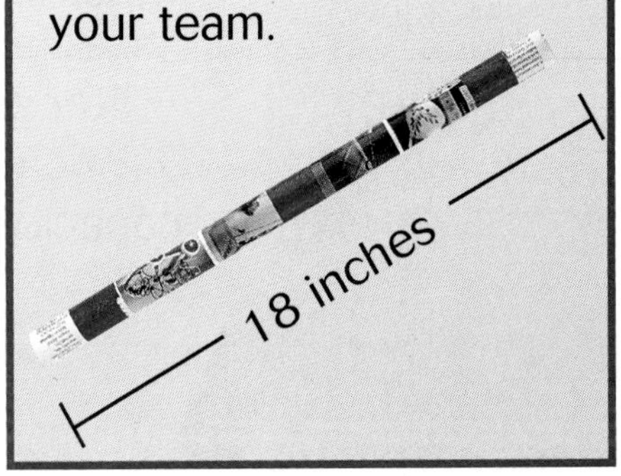

Review and Remember

Add or subtract.

24. $52.79 − $38.08
25. 70 − 53
26. 4,599 + 1,236
27. 6,046 + 7,814
28. 92 − 33
29. $46.25 + $19.98

Critical Thinking Corner

Visual Thinking

What's Wrong?

Ricki, Joe, and Becky each measured the length of a piece of wood by using a centimeter ruler. The pictures show how they made their measurements. What are they each doing wrong?

1. 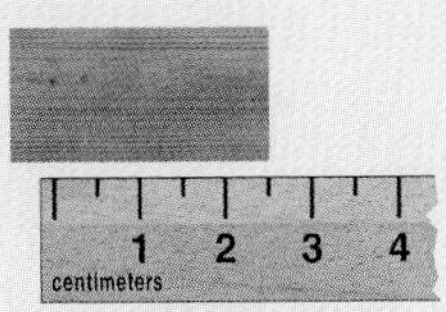

Ricki

2. 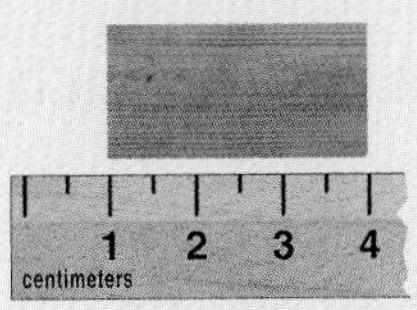

Joe

3. 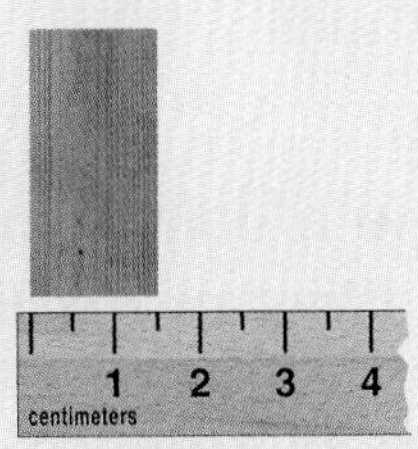

Becky

On the Road

You can use metric units to measure capacity.

This medicine dropper holds about 1 mL.

This water bottle holds about 1 L.

Learning About It

After riding for an hour, the Bicycle Club stops for a drink. Each rider carries 1 liter of water like the one shown.

Word Bank

liter (L)
milliliter (mL)

A **liter** and a **milliliter** are metric units used to measure capacity.

1,000 mL = 1 L

What You Need

For each student:
1-liter container
assorted size containers

- Find three containers that you think will each hold about 1 liter.
- Use water and a 1-liter container to check your estimate.

Think and Discuss Name two items that would have a capacity measured in milliliters.

Try It Out

Using Estimation Does each container hold *more than, less than,* or *about the same as* 1 liter?

1. 

2. 

3. 

4. 

Choose a unit to measure the capacity of each item. Write *liters* or *milliliters*.

5. spoon **6.** bathtub **7.** car gasoline tank

8. drinking glass **9.** swimming pool **10.** soup bowl

Practice

Choose the best estimate.

11. 

1 L or 150 mL

12. 

5 mL or 5 L

13. 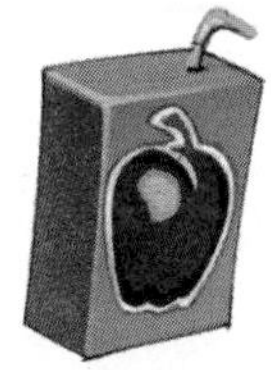

250 mL or 25 L

14. 

40 mL or 40 L

15. 

1 mL or 1 L

16. 

115 mL or 115 L

Choose a unit to measure the capacity of each item. Write *liters* or *milliliters*.

17. soup ladle
18. paint bucket
19. soup can
20. pond
21. perfume bottle
22. pitcher
23. washing machine
24. bottle cap
25. cooler

Problem Solving

26. How many milliliters are in a 5 L container?

27. Suppose you drank 650 mL of water after riding your bicycle. How many more mL would you need to drink to equal 1 liter?

28. Explain If you do not know the capacity of a container, how would you find out how many liters it holds?

Review and Remember

Add or subtract.

29. 7,118 − 6,255
30. 65 + 76
31. 6,794 + 2,363
32. 42 − 21
33. 826 + 108
34. 349 − 149

For Extra Practice, see Set I, page 168.

Grand Grams

Grams and kilograms help you tell how heavy or light objects are.

Learning About It

Some sports equipment is heavy. Some is light. You can use the metric units **grams** and **kilograms** to measure how heavy objects are.

Word Bank
gram (g)
kilogram (kg)

One large paper clip is about 1 gram.

A baseball bat is about 1 kilogram.

1,000 grams = 1 kilogram

- Find three objects that you think would each measure about 1 kilogram.
- Find three objects that you think would each measure about 1 gram.
- Check your estimates by weighing each object.

What You Need

For each class:
balance scale
1-kilogram weight or 400 pennies
1-gram weight or 1 large paper clip

Think and Discuss Which unit would you use to measure how heavy a single golf ball is? a carton of 1,000 golf balls? Give reasons for your choices.

Try It Out

Choose a unit to measure each item.
Write *grams* or *kilograms*.

1. baseball cap **2.** dollar bill **3.** bowling ball **4.** canoe

5. penny **6.** bicycle **7.** piano **8.** golf tee

Practice

Choose the best estimate.

9. 

8 g or 800 g

10. 

1 kg or 1 g

11. 

1 g or 1 kg

12. 

200 kg or 13 kg

13. 

900 kg or 30 g

14. 

5 kg or 550 kg

Using Estimation Is each item *more than, less than,* or *about the same as* 1 kilogram?

15. 

16. 

17. 

Write which measurement is more.

18. 4 kg or 3,500 kg

19. 2,500 g or 2 kg

20. 4,000 g or 4,000 kg

21. 25 g or 1 kg

22. 250 g or 25 kg

23. 3,000 g or 30 kg

Problem Solving

24. One roller skate is about 2 kilograms. How heavy would 2 pairs of skates be?

25. A soccer ball is about 450 grams. How many more grams would it have to be to be 1 kilogram?

Review and Remember

Find each sum.

26. 342 + 904 + 65

27. 2,409 + 371 + 184

28. $18.37 + $52.44 + $85.99

29. 6,435 + 2,114 + 8,790

30. 51 + 49 + 78 + 19

31. 1,234 + 400 + 38

For Extra Practice, see Set J, page 168.

Goose Bumps

You can use a Celsius thermometer (°C) to measure temperature.

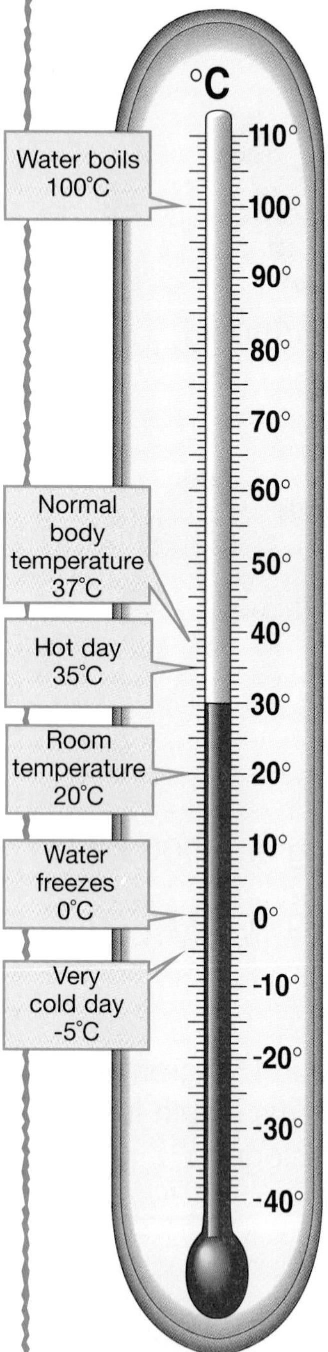

Read: thirty degrees Celsius
Write: 30°C

Learning About It

To measure temperature, you can use **degrees Celsius** (°C).

- The thermometer shows 30°C.
- Water boils at 100°C.
- Water freezes at 0°C.

Estimate the temperature for each of the activities shown. Use the thermometer to help you.

Think and Discuss What would you wear outside if the thermometer measured 10°C? What if it was 35°C?

Try It Out

Write each temperature. Describe the temperature as *hot, cold, warm,* or *cool.*

1. 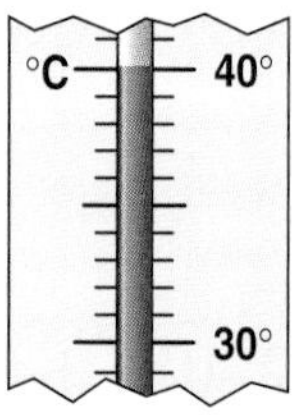

2. 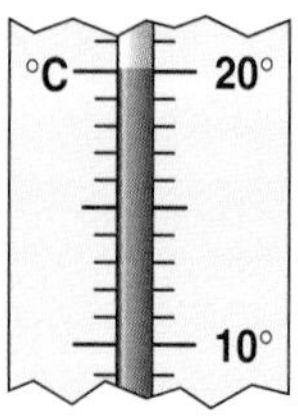

3. 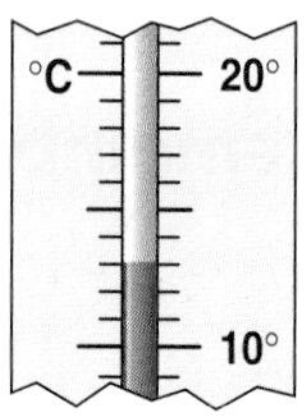

4. 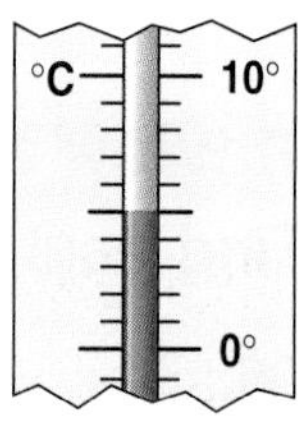

Which temperature is warmer?

5. 18°C or 28°C **6.** 50°C or 60°C **7.** 70°C or 65°C

Practice

Choose the best estimate.

8.

0°C or 20°C

9.

8°C or 100°C

10.

90°C or 32°C

Write each temperature. Describe the temperature as *hot, cold, warm,* or *cool.*

11.

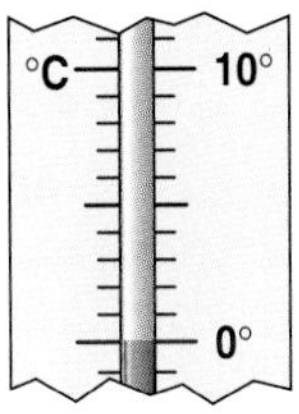

12.

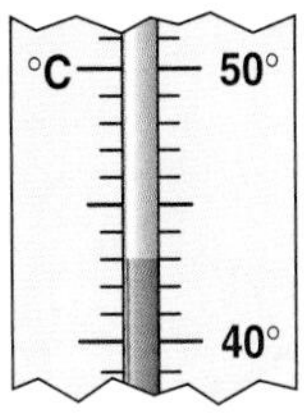

13.

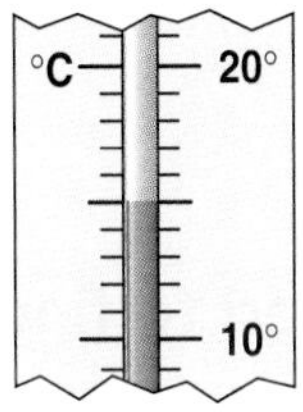

14.

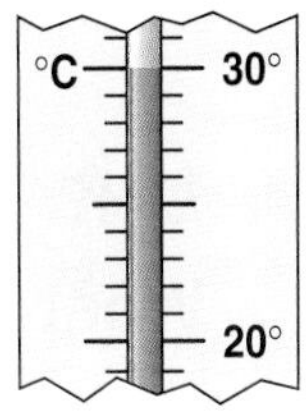

15.

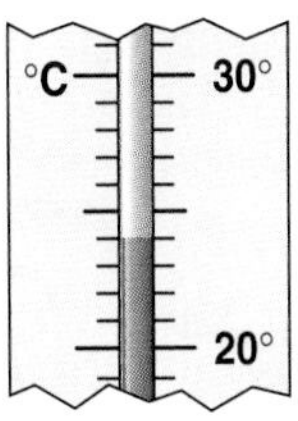

16.

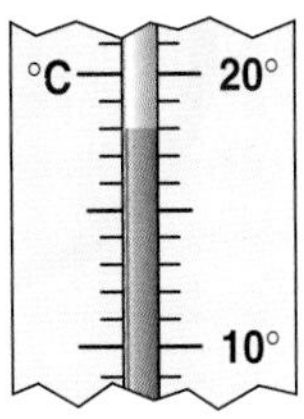

17.

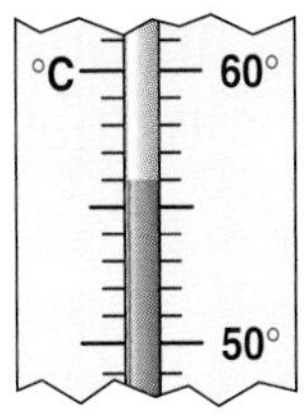

18.

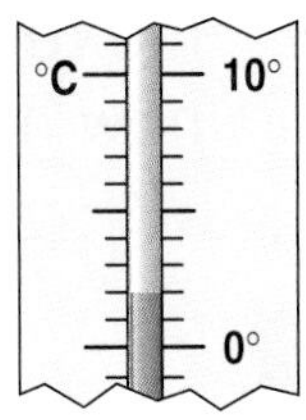

Problem Solving

19. Water is boiling on the stove. Would the water temperature be 212°C or 100°C?

20. A thermometer measures 39°C. Is this warmer or cooler than normal body temperature?

21. **Explain** In Dallas, Texas, the temperature is 34°C. In Chicago, Illinois, the temperature is 15°C. In which city would you be more likely to wear a jacket outside?

22. When Susan woke up yesterday, the temperature outside was 24°C. By noon, the temperature was 7 degrees warmer. What was the temperature at noon?

Review and Remember

www.sbgmath.com

Add or subtract.

23. 39 + 23 **24.** 53 − 11 **25.** 767 − 593 **26.** 384 + 295

27. 88 + 47 **28.** 98 − 59 **29.** 491 + 456 **30.** 685 − 487

For Extra Practice, see Set K, page 168.

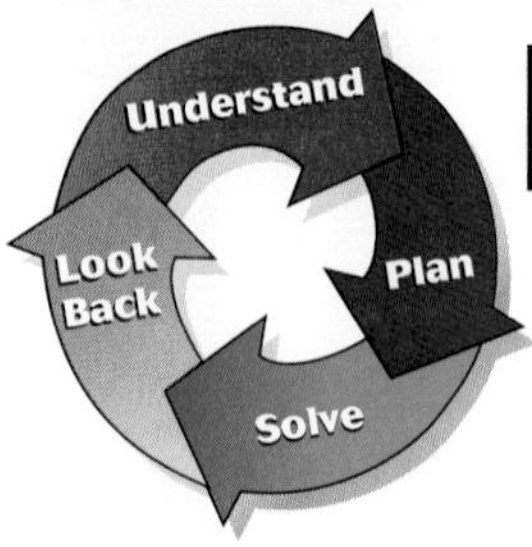

Problem Solving
Using Measurement

Use what you know about measurement to solve problems.

Ginny's class is planning a field day. Her teacher gives her 100 meters of rope. He asks Ginny to make a rectangle on the playground that is 40 meters long and 25 meters wide. Does Ginny have enough rope?

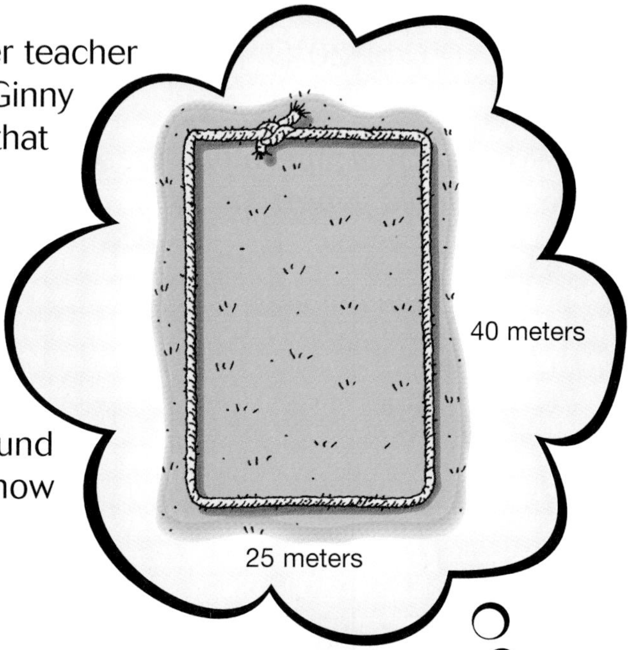

UNDERSTAND

What do you need to find?

You need to find the distance around the rectangle. You also need to know how much rope Ginny has.

PLAN

How can you solve the problem?

You can add the lengths of each side of the rectangle. Then you can compare that sum with the length of the rope.

SOLVE

40 + 40 + 25 + 25 = 130 meters

Ginny needs 130 meters of rope to make the rectangle. She only has 100 meters of rope, so Ginny does *not* have enough rope.

LOOK BACK

Check your answer by adding the sides of the rectangle in a different order.

Show What You Learned

Solve.

1. The 3-kilometer race started at 1:55 P.M. Jed finished the race at 2:10 P.M. How many minutes did Jed run?

2. In the jumping contest, Kamara jumped 2 feet 4 inches. Gwen jumped 2 feet 9 inches. How much farther did Gwen jump?

3. When the field day began, the temperature was 73° Fahrenheit. At noon it was 8° hotter. By 2:00 P.M. the temperature was 2° hotter than it was at noon. What was the temperature at 2:00 P.M.?

4. Ginny hopped the 50-meter sack race in 3 minutes. Suppose she hopped at the same speed in a 100-meter sack race. How many minutes would it take her to finish the race?

5. In one game, Nat's team had to fill a gallon jug with water using a measuring cup. Nat went last. The jug was 3 quarts full. How many cups did Nat have to pour in?

6. **Create Your Own** Write a word problem about a relay race that can be solved using units of measurement. Give it to a classmate to solve.

Use the chart below to answer Questions 7–10.

Race Results		
Runner	50-Meter Race	200-Meter Race
Jake	14 seconds	54 seconds
Scott	12 seconds	52 seconds
Latanya	15 seconds	50 seconds

7. Write the order in which the three runners finished the 50-meter race.

8. Write the order in which the three runners finished the 200-meter race.

9. Rachel also ran in the 50-meter race. If she was 4 seconds slower than the winner, what was her time?

10. **Analyze** When Rachel ran the 200-meter race she was 2 seconds slower than the person who came in third. What was her time?

Checkpoint

Measurement

Use an inch ruler. Draw each length. (pages 140–143)

1. 4 in. **2.** $2\frac{1}{2}$ in. **3.** $4\frac{1}{4}$ in. **4.** $2\frac{3}{4}$ in.

Write the weight that is more. (pages 146–147, 158–159)

5. 1 lb 8 oz or 26 oz **6.** 1 kg or 900 g **7.** 3 kg or 3,100 g

Write each temperature. Describe the temperature as *hot, cold, warm,* or *cool.* (pages 148–149, 160–161)

8.
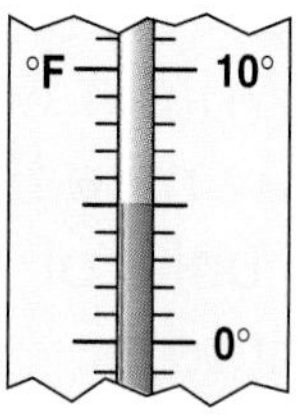

9.
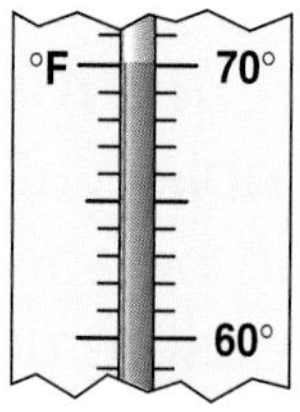

10.
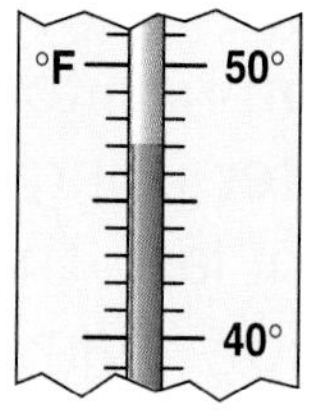

11.
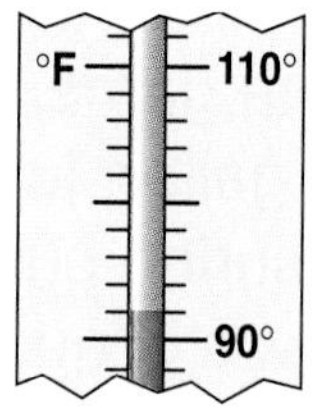

Estimate and measure to the nearest centimeter. (pages 152–155)

12.
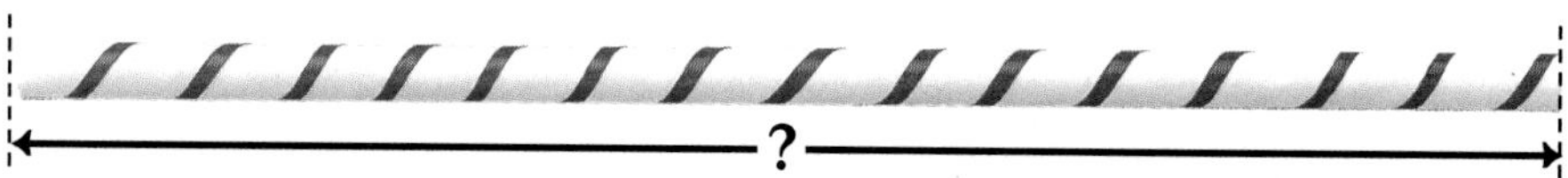

13.
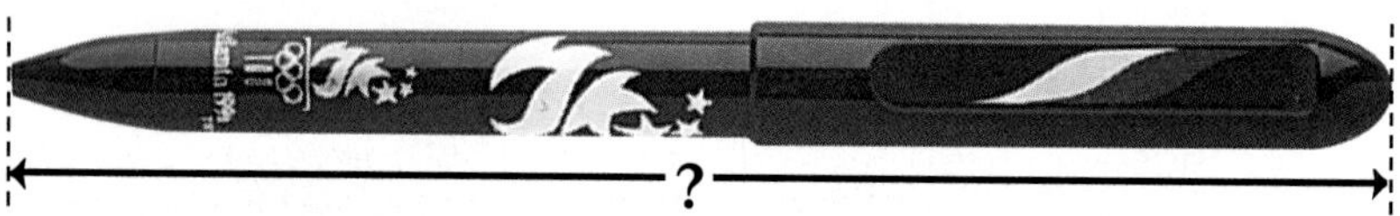

What unit would you use to measure each item? Write *centimeter, decimeter, meter,* or *kilometer.* (pages 152–155)

14. length of a baseball bat

15. distance you could walk in 2 hours

16. length of a swimming pool

17. distance you could throw a ball

What unit would you use to measure the capacity of each item? Write *liters* or *milliliters.* (pages 156–157)

18. pitcher

19. small juice can

20. lake

21. drinking glass

Problem Solving

22. Which is a better outdoor temperature for a picnic, 20°C or 45°C?

23. Suppose it takes 30 minutes to drive in a car from your house to the park. Would the distance be measured in feet, yards, or miles?

24. Carrie walks 2 kilometers every day. How many kilometers does she walk in a week? in 2 weeks?

25. The temperature at noon was 74°F. At night, the temperature was 58°F. How much colder was the temperature at night?

What do you think?

What unit of measure would you use to measure short lengths? Explain your choice.

Journal Idea Write a short, funny story about what happens when someone uses a ruler incorrectly. Tell what is measured incorrectly and why the result is funny.

Project Wrap-Up

On Your Marks! Get Set! Go!

You're ready to race, one team at a time!

- The runner for the first part, or leg, of the relay will start when your teacher says "GO!"
- Record each runner's time. Then find the total team time.

Make a record of your race for your classroom. Work as a class to make a bar graph that shows how the race turned out.

Extra Practice

Set A (pages 128–129)

Write each time using numbers.

1. quarter to three **2.** six forty-five **3.** thirty minutes after three

4. quarter past two **5.** eight-fifteen **6.** eleven o'clock

7. nine-thirty **8.** half past four **9.** forty-five minutes after one

Set B (pages 130–131)

Write each time in two ways.

1. 

2. 

3. 

4. 

Set C (pages 132–133)

Write how much time has passed.

1. 8:10 A.M. and 11:10 A.M. **2.** 9:17 P.M. and 10:17 P.M.

3. 5:20 A.M. and 5:30 A.M. **4.** 6:05 P.M. and 7:00 P.M.

5. Soccer practice starts at 4:00 P.M. and ends at 5:45 P.M. How long is soccer practice?

Set D (pages 136–137)

Use the calendar page for Exercises 1–4.

1. What is the date of the football game?

2. How many Saturdays are there?

3. What day of the week is November 10?

4. On what day of the week is Thanksgiving?

November

Sunday	Monday	Tuesday	Wednesday	Thursday	Friday	Saturday
	1	2	3	4	5	6
7	8	9	10	11	12	13
14 Football Game	15	16	17	18	19	20
21	22	23	24	25 Thanksgiving	26	27 Karate Class
28	29	30				

Extra Practice

Set E (pages 140–143)

Use an inch ruler. Draw each length.

1. 3 in.
2. $5\frac{1}{2}$ in.
3. $2\frac{1}{4}$ in.
4. $3\frac{3}{4}$ in.
5. $1\frac{3}{4}$ in.
6. $4\frac{1}{2}$ in.
7. $2\frac{3}{4}$ in.
8. 5 in.
9. Frank jumped $5\frac{1}{2}$ feet. Is this closer to 1 yard or 2 yards?
10. Would a basketball player be 6 feet tall or 6 yards tall?

Set F (pages 146–147)

Write the weight that is more.

1. 8 ounces or 6 ounces
2. 1 lb 6 oz or 23 oz
3. 1 pound or 18 ounces
4. 2 lb 2 oz or 32 oz
5. 2 lb 11 oz or 40 oz
6. 2 lb 8 oz or 43 oz
7. Colleen's running shoes weigh 20 oz. Kurt's running shoes weigh 1 lb 7 oz. Whose running shoes weigh less?
8. Suppose one red sneaker weighs 1 lb 2 oz. How many ounces does the pair of sneakers weigh?

Set G (pages 148–149)

Write each temperature. Describe the temperature as *hot, cold, warm,* or *cool.*

1. 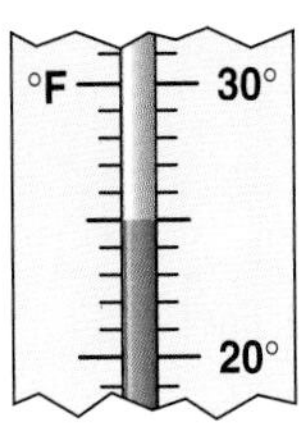

2. 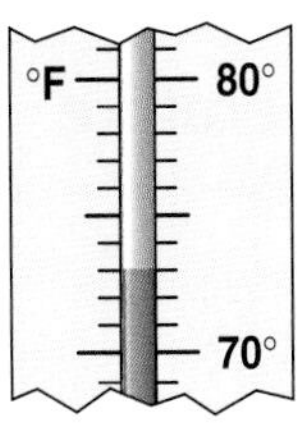

3. 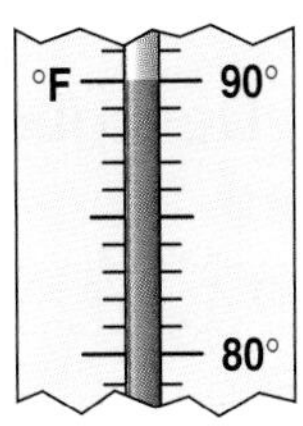

4. 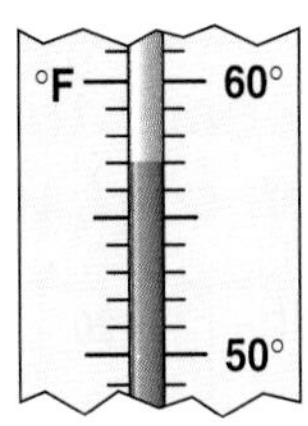

5. The thermometer outside shows 25°F. Will you put on a coat to go out? Why or why not?

Extra Practice

Set H (pages 152–155)

Estimate and measure to the nearest centimeter.

1. 

2. 

3. 

What unit would you use to measure each?
Write *centimeter, decimeter, meter,* or *kilometer.*

4. length of a toothpick
5. height of a mountain
6. height of a flagpole

Set I (pages 156–157)

Choose a unit to measure each item.
Write *liters* or *milliliters*.

1. jug
2. bathtub
3. medicine dropper
4. teacup
5. perfume bottle
6. truck's gasoline tank

Set J (pages 158–159)

Choose the best estimate.

1. 

   50 g or 1 kg

2. 

   10 kg or 100 kg

3. 

   150 kg or 1 kg

Set K (pages 160–161)

Write each temperature. Describe the temperature as *hot, cold, warm,* or *cool.*

1. 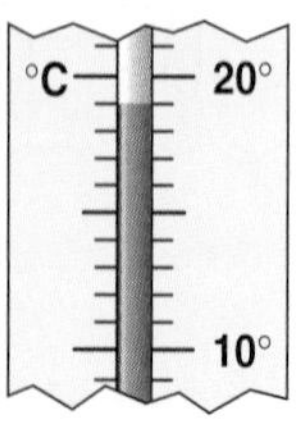

2. 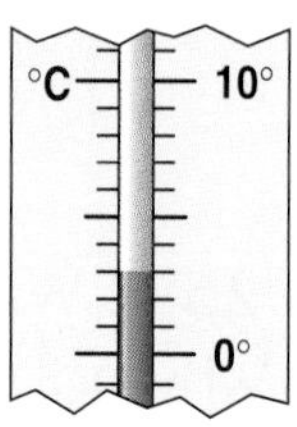

3. 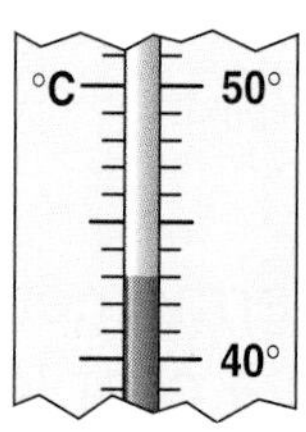

Chapter Test

Write how much time has passed.

1. 

2. 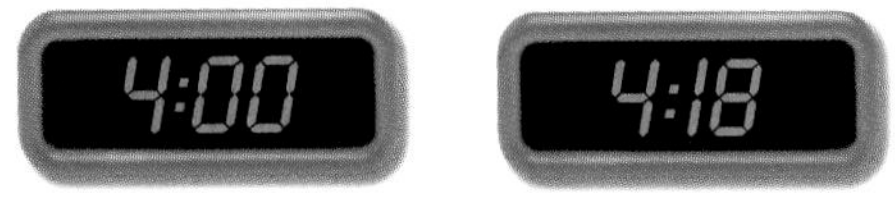

Draw each length.

3. $2\frac{1}{2}$ in. 4. $3\frac{3}{4}$ in. 5. $\frac{1}{4}$ in. 6. 4 cm 7. 10 cm 8. 6 cm

Choose cup, pint, or gallon to measure each item.

9. kitchen sink 10. mug 11. bathtub 12. shampoo bottle

Choose liter or milliliter to measure each item.

13. swimming pool 14. soup spoon 15. medicine dropper

Write each temperature.

16. 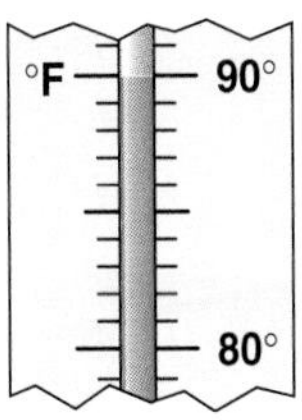

17. 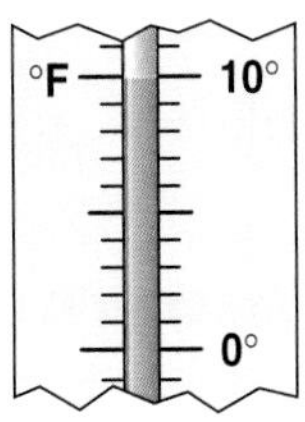

18. 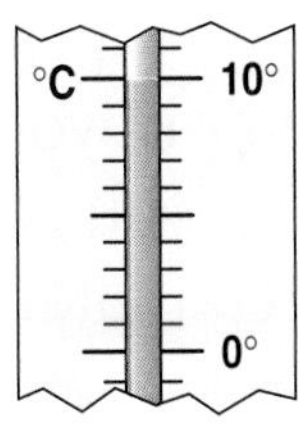

19. 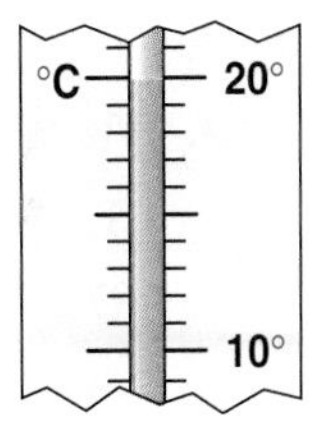

Write the weight that is more.

20. 1 lb or 14 oz 21. 2 lb 3 oz or 40 oz

22. 700 g or 1 kg 23. 5 kg or 4,500 g

24. Bob lost some money. He has $3.50 now. Yesterday he spent $2.50. He started with $10. How much money did Bob lose?

25. It takes Lily 35 minutes to get home. If she leaves at 4:35 P.M., can she be home by 5:00 P.M.? Explain why or why not.

Self-Check
Did you position your ruler correctly for Exercises 3–8?

Performance Assessment

Show What You Know About Time and Measurement

What You Need

rulers
paper clips
string
color tiles
clock

1. Use the chart to answer Questions 1a–1c. Show your answers on a real clock or one you have made or drawn.

   a. You start skating at 3:30 P.M. Show the time that you will be finished.

   b. Some students play 3 games of kickball in a row, without stopping. They start at 10:00 A.M. Show the time that they will be finished.

   c. Basketball starts at 2:25 P.M. The bus will pick up the basketball team 20 minutes after basketball ends. Show the time that the bus will pick up the team.

Playing Time	
Activity	**Minutes**
Basketball	55
Kickball	20
Skating	30

2. Use the materials shown below for Questions 2a–2b.

   a. Measure the cover of your math book in as many ways as you can. Record your results. Which material is best for measuring your book? Explain your thinking.

   b. Repeat the activity, measuring two other items in the classroom. For each item, explain which material is best for measuring.

Self-Check

For Question 1c, did you remember to add the amount of time spent playing basketball to the starting time?

For Question 2a, did you find more than one way to measure your book?

Extension

Making a Schedule

A schedule shows when events or activities will happen. Here's a schedule showing the times for team tryouts.

Use the schedule to answer these questions.

Team Tryouts

Time	Activity
10:30 – 12:30	baseball team
1:00 – 3:00	soccer team
3:30 – 4:30	volleyball team
4:00 – 5:30	swim team

1. What time do swim tryouts start?
2. Could you attend both the soccer and the volleyball tryouts? Why or why not?
3. How much time is there for baseball tryouts?
4. **Create Your Own** Write a schedule for a class picnic. Include time to eat lunch, play games, and clean up.
   - Make two columns. Write *Time* at the top of one column and *Activity* at the top of the other.
   - Under *Activity,* list each of the activities in the order in which they will happen.
   - Under *Time,* write the time each activity will begin and end.
5. Why would students at the picnic want to see the schedule at the start of the picnic?

Chapter 5

Multiplication Concepts

Chapter Theme: SCHOOL ACTIVITIES

Career Spotlight Meet Caryl Williams, a teacher in an elementary school. She gets her students excited about reading all kinds of books—from true stories about desert animals to tales about mice who ride motorcycles!

Reading teachers use math, too. They can use multiplication to figure out how much paper will be needed for book reports.

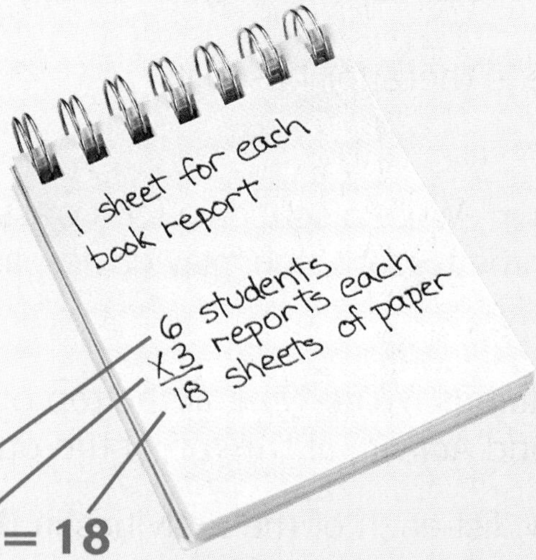

$6 \times 3 = 18$

Chapter Project

Create a Bookworm

Get ready to read, write, and draw! You and your classmates are going to create a giant bookworm! To get started, follow these steps.

- Make the worm's head. What materials will you use?
- Attach the worm's head to the wall. You will add a part to the worm each time one of you finishes reading a book. Make sure there is plenty of room behind the head for you to attach your worm parts.
- Start thinking about books you might like to read.

Kids are Special people
I read
Sylvester and the Magic Pebble
by
William Steig
Maria read
My Father's Dragon
by
Ruth Stiles Gannett
Manuel read
Miss Rumphius
by
Barbara Cooney
Sarah read
Charlotte's Web
by
E.B White
Lin read
Amelia Bedelia
by
Peggy Parish
Onawa read
A Bear Called Paddington
by
Michael Bond
Chung read
The Kingdom of Wolves
by
Scott Barry
A BEAR CALLED PADDINGTON
MICHAEL BOND
MY FATHER'S DRAGON

Counting Counters

Multiplying is like adding equal groups.

Learning About It

Work with your partner. Find out how many counters you need to make 4 groups of 6 counters.

Step 1 Use 4 paper plates. Put 6 counters on each plate. How many counters are there altogether?

> When you have equal groups of objects, you can add or you can **multiply** to find the total number of objects.
>
> $6 + 6 + 6 + 6 = 24$ counters
>
> 4 groups of $6 = 24$ counters
>
> $4 \times 6 = 24$ counters

Word Bank

multiply

What You Need

For each pair:
12 index cards
6 paper plates
36 counters

Step 2 Use the counters and paper plates to make other equal groups. First write the numbers from 1 to 6 on two sets of index cards.

Step 3 Pick a card from one set to find how many plates you need. Pick a card from the other set to find how many counters to put on each plate.

- What could you do to find out how many counters you need for all the plates?

Step 4 Repeat Step 3 five or more times.
Record your work in a chart like the one below.

Draw	Think	Write
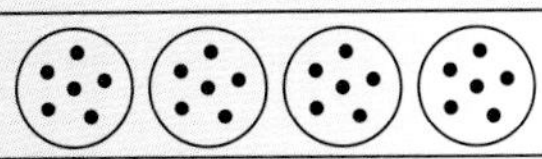	4 groups of 6 = 24	$4 \times 6 = 24$

Think and Discuss Suppose you have 8 boxes of crayons. What must you know before you can multiply to find how many crayons you have in all?

Practice

Write a multiplication sentence for each picture.

1. 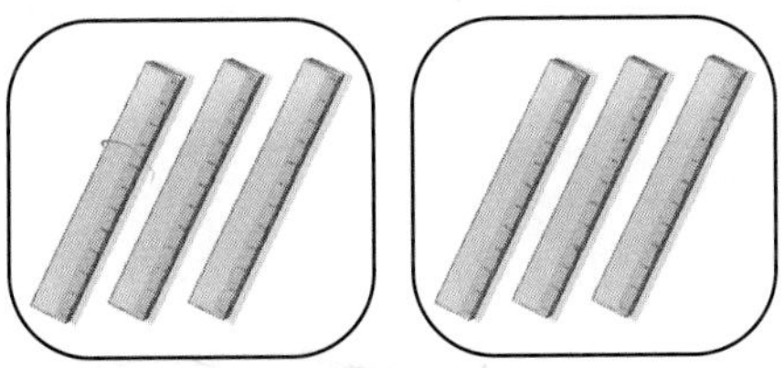

2. 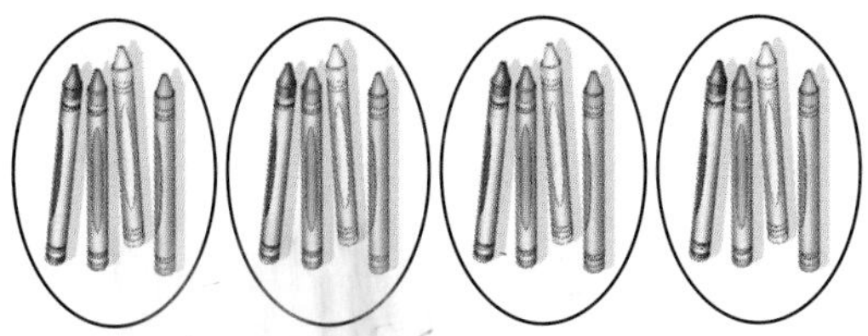

3. 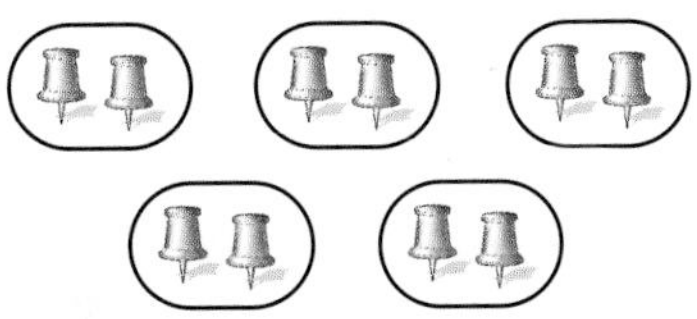

4. 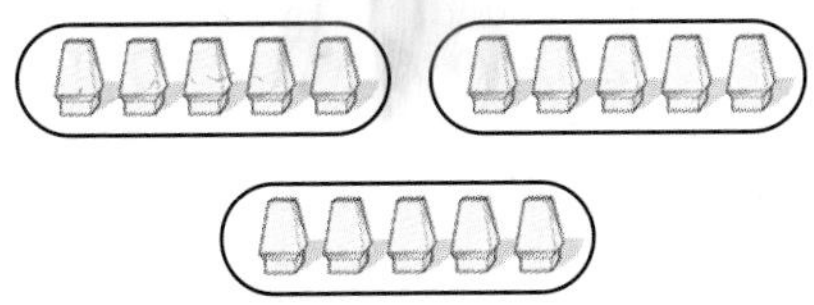

For each picture tell whether or not you can write a multiplication sentence. Explain why or why not.

5. 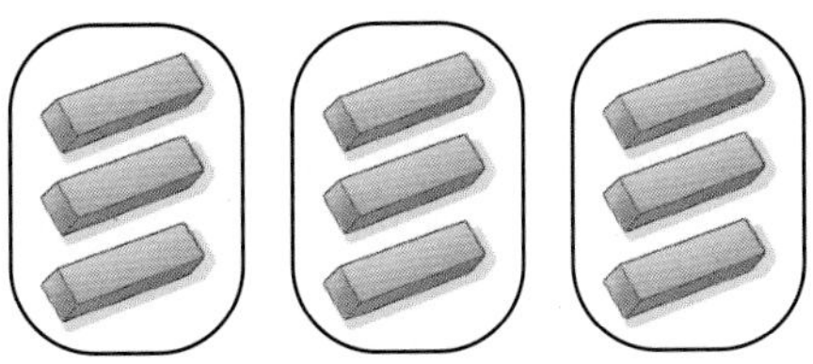

6. 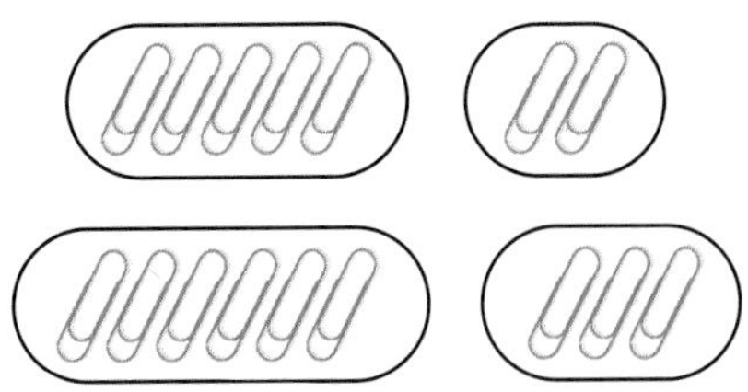

7. 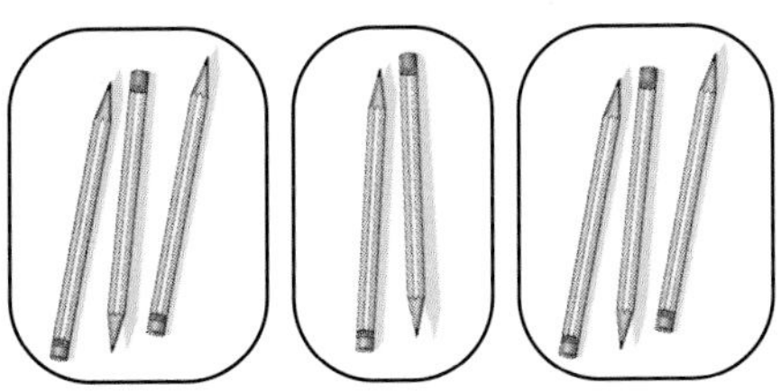

8. 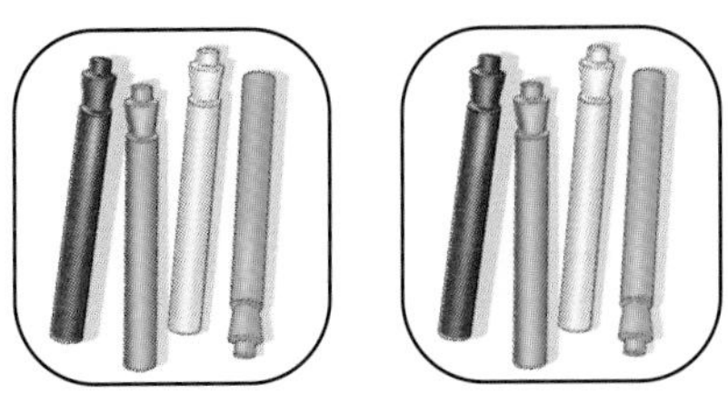

Book Fair

Multiplying can be like using repeated addition.

Learning About It

Word Bank
factors
product

The book fair is here! Each of the 4 shelves in this bookcase holds 8 books. How many books are in the bookcase?

You can add to find out.

$8 + 8 + 8 + 8 = 32$

Whenever you add the same number again and again, you can also multiply.

$8 + 8 + 8 + 8 = 32$

4 groups of 8 = 32

So $4 \times 8 = 32$

(4 and 8: factors; 32: product)

There are 32 books in the bookcase.

> The numbers you multiply are called **factors.**
>
> The answer you get when you multiply is called the **product**.

More Examples

A.

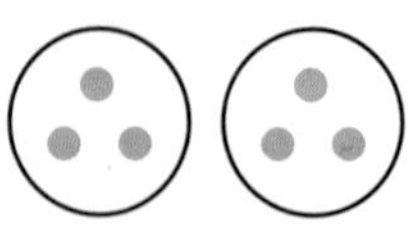

$3 + 3 = 6$
2 groups of 3 = 6
$2 \times 3 = 6$

B.

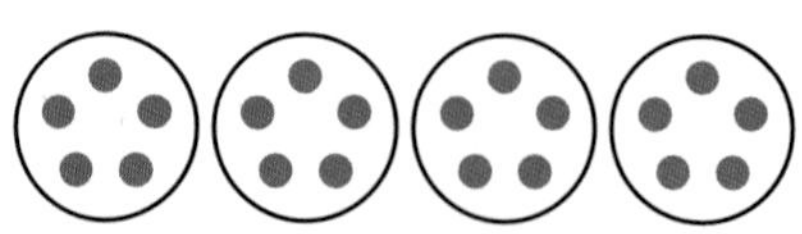

$5 + 5 + 5 + 5 = 20$
4 groups of 5 = 20
$4 \times 5 = 20$

Think and Discuss What multiplication sentence could you use to show $7 + 7 + 7 + 7 + 7 + 7$?

Try It Out

Write a multiplication sentence for each addition sentence.

1. 3 + 3 + 3 + 3 + 3 + 3 = 18 **2.** 5 + 5 = 10 **3.** 7 + 7 + 7 = 21

4. 4 + 4 + 4 + 4 = 16 **5.** 1 + 1 + 1 = 3 **6.** 0 + 0 = 0

Practice

Write an addition sentence and a multiplication sentence for each set of pictures.

7.

8.

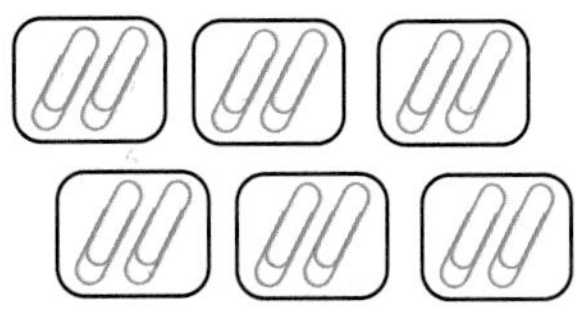

9.

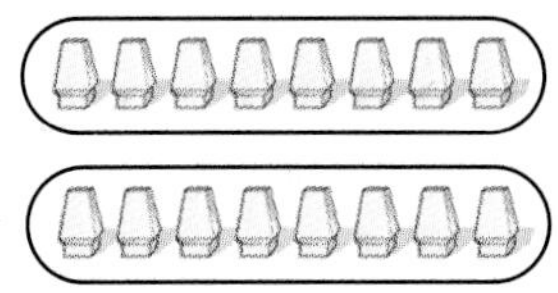

Write a multiplication sentence for each addition sentence.

10. 2 + 2 + 2 + 2 = 8 **11.** 8 + 8 = 16 **12.** 9 + 9 + 9 = 27

13. 7 + 7 + 7 + 7 + 7 = 35 **14.** 5 + 5 + 5 = 15 **15.** 1 + 1 + 1 + 1 = 4

Problem Solving

Use the chart for Problems 16–19.

16. How much do 3 picture books cost?

17. Suppose you have $27. Can you buy 5 storybooks? Explain your answer.

18. Which costs less, 9 comic books or 9 picture books?

19. On the last day of the book fair, storybooks go on sale for $4 each. How much money can you save if you buy 6 storybooks on the last day?

Review and Remember

Add or subtract.

20. 34 + 28

21. 181 + 125

22. 9,004 − 2,506

23. 372 − 164

24. 1,287 − 489

For Extra Practice, see Set A, page 204.

Using Algebra

Hurray for Arrays!

Drawing arrays can help you think about multiplication.

Word Bank

array

Learning About It

It's United Nations Day! You are putting up a display of flags from around the world on your classroom wall. How many flags are in the display?

Wait! Before you start counting, look at how the flags are placed.

The flags form an **array.** An array shows objects in rows and columns.

There are 3 columns.

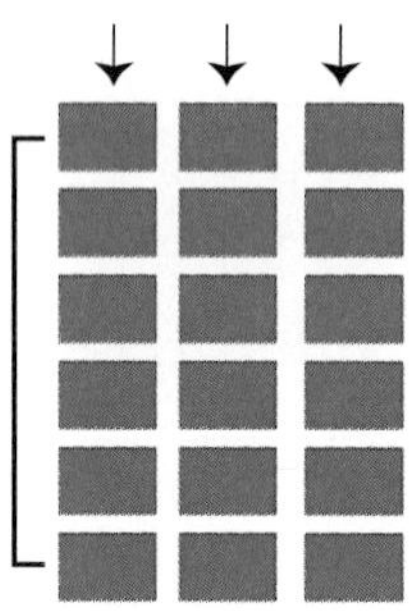

There are 6 rows.

www.sbgmath.com

Since an array is made of equal groups, you can multiply to find how many objects are in it.

There are 6 rows.
There are 3 flags in each row.
$6 \times 3 = 18$

There are 18 flags in the display.

Oh no! The display was put up sideways!
Are there still 18 flags?

Compare the two arrays.

How many rows?
How many flags in each row?
How many in all?
$6 \times 3 = 18$

How many rows?
How many flags in each row?
How many in all?
$3 \times 6 = 18$

Yes, both arrays have 18 flags.

> The order in which you multiply factors does not change the product.

More Examples

A.

$4 \times 2 = 8$

$2 \times 4 = 8$

B.

$5 \times 3 = 15$

$3 \times 5 = 15$

Think and Discuss If you know that $4 \times 8 = 32$, how can that help you find the product of 8×4?

Try It Out

Complete the multiplication sentence for each array.

1. 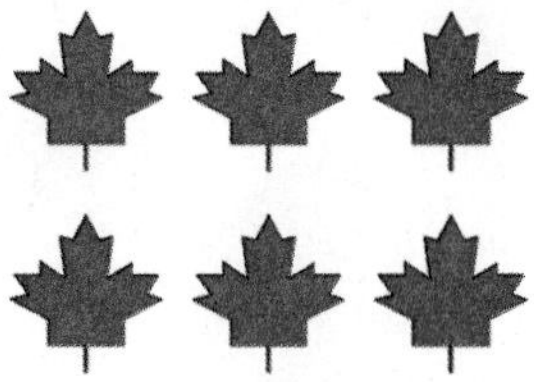

2 × 3 = ■

2. 

3 × 6 = ■

3. 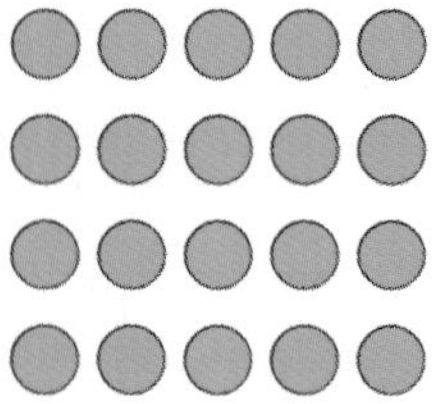

4 × 5 = ■

Practice

Write a multiplication sentence for each array.

4. 

5. 

6. 

7. 

8. 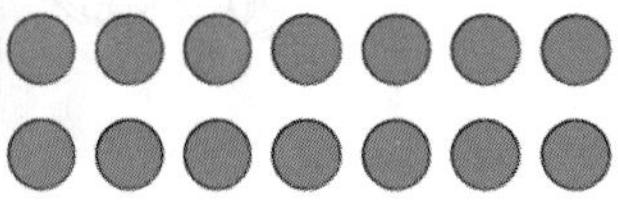

9. 

Draw an array for each multiplication sentence. Then find the product.

10. 3 × 4 **11.** 4 × 3 **12.** 2 × 5 **13.** 5 × 2

14. 8 × 3 **15.** 3 × 8 **16.** 1 × 9 **17.** 9 × 1

Using Algebra **Write the number that belongs in each ■.**

18. 4 × 6 = 24, so 6 × 4 = ■

19. 9 × 7 = 63, so 7 × 9 = ■ 63

20. 5 × 6 = 30, so ■ × 5 = 30

21. 7 × 4 = 28, so ■ × 7 = 28

22. ▼ × ● = 35, so ● × ▼ = ■

23. ▲ × ● = 12, so ● × ▲ = ■

6 × 2 = 12 2 × 6 = 12
4 × 3 = 12, 3 × 4 = 12
1 × 12 = 12, 12 × 1 = 12

Problem Solving

24. Mr. Swinton's class made classroom mailboxes. There are 7 rows. There are 4 mailboxes in each row. How many mailboxes did the class make?

25. A flag store has many flags displayed in an array. There are 3 rows of state flags and 3 rows of flags from other countries. If there are 8 flags in each row, how many flags are on display?

26. Social Studies Connection In 1945, there were 51 countries that belonged to the United Nations. By 1996 there were 185 countries. How many more countries belonged in 1996 than in 1945?

The United Nations headquarters is in New York City. Its goals include peace, health, and education for all people. Flags of the member countries fly in front of its buildings.

Review and Remember

Give the place value of the underlined digit.

27. $\underline{1}8$ **28.** $3\underline{4}$ **29.** $\underline{1}23$ **30.** $8\underline{0}6$ **31.** $\underline{2},970$ **32.** $\underline{4}5,310$

Time for Technology

Using CD-ROM

Making Arrays

Use frames to make an array that shows 8 x 9.

- Open a frames space. Link it to two number spaces.
- Click-drag the right bar until 9 frames show. Then click-drag the top bar until 8 frames show.
- Click a catalog item to fill the array. Click one number space. Then, click =.
- Follow the steps to make another array to show 9 x 8.

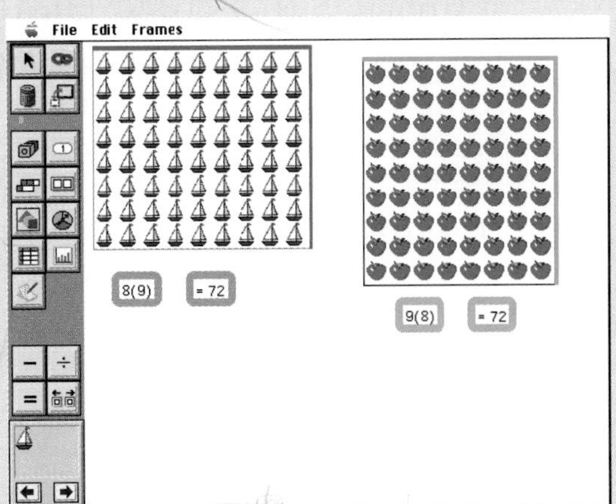

For Extra Practice, see Set B, page 204.

Developing Skills for Problem Solving

First read for understanding and then focus on whether answers are reasonable or not.

READ FOR UNDERSTANDING

Mr. Morgan's class is going on a field trip to the science museum. He is putting students in groups of 4. There are 8 groups of students. One adult volunteer will stay with each group.

1. How many groups are there?
2. How many students are in each group?
3. How many adult volunteers will there be on the trip?

THINK AND DISCUSS

MATH FOCUS

Reasonable Answers Whenever you answer a question, always check that your answer is reasonable. Look at the facts that are given. Then make sure your answer makes sense compared with those facts.

Reread the paragraph at the top of the page.

4. Would it be reasonable to say that 8 students are going on the trip? Explain why or why not.
5. How many people (including Mr. Morgan) are going on the trip? Would 32 people be a reasonable answer?
6. What should you do if your answer is not reasonable?

Show What You Learned

Answer each question. Give a reason for your choice.

The students visit the Rock and Mineral Exhibit, where they see a rock collection. The rocks are arranged in 6 rows with 4 rocks in each row. Four of the rocks are green.

1. How could you find the number of rocks that are *not* green?
   - **a.** Find the total number of rocks.
   - **b.** Find the total number of rocks. Then add 4.
   - **c.** Find the total number of rocks. Then subtract 4.

2. If someone wanted to know how many rocks are *not* green, would 24 be a reasonable answer?
   - **a.** Yes, because there are 24 rocks in all.
   - **b.** No, the answer must be greater than 24.
   - **c.** No, the answer must be less than 24.

The Electricity Exhibit shows 6 videos every day. Five of the videos are each 3 minutes long. The other video is 7 minutes long.

3. What could you do to find the total number of minutes it would take to watch all the videos?
   - **a.** Find $7 + 3$. Then multiply by 6.
   - **b.** Find 5×3. Then add 7.
   - **c.** Find 6×3. Then add 7.

4. **Explain** Would it be reasonable to say that it takes 15 minutes to watch all the videos? Why or why not?

Music Assembly

There are lots of ways to multiply by 2.

Learning About It

The music assembly is starting! Your class has 7 pairs of maracas to use in the show. How many maracas does your class have?

$7 \times 2 = \blacksquare$ or $\begin{array}{r} 2 \\ \times\, 7 \\ \hline \end{array}$

factors   factors

THERE'S ALWAYS A WAY!

- **One way** to find the product is to use repeated addition.

  $2 + 2 + 2 + 2 + 2 + 2 + 2 = 14$

Maracas are rattles that come from South America. They are usually made from gourds or wood. The insides are filled with seeds or beads.

- **Another way** is to skip count.

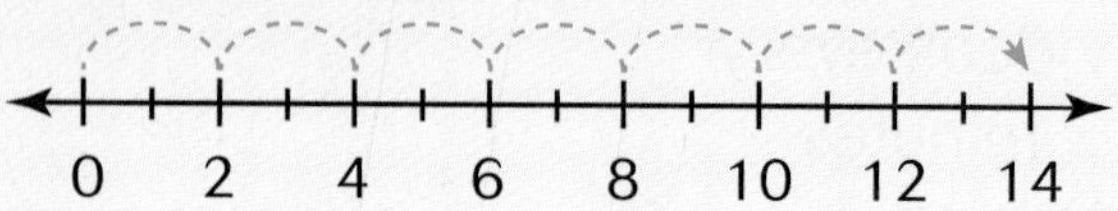

Count by 2s until you have said 7 numbers.

2, 4, 6, 8, 10, 12, 14

- **Another way** is to use doubles.

  Think: $7 \times 1 = 7$
  Double 7 to make 14.
  So, $7 \times 2 = 14$

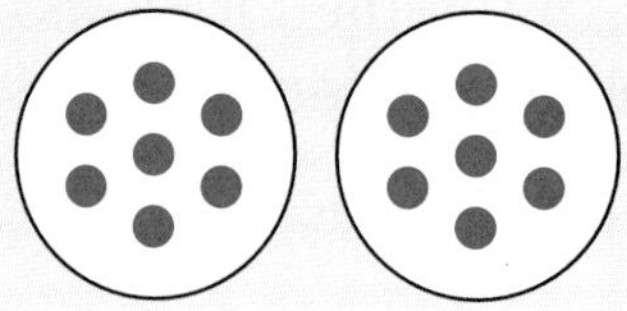

$7 \times 1 = 7$ $7 \times 1 = 7$

Your class has 14 maracas.

Think and Discuss How could you use doubles to find 6×2?

Try It Out

Complete each multiplication sentence.

1.

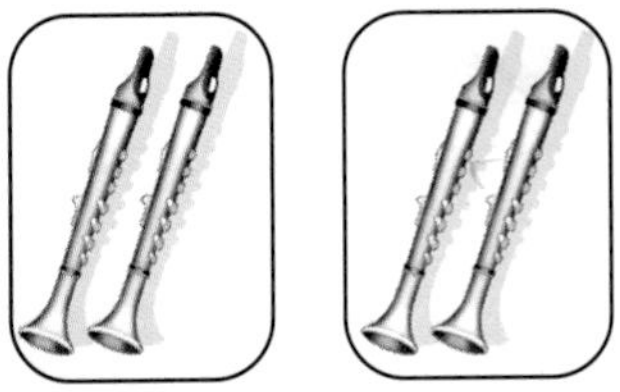

$2 \times 2 =$ ■

2.

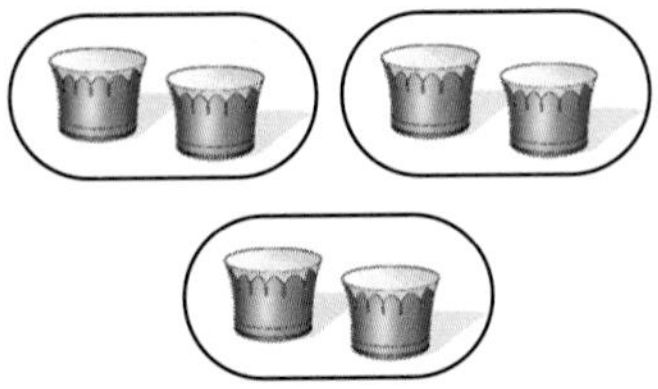

$3 \times 2 =$ ■

3.

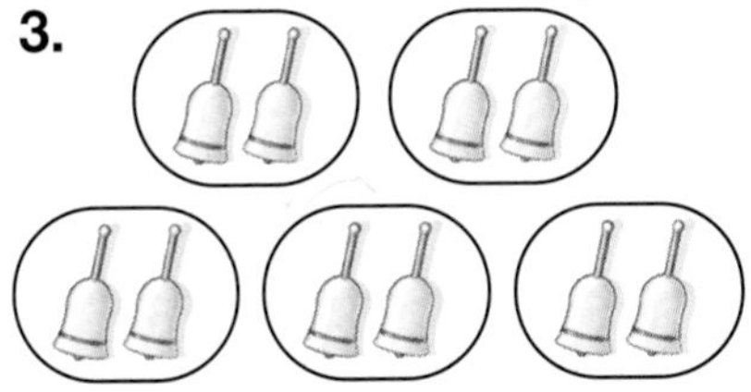

■ × ■ = ■

Practice

Multiply.

4. 2×3	**5.** 4×2	**6.** 2×9	**7.** 7×2	**8.** 5×2	**9.** 3×2
10. 6×2	**11.** 2×1	**12.** 2×2	**13.** 2×5	**14.** 2×8	**15.** 2×7

16. 9×2 **17.** 2×6 **18.** 1×2 **19.** 2×4 **20.** 8×2

Problem Solving

21. A tape of the music assembly is on sale for $2. Is $13 enough to buy 6 tapes?

22. The school band has 4 trumpets, 3 flutes, and 5 clarinets. How many trumpets and flutes are in the school band?

23. **Fine Arts Connection** One class learned how to play tabla drums for the assembly. If the class had 3 pairs of drums, how many drums did they have in all?

Kid Connection Maulik Zaveri, of Maryland, has played the tabla drums since age 5. He has performed in many different countries.

Review and Remember

Estimate. Then use a calculator to find each sum or difference.

24. $356 + 125$	**25.** $641 - 524$	**26.** $387 + 349$	**27.** $972 - 684$	**28.** $793 + 648$

For Extra Practice, see Set C, page 205.

Art Class

Skip counting can help you multiply by 5.

Learning About It

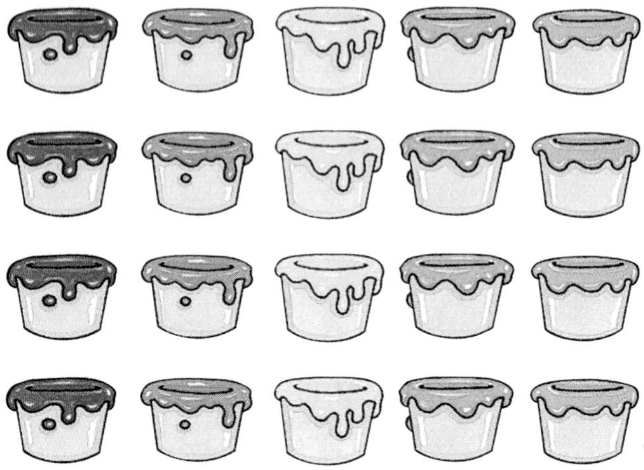

You are getting paint ready for art class. There are 4 groups of students. Each group needs 5 different colors of paint. How many dishes of paint do you need?

4 × 5 = ■ or $\begin{array}{r} 5 \\ \times 4 \\ \hline \end{array}$

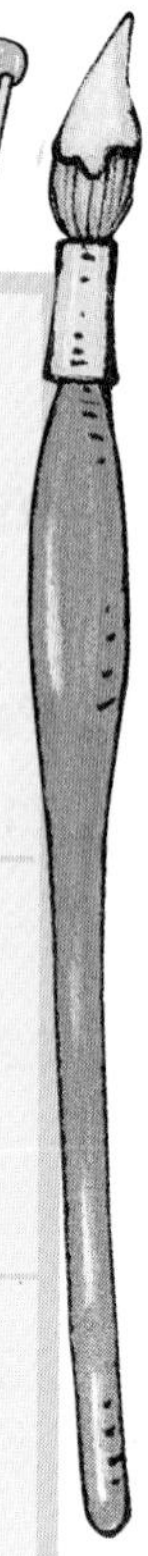

THERE'S ALWAYS A WAY!

- **One way** to find the product is to skip count.

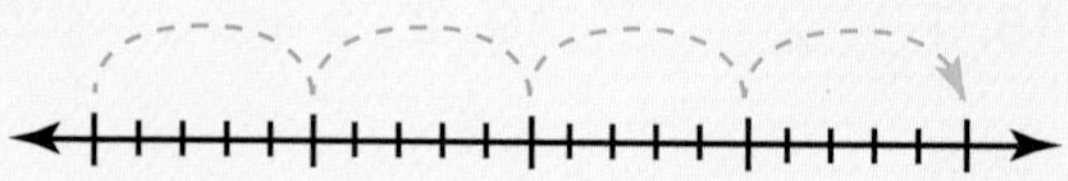

Count by 5s until you have said 4 numbers.

5, 10, 15, 20

- **Another way** is to draw a picture. Show 4 groups of 5.

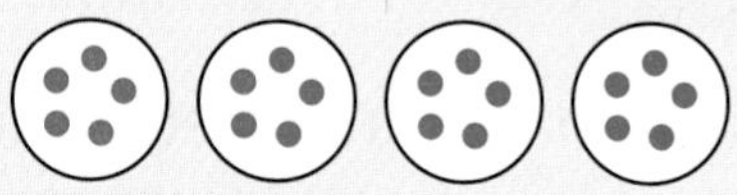

20 dishes in all

- **Another way** is to use a multiplication fact.

4 × 5 = 20

You need 20 dishes of paint.

Think and Discuss How would you use skip counting to find 6 × 5?

www.sbgmath.com

Try It Out

Draw a picture to show each multiplication sentence.

1. 5 × 3 **2.** 7 × 5 **3.** 2 × 5 **4.** 5 × 4 **5.** 5 × 1

Practice

Multiply.

6. 5×7	**7.** 6×5	**8.** 8×5	**9.** 5×4	**10.** 3×5	**11.** 5×6
12. 1×5	**13.** 5×3	**14.** 9×5	**15.** 5×2	**16.** 5×5	**17.** 7×5

18. 5×1 **19.** 5×5 **20.** 5×8 **21.** 5×3 **22.** 5×9

Using Algebra **Complete each pattern.**

23. 5, 10, 15, ■, ■, ■, ■

24. 25, 30, ■, ■, 45, ■, ■

25. 40, 35, 30, ■, ■, ■, ■

26. 4, 6, 8, ■, ■, ■, ■

27. 20, 18, ■, ■, 12, 10, ■

28. 6, 9, ■, ■, ■, 21, ■

Problem Solving

29. Sasha bought 5 sheets of posterboard. She cut each poster into 4 pieces. How many pieces does she have?

30. Mr. Connor buys 8 boxes of colored chalk for his class. Each box has 5 pieces of chalk in it. He puts 9 pieces on the chalkboard tray and saves the rest. How many pieces of chalk does he save?

31. Analyze Any time 5 is a factor, what digits can be in the ones place of the product?

Project Link

Have you chosen some books to read?

- If each person in your class read 2 books, how many parts would be added to the bookworm?
- How many parts would be added to the bookworm if each person in your class read 5 books?

Review and Remember

Using Estimation **Estimate each answer by rounding to the nearest hundred.**

32. $342 + 598$	**33.** $308 - 120$	**34.** $685 + 602$
35. $890 - 476$	**36.** $962 - 676$	**37.** $588 + 324$

Checkpoint

Understanding Multiplication

Write a multiplication sentence for each picture. (pages174–175)

1. 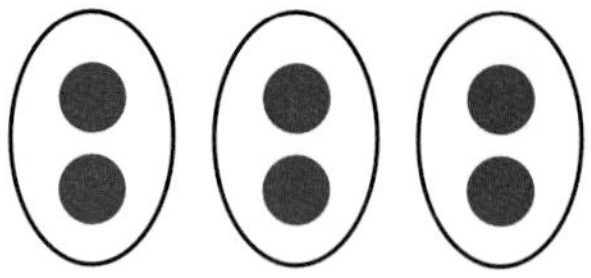

2. 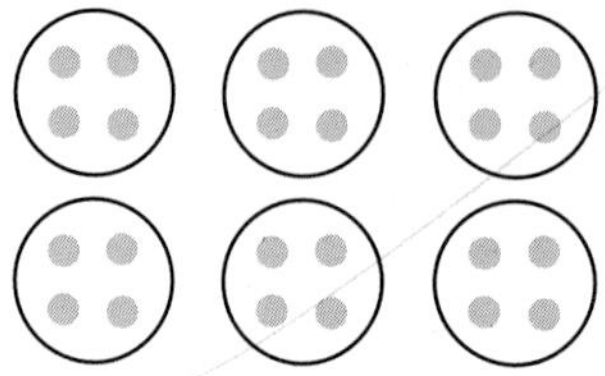

3. 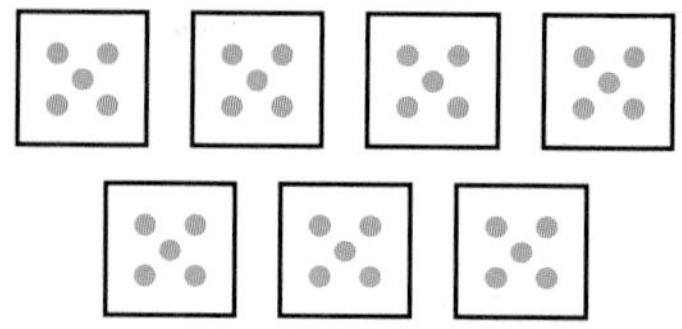

Write a multiplication sentence for each addition sentence. (pages 176–177)

4. $2 + 2 + 2 + 2 + 2$

5. $7 + 7 + 7$

6. $5 + 5 + 5 + 5$

7. $9 + 9 + 9 + 9$

8. $6 + 6$

9. $4 + 4 + 4 + 4 + 4 + 4$

10. $4 + 4$

11. $8 + 8 + 8$

12. $3 + 3 + 3 + 3 + 3 + 3 + 3$

Using Algebra

Write a multiplication sentence for each array. (pages 178–181)

13. 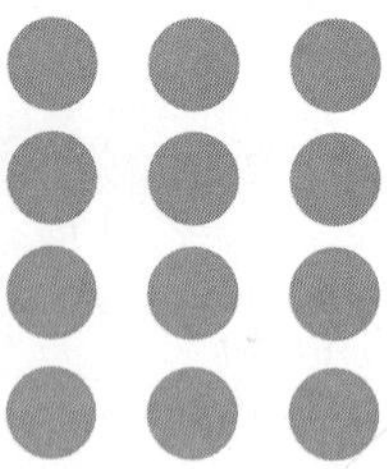

14. 

15. 

Using Algebra

Draw an array for each multiplication sentence. (pages 178–181)

16. 2×5

17. 4×3

18. 2×2

19. 6×6

20. 8×2

21. 3×4

Find each product. (pages 184–187)

22. 2×7

23. 4×2

24. 6×5

25. 9×5

26. 5×3

27. 4×5

28. 2×6

29. 7×2

30. 9×2

31. 6×2

Problem Solving

32. The Bay School computer lab has 9 tables. There are 5 computers on each of 6 tables. How many computers are in the lab?

33. Mrs. Goodman gave 2 pencils to each of 4 students. Mr. Witt gave 3 pencils to each of 5 students. Who gave out more pencils?

34. Jackie has 3 boxes of markers. Each box has 8 markers in it. Jackie takes 2 markers out of each box. How many markers are still in the boxes?

35. **Analyze** Mrs. Butler wants to put her students into groups of 5. She makes 4 groups. Three students are left. How many students are in Mrs. Butler's class?

What do you think?

Does the order in which you multiply factors change the product?

Journal Idea Write two addition sentences—one that can be solved by multiplying and one that cannot.

Critical Thinking Corner

Using Algebra **Visual Thinking**

An Array Puzzle

- You can use arrays to make a puzzle!
- Use grid paper. Make arrays to show these multiplication examples.

2×7	3×2	8×5
4×5	4×2	3×4

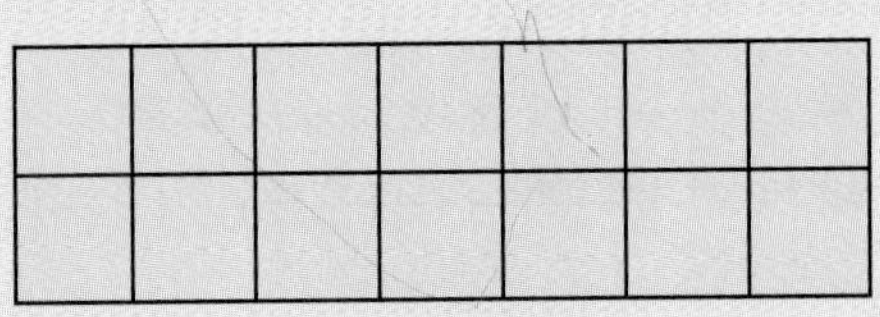

2×7

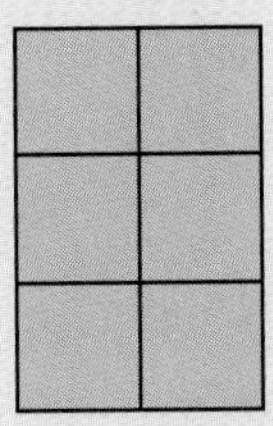

3×2

- Cut out each of your arrays. Put them together to make an array that shows the multiplication example 10×10.

How many squares are in a 10×10 array?

Jump for Recess

Repeated addition and skip counting can help you multiply by 3.

Learning About It

It's time for recess! There are only 4 jump ropes. If 3 students share each jump rope, how many students can jump rope at one time?

$4 \times 3 = \blacksquare$ or $\begin{array}{r} 3 \\ \times\, 4 \\ \hline \end{array}$

THERE'S ALWAYS A WAY!

- **One way** to find the product is to draw a picture. Show 4 groups of 3.

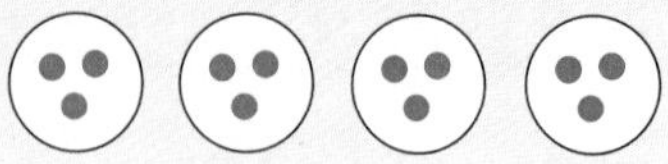

12 students in all

- **Another way** is to use repeated addition.

$3 + 3 + 3 + 3 = 12$

- **Another way** is to skip count.

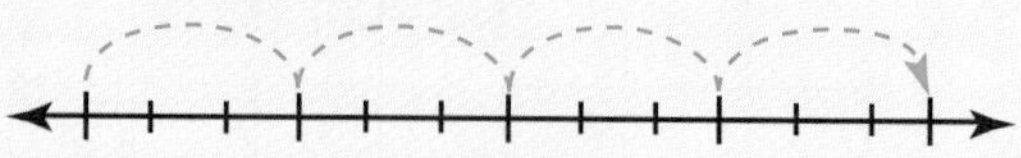

Count by 3s until you have said 4 numbers.

3, 6, 9, 12

- **Another way** is to use a multiplication fact.

$4 \times 3 = 12$

12 students share the jump ropes.

Think and Discuss How can knowing $4 \times 3 = 12$ help you find 5×3?

Try It Out

Multiply.

1. $\begin{array}{r} 3 \\ \times\ 5 \\ \hline \end{array}$ 2. $\begin{array}{r} 3 \\ \times\ 1 \\ \hline \end{array}$ 3. $\begin{array}{r} 4 \\ \times\ 3 \\ \hline \end{array}$ 4. $\begin{array}{r} 3 \\ \times\ 6 \\ \hline \end{array}$ 5. $\begin{array}{r} 3 \\ \times\ 9 \\ \hline \end{array}$ 6. $\begin{array}{r} 8 \\ \times\ 3 \\ \hline \end{array}$

Practice

Multiply.

7. $\begin{array}{r} 2 \\ \times\ 3 \\ \hline \end{array}$ 8. $\begin{array}{r} 3 \\ \times\ 0 \\ \hline \end{array}$ 9. $\begin{array}{r} 6 \\ \times\ 3 \\ \hline \end{array}$ 10. $\begin{array}{r} 3 \\ \times\ 7 \\ \hline \end{array}$ 11. $\begin{array}{r} 3 \\ \times\ 3 \\ \hline \end{array}$ 12. $\begin{array}{r} 9 \\ \times\ 3 \\ \hline \end{array}$

13. 3×1 14. 3×3 15. 9×3 16. 0×3 17. 3×9

18. 7×3 19. 5×3 20. 3×8 21. 3×4 22. 3×6

Using Algebra **Follow each rule to complete each table.**

Rule: Multiply by 3

	Input	Output
	7	21
23.	6	
24.	4	
25.	9	

Rule: Multiply by 5

	Input	Output
	3	15
26.	6	
27.	2	
28.	8	

Problem Solving

29. At Washington School, 8 classes go to early recess. The other 7 classes go to late recess. How many classes are there at Washington School?

30. Each year there is a Double Dutch World Tournament. Each singles team has 3 people. How many people are needed to make 5 singles teams for the tournament?

Kid Connection Jasmine Manns, Latasha Burnett, and Shaquannah Floyd practice for the Double Dutch World Tournament. Their team, coached by Geraldine Code, is from New Jersey.

Review and Remember

Find each sum or difference.

31. $\begin{array}{r} 56 \\ +\ 43 \\ \hline \end{array}$ 32. $\begin{array}{r} 693 \\ -\ 212 \\ \hline \end{array}$ 33. $\begin{array}{r} 682 \\ +\ 320 \\ \hline \end{array}$ 34. $\begin{array}{r} 7{,}043 \\ -\ 2{,}578 \\ \hline \end{array}$ 35. $\begin{array}{r} 8{,}234 \\ +\ 6{,}918 \\ \hline \end{array}$

For Extra Practice, see Set E, page 206.

Computer Lab

There are many ways to multiply by 4.

Learning About It

Your school has a new computer lab. There are 5 rows of computers. There are 4 computers in each row. How many computers are there in the computer lab?

$5 \times 4 = \blacksquare$ or $\begin{array}{r} 4 \\ \times 5 \\ \hline \end{array}$

THERE'S ALWAYS A WAY!

- **One way** to find the product is to draw a picture. Show 5 groups of 4.

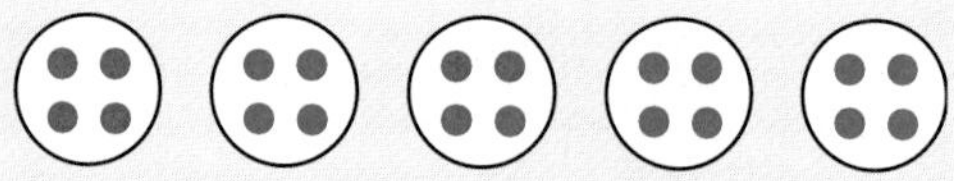

20 computers in all

- **Another way** is to skip count.

4, 8, 12, 16, 20

- **Another way** is to change the order of the factors.

If you know $4 \times 5 = 20$, then you know $5 \times 4 = 20$.

- **Another way** is to use repeated addition.

$4 + 4 + 4 + 4 + 4 = 20$

- **Another way** is to use a multiplication fact.

$5 \times 4 = 20$

There are 20 computers in the lab.

Think and Discuss Which way of finding a product do you like best?

Try It Out

Multiply. Tell how you found the product.

1. 4×3 **2.** 6×4 **3.** 1×4 **4.** 7×4 **5.** 9×4

Practice

Find each product.

6. 4×8 **7.** 4×1 **8.** 9×4 **9.** 4×7 **10.** 8×4 **11.** 1×4

12. 4×4 **13.** 3×4 **14.** 4×5 **15.** 4×6 **16.** 2×4 **17.** 7×4

Problem Solving

18. Four groups of students use the class computer each day. Two students work on the computer at a time. How many students use the computer each day?

19. The computer teacher had 49 CDs. She bought 3 boxes of new CDs. Each box has 4 CDs in it. How many CDs does she have now?

Review and Remember

20. $346 + 694$ **21.** $74 - 18$ **22.** $415 + 987$ **23.** $561 - 284$

Critical Thinking Corner

Visual Thinking

Match It!

Match each set of pictures with its number sentence.

1. 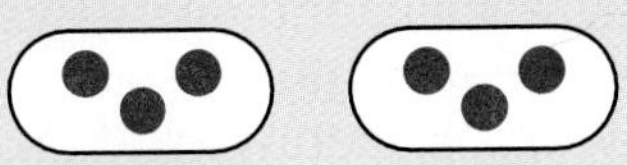

2. 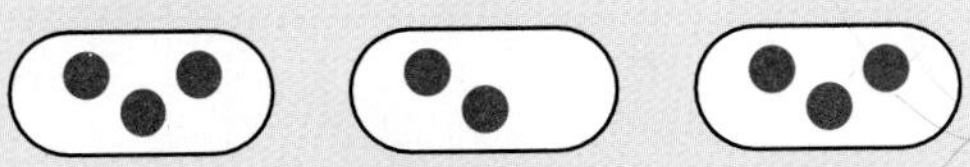

3 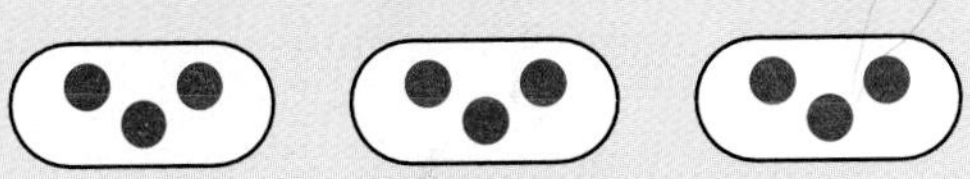

a. 3×3

b. 2×3

c. $3 + 2 + 3$

For Extra Practice, see Set F, page 206.

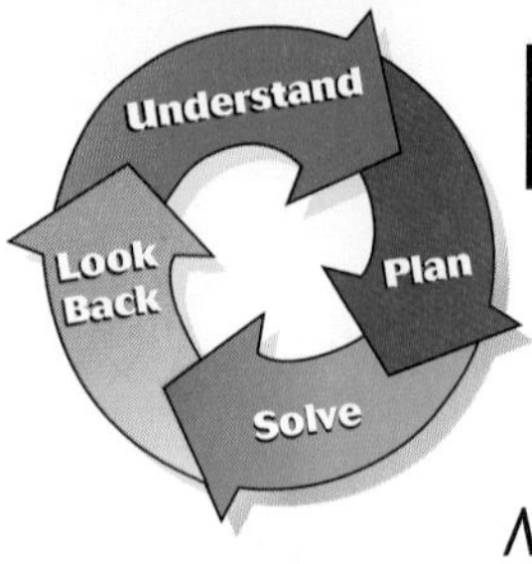

Problem Solving
Make a List

Making a list can sometimes help you solve a problem.

Mr. Weaver is taking a picture of Jenny, Liza, and Ryan for the class scrapbook. He asks them, "How many different ways could you three students stand in a line?"

UNDERSTAND

What do you need to know?

You need to know that any of the students can be first, second, or third.

PLAN

How can you solve the problem?

You can **make a list** to help you find all the different ways. Choose one student to be first and another to be second. The last one will be third.

SOLVE

When you make your list, you will notice that there are 2 ways for Jenny to be first, 2 ways for Liza to be first, and 2 ways for Ryan to be first.

So, there are 6 ways that the students could stand in line.

First	Second	Third
Jenny	Liza	Ryan
Jenny	Ryan	Liza
Liza	Ryan	Jenny
Liza	Jenny	Ryan
Ryan	Jenny	Liza
Ryan	Liza	Jenny

LOOK BACK

How is making a list helpful when you want to know if you covered all the ways?

Using the Strategy

Make a list to help you solve Problems 1–4.

1. Rudy must decide what to wear for his school picture. He likes his blue shirt and his yellow shirt. He likes his black pants and his brown pants. What are the ways Rudy could choose a shirt and pair of pants to wear?

2. Students get to pick the background for their school pictures. They can choose blue, green, or tan. The color can be solid or striped. List all the different background choices that the students have.

3. The photographer needs to take class pictures for Grades 1, 2, and 3. What are all the different orders that the grades could come in to have their pictures taken?

4. Jan, Carl, and Peter are standing in line to get their picture taken. What are all the different ways they can stand in line?

Mixed Strategy Review

Try these or other strategies you have learned.

- *Make a List*
- *Use Logical Reasoning*
- *Work Backwards*
- *Guess and Check*

5. Jeff is taller than Alan. Sue is shorter than Alan. Gayle is taller than Jeff. The school photographer wants the 4 students to stand in line from tallest to shortest. In what order should they stand?

6. The photographer sold 10 picture frames. She sold 4 more wooden frames than plastic frames. How many of each kind of frame did she sell?

7. Joan had \$2.05 when she got home from school. She had paid \$14.95 for her school pictures. She also bought a new pen at the school store for \$3.00. How much money did Joan have to start with?

Lunch Line

Follow the rules to multiply by 1 or 0.

Learning About It

It's lunchtime! There are 4 plates on the counter. Each plate has 1 cheeseburger on it. How many cheeseburgers are there?

4 × 1 = ■
4 × 1 = 4

There are 4 cheeseburgers.

When 1 is a factor, the product is always the same as the other factor.

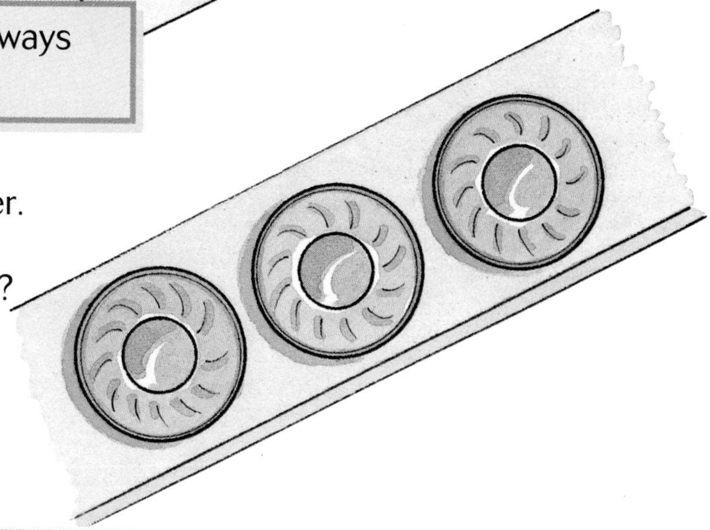

There are 3 plates on another counter. There are no hot dogs on any of the plates. How many hot dogs are there?

3 × 0 = ■
3 × 0 = 0

There are 0 hot dogs.

When 0 is a factor, the product is always 0.

Think and Discuss Is it easier to multiply 3 × 1 than it is to multiply 345 × 1? Explain your thinking.

Try It Out

Multiply.

1. 8 × 1 **2.** 0 × 9 **3.** 1 × 1 **4.** 6 × 0 **5.** 2 × 1

6. 4 × 0 **7.** 8 × 0 **8.** 1 × 9 **9.** 5 × 1 **10.** 7 × 1

Practice

Find each product.

11. 1×6 **12.** 9×0 **13.** 1×7 **14.** 2×0 **15.** 1×0 **16.** 5×0

17. 0×3 **18.** 1×2 **19.** 7×0 **20.** 9×1 **21.** 1×5 **22.** 4×1

23. 1×8 **24.** 0×8 **25.** 0×9 **26.** 1×6 **27.** 3×1

Problem Solving

Use the menu to solve Problems 28–30.

28. How much do 7 tacos cost?

29. You don't buy any sandwiches. How much money do you spend on sandwiches?

30. **Create Your Own** Use the menu to write a multiplication problem of your own.

Review and Remember

Using Algebra

Compare. Use >, <, or = for each ●.

31. 6 + 6 ● 9 + 3 **32.** 11 − 8 ● 13 − 9 **33.** 12 − 5 ● 8 + 6

34. 7 + 8 ● 5 + 9 **35.** 16 − 9 ● 15 − 8 **36.** 9 + 2 ● 2 + 9

Project Link

For each book you read, follow these steps to make a part for the bookworm.

- Use a square of paper that is 7 inches long and 7 inches wide. Write your name on it.
- Under your name, write the title of the book you read. Write the name of the author, too.
- Draw a picture that shows something interesting from the book.

How many worm parts did you make? How many inches will you add to the worm?

Using Algebra

Ready, Set, Multiply!

Multiplication tables are filled with patterns.

Learning About It

What patterns can you find in a multiplication table?

Work with your partner.

Step 1 Make a table like the one at the right.

Find the row marked 3. Then find the column marked 2. In the box where the row and column meet, write the product for 3 × 2.

Step 2 Fill in all of the other boxes in the table with the correct products.

column ↓ (2)

row → (3)

x	0	1	2	3	4	5
0						
1						
2						
3			6			
4						
5						
6						
7						
8						
9						

$3 \times 2 = 6$

Step 3 Make a chart like the one below. For each product listed, record how many times it appears in your multiplication table. Then write as many multiplication sentences as you can for each product.

Product	Number of Times Product Appears	Multiplication Sentence
4	3	$1 \times 4 = 4$ $2 \times 2 = 4$ $4 \times 1 = 4$
10		
15		
8		

Step 4 Look for patterns in your multiplication table. Which columns have only even numbers? Which rows have only even numbers? Can you find a row or a column that has only odd numbers?

Think and Discuss If a product is an odd number, are its factors even or odd?

Practice

Complete each sentence. Use your table to help you.

1. When you multiply by ___?___, the product is always 0.
2. When you multiply by ___?___, the product is always double the number you multiplied.
3. When you multiply by ___?___, the product is always the same as the number you multiplied.
4. **Explain** You multiply a mystery number by 5. The product has a 0 in the ones place. Is the mystery number even or odd? Explain your thinking.

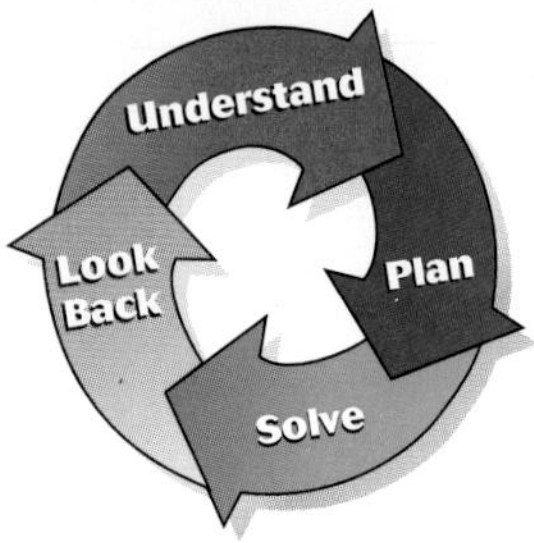

Problem Solving
Using Data From Pictures

Use what you know about problem solving to solve problems involving money.

Lisa is going to the school store to buy some pencils. If she buys 4 or more pencils, she will save 6¢ a pencil. Lisa decides to buy 5 pencils. How much money does she save?

UNDERSTAND

What do you need to know?

First you need to know whether or not Lisa is buying 4 or more pencils. If she is buying 4 or more pencils, you need to know that she saves 6¢ on each pencil she buys.

PLAN

How can you solve the problem?

You can **write a number sentence**. Since Lisa is buying more than 4 pencils, you can multiply 6¢ by 5 to find how much money she saves.

SOLVE

6¢ × 5 = 30¢

(6¢: Savings for 1 Pencil; 5: Number of Pencils; 30¢: Total Savings)

Lisa saves 30¢.

LOOK BACK

How could you use addition to check your answer?

Show What You Learned

Use the information below to answer each question.

1. How much do 2 pens and 3 stickers cost?

2. How much money will Tamara pay for a calculator and 2 pens?

3. Maya buys 4 note pads on sale. How much money does she save?

4. Paul and Karen each need 2 erasers. They decide to buy the erasers together. How much money will each of them save?

5. Which costs more, 10 pens or 2 calculators?

6. Mrs. Smith wants to buy 4 calculators for her classroom. She has $25. What other items could she buy with the money she has left?

7. **Analyze** You have $1 to spend at the school store. You buy a note pad. Do you have enough money left to buy 4 stickers? How do you know?

8. **Create Your Own** Use the information in the picture above to write a problem. Give it to a classmate to solve.

Checkpoint

Multiplication

Follow each rule to complete each table. (pages 190–193; 196–197)

Rule: Multiply by 3

	Input	Output
1.	4	
2.	1	
3.	5	
4.	8	
5.	7	

Rule: Multipy by 4

	Input	Output
6.	4	
7.	2	
8.	5	
9.	9	
10.	8	

Rule: Multiply by 2

	Input	Output
11.	4	
12.	6	
13.	3	
14.	8	
15.	9	

Rule: Multiply by 1

	Input	Output
16.	2	
17.	5	
18.	8	
19.	0	
20.	6	

Rule: Multiply by 0

	Input	Output
21.	3	
22.	9	
23.	6	
24.	5	
25.	8	

Rule: Multiply by 5

	Input	Output
26.	2	
27.	0	
28.	6	
29.	5	
30.	7	

Continue each pattern. (pages 198–199)

31. 3, 6, 9, ■, ■, ■

32. 4, 8, 12, ■, ■, ■

33. 1, 2, 3, ■, ■, ■

34. 5, 10, 15, ■, ■, ■

Mixed Practice

Multiply.

35. 3×2

36. 4×5

37. 3×6

38. 4×9

39. 4×4

40. 3×8

41. 6×4

42. 3×3

43. 7×0

44. 7×4

45. 1×9

46. 5×5

47. 3×5

48. 4×8

49. 6×1

50. 3×7

51. 3×9

52. 5×9

Problem Solving

53. Suppose you are having a bad day at school. In art class, you trip while carrying 3 jars of paint in each hand. If you drop all the jars, how many jars do you drop?

54. You are last in line for lunch. You want 2 hot dogs. They cost $1 each. There are no more hot dogs left. How much money do you spend for hot dogs?

55. You are last to arrive in the computer lab. There are 24 other students in your class. There are 6 tables. Each table has 4 computers. Do you get a computer of your own or do you have to share?

What do you think?

Can you use mental math to find this product?

$9 \times 8 \times 6 \times 0 \times 5$

Explain why or why not.

Journal Idea Write a word problem about a bad day at school. Use the factors 0, 1, 3, or 4 in your problem.

Project Wrap-Up

See How It Grows!

Attach your parts to the bookworm and watch it grow! Then answer these questions.

- How much length did each person add to the bookworm?
- How long is the whole bookworm?

You can make your bookworm grow even longer by reading more books!

Extra Practice

Set A (pages 176–177)

Write an addition sentence and a multiplication sentence for each set of pictures.

1. 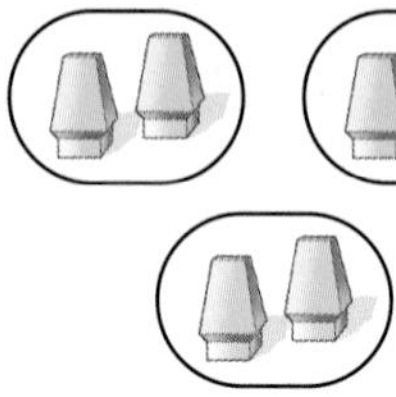

2. 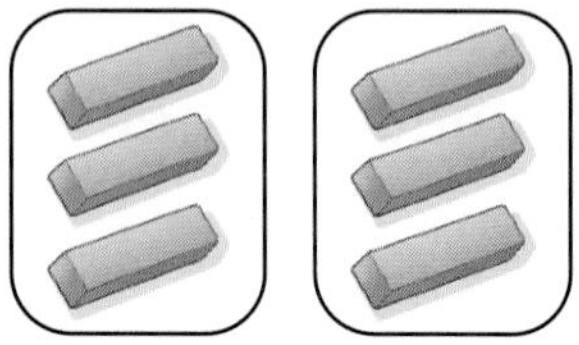

3. 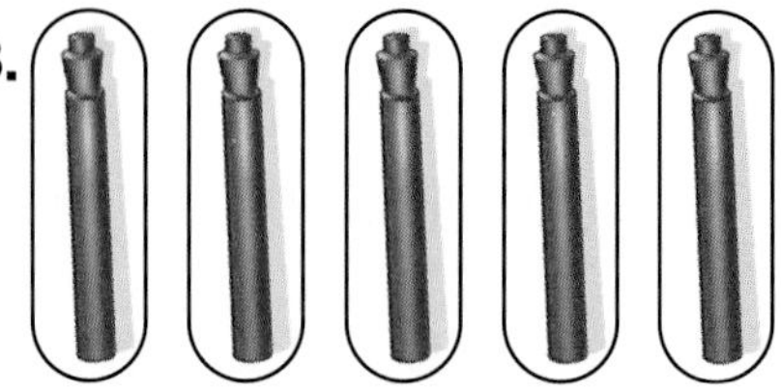

Write a multiplication sentence for each addition sentence.

4. $8 + 8 + 8 = 24$

5. $6 + 6 + 6 + 6 = 24$

6. $1 + 1 + 1 = 3$

7. $4 + 4 + 4 + 4 + 4 = 20$

8. $5 + 5 + 5 + 5 + 5 + 5 = 30$

9. $2 + 2 + 2 + 2 + 2 + 2 = 12$

10. One book costs $4. How much money do 5 books cost?

11. One shelf holds 9 books. How many books can 3 shelves hold?

Using Algebra

Set B (pages 178–181)

Write a multiplication sentence for each array.

1. 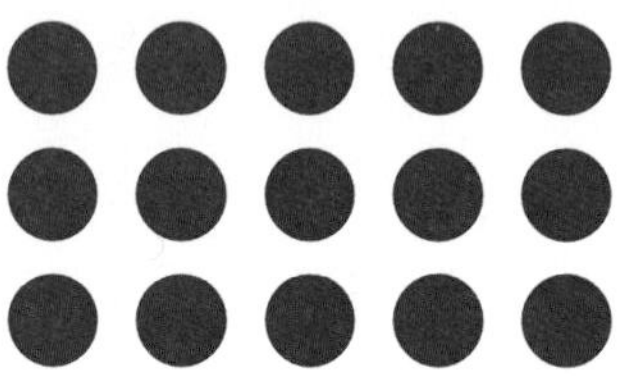

2. 

3. 

Draw an array to show each multiplication problem. Then find the product.

4. 1×6

5. 7×4

6. 2×3

7. 6×2

8. 4×2

9. 3×5

10. The music classroom has 5 rows of bells. Each row has 6 bells. How many bells are there in the music classroom?

11. In the gym there are 4 rows of mats. There are 8 mats in each row. How many mats are there?

Extra Practice

Set C (pages 184–185)

Multiply.

1. 2×4 **2.** 2×3 **3.** 2×9 **4.** 2×8 **5.** 2×6 **6.** 9×2

7. 1×2 **8.** 2×0 **9.** 7×2 **10.** 2×8 **11.** 5×2

Using Algebra **Follow each rule to complete each table.**

Rule: Multiply by 2

	Input	Output
12.	5	
13.	8	
14.	2	
15.	4	

Rule: Multiply by 2

	Input	Output
16.	1	
17.	3	
18.	8	
19.	6	

20. The computer lab received 7 new computer games. Two people are needed to play each game. How many people can play in all?

Set D (pages 186–187)

Multiply.

1. 5×3 **2.** 5×2 **3.** 4×5 **4.** 6×5 **5.** 5×5 **6.** 8×5

7. 5×6 **8.** 2×5 **9.** 5×4 **10.** 5×1 **11.** 3×5 **12.** 7×5

13. 5×9 **14.** 8×5 **15.** 9×5 **16.** 5×1 **17.** 5×0

18. A teacher is putting 5 paintings on each bulletin board. After finishing 4 bulletin boards, he has only 2 paintings left. How many paintings did the teacher start with?

19. The art teacher needs 35 paintbrushes. They come in packages of 8. Will 5 packages be enough? Explain.

Extra Practice

Set E (pages 190–191)

Multiply.

1. 3×2
2. 5×3
3. 3×5
4. 3×8
5. 4×3
6. 8×3
7. 3×3
8. 9×3
9. 6×3
10. 7×3
11. 3×6
12. There are 3 buckets of balls on the playground. Each bucket has 7 balls. Kari takes 4 balls out of one bucket. How many balls are left in the buckets?
13. There are 3 relay teams. There are 7 students and 2 teachers on each team. How many students are there in all?

Set F (pages 192–193)

Find each product.

1. 8×4
2. 6×4
3. 2×4
4. 4×4
5. 5×4
6. 4×6
7. 4×1
8. 4×3
9. 3×4
10. 9×4
11. 7×4

Set G (pages 196–197)

Find each product.

1. 3×0
2. 7×1
3. 1×2
4. 0×6
5. 7×0
6. 5×1
7. 9×0
8. 1×6
9. 9×1
10. 1×3
11. 3×8
12. The school store sells colored-pencil sets. How much money would 9 colored-pencil sets cost?
13. How much money would 3 highlighters cost at the school store?

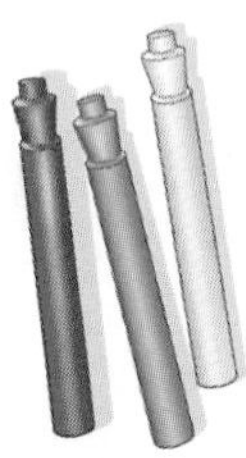

School-Store Sale

Colored-Pencil Sets	$1 each
Highlighters	$2 each
Marker Sets	$3 each
Binders	$5 each

Chapter Test

Write a multiplication sentence. Then find the product.

1. $4 + 4 + 4$

2. $6 + 6 + 6 + 6 + 6 + 6$

3. $5 + 5 + 5 + 5$

4. $7 + 7 + 7 + 7 + 7$

Draw an array for each multiplication exercise.

5. 9×3

6. 7×5

Find each product.

7. $\begin{array}{r} 3 \\ \times\ 4 \\ \hline \end{array}$

8. $\begin{array}{r} 5 \\ \times\ 6 \\ \hline \end{array}$

9. $\begin{array}{r} 5 \\ \times\ 9 \\ \hline \end{array}$

10. $\begin{array}{r} 2 \\ \times\ 6 \\ \hline \end{array}$

11. $\begin{array}{r} 2 \\ \times\ 9 \\ \hline \end{array}$

12. $\begin{array}{r} 5 \\ \times\ 5 \\ \hline \end{array}$

13. $\begin{array}{r} 4 \\ \times\ 9 \\ \hline \end{array}$

14. $\begin{array}{r} 3 \\ \times\ 8 \\ \hline \end{array}$

15. $\begin{array}{r} 3 \\ \times\ 6 \\ \hline \end{array}$

16. $\begin{array}{r} 7 \\ \times\ 3 \\ \hline \end{array}$

17. 0×9

18. 1×5

19. 9×1

Continue each pattern.

20. 2, 4, 6, 8, ■, ■, ■

21. 5, 10, 15, 20, ■, ■, ■

22. 4, 8, 12, 16, ■, ■, ■

23. 3, 6, 9, 12, ■, ■, ■

Solve.

24. There are 7 groups of students. Each group has 4 students. Suppose you collect 2 papers from each student. How many papers will you collect?

25. In the cafeteria you can buy a vanilla, chocolate, or strawberry frozen yogurt with sprinkles or nuts. What are the different ways you can buy a frozen yogurt with a topping?

Self-Check

Look back at Exercise 1. Is the number of addends one of the factors in the multiplication sentence that you wrote?

Performance Assessment

Show What You Know About Multiplication

What You Need

12 counters

1. Use 12 counters for Questions 1a and 1b.

   a. Put the counters into equal groups. Write a multiplication sentence to show how many groups you made and how many counters are in each group. Find as many other ways as you can to put the counters into equal groups. For each way you find, write a multiplication sentence that describes it.

   b. Arrange the counters in as many different arrays as you can. Write a multiplication sentence for each array.

2. Use the chart to answer the questions below. Use numbers, words, or pictures to show your work.

   a. You want to buy 4 medium note pads. How much money will you spend?

   b. You bought 5 boxes of the same size box of crayons. What's the most amount of money you could have spent? What's the least amount?

School Supplies	Price
Small note pad	$2
Medium note pad	$3
Large note pad	$4
Small box of crayons	$3
Medium box of crayons	$4
Large box of crayons	$5

Self-Check

For Question 1b, check that you made all of the possible arrays.

For Questions 2a and 2b, make sure that you multiplied correctly.

Using Algebra

Extension

What's the Rule?

Look at this multiplying machine! Whatever is put in the top is multiplied by a certain number. This machine multiplies by 2.

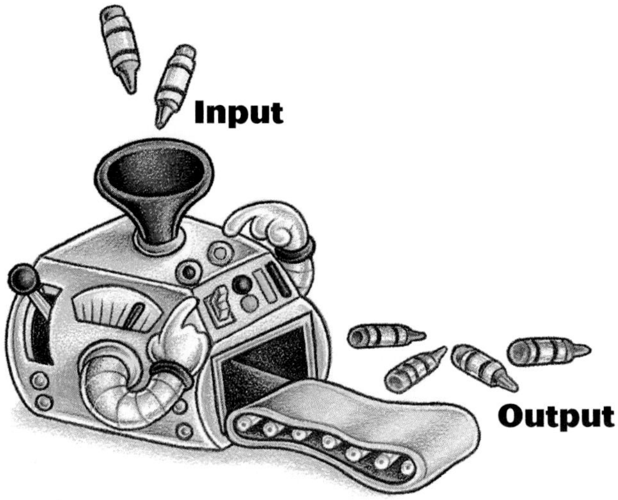

Rule: Multiply by 2

Input	Output
1	2
2	4
3	6
4	8

Here are some more multiplying machines! Look at each machine and table. Write the rule for each machine. Then complete each table.

1. Rule: ____?____

	Input	Output
	1	4
	2	8
2.	3	
3.	4	

4. Rule: ____?____

	Input	Output
	1	5
5.	2	
6.	3	
7.	4	

8. Rule: ____?____

	Input	Output
9.	0	
10.	1	
	2	6
11.	3	

12. Create Your Own Draw your own multiplying machine and make a table that goes with it. Then ask a classmate to guess the rule for your machine.

Chapter 6 Multiplication Facts

Chapter Theme: TRANSPORTATION

Career Spotlight Meet Sandy Elles, a ferry captain in San Francisco Bay. It is her job to steer the ferry from port to port. She makes sure that the ride is as smooth, quick, and safe as possible.

Ferryboats come in different sizes. A small one might carry only 6 cars on each trip.

$2 \times 6 = 12$

Captain's Log

Number of Trips	Number of Cars
1	6
2	12
3	18
4	24
5	30

Chapter Project

Make a Transportation Chart

Work as a class to make a chart about transportation. The chart will show different vehicles that people use to get from one place to another. To begin the project, follow these steps.

- Make a list of all kinds of vehicles—from cars to dog sleds!
- Decide which vehicles you will put on your chart.
- Decide what things you will tell about each vehicle. You might want to use the headings below for the columns on the chart.

Type of Vehicle	Number of People It Holds	Where It Is Used	Who Uses It

Coming and Going

Drawing arrays can help you multiply.

Learning About It

Word Bank
square number

If you lived on an island, you might use a ferryboat to go to other places. Ferryboats carry people and cars over the water. The 12 cars on the ferryboat below form an array. There are 4 rows. There are 3 cars in each row.

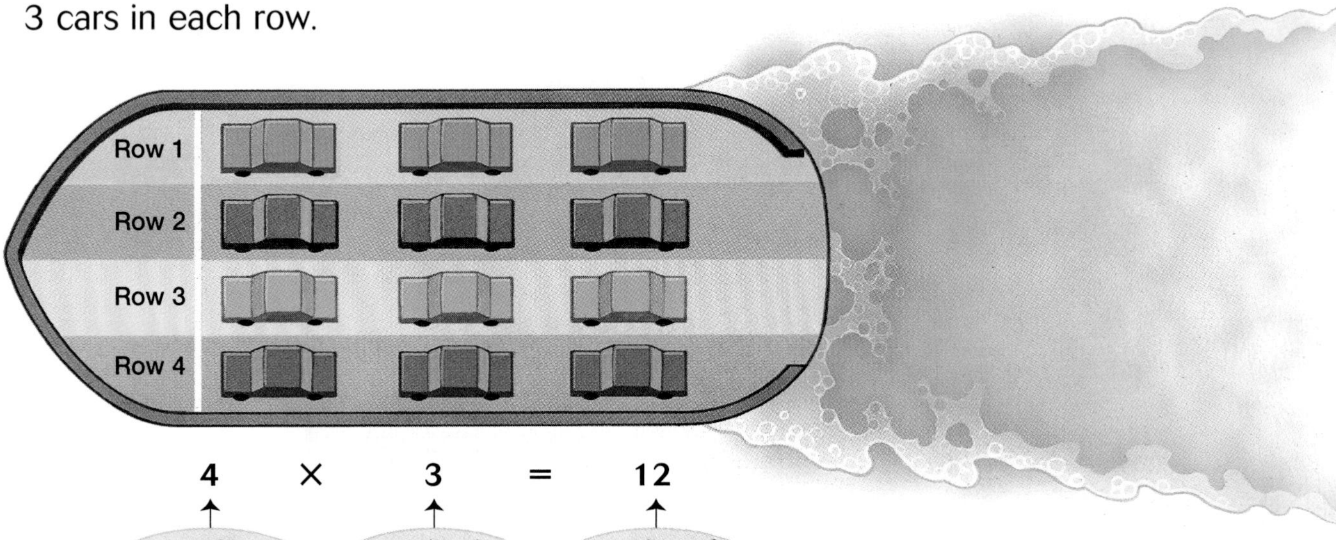

$4 \times 3 = 12$

4 ↑ number of rows; 3 ↑ number in each row; 12 ↑ number of cars in all

What You Need
For each group:
16 color tiles

Work with your group.

Use 12 tiles. Make as many arrays as you can. Record your arrays in a chart like the one below.

Drawing	Number of Rows	Number in Each Row	Multiplication Sentence
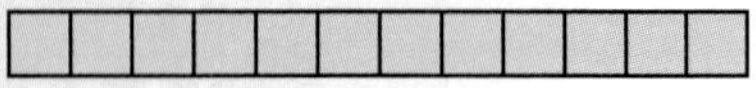	1	12	$1 \times 12 = 12$
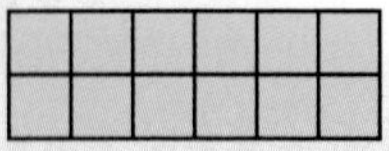	2	6	$2 \times 6 = 12$

How can you be sure you made all the arrays for 12 tiles? What shape is each of your arrays?

Connecting Ideas

All the arrays you made on page 212 were rectangles. But you can also make square arrays.

Look at the arrays at the right. One of them is a square. Look at its factors. What do you notice about the factors?

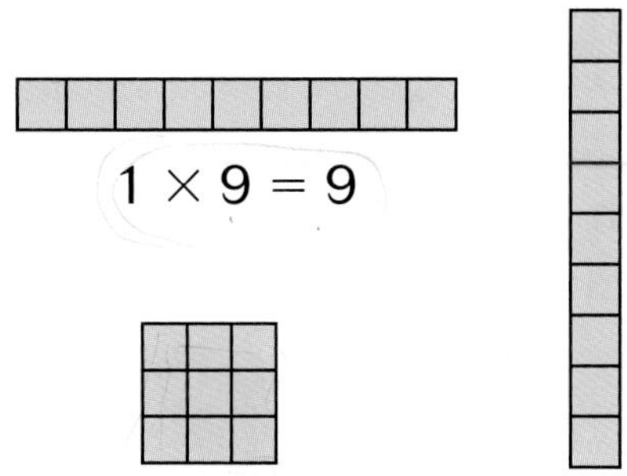

$1 \times 9 = 9$

$3 \times 3 = 9$

$9 \times 1 = 9$

When both factors in a multiplication sentence are the same, the product is called a **square number.** So 9 is a square number, since $3 \times 3 = 9$.

Think and Discuss Suppose you make an array that forms a square. What do you know about the number of rows and the number of columns in the array?

Try It Out

Write a multiplication sentence for each array.

1. 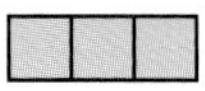

2. 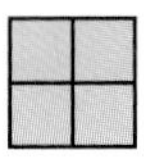

3. 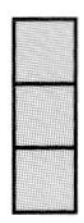

4. 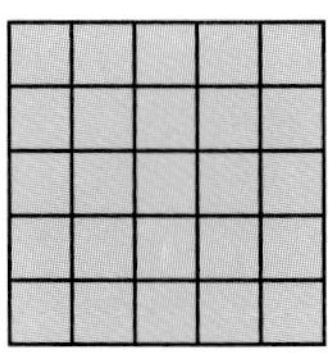

5. 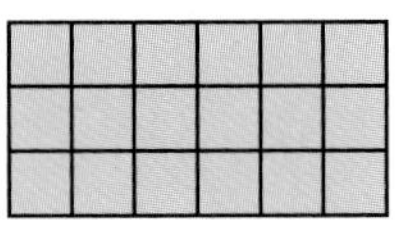

6. 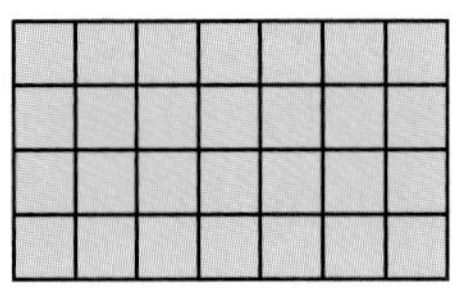

7. Which of the arrays in Exercises 1–6 are squares?

Practice

Use tiles. Make as many arrays as you can for each number shown. Record your work in charts like the ones below.

6

	Drawing	Multiplication Sentence
	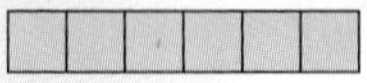	1 × 6 = 6
8.		2 × ■ = ■
9.		3 × ■ = ■
10.		6 × ■ = ■

13

	Drawing	Multiplication Sentence
11.		1 × 13 = 13
12.		■ × ■ = ■

15

	Drawing	Multiplication Sentence
13.		1 × 15 = 15
14.		■ × ■ = ■
15.		■ × ■ = ■
16.		■ × ■ = ■

16

	Drawing	Multiplication Sentence
17.		1 × 16 = 16
18.		2 × ■ = ■
19.		4 × ■ = ■
20.		■ × ■ = ■
21.		■ × ■ = ■

22. Look back at your charts for the numbers 6, 13, 15, and 16. Are there always more arrays for greater numbers than for lesser numbers? Give an example to prove your answer.

23. Look again at your charts. Do you see any square numbers? How do you know?

Problem Solving

24. There are 8 rows of parking spaces with 5 spaces in each row. There are only 3 spaces left open. How many cars are already parked?

25. Megan took 28 trips on the ferry last month and 34 trips this month. How many trips did she take on the ferry in the 2 months?

26. **Analyze** Draw arrays to show all the different ways you could arrange 36 cars on a ferry. Which of the arrays do you think is the best use of space?

Social Studies Connection
The Ocracoke Island Ferry off North Carolina has been carrying cars and passengers since 1953.

Review and Remember

Add or subtract.

27. $920 - 457$

28. $4{,}847 + 8{,}625$

29. $28 + 39$

30. $486 - 232$

31. $3{,}695 - 1{,}809$

Time for Technology

Using a Calculator

Pressing for Products

Use your calculator to compare addition and multiplication.

Press: 7 + 7 + 7 =

What is your answer?

Press: 3 × 7 =

What is your answer?

First add on your calculator. Then multiply.
Write the multiplication sentence you used.

1. Press: 6 + 6 =
2. Press: 2 + 2 + 2 + 2 =
3. Press: 9 + 9 + 9 + 9 + 9 + 9 =

For Extra Practice, see Set A, page 242.

Using Algebra

Double Play

Doubling helps you to learn multiplication facts.

Learning About It

Work with your partner.

Look at the numbers circled in red on the chart. These are the numbers you say when you start at 0 and skip count by 3s. They are also the products for the 3s facts.

$0 \times 3 = \mathbf{0}$ $1 \times 3 = \mathbf{3}$ $2 \times 3 = \mathbf{6}$

What You Need

For each pair:
two 0–99 charts
red and blue crayons

Step 1 Use a 0–99 chart. Circle the products for the first ten 3s facts with a red crayon. Your chart should look like the one shown.

Step 2 Now start at 0 and skip count by 6s. Use a blue crayon. Circle the first ten numbers you say. The numbers you circle are products for the 6s facts.

0	1	2	**3**	4	5	**6**	7	8	**9**
10	11	**12**	13	14	**15**	16	17	**18**	19
20	**21**	22	23	**24**	25	26	**27**	28	29
30	31	32	33	34	35	36	37	38	39
40	41	42	43	44	45	46	47	48	49
50	51	52	53	54	55	56	57	58	59
60	61	62	63	64	65	66	67	68	69
70	71	72	73	74	75	76	77	78	79
80	81	82	83	84	85	86	87	88	89
90	91	92	93	94	95	96	97	98	99

Step 3 Look at the numbers you circled. Write the products for the 3s facts and 6s facts on a chart like the one shown.

Step 4 Compare the products of the 3s facts and the 6s facts. What do you notice?

Step 5 Use a new 0–99 chart. Repeat steps 1 through 4, circling the products of the 4s and 8s facts. Compare the products. What pattern do you notice?

Think and Discuss How could knowing $4 \times 5 = 20$ help you find 4×10?

3s Facts	6s Facts
$0 \times 3 = 0$	$0 \times 6 = 0$
$1 \times 3 = 3$	$1 \times 6 =$ ■
$2 \times 3 = 6$	$2 \times 6 =$ ■
$3 \times 3 = 9$	$3 \times 6 =$ ■
$4 \times 3 =$ ■	$4 \times 6 =$ ■
$5 \times 3 =$ ■	$5 \times 6 =$ ■
■ × ■ = ■	■ × ■ = ■

Practice

Use the first fact to help you multiply the second fact.

1. $2 \times 3 = 6$
$2 \times 6 =$ ■

2. $5 \times 3 = 15$
$5 \times 6 =$ ■

3. $7 \times 3 = 21$
$7 \times 6 =$ ■

4. $8 \times 3 = 24$
$8 \times 6 =$ ■

5. $7 \times 4 = 28$
$7 \times 8 =$ ■

6. $4 \times 4 = 16$
$4 \times 8 =$ ■

7. $6 \times 4 = 24$
$6 \times 8 =$ ■

8. $9 \times 4 = 36$
$9 \times 8 =$ ■

Critical Thinking Corner

Number Sense

Even and Odd

Look at the examples. Then write *even* or *odd* to complete the sentences.

1. If you multiply 2 odd numbers, the product is ___?___.

2. If you multiply 2 even numbers, the product is ___?___.

3. If you multiply an even number and an odd number, the product is ___?___.

$4 \times 2 = 8$
$6 \times 4 = 24$
$3 \times 5 = 15$
$7 \times 3 = 21$
$5 \times 8 = 40$
$2 \times 5 = 10$

Flying Colors

Doubling the 3s facts can help you learn the 6s facts.

Learning About It

Wouldn't it be fun to ride in a hot-air balloon? Six people are riding in each of these balloons. How many people are in all of the balloons?

4 × 6 = ■ or $\begin{array}{r} 6 \\ \times\ 4 \\ \hline \end{array}$

THERE'S ALWAYS A WAY!

- **One way** to find the product is to use doubles.

Think: 4 × 3 = 12
Double 12 to make 24.

So 4 × 6 = 24.

- **Another way** is to skip count by 6s on a number line.

4 × 6 = 24

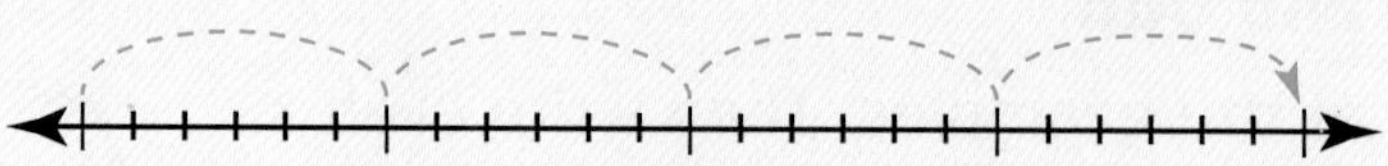

- **Another way** is to remember the 6s fact.

4 × 6 = 24

The 4 hot-air balloons are carrying 24 people in all.

Think and Discuss Compare 7 × 3 and 7 × 6. How are the factors related? How are the products related?

Try It Out

Use the first fact to help you multiply the second fact.

1. $3 \times 3 = ■$
$3 \times 6 = ■$

2. $8 \times 3 = ■$
$8 \times 6 = ■$

3. $4 \times 3 = ■$
$4 \times 6 = ■$

4. $5 \times 3 = ■$
$5 \times 6 = ■$

Practice

Multiply.

5. 9×6 **6.** 7×3 **7.** 7×6 **8.** 6×5 **9.** 3×3 **10.** 9×3

11. 3×6 **12.** 3×4 **13.** 6×6 **14.** 3×8 **15.** 6×8 **16.** 5×3

17. 6×4 **18.** 3×9 **19.** 6×7 **20.** 8×3 **21.** 8×6 **22.** 6×9

Problem Solving

23. Six hot-air balloons are each carrying 9 students. How many students are in the hot-air balloons?

24. The pilot of a hot-air balloon gives rides 6 times a day. How many rides does the pilot give in 3 days?

25. **Analyze** Lauren has 3 ten-dollar bills. She thought that a hot-air balloon ride would cost \$20. It actually costs twice that amount. Does Lauren have enough money for a ride? Explain why or why not.

Project Link

Start your chart now.

- Make rows and columns for the information the chart will show.
- Write in the vehicle names and the headings for the columns.

Review and Remember

Estimate to the nearest hundred first. Then use a calculator to solve.

26. 473 + 618 **27.** 899 − 276 **28.** 954 − 796

29. 678 + 439 **30.** 487 + 395 **31.** 954 − 865

For Extra Practice, see Set B, page 242.

It's in the Mail!

Double the 4s facts to help you learn the 8s facts.

Learning About It

Planes bring letters from far-away places. A third-grade class got 8 letters from each of their 5 pen-pal schools. How many letters did they get?

$5 \times 8 = \blacksquare$ or $\begin{array}{r} 8 \\ \times 5 \\ \hline \end{array}$

THERE'S ALWAYS A WAY!

- **One way** to find the product is to use doubles.

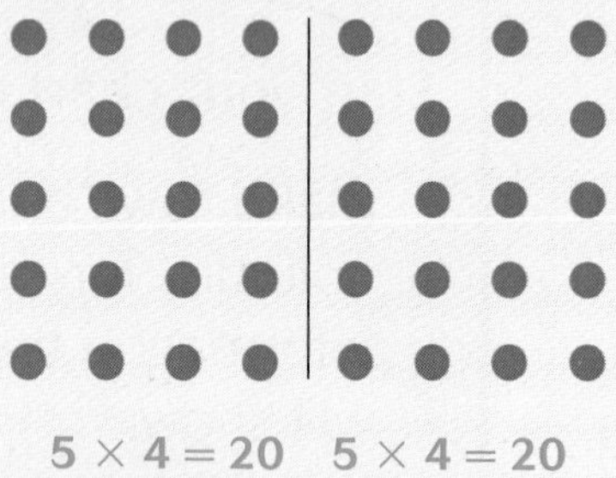

Think: $5 \times 4 = 20$
Double 20 to make 40.

So, $5 \times 8 = 40$.

- **Another way** is to use repeated addition.

$8 + 8 + 8 + 8 + 8 = 40$

- **Another way** is to remember the 8s fact.

$5 \times 8 = 40$

The third-grade class received 40 letters.

Think and Discuss Which of the above ways do you like best? Tell why.

Try It Out

Use the first fact to help you multiply the second fact.

1. $8 \times 4 = \blacksquare$
   $8 \times 8 = \blacksquare$

2. $7 \times 4 = \blacksquare$
   $7 \times 8 = \blacksquare$

3. $6 \times 4 = \blacksquare$
   $6 \times 8 = \blacksquare$

4. $9 \times 4 = \blacksquare$
   $9 \times 8 = \blacksquare$

Practice

Find each product.

5. $\begin{array}{r} 8 \\ \times\ 9 \\ \hline \end{array}$

6. $\begin{array}{r} 8 \\ \times\ 4 \\ \hline \end{array}$

7. $\begin{array}{r} 8 \\ \times\ 8 \\ \hline \end{array}$

8. $\begin{array}{r} 2 \\ \times\ 8 \\ \hline \end{array}$

9. $\begin{array}{r} 3 \\ \times\ 4 \\ \hline \end{array}$

10. $\begin{array}{r} 7 \\ \times\ 8 \\ \hline \end{array}$

11. $\begin{array}{r} 4 \\ \times\ 4 \\ \hline \end{array}$

12. $\begin{array}{r} 6 \\ \times\ 8 \\ \hline \end{array}$

13. $\begin{array}{r} 8 \\ \times\ 3 \\ \hline \end{array}$

14. $\begin{array}{r} 4 \\ \times\ 8 \\ \hline \end{array}$

15. $\begin{array}{r} 7 \\ \times\ 4 \\ \hline \end{array}$

16. $\begin{array}{r} 9 \\ \times\ 4 \\ \hline \end{array}$

Using Algebra Write >, <, or = for each ●.

17. 3×8 ● 16
18. 3×4 ● 24
19. 16 ● 4×4
20. 4×3 ● 3×4
21. 1×2 ● 9×0
22. 4×8 ● 5×8

Problem Solving

23. Suppose the class writes letters to a school in Mexico. They write 8 letters each week for 3 weeks. How many letters do they write?

24. A plane from South Africa is carrying 1,509 letters. If 187 are pen-pal letters, how many letters are not pen-pal letters?

25. A student mails 4 envelopes to friends. Each envelope contains 8 pictures. How many pictures did the student send?

26. **Create Your Own** Write a multiplication word problem that uses either 4 or 8 as a factor. Give it to a classmate to solve.

Review and Remember

Choose a Method **Use mental math, paper and pencil, or a calculator to find each answer. Tell which method you chose.**

27. 40 + 50
28. 590 − 210
29. 6,000 − 1,799
30. 2,385 + 4,000
31. 4,385 − 2,179
32. 984 − 206

For Extra Practice, see Set C, page 243.

Developing Skills for Problem Solving

First read for understanding and then focus on whether there is too much or too little information to solve a problem.

READ FOR UNDERSTANDING

The Cole family is taking a 30-minute taxi ride to the airport. Ed and his mother are going on a trip. Mr. Cole will take a taxi home after saying goodbye to his family. There is a 75¢ toll on the way to the airport. There is no toll on the way home.

1. How long is the taxi ride to the airport?
2. How much is the toll on the way to the airport?
3. Is there a toll on the way home from the airport?

THINK AND DISCUSS

MATH FOCUS

Too Much or Too Little Information
Before you solve a problem, you need to decide whether you have too much or too little information.

Reread the paragraph at the top of the page.

4. Do you have enough information to find the total cost for the toll? Why or why not?
5. How much will the taxi ride cost? Is there too much or too little information to solve the problem?
6. What information in the paragraph is *not* needed to solve Problem 5? What information is needed?

Show What You Learned

Answer each question. Give a reason for your choice.

A taxi driver charges $9 for a trip to the airport. She charges $5 for a trip to the bus station. How much money does she charge for 3 trips to the airport?

1. What information do you *not* need to solve the problem?
   - **a.** the number of trips to the airport
   - **b.** the charge for one trip to the bus station
   - **c.** the charge for one trip to the airport

2. Which number sentence could you use to solve the problem?
   - **a.** $9 + $5 = ■
   - **b.** 3 × $9 = ■
   - **c.** 3 × $5 = ■

A taxi driver gave rides to 60 people on Monday, 48 people on Tuesday, and 54 people on Wednesday. He did not drive the taxi on Thursday or Friday. How many more people rode with him on Monday than on Tuesday?

3. What information do you *not* need to solve the problem?
   - **a.** the number of people who rode on Monday
   - **b.** the number of people who rode on Tuesday
   - **c.** the number of people who rode on Wednesday

4. **Explain** Is there enough information to solve the problem? Why or why not? If not, what else do you need to know to solve the problem?

5. **Explain** Is there enough information to tell how much money the taxi driver collected on Monday and Tuesday? Why or why not?

Checkpoint

Multiplication Facts

Write a multiplication sentence for each array.
(pages 212–215)

1. 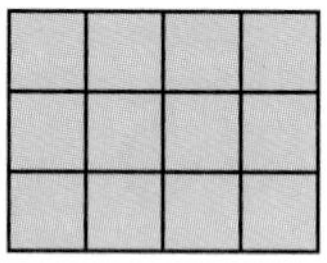

2. 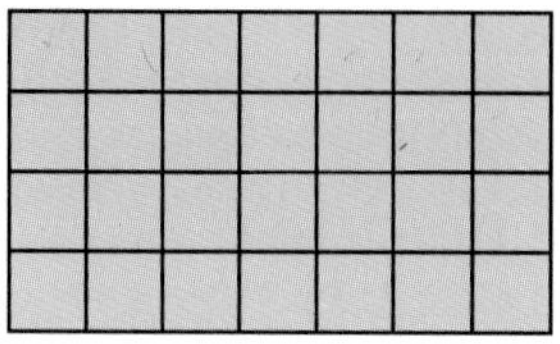

3. 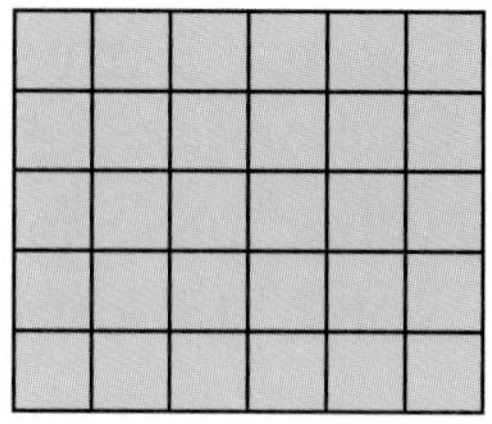

4. 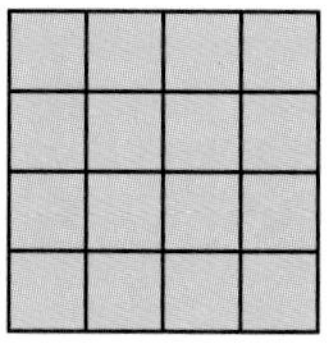

5. 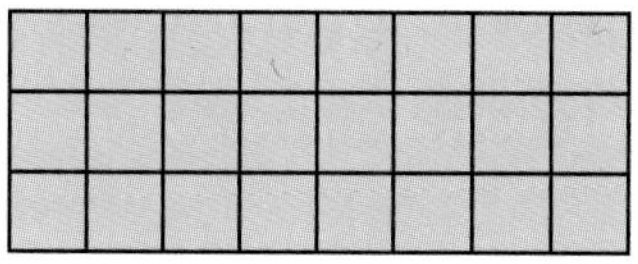

6. 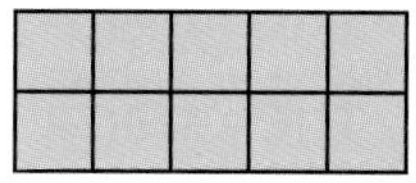

Use the first fact to help you multiply the second fact.
(pages 216–221)

7. 4×3
4×6

8. 5×3
5×6

9. 8×3
8×6

10. 6×4
6×8

11. 9×4
9×8

12. 7×4
7×8

Find the product. (pages 218–221)

13. 4×6 **14.** 6×8 **15.** 4×2 **16.** 8×2 **17.** 4×5 **18.** 8×5

19. 4×7 **20.** 0×8 **21.** 8×7 **22.** 3×9 **23.** 6×9 **24.** 7×3

25. 1×4 **26.** 7×6 **27.** 1×8 **28.** 0×6 **29.** 4×3 **30.** 3×8

31. 8×9 **32.** 5×3 **33.** 6×5 **34.** 8×6 **35.** 9×3 **36.** 6×7

Problem Solving

37. There are 6 rows in Mel's parking lot. He can park 8 cars in each row. If all the rows are filled, how many cars are parked in his lot?

38. Three skiers fit on one chair of a chair lift. How many skiers can fit on 9 chairs?

39. Five groups of 8 students take the bus to school. Twice that many students walk to school. How many students walk to school?

40. **Analyze** Your father bought 3 packs of amusement ride tickets. There are 6 tickets in each pack. Your brother used half of the tickets. How many tickets are left?

What do you think?

Could you write a multiplication sentence for $6 + 6 + 6 + 3$? Explain why or why not.

Journal Idea Explain how knowing $4 \times 5 = 20$ can help you find 8×5.

Critical Thinking Corner

Using Algebra **Logical Thinking**

Number Puzzler

1. Look at the exercises below. Each shape stands for a different number. Find the number for each shape so that all the exercises are correct.

   a. ★ × ★ = 9

   b. ▲ × ★ = 12

   c. ★ × ■ = 15

   d. ■ × ▲ = 20

2. **Create Your Own** Make up your own puzzle. Use the same shapes as above or invent your own shapes. Give your puzzle to a friend to solve.

River Boats

You can multiply by 7 in different ways.

Learning About It

In Brazil, people sometimes ride in boats down the Amazon River. Suppose there are 3 boats on the river and each boat has 7 people in it. How many people are there in all 3 boats?

3 × 7 = ■ or $\begin{array}{r} 7 \\ \times\ 3 \\ \hline \end{array}$

THERE'S ALWAYS A WAY!

- **One way** to find the product is to skip count by 7s on a number line.

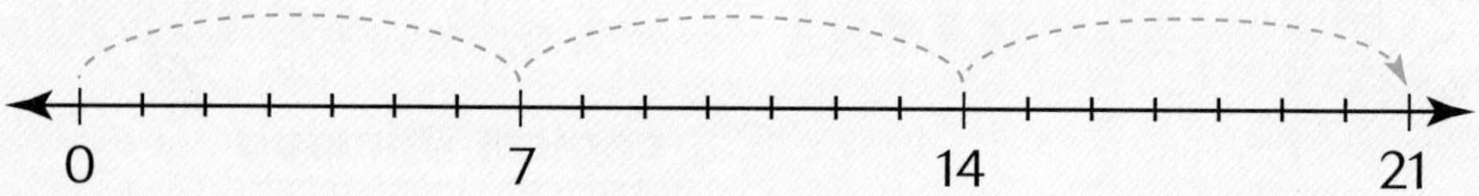

3 × 7 = 21

- **Another way** is to draw an array.

3 × 7 = 21

- **Another way** is to change the order of the factors.

If you know 7 × 3 = 21, then you know 3 × 7 = 21.

There are 21 people in the boats.

Think and Discuss How would skip counting on a number line be different for 7 × 3?

Try It Out

Use the first fact to help you multiply the second fact.

1. $\begin{array}{r}2\\ \times 7\\ \hline\end{array}$ $\begin{array}{r}7\\ \times 2\\ \hline\end{array}$ **2.** $\begin{array}{r}5\\ \times 7\\ \hline\end{array}$ $\begin{array}{r}7\\ \times 5\\ \hline\end{array}$ **3.** $\begin{array}{r}4\\ \times 7\\ \hline\end{array}$ $\begin{array}{r}7\\ \times 4\\ \hline\end{array}$ **4.** $\begin{array}{r}8\\ \times 7\\ \hline\end{array}$ $\begin{array}{r}7\\ \times 8\\ \hline\end{array}$

Practice

Multiply.

5. $\begin{array}{r}0\\ \times 7\\ \hline\end{array}$ **6.** $\begin{array}{r}7\\ \times 1\\ \hline\end{array}$ **7.** $\begin{array}{r}7\\ \times 3\\ \hline\end{array}$ **8.** $\begin{array}{r}7\\ \times 7\\ \hline\end{array}$ **9.** $\begin{array}{r}7\\ \times 4\\ \hline\end{array}$ **10.** $\begin{array}{r}7\\ \times 6\\ \hline\end{array}$

11. $\begin{array}{r}0\\ \times 7\\ \hline\end{array}$ **12.** $\begin{array}{r}8\\ \times 7\\ \hline\end{array}$ **13.** $\begin{array}{r}5\\ \times 7\\ \hline\end{array}$ **14.** $\begin{array}{r}1\\ \times 7\\ \hline\end{array}$ **15.** $\begin{array}{r}6\\ \times 7\\ \hline\end{array}$ **16.** $\begin{array}{r}7\\ \times 9\\ \hline\end{array}$

17. 8×9 **18.** 7×4 **19.** 7×9 **20.** 8×5

21. 6×8 **22.** 7×7 **23.** 8×3 **24.** 5×9

25. 0×7 **26.** 8×7 **27.** 9×5 **28.** 8×8

Problem Solving

29. A group of travelers spends 8 weeks exploring the Amazon River. How many days long is their trip?

30. Analyze Three boats are each 7 feet long. The dock is 3 feet longer than all 3 boats placed end to end. How long is the dock?

www.sbgmath.com

Review and Remember

Using Mental Math **Find each answer.**

31. 80 − 30 **32.** 5,000 − 2,000 **33.** 690 − 30 **34.** 250 − 40

35. 300 − 150 **36.** \$3,000 + \$5,000 **37.** 470 + 210 **38.** 75 + 25

For Extra Practice, see Set D, page 243.

Getting Around

The number facts you already know will help you learn the 9s facts.

Learning About It

One of the best seats on a double-decker bus is a window seat on top. On each side of this bus there are 2 rows of windows. Each row has 9 windows. How many windows are there on one side?

$2 \times 9 = \blacksquare$ or $\begin{array}{r} 9 \\ \times\ 2 \\ \hline \end{array}$

THERE'S ALWAYS A WAY!

- **One way** to find the product is to change the order of the factors.

  If you know $9 \times 2 = 18$, then you know $2 \times 9 = 18$.

- **Another way** is to use a 10s fact. Find 2×10. Then subtract one 2.

  $2 \times 10 = 20$
  $20 - 2 = 18$
  So, $2 \times 9 = 18$

There are 18 windows on one side of the bus.

Think and Discuss Suppose you know that $5 \times 10 = 50$. How can that help you find 5×9?

Try It Out

Use the first fact to help you multiply the second fact.

1. 9×4
4×9

2. 9×6
6×9

3. 9×1
1×9

4. 9×3
3×9

5. 9×0
0×9

6. 9×7
7×9

7. 9×5
5×9

8. 9×8
8×9

Practice

Find the product.

9. 9×5 **10.** 9×9 **11.** 6×9 **12.** 0×9 **13.** 8×9 **14.** 9×7

15. 9×8 **16.** 9×1 **17.** 2×9 **18.** 9×6 **19.** 7×9 **20.** 9×3

21. 2×9 **22.** 9×3 **23.** 4×9 **24.** 9×5

Using Algebra **Follow each rule to complete each table.**

Rule: Multiply by 4

	Input	Output
25.	2	
26.	9	
27.	7	

Rule: Multiply by 9

	Input	Output
28.	9	
29.	3	
30.	6	

Rule: Multiply by 7

	Input	Output
31.	9	
32.	7	
33.	6	

Problem Solving

34. Sarah takes the bus 6 times a week. How many bus trips does she take in 9 weeks?

35. Suppose Kumar's family traveled 600 miles on a plane and 17 miles on a bus. How many more miles did the family travel by plane?

36. **Analyze** James travels 9 miles to school by bus. How many miles does he travel to school and home again in 2 days?

Social Studies Connection
Double-decker buses can be found in cities around the world. This picture shows a double-decker bus in London.

Review and Remember

Find the total amount of each.

37. 5 pennies
2 dimes
3 quarters

38. 10 nickels
2 quarters
4 dollars

39. 6 pennies
6 dimes
3 quarters

40. 5 dimes
1 quarter
3 dollars

Subways

There are many ways to find a product.
The way you do it is up to you.

Learning About It

Subway trains roar in and out of the station. This train has 4 cars. There are 8 people riding in each car. How many people are riding in all?

$4 \times 8 = \blacksquare$ or $\begin{array}{r} 8 \\ \times 4 \\ \hline \end{array}$

THERE'S ALWAYS A WAY!

There are many strategies you can use.

- You can **draw an array**.

$4 \times 8 = 32$

- You can **change the order** of the factors.

If you know $8 \times 4 = 32$, then you know $4 \times 8 = 32$.

- You can **skip count** by 8s.

8, 16, 24, 32

- You can use a **multiplication chart**.

x	0	1	2	3	4	5	6	7	8	9
0	0	0	0	0	0	0	0	0	0	0
1	0	1	2	3	4	5	6	7	8	9
2	0	2	4	6	8	10	12	14	16	18
3	0	3	6	9	12	15	18	21	24	27
4	0	4	8	12	16	20	24	28	**32**	36
5	0	5	10	15	20	25	30	35	40	45
6	0	6	12	18	24	30	36	42	48	54
7	0	7	14	21	28	35	42	49	56	63
8	0	8	16	24	32	40	48	56	64	72
9	0	9	18	27	36	45	54	63	72	81

$4 \times 8 = 32$

There are 32 people in the 4 subway cars.

Think and Discuss Which strategy do you like best? Would you always use the same strategy? Why or why not?

Try It Out

Multiply.

1. 9×2
2. 9×9
3. 3×8
4. 4×7
5. 0×7
6. 8×6

Practice

Find each product.

7. 7×5
8. 7×9
9. 0×9
10. 8×7
11. 7×6
12. 3×9
13. 5×8
14. 4×9
15. 6×9
16. 7×7
17. 5×9
18. 3×5
19. 6×5
20. 3×7
21. 8×4
22. 9×8
23. 7×6
24. 6×4
25. 4×9
26. 8×8

Problem Solving

27. Suppose you wanted to ride on all the subway lines in New York City. You estimate that you could do it in 3 days if you rode 8 hours each day. How many hours would that be?

28. Each week you use 6 subway tokens. How many tokens would you use in 7 weeks?

29. There are a total of 136 stations in the Moscow subway system. If 24 of the stations are being painted, how many stations are not being painted?

Social Studies Connection
The Moscow subway system is the busiest subway system in the world. Over 5 million people ride it every day.

www.sbgmath.com

Review and Remember

Using Estimation Estimate each answer to the greatest place value.

30. $175 + 432$
31. $59 + 67$
32. $45 - 17$
33. $721 + 819$
34. $645 - 195$

For Extra Practice, see Set F, page 244.

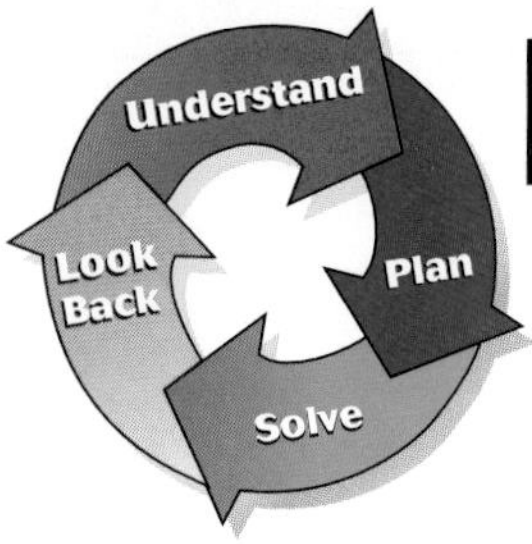

Problem Solving
Choose a Strategy

There is often more than one strategy that can help you solve a problem.

Some students are exploring a streetcar at the transportation museum. They sit in 6 seats. Each seat holds 2 people. How many students are sitting on the streetcar?

▲ **Social Studies Connection**
An electric streetcar from the late 1800s

UNDERSTAND

What do you need to find?

You need to find the total number of students sitting on the streetcar.

PLAN

How can you solve the problem?

You can often use more than one strategy to solve a problem. For this problem, you could **draw a picture** or **write a number sentence**.

SOLVE

Draw a Picture

- Draw 6 lines to stand for the seats.
- Draw 2 Xs on each line. Then count the Xs.

XX XX XX XX XX XX

Write a Number Sentence

$6 \times 2 = \blacksquare$

6 ↑ number of seats
2 ↑ number of students in each seat
■ ↑ total number of students

$6 \times 2 = 12$

There are 12 students sitting on the streetcar.

LOOK BACK

Can you think of another way to solve the problem?

Using Strategies

Solve these problems using these or other strategies you have learned.

THERE'S ALWAYS A WAY!

- *Use Logical Reasoning*
- *Make a Table*
- *Make a List*
- *Work Backwards*
- *Act It Out*
- *Write a Number Sentence*

1. In the museum there are 3 rows of airplane pictures and 5 rows of train pictures. How many more rows are there of train pictures than of airplane pictures?

2. There are 7 tables in the activity room where students can make model cars. If 4 students work at each table, how many students can make model cars?

3. Jim is next in line to ring the bell on the streetcar. Ramón is standing behind Jim but in front of Melody. In what order are the students waiting in line?

4. You are putting together 6 model trucks. Each truck needs 6 wheels. How many wheels do you need in order to put together all 6 trucks?

5. Ben, Dan, and Will wrote their names on cards. They put the cards in a hat. Then they each took out one card. No one had his own name. Ben picked Dan. What name did Will pick?

6. In front of the museum, a model streetcar moves around a tiny town. The streetcar can travel 100 feet in 2 minutes. How long does it take the streetcar to travel 1,000 feet?

7. When Nora got to the museum, she looked at cars for an hour. Next, she watched a 30-minute movie about trains. The movie ended at 1:15 P.M. When did Nora get to the museum?

8. You put 14 model train cars down on a track. Your friend picks up 4 cars. You put down 5 cars. Your friend picks up 6 cars. Then you put down 3 cars. How many cars are on the track now?

In-line Numbers

You can multiply 3 numbers in any order.

Learning About It

The race is on! Each of the 3 skaters is wearing 2 skates. There are 4 wheels on each skate. How many wheels are there in all?

$3 \times 2 \times 4 = \blacksquare$

- 3 → skaters
- 2 → skates on each skater
- 4 → wheels on each skate
- ■ → product

THERE'S ALWAYS A WAY!

- **One way** to find the product is to multiply 3×2 first.

  $(3 \times 2) \times 4 = \blacksquare$

  $6 \times 4 = 24$

- **Another way** to find the product is to multiply 2×4 first.

  $3 \times (2 \times 4) = \blacksquare$

  $3 \times 8 = 24$

There are 24 wheels in all.

Think and Discuss What is another way to multiply $3 \times 2 \times 4$? Remember, you can multiply factors in any order.

Try It Out

Using Algebra

Find the product. Multiply factors in the parentheses ( ) first.

1. $(2 \times 3) \times 1 = \blacksquare$
   $2 \times (3 \times 1) = \blacksquare$
2. $4 \times (2 \times 3) = \blacksquare$
   $(4 \times 2) \times 3 = \blacksquare$
3. $(1 \times 4) \times 2 = \blacksquare$
   $1 \times (4 \times 2) = \blacksquare$
4. **Explain** Choosing the right order can make multiplying easier. Look back at Exercise 2. Which way was easier for you? Tell why.

Practice

Using Algebra

Multiply in any order.

5. 9 × 1 × 7 = ■
6. 2 × 3 × 3 = ■
7. 5 × 6 × 1 = ■
8. 8 × 0 × 9 = ■
9. 3 × 3 × 2 = ■
10. 3 × 2 × 4 = ■
11. 4 × 2 × 3 = ■
12. 1 × 7 × 9 = ■
13. 2 × 1 × 4 = ■
14. 2 × 2 × 4 = ■
15. 1 × 5 × 3 = ■
16. 2 × 6 × 1 = ■

Using Algebra

Write >, <, or = for each ●.

17. (2 × 3) × 2 ● 14
18. 4 × (1 × 5) ● 20
19. (3 × 3) × 4 ● 9 × 4
20. 2 × (3 × 3) ● 2 × 3

Problem Solving

21. A park has 4 skate paths. each path is 3 miles long. How many miles long are all the paths?
22. Elbow pads are on sale for $5 each. How much would it cost to buy 4 *pairs* of elbow pads?
23. Your mom, dad, and two grandparents each have a pair of 5-wheel skates. How many wheels is that in all?
24. Suppose secondhand skates cost $35. You have $29.14. How much more money do you need to buy the skates?

Review and Remember

Write *inches, feet,* or *miles.*

25. Your skates might add 2 __?__ to your height.
26. You might ride your bike for 2 __?__.
27. You might have grown 4 __?__ since birth.
28. Your finger might be 2 __?__ long.

For Extra Practice, see Set G, page 244.

Using Algebra

Flying Factors

Remembering the multiplication facts can help you find a missing factor.

Learning About It

Twenty-eight people wait on the helicopter pad. Seven people can fit in each helicopter. How many helicopters are needed?

Write: ■ × 7 = 28.

Then find the missing factor.

THERE'S ALWAYS A WAY!

- **One way** to find the missing factor is to skip count by 7s until you reach 28.

  7, 14, 21, 28

  You counted 4 numbers.

- **Another way** is to list the 7s facts until you reach 28.

  1 × 7 = 7
  2 × 7 = 14
  3 × 7 = 21
  4 × 7 = 28

The number 4 is the missing factor.
So 4 helicopters are needed for 28 people.

Think and Discuss How do you know that the missing factor in 4 × ■ = 12 is more than 2?

Try It Out

Find each missing factor.

1. 8 × ■ = 24 **2.** ■ × 7 = 56 **3.** 6 × ■ = 30

4. 5 × ■ = 25 **5.** 3 × ■ = 21 **6.** ■ × 2 = 18

Practice

Find each missing factor.

7. $9 \times ■ = 63$ **8.** $5 \times ■ = 45$ **9.** $■ \times 4 = 28$

10. $1 \times ■ = 6$ **11.** $2 \times ■ = 12$ **12.** $9 \times ■ = 36$

13. $■ \times 3 = 27$ **14.** $9 \times ■ = 0$ **15.** $■ \times 7 = 35$

16. $■ \times 5 = 40$ **17.** $■ \times 9 = 54$ **18.** $9 \times ■ = 81$

Problem Solving

Write a multiplication sentence to solve each problem.

19. A company has 2 pilots for each helicopter it owns. If there are 14 pilots, how many helicopters does the company own?

20. Suppose each helicopter has 3 passenger seats. How many passengers could ride in 8 helicopters?

21. Every hour a helicopter pilot gives 4 rides. How many rides does she give in 8 hours?

22. If 3 people can ride in each helicopter, how many helicopters are needed for 15 people?

Review and Remember

Using Estimation **Estimate each answer to the nearest 10.**

23. $57 - 32$ **24.** $72 + 55$ **25.** $79 + 48$ **26.** $89 - 76$

27. $48 + 39$ **28.** $67 - 42$ **29.** $95 + 45$ **30.** $62 - 38$

Project Link

You have already made the rows and columns for your chart. Now figure out how many people can travel in each vehicle at one time. Fill in that column on your chart.

Then multiply to figure out how many people two, three, and four of the vehicles would hold.

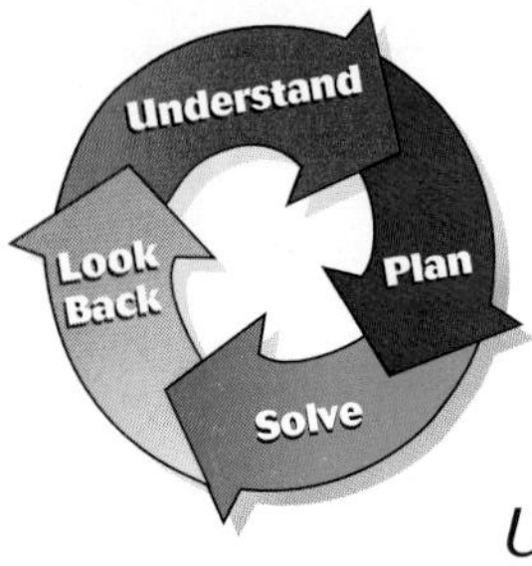

Problem Solving
Using a Pictograph

Using data in a pictograph can help you solve problems.

Suppose a train makes three stops while going from Miami, Florida, to Jacksonville, Florida. The pictograph shows the number of people who get on the train at each stop. How many people get on at Orlando?

People Boarding the Train

Miami	🚶🚶🚶🚶🚶🚶
Ft. Lauderdale	🚶🚶🚶🚶🚶
West Palm Beach	🚶🚶🚶🚶🚶🚶🚶🚶
Orlando	🚶🚶🚶🚶🚶🚶🚶
Jacksonville	🚶🚶🚶🚶

Each 🚶 stands for 5 people.

UNDERSTAND

What do you need to know?

First you need to know which row of 🚶 shows the people getting on at Orlando. Then you need to know how many people each 🚶 stands for.

PLAN

How can you solve the problem?

Count the pictures in the row for Orlando. Then look at the key to see how many people each 🚶 stands for. Then multiply the two numbers.

SOLVE

The row for Orlando has 7 pictures. Each picture stands for 5 people.

$7 \times 5 = 35$ people

So, 35 people got on the train at Orlando.

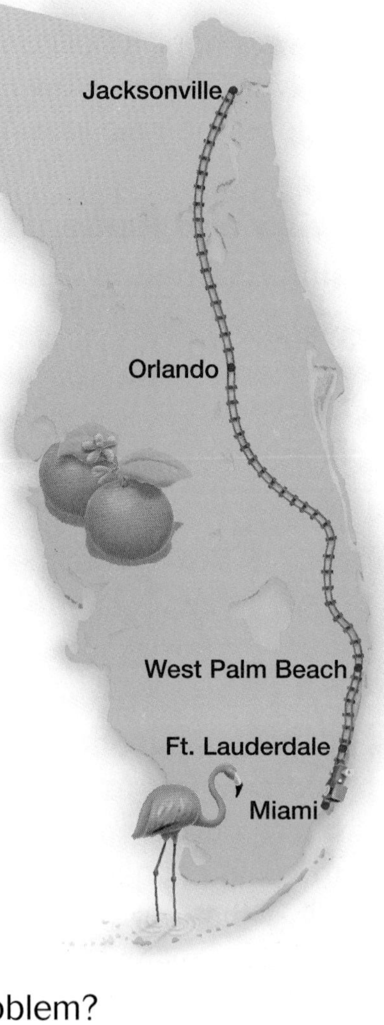

LOOK BACK

Can you think of another way to solve the problem?

Show What You Learned

Use the pictograph at the right to answer Problems 1–4.

There are different kinds of cars on the train. The pictograph at the right shows some of the kinds of cars and how many of each kind there are.

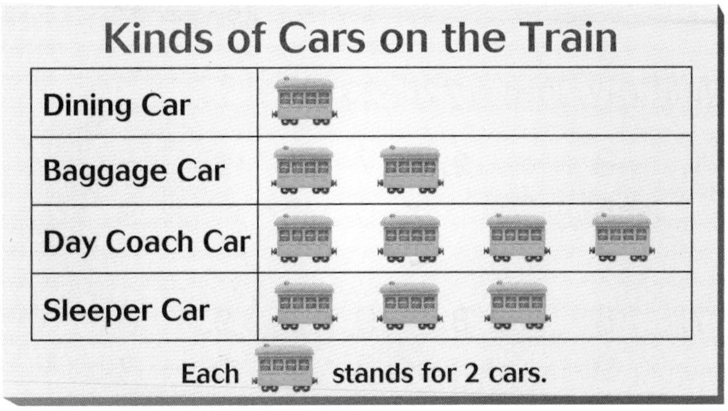

1. Which kind of car makes up the greatest number of cars?

2. Which kind of car makes up the least number of cars?

3. How many sleeper cars are there?

4. How many more day coach cars are there than sleeper cars?

Use the pictograph at the right to answer Problems 5–10.

There are 4 sections in each dining car. The pictograph shows the number of people that are sitting in each section of one of the dining cars.

5. How many people are sitting in Section 3?

6. Which section has half as many people as Section 2?

7. How many people are sitting in all 4 sections of the dining car?

8. All but 3 people in Section 4 ask for salad. How many salads must the waiter bring?

9. **Analyze** Each section of the dining car can seat 24 people. A group of 8 more people come in. They want to sit together. In which sections could they sit?

10. **Create Your Own** Write a word problem using one of the pictographs in this lesson. Give your problem to a classmate to solve.

Checkpoint

More Multiplication

Multiply. (pages 226–231)

1. 8×5
2. 7×6
3. 5×9
4. 4×7
5. 7×5
6. 7×3
7. 8×9
8. 9×2
9. 8×3
10. 8×7
11. 2×8
12. 7×2
13. 9×9
14. 6×9
15. 8×8
16. 2×9
17. 6×8
18. 0×7

Multiply in any order. (pages 234–235)

19. $2 \times 1 \times 8$
20. $2 \times 3 \times 3$
21. $2 \times 1 \times 7$
22. $4 \times 2 \times 4$
23. $8 \times 7 \times 0$
24. $6 \times 1 \times 8$
25. $3 \times 4 \times 1$
26. $6 \times 1 \times 3$
27. $5 \times 0 \times 2$

Using Algebra

Find each missing factor. (pages 236–237)

28. ■ × 6 = 18
29. 7 × ■ = 21
30. 8 × ■ = 56
31. 9 × ■ = 81
32. ■ × 5 = 45
33. ■ × 9 = 72
34. ■ × 4 = 36
35. 7 × ■ = 63
36. 8 × ■ = 40

Using Algebra

Mixed Practice

Follow each rule to complete each table.

Rule: Multiply by 6

	Input	Output
37.	3	
38.	7	
39.	8	
40.	9	
41.	6	

Rule: Multiply by 9

	Input	Output
42.	4	
43.	9	
44.	5	
45.	8	
46.	7	

Rule: Multiply by 7

	Input	Output
47.	4	
48.	7	
49.	3	
50.	6	
51.	8	

Problem Solving

52. A monorail has 5 cars. Each car can carry 8 passengers. If the monorail is exactly half full, how many people are on the monorail?

53. There are 9 players and 2 coaches on a baseball team. Five teams are going to a tournament. Can all the teams ride on a bus that can carry up to 45 people? Explain your answer.

54. On Saturday, Mr. Fenton gave carriage rides for $2 a ride. Terry, Liza, Alex, and Roy each had 2 rides. How much money did the children spend on rides?

55. Using Algebra **Analyze** Danielle rode 2 miles in her first bike race. Every race after that she rode 2 miles more than she rode in the race before. How many miles did she ride in her fifth race?

Journal Idea Suppose you don't remember the product of 8 × 5. List some things you could do to help you find the answer.

What do you think?

Which multiplication facts are the easiest for you to remember? Explain why.

Project Wrap-Up

Follow these steps to finish the project.

- Work with your classmates to fill in the rest of the chart.
- Add art or other decorations to make the chart look nice.
- Take turns asking questions about the chart. Invite volunteers to use the chart to answer the questions.

Fill in the Blanks

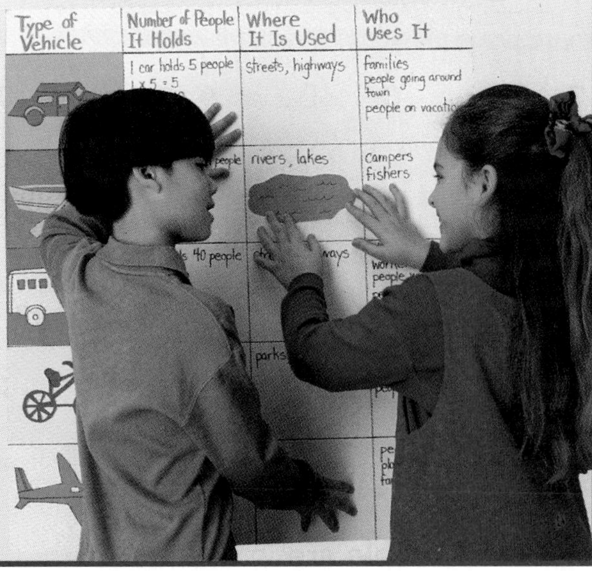

Extra Practice

Set A (pages 212–215)

Write a multiplication sentence for each array.

1. 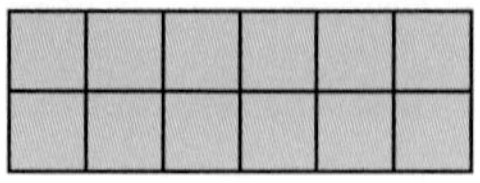

2. 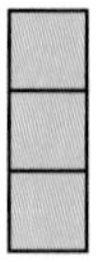

3. 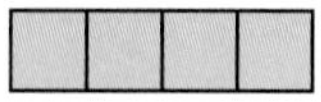

4. 

5. 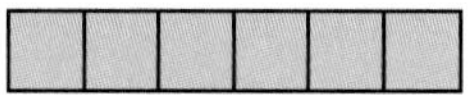

6. 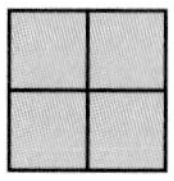

7. 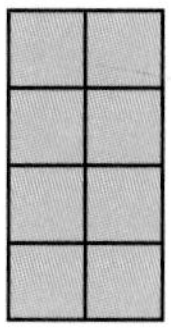

8. 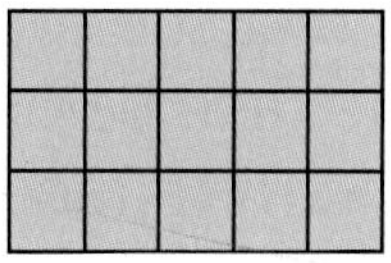

9. 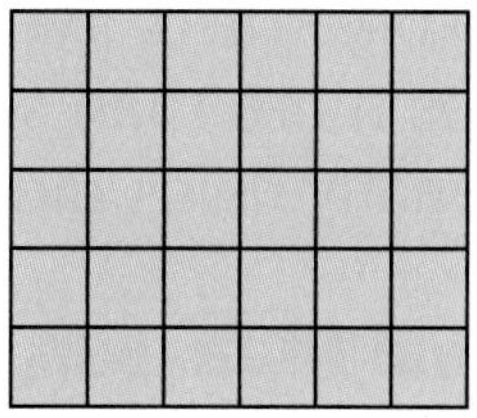

Set B (pages 218–219)

Find each product.

1. 6×2
2. 6×8
3. 4×6
4. 9×3
5. 6×9
6. 3×7
7. 5×6
8. 6×6
9. 3×4
10. 9×6
11. 7×6
12. 6×1
13. 5×3
14. 4×6
15. 6×3
16. 3×8
17. 2×3
18. 3×3
19. 1×3
20. 4×3
21. There are 24 balloons at a hot-air balloon festival. Six balloons enter a race. Each balloon carries 2 people. How many people are in the race?
22. Mr. Peterson is preparing for a trip in his hot-air balloon. Each day for a week he travels 6 miles in the balloon. How many miles does he travel?

Extra Practice

Set C (pages 220–221)

Multiply.

1. 8×8
2. 3×8
3. 8×9
4. 5×8
5. 4×6
6. 8×6
7. 8×4
8. 7×8
9. 5×4
10. 4×9
11. 4×4
12. 3×4

13. Five buses are leaving for Dallas. There are 8 empty seats on each bus. If 17 more people get on the buses, how many seats are still empty?

Set D (pages 226–227)

Find each product.

1. 7×6
2. 5×7
3. 3×7
4. 8×7
5. 7×4
6. 7×9
7. 7×2
8. 0×7
9. 4×7
10. 7×7
11. 6×7
12. 7×1

Set E (pages 228–229)

Find each product.

1. 9×5
2. 9×4
3. 9×8
4. 3×9
5. 7×9
6. 9×6
7. 6×9
8. 9×9
9. 2×9
10. 5×9
11. 9×7
12. 0×9

13. Can 37 people row across a lake in 9 rowboats that hold 4 people each? Explain your answer.

Extra Practice

Set F (pages 230–231)

Find each product.

1. $\begin{array}{r} 5 \\ \times\ 9 \\ \hline \end{array}$ 2. $\begin{array}{r} 4 \\ \times\ 7 \\ \hline \end{array}$ 3. $\begin{array}{r} 8 \\ \times\ 4 \\ \hline \end{array}$ 4. $\begin{array}{r} 9 \\ \times\ 8 \\ \hline \end{array}$ 5. $\begin{array}{r} 6 \\ \times\ 7 \\ \hline \end{array}$ 6. $\begin{array}{r} 7 \\ \times\ 5 \\ \hline \end{array}$

7. $\begin{array}{r} 6 \\ \times\ 5 \\ \hline \end{array}$ 8. $\begin{array}{r} 7 \\ \times\ 7 \\ \hline \end{array}$ 9. $\begin{array}{r} 9 \\ \times\ 3 \\ \hline \end{array}$ 10. $\begin{array}{r} 8 \\ \times\ 8 \\ \hline \end{array}$ 11. $\begin{array}{r} 7 \\ \times\ 9 \\ \hline \end{array}$ 12. $\begin{array}{r} 4 \\ \times\ 6 \\ \hline \end{array}$

13. Mrs. Lee rides a subway to and from work 5 days a week. Each ride is 7 miles long. How many miles does she travel each week?

Set G (pages 234–235)

Using Algebra

Multiply in any order.

1. $8 \times 1 \times 5$ 2. $3 \times 3 \times 3$ 3. $5 \times 3 \times 1$ 4. $1 \times 2 \times 9$

5. $9 \times 0 \times 5$ 6. $3 \times 2 \times 4$ 7. $2 \times 3 \times 3$ 8. $2 \times 3 \times 1$

9. $4 \times 3 \times 1$ 10. $2 \times 3 \times 2$ 11. $9 \times 9 \times 0$ 12. $7 \times 1 \times 3$

13. Amy, Ron, and Chris each bought 1 pair of 5-wheel skates. They counted all the wheels. How many wheels did they count?

Set H (pages 236–237)

Using Algebra

Find the missing factor.

1. $5 \times ■ = 40$ 2. $7 \times ■ = 42$ 3. $9 \times ■ = 27$ 4. $■ \times 6 = 30$

5. $4 \times ■ = 32$ 6. $■ \times 8 = 48$ 7. $■ \times 7 = 56$ 8. $■ \times 9 = 81$

9. $■ \times 4 = 36$ 10. $■ \times 5 = 45$ 11. $3 \times ■ = 21$ 12. $4 \times ■ = 24$

13. Forty-eight people need to ride in helicopters to the airport. Each helicopter can hold 8 people. How many helicopters are needed?

Chapter Test

Write a multiplication sentence for each array.

1. 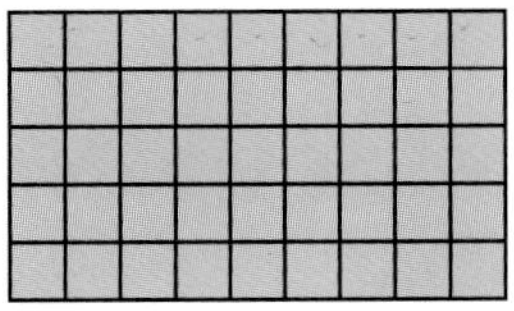

2. 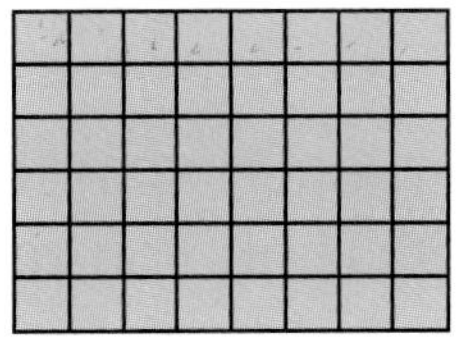

Multiply.

3. $\begin{array}{r} 3 \\ \times\ 9 \\ \hline \end{array}$
4. $\begin{array}{r} 3 \\ \times\ 8 \\ \hline \end{array}$
5. $\begin{array}{r} 8 \\ \times\ 7 \\ \hline \end{array}$
6. $\begin{array}{r} 9 \\ \times\ 5 \\ \hline \end{array}$
7. $\begin{array}{r} 7 \\ \times\ 7 \\ \hline \end{array}$
8. $\begin{array}{r} 8 \\ \times\ 4 \\ \hline \end{array}$
9. $\begin{array}{r} 6 \\ \times\ 6 \\ \hline \end{array}$
10. $\begin{array}{r} 4 \\ \times\ 7 \\ \hline \end{array}$
11. $\begin{array}{r} 0 \\ \times\ 7 \\ \hline \end{array}$
12. $\begin{array}{r} 8 \\ \times\ 8 \\ \hline \end{array}$
13. $\begin{array}{r} 6 \\ \times\ 9 \\ \hline \end{array}$
14. $\begin{array}{r} 4 \\ \times\ 4 \\ \hline \end{array}$

15. $2 \times 1 \times 9$
16. $3 \times 2 \times 4$
17. $3 \times 9 \times 1$

Find the missing factor.

18. $7 \times \blacksquare = 56$
19. $\blacksquare \times 6 = 54$
20. $\blacksquare \times 8 = 72$
21. $3 \times \blacksquare = 21$
22. $\blacksquare \times 4 = 28$
23. $9 \times \blacksquare = 81$

Solve.

24. Cathy rode her bike for 5 hours. She rode 7 miles each hour. Brandon rode his bike for 6 hours. He rode 6 miles each hour. Who rode farther?

25. Gina will earn $1 this week, $2 next week, and $3 the week after that. Suppose she keeps earning $1 more than the week before. How much money will she have earned after 6 weeks?

Self-Check

Look back at Exercises 15–17. Multiply the factors in a different order to see if your answers are correct.

Performance Assessment

Show What You Know About Multiplication

What You Need

2 spinners

① Suppose you spin each spinner shown once to get two numbers. Then you multiply the two numbers that the spinners land on.

a. What is the greatest product you could get? What is the least product you could get?

b. Suppose you get a product of 12. What two numbers could the spinners have landed on?

c. Could the product of the two numbers that the spinners land on be 1? Why or why not?

Spinner A

② Make two spinners like the ones shown.

a. Spin each spinner once to get two numbers. Then write as many multiplication sentences as you can to show the product of the two numbers.

b. Make a chart like the one below. Spin each spinner 5 more times. Use the 5 pairs of numbers you get to complete the chart.

Spinner B

Spinner A	Spinner B	Multiplication Sentences
0	4	$0 \times 4 = 0$ or $4 \times 0 = 0$

Self-Check

For Question 1a, did you find the two numbers that make the greatest product and the least product?

For Questions 2a and 2b, did you multiply correctly in each multiplication sentence?

Using Algebra

Extension

Multiplication Mysteries

Work with a partner. Follow the clues below to find each mystery number on the chart.

What is the mystery number?

You will say it if you count by 7s.

5 is one of its factors.

The sum of its digits is an even number.

What is the mystery number?

It is greater than 7×7.

It is the product of 2 factors that are the same.

It is an odd number.

What is the mystery number?

You will say it if you count by 3s.

You will say it if you count by 5s.

It has a 4 in the tens place.

0	1	2	3	4	5	6	7	8	9
10	11	12	13	14	15	16	17	18	19
20	21	22	23	24	25	26	27	28	29
30	31	32	33	34	35	36	37	38	39
40	41	42	43	44	45	46	47	48	49
50	51	52	53	54	55	56	57	58	59
60	61	62	63	64	65	66	67	68	69
70	71	72	73	74	75	76	77	78	79
80	81	82	83	84	85	86	87	88	89
90	91	92	93	94	95	96	97	98	99

Create Your Own Now make up a multiplication mystery of your own. Give it to a friend to solve.

Cumulative Review

Preparing for Tests

Choose the letter for the correct answer.

1. 9×7

A. 16
B. 54
C. 63
D. 72
E. none of these

2. $\$10.00 - 5.48$

A. $15.48
B. $40.52
C. $14.52
D. $0.52
E. none of these

3. 4×5

A. 20
B. 9
C. 15
D. 25
E. none of these

4. $800 + 40 + 6$

A. 846
B. 540
C. 900
D. 126
E. none of these

5. $8 \times 1 \times 8$

A. 8
B. 64
C. 16
D. 32
E. none of these

6. $5 \times 7 \times 0$

A. 30
B. 35
C. 12
D. 45
E. none of these

7. $1 \times 9 \times 3$

A. 12
B. 27
C. 28
D. 13
E. none of these

8. $\blacksquare - 6 = 5$

A. 6
B. 9
C. 1
D. 11
E. none of these

9. $9 \times \blacksquare = 54$

A. 6
B. 7
C. 45
D. 9
E. none of these

10. $\blacksquare \times 8 = 64$

A. 6
B. 8
C. 56
D. 9
E. none of these

11. $486 + 254$

A. 630
B. 61,310
C. 740
D. 232
E. none of these

12. $124 + 236 + 174$

A. 562
B. 534
C. 4,714
D. 196
E. none of these

13. Which set of coins makes 57¢?

A. 5 dimes, 1 nickel, 2 pennies
B. 2 dimes, 1 nickel, 2 pennies
C. 1 quarter, 1 dime, 7 pennies
D. 5 nickels, 7 pennies

14. Which height might a third-grade student be?

A. 4 yd
B. 4 in.
C. 4 cm
D. 4 ft

15. Which item weighs more than a pound?

A. paper clip
B. feather
C. computer
D. sheet of paper

16. How much time has passed?

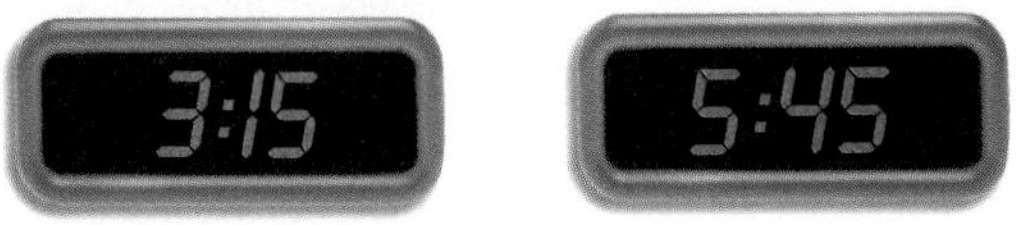

A. 2 hours
B. 2 hours and 45 minutes
C. 2 hours and 15 minutes
D. 2 hours and 30 minutes

17. Which is the coldest temperature?

A. 20°F
B. 1°F
C. 57°F
D. 32°F

This table shows the length of different rivers in the United States. Study the table. Then answer Questions 18–20.

Name of River	Length of River in Miles
Columbia River	1,214
Mississippi River	2,340
Ohio River	981
Tennessee River	650
Shenandoah River	172

18. Which river is the longest?

A. the Ohio
B. the Mississippi
C. the Tennessee
D. the Shenandoah

19. Which rivers are longer than the Ohio?

A. the Tennessee and the Shenandoah
B. the Columbia and the Mississippi
C. the Tennessee and the Columbia
D. the Mississippi and the Shenandoah

20. How many rivers are shorter than the Columbia?

A. 3
B. 2
C. 4
D. 1

Chapter 7 Using Data and Probability

Chapter Theme: OUR EARTH

Career Spotlight Meet Jim Gary. He is a sculptor who uses the parts from old cars to make "twentieth-century dinosaurs." He uses eight cars to make one giant dinosaur sculpture!

Sculptors use special materials to make their sculpture pieces. Jim Gary, for example, needs to keep track of how many of each car part he has.

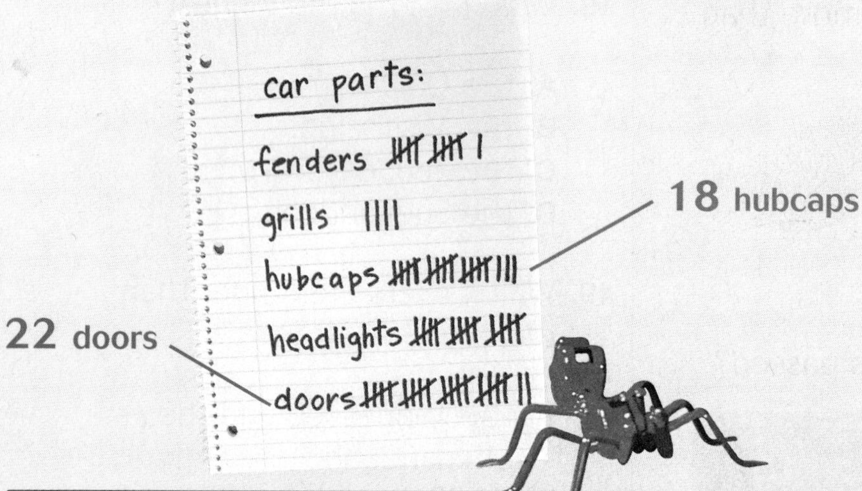

Chapter Project

Create a Recycled Creature

Many artists take old material and use it again in some way. In this project, you will design and create a creature from recyclable materials.

- Talk with your classmates. Think about materials you could use to make your creatures. Aluminum cans and foil, used paper, and old plastic containers are some ideas.
- Decide what kind of creature you will make. It can be a real animal or a creature you make up.

Auto Lamp Bulbs

Places to Go!

You can organize data in different ways.

Learning About It

Word Bank
tally chart
data

Which of these places would your classmates pick to visit?

Work with your group to find out.

Step 1 Ask your classmates which place they would like to visit most. Record their votes in a **tally chart** like the one below.

- Mark a tally for each vote like this: |
- Make a group of 5 tally marks like this: ~~||||~~

Places to Visit	Votes
Plains	|||
Mountains	~~||||~~
Rain Forest	|

PLAINS
Amboseli National Park, Kenya

MOUNTAINS
Mount Everest, Nepal

Step 2 After you have recorded everyone's vote, look at the tallies. Which place got the most votes? Which place got the least number of votes?

RAIN FOREST
Monteverde, Costa Rica

All the pieces of information you collected are called **data**. Data can also be shown in other ways. One way is to make a table.

Step 3 Count the tallies in each row of your tally chart. Then record the number for each row in a table like the one shown.

Places to Visit	Votes
Plains	3
Mountains	5
Rain Forest	1

Step 4 Compare the information in the tally chart and in the table. Which is easier to read?

Think and Discuss If you had to record 300 votes one at a time, would you use tallies or a table?

Practice

1. Make a tally chart to record the information shown at the right.

2. Use the number of tallies in your tally chart to make a table.

3. **Analyze** What do the tally chart and table tell you about the class's favorite seasons?

4. Pick one of the questions below. Think of four answers people might give. Then ask ten classmates to pick the answer they like best. Record their choices in a tally chart and table.

Our Class's Favorite Seasons

Macy	fall
Ron	summer
Clara	fall
Maizie	spring
Nick	summer
Ping	winter
Jenny	summer
Jill	summer
Steven	spring
Toby	summer

Developing Skills for Problem Solving

First read for understanding and then focus on whether an estimate is enough to solve a problem.

READ FOR UNDERSTANDING

The third-grade Recycling Club collects soda cans around the school. When at least 400 cans have been collected, the club takes them to a recycling center. The table at the right shows the number of cans the club has collected in the last 4 weeks.

Number of Cans We Have Collected

Week	Number of Cans
Week 1	89
Week 2	96
Week 3	102
Week 4	75

1. How many cans does the club collect before taking them to a recycling center?
2. How many cans did the club collect each week?

THINK AND DISCUSS

MATH FOCUS

Is an Estimate Enough? Sometimes an estimate is all you need to solve a problem. If you are asked if there is *enough* of something, often you just need to estimate.

Reread the paragraph at the top of the page.

3. Would you estimate or find an exact answer to find the total number of cans that the Recycling Club has collected?
4. Does the club have enough cans to take to the recycling center? How could an estimate help you decide?
5. Why can it be helpful to estimate to find answers?

Show What You Learned

Answer each question. Give a reason for your choice.

A company orders special recycled paper. The paper comes in cartons of 475 sheets. Each carton of paper costs $65.

1. Which of these problems needs an exact answer to be solved?
   - **a.** Is $200 enough to pay for 2 cartons of paper?
   - **b.** How much do 2 cartons of paper cost?
   - **c.** Will 2 cartons be enough to buy if the company needs 725 sheets of paper?

2. Which of these problems can be solved by using an estimate?
   - **a.** How much do 5 cartons of paper cost?
   - **b.** How many sheets are there in 2 cartons?
   - **c.** Will 2 cartons be enough to buy if the company needs 775 sheets of paper?

The Royal Recycling Center can start to recycle paper every time it has 1,500 pounds of paper. One day the center collects 882 pounds of paper. The next day it collects 492 pounds of paper.

3. Which number sentence could you use to estimate how much paper the center has?
   - **a.** $882 + 492 = \blacksquare$
   - **b.** $900 + 500 = \blacksquare$
   - **c.** $900 - 500 = \blacksquare$

4. Which number sentence would you use to find exactly how much paper the center has?
   - **a.** $882 + 492 = \blacksquare$
   - **b.** $900 + 500 = \blacksquare$
   - **c.** $882 - 492 = \blacksquare$

5. **Explain** Can you estimate to find out if the center has enough paper to begin recycling? Why or why not?

Where to Park?

Bar graphs help you organize and compare data.

Learning About It

Hiking trails, campgrounds, and much more can be found in national parks. The **bar graph** below shows how many campgrounds there are at some of our national parks.

Word Bank

bar graph

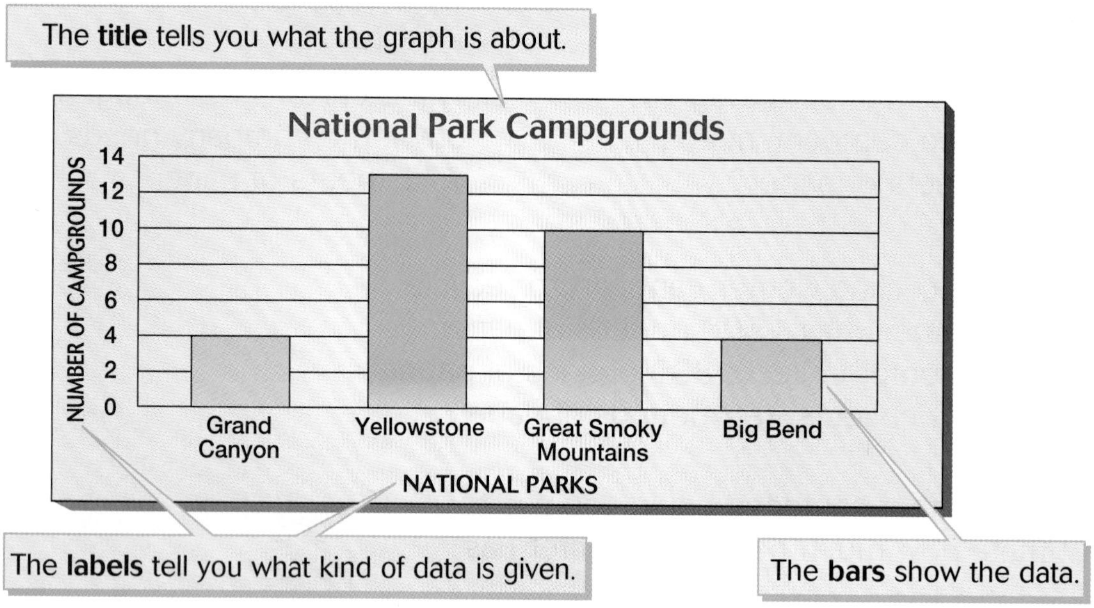

Look at the bars to read and compare the data.

- **Which park has 10 campgrounds?** The bar for Great Smoky Mountains stops at the number 10, so there are 10 campgrounds at Great Smoky Mountains Park.
- **How many campgrounds does Yellowstone have?** The bar for Yellowstone stops halfway between the numbers 12 and 14, so there are 13 campgrounds at Yellowstone.
- **Which park has more campgrounds, Yellowstone or Big Bend?** The bar for Yellowstone is taller, so there are more campgrounds at Yellowstone.

Connecting Ideas

You have been *reading* bar graphs to compare data. You can also *make* bar graphs to organize data.

What You Need

For each student:
graph paper

The table below shows the number of people that signed up for park activities. You can show this information in a bar graph like the one started below.

People Signed Up for Park Activities

Rafting	40 people
Hiking	35 people
Swimming	50 people
Biking	20 people

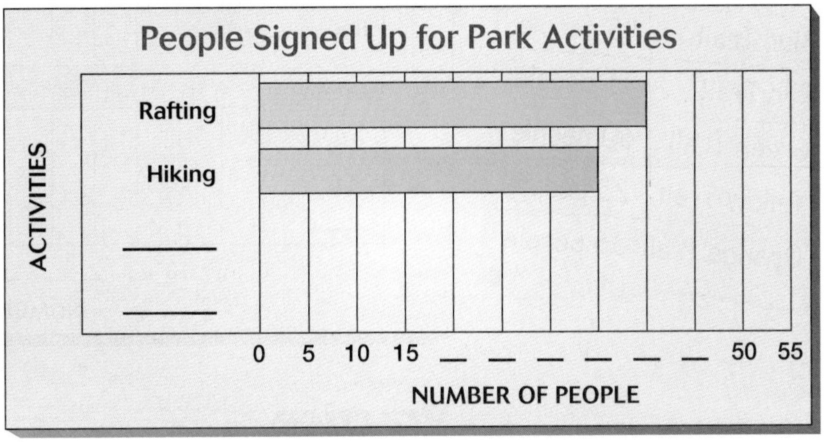

Copy the bar graph on graph paper. Then finish it.

- Write the activities along the side of the graph.
- Write the missing numbers along the bottom of the graph.
- Draw the missing bars.

Think and Discuss Look at the graphs on these pages. How are they the same? How are they different?

www.sbgmath.com

Social Studies Connection In 1872, Yellowstone National Park became the first national park in the world. The park is located in Wyoming, Montana, and Idaho. It is famous for its many geysers.

Try It Out

1. The table below shows the number of people using hiking trails. Make a bar graph to show the data. The graph has been started for you.

Number of People Using Hiking Trails	
Blue Trail	45 people
Red Trail	15 people
Green Trail	60 people
Yellow Trail	25 people
Orange Trail	35 people

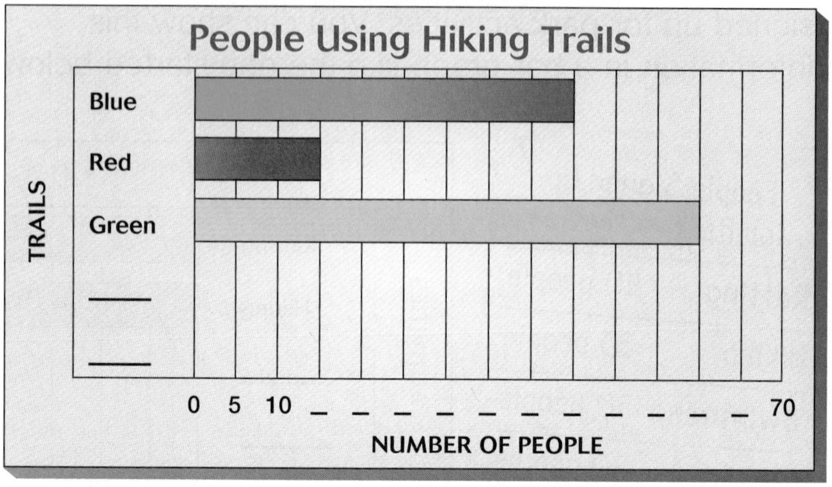

Practice

Use the information in the table to make a bar graph. Then use the graph to answer the questions. The graph below has been started for you.

Animals Seen on a Nature Trail	
Squirrels	4
Raccoons	3
Birds	12
Deer	1
Chipmunks	10

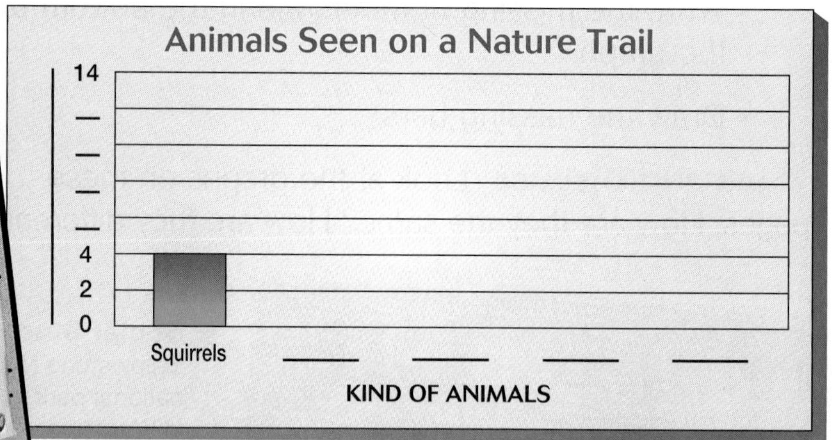

2. Which animal was seen the most?

3. Which animal was seen the least?

4. How many more chipmunks than squirrels were seen?

5. How many animals were seen in all?

Problem Solving

6. **Create Your Own** Make a list of four or five activities that you can do at a park. Ask your classmates to vote for their favorite. Then make a bar graph to show your results.
    - Which activity was chosen the most?
    - Which activity was chosen the least?

Project Link

What kind of creature will you create? What recyclable materials will you use?

- Make a drawing of your creature.
- List the materials you plan to use.
- Make a tally chart to record the materials you collect.

Review and Remember

Find each answer.

7. $24 + 17$
8. 4×2
9. $89 - 56$
10. $70 - 15$
11. 9×6
12. $84 + 67$
13. $7 + 6$
14. $50 - 13$
15. 3×7

Time for Technology

Using CD-ROM

Collecting Cans

You can use a bar graph to show data.

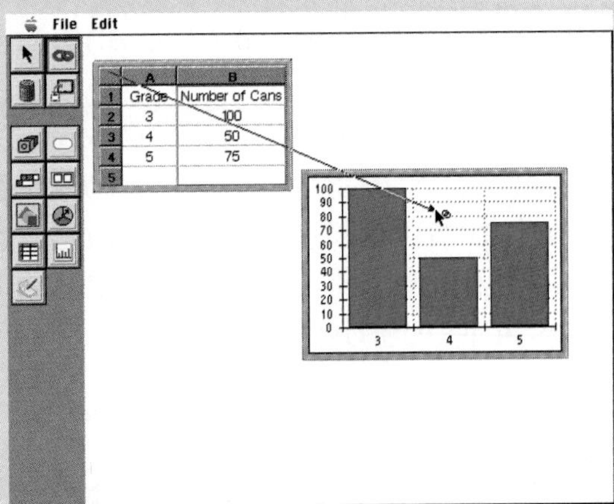

- Click spreadsheet. Then record the data about the number of cans collected for a recycling project.

  Grade 3: 100 cans
  Grade 4: 50 cans
  Grade 5: 75 cans

- Open a bar graph. Be sure to click on the empty cell at the top left, linking the spreadsheet to the bar graph. Which grade has the tallest bar? the shortest bar?

Counting Creatures

Pictographs use pictures to show data.

Learning About It

Word Bank
pictograph

Animals live in many places. Some animals live in zoos. Zoos can help protect animals. The **pictograph** below shows how many leopards there are in four different zoos.

The **title** tells you what the graph is about.

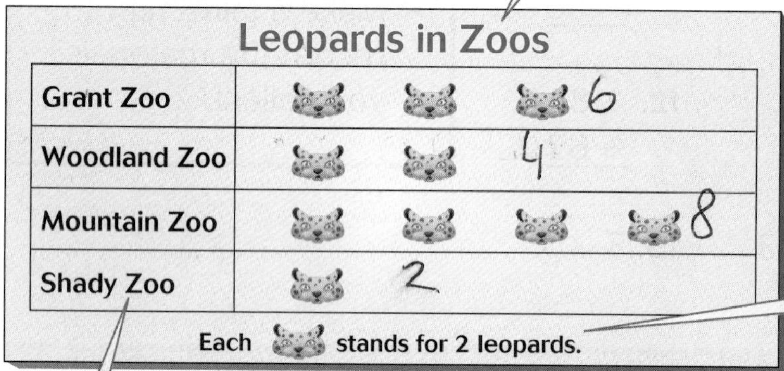

The **key** tells you how many each picture stands for.

The **labels** tell you what information is shown.

Look at the pictures to read and compare the data.

- **How many leopards does Woodland Zoo have?**
There are 2 pictures next to Woodland Zoo. Each picture stands for 2 leopards, so multiply the number of pictures by 2. Woodland Zoo has 4 leopards.

- **Which zoo has 8 leopards?**
Four pictures stand for 8 leopards, so Mountain Zoo has 8 leopards.

- **Which zoo has the fewest leopards?**
Shady Zoo has the fewest pictures, so it has the fewest leopards.

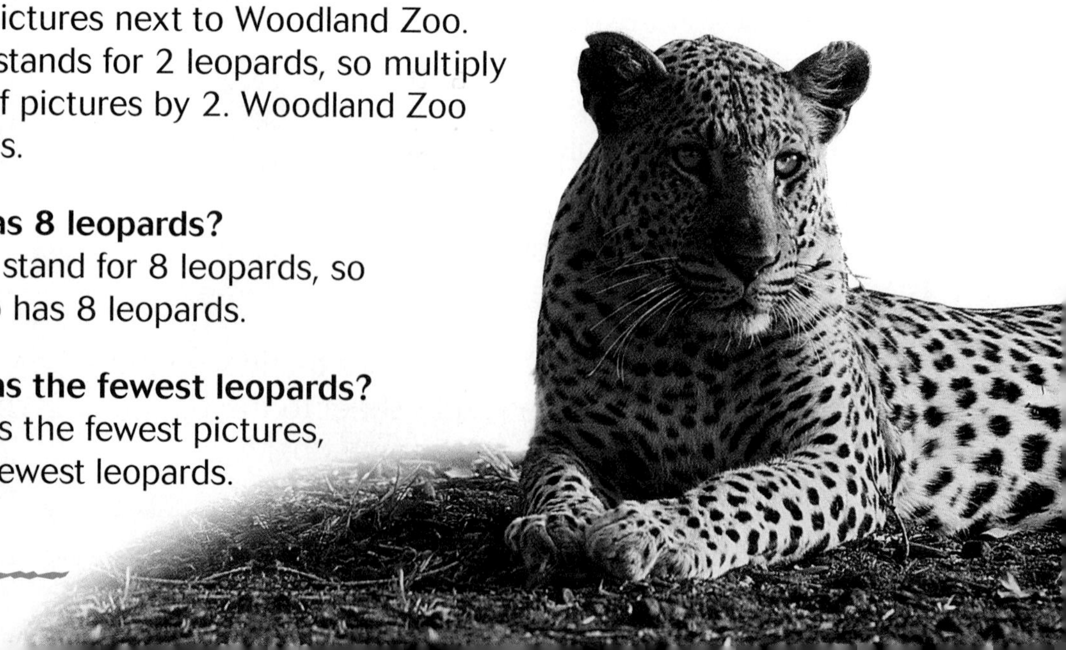

Connecting Ideas

You have been *reading* pictographs to compare data. You can also *make* pictographs to organize data.

What You Need

For each student:
graph paper

www.sbgmath.com

The table shows how many clams a sea otter ate in one week. You can show this information in a pictograph like the one started below.

Ollie the Otter's Clam Diet

Sunday	10
Monday	6
Tuesday	8
Wednesday	11
Thursday	14
Friday	8
Saturday	6

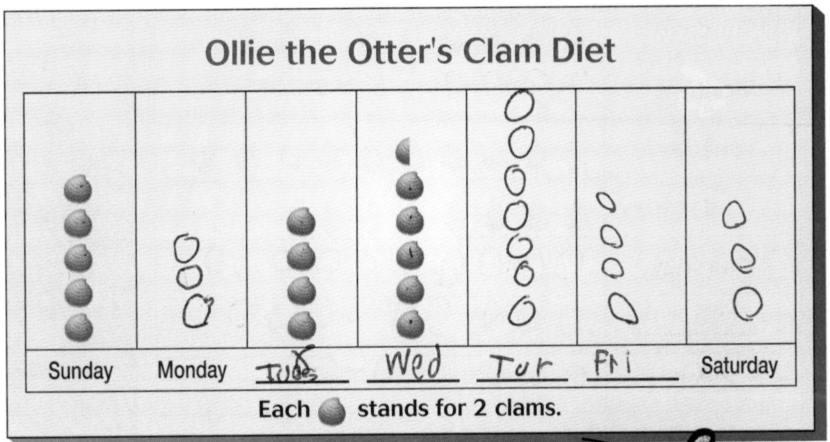

Copy the pictograph on graph paper. Then finish it.

- Write the days of the week at the bottom of the graph.
- Decide how many pictures each day should have. Then draw the pictures above each day.

Think and Discuss Look at the pictograph above. A half picture stands for half of the number given in the key. How many clams did the otter eat on Wednesday?

Science Connection
The leopard is a member of the cat family. Leopards live in parts of Asia and Africa.

Try It Out

1. **Science Connection** Tapirs like to eat bananas, bugs, and leaves. Make a pictograph to show how much food a tapir ate in one week. The graph below has been started for you.

Tapir Food Eaten in One Week

Sunday	18 pounds
Monday	16 pounds
Tuesday	20 pounds
Wednesday	15 pounds
Thursday	19 pounds
Friday	18 pounds
Saturday	14 pounds

Practice

Use this table of a class's favorite animals to make a pictograph. Then answer the questions below.

6 x 12 ~ 18

Class Vote	
Tiger	2
Red Wolf	4
Giant Panda	12
Manatee	8
Elephant	10

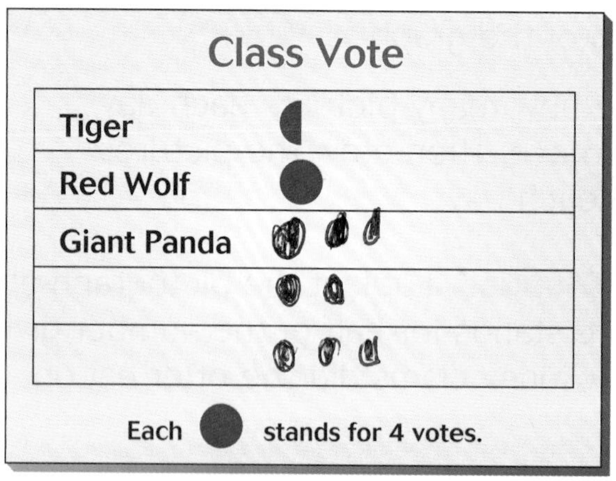

2. How many votes did the tiger get? 2

3. Which animal got the most votes? Panda

4. Which animal got the fewest votes? Tiger

5. Each student voted once. How many students voted in all? 36

Problem Solving

Science Connection **Look at the endangered animals at the right. Then answer Questions 6–9.**

Giant Panda

Koala Bear

Manatee

6. **Create Your Own** Ask your classmates to pick one animal they would like to learn more about. Tally each vote. Then use your data to make a pictograph.
7. What picture did you use to show the votes?
8. What number did each picture stand for?
9. Which animal was chosen the most? the least?

Review and Remember

Estimate first. Then use a calculator to find each answer.

10. $423 - 112$ **11.** $604 + 233$ **12.** $\$9.12 + 7.64$ **13.** $5{,}957 - 2{,}364$ **14.** $\$67.48 - 38.29$

Critical Thinking Corner

Logical Thinking

Reading a Venn Diagram

The animals in the blue circle live on land. The animals in the pink circle live in water. The animal in both circles lives on land *and* in water.

1. How many animals shown live on land? 4
2. Where can a frog live? Bolth
3. How many more animals shown can live on land than in water? 1

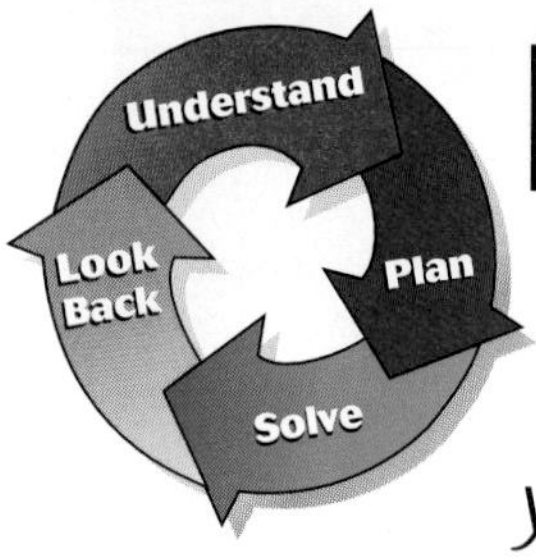

Problem Solving
Make a Graph

You can make a graph to organize data that will help you solve a problem.

Tory's class is voting on a project to help our planet. Four people want to plant trees, 7 want to collect trash, 8 want to donate used toys, 6 want to recycle bottles, and 4 want to learn how to save water. How could Tory organize the data? Which project is the most popular?

Kid Connection These stamps, that were designed by students for the U.S. Postal Service, show two ways to help our planet.

UNDERSTAND

What do you need to find?

You need to find a way for Tory to organize the data. Then you need to find which project got the most votes.

PLAN

How can you solve the problem?

You can **make a bar graph** to organize the data. Then you can compare the bars to see which project is the most popular.

SOLVE

Make the bar graph as shown. Be sure to label the graph.

The "Donate toys" bar is the tallest. So, it is the most popular project.

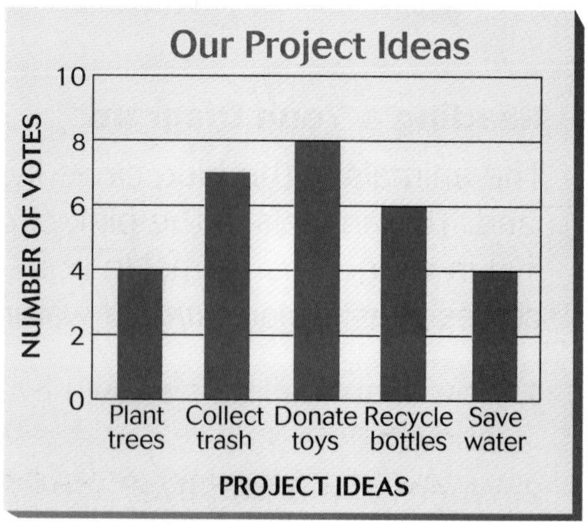

LOOK BACK

Could you have made a pictograph to organize and compare the data? Explain how.

Using the Strategy

Use this chart to answer Problems 1–6.

1. Eric and his classmates decided to collect used toys to give away. Eric made the tally chart at the right to record the number of toys the class has collected so far. Make a bar graph to organize Eric's data.

Kinds of Toys	Number of Toys Collected
Stuffed animals	𝍸 II
Games	𝍸 III
Dolls	𝍸 I
Trucks	IIII
Sporting goods	𝍸 𝍸 I

2. Which kind of toy was collected the most? the least?

3. How many more sporting goods than dolls did the class collect?

4. How many more games than trucks did the class collect?

5. Becky wants to make a list of the kinds of toys collected in order from least to most. How should she order her list?

6. What if the class collects 5 more games and 2 more dolls? How will that change your answers for Problem 2?

Mixed Strategy Review

Try these or other strategies you have learned.

- *Act It Out*
- *Work Backwards*
- *Find a Pattern*
- *Write a Number Sentence*

7. A class collects 4 cans on Monday, 8 cans on Tuesday, and 16 cans on Wednesday. If this pattern continues, how many cans will be collected on Friday?

8. Laura counts 8 glass bottles and 15 cans in the class recycling bin. How many more cans than glass bottles are in the recycling bin?

9. Laura puts some glass bottles in an empty class recycling bin. Later 5 bottles are taken out for a project. At the end of the day, Jonna puts 3 new bottles in the bin and says that now there are 15 bottles in the bin. How many bottles did Laura put in the bin?

Checkpoint

Using Data and Graphs

The tally chart shows the favorite national parks of one third-grade class. Use the tally chart to answer Questions 1–5. (pages 252–253)

1. Which park received the most votes?

2. Which parks received the same number of votes?

3. Which parks received more than 5 votes?

4. How many more students voted for Yellowstone than for the Grand Canyon?

5. How many students voted?

Favorite National Parks	
National Park	**Votes**
Grand Canyon	𝍸
Yellowstone	𝍸 |||
Big Bend	𝍸	
Great Smoky Mountains	||||
Everglades	𝍸	

Use the bar graph to answer Questions 6–10.
(pages 256–259)

6. Which animal runs fastest?

7. Which animal runs slowest?

8. Which two animals run at the same speed?

9. Which animal can run 70 miles per hour?

10. How fast does an elephant run?

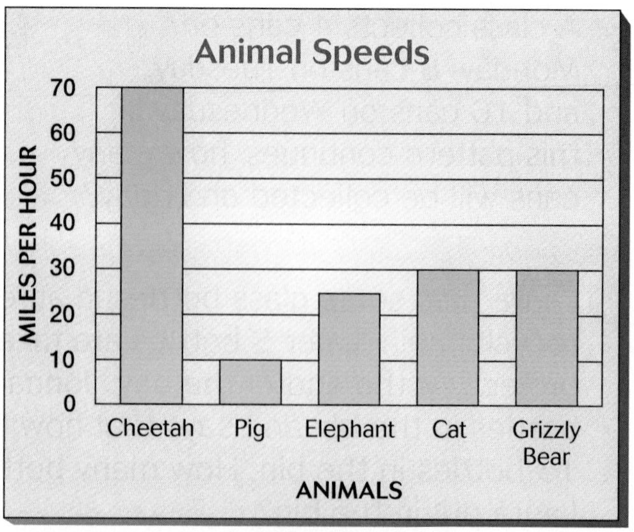

Use the pictograph to answer Questions 11–15. (pages 260–263)

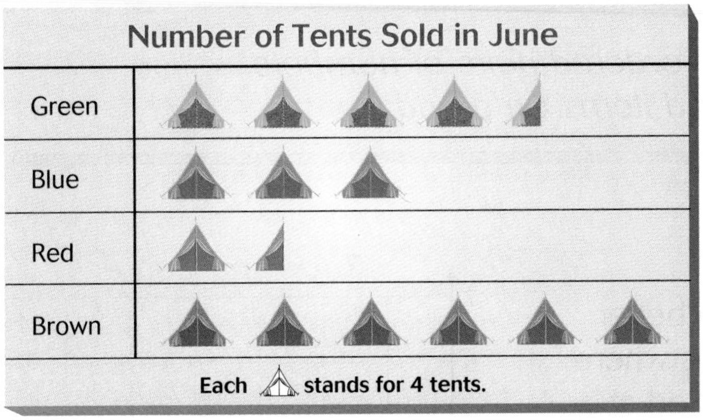

> **What do you think?**
>
> Do you think it's easier to read a pictograph or a bar graph?

11. How many blue tents were sold in June?

12. How many red tents were sold in June?

13. Which color tent was sold the most?

14. Which color tent was sold the least?

15. **Analyze** There were 53 tents sold in May. How many more tents were sold in June than in May?

Journal Idea What kind of graph is easiest for you to make? Why?

Critical Thinking Corner

Using Algebra **Visual Thinking**

Follow That Pattern!

Continue each pattern.

1.  ? ? ?

2. 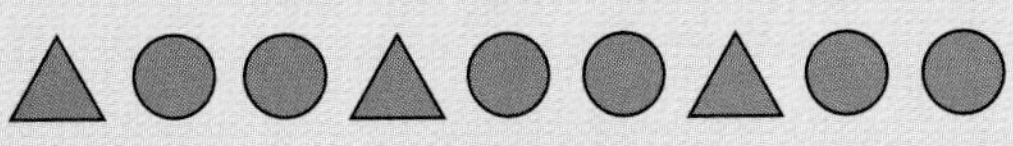 ? ? ?

3. 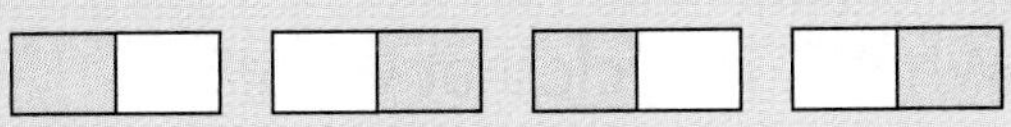 ? ? ?

Using Algebra

Don't Throw It Away!

You can use ordered pairs of numbers to find items on a grid.

Learning About It

Recycling can help make Earth a better place to live. This grid map shows where different kinds of trash are collected at a recycling center.

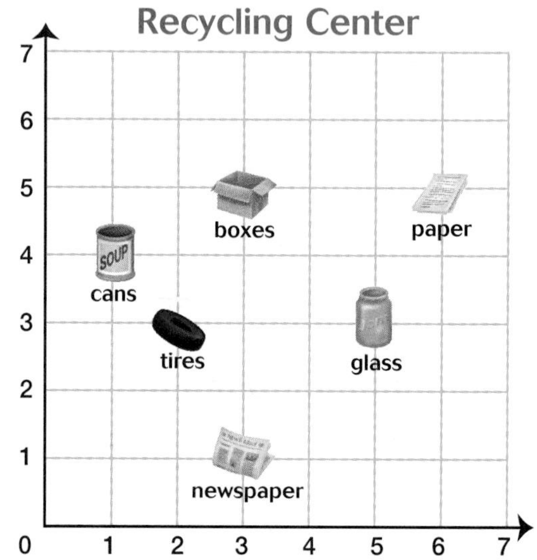

Look at the grid. Where is glass recycled?

- Start at 0.
- Go 5 spaces to the right.
- Go 3 spaces up.

Glass is recycled at the point marked by the **ordered pair** (5, 3).

(5 = spaces to the right; 3 = spaces up)

Another Example

Where are cans recycled?

- Start at 0.
- Go 1 space to the right.
- Go 4 spaces up.

Cans are recycled at (1, 4).

Think and Discuss Is there a difference between the ordered pairs (5, 3) and (3, 5)? Explain.

Fine Arts Connection
Janet Cooper of Sheffield, Massachusetts, uses bottle caps to make all kinds of jewelry and sculptures.

Try It Out

Use the grid above for Exercises 1–4.

1. What is recycled at (3, 1)?

2. What is recycled at (6, 5)?

3. Where are boxes recycled?

4. Where are tires recycled?

Practice

Write the ordered pair for each trash bin.

5.    **6.**    **7.** 

8.    **9.**    **10.** 

What bin is found at each ordered pair?

11. (6, 2)   **12.** (5, 4)   **13.** (1, 1)

14. (4, 1)   **15.** (3, 5)   **16.** (5, 6)

Trash Bin Location

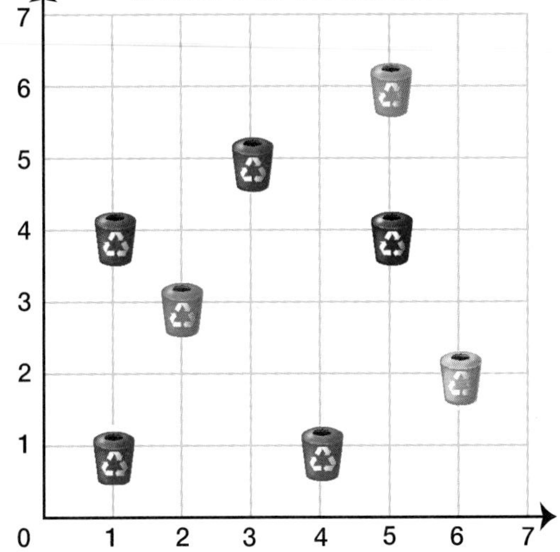

Problem Solving

17. Suppose a gray bin is 2 spaces to the right of the green bin. What ordered pair would name the gray bin's location?

18. Suppose you put a pink bin at (5, 3). What bin would be 3 spaces to the left of the pink bin?

Review and Remember

Using Estimation **Estimate each answer by rounding to the nearest ten.**

19. $62 - 23$

20. $55 + 91$

21. $23 + 56$

22. $86 - 37$

23. $37 + 62$

Now follow these steps.

- Check your tally chart. Decide if you have enough materials to make your creature.
- Collect other things you need.
- Put your creature together. Use tape or glue to keep the pieces in place.

For Extra Practice, see Set C, page 282.

Using Algebra

Trees, Please!

You can use ordered pairs on a grid map to show where things are.

Learning About It

It's Arbor Day! Foster Elementary School is celebrating by planting fruit trees. The grid map shows where each tree will go. Each tree's fruit stands for the tree. Follow these directions to finish the grid.

- Copy the grid on grid paper. Be sure to number the bottom and side of the grid as shown.
- Use the ordered pairs to draw more of these fruits on the grid.

(3, 1)	(4, 7)
(2, 3)	(7, 6)

Remember to follow these steps.

- Start at 0.
- Count the spaces to the right.
- Count the spaces up.
- Draw the item.

Think and Discuss Why is it important to always go over first and *then* up when finding a point?

Kid Connection Arbor Day is a special day for planting trees. Students at Jackson Elementary School in Utah believe every day should be Arbor Day. They have worked to get laws passed that help students raise money to plant trees.

What You Need

For each student:
grid paper
crayons

Arbor Day Planting

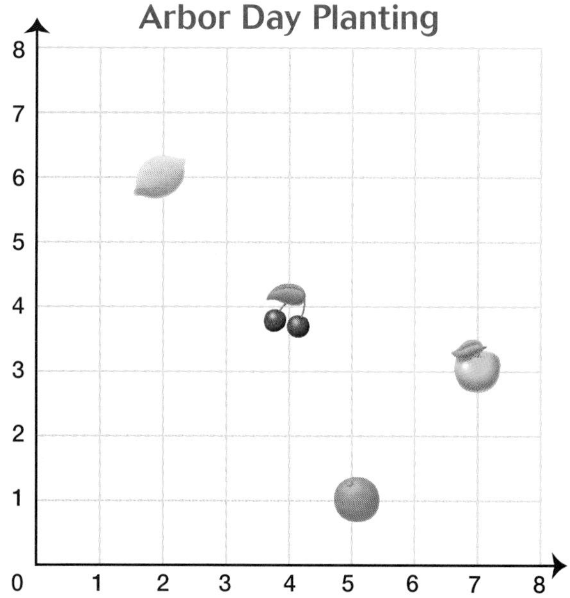

Try It Out

Copy this grid on grid paper. Then draw a point on the grid for each letter below. Use the ordered pairs to put the letters in the right place.

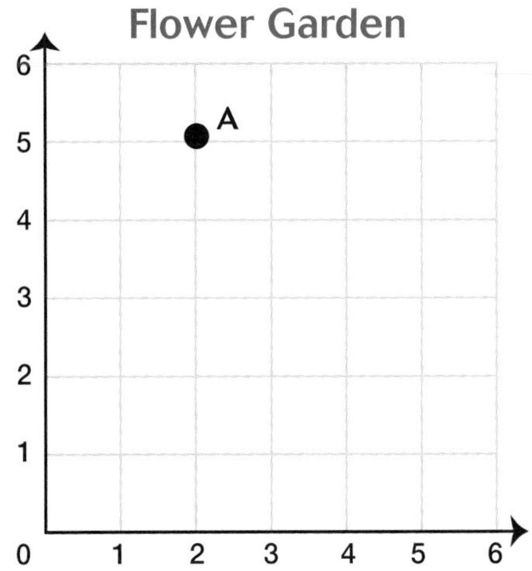

1. A (2, 5) **2.** B (1, 3) **3.** C (3, 4)

4. D (4, 1) **5.** E (4, 5) **6.** F (5, 3)

Practice

Use grid paper to make a grid like the one above. Draw each of these colored dots on the grid.

7. ● (1, 3) **8.** ● (6, 2) **9.** ○ (4, 1) **10.** ● (3, 5)

11. ● (5, 6) **12.** ● (2, 1) **13.** ● (4, 3) **14.** ● (2, 4)

Problem Solving

15. Make a grid map like the one above to show these places in Courtyard Gardens.

Courtyard Gardens

- The entrance is at (3, 1).

- The fountain is 3 spaces above the entrance.

- The roses are 2 spaces to the right of the fountain.

- The daisies are 1 space below the roses.

Review and Remember

Find each answer.

16. $60 + 40$

17. $\$31.08 - 23.06$

18. $300 + 700$

19. $\$97.58 + 24.64$

20. $605 - 299$

For Extra Practice, see Set D, page 282.

Tile After Tile

You can use tiles to explore probability.

Learning About It

Probability tells the chance that something will happen. One way to explore probability is by picking color tiles out of a bag. There is a probability that a certain color will or will not be picked.

Work with your group.

Word Bank

probability
impossible
certain
more likely
less likely
equally likely

What You Need

For each group:
5 red tiles
1 blue tile
1 bag

Step 1 Put 4 red tiles in a bag. Suppose you picked a tile out of the bag without looking. Could you pick a blue tile? Why or why not?

Step 2 Take turns picking 1 tile out of the bag 10 times without looking. Put the tile back in the bag each time. What do you always pick? Why?

- Sometimes it is **impossible** that something will happen.
- Sometimes it is **certain** that something will happen.

Step 3 Now put 5 red tiles and 1 blue tile in a bag. Suppose you picked 1 tile out of the bag 20 times without looking, and that you replaced the tile each time. Predict the color you would pick more often and less often.

Step 4 Take turns picking 1 tile from the bag without looking. Use a tally mark to record the color on a chart like the one below. Then put the tile back in the bag before you choose another. Repeat this step 19 times.

Color	Tally	Total Picked
Red		
Blue		

Which color was picked more often? less often?

Why do you think one color was picked more than the other?

- Sometimes it is **more likely** that something will happen.
- Sometimes it is **less likely** that something will happen.

Think and Discuss Suppose you picked a tile from the bag at the right. Is one color more likely to be picked, or are the chances of picking each color **equally likely**? Why?

Practice

Write whether picking a red tile is *certain* or *impossible*.

1. 

2. 

3. 

Write *more likely, less likely,* or *equally likely* to tell how likely it would be to pick a red tile rather than a blue tile.

4. 

5. 

6. 

What Are the Chances?

You can predict the chance of something happening.

Learning About It

Look at this spinner. There are 4 possible **outcomes** of a spin. The spinner could land on red, green, yellow, or blue.

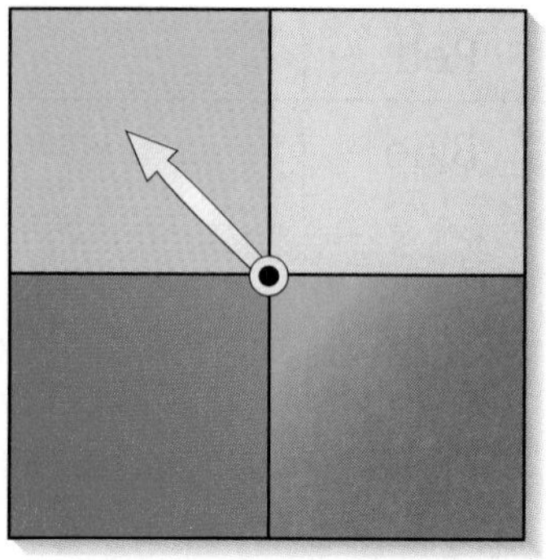

Each colored space is the same size. So, the **chance** that each outcome will happen is the same.

- The chance of spinning red is 1 out of 4.
- The chance of spinning green is 1 out of 4.
- The chance of spinning yellow is 1 out of 4.
- The chance of spinning blue is 1 out of 4.

Word Bank

outcomes
chance

Work with your partner.

Step 1 Think about spinning the spinner 40 times. Predict how many times the spinner would land on each color. Record your predictions in a chart like the one below.

Color	Prediction	Outcome
Red		
Green		
Blue		
Yellow		

What You Need

For each pair:
2 spinners

Step 2 Take turns spinning a spinner, like the one shown, 40 times. Use tally marks to record the outcomes on your chart. How close were the outcomes to your predictions?

www.sbgmath.com

Step 3 Look at this spinner. What are the possible outcomes of a spin? What is the chance that each outcome will happen?

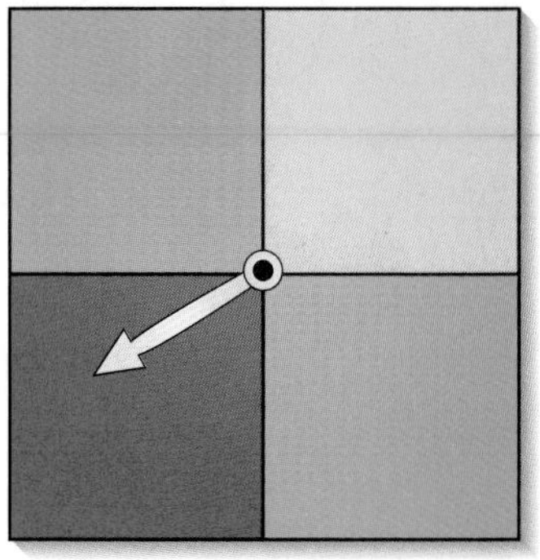

Is the chance of the spinner landing on each color equally likely? Why or why not?

Think about spinning the spinner 40 times. Predict how many times the spinner will land on each color. Record your predictions in a chart like the one below.

Color	Prediction	Outcome
Red		
Green		
Blue		

Step 4 Take turns spinning a spinner, like the one shown, 40 times. Use tally marks to record the outcomes on your chart. How close were the outcomes to your predictions?

Think and Discuss Suppose you picked one tile out of the bag at the right. What is the chance of picking red? of picking blue?

Practice

For each spinner, name all the possible outcomes of a spin. Then write the chance of spinning each outcome.

1. 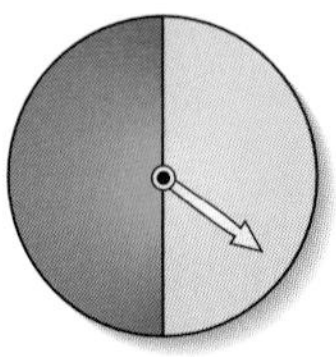

2. 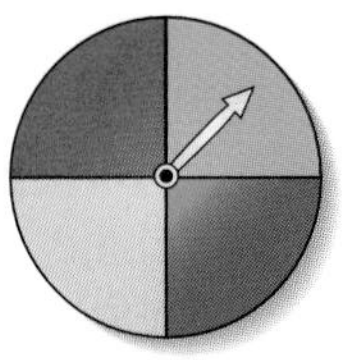

3. 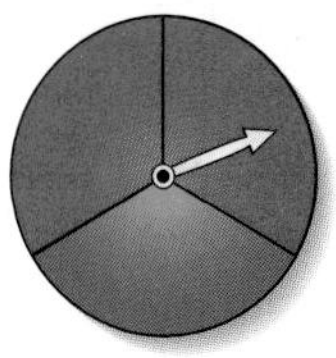

4. 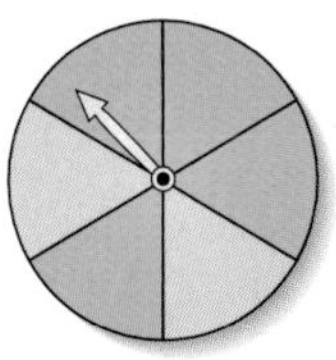

5. 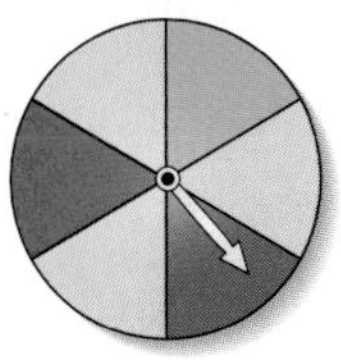

6. 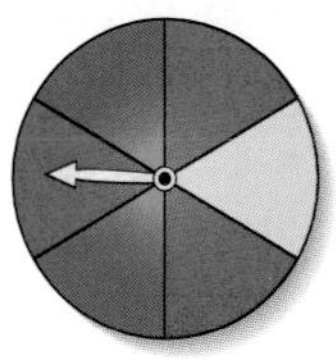

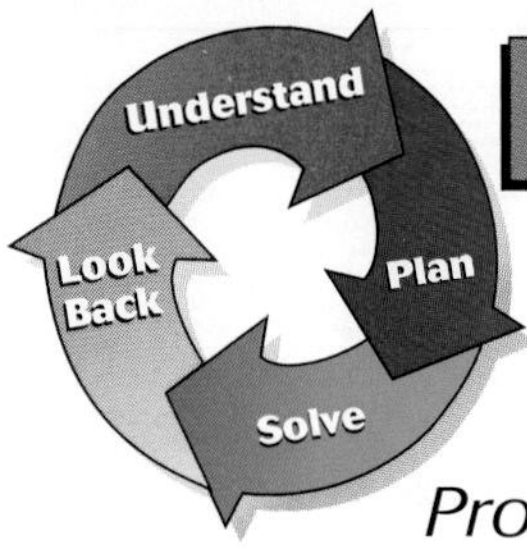

Problem Solving
Fair and Unfair Games

Probability helps you know if a game is fair or unfair.

Ben and Jill are spinning a spinner to play the game at the right. Ben moves a space if he spins blue. Jill moves a space if she spins red. Which spinner below would make the game fair?

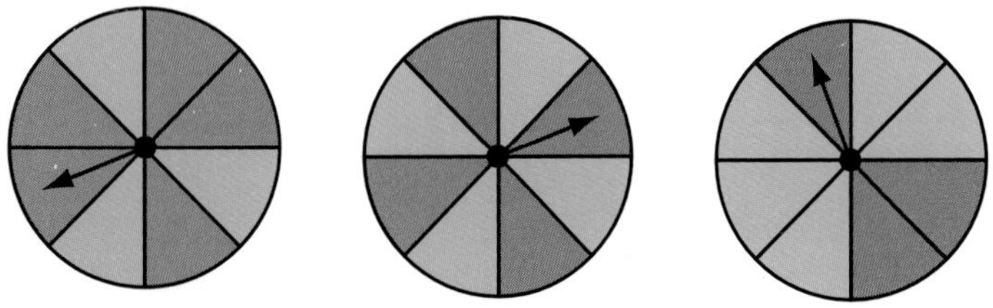

Spinner A　　Spinner B　　Spinner C

Rain Forest Game

First player to reach FINISH wins!

UNDERSTAND

What do you need to find?

You need to find the spinner that is equally likely to land on red or blue.

PLAN

How can you solve the problem?

You can count the spaces on each spinner to find the one that has the same number of red and blue spaces.

SOLVE

Spinner A	Spinner B	Spinner C
3 blue spaces	4 blue spaces	5 blue spaces
5 red spaces	4 red spaces	3 red spaces

Spinner B would make the game fair.

LOOK BACK

Explain which spinner gives Ben an unfair chance to win.

Show What You Learned

Use the spinners at the right to solve Problems 1 – 4.

1. Suppose you play the Rain Forest Game with Spinner D. Would you be more likely to win if you were the blue player or the red player? Is this a fair spinner to use?

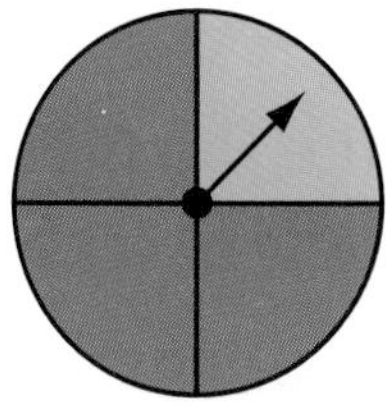

Spinner D

2. Suppose you want to play the Rain Forest Game with Spinner E. One space needs to be filled in with red or blue. Which color should be used to make the spinner fair?

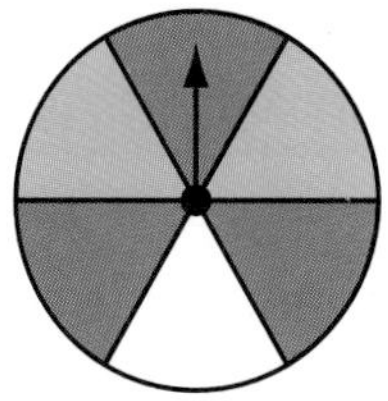

Spinner E

3. Daisy and Hector are playing the Rain Forest Game with Spinner F. Daisy is the red player and Hector is the blue player. Who do you think is more likely to win, Daisy or Hector? Tell why.

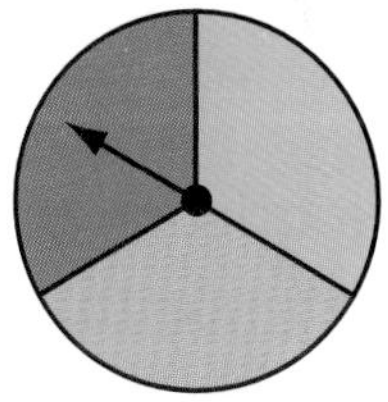

Spinner F

4. Suppose 3 people want to play the Rain Forest Game together. Which spinner should they use if they want the game to be fair?

5. **Explain** Suppose you and a friend play the Rain Forest Game 20 times with a fair spinner. How many games do you think each of you will win? Can you tell ahead of time exactly how many games each of you will win? Explain your thinking.

6. **Create Your Own** Draw three spinners that can be used to play the Rain Forest Game. Make one of the spinners fair. Make the other two spinners unfair.

Checkpoint

Understanding Ordered Pairs and Probability

Using Algebra

Write the ordered pair for each place at Mountain State Park. (pages 268–269)

1. Big Springs **2.** Waterfall

3. Fire Station **4.** High Point

5. Main Meadow **6.** Entrance

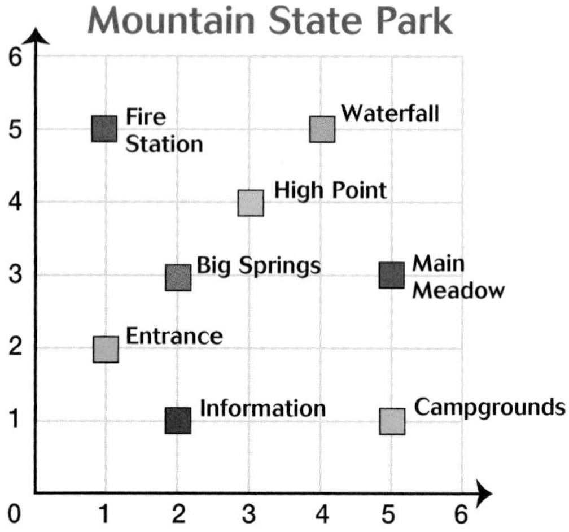

What place is found at each ordered pair? (pages 268–269)

7. (2, 1) **8.** (1, 5) **9.** (5, 1)

Make a grid on grid paper. Then use the ordered pairs to write the names of these places on the grid.
(pages 270–271)

10. food stand (5, 4) **11.** lodge (2, 1) **12.** first-aid station (4, 2)

13. ticket booth (1, 3) **14.** ski lift (2, 4) **15.** pool (4, 6)

Write whether the chance of picking a blue marble rather than a red marble is *more likely, less likely,* or *equally likely*. (pages 272–273)

16.

17.

18.

Name all of the possible outcomes for each spinner. Then write the chance of spinning each outcome.
(pages 274–275)

19.

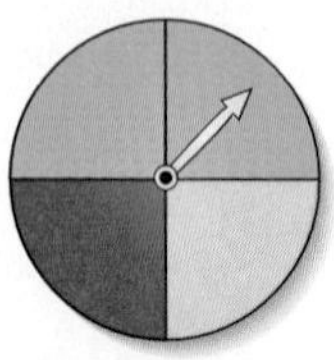

20.

21.

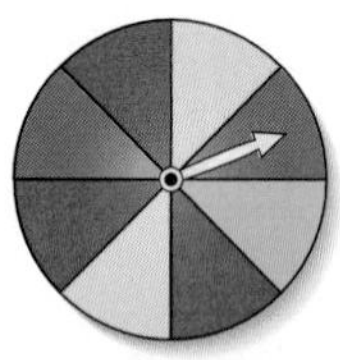

Using Algebra

Problem Solving

Use the grid map on page 278 to answer Questions 22–25.

22. Which is closer to the Entrance, Information or Campgrounds?

23. Gia hiked from the Campgrounds to a point 3 spaces up and 2 spaces to the left. Where did she go?

24. Harper found a lake 2 spaces to the right of the fire station. What ordered pair names where the lake is?

25. **Analyze** Park rangers want to build a first-aid station as close as possible to both Big Springs and High Point. Name an ordered pair where they could build the first-aid station.

What do you think?

Will you end up at the same point on a grid map for the ordered pairs (2, 6) and (6, 2)? Explain your thinking.

Journal Idea Design a fair spinner for a game for 3 players. Draw a picture of the spinner you would make and explain your thinking.

Project Wrap-Up

Feature Your Creatures

When the creatures are finished, meet to talk about your art.

- Make a class chart. Show how much of each type of recyclable material was used.
- Talk about which materials were best to use for making your piece of art.
- Compare all the creatures. Decide what is special about each one.
- Invite another class to come see your recycled material art exhibit. Talk together about other good ways to recycle.

Extra Practice

Set A (pages 256–259)

Use the bar graph to answer Questions 1–4.

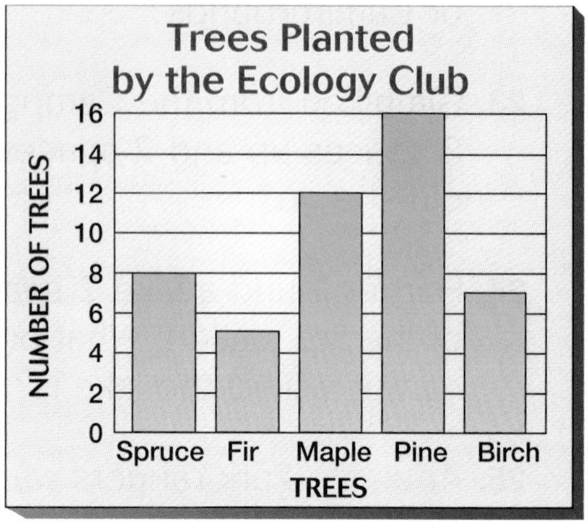

1. What kind of tree was planted the most?
2. How many birch trees were planted?
3. How many more spruce trees than fir trees were planted?
4. How many trees were planted in all?

Use the bar graph to answer Questions 5–8.

5. On which days were the fewest bags collected?
6. How many bags were collected on Thursday?
7. How many more bags were collected on Friday than on Tuesday?
8. How many bags were collected in all?

Use the bar graph to answer Questions 9–12.

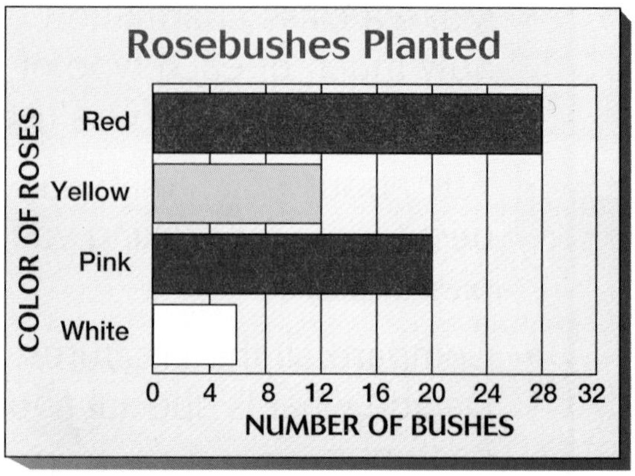

9. What color rosebush was planted the most?
10. What color rosebush was planted the least?
11. How many yellow rosebushes were planted?
12. How many more pink rosebushes than white rosebushes were planted?

Extra Practice

Set B (pages 260–263)

Use the pictograph to answer Questions 1–5.

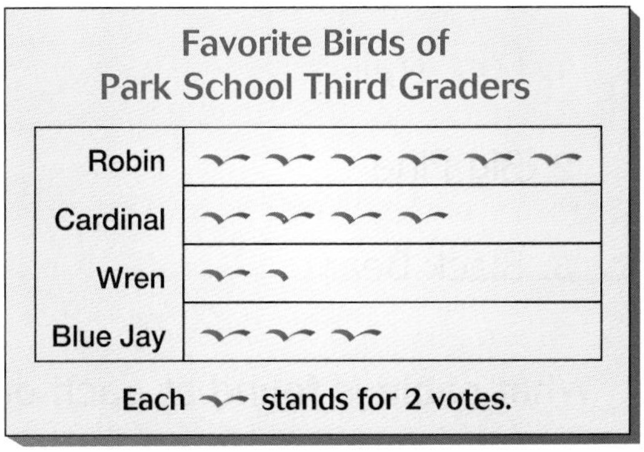

1. Which bird received the most votes?
2. Which bird received the fewest votes?
3. How many students voted for the robin?
4. How many more students voted for the blue jay than for the wren?
5. How many students voted in all?

Use the pictograph to answer Questions 6–9.

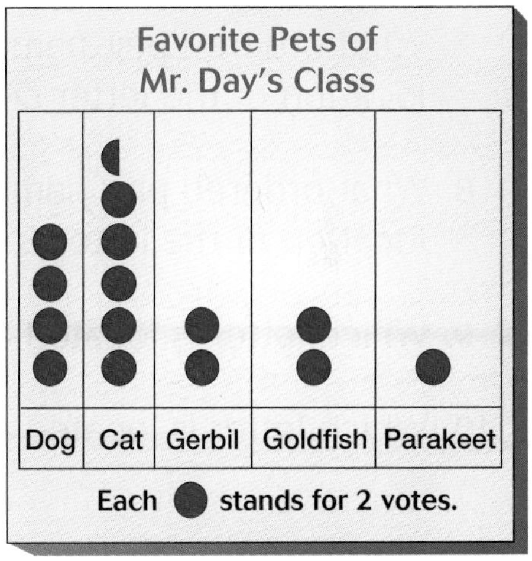

6. Which pet received the most votes?
7. Which pet received the fewest votes?
8. How many students voted for the gerbil?
9. How many more students voted for the cat than for the goldfish?

Use the pictograph to answer Questions 10–13.

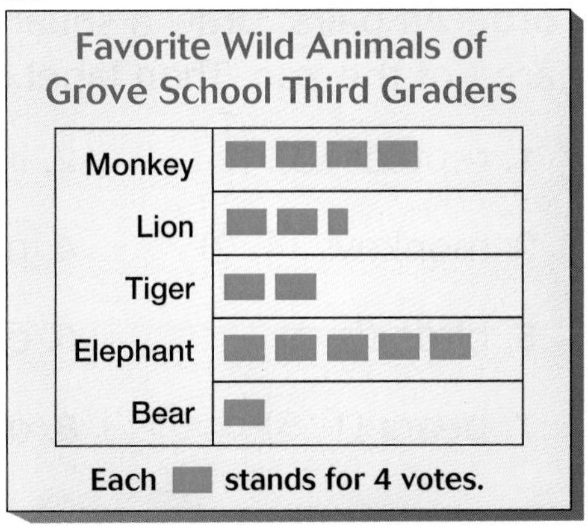

10. Which animal received the most votes?
11. Which animal received the fewest votes?
12. How many students voted for the elephant?
13. How many students voted in all?

Extra Practice

Set C (pages 268–269)

Write the ordered pair that names the location for each cabin.

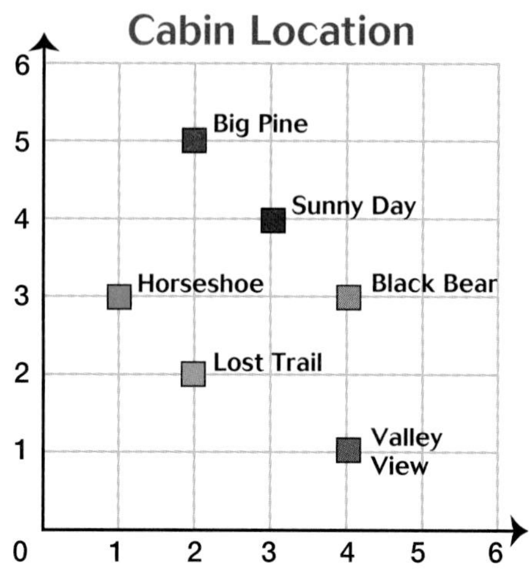

1. Lost Trail

2. Big Pine

3. Black Bear

What cabin is found at each ordered pair?

4. (4, 1) **5.** (1, 3) **6.** (3, 4)

Use the grid at the right to answer Questions 7–10.

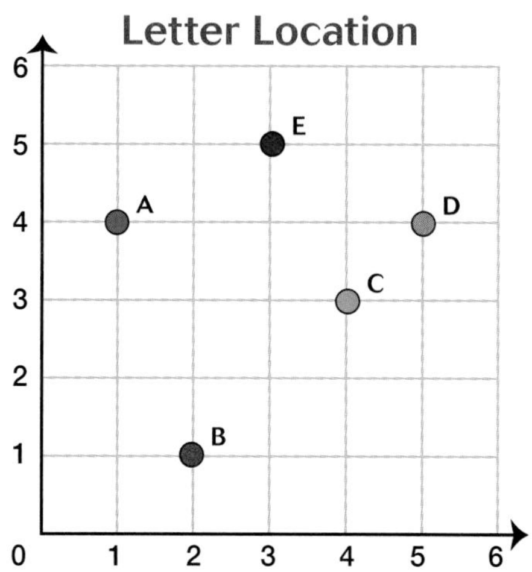

7. What ordered pair names the location of the letter *D*?

8. What ordered pair names the location of the letter *B*?

9. Which letter is located at (3, 5)?

10. Which letter is located at (1, 4)?

Set D (pages 270–271)

Copy the grid at the right. Use the ordered pairs. Draw a square at each animal area of the zoo. Then label each area.

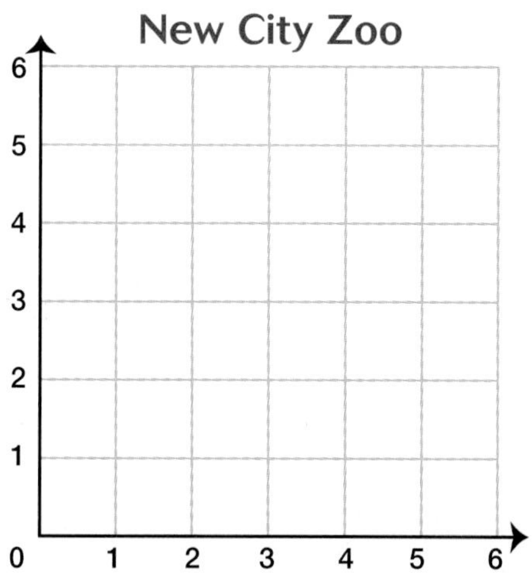

1. reptiles (3, 4) **2.** lions (3, 1)

3. monkeys (4, 2) **4.** pandas (5, 5)

5. birds (5, 1) **6.** entrance (1, 1)

7. bears (1, 5) **8.** otters (1, 2)

Chapter Test

Use the tally chart to answer the questions.

1. Which place received the most votes?
2. How many votes did Rocky Park get?
3. How many more votes did Sand Dune Park receive than Clearwater Beach?

Favorite Places to Visit

Places to Visit	Votes
Clearwater Beach	|||
Rocky Park	𝍸
Sand Dune Park	𝍸 |||
Fun Farm	𝍸 𝍸 ||

Use the graphs to answer the questions.

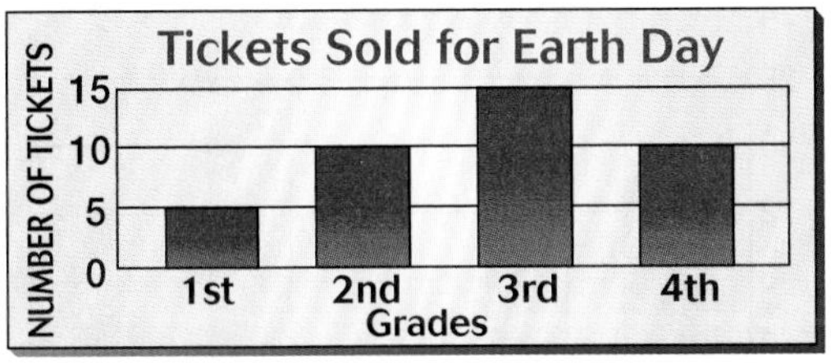

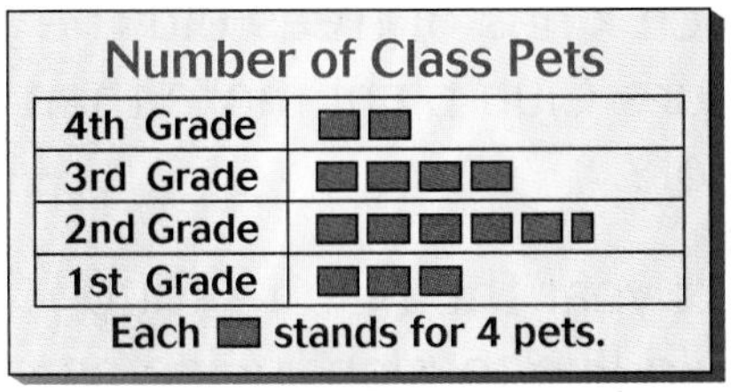

4. Who sold the most tickets?
5. How many tickets did the 4th grade sell?
6. How many tickets were sold?
7. Which grade has the fewest pets?
8. How many pets does the 2nd grade have?
9. How many pets are there in all?

Write the ordered pair for each color.

10. purple **11.** blue **12.** yellow
13. red **14.** orange **15.** green
16. black **17.** pink **18.** gray

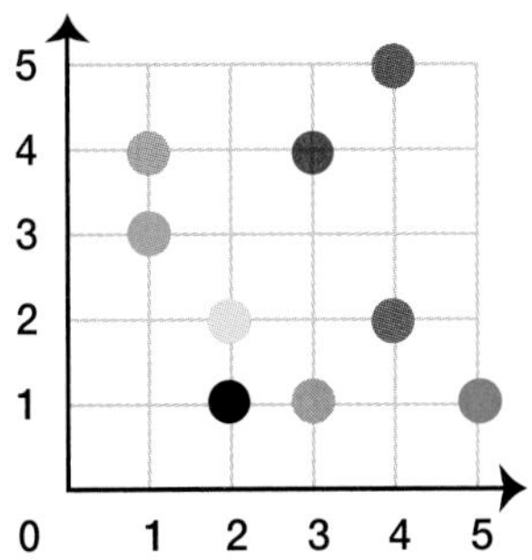

Problem Solving

19. Use the tally chart at the top of the page to make a bar graph or pictograph.

20. What is the chance that this spinner will land on green?

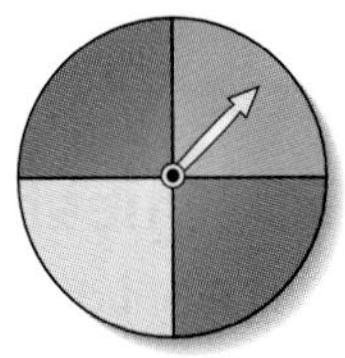

Self-Check

Look back at Exercises 10–18. Did you write the correct number first for each ordered pair?

Performance Assessment

Show What You Know About Using Data

What You Need
graph paper

1. Use the bar graph to answer Questions 1a–1d.
   a. How many different kinds of trees were planted?
   b. Which kind of tree was planted least often?
   c. Which kinds of trees did the Nature Club plant more than 10 of?
   d. Next year the Nature Club would like to plant twice as many trees as they planted this year. How many trees should they plant?

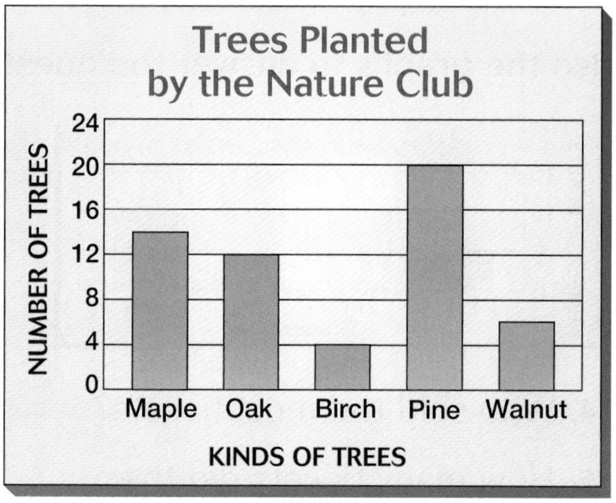

2. Every day a third-grade class collects and recycles the milk cartons they have used. The tally chart below shows how many milk cartons the class collected in one week.
   a. Make a bar graph or a pictograph to show the data.
   b. Write two questions that can be answered by using your graph.

Day	Number of Cartons
Monday	𝍸 𝍸 𝍸 𝍸
Tuesday	𝍸 𝍸 𝍸 𝍷
Wednesday	𝍸 𝍸 𝍸 𝍷𝍷𝍷
Thursday	𝍸 𝍸 𝍸
Friday	𝍸 𝍸 𝍸 𝍸

Self-Check

For Questions 1a and 1b, did you correctly read the number that each bar stands for?

For Question 2a, did you label all the parts of your graph?

Extension

Circle Graphs

Zoos are fun places to visit to see many different animals. At a petting zoo you can pet the animals.

Suppose you visited the Parkland Petting Zoo. This zoo has baby llamas, ponies, baby goats, and piglets.

The graph at the right is called a circle graph. It shows how much space each kind of animal in the zoo has.

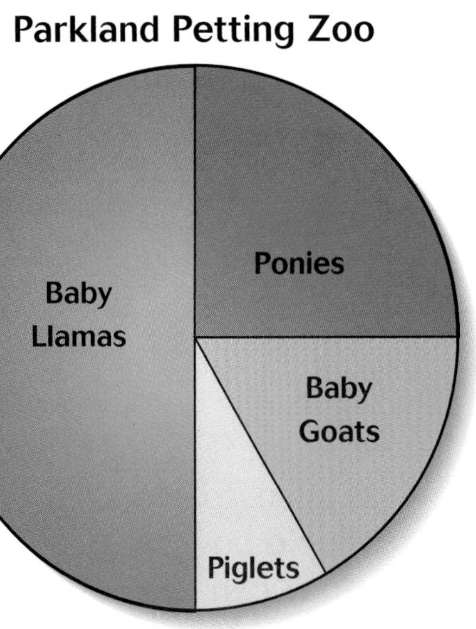

Use the graph to answer the questions.

1. Which kind of animal has the most space?

2. Which kind of animal has the least space?

3. Do the ponies or the baby goats have more space? Explain how you know.

The pens in the zoo are all the same size. The number of pens used by each kind of animal is listed below. Match the number of pens to each kind of animal.

4. 2 pens   **a.** baby llamas

5. 3 pens   **b.** baby goats

6. 6 pens   **c.** piglets

7. 1 pen   **d.** ponies

Chapter 8

Division Concepts

Chapter Theme: COMMUNITIES

Career Spotlight Meet Lisa Geiger. She is a juggler who likes to perform at birthday parties and community shows.

Some jugglers teach other people how to juggle. They can use division to figure out how many classes they need to teach a certain number of students.

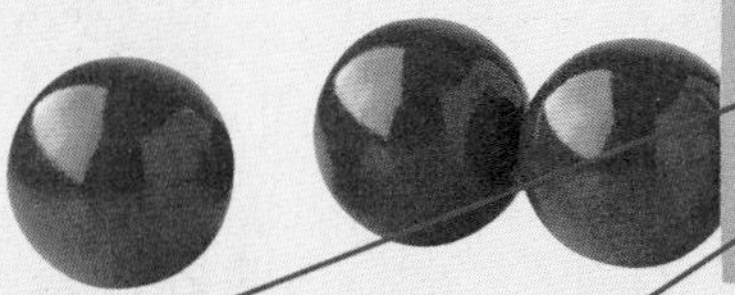

12 students ÷ **4** per class = **3** classes

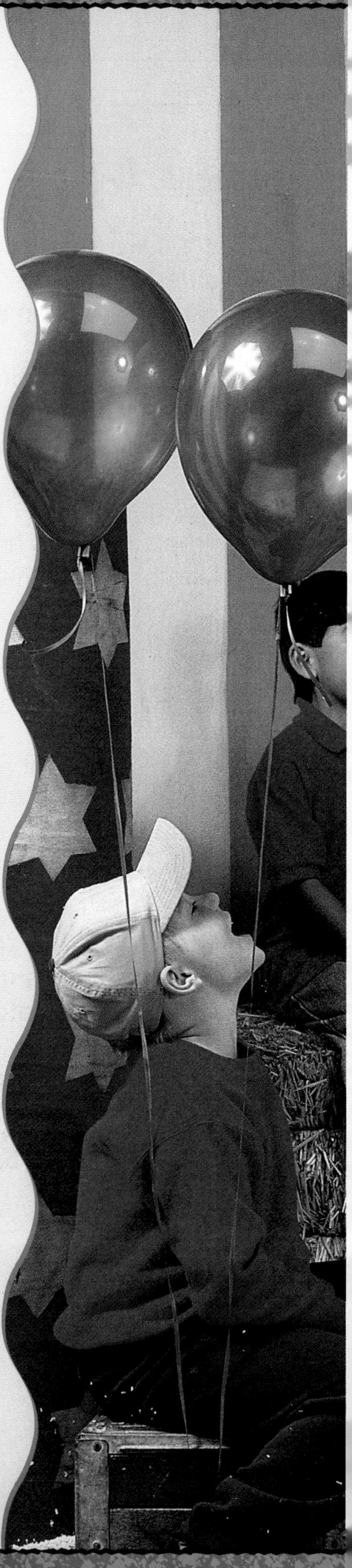

Chapter Project

Plan a School Fair

Working in groups, your class will plan four booths for a school fair. Start by thinking about how to decorate the booths. You could collect balloons and crepe paper or streamers. You could make banners and paper flowers. What else could you do?

When all the decorations are ready, you will divide them into 4 equal groups—1 group for each booth.

An Equal Share

To share a number of items, divide them into equal groups.

Learning About It

Get your tickets for the Community Day Fair! Suppose 12 tickets were bought by 3 families. If each family bought the same number of tickets, how many tickets did each family buy?

Work with your group.

Step 1 Use counters to show how 3 families could share 12 tickets equally. Put the counters into 3 equal groups.

- How many counters are there in all?
- How many groups are there?
- How many counters are in each group?

Word Bank

divide
division

What You Need

For each group:
18 counters

To share objects equally, you **divide.**

A **division** sentence tells how you divide the objects.

Think: Divide 12 objects into 3 equal groups.

Write: $12 \div 3 = 4$ The symbol $\div$ means "divided by."

Read: Twelve divided by three equals four.

Step 2 Now divide 12 counters into 2 equal groups, then into 4 equal groups, and then into 6 equal groups. Record your work in a chart like the one shown.

Number of Counters	Number of Equal Groups	Number in Each Group	Division Sentence
12	2	6	12 ÷ 2 = 6
12	3	4	12 ÷ 3 = 4
12	4	3	12 ÷ 4 = 3
12	6	2	12 ÷ 6 = 2

Step 3 Use 18 counters. Divide them into equal groups in as many different ways as you can. Record your work in a chart like the one shown above.

Think and Discuss Suppose you have 16 tickets for the fair. What must you know before you can divide them into equal groups?

Practice

Use the pictures to answer the questions.

1. a. How many tickets in all? 6
b. How many groups? 3
c. How many in each group? 2
d. 6 ÷ 3 = ■ 2

2. a. How many tickets in all? 12
b. How many groups? 4
c. How many in each group? 3
d. 12 ÷ 4 = ■ 3

3. a. How many tickets in all? 15
b. How many groups? 3
c. How many in each group? 5
d. 15 ÷ 3 = ■ 5

4. Analyze Suppose you divide 36 tickets into 4 equal groups. Then you divide the 36 tickets into 6 equal groups. Which way gives you more tickets in each group?

How Many Groups?

One way to divide a number of objects into equal groups is to use subtraction.

Learning About It

There are 18 game booths at the Community Day Fair. The booths are set up in groups of 3. How many groups are there?

Work with a partner to find out.

18 ÷ 3 = ■

What You Need

For each pair:
18 counters

Step 1 You can use subtraction to help you divide. Use 18 counters to show the booths. Put 3 counters in one group. Continue putting counters in groups of 3 until all of the counters have been used. How many groups of 3 did you make?

Step 2 You can use a number line to show how you subtracted. Start at 18. Jump back by 3s until you reach 0. How many jumps did you make?

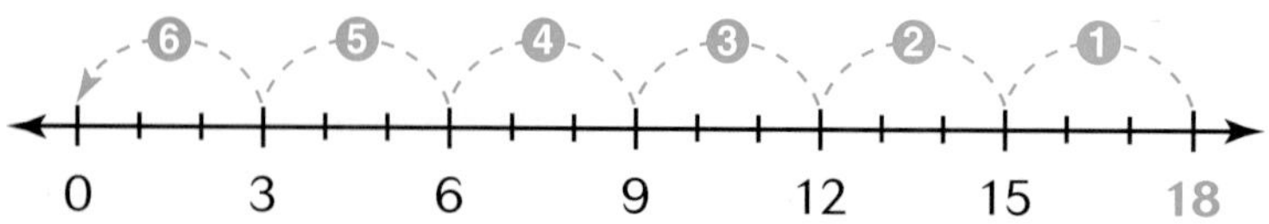

You made 6 jumps.

18 ÷ 3 = 6

There are 6 groups of booths.

Think and Discuss Look back at the number line that shows 18 ÷ 3 = 6. You can show these jumps with 6 subtraction sentences. The first two sentences are shown at the right. What are the next four?

18 − 3 = 15

15 − 3 = 12

Practice

Use the pictures to answer the questions.

1. **a.** How many counters in all?
b. How many in each group?
c. How many groups?

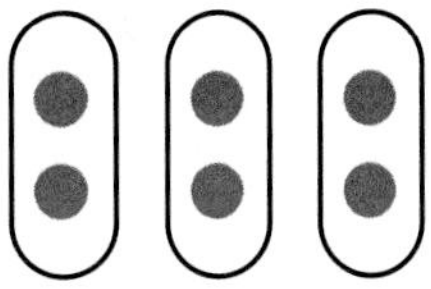

d. Use the number line. How many groups of 2?

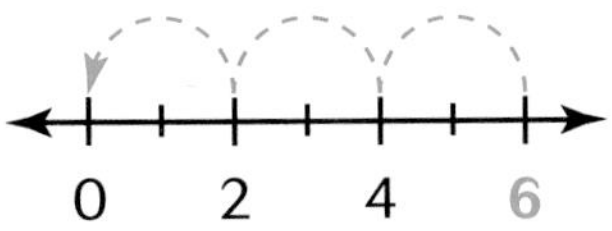

e. 6 ÷ 2 = ■

---

2. **a.** How many counters in all?
b. How many in each group?
c. How many groups?

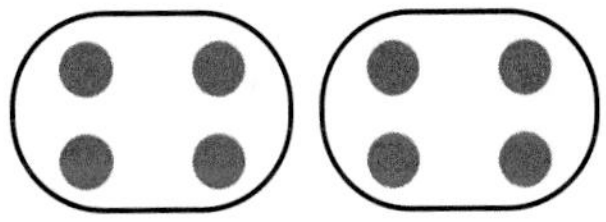

d. Use the number line. How many groups of 4?

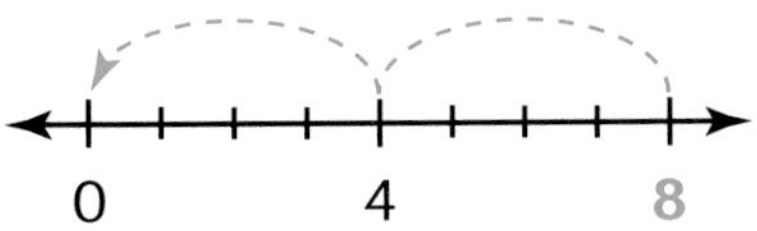

e. 8 ÷ 4 = ■

---

3. **a.** How many counters in all?
b. How many in each group?
c. How many groups?

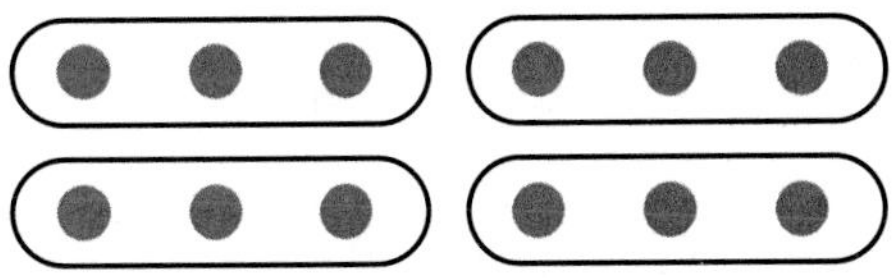

d. Use the number line. How many groups of 3?

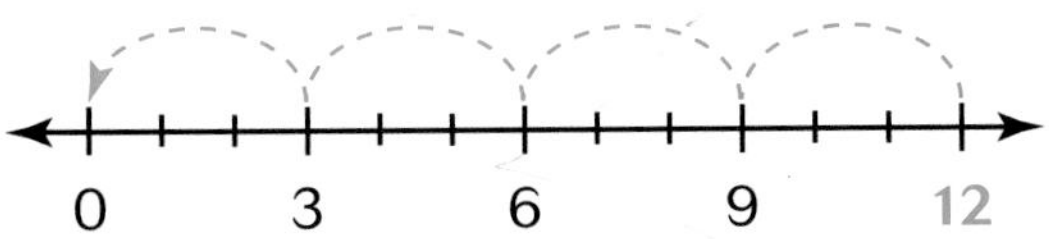

e. 12 ÷ 3 = ■

---

4. **Create Your Own** Draw "jumps" on a number line to show a division example. Then challenge a classmate to write the division sentence that goes with your number line.

Using Algebra

Strike Up the Band!

You can use what you know about multiplying to help you divide.

Learning About It

Here comes the band! The school band is marching in the Community Day Parade. The drummers line up in equal rows.

Word Bank

dividend
divisor
quotient

There are 3 rows with 7 drummers in each row. How many drummers are marching?

Multiply to find the answer.

$$3 \times 7 = 21$$

3 ↑ number of rows; 7 ↑ number in each row; 21 ↑ number in all

There are 21 drummers marching in 3 rows. How many drummers are in each row?

Divide to find the answer.

$$21 \div 3 = 7$$

21 ↑ number in all; 3 ↑ number of rows; 7 ↑ number in each row

How are multiplication and division related? Look at the array and at the number sentences below.

$$3 \times 7 = 21$$

3 and 7: factors; 21: product

$$21 \div 3 = 7$$

21: dividend; 3: divisor; 7: quotient

Math Note

Remember, an array shows objects in rows and columns.

Another Example

Look at the array of horns. There are 15 horns in 5 rows. Each row has the same number of horns. How many horns are in each row?

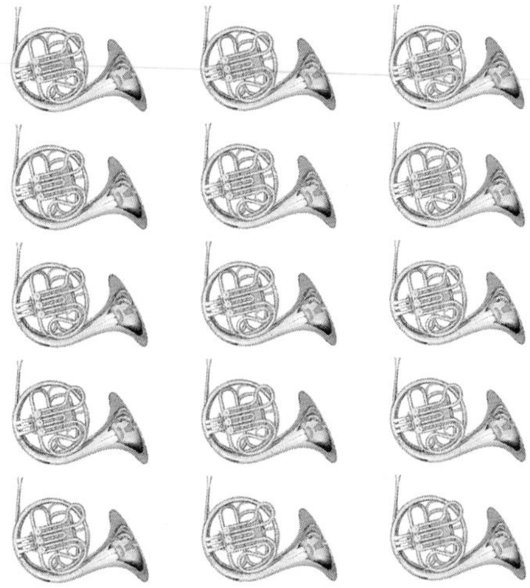

$15 \div 5 = ■$

Use a multiplication fact to help you divide.

Think: 5 times what number equals 15?

$5 \times 3 = 15$

So, $15 \div 5 = 3$

There are 3 horns in each row.

www.sbgmath.com

Think and Discuss Look at the numbers in the multiplication sentence above. Where do you find them in the division sentence?

Try It Out

Use the array to complete each sentence.

1.

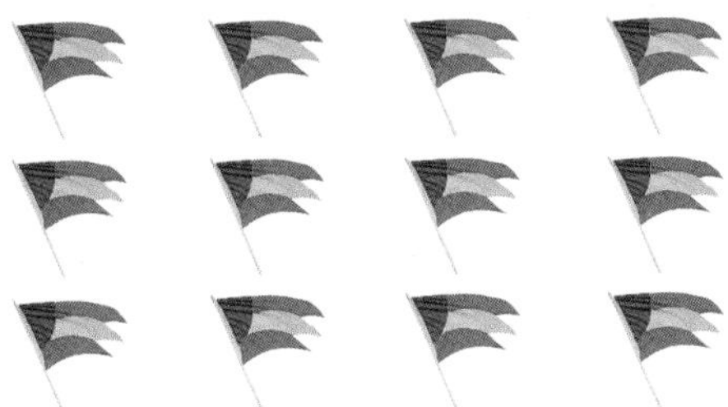

$3 \times 4 = ■$
$12 \div 3 = ■$

2.

$3 \times ■ = 18$
$18 \div 3 = ■$

3.

$2 \times ■ = 10$
$10 \div 2 = ■$

4.

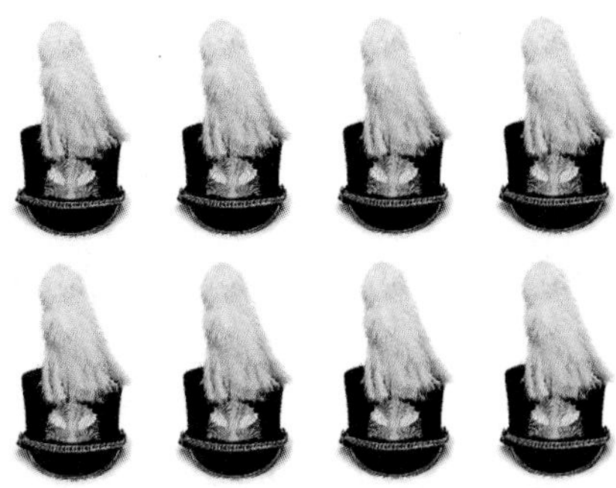

$2 \times ■ = 8$
$8 \div 2 = ■$

Practice

Write a multiplication sentence and a division sentence for each array.

5. 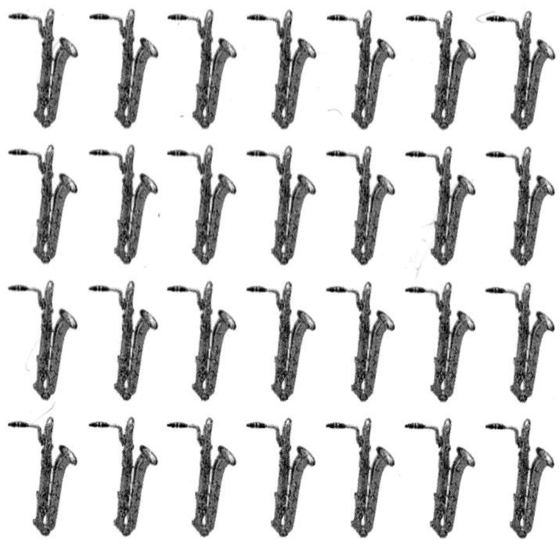

6. 

Draw an array for each pair of number sentences.

7. $3 \times 6 = 18$ $18 \div 3 = 6$	**8.** $4 \times 8 = 32$ $32 \div 4 = 8$	**9.** $2 \times 7 = 14$ $14 \div 2 = 7$	**10.** $4 \times 5 = 20$ $20 \div 4 = 5$
11. $2 \times 5 = 10$ $10 \div 2 = 5$	**12.** $3 \times 9 = 27$ $27 \div 3 = 9$	**13.** $5 \times 5 = 25$ $25 \div 5 = 5$	**14.** $5 \times 6 = 30$ $30 \div 5 = 6$

Write two related division sentences for each multiplication fact.

15. $3 \times 2 = 6$	**16.** $5 \times 8 = 40$	**17.** $4 \times 7 = 28$	**18.** $2 \times 9 = 18$
19. $8 \times 3 = 24$	**20.** $7 \times 2 = 14$	**21.** $9 \times 4 = 36$	**22.** $5 \times 7 = 35$
23. $4 \times 3 = 12$	**24.** $3 \times 7 = 21$	**25.** $2 \times 8 = 16$	**26.** $5 \times 9 = 45$

Problem Solving

27. At a fair, a musician displays Andean panpipes. He has 3 rows with 6 panpipes in each row. Draw an array and write a multiplication sentence to show how many panpipes he has.

28. The musician also has 15 CDs of panpipe music. How can he arrange all of his CDs in an array? Write a division sentence to show one array he might use.

Music Connection ▲
This panpipe is from the Andes Mountains in South America. It is played by blowing across the ends of the pipes. The longer a pipe is, the lower the sound it makes.

29. The school band has 48 members. They march in rows with 6 people in each row. Draw an array and write a division sentence to show how many rows of marchers there are.

30. The Music Club has a float in the parade. They worked on the float for 6 hours on Saturday and for 3 hours on Sunday. How many hours did they work on the float?

Review and Remember

Use the pictograph at the right to answer Questions 31–34.

31. Which is the largest group in the parade?

32. How many 4-H Club members are in the parade?

33. How many more firefighters are there than Boy Scouts?

34. What is the total number of scouts in the parade?

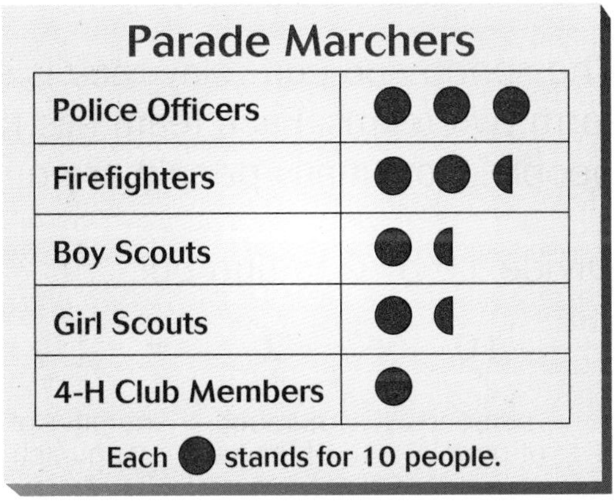

Critical Thinking Corner

Visual Thinking

Join the Parade

A parade is to start at A and finish at G. The diagram shows the streets and the directions the parade could take. Find three different parade routes. Record your routes by writing the letters in the correct order.

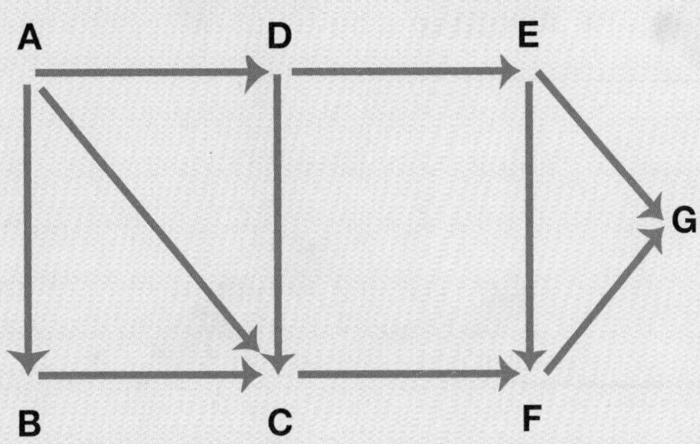

Eggs-actly Two!

You can use counters or use a multiplication fact to help you divide by 2.

Learning About It

The spoon-and-egg relay race is starting! Ten people form two teams. Each team has the same number of people. How many people are on each team?

Divide 10 by 2 to find out.

10	÷	2	=	■
↑ number of people		↑ number of teams		↑ number of people on each team

THERE'S ALWAYS A WAY!

- **One way** to divide is to use counters.
  - Use 10 counters.
  - Put the same number of counters in each of 2 groups.

  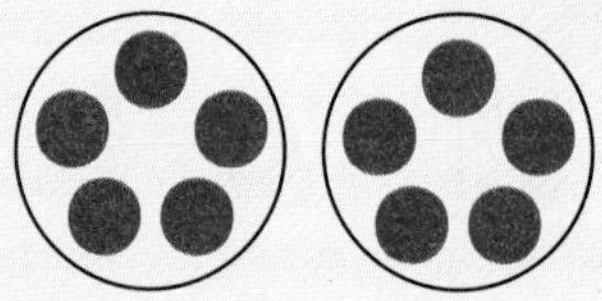

  10 ÷ 2 = 5

- **Another way** to divide is to use a related multiplication fact.

  10 ÷ 2 = ■

  Think: 2 × ■ = 10
  2 × 5 = 10

  So, 10 ÷ 2 = 5
  (10: dividend, 2: divisor, 5: quotient)

There are 5 people on each team.

Think and Discuss Think about finding half of 12. Think about finding 12 ÷ 2. How are they both the same?

Try It Out

Use the picture to find each quotient.

1.
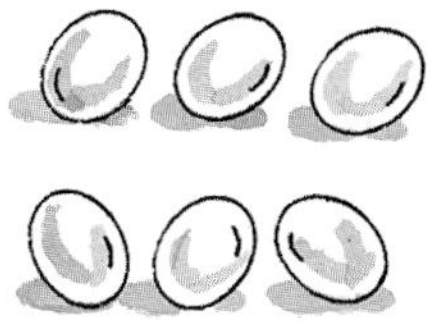
6 ÷ 2 = ■

2.

8 ÷ 2 = ■

3.
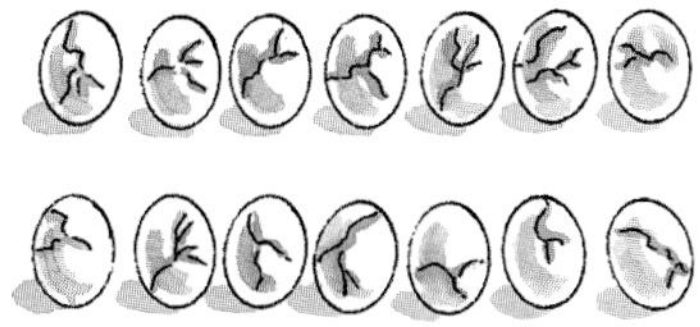
14 ÷ 2 = ■

Practice

Use the multiplication fact to find each quotient.

4. 2 × 2 = 4
4 ÷ 2 = ■

5. 2 × 6 = 12
12 ÷ 2 = ■

6. 2 × ■ = 16
16 ÷ 2 = ■

7. 2 × ■ = 18
18 ÷ 2 = ■

Find each quotient.

8. 10 ÷ 2 **9.** 2 ÷ 2 **10.** 6 ÷ 2 **11.** 8 ÷ 2

12. 4 ÷ 2 **13.** 18 ÷ 2 **14.** 12 ÷ 2 **15.** 16 ÷ 2

16. 14 ÷ 2 **17.** 6 ÷ 2 **18.** 4 ÷ 2 **19.** 18 ÷ 2

Problem Solving

20. There are a dozen eggs in a carton. The eggs are arranged in 2 equal rows. How many eggs are there in each row?

21. **Analyze** The fair lasts 8 hours. Taped music is played for the first 4 hours. A band plays for half of the remaining time. How long does the band play?

Review and Remember

Find each answer.

22. 6 × 7 **23.** 19 − 8 **24.** 9 × 9

25. 8 × 9 **26.** 15 + 46 **27.** 25 − 9

Project Link

How will your group make its booth? You could use

- a table
- a cardboard box
- desks pushed together

Don't forget to divide the decorations equally!

For Extra Practice, see Set B, page 316.

Craft Sale

You can use repeated subtraction to divide by 3.

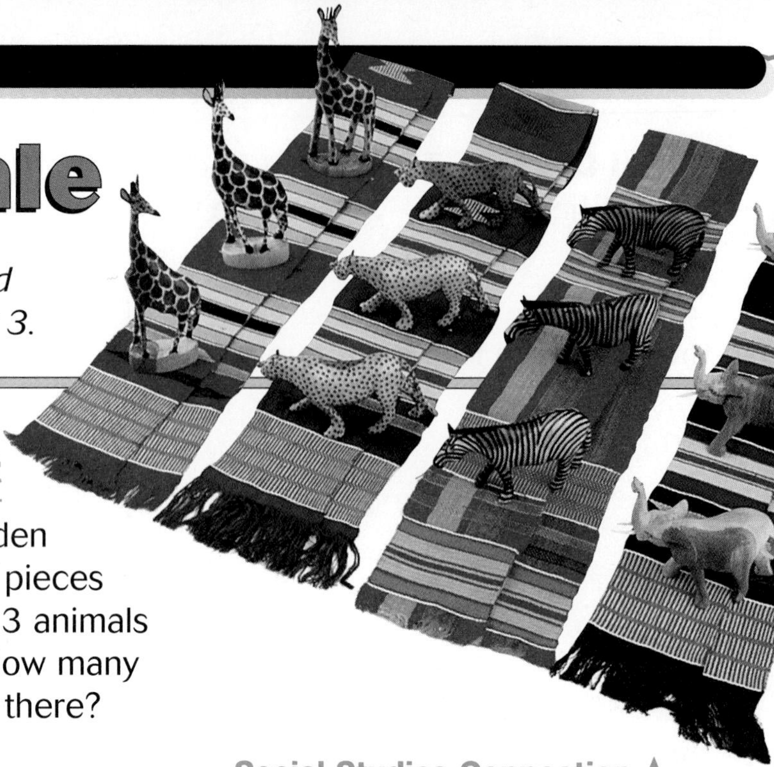

Learning About It

At a craft booth, 12 wooden animals are displayed on pieces of kente cloth. There are 3 animals on each piece of cloth. How many pieces of kente cloth are there?

Divide 12 by 3.

12 ÷ 3 = ■

Social Studies Connection ▲
Kente cloth is made by the Ashanti people of Ghana, West Africa. It is used to make robes, sashes, and head coverings.

THERE'S ALWAYS A WAY!

- **One way** to divide is to use repeated subtraction.

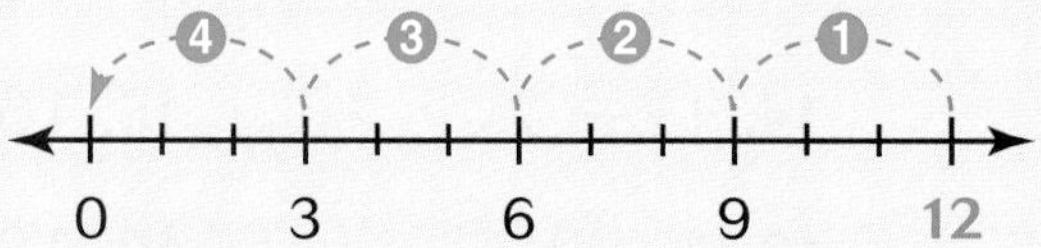

- Start at 12.
- Subtract by 3s until you reach 0.
- Count how many 3s you subtracted.

12 ÷ 3 = 4.

- **Another way** to divide is to use a related multiplication fact.

12 ÷ 3 = ■

Think: 3 × ■ = 12
3 × 4 = 12

So, 12 ÷ 3 = 4

There are 4 pieces of kente cloth.

www.sbgmath.com

Think and Discuss Suppose you have 15 wooden animals and 4 pieces of kente cloth. You want to display 3 animals on each cloth. Do you have enough pieces of kente cloth to display all the animals? Explain.

Try It Out

Use the picture to find each quotient.

1. 

$6 \div 3 = ■$

2. 

$9 \div 3 = ■$

3. 

$15 \div 3 = ■$

Practice

Using Algebra

Find the missing factor. Use it to help you divide.

4. $3 \times ■ = 18$
$18 \div 3 = ■$

5. $3 \times ■ = 24$
$24 \div 3 = ■$

6. $3 \times ■ = 21$
$21 \div 3 = ■$

Find the quotient.

7. $12 \div 3$ **8.** $3 \div 3$ **9.** $9 \div 3$ **10.** $27 \div 3$

11. $6 \div 3$ **12.** $15 \div 3$ **13.** $14 \div 2$ **14.** $24 \div 3$

15. $18 \div 3$ **16.** $21 \div 3$ **17.** $16 \div 2$ **18.** $12 \div 3$

Problem Solving

19. An artist has 9 wooden animals to pack in boxes. If each box holds 3 animals, how many boxes does she need?

20. Handmade baskets from Chad are displayed on 3 craft tables. There are 8 baskets on each table. How many baskets are there?

21. Create Your Own Write a division sentence that uses 3 as a divisor. Then draw a picture to show your sentence.

Fine Arts Connection
A craftsman from Chad, Africa, makes baskets out of grass.

Review and Remember

Using Estimation **Round to the nearest ten to estimate each answer.**

22. $32 + 16$ **23.** $35 - 19$ **24.** $62 - 28$ **25.** $44 + 34$

For Extra Practice, see Set C, page 317.

Developing Skills for Problem Solving

First read for understanding and then focus on solving problems that have more than one step.

READ FOR UNDERSTANDING

The 4-H Club grew 16 outdoor plants and 12 houseplants. They sold half of the outdoor plants at the community fair. They only sold 3 of the houseplants. After the fair they donated all the leftover plants to a local hospital.

1. How many houseplants did the 4-H Club grow?

2. How many houseplants were sold?

THINK AND DISCUSS

MATH FOCUS **Multistep Problems** Sometimes more than one step is needed to solve a problem. To solve the problem you must decide not only *what* to do, but in what *order* you should do it.

Reread the paragraph at the top of the page.

3. What information do you need in order to find out how many plants the 4-H Club donated?

4. How many plants did the 4-H Club donate? Write number sentences to show the steps you used to find the answer.

5. Look back at your answer to Problem 4. Could you have done the steps in a different order? Why or why not?

Show What You Learned

Answer each question. Give a reason for your choice.

A club planted a neighborhood vegetable garden. They had 4 rows of tomato plants and 2 rows of bean plants. They put 8 plants in each row. How many more tomato plants than bean plants were there?

1. Which would you do first to solve the problem?
   - **a.** Find the total number of tomato plants.
   - **b.** Subtract the number of bean plants from the number of tomato plants.
   - **c.** Add the tomato plants to the bean plants.

2. What else do you need to find in order to solve the problem?
   - **a.** the number of bean plants
   - **b.** the total number of rows
   - **c.** the total number of plants

3. What is the final step you need to do to solve the problem?
   - **a.** Find 4×8.
   - **b.** Find $32 - 16$.
   - **c.** Find 2×8.

Scott, Alison, and Miles are working on a cleanup project. They have volunteered to fill 15 bags of trash. So far they have filled 3 bags with trash. If they each want to fill the same number of the remaining bags, how many bags does each person need to fill?

4. Which number sentence tells how many bags there are left to fill?
   - **a.** $15 - 3 = 12$ bags
   - **b.** $15 + 3 = 18$ bags
   - **c.** $15 - 12 = 3$ bags

5. Which number sentence tells how many bags there are left for each person to fill?
   - **a.** $3 \div 3 = 1$ bag
   - **b.** $18 \div 3 = 6$ bags
   - **c.** $12 \div 3 = 4$ bags

6. **Explain** What if the 3 students had volunteered to fill 21 bags of trash? Would the steps needed to solve the problem change?

Checkpoint

Understanding Division

Word List

divide
dividend
divisor
product
quotient

Complete. Use words from the list.

1. The answer in division is called the __?__.
2. When you share objects equally, you __?__.
3. The answer in multiplication is called the __?__.
4. The number to be divided is called the __?__.
5. The __?__ is the number you divide by.

Using Algebra **Use the array to complete each sentence.** (pages 292–295)

6. 

$3 \times \blacksquare = 15$
$15 \div 3 = \blacksquare$

7. 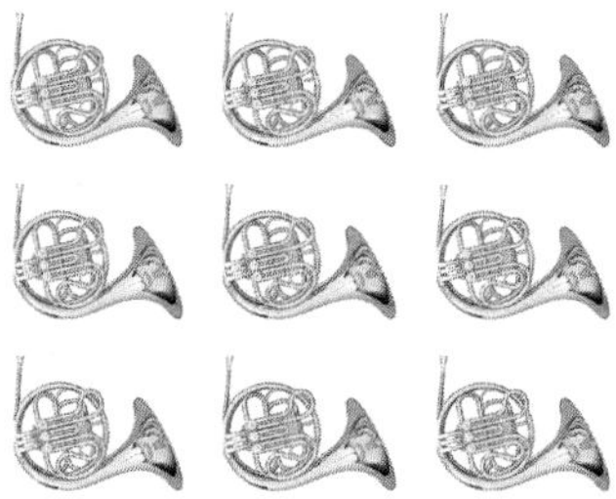

$3 \times \blacksquare = 9$
$9 \div 3 = \blacksquare$

8. 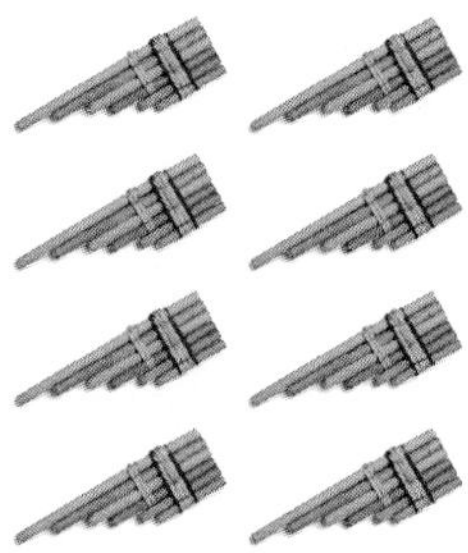

$4 \times \blacksquare = 8$
$8 \div 4 = \blacksquare$

Using Algebra **Use the multiplication fact to find each quotient.** (pages 296–299)

9. $3 \times \blacksquare = 18$
   $18 \div 3 = \blacksquare$
10. $2 \times \blacksquare = 8$
    $8 \div 2 = \blacksquare$
11. $3 \times \blacksquare = 12$
    $12 \div 3 = \blacksquare$
12. $2 \times \blacksquare = 12$
    $12 \div 2 = \blacksquare$
13. $3 \times \blacksquare = 27$
    $27 \div 3 = \blacksquare$
14. $2 \times \blacksquare = 6$
    $6 \div 2 = \blacksquare$

Find each quotient. (pages 296–299)

15. $4 \div 2$
16. $9 \div 3$
17. $21 \div 3$
18. $24 \div 3$
19. $16 \div 2$
20. $10 \div 2$
21. $15 \div 3$
22. $14 \div 2$
23. $27 \div 3$
24. $12 \div 2$
25. $18 \div 2$
26. $18 \div 3$

Problem Solving

27. There are 10 students carrying flags in the Community Day Parade. If there are 2 equal rows of students, how many students are in each row?

28. During the parade, 18 clowns hand out balloons. If the clowns walk in groups of 3, how many groups are there?

29. Scout troops march in the parade. If there are 3 troops with 9 scouts in each troop, how many scouts are in the parade?

30. **Analyze** The Korean Club float leads the parade. The club's 21 members are in groups of equal size. One group marches in front of the float. One group marches behind the float. Another group rides on the float. How many club members are on the float?

Journal Idea Division is the opposite of multiplication. Write a few sentences explaining what you think that means.

What do you think?

How can you use the multiplication fact $4 \times 3 = 12$ to help you find $12 \div 3$?

Critical Thinking Corner

Logical Thinking

Floating Around

There are 4 floats in the parade. Read the clues below. Write the order in which the floats will appear in the parade.

- The scout float will be before the library float.
- The library float will not be between other floats.
- The firefighter float will be just behind the soccer float.
- The scout float will be third.

Floating Fours

Multiplication facts for 4 can help you divide by 4.

Learning About It

Here come the clowns! There are 16 balloons and 4 clowns. Each clown has the same number of balloons. How many balloons does each clown have?

You can show 16 divided by 4 by writing **16 ÷ 4 = ■**.

You can show the same thing by writing:

$$\text{divisor} \rightarrow 4\overline{)16} \leftarrow \text{dividend}, \quad ■ \leftarrow \text{quotient}$$

THERE'S ALWAYS A WAY!

- **One way** to divide is to make an array.
  - Draw 16 Xs in 4 rows.
  - Put the same number of Xs in each row.

  X X X X
  X X X X
  X X X X
  X X X X

  16 ÷ 4 = 4 or $4\overline{)16}$ with quotient 4

- **Another way** to divide is to use a related multiplication fact.

  16 ÷ 4 = ■

  Think: 4 × ■ = 16
  4 × 4 = 16

  So, 16 ÷ 4 = 4

Think and Discuss What related multiplication sentence could you use to find 32 ÷ 4?

Try It Out

Using Algebra

Draw an array to help you complete the related facts.

1. 4 × ■ = 36
36 ÷ 4 = ■

2. 4 × ■ = 24
24 ÷ 4 = ■

3. 4 × 7 = ■
28 ÷ 4 = ■

Practice

Divide.

4. $4\overline{)12}$ **5.** $4\overline{)36}$ **6.** $4\overline{)16}$ **7.** $4\overline{)32}$ **8.** $4\overline{)8}$

9. $4\overline{)24}$ **10.** $4\overline{)20}$ **11.** $4\overline{)4}$ **12.** $4\overline{)28}$ **13.** $3\overline{)24}$

14. $8 \div 2$ **15.** $27 \div 3$ **16.** $36 \div 4$ **17.** $32 \div 4$

18. $28 \div 4$ **19.** $20 \div 4$ **20.** $21 \div 3$ **21.** $18 \div 2$

Problem Solving

22. Balloons are sold in bunches of 8 at the fair. If 4 friends share 1 bunch equally, how many balloons will each person get?

23. Four clowns each have 7 paper flowers to give away. If no one is given more than 1 flower, how many people can get a flower?

24. A clown paints 24 stars in all on the faces of 4 children. If each child has the same number of stars, how many stars are painted on each child's face?

25. Using Algebra Look at $28 \div 4$, $12 \div 4$, and $24 \div 4$. Without dividing, how can you tell which has the smallest quotient? the largest quotient? Explain how you know.

Review and Remember

Find each answer.

26. 3×5 **27.** $143 + 254$ **28.** 6×8 **29.** $472 - 396$ **30.** 5×7

Project Link

Keep on planning your booth for the fair.

- Meet with your group to plan contests and games.
- Think about giving prizes. What if you make 15 prizes and give 3 for each contest? How many contests can you have?
- Make a poster for your booth.

For Extra Practice, see Set D, page 317.

Firehouse Five

If you can count backward by fives, you can divide by 5.

Learning About It

Firefighters are giving children rides on an old fire truck. Twenty children want a ride. If 5 children can ride at a time, how many trips will the fire truck make?

Divide 20 by 5.

$20 \div 5 = \blacksquare$ or $5\overline{)20}$ with $\blacksquare$ above

THERE'S ALWAYS A WAY!

- **One way** to divide is to skip count backward on a number line. Count how many jumps you made.

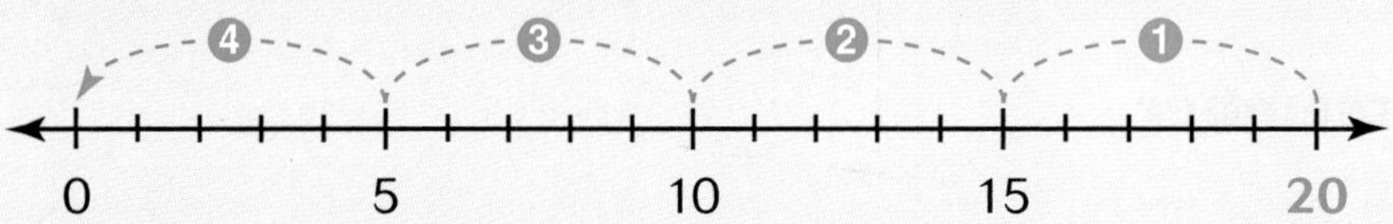

You made 4 jumps.

So, $20 \div 5 = 4$ or $5\overline{)20}$ with 4 above

- **Another way** to divide is to use a related multiplication fact.

$20 \div 5 = \blacksquare$

Think: $5 \times \blacksquare = 20$

$5 \times 4 = 20$

So, $20 \div 5 = 4$ or $5\overline{)20}$ with 4 above

The fire truck will make 4 trips.

Think and Discuss Which number in the division sentence $35 \div 5 = 7$ is the dividend?

Try It Out

Using Algebra

Find the missing factor. Use it to help you divide.

1. $5 \times \blacksquare = 25$
$25 \div 5 = \blacksquare$

2. $5 \times \blacksquare = 15$
$15 \div 5 = \blacksquare$

3. $5 \times \blacksquare = 10$
$10 \div \blacksquare = 2$

Practice

Find each quotient.

4. $5\overline{)20}$ **5.** $5\overline{)5}$ **6.** $5\overline{)25}$ **7.** $5\overline{)40}$ **8.** $5\overline{)15}$

9. $5\overline{)45}$ **10.** $5\overline{)30}$ **11.** $5\overline{)10}$ **12.** $2\overline{)10}$ **13.** $5\overline{)35}$

14. $3\overline{)21}$ **15.** $4\overline{)24}$ **16.** $4\overline{)36}$ **17.** $3\overline{)15}$ **18.** $4\overline{)20}$

Using Algebra

Follow each rule to complete each table.

Rule: Divide by 4.

	Input	Output
	28	7
19.	8	
20.	16	
21.	32	

Rule: Divide by 5.

	Input	Output
	30	6
22.	10	
23.	35	
24.	40	

Rule: Divide by 3.

	Input	Output
	27	9
25.	18	
26.		4
27.		8

Problem Solving

28. Five firefighters each give a 7-mile ride on their fire truck. How many miles do the firefighters drive altogether?

29. The firefighters sound the siren every 5 minutes. How many times does the siren sound in a half hour?

30. Casey and his 3 sisters each have \$5. If they put all their money together, could they buy an \$18 game? Explain.

31. **Analyze** Anne has 25 pennies and 2 dimes. Dylan has the same amount of money, but he only has nickels. How many nickels does Dylan have?

Review and Remember

Look at each pair of times. How much time has passed?

32. 3:15 P.M. and 4:30 P.M.

33. 9:42 A.M. and 10:00 A.M.

34. 6:23 P.M. and 8:23 P.M.

35. 11:05 A.M. and 12 noon

For Extra Practice, see Set E, page 318.

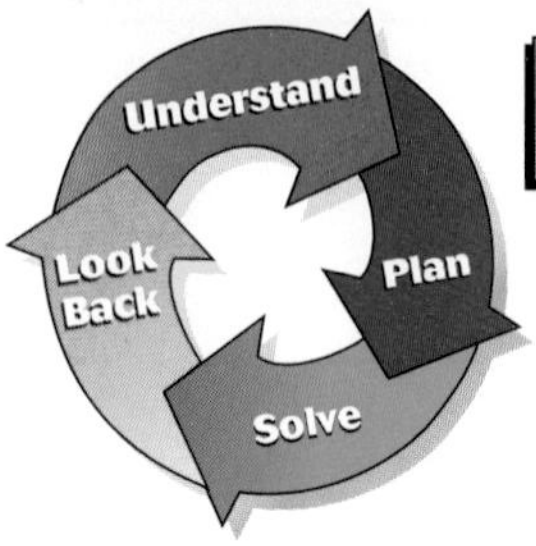

Problem Solving
Write a Number Sentence

You can write a number sentence to help solve a problem.

Bike Safety booklets are free at the Community Day Fair. Twenty-one booklets have been put into 3 equal groups. How many booklets are in each group?

UNDERSTAND

What do you need to know?

You need to know that there are 21 booklets and that they are divided into 3 equal groups.

PLAN

How can you solve the problem?

You can **write a number sentence** to solve the problem. Write a division sentence to divide the booklets into 3 equal groups.

SOLVE

$$21 \div 3 = 7$$

21 → number of booklets in all
3 → number of groups
7 → number of booklets in each group

There are 7 booklets in each group.

LOOK BACK

Explain another strategy you could use to solve the problem.

Using the Strategy

Write a number sentence to solve each problem.

1. Tracey helps out at the Bike Safety table. She fills 2 boxes with helmets. She puts the same number of helmets in each box. There are 16 helmets in all. How many helmets are in each box?

2. A bicycle shop has donated 27 bike horns for the Bike Safety table. Each horn is red, gold, or black. There are the same number of each color horn. How many gold horns were donated?

3. Peter spends $12 for mirrors and $3 for lights. How much money does Peter spend?

4. Mrs. Kane buys 2 reflectors for each of her 3 children. How many reflectors does she buy?

5. The Bike Safety table has 40 reflectors to sell. By noon, 16 are sold. By the end of the day, 12 more are sold. How many reflectors are sold?

6. Sam brought 24 water bottles to sell at the fair. He sold all but 3 water bottles. How many water bottles did Sam sell?

Mixed Strategy Review

Try these or other strategies you have learned.

THERE'S ALWAYS A WAY!

- *Make a List*
- *Find a Pattern*
- *Make a Table*
- *Write a Number Sentence*

7. Eduardo is training for a bike race. The first week he rides 4 miles. Then each week for the next 2 weeks he doubles the number of miles he rides. How many miles does Eduardo ride in the third week?

8. Mary wants to buy a bike helmet. Helmets come in red, green, or blue. Each color comes in small, medium, and large sizes. What helmet choices does Mary have?

9. Paula made first-aid kits to sell at the fair. She made 1 kit on Monday, 2 kits on Tuesday, 3 kits on Wednesday, and so on, until Saturday. How many kits did Paula make on Saturday?

Zero and One

Learning some rules about 0 and 1 can help you divide.

Learning About It

Use counters to find out what is special about dividing with 0 and 1.

What You Need

For each student:
4 counters

Divide 4 counters into 1 group. How many counters are in the group?

$4 \div 1 = ■$

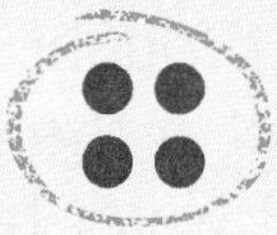

$4 \div 1 = 4$

When you divide a number by 1, the answer is that number.

Divide 4 counters into 4 groups. How many counters are in each group?

$4 \div 4 = ■$

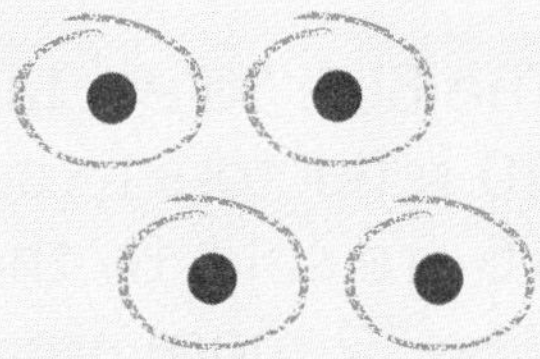

$4 \div 4 = 1$

When you divide any number except zero by itself, the answer is 1.

Divide 0 counters into 4 groups. How many counters are in each group?

$0 \div 4 = ■$

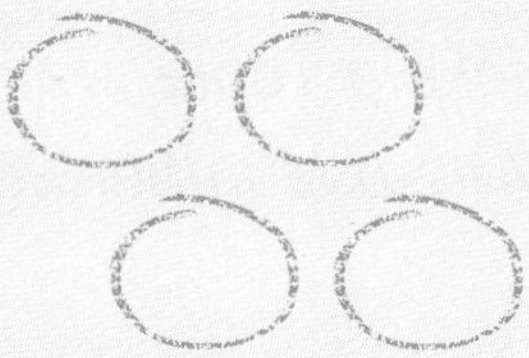

$0 \div 4 = 0$

When you divide 0 by any number except 0, the answer is 0.

Try to divide 4 counters into 0 groups. It's not possible!

$4 \div 0 = ■$ (crossed out with an X)

You cannot divide a number by 0.

Think and Discuss Look at the division sentences at the right. Explain how you could use the rules above to complete them.

486 ÷ 486 = ■

599 ÷ 1 = ■

0 ÷ 954 = ■

Try It Out

Find each quotient.

1. 0 ÷ 5 **2.** 3 ÷ 3 **3.** 2 ÷ 1 **4.** 0 ÷ 4 **5.** 7 ÷ 1

6. 9 ÷ 1 **7.** 1 ÷ 1 **8.** 0 ÷ 1 **9.** 6 ÷ 6 **10.** 0 ÷ 8

Practice

Find each quotient.

11. $1\overline{)3}$ **12.** $2\overline{)0}$ **13.** $5\overline{)5}$ **14.** $7\overline{)0}$ **15.** $2\overline{)2}$

16. $1\overline{)5}$ **17.** $7\overline{)7}$ **18.** $4\overline{)0}$ **19.** $1\overline{)9}$ **20.** $3\overline{)0}$

21. $4 \div 4$ **22.** $0 \div 6$ **23.** $8 \div 8$ **24.** $4 \div 1$ **25.** $3 \div 3$

Problem Solving

26. At the end of the fair, a total of 5 prizes were given to 5 people. Each person got the same number of prizes. How many prizes did each person get?

27. There were 3 first-place prizes, 6 second-place prizes, and 8 third-place prizes. How many first- and second-place prizes were there altogether?

Review and Remember

Choose a Method **Use mental math or paper and pencil to find each answer. Tell which method you used.**

28. \$3.40 − \$1.20 **29.** $3 \times 1 \times 4$ **30.** \$10.75 − \$7.30

31. 410 + 286 **32.** $4 \times 2 \times 5$ **33.** 635 + 322

Time for Technology

Using a Calculator

Calculator Memories

Use a calculator to find 27 ÷ 3.

Press: 2 7 ÷ 3 = .

Now, to find 12 ÷ 3, just press: 1 2 = .

Your calculator remembers you are dividing by 3!

Use your calculator's memory to divide the numbers below by 3. Just press the number and = .

1. 9 **2.** 6 **3.** 21 **4.** 30 **5.** 291

For Extra Practice, see Set F, page 318.

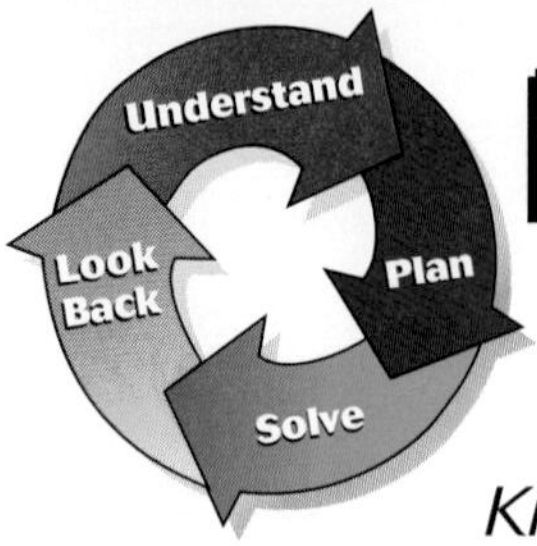

Problem Solving
Using Money

Knowing how to add, subtract, multiply, and divide can help you solve money problems.

Puzzling 3-D puzzles are popular at the fair! Large puzzles cost \$18 each. If Carly and her two sisters want to share the cost of a large puzzle equally, how much money will each girl need?

UNDERSTAND

What do you need to know?

First you need to know the cost of the puzzle. Then you need to know how many girls are sharing the cost.

PLAN

How can you solve the problem?

Divide \$18 by 3 to find how much money each girl needs to buy the puzzle.

SOLVE

$$\$18 \div 3 = \$6$$

- \$18: cost of the puzzle
- 3: number of people sharing the cost
- \$6: cost for each person

Each girl needs \$6 to buy the puzzle.

LOOK BACK

Write a number sentence to show how you could check your answer by multiplying.

Show What You Learned

Solve

1. Mrs. Falvey wants to buy 6 glasses. Small glasses cost $8 each. Large glasses cost $12 each. How much money does Mrs. Falvey save by buying all small glasses instead of all large ones?

2. John bought a cap for $6 and a picture for $8.50. How much money does he have left if he started with $20?

3. James has $12. He wants to buy as many key chains as he can. Each key chain costs $2.50. How many key chains can James buy?

4. Mattie is looking at bracelets that cost two for $14. She wants to buy only one bracelet. She can buy one bracelet for half the price. How much money will Mattie pay for one bracelet?

5. You can buy 2 rings for $3.00. If Kamara spent $12.00 for rings, how many rings did she buy?

6. Jill decides to buy some candles for her mother. The candles cost $3 a pair. How many candles can Jill buy with $9?

7. Nelson spent $16 on 4 bags of marbles. If each bag costs the same amount, how much did each bag of marbles cost?

8. Meg made 8 potholders to sell at the fair. If she sells each one for $2, how much money will she earn?

9. **Create Your Own** Write a word problem that can be solved either by multiplying or dividing money.

Checkpoint

Division Facts

Using Algebra

Follow each rule to complete each table.
(pages 304–307, 310–311)

Rule: Divide by 4

	Input	Output
	32	8
1.	16	
2.		7
3.	24	

Rule: Divide by 5

	Input	Output
	20	4
4.	25	
5.		9
6.	15	

Rule: Divide by 1

	Input	Output
7.	8	
8.		3
9.	6	
10.		5

Use the number 1 or 0 to complete each sentence.
(pages 310–311)

11. When you divide any number except zero by itself, the quotient is always __?__.

12. When you divide 0 by any number except zero, the answer is always __?__.

13. You cannot divide a number by __?__.

Mixed Practice

Find each quotient.

14. $5\overline{)15}$ **15.** $4\overline{)32}$ **16.** $3\overline{)6}$ **17.** $4\overline{)24}$

18. $5\overline{)35}$ **19.** $5\overline{)30}$ **20.** $3\overline{)18}$ **21.** $5\overline{)25}$

22. $2\overline{)16}$ **23.** $4\overline{)16}$ **24.** $2\overline{)8}$ **25.** $3\overline{)27}$

26. $5\overline{)10}$ **27.** $4\overline{)12}$ **28.** $4\overline{)4}$ **29.** $1\overline{)5}$

30. $21 \div 3$ **31.** $14 \div 2$ **32.** $36 \div 4$ **33.** $28 \div 4$

34. $20 \div 4$ **35.** $45 \div 5$ **36.** $20 \div 5$ **37.** $18 \div 2$

38. $8 \div 4$ **39.** $5 \div 5$ **40.** $24 \div 3$ **41.** $0 \div 1$

Problem Solving

42. Red balloons are sold in packs of 4. Blue balloons are sold in packs of 5. Jan buys 9 packs of red balloons and 8 packs of blue balloons. Does she get more red or more blue balloons? How many more?

43. Each clown wears a pair of funny shoes. If there are 8 clowns, how many single shoes are they wearing altogether?

44. **Explain** John and 3 friends want to ride on the merry-go-round. Each person needs 4 tickets for the ride. If John has 18 tickets, will they have enough tickets for the ride? How do you know?

45. **Analyze** A clown has 18 balloons. What are two different ways she can tie them in equal groups?

What do you think?

Without dividing, what rule helps you complete the following division sentence?

$851 \div 851 = \blacksquare$

Journal Idea Write a problem in which you can use the special rules for dividing with 0 or 1 to find the answer. Share your problem with a classmate.

Project Wrap-Up

Fair Play

It's time for the fair!

- Choose a date and time for the fair.
- Make posters to advertise the fair. Make one poster for each class in your school. How many posters does each group have to make?

During the fair, give each person in your group some time off to visit the other booths.

Extra Practice

Set A (pages 292–295)

Using Algebra

Write a multiplication sentence and a division sentence for each array.

1. 

2. 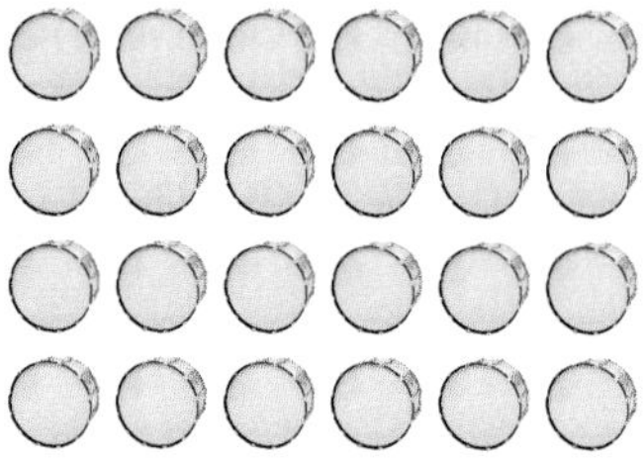

3. 

4. There are 36 members in the school band. They are sitting in 4 equal rows. How many band members are in each row?

5. Three students made 21 posters for the fair. They each made the same number of posters. How many posters did each student make?

Set B (pages 296–297)

Use the multiplication fact to find the quotient.

1. $2 \times 3 = 6$
   $6 \div 2 = \blacksquare$

2. $2 \times 9 = 18$
   $18 \div 2 = \blacksquare$

3. $2 \times 5 = 10$
   $10 \div 2 = \blacksquare$

4. $2 \times 7 = 14$
   $14 \div 2 = \blacksquare$

5. $2 \times \blacksquare = 16$
   $16 \div 2 = \blacksquare$

6. $2 \times \blacksquare = 4$
   $4 \div 2 = \blacksquare$

Divide.

7. $2\overline{)18}$
8. $2\overline{)6}$
9. $2\overline{)12}$
10. $2\overline{)14}$
11. $2\overline{)8}$
12. $2\overline{)2}$
13. $2\overline{)10}$
14. $2\overline{)4}$
15. $2\overline{)16}$
16. $2\overline{)12}$

17. At a food booth, Jason has 14 jars of homemade jelly to sell. He puts the jars in 2 equal rows. How many jars are in each row?

18. Kyla is selling oatmeal muffins at the bakery booth. She puts 2 muffins in each package. How many packages can she make with 16 muffins?

Extra Practice

Set C (pages 298–299)

Using Algebra

Find the missing factor. Use it to help you divide.

1. $3 \times ■ = 12$
   $12 \div 3 = ■$
2. $3 \times ■ = 27$
   $27 \div 3 = ■$
3. $3 \times ■ = 15$
   $15 \div 3 = ■$
4. $3 \times ■ = 6$
   $6 \div 3 = ■$
5. $3 \times ■ = 18$
   $18 \div 3 = ■$
6. $3 \times ■ = 9$
   $9 \div 3 = ■$

Find each quotient.

7. $3\overline{)3}$
8. $3\overline{)27}$
9. $3\overline{)9}$
10. $3\overline{)24}$
11. $3\overline{)6}$
12. $3\overline{)18}$
13. $3\overline{)12}$
14. $3\overline{)15}$
15. $3\overline{)21}$
16. $2\overline{)14}$
17. The baseball toss booth has 12 small buckets on a table. The buckets are in 4 rows. If each row has the same number of buckets, how many buckets are in each row?
18. Cassie makes costumes for the parade. She has 15 beads to glue on 3 costumes. If she divides the beads equally, how many beads can she glue on each costume?

Set D (pages 304–305)

Divide.

1. $4\overline{)16}$
2. $4\overline{)4}$
3. $4\overline{)32}$
4. $4\overline{)8}$
5. $4\overline{)12}$
6. $4\overline{)20}$
7. $4\overline{)28}$
8. $4\overline{)36}$
9. $4\overline{)24}$
10. $3\overline{)21}$
11. $2\overline{)16}$
12. $3\overline{)15}$
13. $2\overline{)12}$
14. $3\overline{)27}$
15. $2\overline{)18}$
16. The food booth sells a basket with 28 pieces of fruit. There are an equal number of oranges, pears, apples, and bananas in the basket. How many apples are there?
17. At the crafts booth you can make a sand painting for $4. If you have $12, how many sand paintings can you make?

Extra Practice

Set E (pages 306–307)

Find each quotient.

1. 5)25	**2.** 5)15	**3.** 5)45	**4.** 5)35	**5.** 5)5
6. 5)10	**7.** 5)30	**8.** 5)40	**9.** 5)20	**10.** 4)12
11. 4)16	**12.** 4)8	**13.** 4)24	**14.** 4)32	**15.** 4)28

Using Algebra **Follow each rule to complete each table.**

Rule: Divide by 3

	Input	Output
	9	3
16.	21	
17.	15	
18.	12	

Rule: Divide by 4

	Input	Output
	12	3
19.	24	
20.	20	
21.	36	

Rule: Divide by 5

	Input	Output
	45	9
22.		3
23.		8
24.	30	

25. Firefighters handed out fire safety books to 5 groups of school children. If they gave 8 books to each group, how many books did they hand out?

Set F (pages 310–311)

Find each quotient.

1. 1)5	**2.** 1)9	**3.** 6)0	**4.** 3)3	**5.** 2)0
6. 4)0	**7.** 7)7	**8.** 1)4	**9.** 6)6	**10.** 1)8
11. 5 ÷ 5	**12.** 0 ÷ 5	**13.** 6 ÷ 1	**14.** 0 ÷ 3	**15.** 7 ÷ 1
16. 0 ÷ 1	**17.** 8 ÷ 8	**18.** 2 ÷ 1	**19.** 9 ÷ 9	**20.** 0 ÷ 8

21. The 4-H Club is having a bake sale. Roger sells 9 loaves of banana bread. How many bags does he use if he puts 1 loaf of bread in each bag?

22. Shannon sold a total of 4 cakes to 4 people. Each person bought the same number of cakes. How many cakes did each person buy?

Chapter Test

Write a division sentence for each number line.

1.

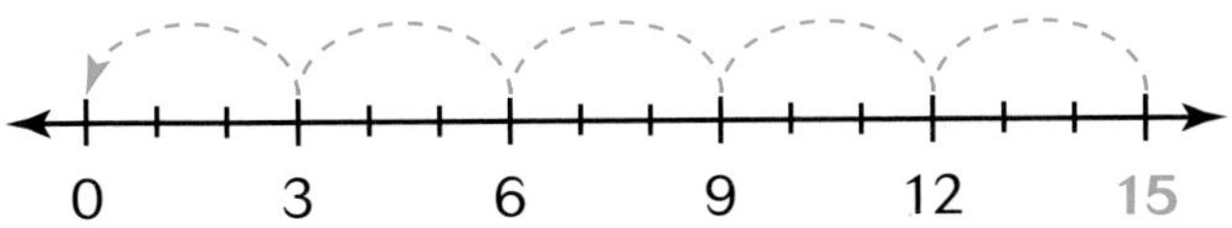

2.

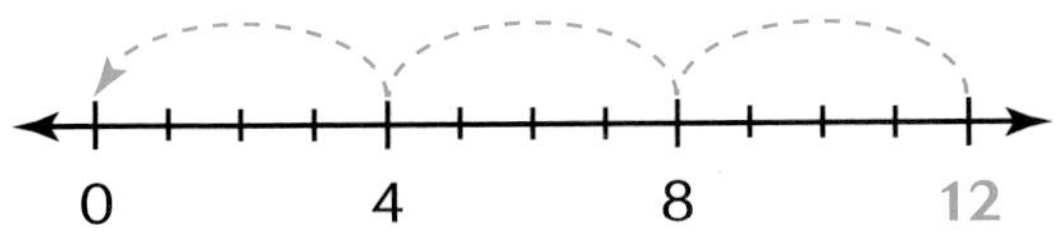

Write a multiplication and a division sentence for each array.

3.

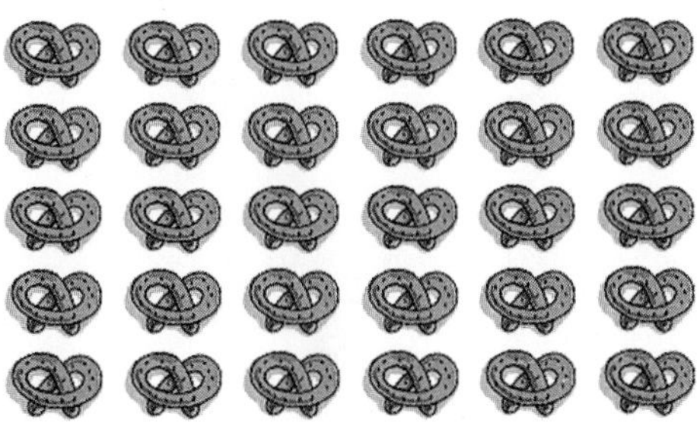

4.

Find each quotient.

5. $4\overline{)36}$ **6.** $5\overline{)45}$ **7.** $3\overline{)21}$ **8.** $2\overline{)16}$ **9.** $5\overline{)25}$

10. $5\overline{)20}$ **11.** $4\overline{)24}$ **12.** $2\overline{)14}$ **13.** $3\overline{)27}$ **14.** $2\overline{)8}$

15. $4\overline{)20}$ **16.** $2\overline{)12}$ **17.** $3\overline{)24}$ **18.** $4\overline{)16}$ **19.** $3\overline{)9}$

20. $40 \div 5$ **21.** $18 \div 2$ **22.** $32 \div 4$ **23.** $18 \div 3$

Solve.

24. The 35 baton twirlers from Jefferson High School march in the parade. There are 5 twirlers in each row. How many rows of twirlers are there?

25. The flag bearers march in 9 rows, with 5 people in each row. Each person is carrying a flag. Write a number sentence to show how many flags there are.

Self-Check Look back at Exercises 20–23. Use a related multiplication sentence to check your answer.

Performance Assessment

Show What You Know About Division

① Use 24 counters. Make as many different arrays as you can with the counters. For each array, write two division sentences that describe the array. You can use pictures, counters, numbers, or words to show your work.

What You Need

24 counters

② Keiko has taken 36 photos at the Street Fair. She wants to buy an album for her photos. Use the chart below to answer Questions 2a–2b.

Photo Album Choices		
Size	**Number of pages in the album**	**Number of photos that fit on a page**
Small	6	4
Medium	8	6
Large	10	12

a. How many pages of each size album would Keiko need for her photos?

b. Which album should Keiko buy? Explain your choice.

Self-Check

For Question 1, did you check that each array you found is a different one?

For Question 2b, did you make sure that all 36 photos will fit in Keiko's album?

Extension

Division Match Game

Here's a fun game to play that will help you learn division facts.

Play the game with a classmate.

What You Need

For each pair:
24 index cards or sheets of paper

Step 1 Use 24 index cards. Copy each of the division facts below on a different card.

8 ÷ 2	12 ÷ 3	16 ÷ 4	20 ÷ 5
10 ÷ 2	15 ÷ 3	20 ÷ 4	25 ÷ 5
12 ÷ 2	18 ÷ 3	24 ÷ 4	30 ÷ 5
14 ÷ 2	21 ÷ 3	28 ÷ 4	35 ÷ 5
16 ÷ 2	24 ÷ 3	32 ÷ 4	40 ÷ 5
18 ÷ 2	27 ÷ 3	36 ÷ 4	45 ÷ 5

Step 2 Mix up the cards. Place them face down in 4 rows. Put 6 cards in each row.

Step 3 Take turns. Turn over two cards at a time.

- If the cards have the same quotient, you can keep the cards and take another turn.
- If the cards do not have the same quotient, turn the cards face down again. Then the other person takes a turn.

Step 4 Continue playing until all the cards have been taken. The person with the most cards wins.

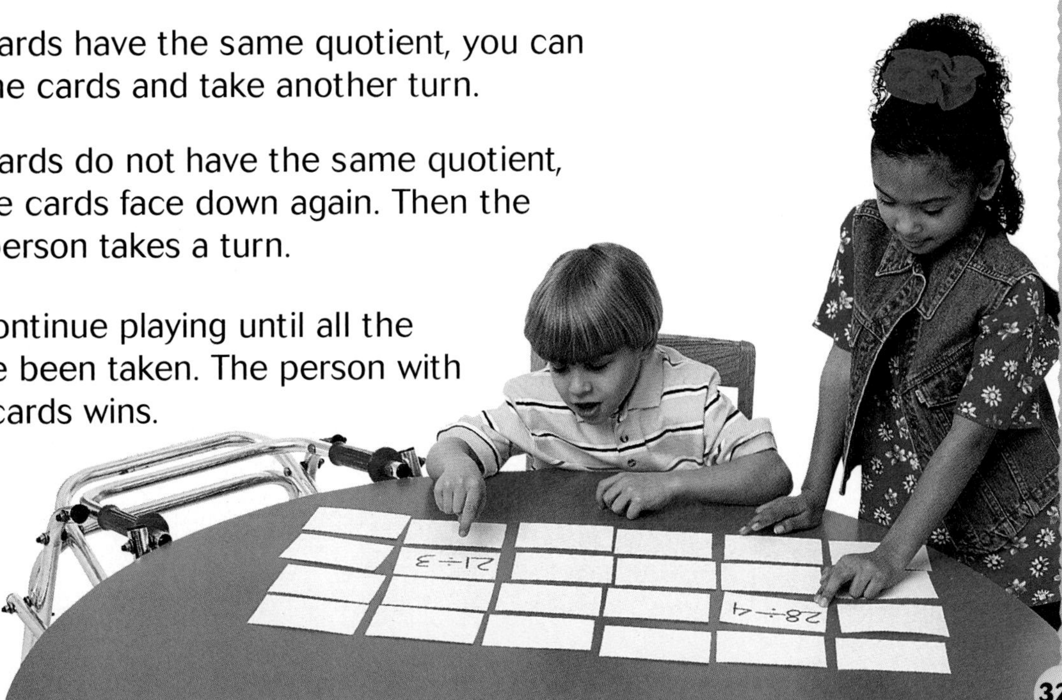

Chapter 9 Division Facts

Chapter Theme: PERFORMING ARTS

Career Spotlight Meet Susan Marcus, a puppeteer. She travels to schools, fairs, libraries, and other places to put on puppet shows.

Puppeteers might need to figure out how many puppets they will each handle. They would use division to do this.

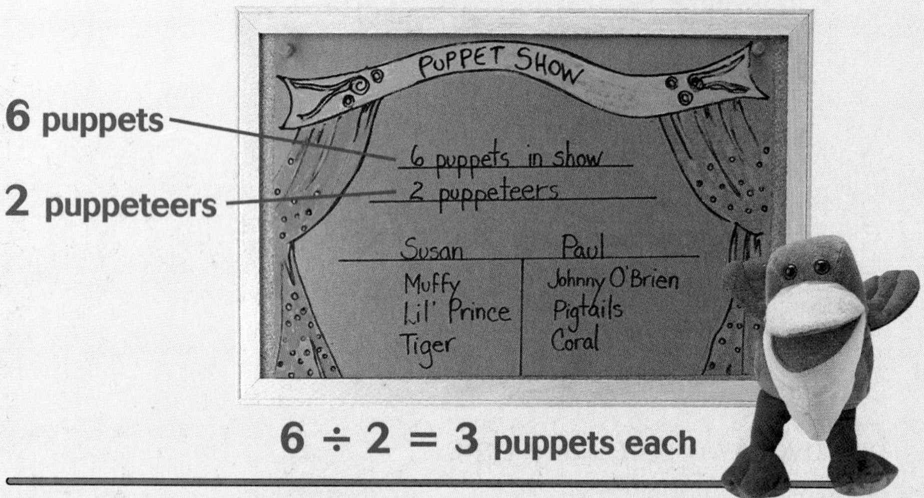

$6 \div 2 = 3$ puppets each

Chapter Project

Put On a Puppet Show

With a group of your classmates, make puppets and put on a show. Here are some things to decide.

- What will your puppet show be about? Talk with your group about story ideas. Then pick the best one.
- What will your puppets be? They might be people, animals, or imaginary creatures.
- Each person in your group will make one puppet. Decide which puppet each person will make. That person will be in charge of that puppet.

Dancing Division

Fact families show you how division and multiplication are related.

Learning About It

Word Bank

fact family

Swing your partner! Eight people wait to dance at the Division Street Theater. When they dance, they can arrange themselves in different ways.

They can make an array of 4 rows with 2 people in each row.

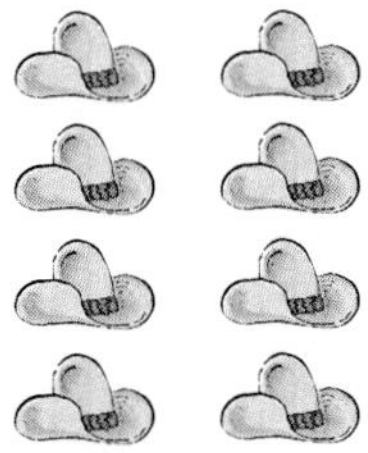

4 × 2 = 8 people

They can make an array of 2 rows with 4 people in each row.

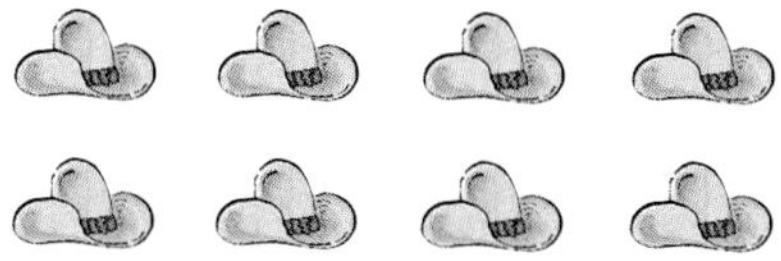

2 × 4 = 8 people

They can divide themselves into 4 groups of 2 people.

8 ÷ 4 = 2 people

They can divide themselves into 2 groups of 4 people.

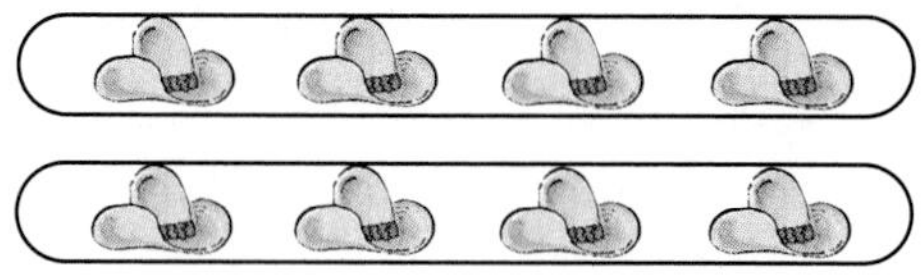

8 ÷ 2 = 4 people

The numbers 2, 4, and 8 form a **fact family**. Fact families show how division and multiplication are related.

4 × 2 = 8   **2 × 4 = 8**

8 ÷ 4 = 2   **8 ÷ 2 = 4**

www.sbgmath.com

Think and Discuss Look back at the arrays for 4×2 and 2×4. How are the two arrays the same? How are they different?

Try It Out

Use each array to complete each fact family.

1.

$3 \times 4 = \blacksquare$
$4 \times 3 = \blacksquare$
$12 \div 3 = \blacksquare$
$12 \div 4 = \blacksquare$

2.

$3 \times 5 = \blacksquare$
$5 \times 3 = \blacksquare$
$15 \div 3 = \blacksquare$
$15 \div 5 = \blacksquare$

3.

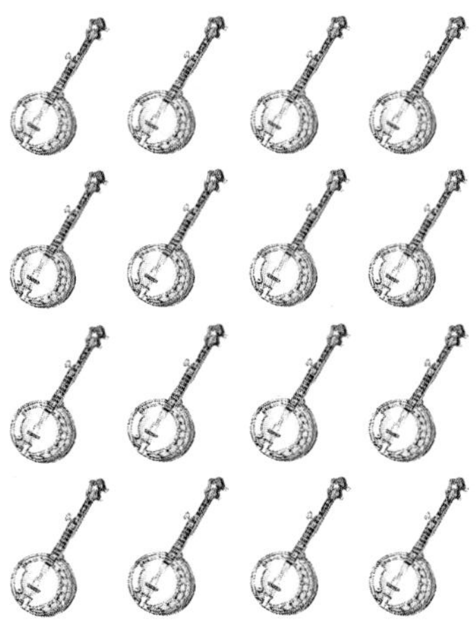

$4 \times 4 = \blacksquare$
$16 \div 4 = \blacksquare$

4.

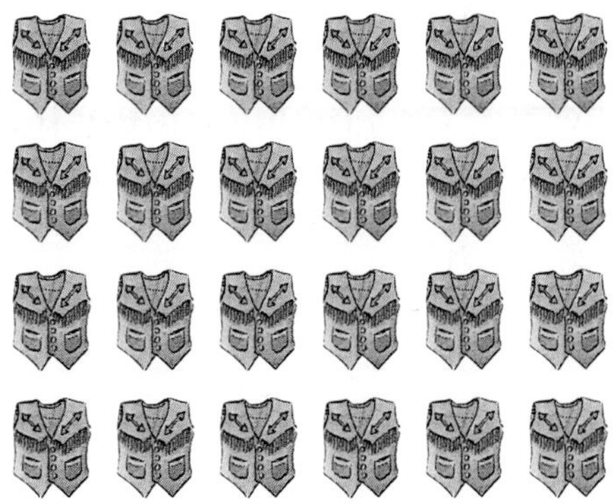

$4 \times 6 = \blacksquare$
$6 \times 4 = \blacksquare$
$24 \div 4 = \blacksquare$
$24 \div 6 = \blacksquare$

5. Analyze Why is there only one multiplication sentence and one division sentence in Exercise 3?

Practice

Write a multiplication sentence and a division sentence to finish the fact family for each array.

6.

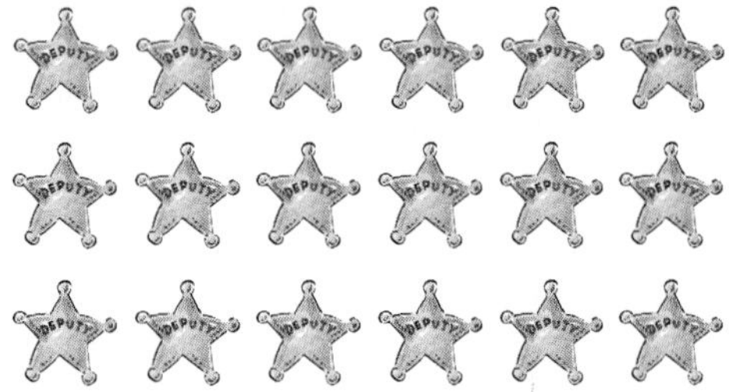

$3 \times 6 = 18$
$18 \div 3 = 6$

7.

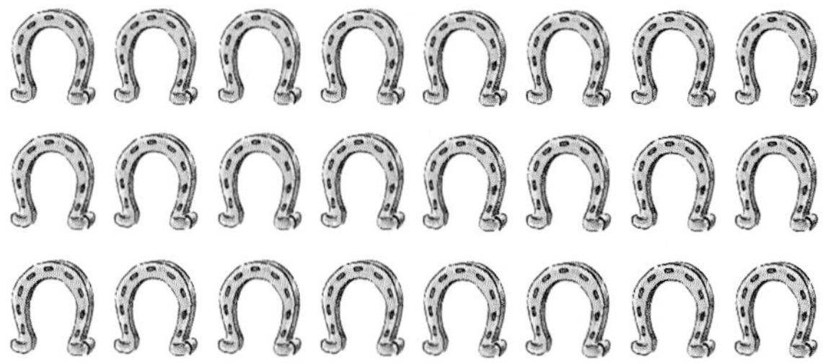

$3 \times 8 = 24$
$24 \div 3 = 8$

Using Algebra **Copy and complete each fact family.**

8. $4 \times 8 = 32$
■ $\times 4 = 32$
$32 \div 4 =$ ■
$32 \div$ ■ $= 4$

9. $3 \times 9 = 27$
■ $\times 3 = 27$
$27 \div 3 =$ ■
$27 \div$ ■ $= 3$

10. $2 \times 7 = 14$
■ $\times 2 = 14$
$14 \div 2 =$ ■
$14 \div$ ■ $= 2$

11. $2 \times 5 = 10$
■ $\times 2 = 10$
$10 \div 2 =$ ■
$10 \div$ ■ $= 2$

12. $4 \times 9 = 36$
■ $\times 4 = 36$
$36 \div 4 =$ ■
$36 \div$ ■ $= 4$

13. $5 \times 8 = 40$
■ $\times 5 = 40$
$40 \div 5 =$ ■
$40 \div$ ■ $= 5$

Write the fact family for each set of numbers. If you wish, make an array to help you.

14. 4, 5, 20
15. 2, 3, 6
16. 6, 9, 54
17. 5, 7, 35
18. 5, 6, 30
19. 3, 3, 9
20. 8, 9, 72
21. 5, 5, 25

Problem Solving

22. There are 20 people line dancing. For part of the dance they form 5 lines. Each line has the same number of people. Draw an array to show how many people are in each line.

23. Four friends take dance lessons with 12 other people. How could they form groups so there are the same number of people in each group?

24. There are 5 rows of 6 dancers on the dance floor. Then 4 more people join them. How many people are dancing now?

25. Suppose 18 people want to dance in circles of 4 or more. How could all 18 people make at least 2 circles so that each circle has the same number of people?

26. **Analyze** There are 2 groups of dancers on the dance floor. Each group has 8 dancers. Then all the dancers change places and make 4 equal groups. How many dancers are in each new group?

Social Studies Connection
Line dancing has its roots in many American folk dances. The dancers pictured above are performing at the Fiddler's Jamboree Country Music Festival in Smithville, Tennessee.

Review and Remember

Using Estimation Estimate each answer by rounding to the nearest hundred.

27. 486 + 612 **28.** 985 − 463 **29.** 349 − 221 **30.** 274 + 399

31. 722 − 439 **32.** 117 + 906 **33.** 492 + 877 **34.** 656 − 507

Time for Technology

Surf the Net

Dancing Databases

What's square dancing? What's the difference between modern dancing and ballet? To find the answers to questions like these about dancing, you can explore one of these sites on the Internet.

www.abt.org **www.danceonline.com** **www.dosado.com**

Share what you find with your class.

For Extra Practice, see Set A, page 352.

Crossroads

Using Algebra

You can use a multiplication table to help you divide.

Learning About It

Work with your partner.

Use the multiplication table at the right to find the quotient of 12 ÷ 3.

Step 1 Point to the row for the divisor 3. Move across the row until you come to the dividend 12. Then move up to the top of the column to find the quotient.

So, 12 ÷ 3 = 4.

Step 2 Now use your own multiplication table. Find 15 in your table.

- Color the row red where you find 15. What number is at the beginning of the row? Use that number as the divisor.
- Now use blue to color the column above 15. What number is at the top of the column? Use that number as the quotient.
- Write a division sentence to show what you did.

Step 3 Think of other division examples that can be solved by using your multiplication table. Challenge your partner to find each quotient.

Think and Discuss Describe how you could use a multiplication table to find 25 ÷ 5.

What You Need

For each pair:
multiplication table
crayons

column

row

x	0	1	2	3	4	5
0	0	0	0	0	0	0
1	0	1	2	3	4	5
2	0	2	4	6	8	10
3	0	3	6	9	12	15
4	0	4	8	12	16	20
5	0	5	10	15	20	25

Practice

Use the multiplication table to help you answer Questions 1–12.

1. 8 ÷ 2 **2.** 6 ÷ 3

3. 5 ÷ 1 **4.** 3 ÷ 3

5. 10 ÷ 5 **6.** 12 ÷ 4

7. 16 ÷ 4 **8.** 20 ÷ 5

9. 20 ÷ 4 **10.** 25 ÷ 5

11. Find the number 1 at the side of the table. Look at the numbers across. What rule about dividing a number by 1 does this row of numbers help you remember?

12. Look at the row that begins with the number 2. Are the numbers in the row even or odd? How does this pattern help you know that 21 cannot be divided evenly by 2?

Project Link

Begin to make your puppets.

- Draw a sketch of what your puppet will look like.
- Gather materials to use, such as buttons, yarn, sequins, and cotton balls.
- Count the pieces of material you have. How could you divide these materials equally among all puppets?

Tune Up

You can use counters or related division facts to help you divide.

Learning About It

What's that sound? It's cello practice in the Division Street Theater music room. There are 18 cellos in 6 groups of equal size. How many cellos are in each group?

18 ÷ 6 = ■ or $6\overline{)18}$ (quotient: ■)

THERE'S ALWAYS A WAY!

- **One way** to divide is to use counters.
  - Use 18 counters.
  - Put the same number of counters into each of 6 groups.

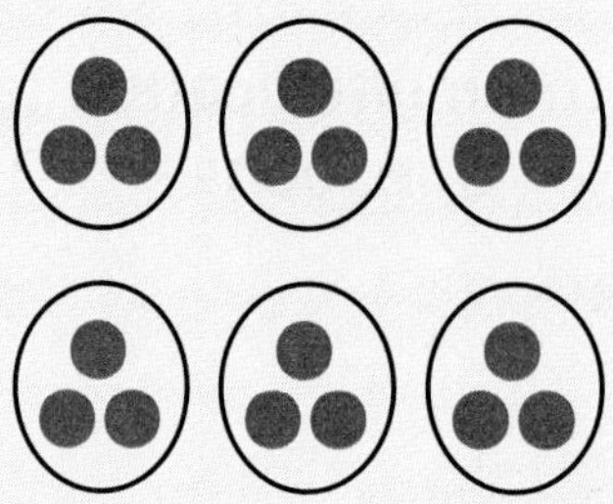

How many counters are in each group?

18 ÷ 6 = 3 or $6\overline{)18}$ (quotient: 3)

- **Another way** to divide is to think of a related division fact.

If you know 18 ÷ 3 = 6,
then you know 18 ÷ 6 = 3.

There are 3 cellos in each group.

Think and Discuss Suppose you know that 24 ÷ 4 = 6. How could that help you find 24 ÷ 6?

Try It Out

Write a related division fact for each.

1. 12 ÷ 2 = 6 **2.** 30 ÷ 5 = 6 **3.** 6 ÷ 1 = 6 **4.** 42 ÷ 7 = 6

Practice

Complete the division fact for each picture.

5.

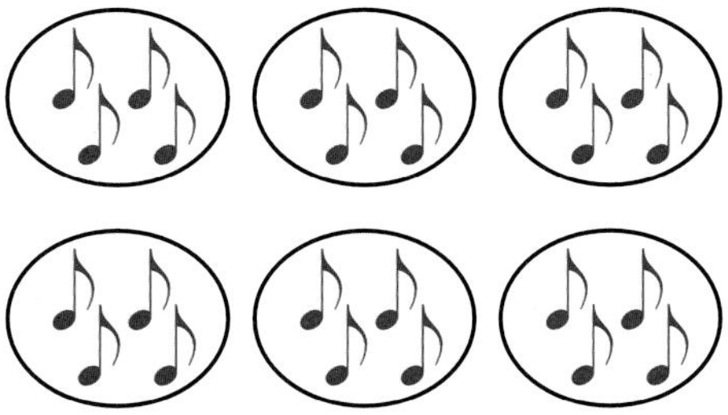

24 ÷ 6 = ■

6.

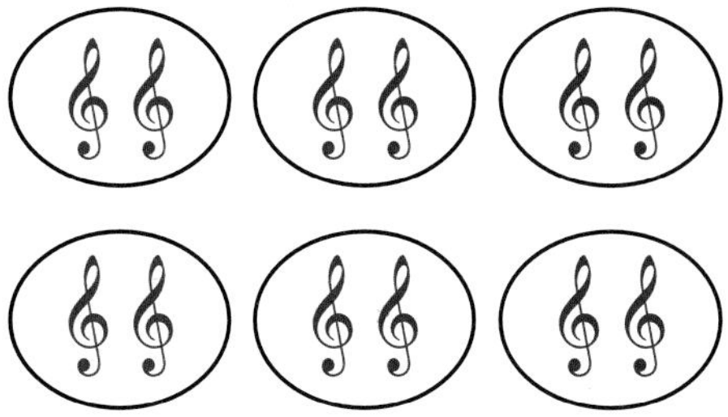

12 ÷ 6 = ■

Divide.

7. $6\overline{)42}$ **8.** $6\overline{)48}$ **9.** $6\overline{)18}$ **10.** $6\overline{)54}$ **11.** $6\overline{)0}$

12. $6\overline{)6}$ **13.** $6\overline{)12}$ **14.** $6\overline{)36}$ **15.** $6\overline{)24}$ **16.** $6\overline{)30}$

17. $5\overline{)45}$ **18.** $4\overline{)24}$ **19.** $5\overline{)35}$ **20.** $5\overline{)30}$ **21.** $3\overline{)21}$

22. 6 ÷ 6 **23.** 30 ÷ 6 **24.** 18 ÷ 6 **25.** 42 ÷ 6

26. 24 ÷ 6 **27.** 48 ÷ 6 **28.** 36 ÷ 6 **29.** 54 ÷ 6

Problem Solving

30. An orchestra has 18 violinists who sit in 3 rows. If the same number of violinists sit in each row how many violinists are in each row?

31. A band practiced 6 songs. If they practiced each song for 5 minutes, how many minutes did they practice?

32. Mr. Little is putting new strings on some guitars. He has 48 new guitar strings. Each guitar needs 6 strings. On how many guitars can he put new strings?

33. **Create Your Own** Write a division problem that uses the numbers 24, 4, and 6. Ask a classmate to solve your problem.

Using Algebra

Review and Remember

Write the missing numbers.

34. 30, 41, 52, ■, ■, ■

35. 568, 468, 368, ■, ■, ■

36. 485, 490, 495, ■, ■, ■

37. 63, 60, 57, ■, ■, ■

For Extra Practice, see Set B, page 352.

Top Hat Tappers

You already know multiplication facts that will help you divide by 7.

Learning About It

The Top Hat tap dancers have gone on stage! There are 14 dancers in the group. They dance in rows of 7. How many rows are there?

$14 \div 7 = \blacksquare$ or $7\overline{)14}$ with ■ above

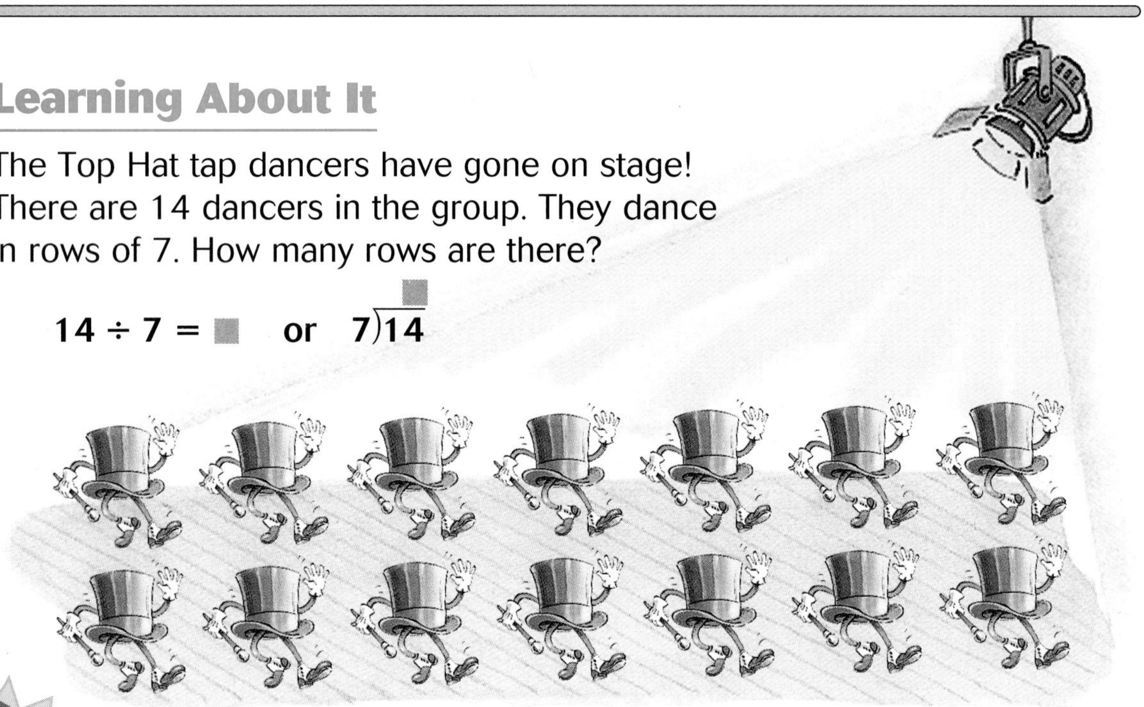

THERE'S ALWAYS A WAY!

- **One way** to divide is to use repeated subtraction.
  - Start at 14.
  - Subtract by 7s until you reach 0.
  - Count how many 7s you subtracted.

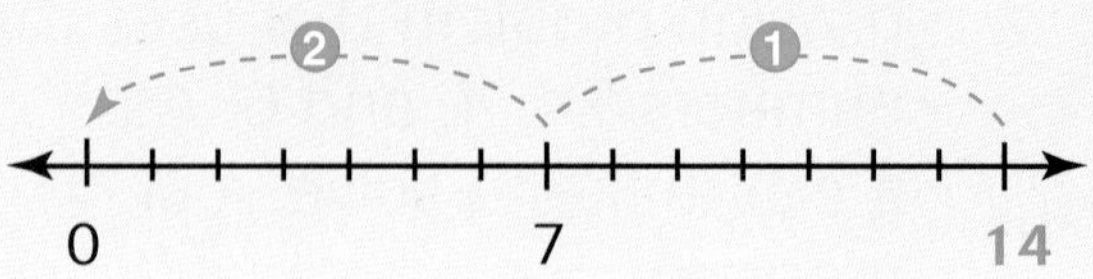

So, $14 \div 7 = 2$ or $7\overline{)14}$ with 2 above

- **Another way** is to use a related multiplication fact.

$14 \div 7 = \blacksquare$

Think: $7 \times \blacksquare = 14$
$7 \times 2 = 14$

So, $14 \div 7 = 2$

There are 2 rows of dancers.

Think and Discuss Suppose you know that $7 \times 9 = 63$. Explain how that fact could help you find $63 \div 7$.

Try It Out

Using Algebra

Find each missing factor. Then use it to find the quotient.

1. $7 \times ■ = 42$
$42 \div 7 = ■$

2. $7 \times ■ = 56$
$56 \div 7 = ■$

3. $7 \times ■ = 35$
$35 \div 7 = ■$

Practice

Find each quotient.

4. $7\overline{)49}$ **5.** $7\overline{)35}$ **6.** $7\overline{)0}$ **7.** $7\overline{)42}$ **8.** $7\overline{)7}$

9. $7\overline{)21}$ **10.** $7\overline{)63}$ **11.** $7\overline{)14}$ **12.** $7\overline{)28}$ **13.** $7\overline{)56}$

14. $6\overline{)54}$ **15.** $1\overline{)7}$ **16.** $5\overline{)35}$ **17.** $4\overline{)32}$ **18.** $4\overline{)36}$

19. $28 \div 7$ **20.** $21 \div 7$ **21.** $49 \div 7$ **22.** $63 \div 7$

Problem Solving

23. There are 21 tap dancers on stage. They dance in groups of 7. How many groups of dancers are there?

24. In the costume room there are 20 red hats and 15 blue hats. The hats are hung in 7 equal rows. How many hats are in each row?

Review and Remember

Find each answer.

25. 7×3 **26.** $14 + 62$ **27.** $35 - 9$ **28.** $32 \div 8$ **29.** 6×8

Critical Thinking Corner

Number Sense

What Went Wrong?

Sumita wanted her dancers to be in 6 groups of equal size. At the first rehearsal she said, "Please get into 6 groups." The dancers did as she asked, but it wasn't what Sumita wanted! What do you think went wrong?

Developing Skills for Problem Solving

First read for understanding and then focus on which operation to use to solve a problem.

READ FOR UNDERSTANDING

The Division Street Theater is getting ready for the next play. Six people are making costumes. They need to make a total of 24 costumes. Five different scenes for the play are being painted. Three people are painting each scene.

1. How many people are making costumes?
2. How many scenes are being painted?

THINK AND DISCUSS

MATH FOCUS

Choose the Operation You can add to put groups together. You can subtract to find out how many more are in one group than in another. You can multiply to combine equal groups. You can divide to separate items into equal groups.

Reread the paragraph at the top of the page.

3. Which operation would you use to find the total number of people painting scenery? Explain why.
4. How many more people are painting scenery than making costumes? Which operation did you use to find the answer? Explain why.
5. Explain how you know whether to multiply or divide.

Show What You Know

Answer each question. Give a reason for your choice.

Alyssa and Peter are making programs and posters for the play. They want to make 100 programs for the ushers to hand out. They also need a total of 10 posters to place in stores around town.

1 Which operation would you use to find out how many programs and posters they are making?

a. Addition

b. Subtraction

c. Multiplication

2 Which number sentence tells you how many programs and posters they are making?

a. $100 - 10 = \blacksquare$

b. $100 \times 10 = \blacksquare$

c. $100 + 10 = \blacksquare$

3 Which operation would you use to find out how many more programs they are making than posters?

a. Addition

b. Subtraction

c. Division

4 Which number sentence tells you how many more programs they are making than posters?

a. $100 - 10 = \blacksquare$

b. $100 \div 10 = \blacksquare$

c. $100 + 10 = \blacksquare$

The play tickets are finally on sale! So far 58 tickets have been sold. There are 42 tickets left to sell. Six people have promised to sell the rest of the tickets. Suppose they each sell the same number of tickets.

5 Which operation would you use to find out how many tickets each person will sell?

a. Subtraction

b. Division

c. Multiplication

6 Which number sentence tells you the number of tickets each person will sell?

a. $42 \div 6 = \blacksquare$

b. $42 - 6 = \blacksquare$

c. $58 \div 6 = \blacksquare$

7 **Explain** Suppose you wanted to know the total number of tickets. How would you solve the problem?

Checkpoint

Fact Families and Division

Write the fact family for each set of numbers.
(pages 324–327)

1. 7, 9, 63 **2.** 6, 6, 36 **3.** 3, 6, 18

4. 6, 8, 48 **5.** 4, 7, 28 **6.** 5, 5, 25

Complete the division fact for each picture.
(pages 330–331)

7.

$18 \div 6 = ■$

8.

$30 \div 6 = ■$

Using Algebra

Find each missing factor. Then use it to find the quotient. (pages 332–333)

9. $7 \times ■ = 28$
$28 \div 7 = ■$

10. $7 \times ■ = 14$
$14 \div 7 = ■$

11. $7 \times ■ = 42$
$42 \div 7 = ■$

12. $7 \times ■ = 63$
$63 \div 7 = ■$

13. $7 \times ■ = 49$
$49 \div 7 = ■$

14. $7 \times ■ = 35$
$35 \div 7 = ■$

Mixed Practice

Divide.

15. $7\overline{)35}$ **16.** $6\overline{)36}$ **17.** $6\overline{)42}$ **18.** $7\overline{)49}$

19. $6\overline{)30}$ **20.** $7\overline{)0}$ **21.** $6\overline{)6}$ **22.** $6\overline{)48}$

23. $18 \div 6$ **24.** $56 \div 7$ **25.** $28 \div 7$ **26.** $12 \div 6$

27. $21 \div 7$ **28.** $63 \div 7$ **29.** $54 \div 6$ **30.** $42 \div 7$

Problem Solving

31. At the folk festival, 42 people dance in groups. If 6 people are in each group, how many groups are there?

32. There is room for 8 autographs on each page of Dwayne's autograph book. If 4 pages of his book are filled, how many autographs does Dwayne have in his book?

33. Suppose there are 35 people dancing. They form 7 circles with the same number of people in each circle. How many people are in each circle?

34. Kit plays a videotape of her favorite singing group. The tape has 9 songs. Each song lasts 5 minutes. How long is the tape?

35. **Analyze** Tickets for the Division Street Theater cost $7 each. A book of 6 tickets costs $30. How much money do you save on each ticket when you buy a book?

What do you think?

How does knowing $7 \times 4 = 28$ help you solve $28 \div 7$? Explain your thinking.

Journal Idea Write the division and multiplication sentences for any fact family. Then draw arrays to model your sentences.

Critical Thinking Corner

Logical Thinking

Change Partners

There are 4 people in a singing class. Each person wants to sing 1 song with each of the other people in the class. How many songs will be sung in all? Draw a picture or make a list to help you find the answer.

Give 'Em a Hand

Knowing the multiplication facts for 8 will help you divide by 8.

Learning About It

A puppeteer uses 16 finger puppets to tell a story in 8 scenes. Each puppet appears in only 1 scene. The same number of puppets are used in each scene. How many puppets are in each scene?

$16 \div 8 = ■$ or $8\overline{)16}$ (quotient ■)

THERE'S ALWAYS A WAY!

- **One way** to divide is to draw a picture using 16 Xs.
  - Draw a circle for each scene.
  - Put the same number of Xs in each circle.

(XX) (XX) (XX) (XX) (XX) (XX) (XX) (XX)

So, $16 \div 8 = 2$ or $8\overline{)16}$ (quotient 2)

- **Another way** to divide is to use a related multiplication fact.

$16 \div 8 = ■$

Think: $8 \times ■ = 16$
$8 \times 2 = 16$

So, $16 \div 8 = 2$.

There are 2 puppets in each scene.

Think and Discuss Explain how you could draw a picture to find $32 \div 8$.

Using Algebra

Try It Out

Find each missing factor. Use it to help you divide.

1. $8 \times ■ = 64$
$64 \div 8 = ■$

2. $8 \times ■ = 56$
$56 \div 8 = ■$

3. $8 \times ■ = 48$
$48 \div 8 = ■$

Practice

Divide.

4. $8\overline{)72}$ **5.** $8\overline{)8}$ **6.** $8\overline{)0}$ **7.** $8\overline{)40}$ **8.** $8\overline{)16}$

9. $8\overline{)32}$ **10.** $8\overline{)48}$ **11.** $8\overline{)56}$ **12.** $8\overline{)24}$ **13.** $8\overline{)64}$

14. $7\overline{)56}$ **15.** $6\overline{)36}$ **16.** $6\overline{)48}$ **17.** $7\overline{)49}$ **18.** $1\overline{)8}$

Write × or ÷ for each ●.

19. 8 ● 8 = 64 **20.** 56 ● 8 = 7 **21.** 24 ● 8 = 3

22. 5 ● 8 = 40 **23.** 8 ● 4 = 32 **24.** 72 ● 8 = 9

Problem Solving

25. A puppeteer is putting away 32 puppets in boxes. Each box holds 8 puppets. How many boxes does he use?

26. The theater has 48 shadow puppets from Thailand. The puppets are displayed in 8 groups of equal size. How many puppets are in each group?

27. **Analyze** Each day there are 6 puppet shows. How many shows are there in 2 weeks?

Fine Arts Connection
In Thailand, shadow puppets are made from wood and leather. The puppets cast shadows from behind a lighted screen.

Review and Remember

Choose a Method Use paper and pencil or mental math to solve. Tell which method you used.

28. 987 − 400 **29.** 679 + 385 **30.** 486 − 395 **31.** 1,200 + 800

Spring Concert

You already know multiplication and division facts that will help you divide by 9.

Learning About It

The third-grade chorus is getting ready for their spring concert. They are making flower costumes. They need 9 petals for each flower. They have cut out 27 petals so far. How many flowers can they make?

27 ÷ 9 = ■ or $9\overline{)27}$ ■

THERE'S ALWAYS A WAY!

- **One way** to divide is to use a related multiplication fact.

  27 ÷ 9 = ■

  Think: 9 × ■ = 27
  9 × 3 = 27

  So, 27 ÷ 9 = 3.

- **Another way** to divide is to use a related division fact.

  If you know 27 ÷ 3 = 9, then you know 27 ÷ 9 = 3.

They can make 3 flowers.

Think and Discuss What related multiplication fact would you use to help you divide 63 ÷ 9?

Try It Out

Write two related division sentences for each multiplication sentence.

1. 9 × 2 = 18 **2.** 9 × 8 = 72 **3.** 9 × 5 = 45

4. 9 × 6 = 54 **5.** 9 × 4 = 36 **6.** 9 × 7 = 63

Practice

Divide.

7. $9\overline{)0}$ **8.** $9\overline{)45}$ **9.** $9\overline{)63}$ **10.** $9\overline{)18}$ **11.** $9\overline{)54}$

12. $9\overline{)9}$ **13.** $9\overline{)27}$ **14.** $9\overline{)81}$ **15.** $9\overline{)36}$ **16.** $9\overline{)72}$

17. $8\overline{)48}$ **18.** $7\overline{)21}$ **19.** $1\overline{)9}$ **20.** $8\overline{)64}$ **21.** $6\overline{)24}$

Using Algebra **Follow the rule to complete each table.**

Rule: Divide by 9

	Input	Output
22.	36	
23.	9	
24.	54	
25.	72	

Rule: Divide by 7

	Input	Output
26.	28	
27.	35	
28.	63	
29.	49	

Rule: Divide by 8

	Input	Output
30.	64	
31.	48	
32.	16	
33.	56	

Problem Solving

34. There are 72 people in the chorus. They form 9 groups to practice. Each group has the same number of people in it. How many people are in each group?

35. The chorus is making cassette tapes of their favorite songs. They sing 9 songs for each tape. How many songs will be on 2 tapes?

36. Nine people cut out 81 stars to decorate the stage. Everyone makes the same number of stars. How many stars does each person make?

Kid Connection The Harlem Boys Choir of New York City sings all around the world. Members of this famous choir range in age from 8 to 18. The choir has received many awards for its performances.

Review and Remember

Find each answer.

37. 9×9 **38.** $285 + 396$ **39.** $487 - 295$ **40.** 8×4

41. 6×8 **42.** $1{,}246 - 254$ **43.** $691 + 509$ **44.** $32 \div 4$

For Extra Practice, see Set E, page 354.

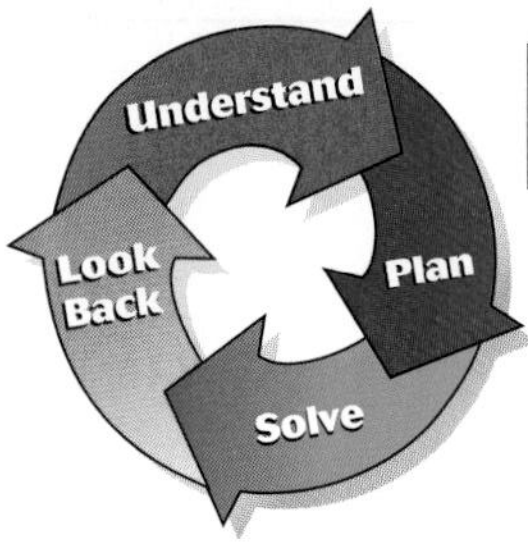

Problem Solving

Guess and Check

You can guess and then check to help you solve a problem.

On stage are 28 juggling jugglers and clowning clowns! There are 2 more jugglers than clowns. How many jugglers are there? How many clowns are there?

UNDERSTAND

What do you need to know?

You need to know that there are 28 jugglers and clowns altogether. You also need to know that there are 2 more jugglers than clowns.

PLAN

How can you solve the problem?

You can **guess and check** to find two numbers with a sum of 28 *and* a difference of 2. If your first guess does not work, try two different numbers.

SOLVE

First guess	**Second guess**
16 jugglers, 12 clowns	15 jugglers, 13 clowns
Check	**Check**
$16 + 12 = 28$	$15 + 13 = 28$
$16 - 12 = 4$ ← 4 more jugglers than clowns.	$15 - 13 = 2$ ← 2 more jugglers than clowns.
These numbers don't work!	These numbers do work!

There are 15 jugglers and 13 clowns.

LOOK BACK

How did your first guess help you make the second guess?

Using the Strategy

Use guess and check to solve each problem.

1. Tickets for an acrobat show cost \$3 for adults and \$2 for children. Harper sells the same number of adult tickets and child tickets. She collects \$25. How many of each kind of ticket does Harper sell?

2. A juggler juggles pins and then beanbags for 9 minutes. She juggles the pins 5 minutes longer than she does the beanbags. How long does she juggle pins? How long does she juggle beanbags?

3. Together, Jared and Jim sold 12 show tickets. Jared sold 2 more tickets than Jim. How many tickets did each boy sell?

4. Tyrone and Shirlee fold 133 show programs. Tyrone folds 9 more programs than Shirlee. How many programs does each person fold?

5. Kay says, "Divide my two numbers and the quotient is 3. Subtract my numbers and the difference is 10." What are Kay's numbers?

6. Holly says, "Add my two numbers and the sum is 17. Multiply my numbers and the product is 72. The lesser of the two numbers is my age." How old is Holly?

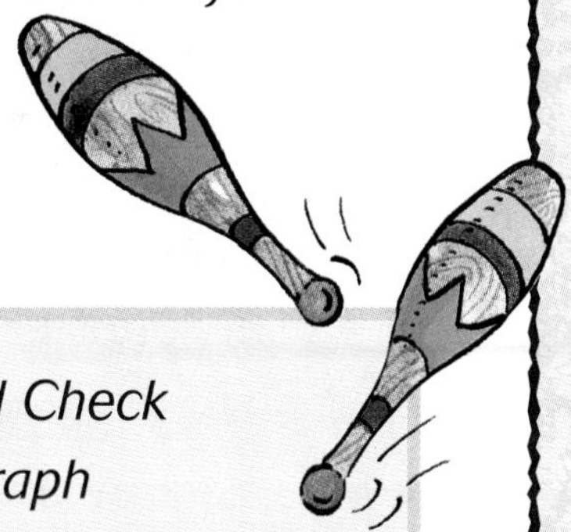

Mixed Strategy Review

Try these or other strategies you have learned.

THERE'S ALWAYS A WAY!

- *Work Backwards*
- *Write a Number Sentence*
- *Guess and Check*
- *Make a Graph*

7. After the show, the clowns had a pizza party. They spent \$48 for pizza. If each pizza cost \$6, how many pizzas did the clowns buy?

8. Jenny and Cheri have juggled for a total of 8 years. Jenny has juggled for 2 more years than Cheri. How many years has each girl been juggling?

9. **Analyze** Chris buys 3 sets of markers to make signs for the show. Each set of markers is the same price. He pays with a \$20 bill and receives \$11 in change. How much does each set of markers cost?

www.sbgmath.com

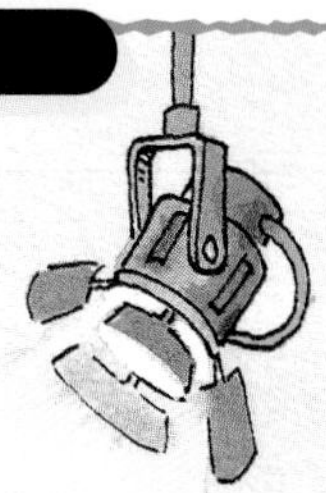

Take a Bow

You can use many different strategies to divide.

Learning About It

The show is over! Eighteen of the performers are back on stage for a final bow. They line up in rows of 6. How many rows are there?

There are many ways to help you divide 18 by 6.

18 ÷ 6 = ■ or $\overset{■}{6\overline{)18}}$

THERE'S ALWAYS A WAY!

- **One way** to divide is to draw an array.
  - Draw 18 Xs.
  - Put 6 Xs in each row.
  - How many rows are there?

X X X X X X
X X X X X X
X X X X X X

18 ÷ 6 = 3 or $\overset{3}{6\overline{)18}}$

- **Another way** to divide is to use repeated subtraction.

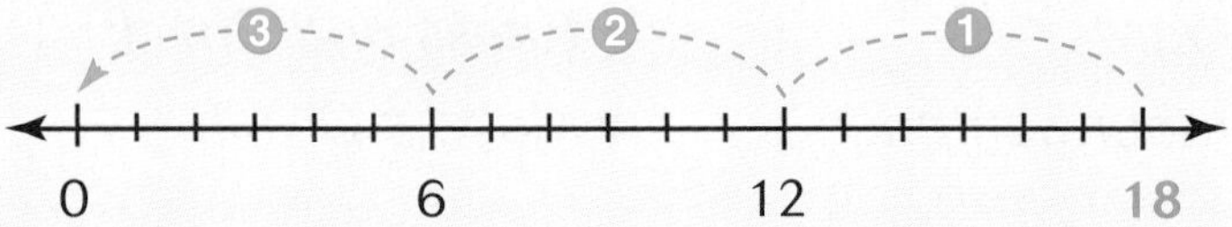

18 ÷ 6 = 3

- **Another way** is to use a related multiplication fact.

18 ÷ 6 = ■

Think: 6 × ■ = 18
6 × 3 = 18

So, 18 ÷ 6 = 3.

- **Another way** is to use a related division fact.

If you know 18 ÷ 3 = 6, then you know 18 ÷ 6 = 3.

There are 3 rows of performers.

Think and Discuss Which of the ways to divide shown on page 344 do you like best? Why?

Try It Out

Find each quotient.

1. $14 \div 7$ **2.** $42 \div 7$ **3.** $18 \div 6$ **4.** $40 \div 8$

5. $45 \div 9$ **6.** $30 \div 6$ **7.** $27 \div 9$ **8.** $24 \div 8$

Practice

Divide.

9. $8\overline{)72}$ **10.** $8\overline{)64}$ **11.** $9\overline{)54}$ **12.** $6\overline{)48}$ **13.** $8\overline{)56}$

14. $9\overline{)72}$ **15.** $7\overline{)63}$ **16.** $9\overline{)18}$ **17.** $7\overline{)7}$ **18.** $8\overline{)0}$

19. $7\overline{)35}$ **20.** $6\overline{)24}$ **21.** $6\overline{)36}$ **22.** $9\overline{)81}$ **23.** $7\overline{)49}$

Using Algebra **Compare. Write >, <, or = for each ●.**

24. $18 \div 6$ ● 8 **25.** $12 \div 6$ ● 2 **26.** $27 \div 9$ ● 3

27. $28 \div 4$ ● 4 **28.** $8 \div 2$ ● 2×8 **29.** $10 \div 5$ ● 5×2

Problem Solving

30. The chart lists the ticket prices for the Division Street Theater show. You sell \$49 worth of student tickets and \$54 worth of adult tickets. How many of each kind of ticket do you sell?

31. **Create Your Own** Write a division word problem that uses the information in the chart. Give it to a classmate to solve.

Show Tickets	
Child under 6	\$2
Student	\$7
Adult	\$9
Senior citizen	\$4

Review and Remember

Find each answer.

32. 8×9 **33.** $423 + 94$ **34.** $52 - 37$ **35.** $36 \div 4$

36. $89 + 63$ **37.** 6×7 **38.** $21 \div 3$ **39.** $356 - 138$

For Extra Practice, see Set F, page 354.

What's Left?

Sometimes when you divide, you can't put everything into equal groups.

Word Bank

remainder

Learning About It

Work with your partner.

Step 1 Divide 21 counters into groups of 8.

- How many groups of 8 did you make?
- Are there any counters left over?
- If so, how many counters are left over?

What You Need

For each pair:
28 counters

► In division, the number left over is called the **remainder**.

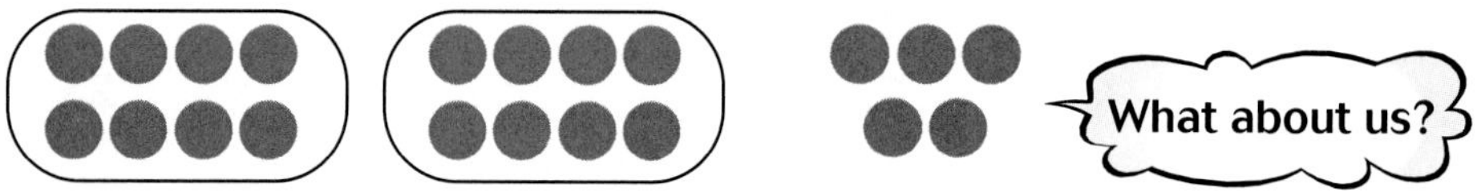

Step 2 Divide 21 counters in other ways to see if you have a remainder. Record your work in a chart like the one below.

Total Number of Counters (Dividend)	Number in Each Group (Divisor)	Number of Groups (Quotient)	What's Left Over? (Remainder)
21	8	2	5
21	7		
21	6		
21	5		
21	4		
21	3		

Step 3 Try to divide 18 counters into equal-size groups. Make a chart like the one above to record your work. Then look back at your completed chart. When do you have a remainder greater than 0?

Think and Discuss Is the remainder always less than or greater than the divisor? Explain.

Practice

Tell which division sentence goes with each picture.

1. 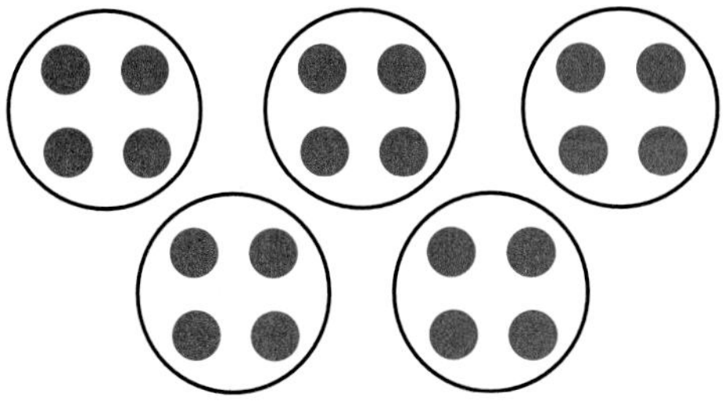

a. 20 ÷ 4 = 5

b. 20 ÷ 6 = 3 Remainder 2

2. 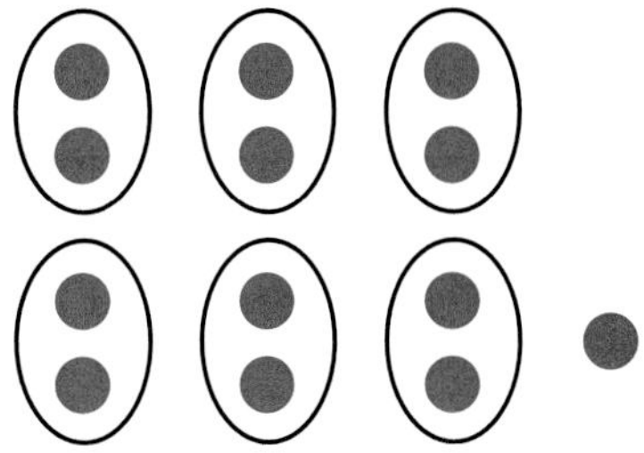

a. 13 ÷ 2 = 7

b. 13 ÷ 2 = 6 Remainder 1

3. Which picture correctly shows 17 ÷ 5?

a. 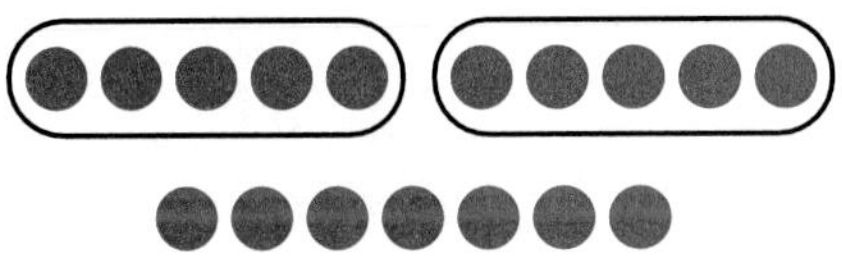

17 ÷ 5 = 2 Remainder 7

b. 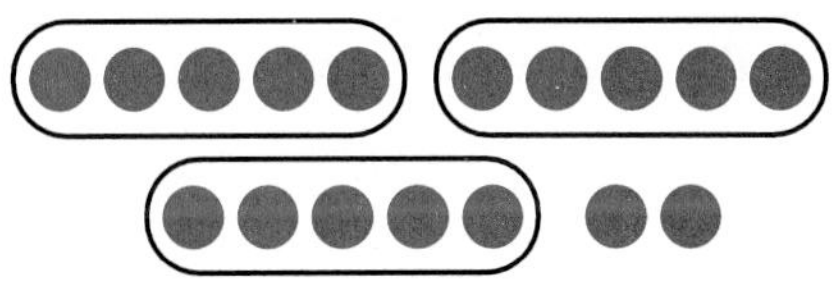

17 ÷ 5 = 3 Remainder 2

4. What is the largest remainder you can have if you divide any number by 8?

When your group's puppets are finished, start practicing for the puppet show. Make a schedule for the show, too.

- Find out how many groups will be performing.
- If the whole show lasts 40 minutes, how many minutes would each of 4 groups have? each of 5 groups?

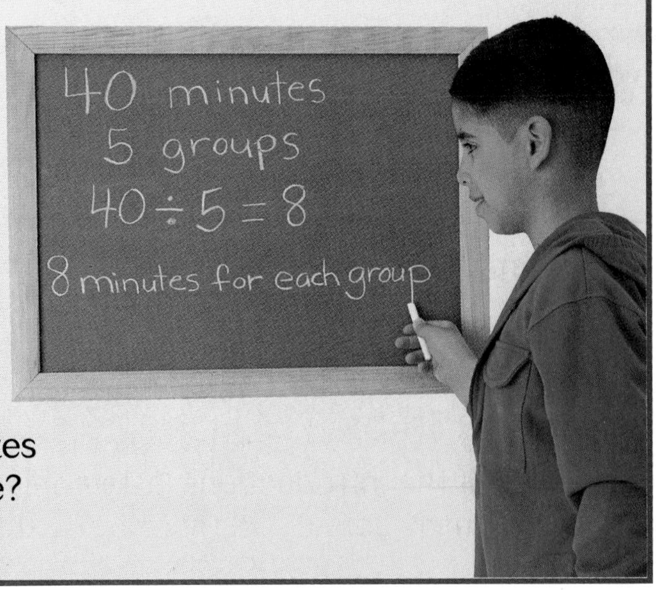

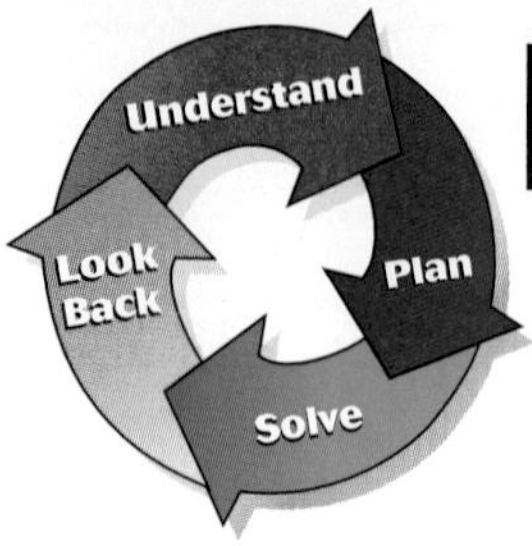

Problem Solving
Using Operations

Knowing how to add, subtract, multiply, and divide can help you solve problems.

The school talent show is from 1:00 P.M. to 2:00 P.M. Students have 5 minutes to perform each act. Fifteen minutes have been planned for introductions. How many acts can be in the talent show?

UNDERSTAND

What do you need to know?

You need to know how long the show lasts, the number of minutes for introductions, and the number of minutes for each act.

PLAN

How can you solve the problem?

First find the total number of minutes the show will last. Then subtract 15 minutes for introductions. Finally, divide the remaining minutes by 5 to find the number of acts.

SOLVE

Step 1 1:00 P.M. to 2:00 P.M. = 60 min

Step 2 60 min − 15 min = 45 min

Step 3 45 ÷ 5 = 9 acts

There can be 9 acts in the talent show.

LOOK BACK

What if the introductions lasted only 5 minutes? How many acts could there be? Explain.

Show What You Learned

Solve.

1. This year, the talent show is 60 minutes long. Last year, the show was twice as long. How long was last year's show?

2. Marisa is performing in 3 acts. Each act lasts 5 minutes. For how many minutes will Marisa perform in the talent show?

3. Rich and Jess have a juggling act. Rich has 14 pins. Jess has 4 pins. They need to have the same number of pins to begin their act. How many pins should Rich give to Jess?

4. Sarah bought a costume for $19.99. She also paid $3.79 for a hat. Becky spent a total of $23.99 for her costume and hat. About how much did each girl spend?

5. There are 6 students on stage tap-dancing. Seven more students join them. Then 3 students leave. How many students are dancing now?

6. There are 9 acts in the talent show. Three of the acts do not include music. How many acts in the talent show do include music?

7. Ali practices playing the piano for 20 minutes each day. How many minutes does she practice in 3 days?

8. **Create Your Own** Write a problem about the talent show. Give it to a classmate to solve.

9. Jerome and Derek buy 2 hats and some funny ties for their comedy act. The hats cost $2.50 each, and the ties cost $3.00 altogether. If they share the total cost equally, how much money will each boy have to pay?

10. **Analyze** Fifteen minutes is set aside at the end of a talent show for comedy acts. The first 2 acts last 4 minutes each. The third act lasts 5 minutes. Is there enough time left for a 3-minute act? Explain why or why not.

Checkpoint

Division Facts

Choose the related multiplication sentence that could help you find the quotient. (pages 338–341, 344–345)

1. $72 \div 9$

2. $54 \div 9$

3. $63 \div 9$

4. $48 \div 8$

5. $64 \div 8$

a. $9 \times 7 = 63$

b. $8 \times 8 = 64$

c. $9 \times 8 = 72$

d. $8 \times 6 = 48$

e. $9 \times 6 = 54$

Divide. (pages 338–341, 344–345)

6. $8\overline{)72}$	**7.** $9\overline{)36}$	**8.** $9\overline{)18}$	**9.** $8\overline{)40}$
10. $9\overline{)0}$	**11.** $8\overline{)48}$	**12.** $8\overline{)16}$	**13.** $9\overline{)54}$
14. $8\overline{)32}$	**15.** $9\overline{)81}$	**16.** $8\overline{)56}$	**17.** $9\overline{)72}$
18. $9 \div 9$	**19.** $8 \div 8$	**20.** $24 \div 8$	**21.** $63 \div 9$
22. $27 \div 9$	**23.** $45 \div 9$	**24.** $36 \div 9$	**25.** $56 \div 8$
26. $0 \div 8$	**27.** $40 \div 8$	**28.** $64 \div 8$	**29.** $72 \div 8$

Tell which division sentence goes with each picture.
(pages 346–347)

30.

a. $16 \div 8 = 2$

b. $16 \div 5 = 3$ Remainder 1

31.

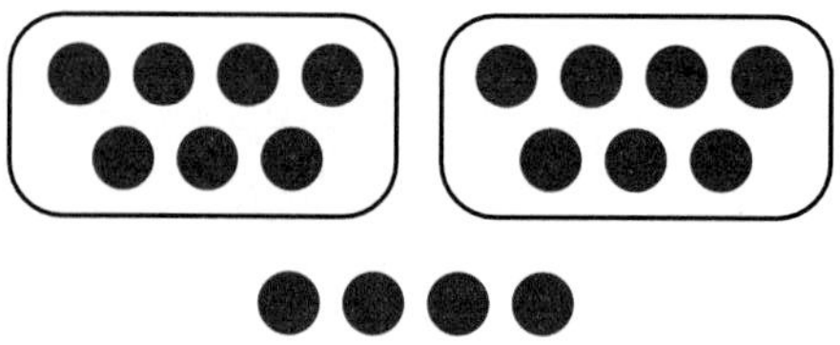

a. $18 \div 9 = 2$

b. $18 \div 7 = 2$ Remainder 4

Problem Solving

32. There are 45 seats in one part of the theater. The seats are arranged in 9 equal rows. How many seats are in each row?

33. There are 5 sections of seats in the Division Street Theater. If 4 ushers work in each section, how many ushers are there?

34. Explain Forty-two students are being driven to the theater in vans. Each van holds 8 students. Will 5 vans be enough to take all the students? Explain why or why not.

35. Explain Alex sells fruit drinks during intermission at the play. There are 6 drinks in a package. How many packages did he open if he sold 43 drinks? Explain your answer.

What do you think?

Is it possible to divide 19 counters into equal groups without any counters being left over? Explain why or why not.

Journal Idea Suppose you cannot remember the quotient for $56 \div 8$. List four things that you could do to find the answer.

Project Wrap-Up

Puppet Performances

It's time to put on your puppet shows.

- Set up a stage where groups can perform.
- When it is your turn, tell the class who your characters are. Tell what your show will be about. Then put on the show for your audience!

Extra Practice

Using Algebra

Set A (pages 324–327)

Copy and complete each fact family.

1. $5 \times 7 = 35$
$■ \times 5 = 35$
$35 \div 5 = ■$
$35 \div 7 = ■$

2. $9 \times 6 = 54$
$■ \times 9 = 54$
$54 \div 9 = ■$
$54 \div 6 = ■$

3. $7 \times 8 = 56$
$■ \times 7 = 56$
$56 \div 7 = ■$
$56 \div 8 = ■$

4. $9 \times 7 = 63$
$■ \times 9 = 63$
$63 \div 9 = ■$
$63 \div 7 = ■$

5. $6 \times 5 = 30$
$■ \times 6 = 30$
$30 \div 6 = ■$
$30 \div 5 = ■$

6. $7 \times 6 = 42$
$■ \times 7 = 42$
$42 \div 7 = ■$
$42 \div 6 = ■$

Write the fact family for each set of numbers.

7. 5, 9, 45 **8.** 3, 4, 12 **9.** 6, 8, 48 **10.** 6, 7, 42

11. 8, 8, 64 **12.** 9, 9, 81 **13.** 2, 8, 16 **14.** 4, 8, 32

Set B (pages 330–331)

Divide.

1. $6\overline{)24}$ **2.** $6\overline{)6}$ **3.** $6\overline{)18}$ **4.** $6\overline{)42}$

5. $6\overline{)12}$ **6.** $6\overline{)30}$ **7.** $6\overline{)36}$ **8.** $6\overline{)54}$

9. $6\overline{)48}$ **10.** $6\overline{)0}$ **11.** $4\overline{)24}$ **12.** $5\overline{)30}$

13. $3\overline{)9}$ **14.** $3\overline{)24}$ **15.** $5\overline{)25}$ **16.** $4\overline{)32}$

17. $12 \div 6$ **18.** $48 \div 6$ **19.** $36 \div 6$ **20.** $18 \div 6$

21. $24 \div 6$ **22.** $54 \div 6$ **23.** $30 \div 6$ **24.** $42 \div 6$

25. Suppose 30 musical instruments are shared equally among 6 classes. How many instruments would each class get?

26. The 24 members of a school band travel in vans. Each van carries 6 passengers. How many vans are needed to carry all the band members?

Extra Practice

Set C (pages 332–333)

Find the quotient.

1. $7\overline{)14}$
2. $7\overline{)63}$
3. $7\overline{)35}$
4. $7\overline{)7}$
5. $7\overline{)28}$
6. $7\overline{)49}$
7. $7\overline{)42}$
8. $7\overline{)56}$
9. $7\overline{)0}$
10. $7\overline{)21}$
11. $6\overline{)36}$
12. $6\overline{)42}$
13. $35 \div 7$
14. $14 \div 7$
15. $28 \div 7$
16. $49 \div 7$
17. $21 \div 7$
18. $56 \div 7$
19. $42 \div 7$
20. $63 \div 7$
21. There are 30 minutes in a talent show for tap dancers to perform alone. Each dancer performs for 5 minutes. How many dancers can perform in the show?
22. **Analyze** Before the show starts, the dance teacher counts 37 tap shoes. What problem did she discover? Explain.

Set D (pages 338–339)

Divide.

1. $8\overline{)16}$
2. $8\overline{)64}$
3. $8\overline{)32}$
4. $8\overline{)48}$
5. $8\overline{)0}$
6. $8\overline{)56}$
7. $8\overline{)40}$
8. $8\overline{)72}$
9. $8\overline{)24}$
10. $8\overline{)8}$
11. $1\overline{)8}$
12. $7\overline{)56}$
13. $32 \div 8$
14. $0 \div 8$
15. $48 \div 8$
16. $56 \div 8$
17. $72 \div 8$
18. $24 \div 8$
19. $40 \div 8$
20. $64 \div 8$
21. There are 32 costumes worn by 8 actors in a play. If each actor wears the same number of costumes, how many costumes does each actor wear?
22. In the play, 1 actress sings 4 songs by herself. The other 8 songs are sung by a group of 5 actors. How many songs are in the play?

Extra Practice

Set E (pages 340–341)

Divide.

1. $9\overline{)27}$
2. $9\overline{)54}$
3. $9\overline{)9}$
4. $9\overline{)72}$
5. $9\overline{)18}$
6. $1\overline{)9}$
7. $9\overline{)45}$
8. $9\overline{)36}$
9. $9\overline{)63}$
10. $9\overline{)81}$
11. $8\overline{)72}$
12. $9\overline{)0}$
13. $36 \div 9$
14. $63 \div 9$
15. $45 \div 9$
16. $54 \div 9$
17. $27 \div 9$
18. $18 \div 9$
19. $0 \div 9$
20. $72 \div 9$
21. The music teacher places her students into groups of 9. If she has 27 students, how many groups can she make?
22. A ticket for a play costs $9. Malik is buying tickets for himself and 6 of his friends. How much will he pay for the tickets?

Set F (pages 344–345)

Find the quotient.

1. $7\overline{)42}$
2. $8\overline{)40}$
3. $9\overline{)63}$
4. $6\overline{)36}$
5. $6\overline{)54}$
6. $9\overline{)45}$
7. $8\overline{)16}$
8. $7\overline{)49}$
9. $9\overline{)27}$
10. $7\overline{)21}$
11. $8\overline{)24}$
12. $9\overline{)81}$
13. $35 \div 7$
14. $56 \div 8$
15. $64 \div 8$
16. $72 \div 8$
17. $30 \div 6$
18. $36 \div 9$
19. $28 \div 7$
20. $18 \div 6$
21. At the theater the musicians sit on 36 chairs arranged in equal rows. Describe two ways the chairs could be arranged.
22. The theater manager gave 42 free tickets to 6 equal groups of students. How many tickets did each group get?

Chapter Test

Write the fact family for each set of numbers.

1. 7, 8, 56 **2.** 4, 6, 24 **3.** 4, 4, 16

4. 6, 9, 54 **5.** 8, 8, 64 **6.** 3, 7, 21

Find each quotient.

7. $7\overline{)49}$ **8.** $8\overline{)64}$ **9.** $6\overline{)42}$

10. $9\overline{)36}$ **11.** $8\overline{)72}$ **12.** $7\overline{)63}$

13. $6\overline{)54}$ **14.** $9\overline{)63}$ **15.** $8\overline{)40}$

16. $42 \div 7$ **17.** $32 \div 8$ **18.** $28 \div 7$

19. $36 \div 6$ **20.** $72 \div 9$ **21.** $81 \div 9$

Write a division sentence to go with each picture.

22.

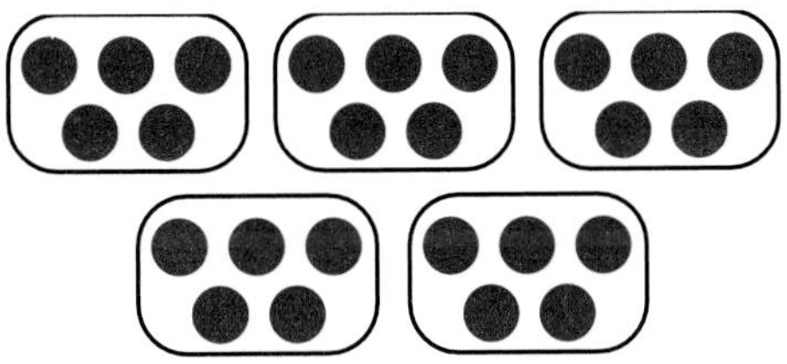

23.

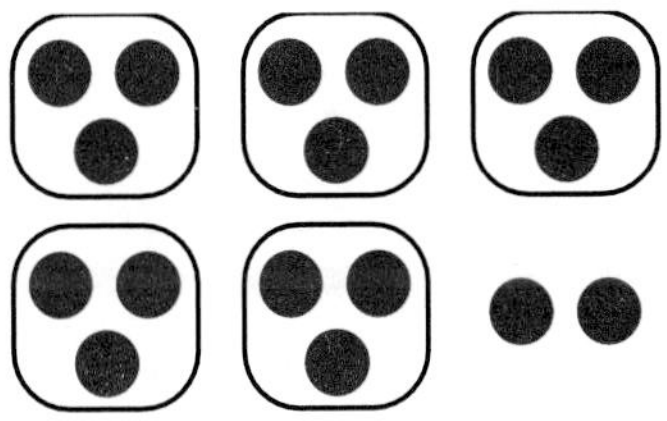

Solve.

24. Carmen collected 48 pictures of famous people. She put 8 pictures on each page of a photo album. How many pages of the album did she fill?

25. There are 7 coins on a table. Some are dimes and some are nickels. Their total value is 55¢. How many of each kind of coin are on the table?

Self-Check Look back at Exercises 16–21. Use a related multiplication fact to check each quotient.

Performance Assessment

Show What You Know About Division

What You Need

27 counters

1. Use counters for Questions 1a and 1b.

   a. Divide 27 counters into equal groups with no counters left over. Do this in as many different ways as you can. Write a division sentence to show each way you find.

   b. Repeat the above activity with 18 counters.

2. Use the red and blue numbers below to answer Question 2a.

   a. Fill the boxes to make division sentences that have remainders of 0. To fill the red boxes, choose from the red numbers. To fill the blue boxes, choose from the blue numbers. Use each number only once.

$\square \div \square = \square$

$\square \div \square = \square$

$\square \div \square = \square$

$\square \div \square = \square$

18 32 28 36

6 8 9 7

Self-Check

For Questions 1a and 1b, did you make sure that you wrote all of the possible division sentences?

For Question 2a, did you check that each division sentence has a remainder of 0?

Extension

A Logical Play

Miss Kopp's third-grade class is putting on a play. There are so many things to think about!

- All students will wear an animal costume.
- Some students will wear a lizard costume.
- No students will wear a dog costume.

1. Will all students wear a lizard costume?

2. Andy has a dog costume and a cat costume. Which one could he wear for this play?

- No students who play parrots use makeup.
- Some students who play tigers use makeup.
- Students who play all the other animals use makeup.

3. May is playing a zebra. Does she need makeup?

4. Stef and Gracie are the same animal. Stef needs makeup and Gracie does not. What animal are they playing?

- There are no lizards in the first act.
- There are some zebras in the second act.
- All the parrots are in the third act.

5. Dirk is playing a parrot. Which act is he definitely in?

6. Cheri is in the first act. Could she be a lizard?

7. Bobby is playing a zebra. Could he be in the second act?

Cumulative Review

Preparing for Tests

Choose the letter for the correct answer.

1. $\begin{array}{r} 592 \\ +\ 284 \\ \hline \end{array}$

A. 776
B. 876
C. 7,176
D. 312
E. none of these

2. 839 – 654

A. 185
B. 285
C. 2,493
D. 225
E. none of these

3. $\begin{array}{r} \$28.10 \\ 74.99 \\ +\ 61.25 \\ \hline \end{array}$

A. 16,434
B. 15,439
C. $164.34
D. $1,643.40
E. none of these

4. What is the value of the digit 5 in 23,570?

A. 50
B. 500
C. 5
D. 5,000
E. none of these

5. Which number sentence is true?

A. $6 \times 3 < 3 \times 6$
B. $6 \times 3 > 3 \times 6$
C. $6 \times 3 = 3 \times 6$
D. $3 \times 6 < 6 \times 3$
E. none of these

6. $\begin{array}{r} 4{,}502 \\ -\ 1{,}916 \\ \hline \end{array}$

A. 6,418
B. 2,696
C. 2,586
D. 3,586
E. none of these

7. Estimate the sum.
72 + 29

A. 100
B. 40
C. 70
D. 200
E. none of these

8. $72 \div 9$

A. 63
B. 81
C. 7
D. 8
E. none of these

9. 4×6

A. 32
B. 10
C. 18
D. 20
E. none of these

10. $5 \times 2 \times 7$

A. 70
B. 17
C. 10
D. 35
E. none of these

11. $\begin{array}{r} \$78.99 \\ -\ 40.00 \\ \hline \end{array}$

A. $38.99
B. $74.99
C. $111.89
D. $118.99
E. none of these

12. Which shows the numbers in order from least to greatest?

A. 437, 374, 347
B. 347, 437, 374
C. 347, 374, 437
D. 374, 347, 437
E. none of these

13. What comes next in the pattern?

A. 

B. 

C. 

D. 

14. Ron has enough money in his pocket to buy 2 pens. Each pen costs 47¢. Which group of coins below shows how much money Ron has?

A. 2 quarters, 4 dimes, 1 penny
B. 3 dimes, 1 nickel, 3 pennies
C. 3 quarters, 3 dimes
D. 5 dimes, 2 nickels, 8 pennies

15. What is the chance that the spinner will land on an even number?

A. 1 chance out of 4
B. 2 chances out of 4
C. 3 chances out of 4
D. none of these

16. A running race began at 1:15 P.M. The last runner went across the finish line at 4:25 P.M. How long did it take the last runner to run the race?

A. 2 hours 10 minutes
B. 3 hours
C. 2 hours 50 minutes
D. none of these

Use the graph to answer Questions 17–20.

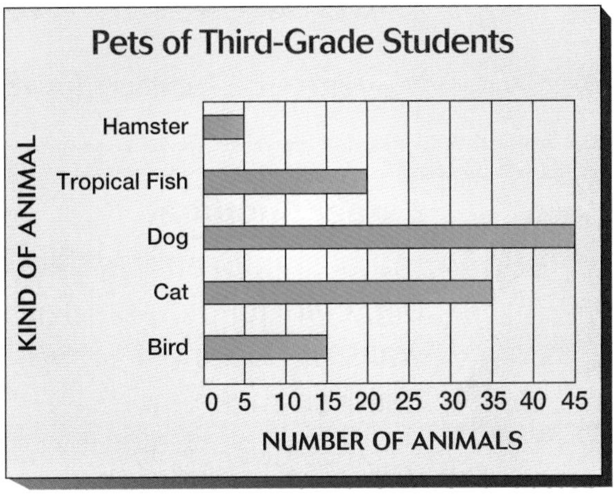

17. What kind of pet is the most popular?

A. Cat
B. Bird
C. Fish
D. Dog

18. How many third-grade students have cats?

A. 25
B. 30
C. 35
D. 40

19. How many more dogs than birds do third-grade students have?

A. 5
B. 10
C. 15
D. 30

20. How many tropical fish and hamsters do the students have in all?

A. 5
B. 15
C. 20
D. 25

Chapter 10

Geometry

Chapter Theme: FINE ARTS

Career Spotlight Meet William Walsh, a muralist in Brooklyn, New York. He paints big, colorful pictures—all on the sides and walls of buildings! Sometimes he helps children make murals in their schools.

Some murals have geometric shapes in them.

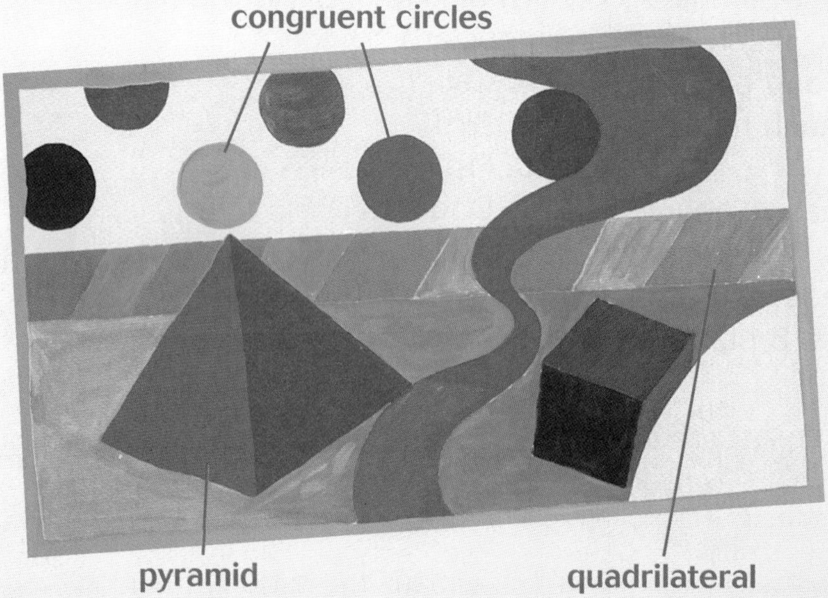

Chapter Project

Make a Mural

Like William Walsh, you and your classmates can plan and create a colorful mural. Before you begin, make these decisions.

- How big will your mural be?
- How will you divide the work?
- Will your mural have a theme, such as "After-School Fun" or "Music in the Air"?

Speller

Getting Into Shapes

You can tell what a figure is by looking at its sides and corners.

Learning About It

Figures come in all shapes and sizes. The figures below are all flat. They are called **plane figures.**

Plane Figures

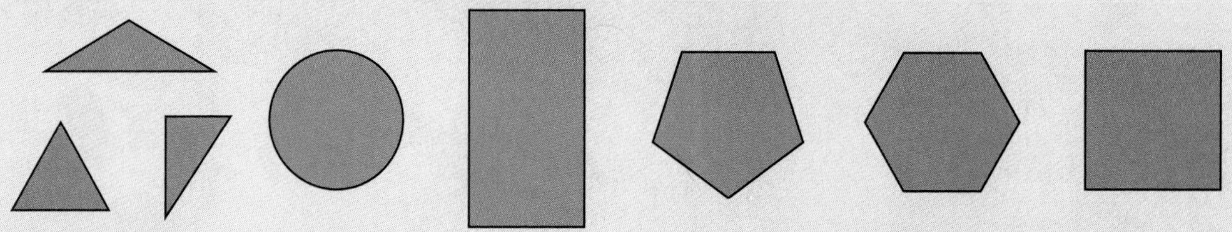

triangles circle rectangle pentagon hexagon square

Look at the pentagon at the right. It has 5 sides and 5 corners.

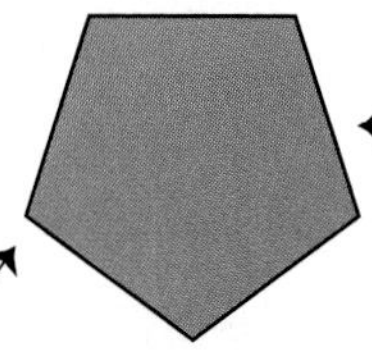

Count the number of sides and corners of each figure shown above. Then copy and fill in the chart below.

Figure	Number of Sides	Number of Corners
Triangle	3	3
Circle	0	0
Rectangle		
Pentagon		
Hexagon		
Square		

What do you notice about the number of sides and corners of each figure?

Connecting Ideas

You have seen how sides and corners help name figures. Now look at these special plane figures called quadrilaterals.

All of the figures above are **quadrilaterals.** What do you think makes a figure a quadrilateral?

www.sbgmath.com

How many sides and corners does each quadrilateral have?

- The rectangle at the right is a special kind of quadrilateral. What makes a rectangle different from other quadrilaterals?

- The square at the right is also a special kind of quadrilateral. What makes a square different from other quadrilaterals?

- Which of the quadrilaterals above looks like a kite?

Look at the quilt at the right. How many different kinds of quadrilaterals can you find in it?

Think and Discuss Look back at the square and the rectangle above. Could you also call a square a rectangle? Explain why or why not.

Fine Arts Connection ➤
This quilt is made from different shapes of material. It was crafted in the same way that American quilt makers used in the 1800s.

Try It Out

Name the plane figure that each object looks like.

1. 

2. 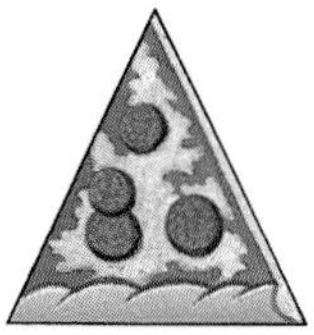

3. 

4. 

5. 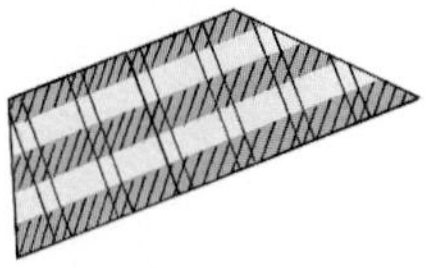

6. 

7. 

8. 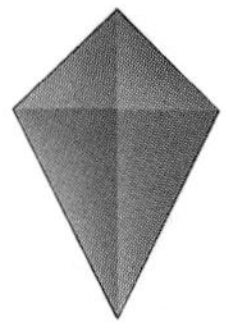

Practice

Tell whether each plane figure is a quadrilateral.

9. 

10. 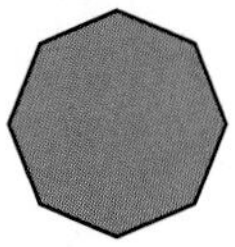

11. 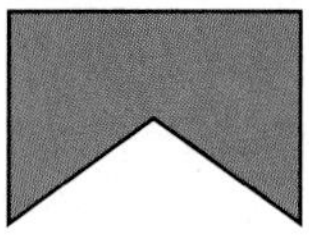

12. 

Name each plane figure. Then tell the number of sides and the number of corners each figure has.

13. 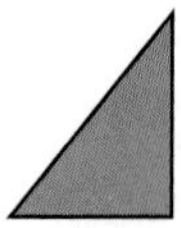

14. 

15. 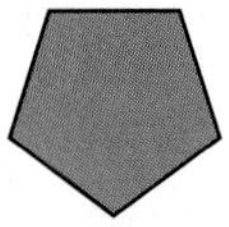

16. 

17. 

18. 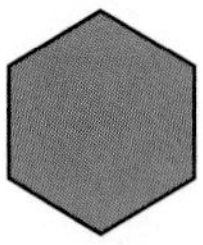

19. 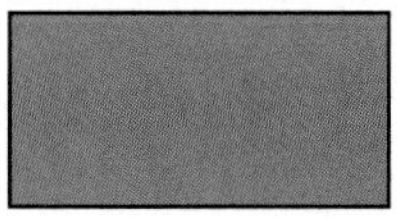

20. 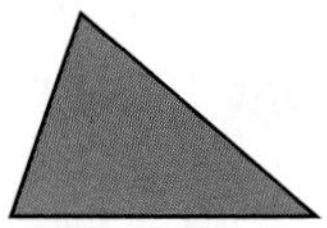

Problem Solving

21. An octagon has 8 sides and 8 corners. Which figure in Exercises 1–12 is an octagon?

22. Look at the signs at the right. Which is the octagon? Which is the circle? Which is the rectangle?

Problem Solving

23. What kinds of plane figures can you find in the quilt at the right?

24. **Analyze** Look back at the square and the rectangle on page 362. How are they the same? How are they different?

25. **Generalize** Are all quadrilaterals rectangles? Why or why not?

26. **Generalize** Are all rectangles quadrilaterals? Why or why not?

Social Studies Connection
This African American quilt uses many plane figures to create a colorful design.

Review and Remember

Using Mental Math Use mental math to find each sum or difference.

27. 340 + 50
28. 2,000 − 600
29. 400 − 100
30. 75 − 25
31. 900 + 400
32. 2,000 + 5,004

Critical Thinking Corner

Visual Thinking

Tangram Shapes

According to a Chinese legend, a man named Tan had a square tile. The tile fell and broke into the 7 pieces shown at the right. The pieces are called **tans**.

Trace the tangram pieces and cut them out. Use all of the pieces to make each of the shapes below.

1.

2.

3.

www.sbgmath.com

What's Your Angle?

Many shapes are made from line segments and angles.

Learning About It

Lines are everywhere. Can you find anything that looks like lines or line segments in this Navajo blanket?

A **line** is straight. It goes on and on in both directions.

A **line segment** is part of a line. It has 2 endpoints.

A **ray** is part of a line. It has one endpoint. It goes on and on in one direction.

An angle is formed when 2 rays meet.

Right angles form square corners.

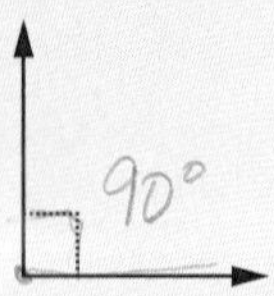

Some angles are less than right angles.

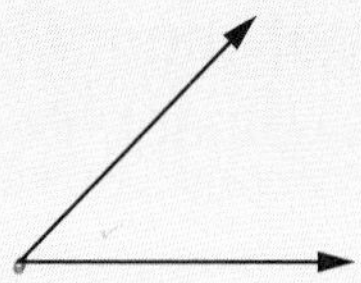

Some angles are greater than right angles.

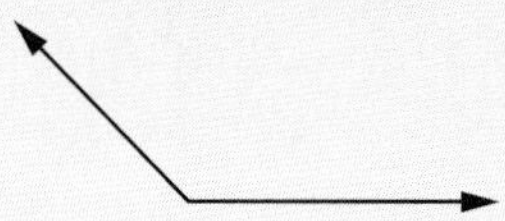

Look around the classroom. Find as many line segments and angles as you can.

Think and Discuss How many different kinds of angles can you find in the Navajo blanket above?

Try It Out

Match each figure with its correct name.

1. 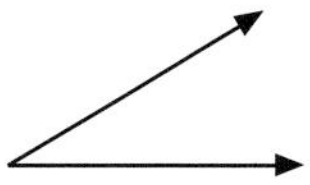

2. 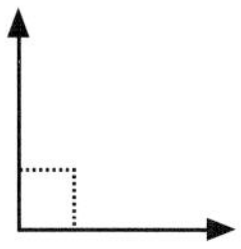

3. 

4. 

5.

6. 

a. right angle
b. line
c. line segment
d. less than a right angle
e. ray

Practice

Tell whether each figure is a line, line segment, or ray.

7. 

8. 

9. 

10. 

Write *right angle, less than a right angle,* or *greater than a right angle* to name each angle.

11. 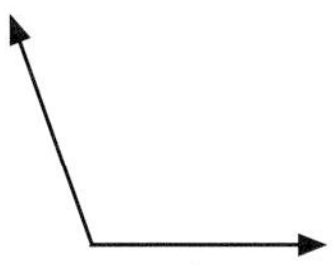

12. 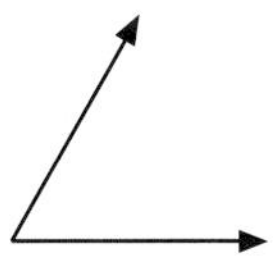

13. 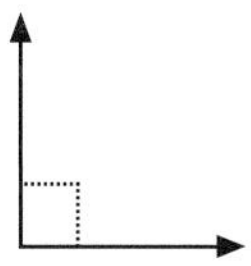

14. 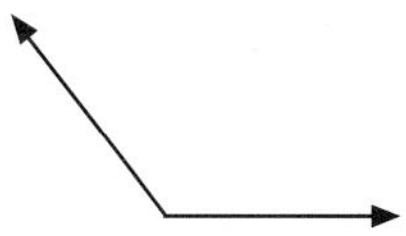

Problem Solving

15. Joshua used 22 craft sticks to make separate triangles. What is the greatest number of triangles he could make?

16. **Analyze** A figure is made with 4 equal line segments. All of its angles are right angles. What is the name of the figure?

17. Draw a square and a triangle. How many angles did you draw?

18. What kind of angle do the hands of a clock show at 9:00?

Review and Remember

Choose a Method Use mental math or paper and pencil to find each answer. Tell which method you used.

19. $\begin{array}{r} 3{,}429 \\ +\ 6{,}587 \\ \hline \end{array}$ **20.** $\begin{array}{r} 890 \\ -\ 400 \\ \hline \end{array}$ **21.** $\begin{array}{r} 7{,}457 \\ +\ 3{,}286 \\ \hline \end{array}$ **22.** $\begin{array}{r} 500 \\ +\ 510 \\ \hline \end{array}$ **23.** $\begin{array}{r} 7{,}444 \\ -\ 5{,}000 \\ \hline \end{array}$

For Extra Practice, see Set B, page 394.

Developing Skills for Problem Solving

First read for understanding and then look at figures to find shapes and patterns.

READ FOR UNDERSTANDING

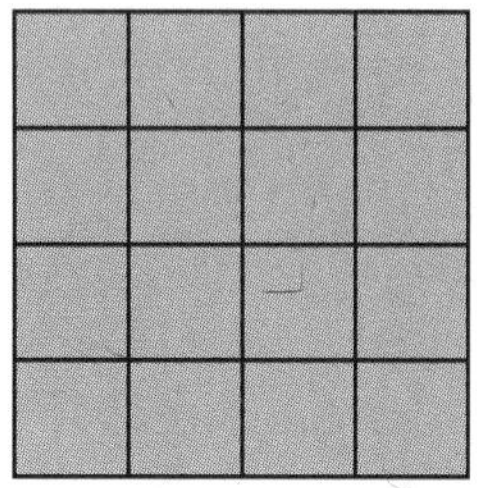

James looked at the figure at the right. Then he showed it to Annie and told her that there are 16 squares in it. Annie looked at the figure and said she could see more than 16 squares.

1. How many squares did James see in the figure?
2. How many squares did Annie see?

THINK AND DISCUSS

MATH FOCUS

Spatial Reasoning If you look at a figure carefully, sometimes you can find geometric shapes and patterns. These shapes and patterns may be able to help you solve problems.

Look again at the figure at the top of the page.

3. How many squares of this size can you find?

4. How many squares of this size can you find?

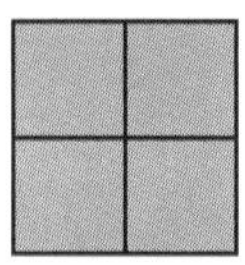

5. How many squares of this size can you find?

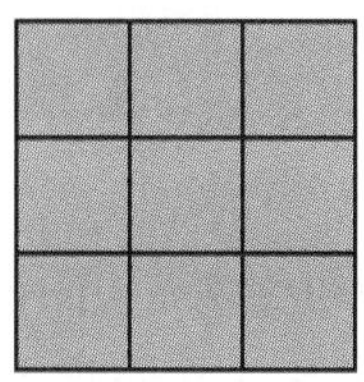

6. What is the biggest square you can find?
7. How many squares can you find in the figure?
8. Why do you think James counted only 16 squares?

Show What You Learned

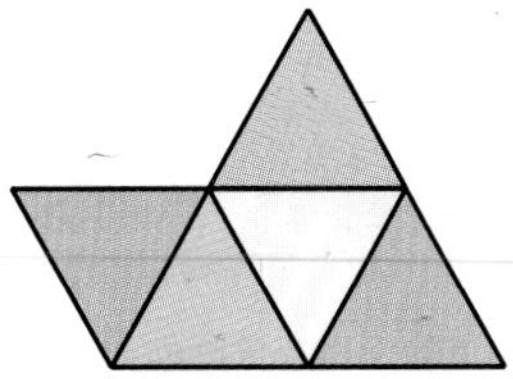

Use the figure at the right to answer Problems 1–3. Give a reason for your choice.

1. How many triangles are there in the design?
   a. 6
   b. 7
   c. 5

2. How many quadrilaterals are there in the design?
   a. 6
   b. 9
   c. 8

3. Which of these shows the above design from a different position?

a. 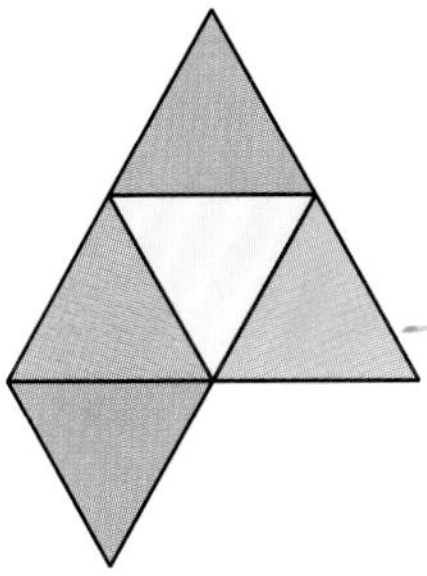

b. 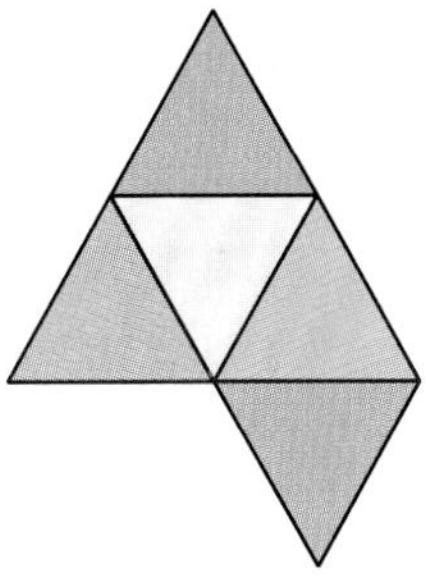

c. 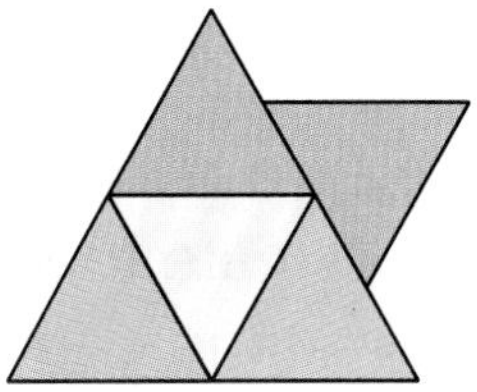

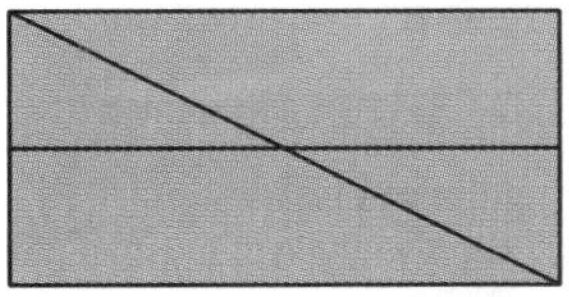

Use the figure at the right to answer Problems 4–5. Give a reason for your choice.

4. How many rectangles are there in the design?
   a. 4
   b. 3
   c. 5

5. How many triangles are there in the design?
   a. 2
   b. 5
   c. 4

6. **Explain** Henna says she can make 9 rectangles with 6 popsicle sticks. Draw a picture to show how she could do it.

All the Same to Me!

Some plane figures are the same size and shape.

Learning About It

Look at this potato stamp design.
All of the stars are the same.

Figures with the same size and shape are **congruent.**

Work with your partner.

- Draw a rectangle on dot paper. Then ask a classmate to make another rectangle that is the same size and shape. Cut out the rectangles and compare them. Are they congruent?
- Take turns. Draw other figures on the dot paper. Then draw a congruent figure for each one. Cut out the figures to see if they match.

What You Need

For each pair:
dot paper

More Examples

A. 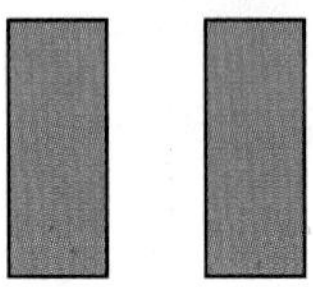

Congruent

B. 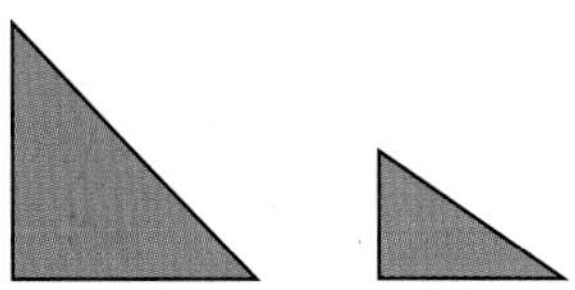

Not congruent

C. 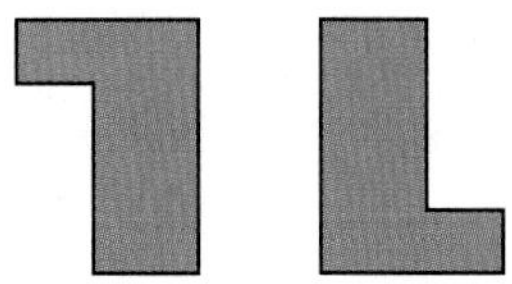

Congruent

Think and Discuss Could a triangle and square ever be congruent? Explain your answer.

Try It Out

Are the figures in each pair congruent?

1. 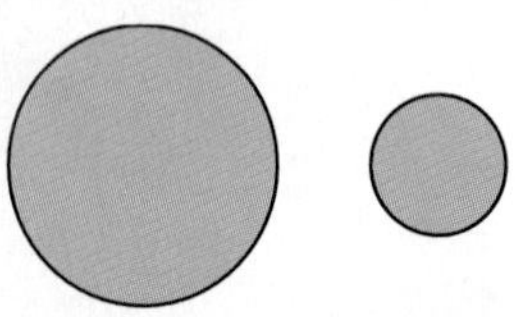

2. 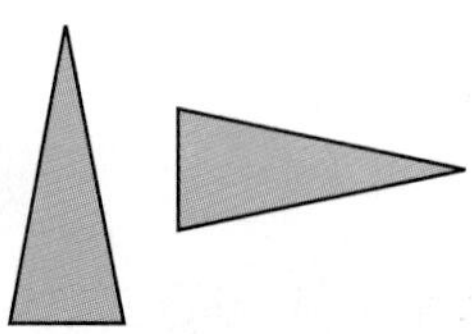

3. 

Practice

Are the figures in each pair congruent?

4. 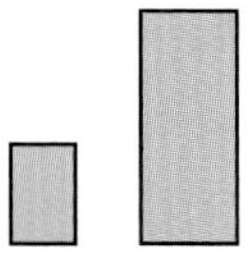

5. 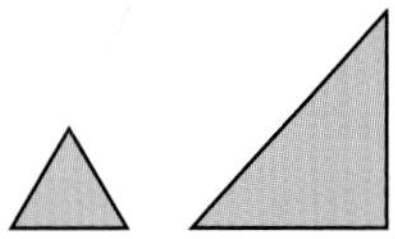

6. 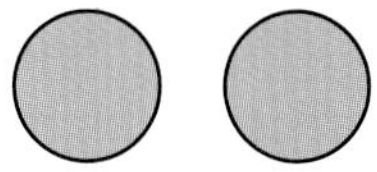

7. 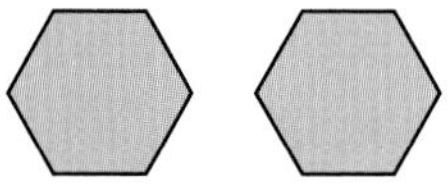

8. 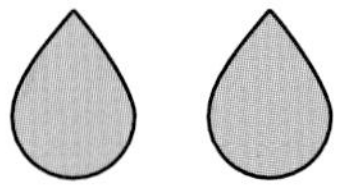

9. 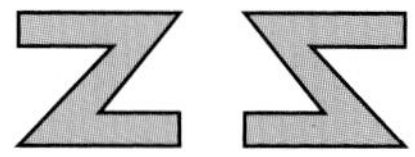

10. 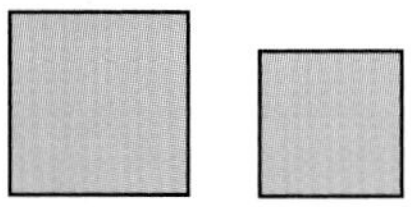

11. 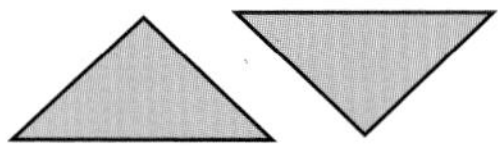

12. 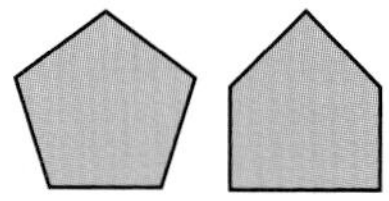

Problem Solving

13. **Social Studies Connection** Look at the American flag in your classroom. Are the stars congruent? Are the stripes congruent?

14. **Analyze** Suppose you had two squares. How could you decide if they are congruent without tracing them and cutting them out?

15. **Create Your Own** Cut out a pair of congruent figures. Then cut out 3 more figures that are not congruent. Mix up all of the figures. Ask a classmate to find the pair of congruent figures.

Using Algebra

Review and Remember

What number does the triangle stand for in each number sentence?

16. 8 + ▲ = 12

17. 14 − ▲ = 6

18. ▲ + 0 = 25

19. 3 × ▲ = 3

20. ▲ ÷ 2 = 4

21. 4 × ▲ = 12

22. ▲ + 7 = 11

23. 16 ÷ ▲ = 4

Project Link

How can geometric figures help you plan your mural?

- You might draw circles for the wheels of a car or a bus.
- You might draw a rectangle for a window.

Think of ways to use shapes, lines, and angles in your work.

For Extra Practice, see Set C, page 395.

Big Shape, Little Shape

Some figures are the same shape but different sizes.

Learning About It

Congruent figures have the same shape *and* the same size. Sometimes though, figures have the same shape but *different* sizes.

What You Need

For each pair:
grid paper in two sizes

Work with your partner.

Step 1 Number a sheet of grid paper as shown at the right. Then make a design like the one shown.

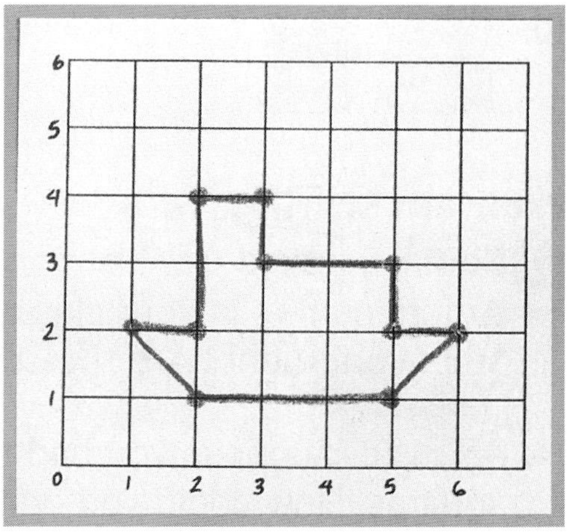

Step 2 Repeat Step 1, only this time use grid paper that has smaller squares. Compare the two designs. How are they the same? How are they different?

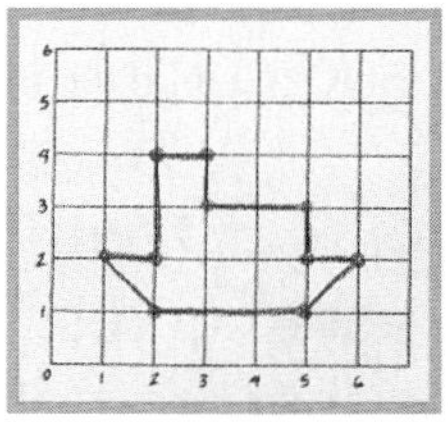

▶ Figures that are the same shape are **similar**. They do not have to be the same size.

Step 3 Repeat Steps 1 and 2 at least four times. Draw different sets of similar figures each time.

Step 4 Mix up all your figures. Challenge another pair of students to match the similar figures.

Think and Discuss

How are similar figures different from congruent figures?

Practice

Which pairs are similar? Which pairs are congruent?

1. 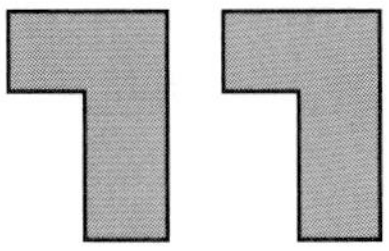

2. 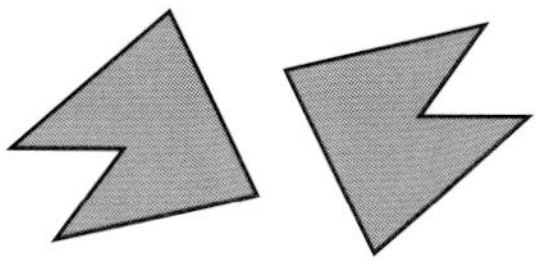

3. 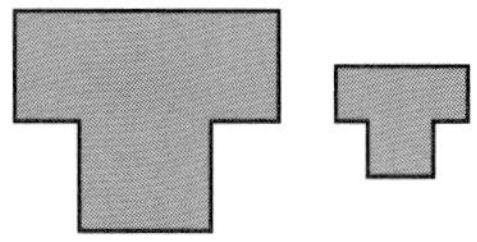

4. 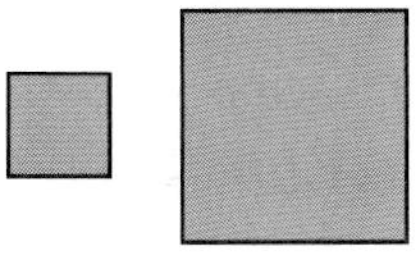

5. 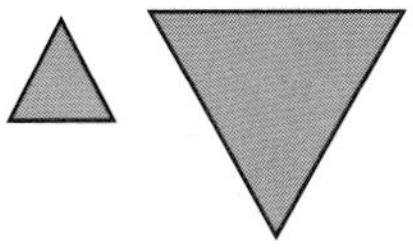

6. 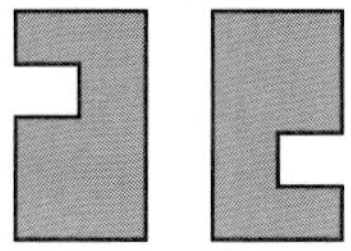

7. 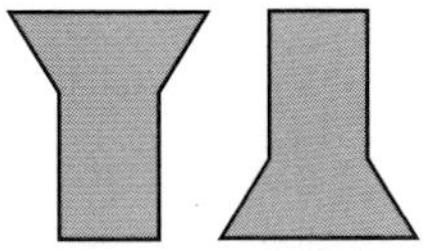

8. 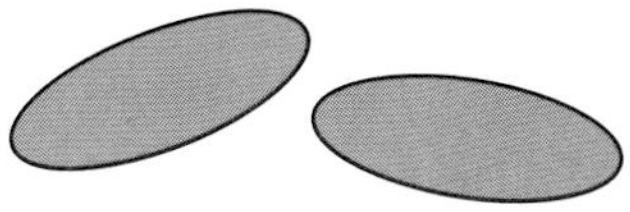

9. 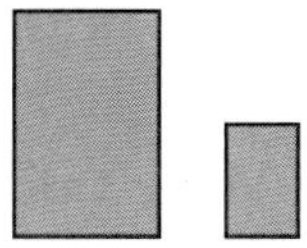

10. Can you draw circles that are not similar? Explain your answer.

11. Can you draw squares that are not similar? Explain your answer.

Time for Technology

Using CD-ROM

Making Similar Triangles

You can use the geometry tool to show similar figures.

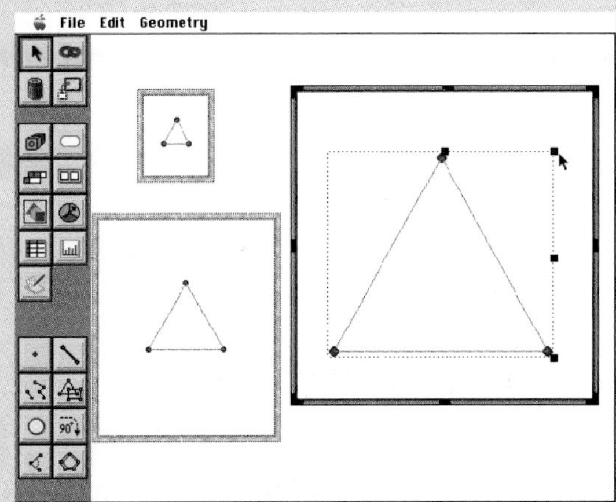

- Open a geometry space. Make the space small.
- Click and make a triangle.
- Open another geometry space and make it larger than the first. Make a triangle in it.
- Open a third geometry space and make it very large. Make another triangle in it.

Look at the triangles. Are they all similar? How do you know?

A Mirror Image

Sometimes half of a figure matches the other half.

Learning About It

Work with your group.

Step 1 Take a sheet of paper and fold it in half. Then cut out a figure like the one shown. Make sure to begin and end along the folded edge of the paper.

Look at your cutout figure. The fold divides the figure in half. Is the figure the same on both sides of the fold?

- A figure is **symmetric** if both sides match each other exactly.
- The line that divides the figure into matching parts is a **line of symmetry**.

Step 2 Repeat Step 1 at least four more times. Each time, look to see how each side of your cutout figure matches the other side.

What You Need

For each group:
scissors
construction paper

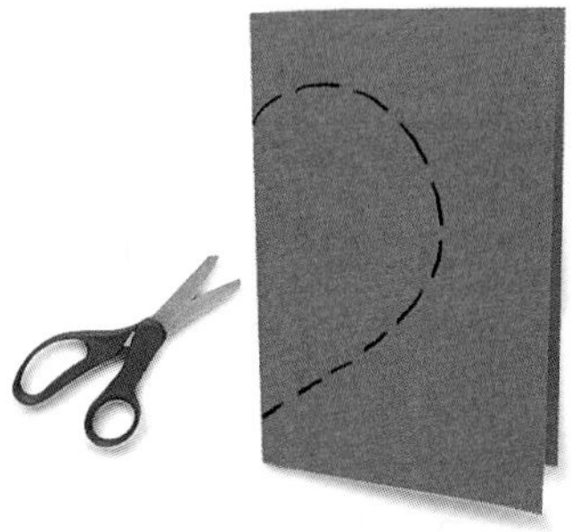

Step 3 Trace each of the figures at the right. Then cut them out. Fold each shape to try to find a line of symmetry.

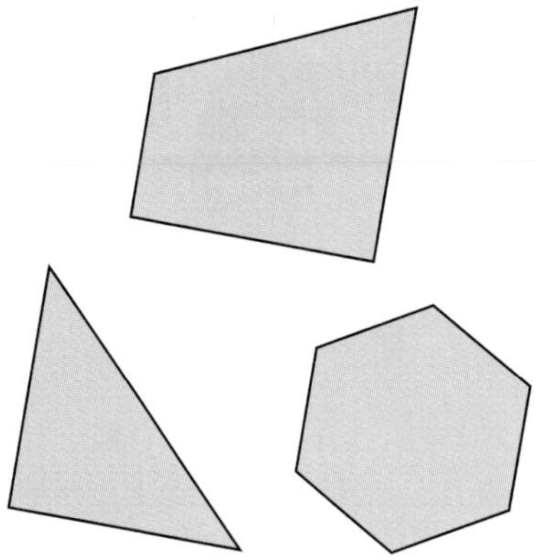

- Which of the figures at the right have lines of symmetry?
- Which of the figures has more than one line of symmetry?

Think and Discuss How many lines of symmetry do you think a circle has?

Practice

Look at each figure. Tell whether the dotted line is a line of symmetry.

1. 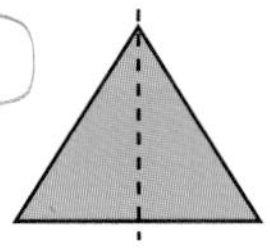
2. 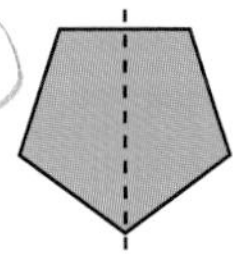
3. 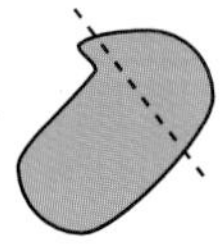
4. 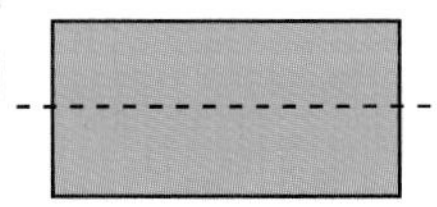
5. 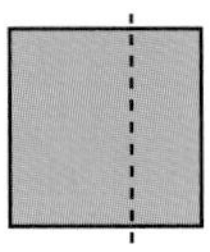
6. 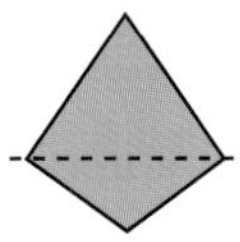
7. 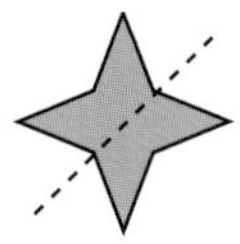
8. 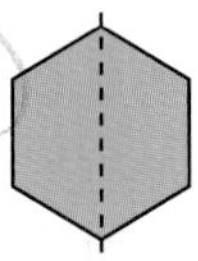

Trace each figure. Then draw a line of symmetry.

9. 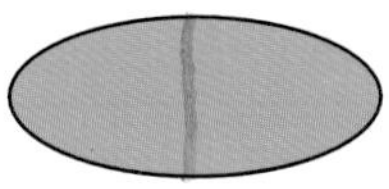
10. 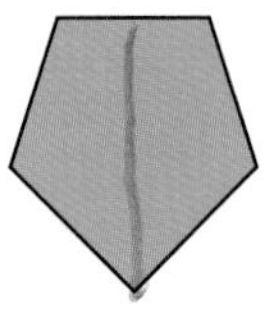
11. 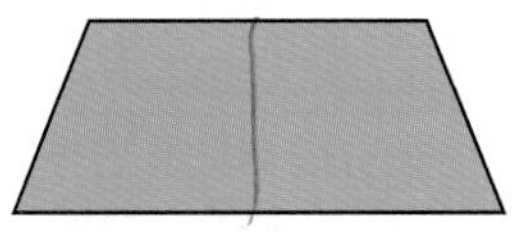

12. Which figure below has no line of symmetry?

a. 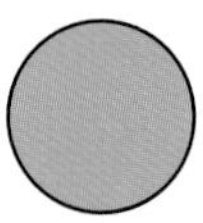

b. 

c. 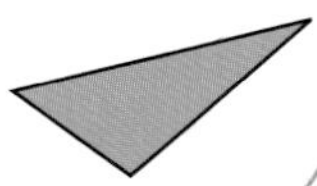

Fine Arts Connection Ukrainian eggs like this one are famous for their beautiful designs. Often the decorated eggs show symmetry. To make a design, an egg is dipped into different colored dyes. Each time, parts of the egg are covered with wax. Wherever there is wax, the color does not stick.

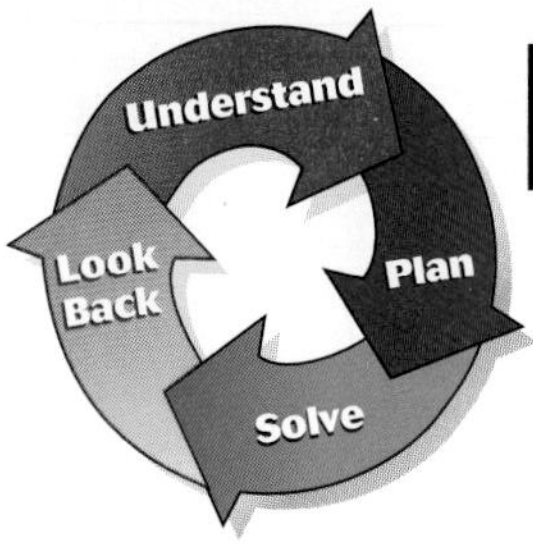

Problem Solving
Find a Pattern

Sometimes finding a pattern can help you solve a problem.

Becky is making a necklace. Look at the beads she has put on the necklace so far. If she continues the pattern, what color will the 20th bead be?

UNDERSTAND

What do you need to know?

You need to know the order in which the colored beads are put on the necklace.

PLAN

How can you solve the problem?

You can **find a pattern** by looking at how the beads have been put on the necklace. Then continue the pattern up to the 20th bead.

SOLVE

Becky puts on 1 bead of each color, then 2 beads of each color, and then 3 beads of each color. She always puts the colors in the same order.

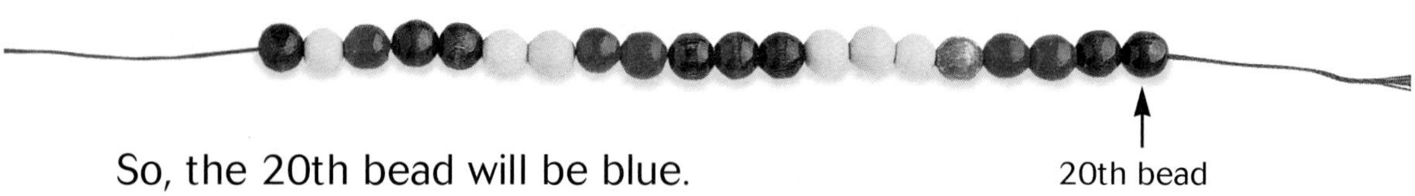

So, the 20th bead will be blue.

LOOK BACK

If the beads were not put on in a pattern, could you still tell what color the 20th bead would be? Explain.

Using the Strategy

Find a pattern to solve each problem.

1. Daniel drew the pattern shown at the right. Draw the next two figures in the pattern.

2. Nadine made the pattern at the right using plane figures. Draw the next four figures in the pattern.

3. Tom wrote the numbers 3, 6, 9, 12, and 15. If he continues the pattern, what are the next five numbers Tom should write?

4. Ms. Martin gave her students a number pattern. She said, "5, 10, 8, 13, 11, 16, 14." What are the next six numbers in her pattern?

5. A dance teacher calls out dance moves: "left, right, forward, back, left, right, forward, back!" If these moves keep repeating, what will the 11th move be?

6. Ellie wrote the following letters: A B B C D A B B C D A B B C D A B B. If she continues the pattern, what will the next four letters be?

Mixed Strategy Review

Try these or other strategies you have learned.

- *Guess and Check*
- *Make a Graph*
- *Act It Out*
- *Find a Pattern*

7. Wendy recorded the number of shapes she found in the classroom. Make a graph to organize the data. How many more squares than triangles did she find?

Shape	Number Found
Circle	𝍸 ||||
Rectangle	𝍸 |||
Triangle	𝍸 𝍸	
Square	𝍸 𝍸 ||

8. Tom has a ball. He passes it to Wally, and Wally passes it to Anne. Anne passes it back to Tom. If they continue in this order, who will catch the ball on the 10th throw?

9. Together, Molly and Zach drew 16 shapes to put on the bulletin board. Molly drew 2 more shapes than Zach drew. How many shapes did they each draw?

Checkpoint

Plane Figures

Name each plane figure. (pages 362–365)

1. 
2. 
3. 
4. 
5. 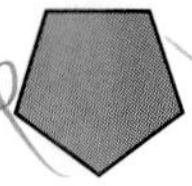
6. 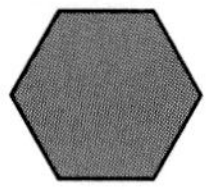

Write *line, line segment,* or *ray* to name each figure. (pages 366–367)

7. 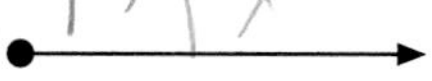
8. 
9. 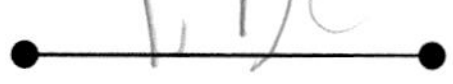

Write *right angle, less than a right angle,* or *greater than a right angle* to name each angle. (pages 366–367)

10. 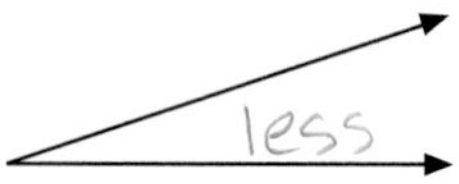
11. 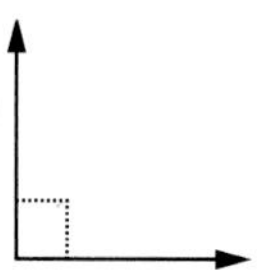
12. 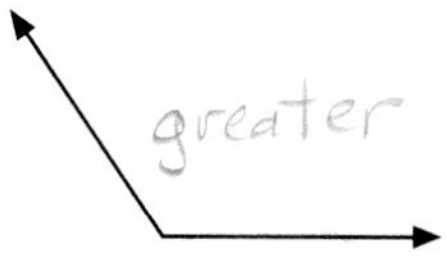

Tell whether each pair of figures is congruent. (pages 370–371)

13. 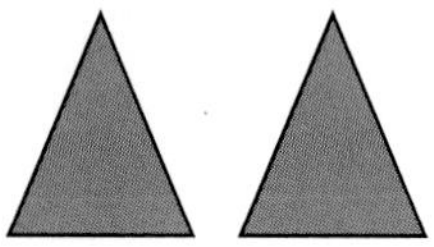
14. 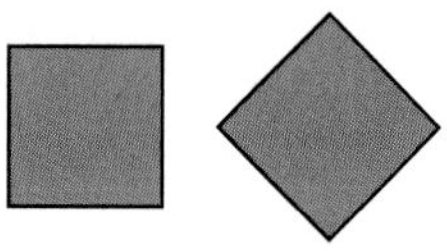
15. 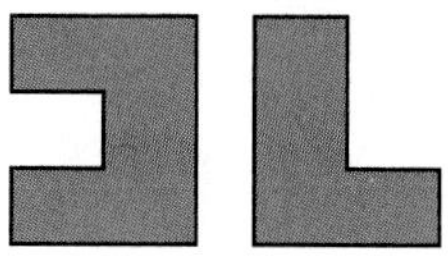

Tell whether each pair of figures is similar. (pages 372–373)

16. 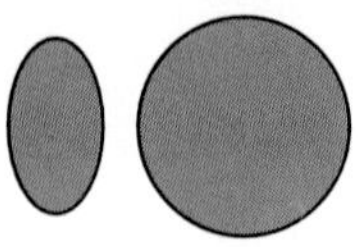
17. 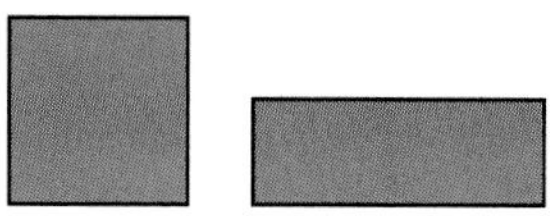
18. 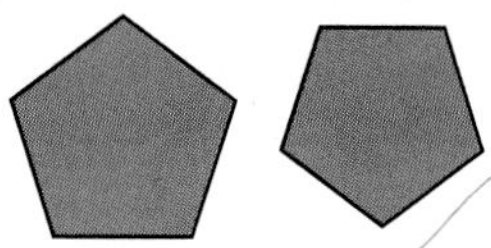

Tell whether each dotted line is a line of symmetry. (pages 374–375)

19. 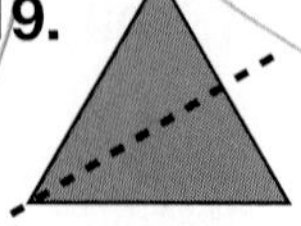
20. 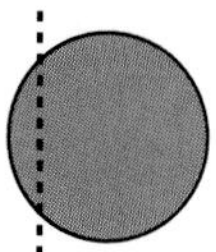
21. 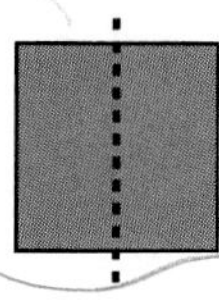

Problem Solving

22. Caroline drew 3 triangles, 3 circles, and 3 squares. How many angles did she draw?

23. Vanessa made a picture with 8 plane figures. Each figure had the same number of sides. She counted 24 sides in all. What plane figures did Vanessa use?

24. Jon draws 2 triangles. Could you tell if the triangles are similar to each other without looking at them? Explain why or why not.

25. How can you tell whether two plane figures are congruent to each other?

Journal Idea Explain to a friend how to draw a pentagon.

What do you think?

Suppose you make a plane figure that has 7 line segments. How many angles does your figure have?

Critical Thinking Corner

Visual Thinking

Shape Hunt

1. How many triangles can you find in the shape below?

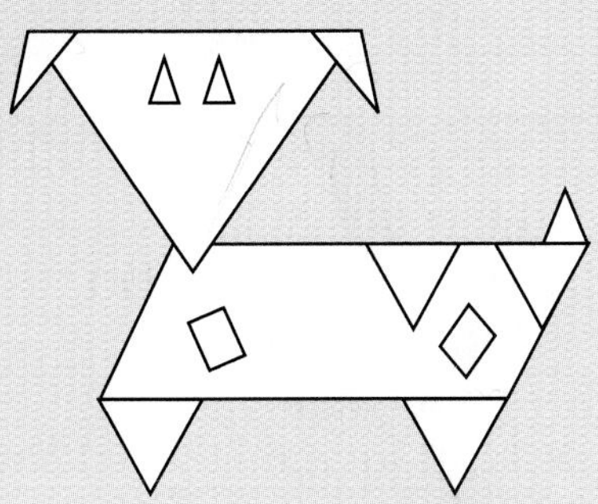

2. How many rectangles can you find in the shape below?

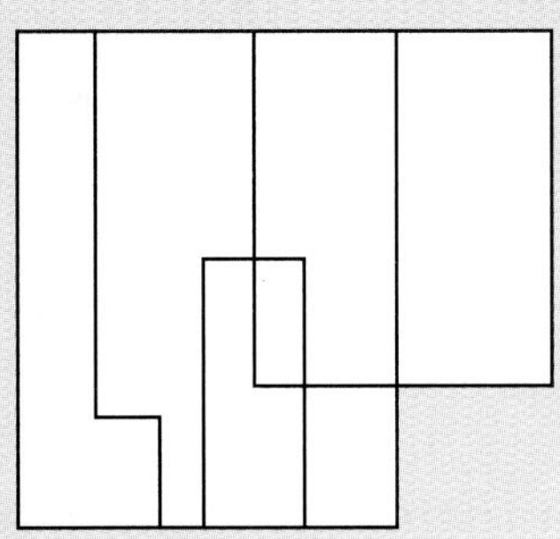

Going the Distance

You can measure the distance around a figure.

Learning About It

What You Need

For each pair:
paper clips

With glue and some fun materials, you can decorate a box. Krista put paper clips around the top of this box. How many paper clips did she use?

▶ The distance around a figure is called its **perimeter.**

Use paper clips to find the perimeter of your math book or desk. How many paper clips did you use?

Using objects like paper clips is one way to find perimeter. But is it the best way?

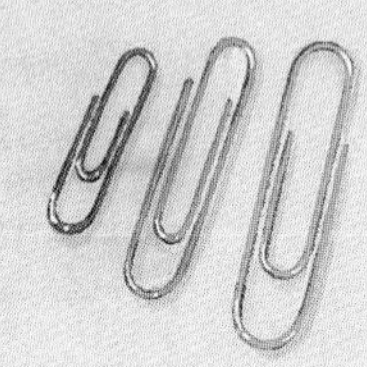

Paper clips can be different sizes, so your answer may be different each time.

Paper clips don't always fit exactly around the edge of a figure.

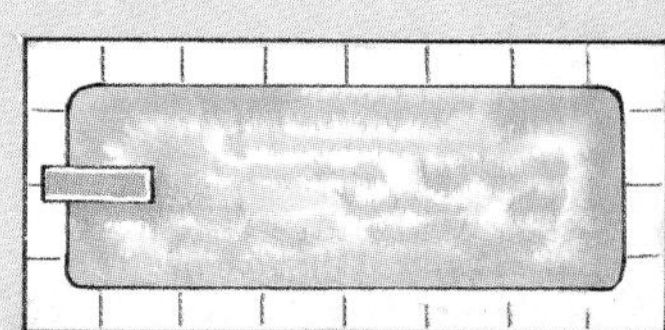

It would be hard to use paper clips to measure the perimeter of large figures.

A more *exact* way to find perimeter is to use a standard measure, like inches or meters.

To find the perimeter of a figure, add the lengths of the sides. The perimeter of the figure at the right is 9 inches.

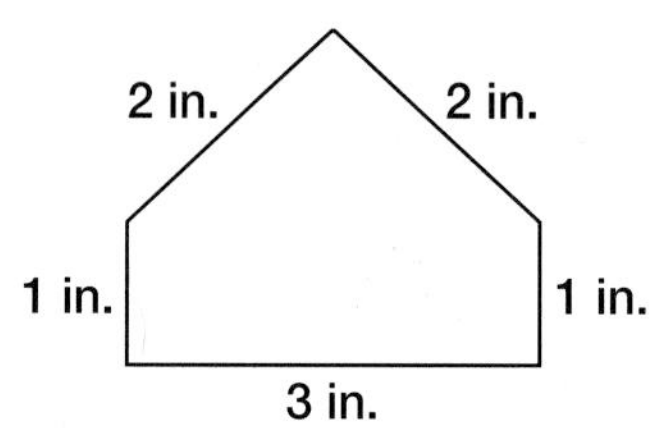

1 + 2 + 2 + 1 + 3 = 9 in.

Think and Discuss Would it be better to use inches or yards to find the perimeter of your school cafeteria? Explain.

Try It Out

Find each perimeter. Label your answer.

1.

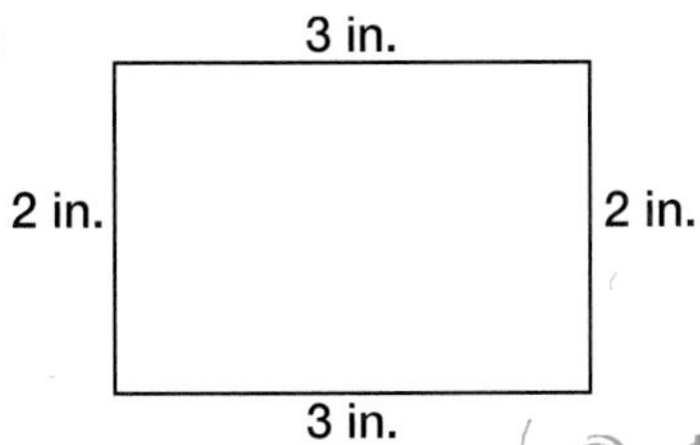

2.

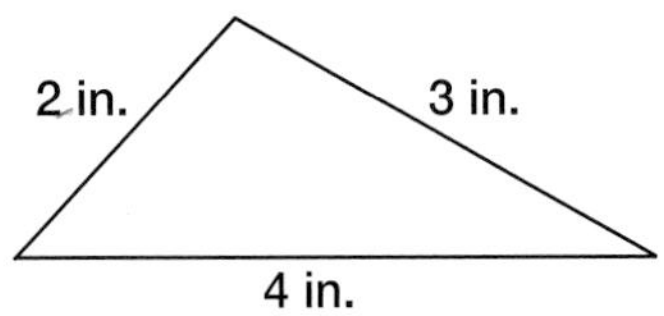

3.

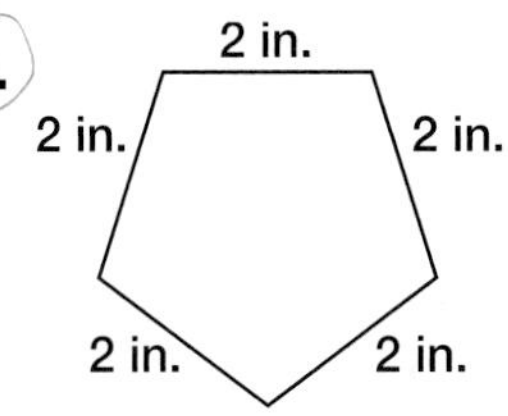

Practice

Find each perimeter. Label your answer.

4.

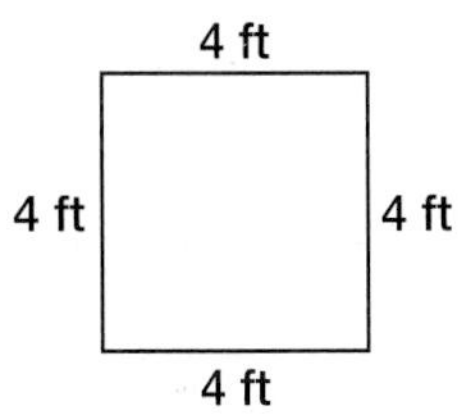

5.

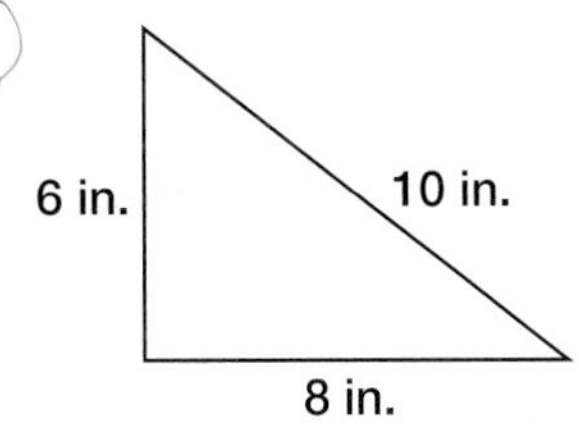

6.

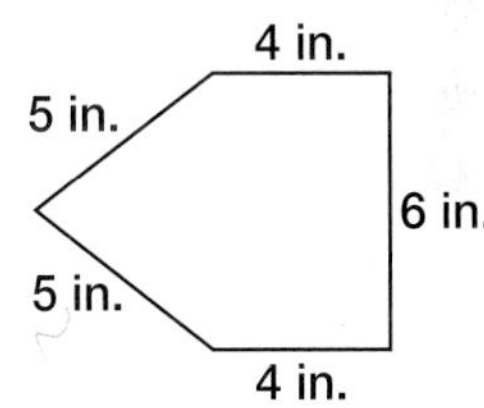

Problem Solving

7. The perimeter of the shape at the right is 26 feet. How long is the left side of the shape?

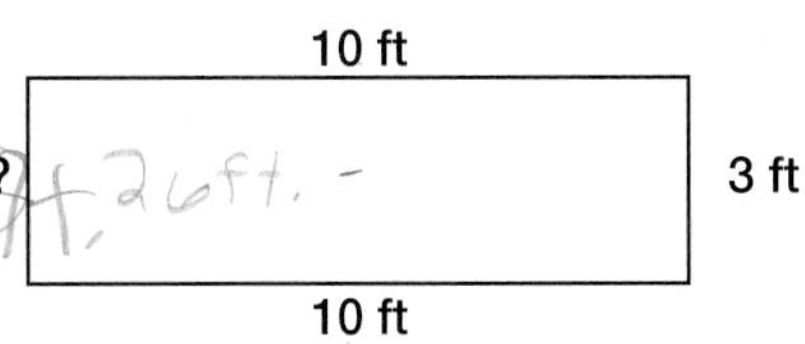

8. Lenny made a square picture. One side is 14 inches long. What is the perimeter of the picture?

9. Use a calculator to find the perimeter of the figure at the right.

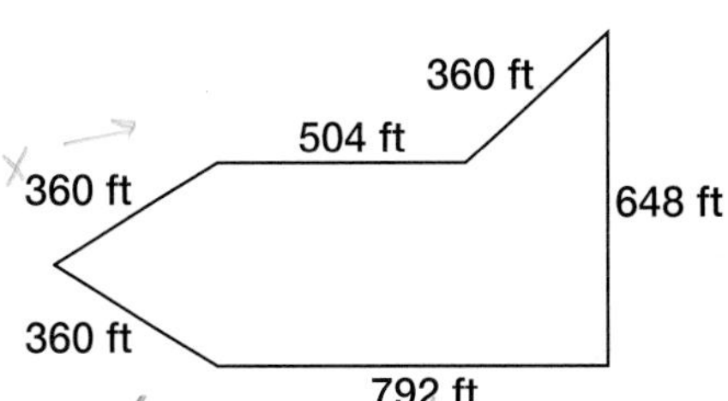

Review and Remember

Find each answer.

10. 840 + 280 **11.** 36 ÷ 9 **12.** 65 − 47 **13.** 4 × 8

14. 756 − 48 **15.** 9 × 5 **16.** 35 + 97 **17.** 56 ÷ 8

For Extra Practice, see Set D, page 395.

Cover Up

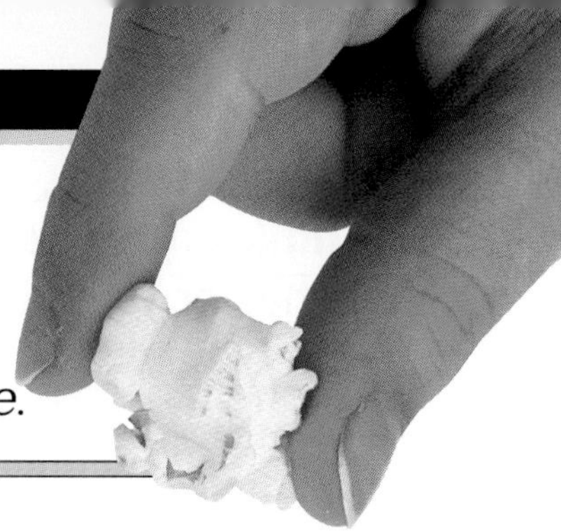

You can find out how many square units cover a figure.

Learning About It

How many pieces of popcorn do you think it would take to cover your hand?

Work with your group.

What You Need

For each group:
popped popcorn
color tiles
one-inch grid paper

Step 1 Trace your hand on paper. Then cover the outline with pieces of popcorn. How many pieces did you use?

Step 2 Use a sheet of one-inch grid paper. Draw a rectangle that is 4 inches by 6 inches. Then cover the rectangle with popcorn.

- How many pieces of popcorn did you use?
- Did you cover the whole grid exactly?
- Did other groups use the same number of pieces?

Step 3 Try covering the grid paper by using square color tiles. How many square tiles do you think it would take to cover the grid?

Estimate first. Then cover the grid with tiles.

- How many tiles did you use?
- Did other groups use the same number of tiles?
- Which covered the grid more completely, popcorn or tiles?

▶ The number of square units needed to cover a figure is called its **area.**

Step 4 Look back at the tiles you used to cover the rectangle. The tiles form an array of square units.

- How many rows of tiles are there?
- How many tiles are in each row?
- What multiplication sentence could you use to find the area in square units?

Think and Discuss What is the difference between area and perimeter?

Practice

Find the area of each figure. Label your answer in square units.

1. 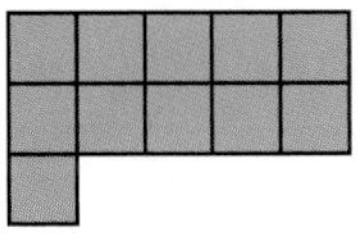

2. 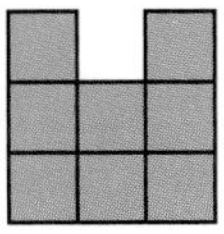

3. 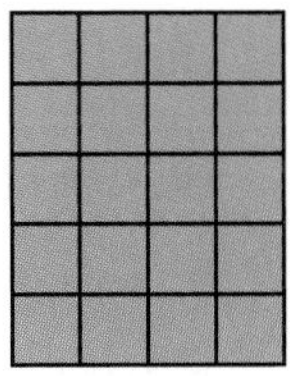

4. 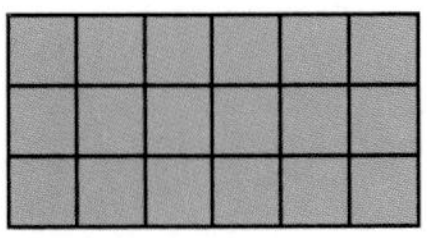

5. 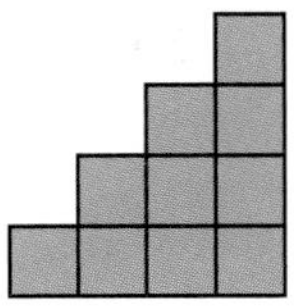

6. 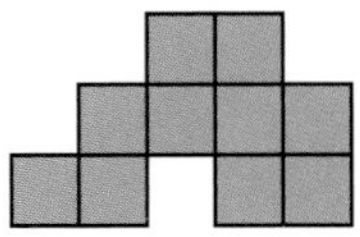

7. 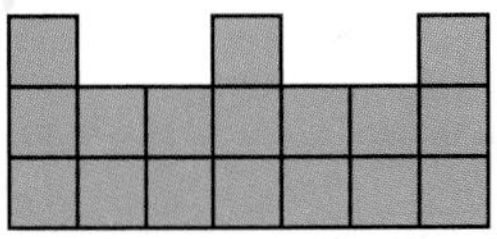

8. 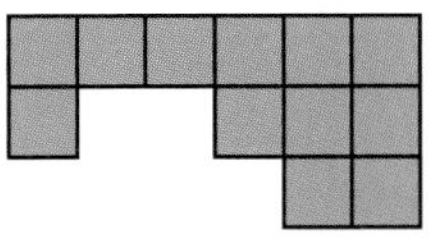

9. 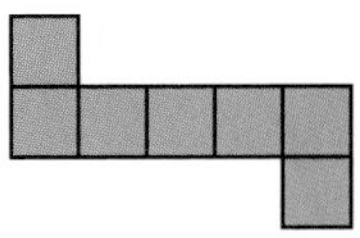

10. Which areas in Exercises 1–9 could be found by multiplying?

11. **Analyze** Which figure below has an area of 12 square units?

a. 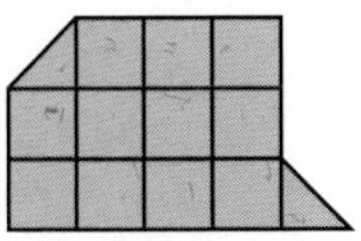

b. 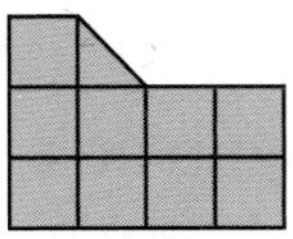

c. 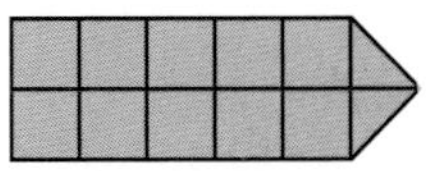

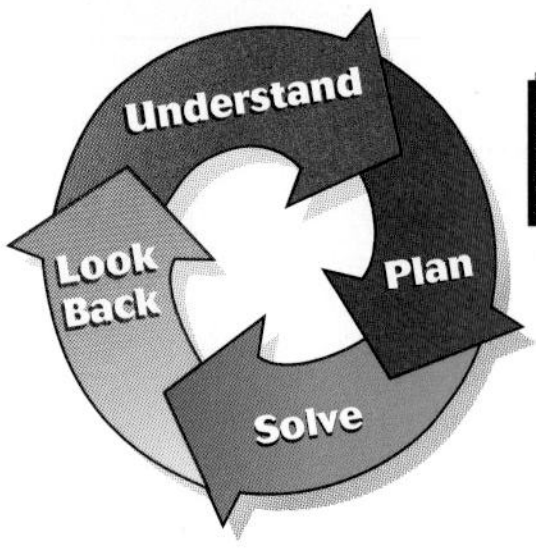

Problem Solving
Using Area and Perimeter

Put your understanding of area and perimeter to work.

Paul drew a picture on a piece of grid paper. He wants to glue a piece of yarn around the outside of his picture. The picture is 7 inches long and 5 inches wide. How much yarn does Paul need?

UNDERSTAND

What do you need to know?

You need to know the distance around Paul's picture, or the perimeter of Paul's picture.

PLAN

How can you solve the problem?

You can find the length of each side of the picture and then add the lengths together.

SOLVE

The lengths of the sides of the picture are 5 inches, 7 inches, 5 inches, and 7 inches.

$5 + 7 + 5 + 7 = 24$ inches

Paul needs 24 inches of yarn.

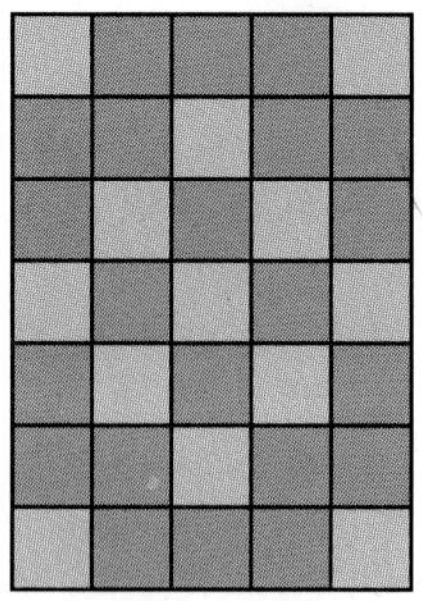

LOOK BACK

Does the order in which you add the sides affect the perimeter? Explain why or why not.

Show What You Learned

Use area and perimeter to answer Problems 1–8.

1. Shelly's flower garden is 4 feet long and 3 feet wide. She divides her garden into 1-foot squares. Shelly is watering her garden. So far she has covered 2 squares with water. How many squares are left to water?

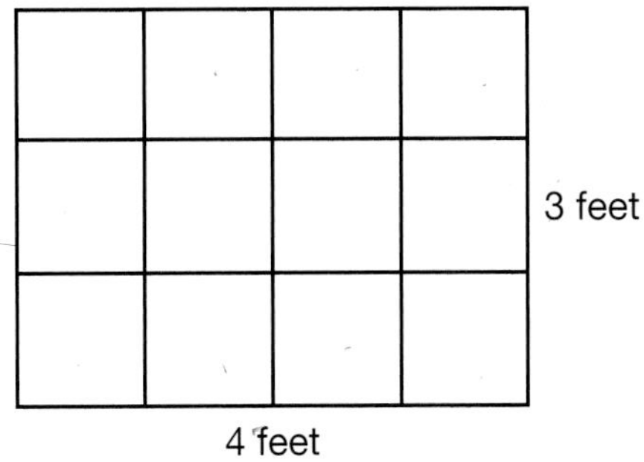

2. Suppose Shelly wants to put a border around her garden. How many feet of border will she need?

3. Jane colored this design on grid paper. What is the area of the colored design?

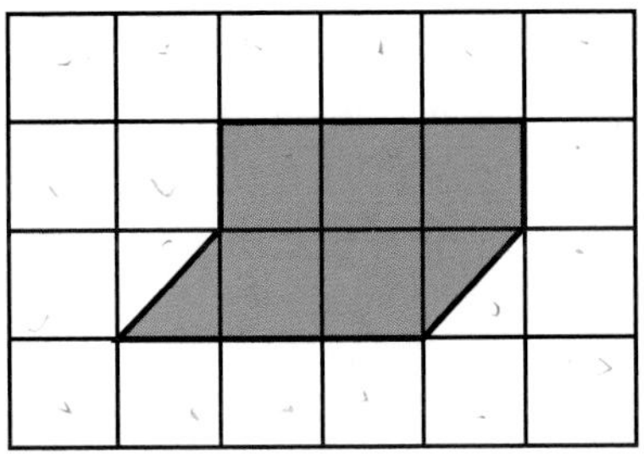

4. What is the area of Jane's grid paper that is not colored?

5. Darlene has a piece of grid paper that is 10 square units long and 4 square units wide. She colors in 18 square units on the grid paper. How many square units on the grid paper are not colored?

6. **Analyze** Harold made a square drawing in art class. He wants to put construction paper around the edge of his drawing. If one side of his drawing is 11 inches long, how many inches of construction paper does Harold need in all?

7. Kate wants to make a tile design that is 6 inches by 4 inches. Each tile is 1 square inch. How many tiles will Kate need to fill the area?

8. **Create Your Own** Write a problem about area or perimeter.

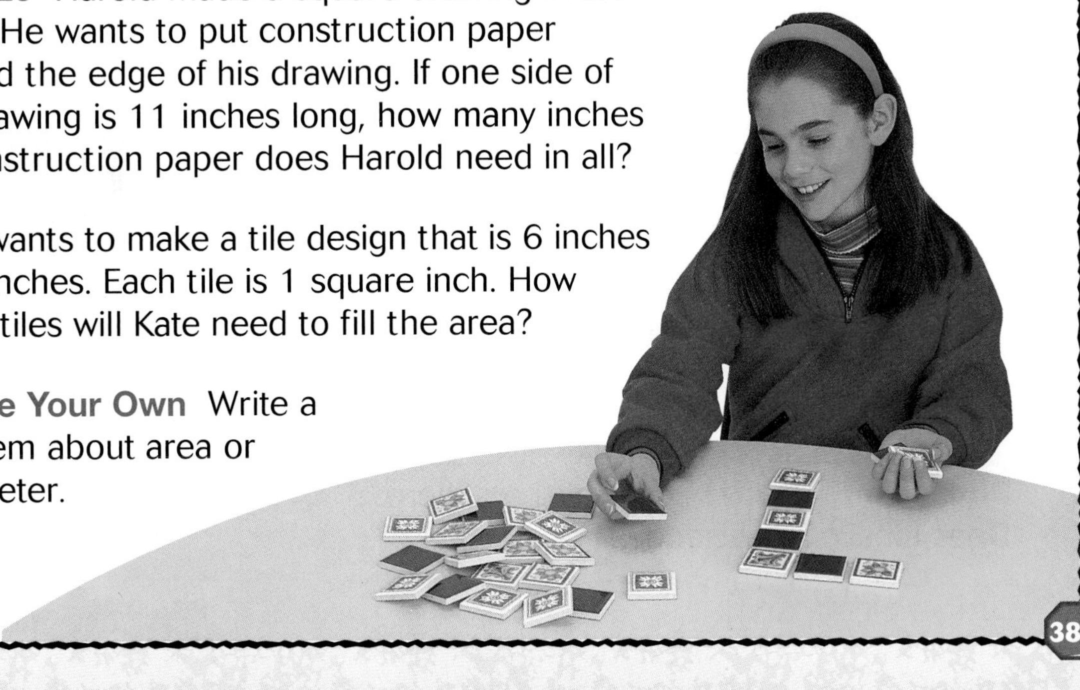

Figure It Out

Faces, edges, and corners can help you name space figures.

Learning About It

Look at the castle sculpture at the right. It is made up of **space figures** like the ones below. Which of the space figures below can you find in the castle?

Space Figures

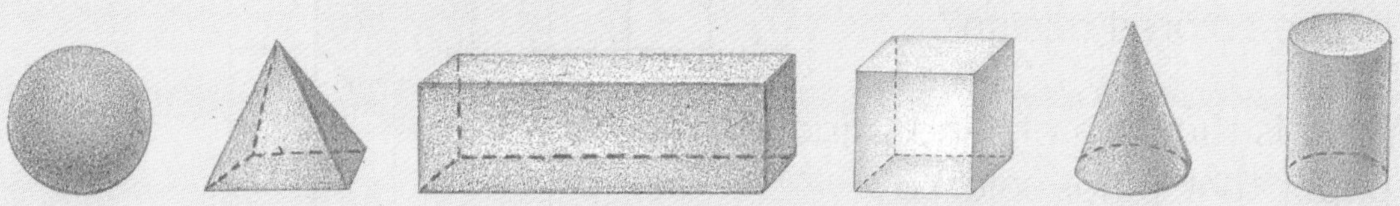

sphere pyramid rectangular prism cube cone cylinder

Many space figures have faces, edges, or corners.

Look at the faces on this cube. Each of the faces is a square.

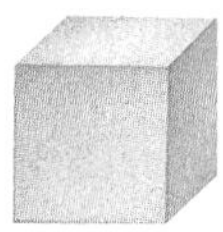

Look at the other space figures above. What plane figures can you see?

Think and Discuss Look at the sphere. Does it have faces? edges? corners?

Try It Out

Name each space figure.

1. 

2. 

3. 

4. 

5. 

6. 

Practice

www.sbgmath.com 

Copy and complete the chart below.

Space Figure	Faces	Edges	Corners
Cube	6	12	8
7. Sphere	0	0	0
8. Pyramid	5	7	5
9. Rectangular prism	6	12	8
10. Cone	1	1	1
11. Cylinder	2	2	0

Name the space figure that each object looks like.

12. 

13. 

14. 

15. 

16. 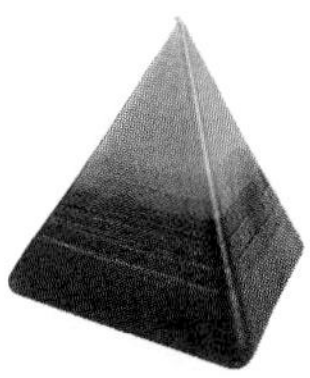

17. 

Use the space figures on page 386 to answer Questions 18–21.

18. Which space figure has 4 faces that are triangles?

19. Which space figure has 6 faces that are squares?

20. Which space figure has no faces?

21. Which space figure has 1 face?

Problem Solving

Match each space figure with the shape being drawn.

22.

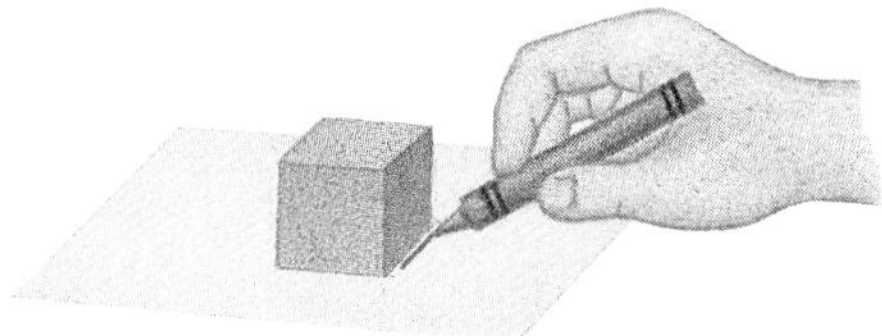

23.

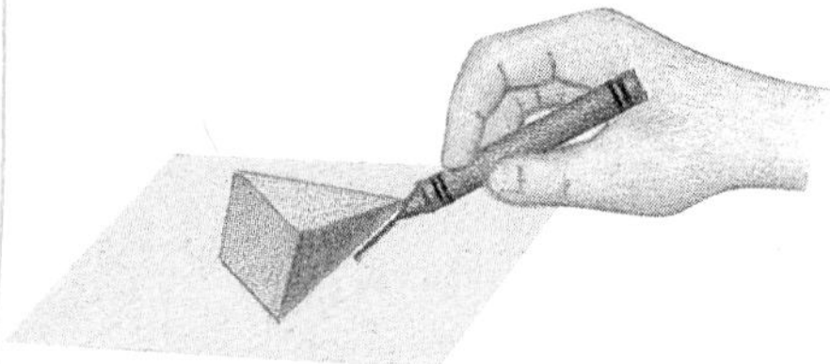

24.

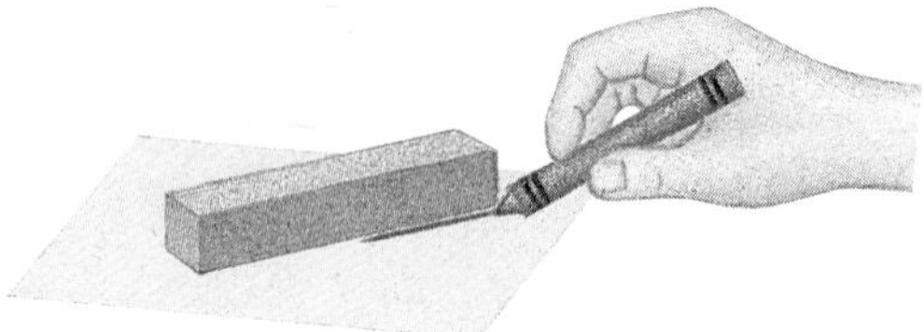

25.

a. 

b. 

c. 

d. 

26. Sophie painted a box shaped like a cube. She used a different color paint for each face of the box. How many colors did she use?

27. Analyze Greg and Cara each have a space figure. All the faces on both space figures are the same shape. Cara's space figure has more faces than Greg's space figure. What space figure does each person have?

Some space figures look different, depending on how you look at them.

28. Look at the cylinder below. What plane figures could you see?

a. 

b. 

c. 

29. Look at the cone below. What plane figures could you see?

a. 

b. 

c. 

Review and Remember

Using Estimation **Estimate each sum or difference by rounding to the greatest place value.**

30. 284 + 495

31. 64 − 23

32. 528 + 671

33. 82 − 53

34. \$7.12 + 8.90

35. 415 + 579

36. \$5.43 − 1.98

37. 74 − 59

38. 392 + 314

39. \$6.42 − 2.12

Project Link

Draw the outline for your mural.

- It's a good idea to use a pencil. Then you can make changes as you go along.
- Take a step back every so often. Is the part you're drawing the right size for the whole picture?
- Use a ruler to help you draw geometric shapes.

Fill It Up!

You can find out how many cubic units fill a space.

Learning About It

Gia's art class is making pompom ball creatures.

Each group has a tissue box filled with pompom balls.

- How many pompom balls do you think fit in the box above?
- Will the pompom balls fill all the space in the box?

What You Need

For each pair:
30 cubes

A more exact way to find the space inside a box is to fill it with cubes. Cubes can be stacked so there isn't any space between them.

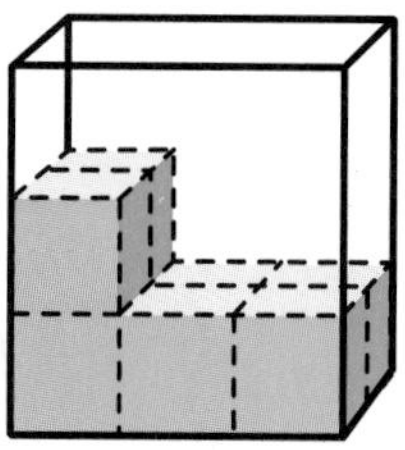

▶ The number of cubic units needed to fill a space figure is called its **volume.**

Work with your partner.

Use cubes to make the figure at the right. Then find the volume of the figure by counting the number of cubes you used.

Think and Discuss Look at the box shown at the right. How many more cubes will it take to completely fill it?

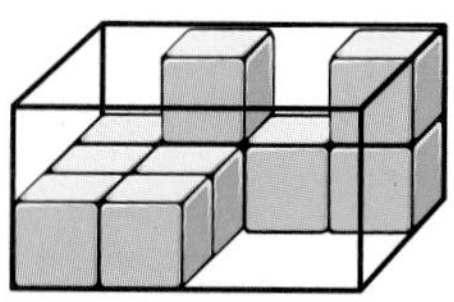

Try It Out

Find the volume of each figure. Use cubes to help you.

1. 

2. 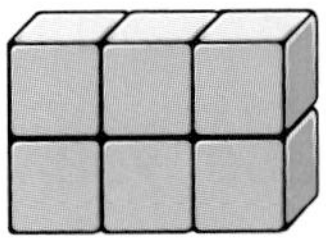

3. 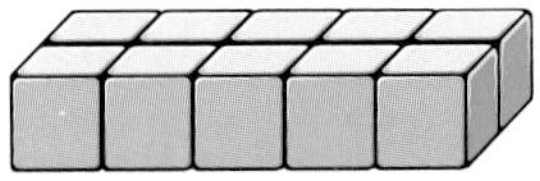

Practice

Find the volume of each figure. Use cubes to help you.

4. 

5. 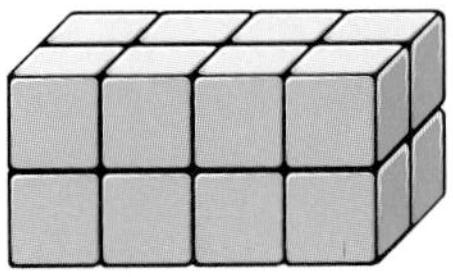

6. 

7. 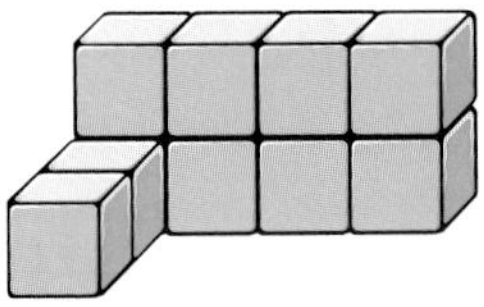

8. 

9. 

Problem Solving

10. Find 4 different ways to make a rectangular prism with 12 cubes.

11. **Analyze** Which paint can do you think has the greater volume? Why?

Gallon Quart

12. **Create Your Own** Make a figure using cubes. Then challenge a classmate to make a different figure with the same volume.

Review and Remember

Write the numbers in order from least to greatest.

13. 32 65 26 **14.** 893 936 386 **15.** 420 240 24

16. 43 28 92 **17.** 541 154 415 **18.** 72 179 291

For Extra Practice, see Set F, page 396.

Checkpoint

Perimeter, Area, and Space Figures

Find the perimeter of each figure. Label your answer.
(pages 380–381)

1.
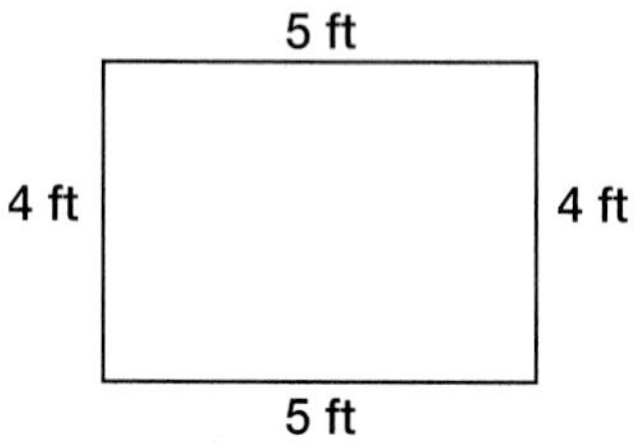

2.
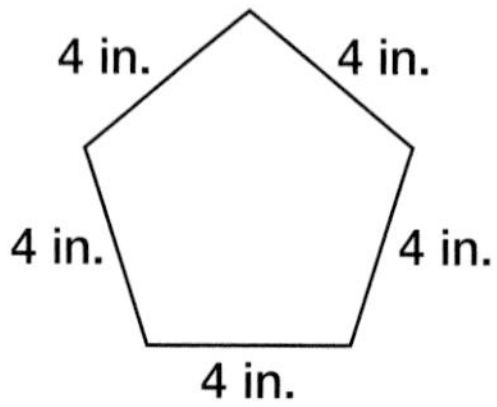

3.
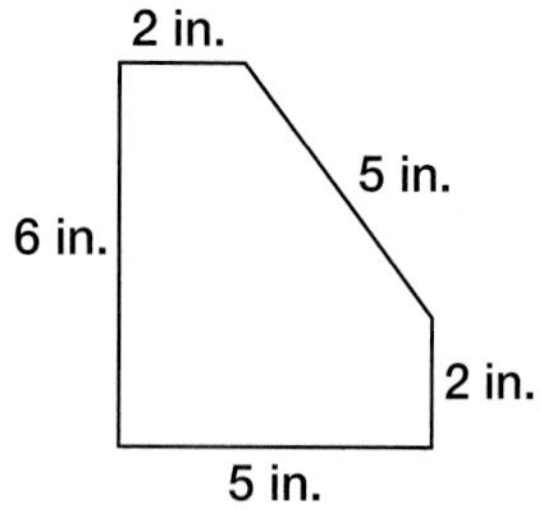

Find the area of each figure. Label your answer in square units. (pages 382–383)

4.
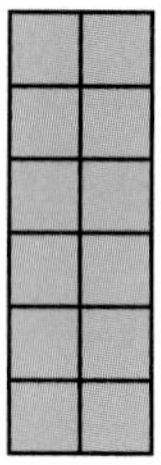

5.
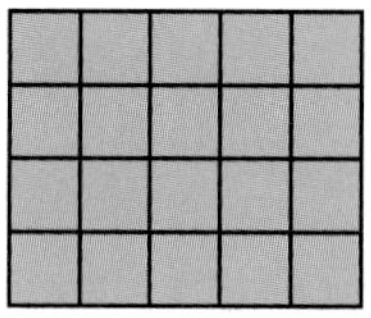

6.
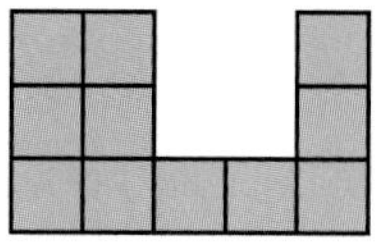

7.
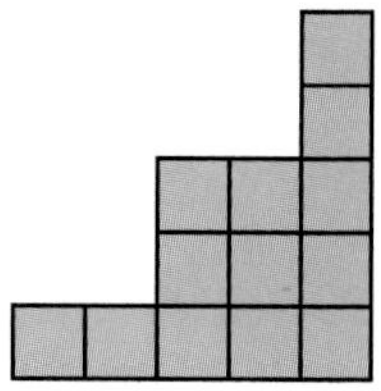

Name each space figure. (pages 386–389)

8.
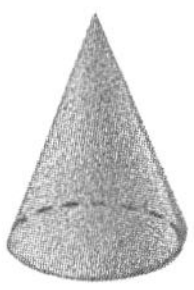

9.
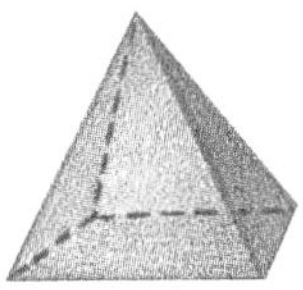

10.
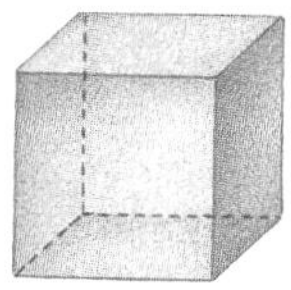

11.
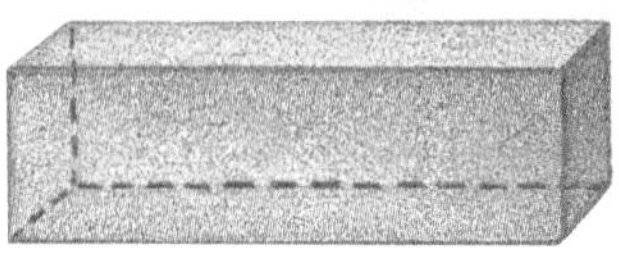

12.

13.

Find the volume of each figure. (pages 390–391)

14.
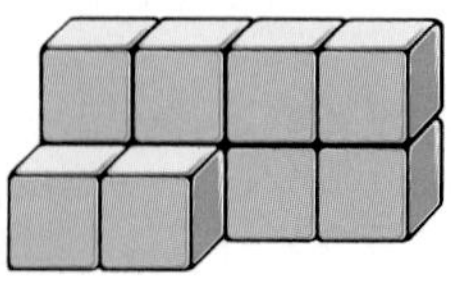

15.

16.

Problem Solving

17. Sarah wanted to design a toy that would roll on a hard surface. Which space figures might she use for her design?

18. Square picture frames come in 2 sizes. The perimeter of a small picture frame is 20 inches. The perimeter of a big picture frame is 32 inches. How much longer is a side of the big picture frame?

19. Savina completely filled her piggy bank with 350 dimes. Then she decided to fill her bank with quarters instead. Could she fit more than or less than 350 quarters into the bank? Explain.

20. Look at the design at the right. Which color squares cover the greatest area? Which color squares cover the least area?

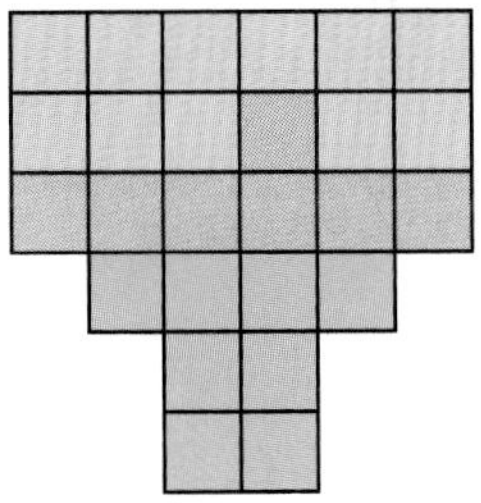

Journal Idea Your class is buying a new carpet to cover your classroom floor. Explain how you would decide what size carpet to buy.

What do you think?

Which do you think is easier to find, the perimeter of a figure or its area? Explain your thinking.

Project Wrap-Up

Finishing Touches

Pick up your brushes. The painting is about to begin!

- When your mural is finished, talk about how it turned out.
- Point out each shape and how it is used.
- Find similar shapes in the mural. Then find congruent shapes.

Extra Practice

Set A (pages 362–365)

Name each figure.

1. 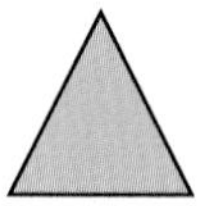
2. 
3. 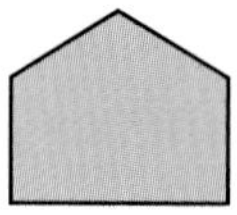
4. 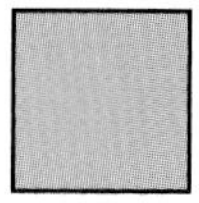

5. 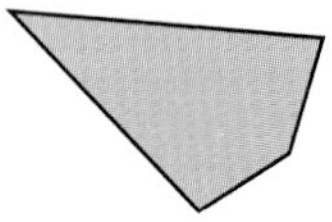
6. 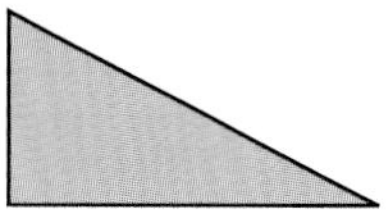
7. 
8. 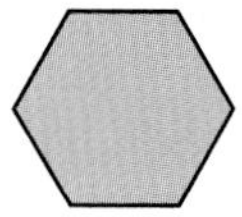

Tell the number of sides and the number of corners for each figure.

9. 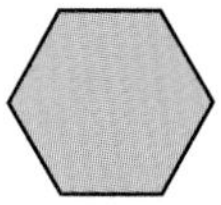
10. 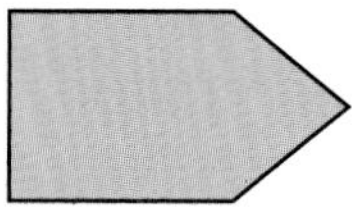
11. 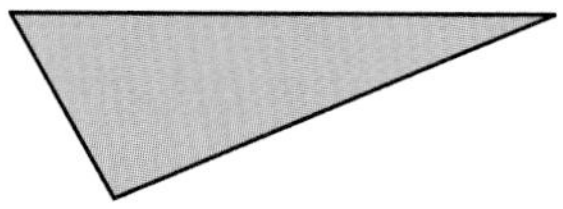
12. 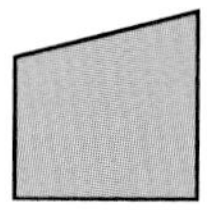

13. Andy cut out some squares. He counted 32 corners in all. How many squares did he cut out?

Set B (pages 366–367)

Tell whether each figure is a line, line segment, or ray.

1. 
2. 
3. 

Tell whether each angle is a right angle, is greater than a right angle, or is less than a right angle.

4. 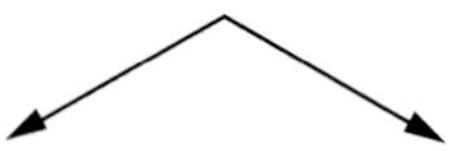
5. 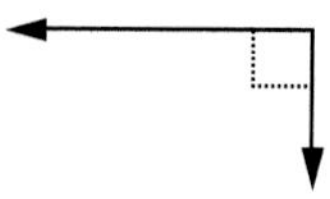
6. 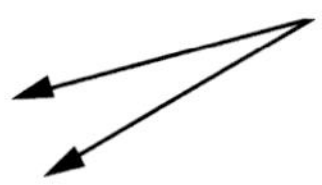

7. 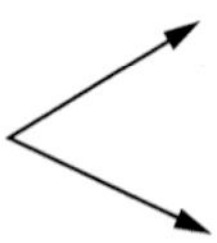
8. 
9. 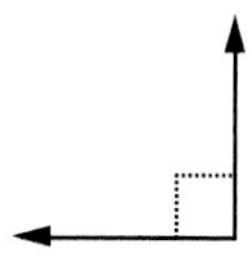

10. A shape has 4 equal line segments and 2 angles that are greater than right angles. Draw a picture of how the shape might look.

Extra Practice

Set C (pages 370–371)

Are the figures in each pair congruent?

1. 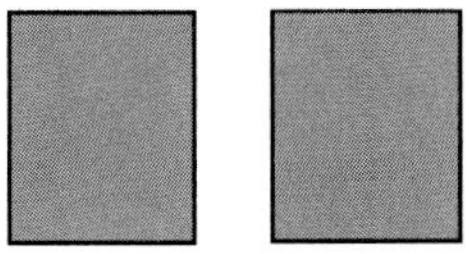

2. 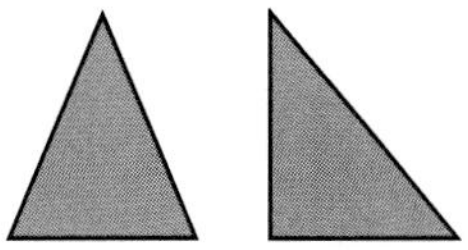

3. 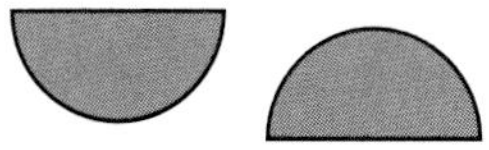

4. 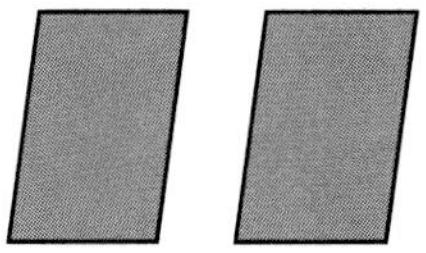

5. 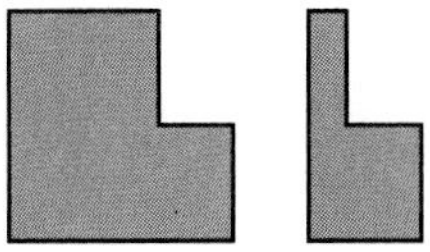

6. 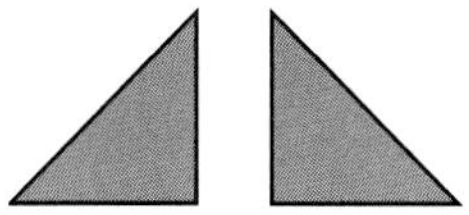

Study the drawing at the right. Then answer Questions 7–10.

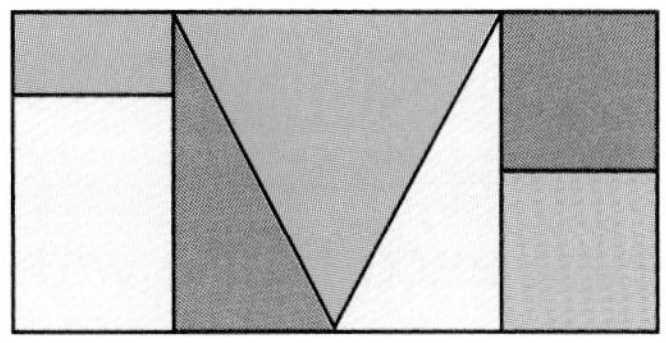

7. Which quadrilaterals are congruent?

8. Which quadrilaterals are not congruent?

9. Which triangles are congruent?

10. Which triangles are not congruent?

Set D (pages 380–381)

Find each perimeter. Label your answer.

1. 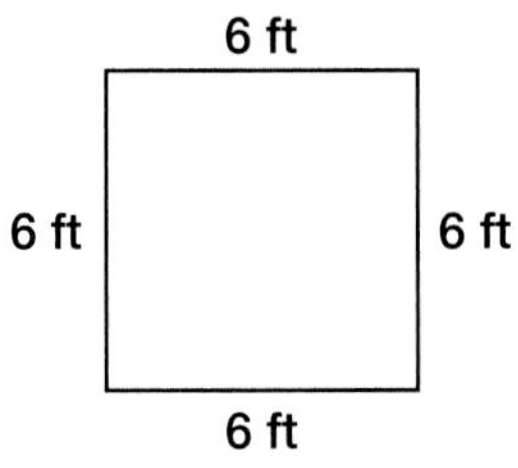

2. 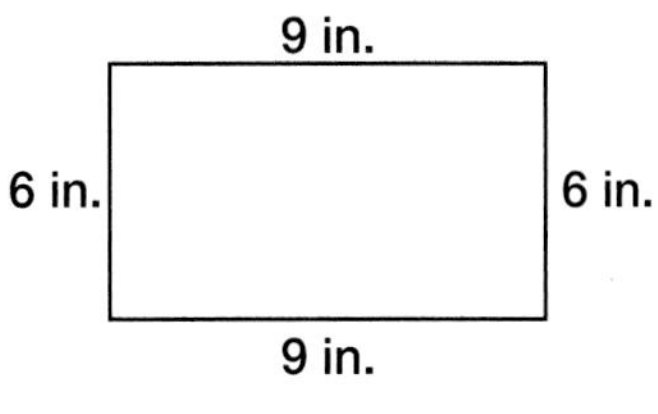

3. 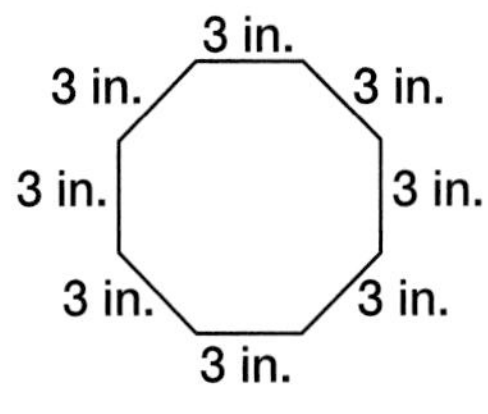

4. 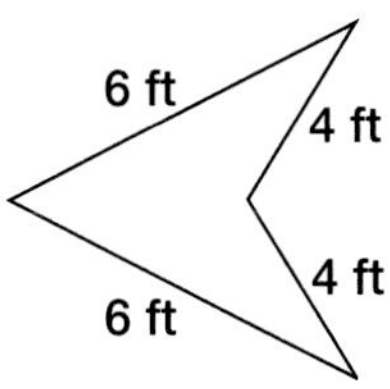

5. 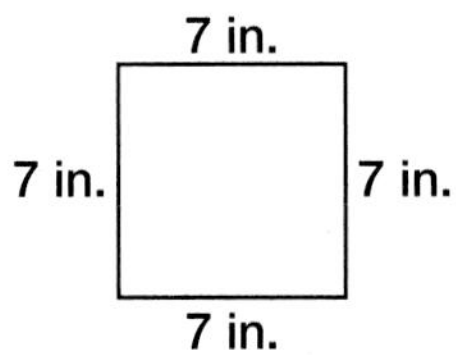

6. 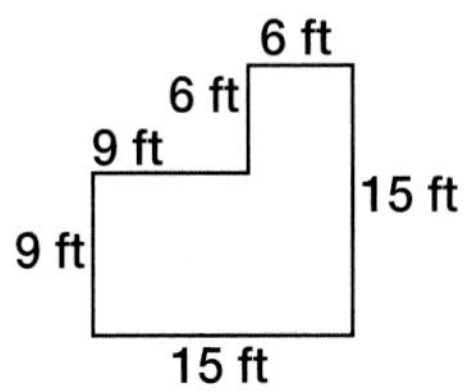

Extra Practice

Set E (pages 386–389)

Name the figure that each object looks like.

1. 

2. 

3. 

4. 

5. 

6. 

Name the space figure each sentence describes.

7. It has no faces, edges, or corners.

8. It has 1 face.

9. It has 6 faces that are squares.

10. It has 2 faces that are circles.

Match each figure with its parts.

11. 

12. 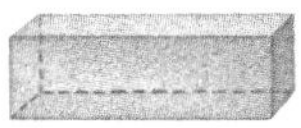

13. 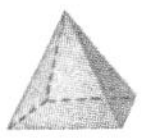

a. 

b. 

c. 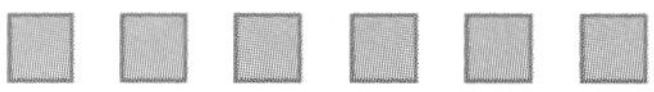

Set F (pages 390-391)

Find the volume of each figure. Use cubes to help you.

1. 

2. 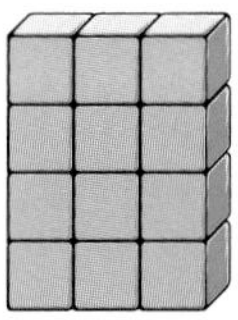

3. 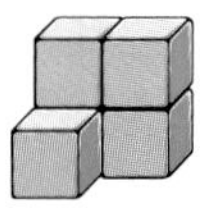

4. 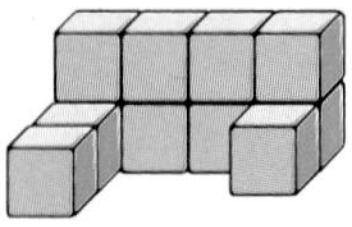

5. 

6. 

Chapter Test

Name each figure.

1. 
2. 
3. 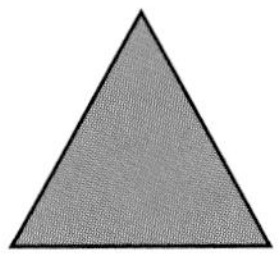
4. 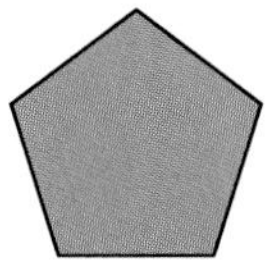
5. 
6. 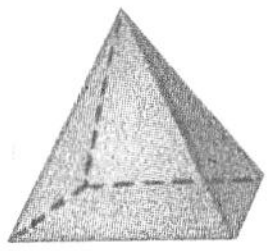
7. 
8. 
9. 
10.
11. 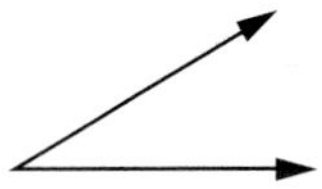

Which pairs are similar? Which pairs are congruent?

12. 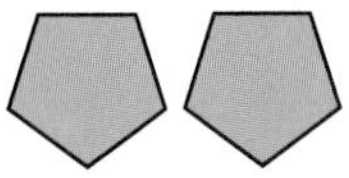
13. 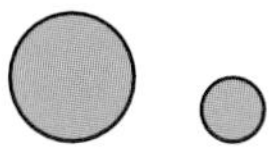

Is the red line a line of symmetry?

14. 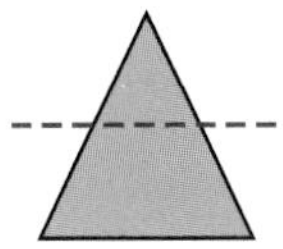
15. 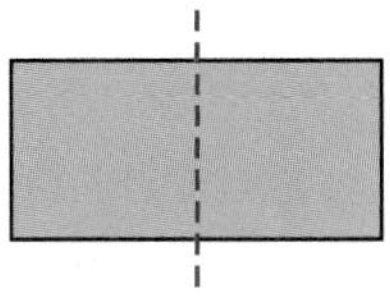

16. Find the perimeter.

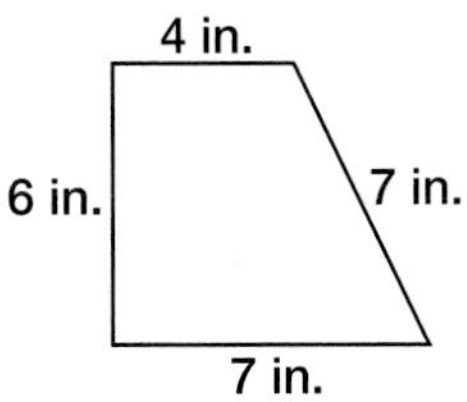

17. Find the area.

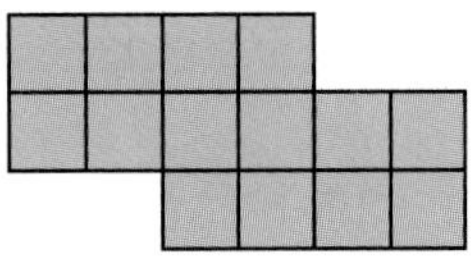

18. Find the volume.

19. A plane figure has 4 equal line segments and 4 right angles. What kind of figure is it?

20. What is the color of the next tile in the pattern?

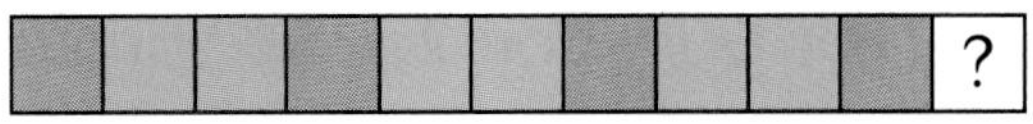

Self-Check Look back at Exercises 16–18. Did you label your answers correctly?

Performance Assessment

Show What You Know About Geometry

What You Need

15 color tiles
1-inch grid paper

1. Use the design below for Questions 1a and 1b.

   a. Describe all the plane figures you see in the design. Use all the geometry words you can.

   b. Describe all the lines and angles you see in the design. Use all the geometry words you can.

2. Make a design on 1-inch grid paper, using 9 or more color tiles. Be sure to place the tiles exactly on the grid squares. Each tile must share at least 1 side with another tile.

   a. Outline your design on the grid paper. Find the perimeter of your design in inches. Record the perimeter on the back of the paper.

   b. Find the area of your design in square units. Record the area on the back of the paper.

Self-Check

For Question 1a, did you describe all the plane figures in the design?

For Question 2a, did you correctly count the number of inches in the perimeter?

Extension

Go Figure!

You can make space figures with paper. Look at the patterns on this page. What shape do you think each pattern will make? Guess first. Then try it!

- Trace and cut out each pattern.
- Fold on the dotted lines.
- Use tape to hold your space figure together.

Was your guess correct?

1

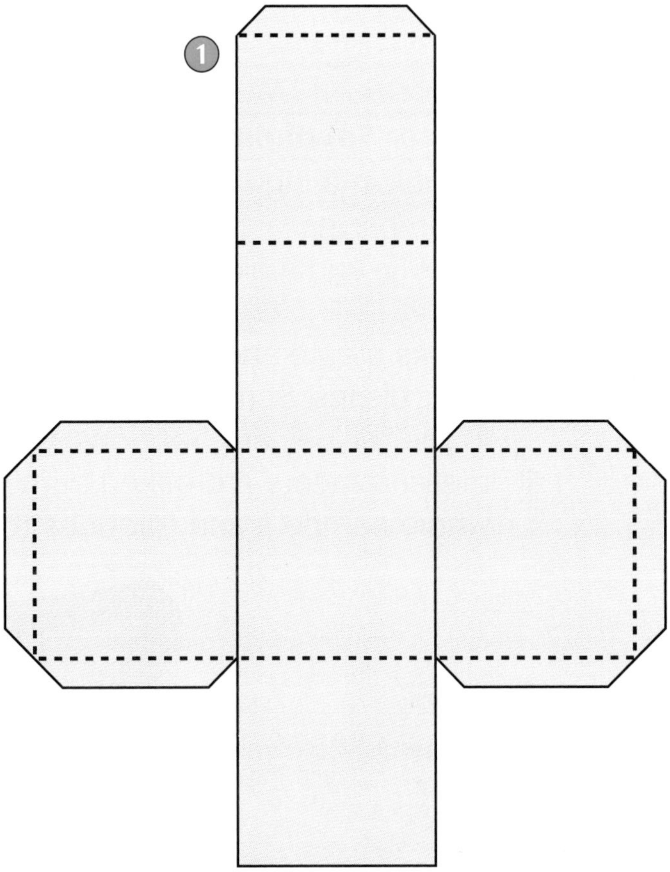

2

Chapter 11 Fractions and Decimals

Chapter Theme: FOOD

Career Spotlight Meet Freddy Calderón, a cook in a big cafeteria. Freddy's job is to prepare a large number of meals very quickly, and make them all taste good!

Cooks create and follow recipes to make their dishes. Some of the measurements in the recipes are fractions. Other measurements are mixed numbers—whole numbers and fractions together.

fraction

mixed number

Chapter Project

Plan a Picnic Menu

Here's your chance to plan a perfect menu for a picnic! Work with a group of classmates.

- Talk about the things you would like to bring on a picnic.
- Will you need recipes for any of the foods and drinks?

Remember to choose things that are easy to pack and to carry!

pelouze

Equal Parts

You can use fractions to name equal parts of regions.

Learning About It

Fold a sheet of paper into 4 equal parts.
Color 1 part orange.

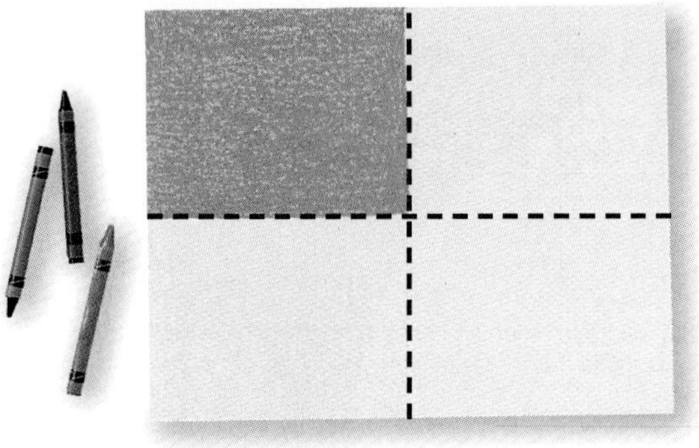

Word Bank

fraction
numerator
denominator

What You Need

For each student:
crayons
sheets of paper

You can use a **fraction** to tell how much you colored.

numerator ⟶ $\frac{1}{4}$ ⟵ orange part
denominator ⟶ ⟵ parts in all

Fold and color paper strips to match these pictures.
What fraction tells how much of each you colored?

More Examples

Here are other ways to divide a whole into equal parts.

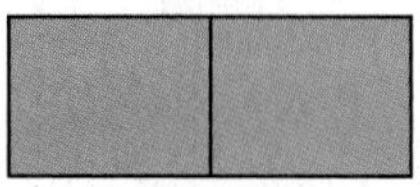

2 equal parts
halves

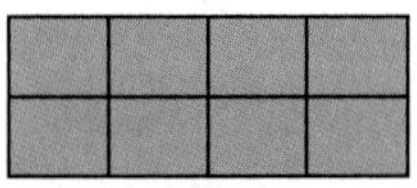

8 equal parts
eighths

6 equal parts
sixths

Think and Discuss What does the word *numerator* mean? What does the word *denominator* mean?

Try It Out

Write a fraction for the shaded part. Then write a fraction for the part that is not shaded.

1. 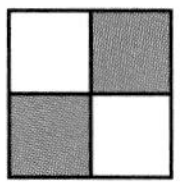

■ shaded parts
4 equal parts

2. 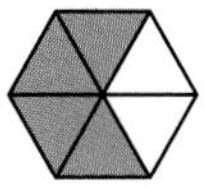

4 shaded parts
■ equal parts

3. 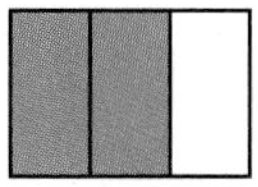

■
3

4. 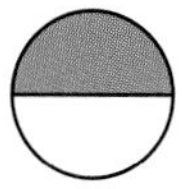

1
■

Practice

Write a fraction for the shaded part.

5. 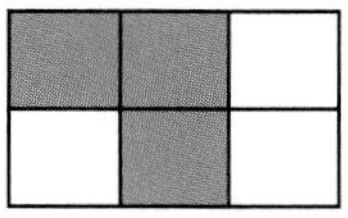

6. 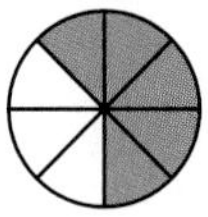

7. 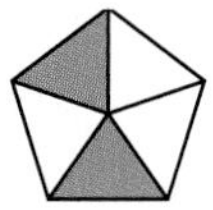

8. 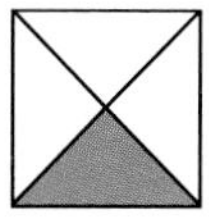

9. 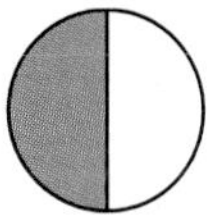

10. 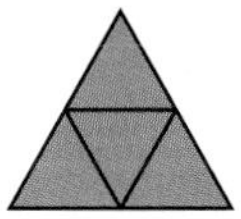

11. 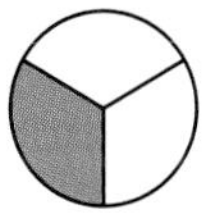

12. 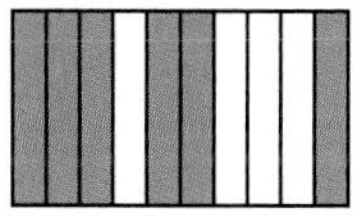

Draw a picture and write a fraction for each fraction name.

13. nine twelfths

14. two eighths

15. one fifth

16. four sixths

Problem Solving

17. Mark folded his paper into 10 equal parts. He colored 7 parts blue and 3 parts red. How many parts did he color?

18. Analyze A striped tent is green and white. If each color has an equal number of stripes, what fraction are green stripes?

Review and Remember

Find each answer.

19. 367 + 122

20. 538 − 467

21. 8 × 6

22. 45 ÷ 9

Project Link

Here are some ideas for finding recipes.

- Ask someone in your family.
- Ask a neighbor or a friend.
- Look in a cookbook or a magazine.

When you find your recipe, you'll probably find some fractions, too!

For Extra Practice, see Set A, page 436.

Using Algebra

What's in a Name?

You can use different fraction names to identify the same part of a region.

Learning About It

Work with a partner.

Step 1 Use fraction pieces to model the sandwiches. Show 1 whole, 2 halves, and 4 fourths. How many fourths are equal to $\frac{1}{2}$?

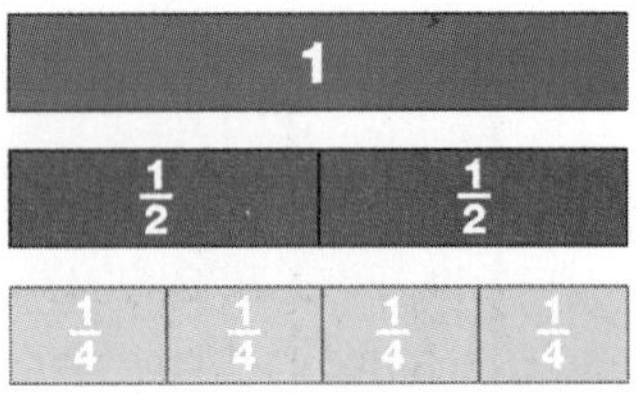

$$\frac{2}{4} = \frac{1}{2}$$

Fractions that name the same parts of a whole are called **equivalent fractions.**

Step 2 Use sixths and eighths. Find other fractions that are equivalent to $\frac{1}{2}$.

$$\frac{1}{2} = \frac{■}{6} = \frac{■}{8}$$

Think and Discuss Look at your fraction pieces. How many twelfths are equal to $\frac{1}{4}$?

Word Bank

equivalent fractions

What You Need

For each pair:
fraction pieces

Try It Out

Use fraction pieces to find equivalent fractions.

1. 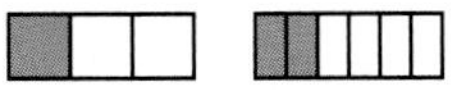

$\frac{\blacksquare}{3} = \frac{\blacksquare}{6}$

2. 

$\frac{\blacksquare}{4} = \frac{\blacksquare}{8}$

3. 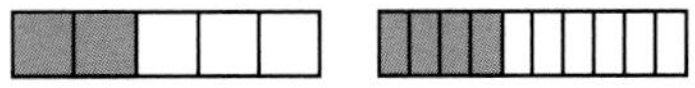

$\frac{\blacksquare}{5} = \frac{\blacksquare}{10}$

Practice

Name the equivalent fraction.

4. 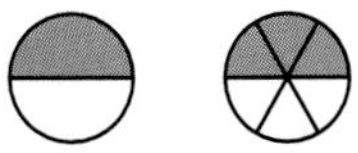

$\frac{1}{2} = \frac{\blacksquare}{6}$

5. 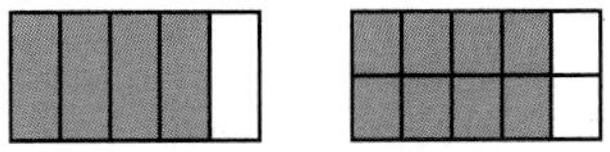

$\frac{4}{5} = \frac{\blacksquare}{10}$

6. 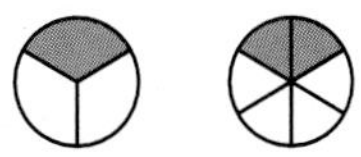

$\frac{1}{3} = \frac{\blacksquare}{\blacksquare}$

7. 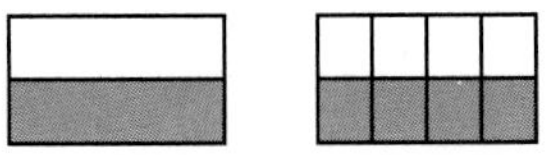

$\frac{1}{2} = \frac{\blacksquare}{\blacksquare}$

8. 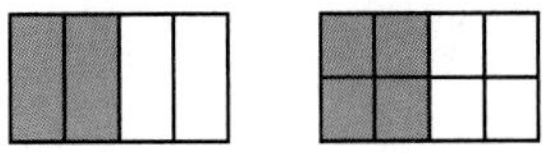

$\frac{2}{4} = \frac{\blacksquare}{\blacksquare}$

9. 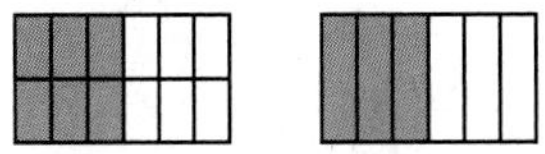

$\frac{\blacksquare}{\blacksquare} = \frac{\blacksquare}{\blacksquare}$

Problem Solving

10. Arnie and Pat had equal-sized hoagies. Arnie ate $\frac{2}{4}$ of his hoagie. Pat ate $\frac{3}{6}$ of his. Who ate more? Explain.

11. How many eighths are in $\frac{1}{2}$ inch? How many eighths are in $\frac{1}{4}$ inch?

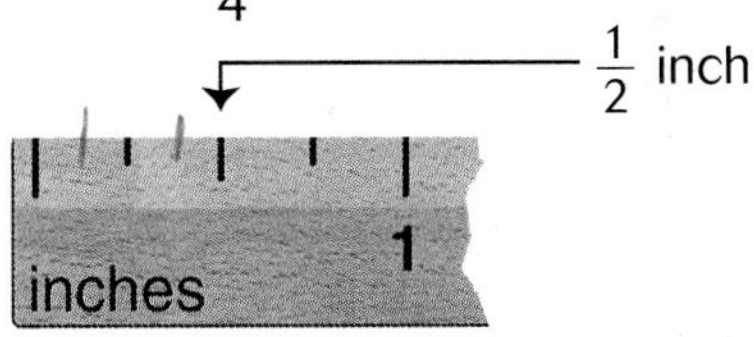

Review and Remember

Find the answer.

12. $16 - 4$

13. 7×4

14. $10 \div 5$

15. $27 - 9$

Critical Thinking Corner

Number Sense

What's Wrong?

Joyce and Richard order a 12-inch pizza for lunch. The cook asks them if they want the pizza cut into 6 pieces or 8 pieces. Joyce answers, "Cut it into 6 pieces because we're not hungry enough to eat 8 pieces." What's wrong with Joyce's answer?

Spice It Up!

Use pictures and fraction pieces to compare fractions.

Learning About It

This spice rack is filled with ground spices. It is divided into 6 equal parts. Is there more red pepper or more ginger?

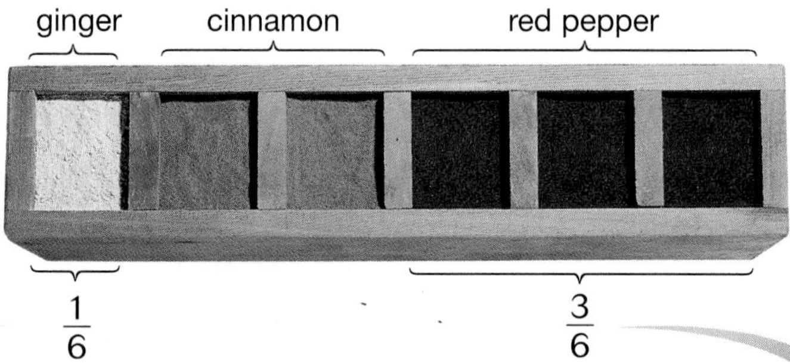

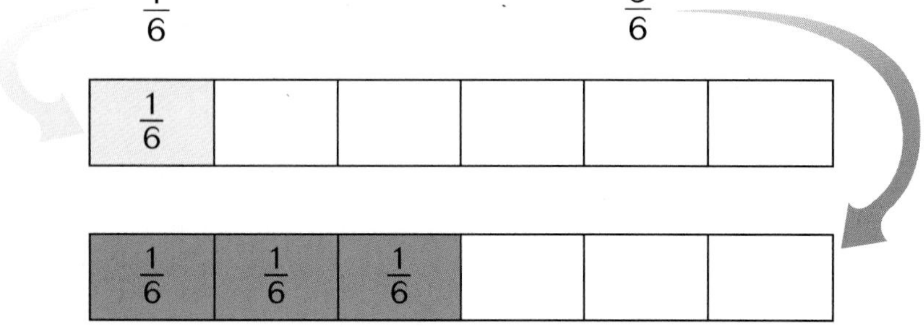

$\frac{1}{6}$ is less than $\frac{3}{6}$ $\quad$ $\frac{3}{6}$ is greater than $\frac{1}{6}$

$\frac{1}{6} < \frac{3}{6}$ $\quad$ $\frac{3}{6} > \frac{1}{6}$

There is more red pepper.

Social Studies Connection Many spices come from India. The picture shows what ginger, pepper, and cinnamon look like before they are ground into powder.

www.sbgmath.com

Another Example

Use the fraction pieces below. Compare them to each other and to the 1 whole strip. Tell which fraction is greater than another.

Think and Discuss Which of the fraction pieces above is the greatest? Look at the denominator. How does it compare to the other denominators?

What You Need

For each student:
fraction pieces

Try It Out

Compare. Write >, <, or = for each ●.

1. 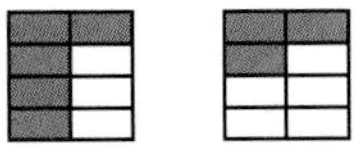

$\frac{5}{8}$ ● $\frac{3}{8}$

2. 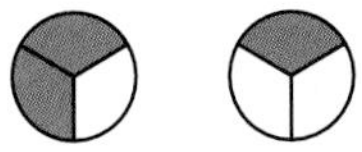

$\frac{2}{3}$ ● $\frac{1}{3}$

3. 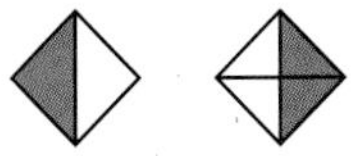

$\frac{1}{2}$ ● $\frac{2}{4}$

Practice

Compare. Write >, <, or = for each ●.

4. 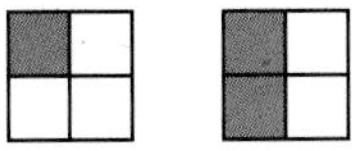

$\frac{1}{4}$ ● $\frac{2}{4}$

5. 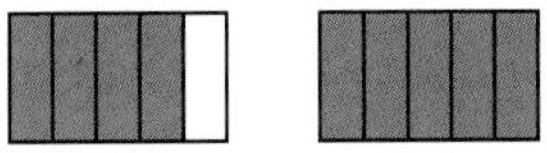

$\frac{4}{5}$ ● $\frac{5}{5}$

6. 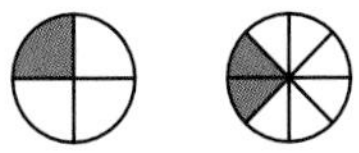

$\frac{1}{4}$ ● $\frac{2}{8}$

7. 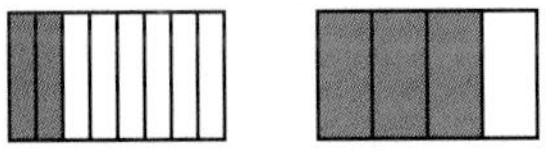

$\frac{2}{8}$ ● $\frac{3}{4}$

8. 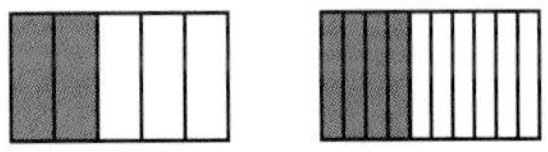

$\frac{2}{5}$ ● $\frac{4}{10}$

9. 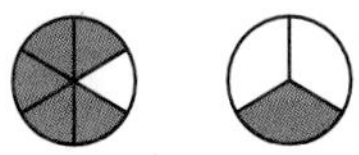

$\frac{5}{6}$ ● $\frac{1}{3}$

10. $\frac{3}{8}$ ● $\frac{7}{8}$

11. $\frac{5}{6}$ ● $\frac{4}{6}$

12. $\frac{2}{4}$ ● $\frac{2}{8}$

13. $\frac{3}{8}$ ● $\frac{3}{6}$

Problem Solving

14. Use fraction pieces to compare the cinnamon and ginger on the spice rack. Which fraction is greater?

15. Samir ate 2 pieces of naan. Rani ate 3 pieces and John ate 1 piece. How many pieces did they all eat?

16. Science Connection Earth is made up of land and water. There is about $\frac{3}{4}$ water and $\frac{1}{4}$ land. Is there more land or water?

Naan is an Indian bread served with spicy foods. Flat circles of dough are baked in an oven, then browned under a hot broiler.

Review and Remember

Write the value of the digit 4 in each number.

17. 456

18. 40

19. 204

20. 4,365

21. 42,131

It's All Set!

You know fractions name equal parts of a region.
Fractions can also name equal parts of a set.

Learning About It

You can use a fraction to name parts of a set.

The ants are carrying 2 red apples and 4 yellow apples. Use counters to find what fraction of the apples are red.

What You Need

For each student:
red counters
yellow counters

numerator

denominator

numerator ⟶ ■ ⟵ red apples
denominator ⟶ ■ ⟵ total number of apples

More Examples

Use counters. What fraction of each set is red?

A. 

$\frac{■}{8}$ ■ red counters / 8 counters in all

B. 

$\frac{■}{6}$ ■ red counters / 6 counters in all

Think and Discuss Suppose you have 8 apples. If 5 of them are red, what fraction of them are not red?

Try It Out

Write a fraction to name the part of each set that is green.

1. 

2. 

3. 

4. 

Practice

Write a fraction that names the part of each set described.

5. red plums

6. purple grapes

7. yellow apples

8. red bananas

9. red apple

10. green pears

Write a fraction for each.

11. 3 out of 8 apples are red.

12. 4 out of 5 peaches are ripe.

13. 9 out of 12 mangoes are ripe.

14. 7 out of 10 bananas are yellow.

Problem Solving

15. Jamal bought 5 oranges. He peeled 2 of them. What fraction of the oranges is peeled?

16. **Analyze** You had 12 cherries. You ate 5, and your brother ate 3. What fraction of the cherries is left?

Review and Remember

Multiply or divide.

17. 6×3

18. $18 \div 6$

19. $18 \div 3$

20. 9×6

For Extra Practice, see Set D, page 437.

Tasty Tacos

You can use counters to help you find fractional parts of a set.

Learning About It

Joan made 8 tacos. If she eats $\frac{1}{4}$ of them, how many tacos will she eat?

What You Need

For each student:
counters

Model the tacos with counters.
Put 8 counters into 4 equal groups.

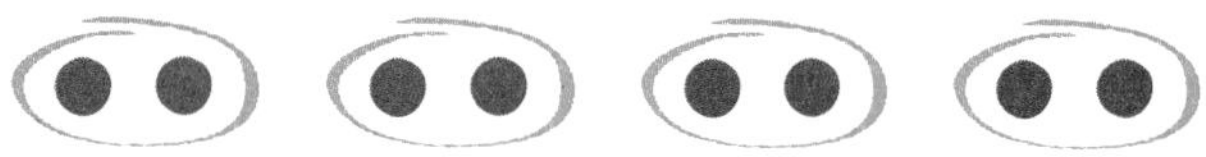

There are 2 counters in each group.

$\frac{1}{4}$ **of 8 = 2**

Joan would eat 2 tacos.

More Examples

A. Find $\frac{1}{2}$ of 6.

Put 6 counters into 2 equal groups.

How many in each group?

$\frac{1}{2}$ of 6 = ■

B. Find $\frac{1}{3}$ of 12.

Put 12 counters into 3 equal groups.

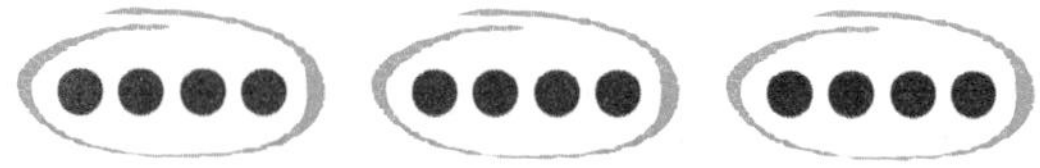

How many in each group?

$\frac{1}{3}$ of 12 = ■

Think and Discuss How would you find $\frac{1}{2}$ of the 8 tacos?

Try It Out

Use counters to find each answer.

1. 

$\frac{1}{3}$ of 9 = ■

2. 

$\frac{1}{2}$ of 8 = ■

3. 

$\frac{1}{5}$ of 10 = ■

Draw a picture to find each answer.

4. $\frac{1}{2}$ of 4 = ■ **5.** $\frac{1}{6}$ of 6 = ■ **6.** $\frac{1}{4}$ of 12 = ■ **7.** $\frac{1}{5}$ of 15 = ■

Practice

Use counters to find each answer.

8. 

$\frac{1}{2}$ of 10 = ■

9. 

$\frac{1}{4}$ of 8= ■

10. 

$\frac{1}{3}$ of 6 = ■

11. $\frac{1}{4}$ of 16 = ■ **12.** $\frac{1}{10}$ of 10 = ■ **13.** $\frac{1}{2}$ of 12 = ■

14. $\frac{1}{3}$ of 15 =■ **15.** $\frac{1}{4}$ of 20 = ■ **16.** $\frac{1}{6}$ of 12 = ■

Problem Solving

17. Marisa has 10 tortillas. If she eats $\frac{1}{5}$ of them, how many will she eat?

18. There are 16 cups in a gallon. How many cups are in $\frac{1}{2}$ gallon?

Using Algebra

Review and Remember

Complete each pattern.

19. 120, 130, 140, ■, ■, ■, ■

20. 30, 60, 90, ■, ■, ■, ■

21. 980, 985, 990, ■, ■, ■, ■

Social Studies Connection
Taco shells are tortillas that Mexican cooks make from corn.

For Extra Practice, see Set E, page 437.

Developing Skills for Problem Solving

First read for understanding and then focus on whether answers are reasonable or not.

READ FOR UNDERSTANDING

Mr. O'Connell sells corn, tomatoes, and beans at a roadside stand. The stand is divided into 4 equal sections. The picture shows how he displays the vegetables.

1. How many equal sections are there?
2. Which two kinds of vegetables cover the same area?
3. Which vegetable covers the most area?

THINK AND DISCUSS

MATH FOCUS

Reasonable Answers Whenever you answer a question, you should check that it is reasonable. Look at the facts that are given. Make sure your answer makes sense compared to those facts.

Reread the paragraph at the top of the page.

4. Is it reasonable to think that $\frac{4}{4}$ of the table is used for corn? Explain why or why not.
5. Is it reasonable to think that $\frac{1}{4}$ of the table is used for corn? Why or why not?
6. Why is it helpful to check to make sure an answer is reasonable?

Show What You Learned

Answer each question. Give a reason for your choice.

One morning, Dolores put 27 tomatoes on a table to sell. At the end of the day, there were 8 tomatoes still on the table.

1. Is it reasonable to say that Dolores has 35 tomatoes left to sell?
   a. Yes; she should have more tomatoes now than when she started.
   b. No; she should have less tomatoes now than when she started.
   c. No; she sold all her tomatoes.

2. Which number sentence shows how many tomatoes Dolores sold?
   a. $27 + 8 = \blacksquare$
   b. $27 - 8 = \blacksquare$
   c. $27 \div 8 = \blacksquare$

3. Is it reasonable to say that Dolores sold about 20 tomatoes?
   a. Yes; 27 − 8 is about 20.
   b. No; 27 + 8 is greater than 20.
   c. No; 27 ÷ 8 is less than 20

Ernie bought a large basket of apples at a roadside stand. He used $\frac{3}{6}$ of them to make apple pies. Then he used 4 apples to make muffins.

4. How many sixths are equal to $\frac{1}{2}$?
   a. 6 sixths
   b. 3 sixths
   c. 2 sixths

5. How many apples did Ernie use for muffins?
   a. $\frac{3}{6}$ of them
   b. 4 apples
   c. 2 apples

6. **Explain** Look back at the information in the problem. Is it reasonable to say that Ernie used only $\frac{1}{2}$ of his apples? Why or why not?

All Mixed Up!

Mixed numbers are whole numbers and fractions together.

Learning About It

Green goo is fun to make. It looks wiggly and gooey, and you can eat it. Look at the recipe. What does $1\frac{1}{2}$ cups mean?

1 cup  + $\frac{1}{2}$ cup  = $1\frac{1}{2}$ cups

Read as one and one half cup.

The number $1\frac{1}{2}$ is a **mixed number.** A mixed number is a whole number and a fraction.

Word Bank

mixed number

More Examples

Mixed numbers are often used when you measure.

A.

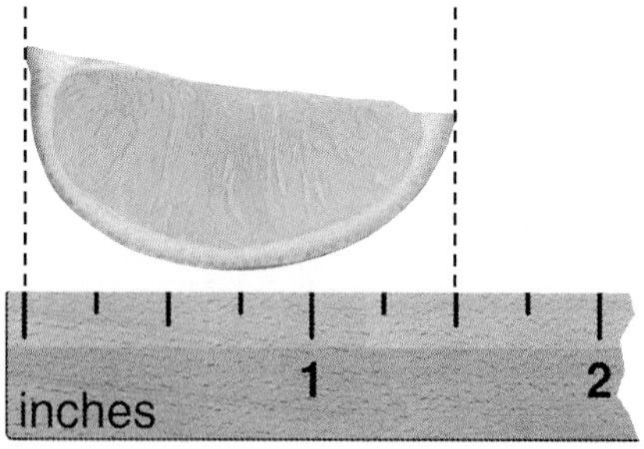

The lime measures $1\frac{1}{2}$ in.

B.

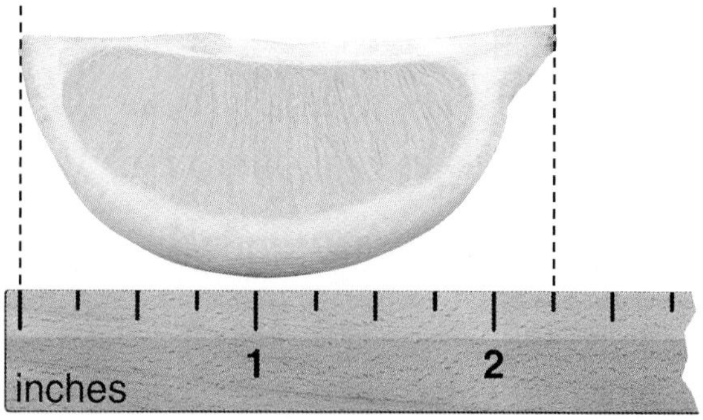

The lemon measures $2\frac{1}{4}$ in.

Think and Discuss How many fourths are in 1 whole? How many fourths are in $1\frac{1}{4}$?

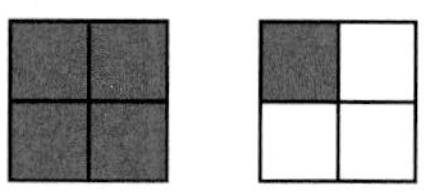

Try It Out

Write a mixed number for the part that is shaded.

1. 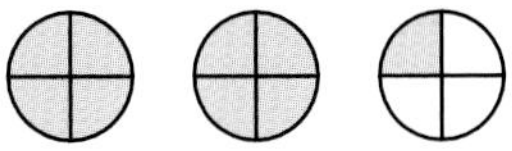

2. 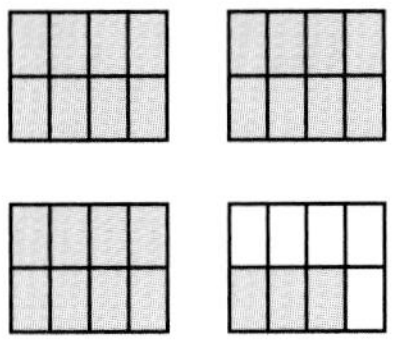

3. 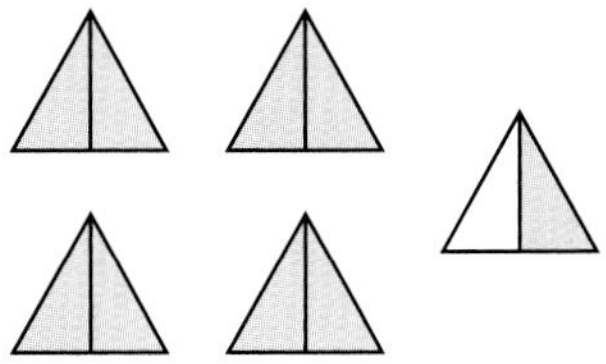

Practice

Write a mixed number for the part that is shaded.

4. 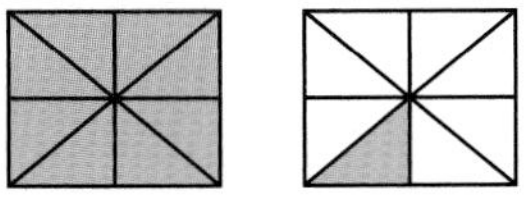

5. 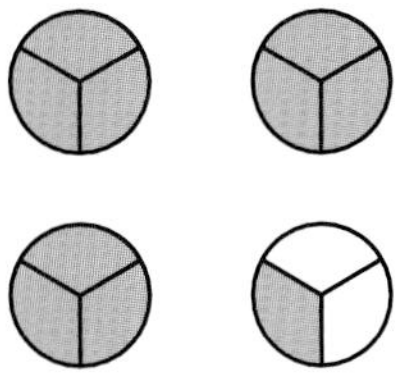

6. 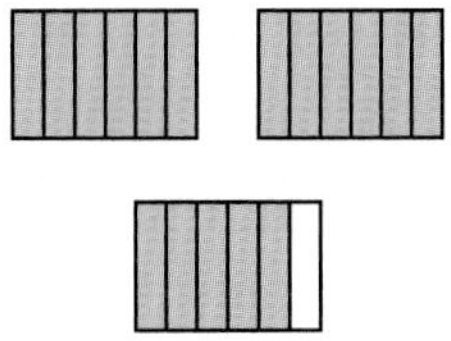

Draw a picture to show each mixed number.

7. $1\frac{1}{2}$ **8.** $2\frac{3}{4}$ **9.** $1\frac{2}{3}$ **10.** $3\frac{1}{5}$ **11.** $1\frac{1}{4}$ **12.** $2\frac{5}{8}$

Measure each object to the nearest quarter inch.

13. 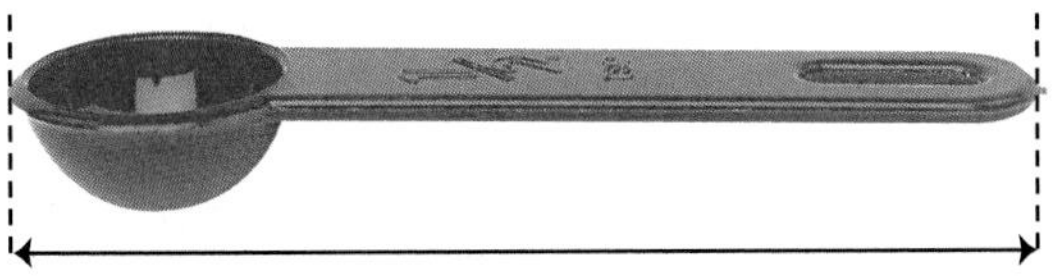

14. 

Problem Solving

15. You need $1\frac{3}{4}$ teaspoons of food coloring. Is that closer to 1 teaspoon or 2 teaspoons?

16. To double the recipe for Green Goo, how many packets of gelatin do you need?

Review and Remember

Estimate. Then use a calculator to add or subtract.

17. 236 + 485 **18.** 684 − 253

19. 754 + 138 **20.** 821 − 465

Project Link

Are your picnic plans perfect yet?

- Have you decided on your main dishes?
- Did you choose a dessert?
- Do you know how much of each food you will need?

For Extra Practice, see Set F, page 437.

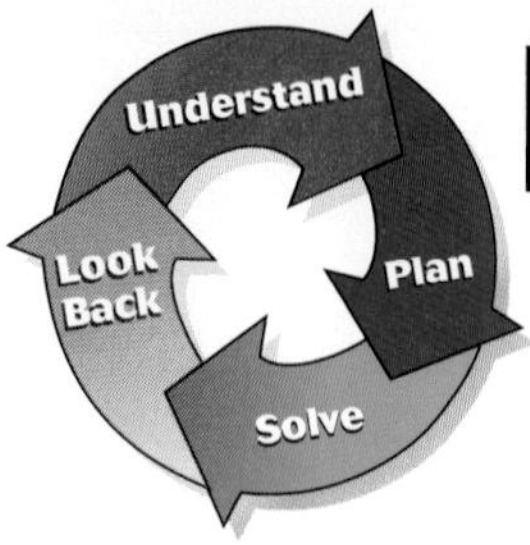

Problem Solving
Draw a Picture

You can draw a picture to help you solve a problem.

At the farmers' market a farmer has 10 bags of potatoes to sell. Each bag weighs 10 pounds. Three of the bags are red potatoes, 3 of the bags are white potatoes, and the rest of the bags are sweet potatoes. What fraction of the total bags of potatoes are sweet potatoes?

UNDERSTAND

What do you need to find?

You need to find how many bags of potatoes there are in all. Then you need to find how many of the bags are sweet potatoes.

PLAN

How can you solve the problem?

You can **draw a picture** to show the information. Then you can use the picture to find the answer.

SOLVE

Draw 10 bags. Label each bag *red, white,* or *sweet.*

$\frac{4}{10}$ of the bags are sweet potatoes.

LOOK BACK

Check to make sure your drawing shows the correct facts from the problem.

Using the Strategy

Draw a picture to help you solve each problem.

1. There are 16 farmers selling food at the market. Only $\frac{1}{4}$ of them are selling corn. How many farmers are selling corn?

2. Kate is selling 6 baskets of onions. She sold $\frac{2}{3}$ of them by noon. How many baskets of onions does she have left to sell?

3. A farmer has 8 boxes of cabbage to sell at the market. She sells 3 boxes in the morning and 2 boxes in the afternoon. What fraction of the boxes of cabbage does she have left to sell?

4. **Analyze** Terry has 5 barrels full of nuts. He has 2 barrels of salted peanuts, 1 barrel of roasted peanuts, 1 barrel of pecans, and 1 barrel of walnuts. What fraction of these barrels contain peanuts?

Mixed Strategy Review

Try these or other strategies you have learned.

THERE'S ALWAYS A WAY!

- *Make a Table*
- *Draw a Picture*
- *Use Logical Reasoning*
- *Act It Out*

5. Margo gives 2 free apples for every 6 apples that a person buys. If you buy 24 apples from Margo, how many free apples will you receive?

6. Greg is selling 12 watermelons at the farmers' market. If he sold $\frac{1}{4}$ of the watermelons by noon, how many watermelons does he have left to sell?

7. A farmer has 15 pounds of turnips. She sells 5 pounds. Later someone returns 2 pounds. How many pounds of turnips does she have left?

Checkpoint

Fractions

Use the word list to complete each sentence.

Word List

denominator
mixed number
numerator

1. In the fraction $\frac{4}{5}$, 4 is the __?__.

2. The bottom number of a fraction is the __?__.

3. One and one-third is a __?__.

Write a fraction for the shaded part. (pages 402–403)

4. 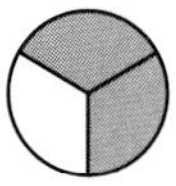

5. 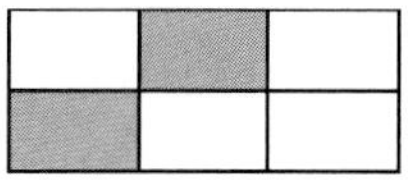

6. 

7. 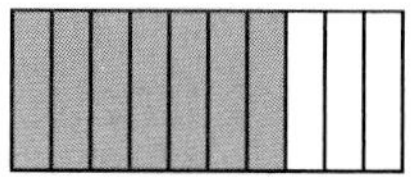

Using Algebra **Write the equivalent fractions.** (pages 404–405)

8. 

$\frac{1}{2} = \frac{■}{4}$

9. 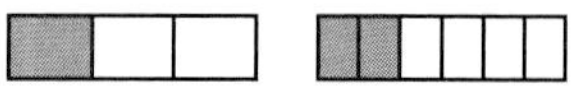

$\frac{1}{3} = \frac{■}{6}$

10. 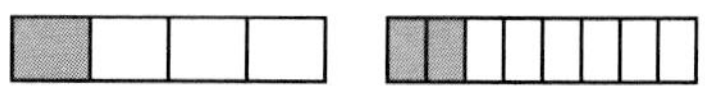

$\frac{1}{4} = \frac{■}{8}$

Compare. Write >, <, or = for each ●. (pages 406–407)

11. 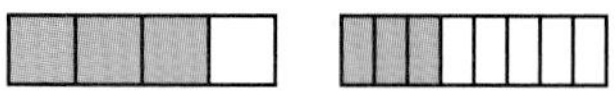

$\frac{3}{4}$ ● $\frac{3}{8}$

12. 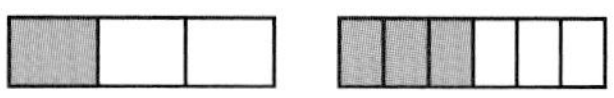

$\frac{1}{3}$ ● $\frac{3}{6}$

13. 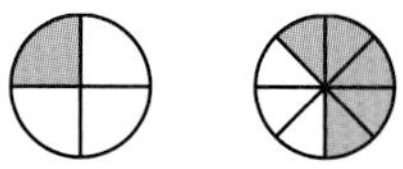

$\frac{1}{4}$ ● $\frac{5}{8}$

Write a fraction for the shaded part of each set. (pages 408–409)

14. 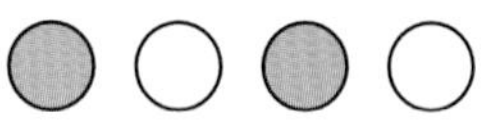

15. 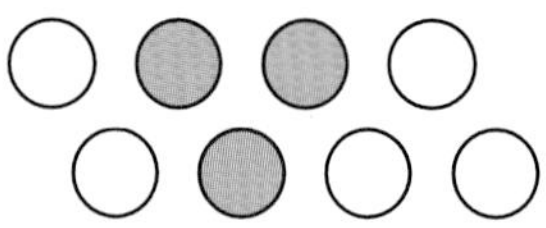

16. 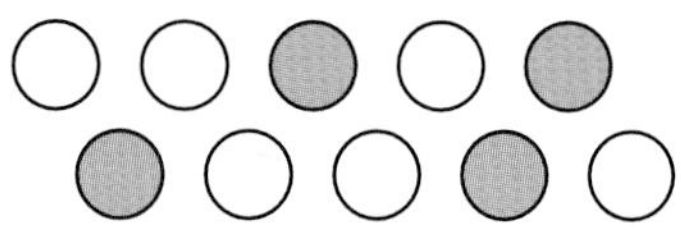

Find each answer. (pages 410–411)

17. $\frac{1}{4}$ of 4 = ■

18. $\frac{1}{3}$ of 15 = ■

19. $\frac{1}{2}$ of 20 = ■

Write a mixed number for the part that is shaded. (pages 414–415)

20. 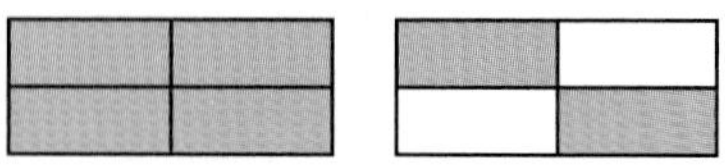

21. 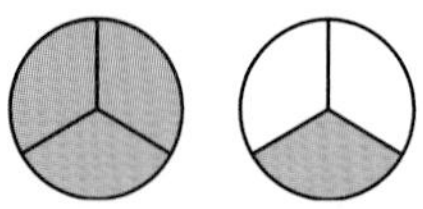

22. 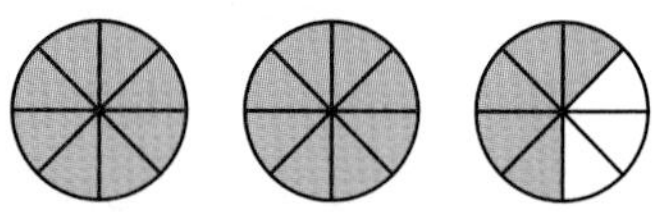

Problem Solving

23. Anthony divided a hoagie into 6 equal parts. He and 2 friends shared the hoagie equally. How many pieces did each of them eat?

24. Jeff has 8 apples to make applesauce. Half are Mclintosh apples and the rest are Empire apples. How many of each kind of apple does he have?

25. Kisha's recipe calls for $\frac{1}{4}$ teaspoon allspice, $\frac{1}{2}$ teaspoon nutmeg, and $1\frac{1}{2}$ teaspoons cinnamon. Does Kisha need more allspice or more nutmeg?

What do you think?

If $\frac{1}{6}$ of a picture is red and the rest is green, how can you tell what fraction of the picture is green?

Journal Idea If you fold a sheet of paper as shown, is each section a fourth? Explain why or why not.

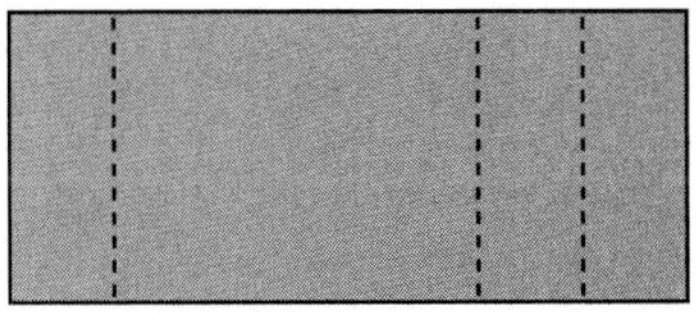

Critical Thinking Corner

Using Algebra **Logical Thinking**

Animal Fractions

Help Farmer Whitney plan a field for his horses, pigs, and chickens. Use the model below.

These are the rules.

- You must use the whole field.
- You may only use whole squares.
- The horses need half the land.
- The chickens and pigs each need the same amount of land.
- Each type of animal must be in a separate square.

How many squares does each type of animal get?

A Garden in Part

Sometimes you can use decimals to name parts of regions or sets.

Learning About It

Look at the plan for a garden. There are 10 equal rows or parts. Each row is $\frac{1}{10}$ of the garden.

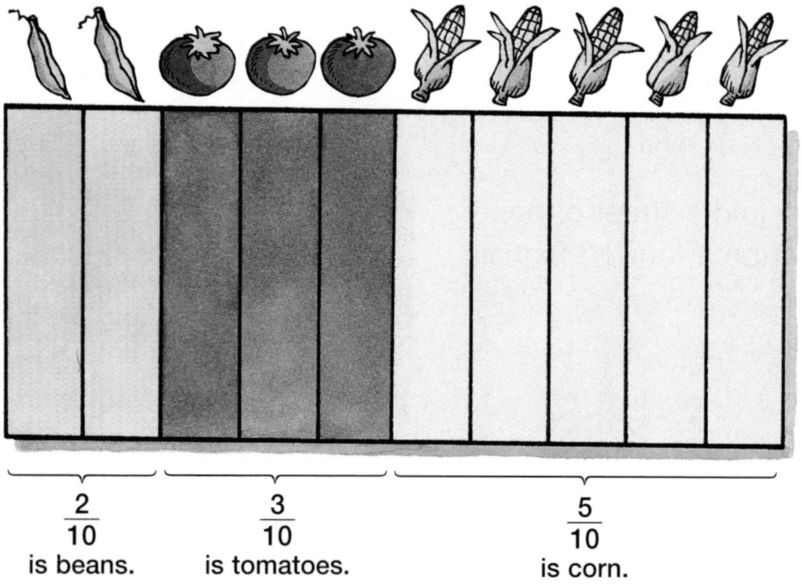

Word Bank

decimal
decimal point

What You Need

For each student:
grid paper
crayons

There is another way to name the parts of the garden. You can use **decimals.** One tenth can be written as $\frac{1}{10}$ or 0.1.

ones		tenths
0	.	1

decimal point

The chart below tells about the parts of the garden in fractions and decimals.

Plants	Color	Fraction	Decimal
green beans	green	$\frac{2}{10}$	0.2
tomatoes	red	$\frac{3}{10}$	0.3
corn	yellow	$\frac{5}{10}$	0.5

Work with a partner.

Step 1 Together choose 3 or 4 vegetables that you will both use in your own garden plans. On grid paper, outline an area that is 10 squares long and 10 squares wide. Divide the area into 10 equal rows.

Step 2 Decide how many rows of each kind of vegetable to plant. Color the rows. Use a different color for each kind of vegetable.

Step 3 Record each plan in a chart like the one on page 420.

▲ **Kid Connection**
Brittany Jones takes part in a program in New Jersey where kids plan, plant, and take care of gardens. They donate some of the vegetables they have grown to a local homeless shelter.

Think and Discuss Suppose 0.2 of a garden was left unplanted. What decimal would describe the planted part?

Practice

1. What decimals are shown in your plan? in your partner's plan?
2. Which vegetable takes up the largest part of your plan? the largest part of your partner's plan?
3. Suppose you want to plant green beans, tomatoes, and corn. You want the same number of rows for tomatoes and corn, but more rows for green beans. How could you plan your garden?

Tasty Tenths

Fractions can be written as decimals.

Learning About It

The menu at the right is divided into 10 equal parts. The 4 hearts show healthy foods. How can you describe the part of the menu marked by hearts?

- You can use a **place-value chart**.

ones		tenths
0	.	4

↑ decimal point

- You can write a **fraction** or **decimal**.

$\frac{4}{10}$ or 0.4

- You can use **words**.

four tenths

0.4 of the menu items is marked by hearts.

More Examples

What part of the shape is shaded?

A. 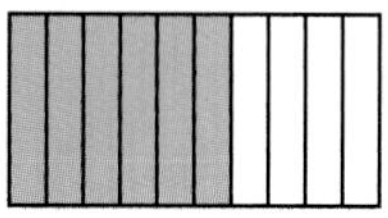

Fraction: $\frac{6}{10}$

Decimal: 0.6

Words: six tenths

B. 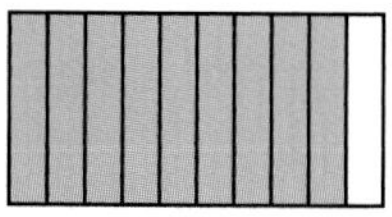

Fraction: $\frac{9}{10}$

Decimal: 0.9

Words: nine tenths

Think and Discuss The fraction name for the entire menu above is $\frac{10}{10}$. The decimal name for all the parts is 1.0. Explain what these names mean.

Try It Out

Write a fraction and a decimal for the shaded part.

1. 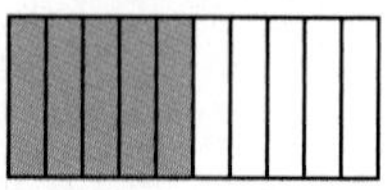

2. 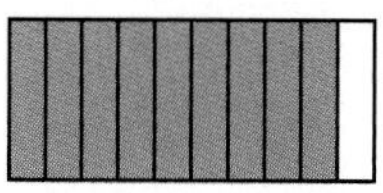

3. 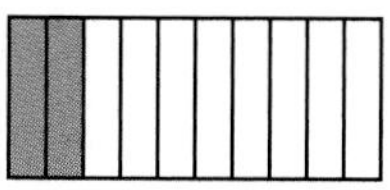

4. 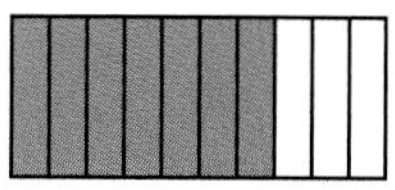

Practice

Write a fraction and a decimal for the shaded part.

5. 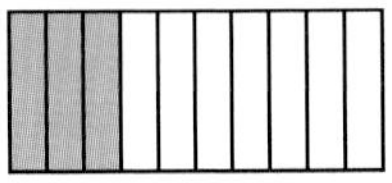

6. 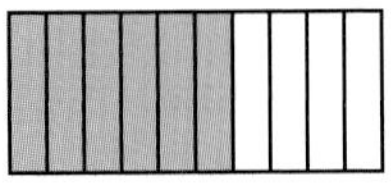

7. 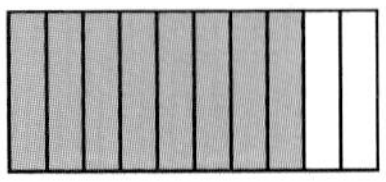

8. 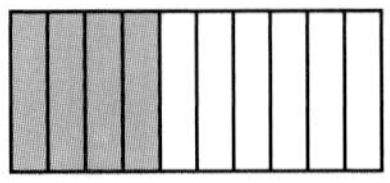

Write each as a decimal.

9. $\frac{4}{10}$ **10.** $\frac{9}{10}$ **11.** $\frac{3}{10}$ **12.** $\frac{7}{10}$ **13.** $\frac{8}{10}$ **14.** $\frac{1}{10}$

15. two tenths **16.** six tenths **17.** three tenths

18. one tenth **19.** nine tenths **20.** five tenths

Problem Solving

21. Which picture shows 1.0 shaded?

a. 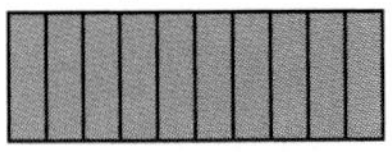

b. 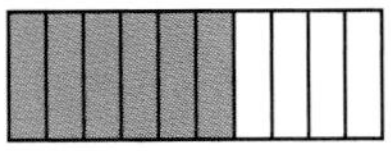

c. 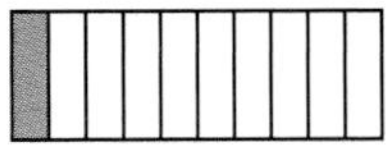

22. Draw a picture to show $\frac{4}{10}$. Then write the decimal shown by your picture.

23. Draw a picture to show 0.9. Then write the fraction shown by your picture.

Review and Remember

Round to the nearest hundred.

24. 432 **25.** 311 **26.** 692 **27.** 750 **28.** 945 **29.** 954

Time for Technology

Using a Calculator

Fractions to Decimals

You can use a calculator to see $\frac{4}{10}$ written as a decimal.

Press: 4 ÷ 1 0 = Display: 0.4

Use a calculator. Write each fraction as a decimal.

1. $\frac{5}{10}$ **2.** $\frac{1}{10}$ **3.** $\frac{3}{5}$ **4.** $\frac{2}{5}$ **5.** $\frac{1}{2}$ **6.** $\frac{4}{5}$

Mooove Over!

Like tenths, hundredths can be written as decimals, too!

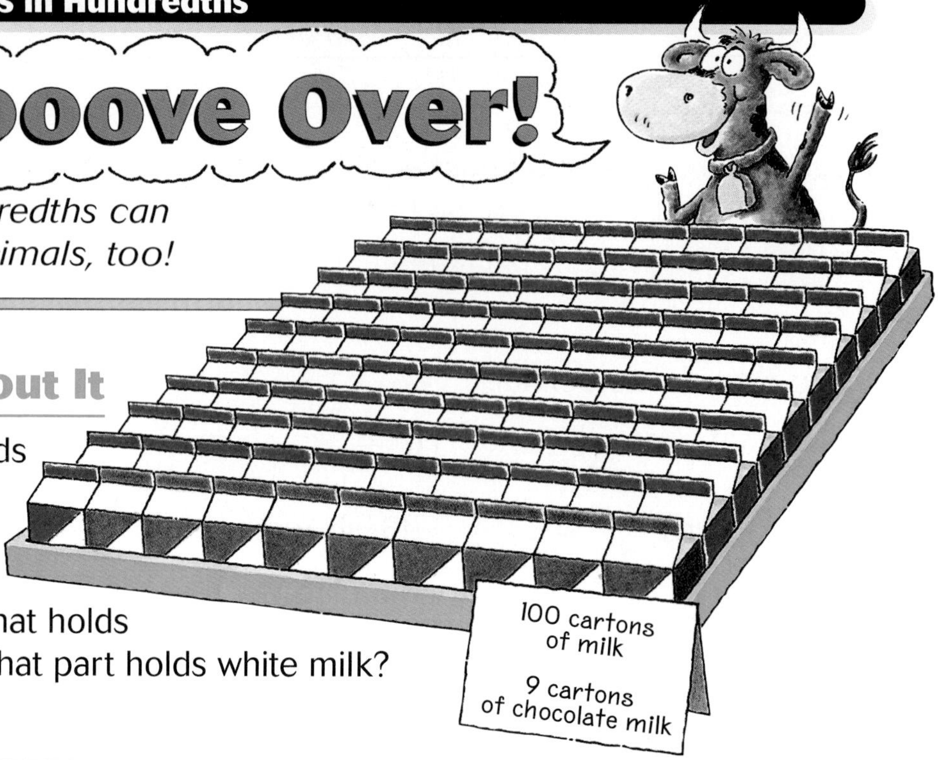

Learning About It

The milk crate holds 100 cartons in all. How can you describe the part of the crate that holds chocolate milk? What part holds white milk?

THERE'S ALWAYS A WAY!

	Chocolate Milk	White Milk
• You can use a **place-value chart**.	ones: 0 . tenths: 0, hundredths: 9 (decimal point)	ones: 0 . tenths: 9, hundredths: 1 (decimal point)
• You can write a **fraction** or **decimal**.	$\frac{9}{100}$ or 0.09	$\frac{91}{100}$ or 0.91
• You can use **words**.	nine hundredths	ninety-one hundredths

0.09 of the crate holds chocolate milk.
0.91 of the crate holds white milk.

More Examples

You use a decimal point and a dollar sign to write money.

A. 24 pennies

Decimal: $0.24

Words: 24 cents

B. 3 dimes, 9 pennies

Decimal: $0.39

Words: 39 cents

A penny is $\frac{1}{100}$ or 0.01 of a dollar.

A dime is $\frac{1}{10}$ or 0.10 of a dollar.

Think and Discuss What decimal would you write to show 9 dimes and 9 pennies?

Try It Out

Write a fraction and a decimal for the shaded part.

1. 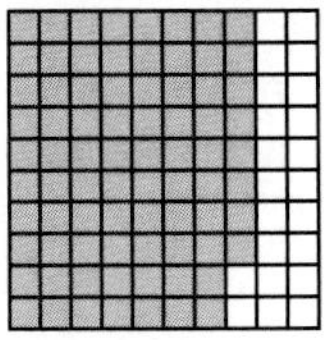

2. 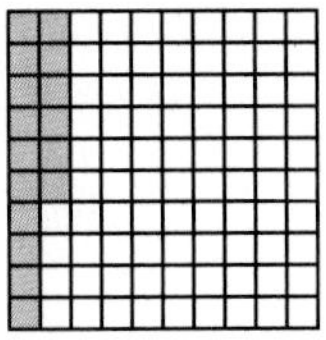

3. 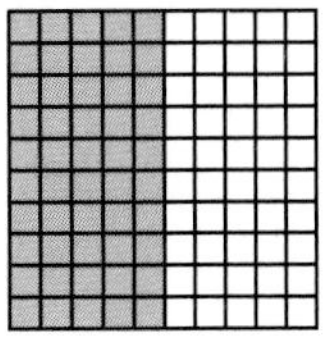

4. 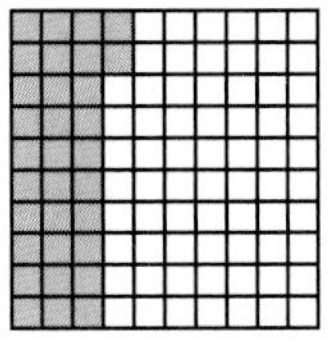

Write each as a decimal.

5. $\frac{11}{100}$ **6.** $\frac{60}{100}$ **7.** $\frac{51}{100}$ **8.** $\frac{12}{100}$ **9.** $\frac{42}{100}$ **10.** $\frac{6}{100}$

11. 5 pennies **12.** 49 pennies **13.** 6 dimes **14.** 5 dimes 8 pennies

Practice

Write each as a decimal.

15. $\frac{79}{100}$ **16.** $\frac{8}{100}$ **17.** $\frac{90}{100}$ **18.** $\frac{9}{100}$ **19.** $\frac{25}{100}$ **20.** $\frac{80}{100}$

21. three hundredths **22.** sixty-two hundredths **23.** four hundredths

24. 87 pennies **25.** 2 dimes, 6 pennies **26.** 4 dimes 9 pennies

What is the value of the digit 3 in each number?

27. 0.83 **28.** 0.53 **29.** 0.30 **30.** $0.32 **31.** $0.03

Problem Solving

32. At the school bake sale, 84 out of 100 muffins were sold. What decimal shows what part of the 100 muffins was sold?

33. Stamps are sold in sheets of 100. Suppose you bought 1.25 sheets of stamps. How many stamps did you buy?

34. Brenda has 7 dimes and 15 pennies. How much money does she have? Write your answer using a dollar sign and decimal point.

Review and Remember

How many line segments are there in each figure?

35. 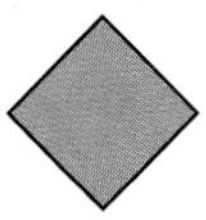

36. 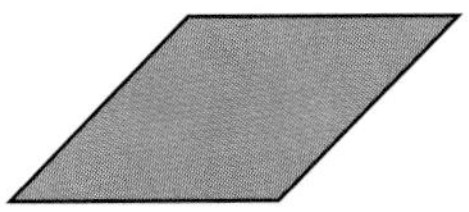

37. 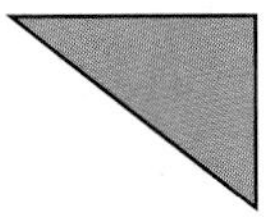

38. 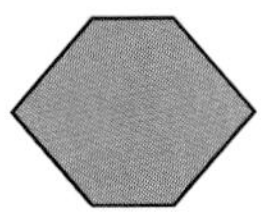

For Extra Practice, see Set H, page 438.

Pizza Pizazz

Decimals can be used to show more than one.

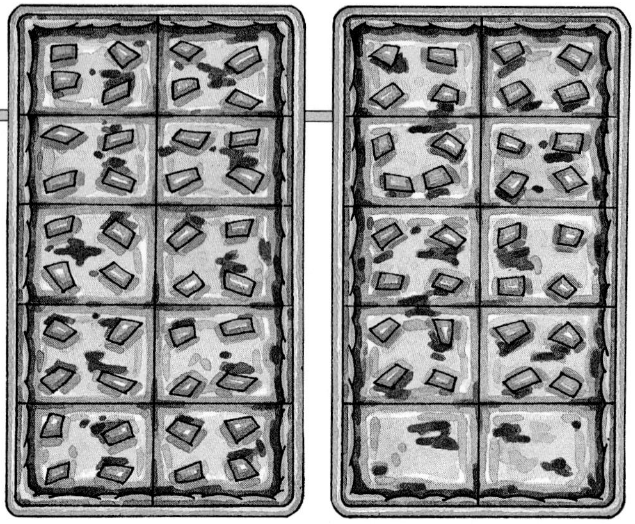

Learning About It

Chuck ordered 2 Sicilian pizzas. Each pizza was cut into 10 equal pieces. There are green pepper strips on 18 of the pieces. There are many ways to describe how much of the pizza has green pepper on it.

THERE'S ALWAYS A WAY!

- You can use a **place-value chart**.

ones		tenths
1	.	8

↑ decimal point

- You can write a **fraction** or **decimal**.

$1\frac{8}{10}$ or 1.8

- You can use **words**.

one and eight tenths

1.8 of the pizza has green peppers on it.

More Examples

A. You can use decimals to describe these grids.

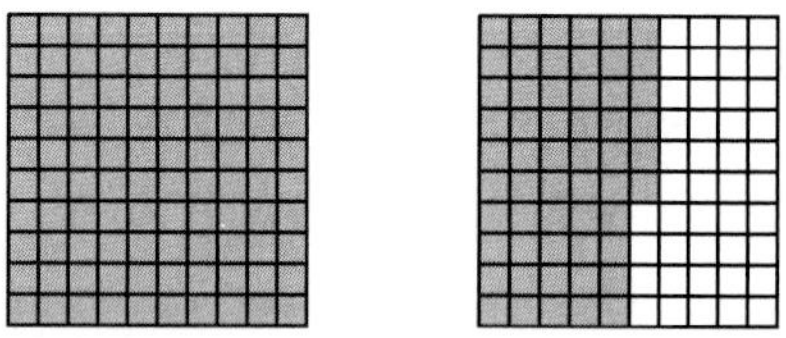

Place-Value Chart:

ones		tenths	hundredths
1	.	5	6

↑ decimal point

Write: $1\frac{56}{100}$ or 1.56

Words: one and fifty-six hundredths

B. You use decimals when you write money.

Write: $2.35

Words: two dollars and thirty-five cents

Think and Discuss Look at the numbers $1\frac{5}{10}$ and 1.5. How are they the same? How are they different?

Try It Out

Write a decimal for the shaded part.

1. 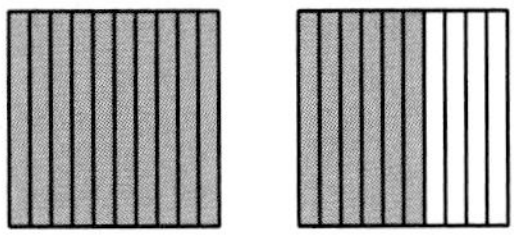

2. 

3. 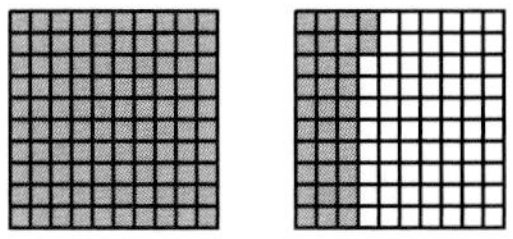

Write each mixed number as a decimal.

4. $6\frac{1}{10}$ **5.** $3\frac{45}{100}$ **6.** $8\frac{7}{10}$ **7.** $1\frac{86}{100}$ **8.** $5\frac{3}{100}$

Practice

Write a decimal for the shaded part.

9. 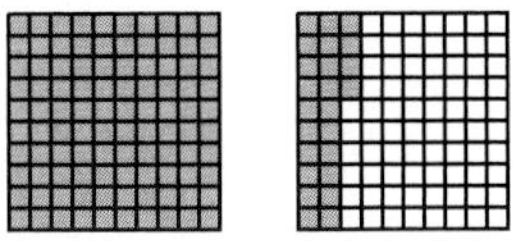

10. 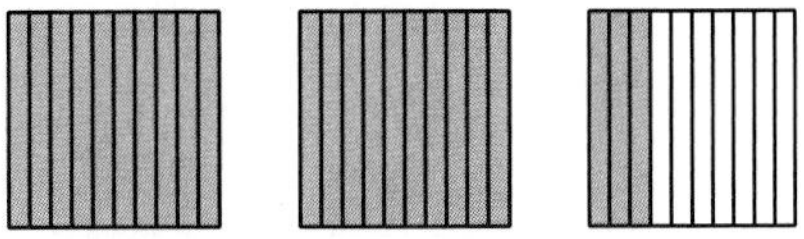

11. 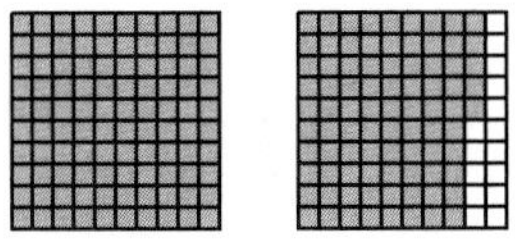

Write each mixed number as a decimal.

12. $3\frac{4}{10}$ **13.** $7\frac{4}{10}$ **14.** $9\frac{61}{100}$ **15.** $4\frac{15}{100}$ **16.** $8\frac{9}{100}$

What is the value of the digit 7 in each number?

17. 2.67 **18.** 4.7 **19.** $7.46

Problem Solving

20. Nan's team had 3 pizzas. Each pizza was cut into 10 equal pieces. The team ate 2 whole pizzas and 3 pieces from the third pizza. Write a mixed number and a decimal to tell how much pizza was eaten.

21. Analyze Add one penny to each amount: 9 cents, $0.99, $9.99. Then write each amount as a decimal.

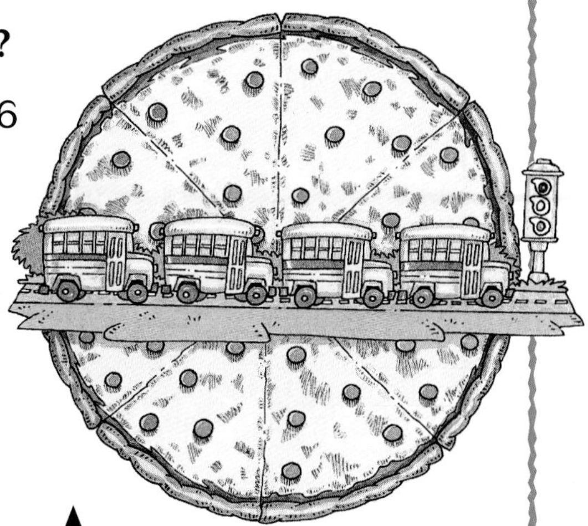

The largest pizza ever made was made in Norwood, South Africa, in 1990. It measured 122 feet 8 inches across. That's about the length of four school buses!

www.sbgmath.com

Review and Remember

Find each answer.

22. 486 + 285 **23.** 354 − 246 **24.** 8 × 9 **25.** 63 ÷ 7

For Extra Practice, see Set I, page 438.

Fruit Toss

You can add and subtract decimals the same way you add and subtract whole numbers.

Learning About It

What You Need

For each student:
decimal models

Brad made a fruit salad for the class picnic. He used 2.6 pounds of watermelon, 1.8 pounds of strawberries, and 3.2 pounds of bananas. How many pounds of melon and strawberries did he use in the salad?

Use decimal models to find the sum.

This is one whole. 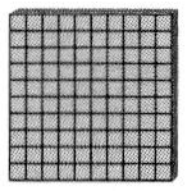 This is one tenth. 

Step 1

Show 2.6 and 1.8 using decimal models.

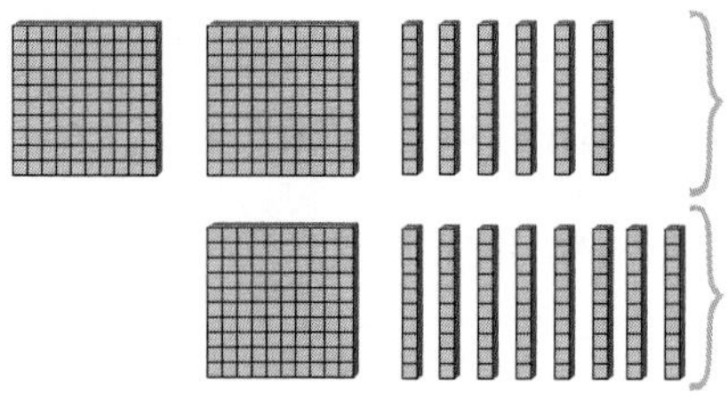

Step 2

Add tenths.
6 + 8 = 14 tenths

Regroup 14 tenths as 1 whole and 4 tenths.

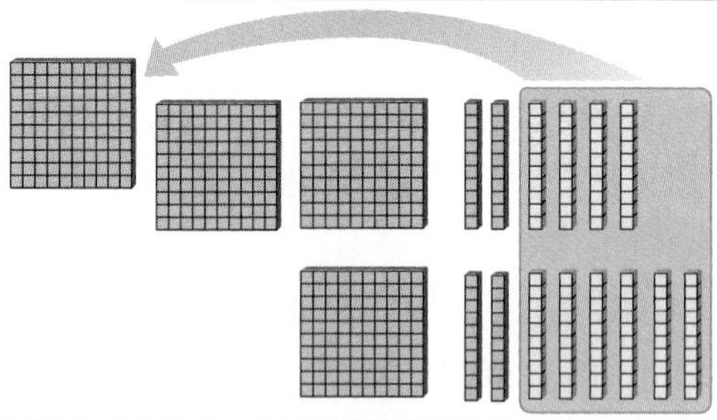

$$\begin{array}{r} {}^{1}\ \ \\ 2.6 \\ +\ 1.8 \\ \hline 4 \end{array}$$

14 tenths

Step 3

Add ones.
1 + 2 + 1 = 4 ones

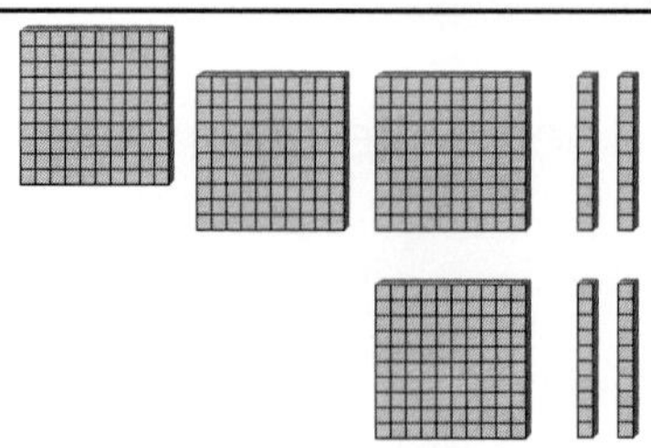

$$\begin{array}{r} {}^{1}\ \ \\ 2.6 \\ +\ 1.8 \\ \hline 4.4 \end{array}$$

Place the decimal point.

Brad used 4.4 pounds of watermelon and strawberries.

Connecting Ideas

So far you have been adding decimals.
Now try subtracting.

How many more pounds of bananas than strawberries did Brad use in his fruit salad?

www.sbgmath.com

Step 1 Show 3.2 using decimal models.	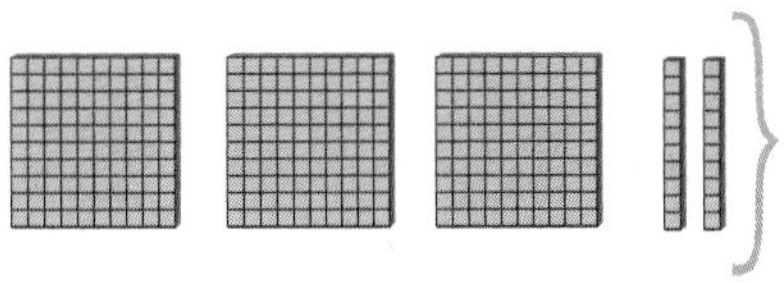	**3.2**
Step 2 You need to subtract 0.8 from 0.2, so you need more tenths to subtract. Regroup 1 one as 10 tenths. Then subtract the tenths. 12 tenths − 8 tenths = 4 tenths	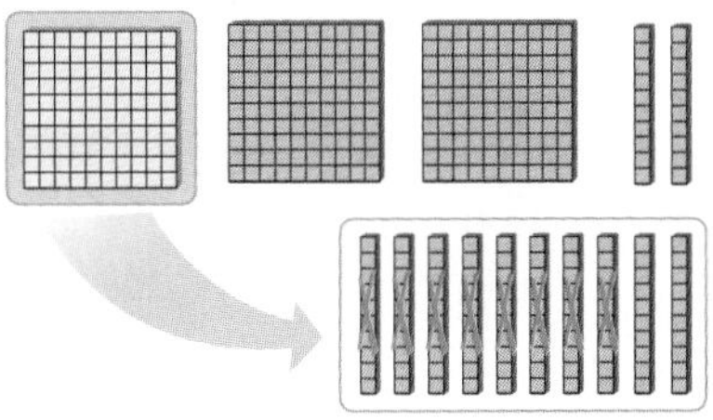	2 12 ~~3~~.~~2~~ − 1.8 4
Step 3 Subtract the ones. 2 ones − 1 one = 1 one	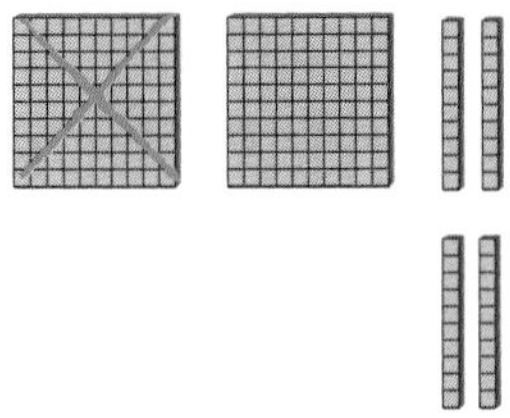	2 12 ~~3~~.~~2~~ − 1.8 1.4 Place the decimal point.

Brad used 1.4 more pounds of bananas.

Another Example

Step 1 Regroup 1 one as 10 tenths. Subtract tenths.	**Step 2** Subtract ones.
$\begin{array}{r} \overset{3\ 13}{\cancel{4}.\cancel{3}} \\ -\ 2.6 \\ \hline 7 \end{array}$ 4 ones 3 tenths = 3 ones 13 tenths; 13 tenths − 6 tenths = 7 tenths	$\begin{array}{r} \overset{3\ 13}{\cancel{4}.\cancel{3}} \\ -\ 2.6 \\ \hline 1.7 \end{array}$ 3 ones − 2 ones = 1 one

Think and Discuss How is subtracting decimals like subtracting whole numbers? How is it different?

Try It Out

Use decimal models to add.

1. 2.3 + 0.1
2. 5.3 + 3.8
3. 3.2 + 0.8
4. 6.1 + 5.3
5. 1.7 + 0.9

Use decimal models to subtract.

6. 1.3 − 0.3
7. 3.1 − 1.1
8. 0.9 − 0.3
9. 4.2 − 2.7
10. 2.6 − 1.9

Practice

Find each sum or difference.

11. 6.2 + 4.8
12. 5.4 − 1.0
13. 5.1 + 6.9
14. 6.1 − 3.2
15. 2.3 − 1.7
16. 4.2 + 2.7
17. 3.4 − 1.5
18. 1.6 + 3.7
19. 8.7 − 7.8
20. 4.4 + 3.9
21. 0.6 + 0.3
22. 1.3 − 0.2
23. 2.3 − 1.4
24. 0.6 + 0.7
25. 4.2 + 3.4

26. 1.5 + 7.5 **27.** 9.5 − 1.7 **28.** 0.6 + 9.4 **29.** 3.8 − 2.9

30. 2.5 + 2.7 **31.** 7.3 − 5.6 **32.** 3.7 − 1.8 **33.** 6.2 + 0.9

Problem Solving

34. Sara rode her bike 0.7 mile to the store. Then she turned around and went home. When she returned home she had ridden 1.5 miles. Did she use the same route going back home?

35. **Create Your Own** Write a problem in which you add or subtract decimals. Exchange problems with a classmate.

36. **Health and Fitness Connection** There is vitamin C in fruits. As part of a healthful diet, Florrie needs 45 milligrams of vitamin C a day. Yesterday, she ate 1 orange. Did she get enough vitamin C for the day? Explain.

Review and Remember

Use the bar graph to answer Questions 37–39.

37. How many students picked plums?

38. Which fruit was the most popular?

39. Which fruits had the same number of votes?

Project Link

Picnic time is getting closer! When your group has finished making its menu, do these things.

- Figure out how you would share the picnic food equally.
- Write down how much of each food each person would get.

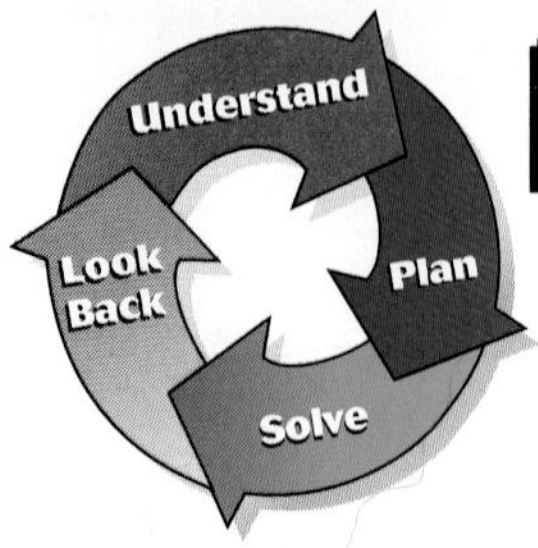

Problem Solving
Using Money

You can add and subtract money to solve problems.

Look at the menu at the right. Suppose you order a roast beef sandwich with Swiss cheese. If you pay with a $5 bill, how much change will you get back?

UNDERSTAND

What do you need to know?

You need to know that a roast beef sandwich costs $3.95 plus $0.65 extra for the Swiss cheese. You also need to know that you paid with a $5 bill.

PLAN

How can you solve the problem?

First add the cost of the sandwich and the cost of the cheese. Then subtract the total cost from the amount you paid.

SOLVE

Step 1

$3.95 (regrouped: 1 1)	← roast beef sandwich
+ .65	← Swiss cheese
$4.60	← total cost

Step 2

$5.00 (regrouped: 4 10)	← what you paid
−4.60	← total cost
$0.40	← change

You will get $0.40 in change.

LOOK BACK

How could you use the act it out strategy to check your answer?

Show What You Learned

Use the information below and on page 432 to solve each problem.

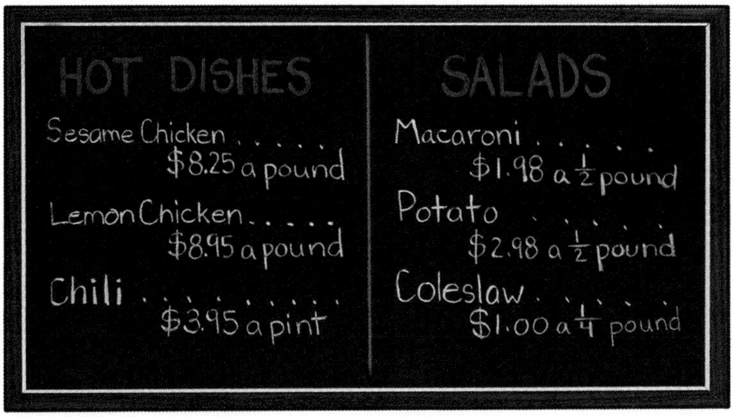

1. Gary buys a chicken salad sandwich with tomatoes and peppers. He pays for the sandwich with a $10 bill. How much change should he get back?

2. **Explain** Sherri wants to spend no more than $25 at the deli. She wants to order as much sesame chicken as she can. How many pounds can she buy? Explain how you know.

3. Kenya orders 2 egg salad sandwiches with tomatoes and a half pound of macaroni salad. She gives the salesperson $10. What is her change?

4. **Analyze** Darrell has $7. He wants a roast beef sandwich with tomatoes. Does he have enough money left to also buy $\frac{1}{2}$ pound of potato salad?

5. Joan orders a tuna salad sandwich with cheese. She gives the clerk three $1 bills and 2 quarters. How much more money does Joan owe?

6. **Analyze** Suppose you ordered $\frac{1}{4}$ pound of coleslaw and 2 egg salad sandwiches with tomatoes and cheese. Which bag at the right holds your order?

7. **Create Your Own** Write a problem using information from the menus. Give it to a classmate to solve.

Checkpoint

Decimals

Write a fraction and a decimal for the shaded part.
(pages 422–427)

1. 

2. 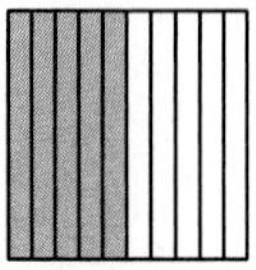

3. 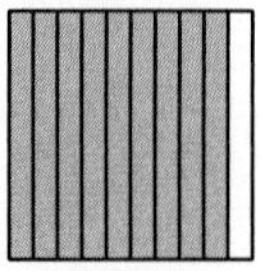

4. 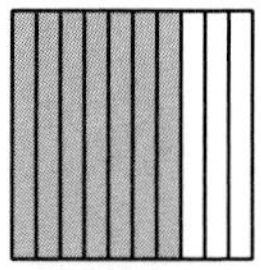

5. 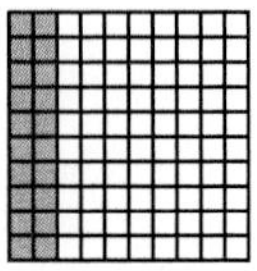

6. 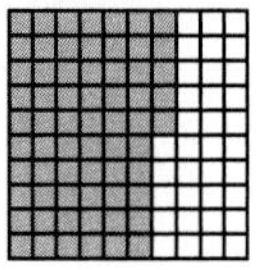

7. 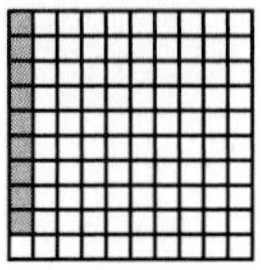

8. 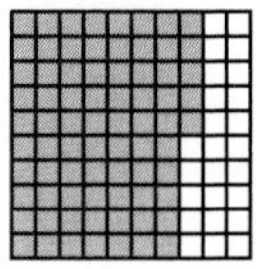

9. 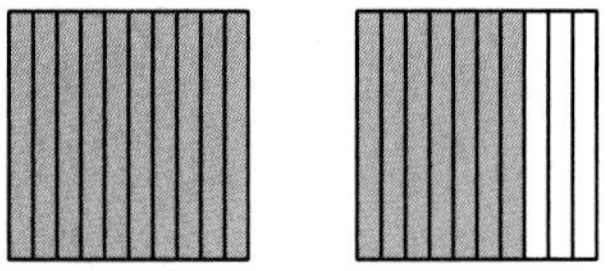

10. 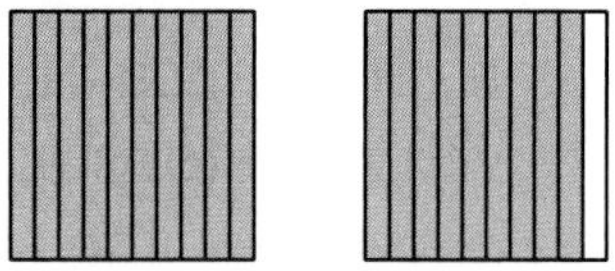

Write each as a decimal. (pages 420–427)

11. $\frac{3}{10}$ **12.** $\frac{8}{10}$ **13.** $\frac{10}{10}$ **14.** $\frac{2}{10}$ **15.** $\frac{7}{10}$

16. $\frac{32}{100}$ **17.** $\frac{6}{100}$ **18.** $\frac{95}{100}$ **19.** $\frac{4}{100}$ **20.** $\frac{58}{100}$

21. $7\frac{3}{10}$ **22.** $4\frac{79}{100}$ **23.** $1\frac{6}{100}$ **24.** $5\frac{9}{10}$ **25.** $8\frac{18}{100}$

26. four tenths

27. one tenth

28. nine hundredths

29. fifteen hundredths

30. eighty-nine hundredths

31. three hundredths

Find each sum or difference. (pages 428–431)

32. $\begin{array}{r} 0.8 \\ +\ 0.1 \\ \hline \end{array}$ **33.** $\begin{array}{r} 1.3 \\ +\ 2.5 \\ \hline \end{array}$ **34.** $\begin{array}{r} 0.7 \\ +\ 0.8 \\ \hline \end{array}$ **35.** $\begin{array}{r} 2.6 \\ +\ 1.4 \\ \hline \end{array}$

36. $\begin{array}{r} 0.7 \\ -\ 0.2 \\ \hline \end{array}$ **37.** $\begin{array}{r} 2.6 \\ -\ 1.3 \\ \hline \end{array}$ **38.** $\begin{array}{r} 1.4 \\ -\ 0.8 \\ \hline \end{array}$ **39.** $\begin{array}{r} 3.6 \\ -\ 1.9 \\ \hline \end{array}$

40. $4.3 + 4.5$

41. $6.9 - 2.8$

Problem Solving

42. Han bought yogurt with 4 quarters and 3 dimes. How much money did he spend?

43. Carlos rode his bicycle 0.6 mile to the store. Then he rode it 0.5 mile to a friend's house. How many miles did he ride?

44. Ruth ran 1.5 miles. Jackie ran 0.9 mile. Who ran farther? how much farther?

45. Flora and her mother used 100 squares of fabric to make a quilt. Forty-five squares are red. The rest are white. What part of the quilt is white? Write your answer as a fraction and a decimal.

What do you think?

How are fractions and decimals alike? How are they different?

Journal Idea When might you use fractions or decimals outside of school?

Project Wrap-Up

Eat Up!

Now that you have finished your menu, you are probably ready to sit down and eat! To wrap up the project, you can:

- Talk together about how knowing fractions helped you in the project.
- Present your picnic plan to the class and ask who would like to come along!

Extra Practice

Set A (pages 402–403)

Write a fraction for the shaded part.

1. 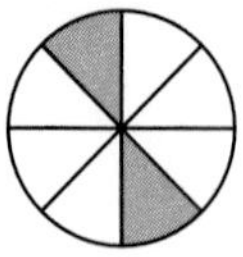

2. 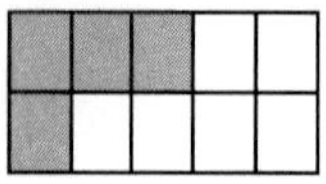

3. 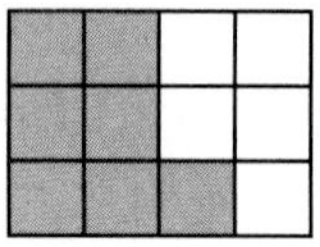

4. 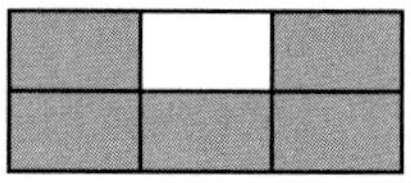

Write a fraction and draw a picture for each.

5. four fifths

6. three eighths

7. two thirds

8. one fourth

9. two tenths

10. five sixths

Using Algebra

Set B (pages 404–405)

Name the equivalent fraction.

1. 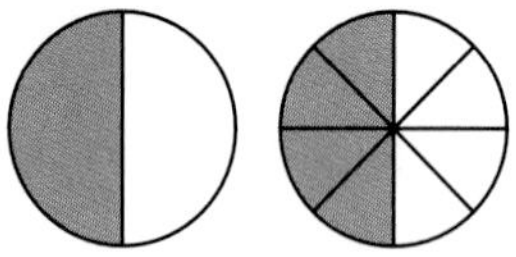

$\frac{1}{2} = \frac{■}{8}$

2. 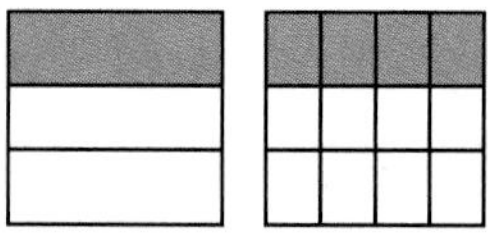

$\frac{1}{3} = \frac{■}{12}$

3. 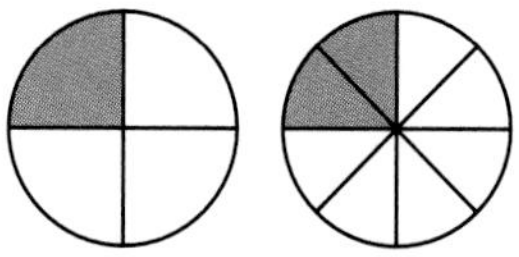

$\frac{1}{4} = \frac{■}{8}$

4. 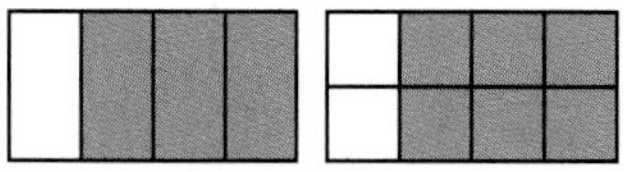

$\frac{3}{4} = \frac{■}{■}$

5. 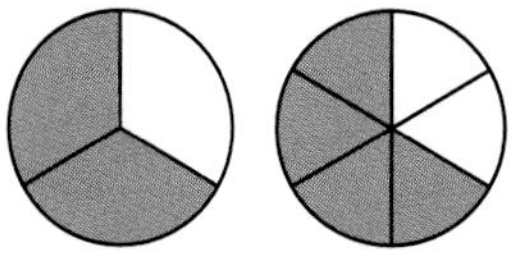

$\frac{2}{3} = \frac{■}{■}$

6. 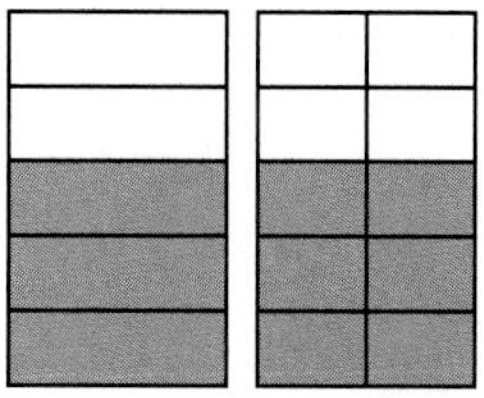

$\frac{3}{5} = \frac{■}{■}$

Set C (pages 406–407)

Compare. Use >, <, or = for each ●.

1. 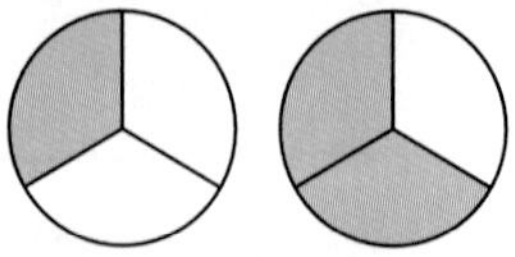

$\frac{1}{3}$ ● $\frac{2}{3}$

2. 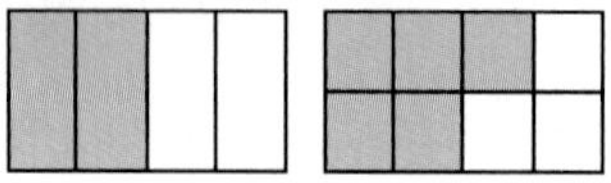

$\frac{2}{4}$ ● $\frac{5}{8}$

3. 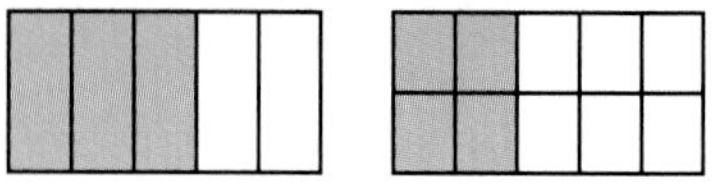

$\frac{3}{5}$ ● $\frac{4}{10}$

4. Anna and Paco each made the same number of pies for a bake sale. Anna sold $\frac{2}{3}$ of her pies. Paco sold $\frac{2}{6}$ of his pies. Who sold more?

Extra Practice

Set D (pages 408–409)

Write a fraction to name the part that is shaded.

1. 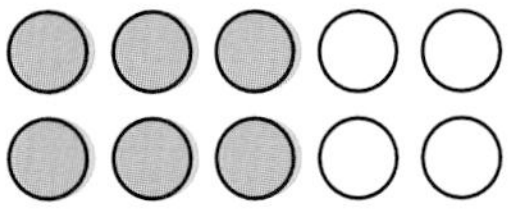

2. 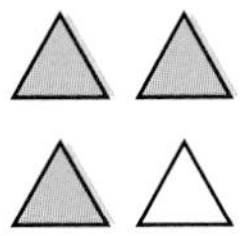

3. 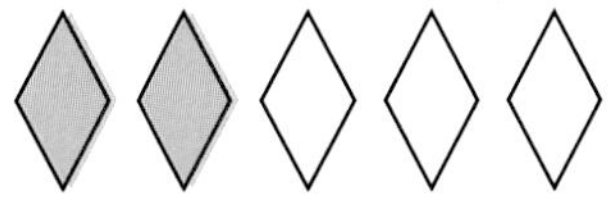

Write a fraction for each.

4. 3 out of 8 hats are purple.

5. 7 out of 12 shirts are yellow.

6. 6 out of 10 coats are red.

7. 4 out of 5 jeans are blue.

Set E (pages 410–411)

Use counters to find each answer.

1. 

$\frac{1}{2}$ of 6 = ■

2. 

$\frac{1}{4}$ of 8 = ■

3. 

$\frac{1}{5}$ of 15 = ■

4. $\frac{1}{6}$ of 12 = ■

5. $\frac{1}{3}$ of 9= ■

6. $\frac{1}{2}$ of 18 = ■

7. $\frac{1}{3}$ of 15 = ■

8. $\frac{1}{4}$ of 16= ■

9. $\frac{1}{6}$ of 36 = ■

Set F (pages 414–415)

Write a mixed number to name the shaded part.

1. 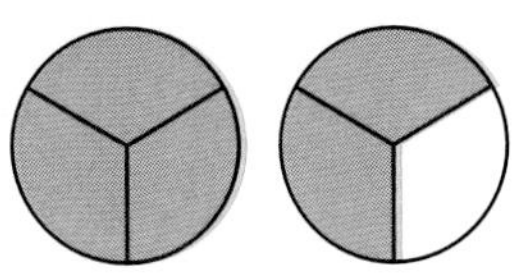

2. 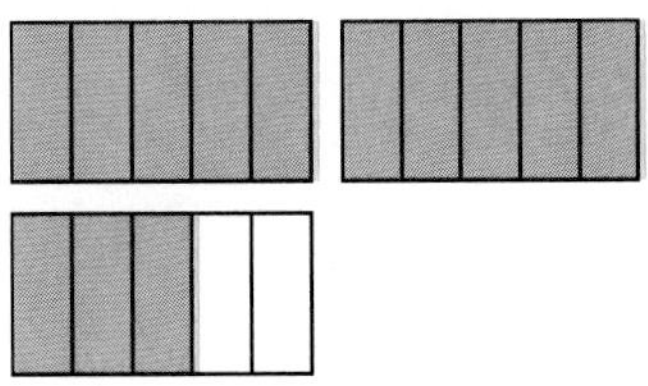

3. 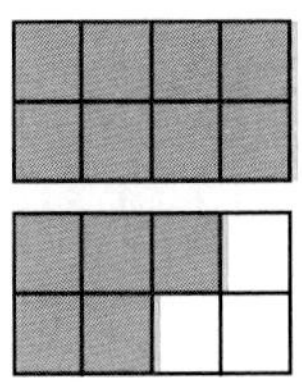

Draw a picture to show each mixed number.

4. $8\frac{7}{10}$

5. $1\frac{2}{5}$

6. $2\frac{1}{6}$

7. $3\frac{1}{2}$

8. $3\frac{3}{4}$

Extra Practice

Set G (pages 422–423)

Write a decimal for each.

1. 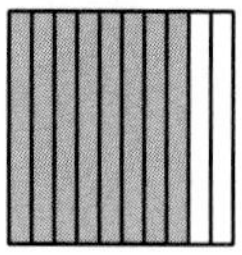
2. 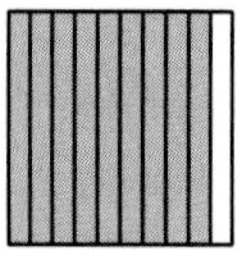
3. 
4. 

5. $\frac{4}{10}$ **6.** $\frac{9}{10}$ **7.** six tenths **8.** two tenths

Set H (pages 424–425)

Write a decimal for each.

1. 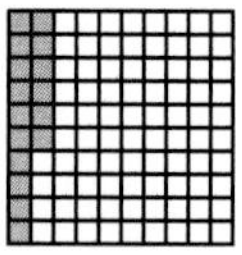
2. 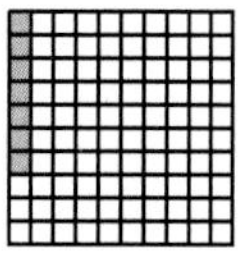
3. 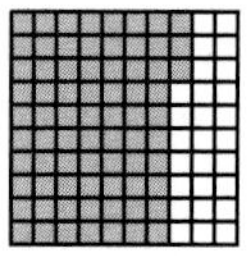
4. 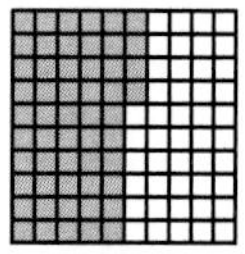

5. $\frac{85}{100}$ **6.** $\frac{37}{100}$ **7.** one hundredth **8.** fifty-two hundredths

Set I (pages 426–427)

Write a decimal for each.

1. 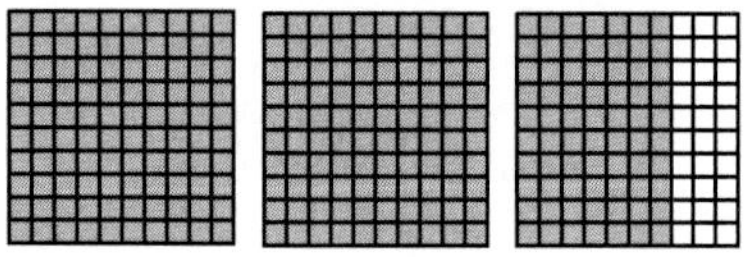
2. 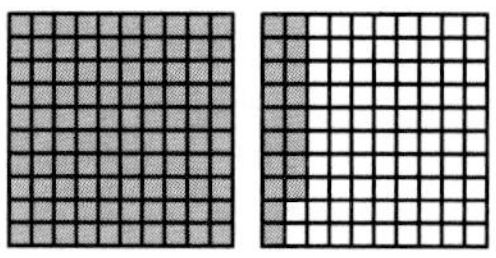
3. 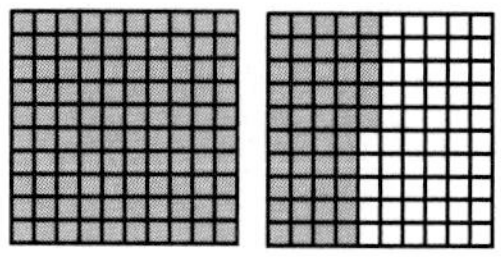

4. $3\frac{2}{10}$ **5.** $14\frac{5}{100}$ **6.** $7\frac{6}{10}$ **7.** $4\frac{81}{100}$

Set J (pages 428–431)

Add or subtract.

1. $\begin{array}{r} 4.6 \\ +\ 3.9 \\ \hline \end{array}$ **2.** $\begin{array}{r} 3.8 \\ -\ 2.4 \\ \hline \end{array}$ **3.** $\begin{array}{r} 7.4 \\ +\ 1.7 \\ \hline \end{array}$ **4.** $\begin{array}{r} 9.3 \\ +\ 2.8 \\ \hline \end{array}$ **5.** $\begin{array}{r} 3.3 \\ -\ 0.7 \\ \hline \end{array}$

6. $8.9 - 3.1$ **7.** $4.4 + 2.4$ **8.** $3.2 + 8.3$ **9.** $6.5 - 2.3$

Chapter Test

Write a fraction for the shaded part.

1. 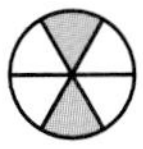

2. 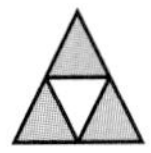

3. 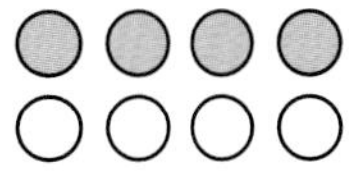

Write the equivalent fraction.

4. 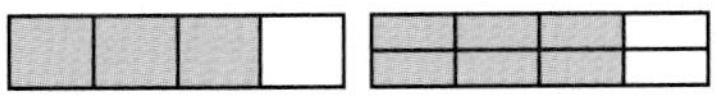

$\frac{3}{4} = \frac{■}{■}$

5. 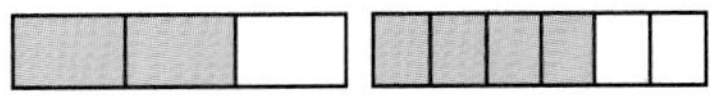

$\frac{2}{3} = \frac{■}{■}$

Compare. Use >, <, or = for each ●.

6. 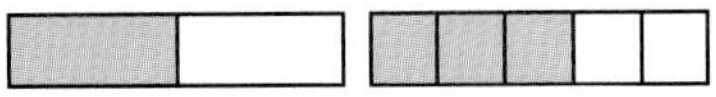

$\frac{1}{2}$ ● $\frac{3}{5}$

7. 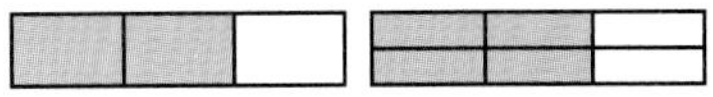

$\frac{2}{3}$ ● $\frac{4}{6}$

Draw a picture to find each answer.

8. $\frac{1}{2}$ of 10 = ■ **9.** $\frac{1}{4}$ of 12 = ■ **10.** $\frac{1}{3}$ of 9 = ■ **11.** $\frac{1}{3}$ of 12 = ■

Draw a picture to show each mixed number.

12. $1\frac{8}{10}$ **13.** $3\frac{4}{5}$ **14.** $2\frac{1}{4}$ **15.** $4\frac{3}{8}$

Write each as a decimal.

16. $\frac{5}{10}$ **17.** $1\frac{59}{100}$ **18.** $\frac{4}{100}$ **19.** $2\frac{8}{10}$

Find each sum or difference.

20. $0.3 + 0.4$ **21.** $0.8 - 0.5$ **22.** $2.3 + 2.7$ **23.** $8.3 - 5.7$

24. Al bought 2.8 pounds of cheese. He ate 0.5 pound of it. How much cheese is left?

25. A carton of 12 eggs fell on the floor. One third of the eggs broke. How many eggs broke?

Self-Check

Look back at Exercises 22 and 23. Check to see that you regrouped correctly each time.

Performance Assessment

Show What You Know About Fractions and Decimals

What You Need

grid paper
red, yellow, green, and blue crayons

1. Use the picture below to answer Questions 1a–1c.

   a. What part of the whole is shaded green?

   b. What part of the whole is *not* shaded green?

   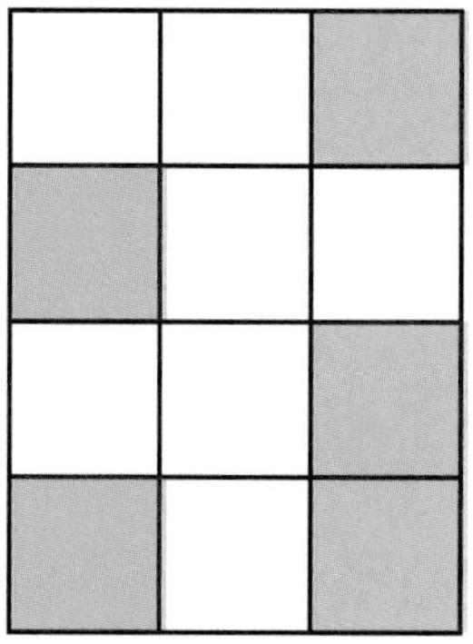

   c. Copy the picture onto grid paper. Color in the remaining squares so that $\frac{1}{3}$ of the whole is blue, $\frac{1}{6}$ is red, and $\frac{1}{12}$ is yellow.

2. Use the menu to the right to answer Questions 2a and 2b. Suppose you have \$3.50 to spend. Choose at least two items to buy.

   a. What will you buy? How much will the items cost? How much money will you have left?

   b. Which is the most costly item on the menu? How many of that item could you buy?

Menu

Sandwiches	
Cheese	\$1.05
Tuna	\$1.55
Chicken	\$1.75
Roast beef	\$2.25
Desserts	
Fruit salad	\$0.95
Rice pudding	\$0.60
Drinks	
Milk	\$0.85
Juice	\$0.55

Self-Check

For Questions 1a and 1b, did you use fractions in your answer?

For Question 2a, did you choose at least two items to buy?

Extension

The Russian Abacus

Social Studies Connection The Russian abacus is used as a counting board. Some boards have 7 wires. The 5th wire from the top has only one bead on it. That bead marks the decimal point.

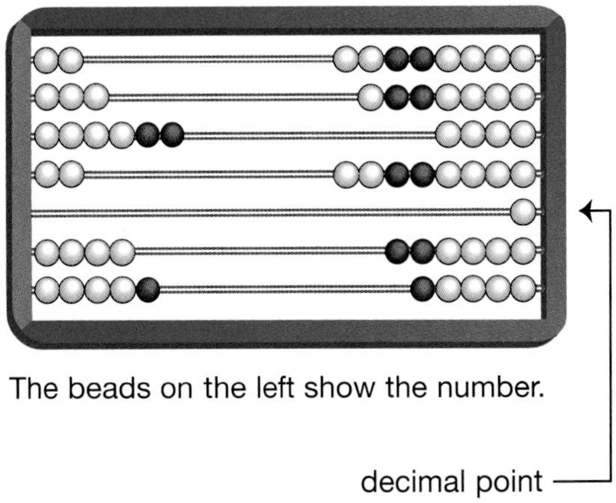

The beads on the left show the number.

decimal point

To show a number, the beads are moved to the left. The abacus in this picture shows the number 2,362.45.

Write the number shown on each abacus.

1. 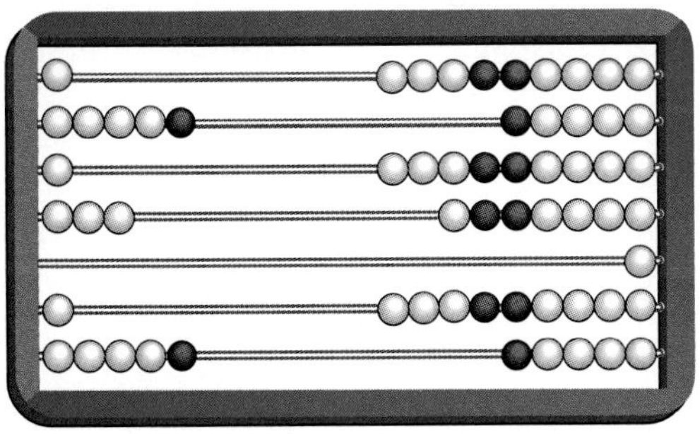

1,513. ___?___

2. 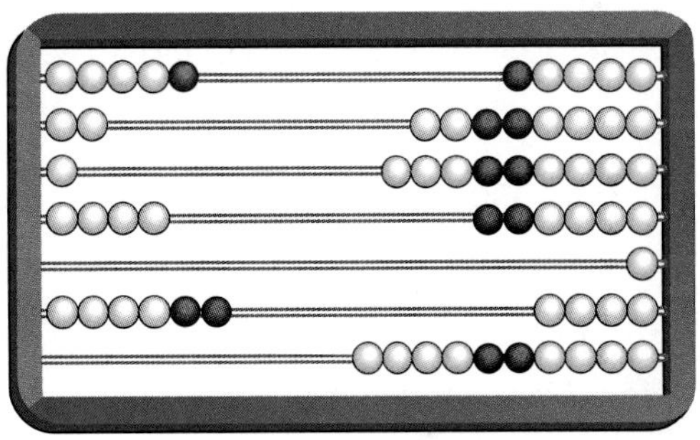

___?___ **.60**

3. 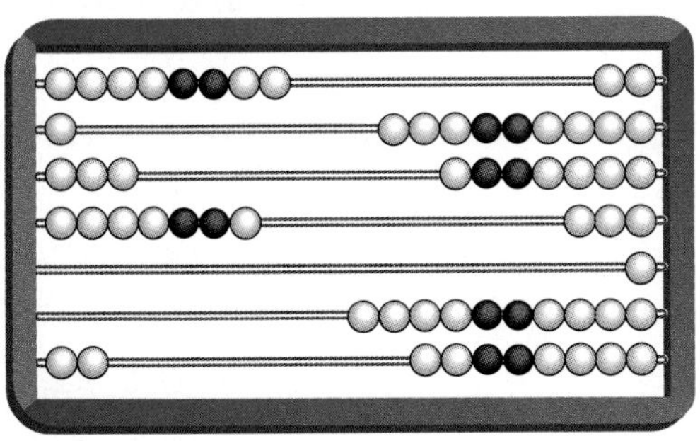

___?___

4. 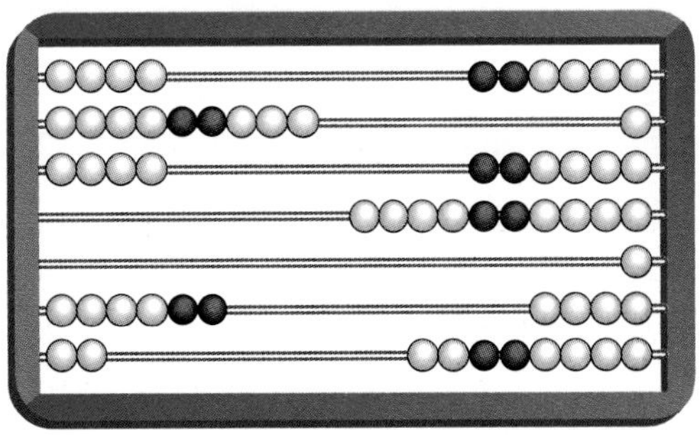

___?___

5. **Create Your Own** You can make your own Russian abacus. Use string for wire and elbow macaroni for beads. Attach the strings to a sheet of cardboard.

Chapter 12

Multiplying and Dividing Greater Numbers

Chapter Theme: THE FUTURE

Career Spotlight Meet Mark C. Lee, an astronaut who has blasted into space four times. On these trips, he gets to do all kinds of things—like spacewalking!

Math plays a part in planning space travel. Multiplication and division could be used to find out how many units are needed to store food on a trip.

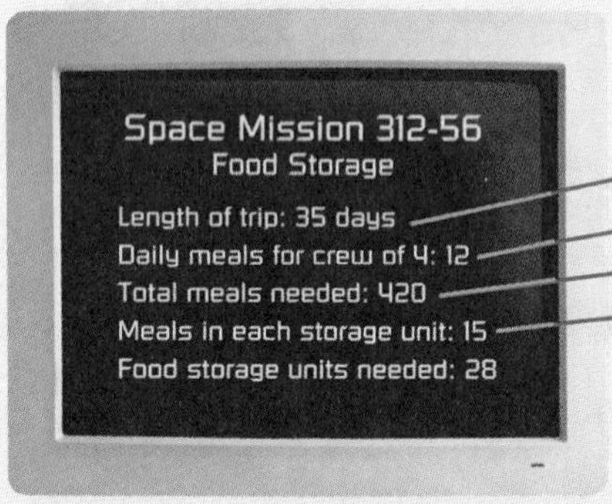

$35 \times 12 = 420$

$420 \div 15 = 28$

Chapter Project

Design a Space Station

Suppose that in the year 2050 people begin to live in outer space. Space stations are popping up everywhere! You are part of a team that is planning a new space station. Your station must follow these rules.

- All of the apartments or living areas are the same size.
- The apartments must be laid out in straight lines.
- Other areas, such as stores, offices, schools, and play areas, must be placed around the apartments.

Meet with your team and start thinking about your station.

Using Algebra

A Place in Space

Sometimes you can use patterns to help you multiply.

Learning About It

It's the year 2050 and you are visiting a space station! There are 5 floors on the station, and 100 people live on each floor. How many people live on all 5 floors?

5 × 100 = ■

Think: 5 × 1 = 5

Think: 5 × 10 = 50

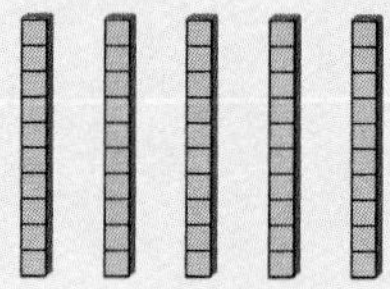

So, 5 × 100 = 500

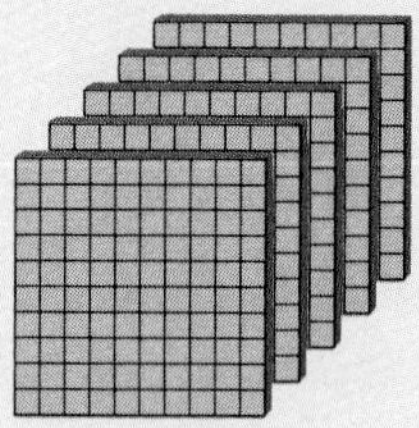

There are 500 people living on the space station.

More Examples

A. 3 × 2 = 6
3 × 20 = 60
3 × 200 = 600

B. 4 × 7 = 28
4 × 70 = 280
4 × 700 = 2,800

C. 5 × 8 = 40
5 × 80 = 400
5 × 800 = 4,000

Think and Discuss Explain how knowing 2 × 8 = 16 can help you find 2 × 80.

Try It Out

Use basic facts and patterns to find each product.

1. $3 \times 3 = \blacksquare$
   $3 \times 30 = \blacksquare$
   $3 \times 300 = \blacksquare$

2. $4 \times 9 = \blacksquare$
   $4 \times 90 = \blacksquare$
   $4 \times 900 = \blacksquare$

3. $7 \times 2 = \blacksquare$
   $7 \times 20 = \blacksquare$
   $7 \times 200 = \blacksquare$

Practice

Using Mental Math **Use mental math to find each product.**

4. 50×3
5. 70×4
6. 400×6
7. 700×5
8. 20×6
9. 80×5
10. 600×3
11. 500×2
12. 30×4
13. 400×2

Problem Solving

14. A robot on the space station can solve 800 math problems in 1 second. How many problems can the robot solve in 6 seconds?

15. The Galaxy space station has 4 floors with 600 people living on each floor. The Comet space station has 7 floors with 300 people on each floor. Which station has more people? how many more?

16. The Russian space station *Mir* was launched in 1986. How many years ago was *Mir* launched?

Science Connection
A United States space shuttle is docked with the Russian space station *Mir*. One meaning of the Russian word *mir* is "peace."

Review and Remember

Compare. Use >, <, or = for ●.

17. 3 ounces ● 3 pounds
18. 6 feet ● 10 inches
19. 2 cups ● 1 pint
20. 24 centimeters ● 14 meters

For Extra Practice, see Set A, page 480.

Block Multiplication

Base-ten blocks can help you explore multiplication.

Learning About It

Work with your partner.

Step 1 Use base-ten blocks to show 3×21.
Start by showing 3 groups of 21.

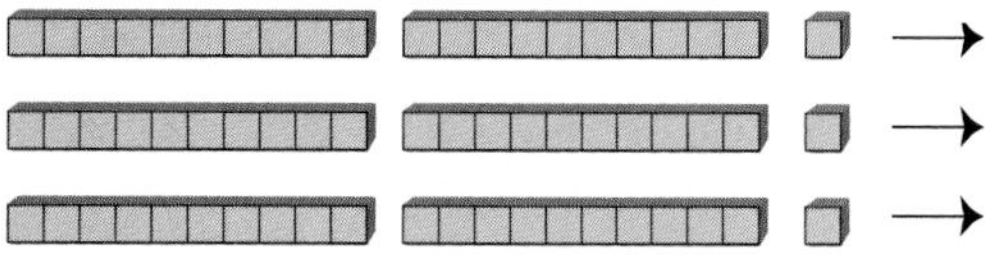

$$\begin{array}{r} 21 \\ 21 \\ +\ 21 \\ \hline \end{array}$$

- What is $21 + 21 + 21$? What is 3×21?
- Did you need to regroup blocks? Why or why not?
- Is 3×21 the same as 3×20 plus 3×1? Explain how you know.

Step 2 Now use the blocks to show 2×18.
Start by showing 2 groups of 18. Regroup if you can.

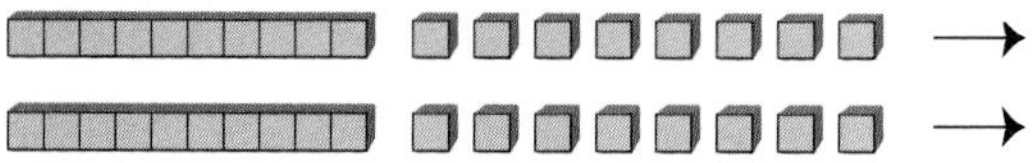

$$\begin{array}{r} 18 \\ +\ 18 \\ \hline \end{array}$$

- What is $18 + 18$? What is 2×18?
- Did you need to regroup blocks? Why or why not?
- Is 2×18 the same as 2×10 plus 2×8?

What You Need

For each pair:
base-ten blocks

Think and Discuss If you use blocks to show 4×38, when do you need to regroup blocks?

Practice

Write an addition sentence and a multiplication sentence for each picture.

1. 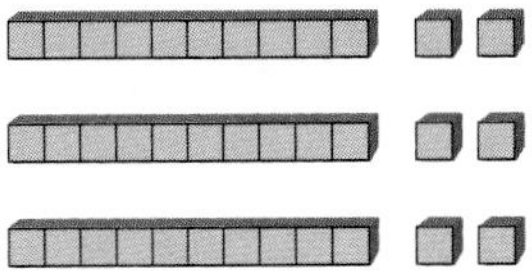

2. 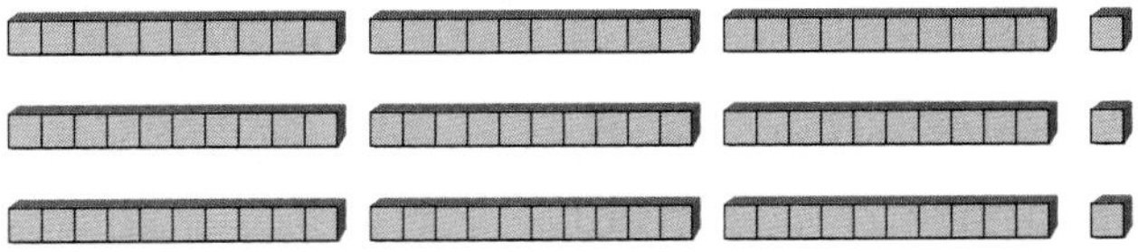

3. 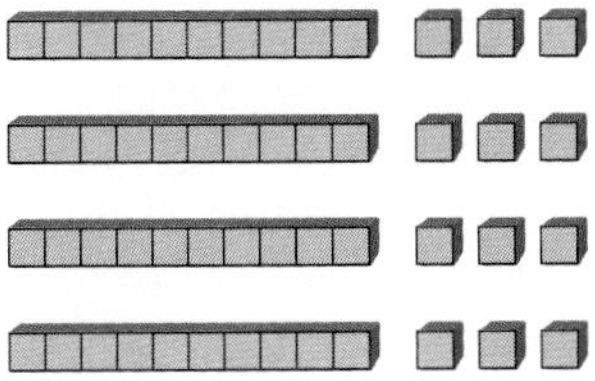

4. 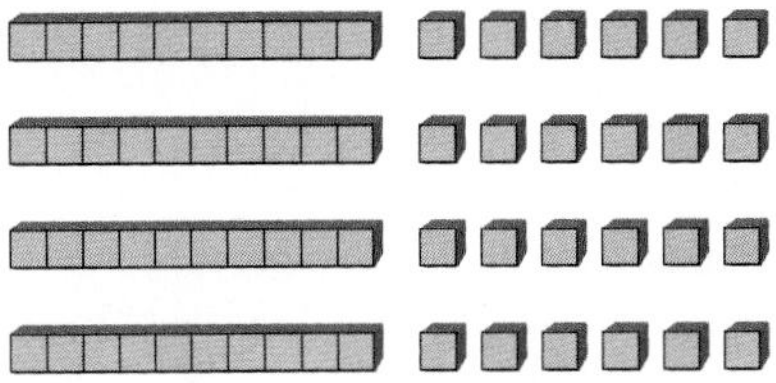

5. 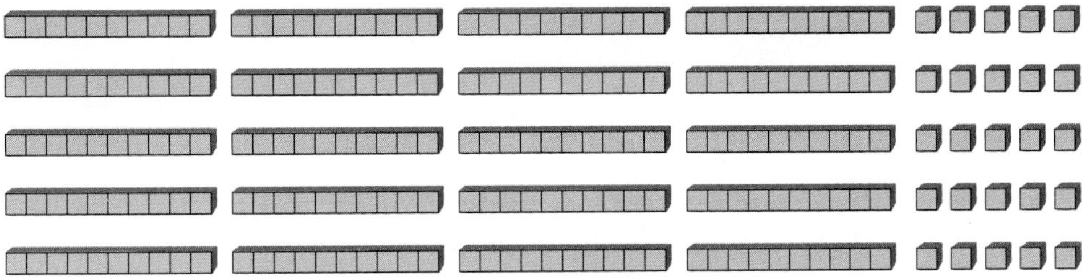

6. 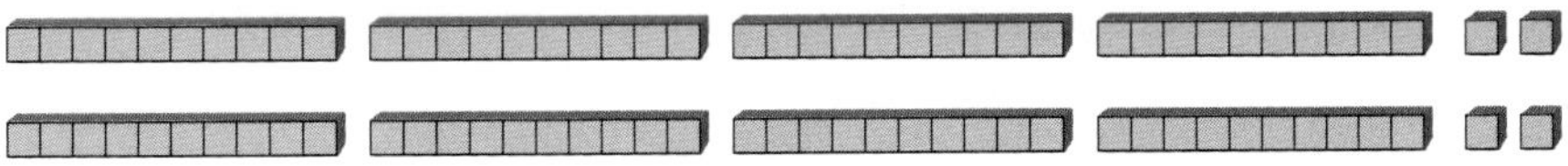

7. Suppose you wanted to show 5×67 with blocks. How many tens rods and ones blocks would you need to show the problem?

8. Use blocks to show 3 groups of 65. When can you regroup? What multiplication sentence can you write to show what you did?

9. **Create Your Own** Show a multiplication example with base-ten blocks. Have your partner write an addition sentence and a multiplication sentence for your example.

Space News!

Sometimes you can regroup when you multiply larger numbers.

Learning About It

Every month you send 15 Space News videos from your space station to each of the 3 nearby space stations. How many videos do you send altogether each month?

What You Need

For each student:
base-ten blocks

$3 \times 15 = ■$

You can use base-ten blocks to find the product.

Step 1
Think about 3 groups of 15.

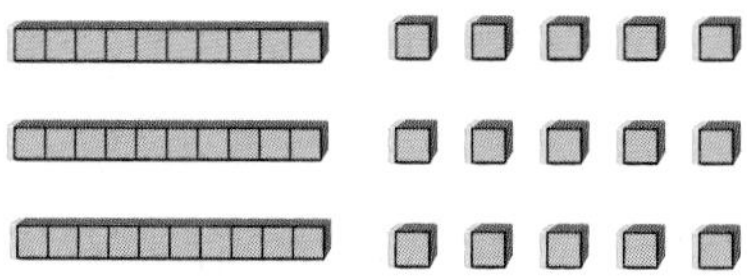

$$\begin{array}{r} 15 \\ \times\ 3 \\ \hline \end{array}$$

Step 2
Multiply ones.
3 × 5 ones = 15 ones

Regroup 15 ones as 1 ten 5 ones.

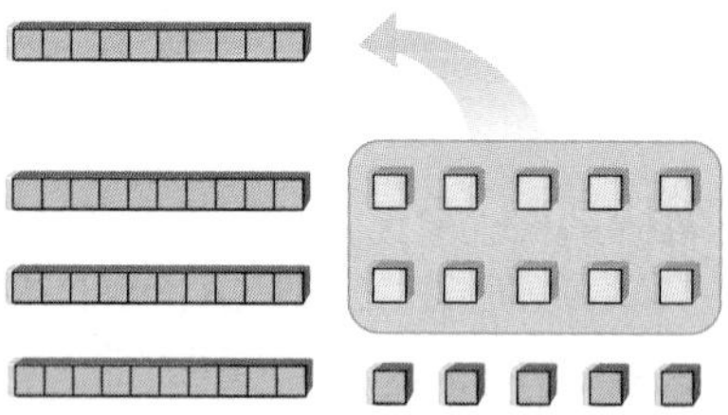

$$\begin{array}{r} {}^{1} \\ 15 \\ \times\ 3 \\ \hline 5 \end{array}$$

15 ones

Step 3
Multiply tens.
3 × 1 ten = 3 tens

Add the 1 regrouped ten.
3 tens + 1 ten = 4 tens

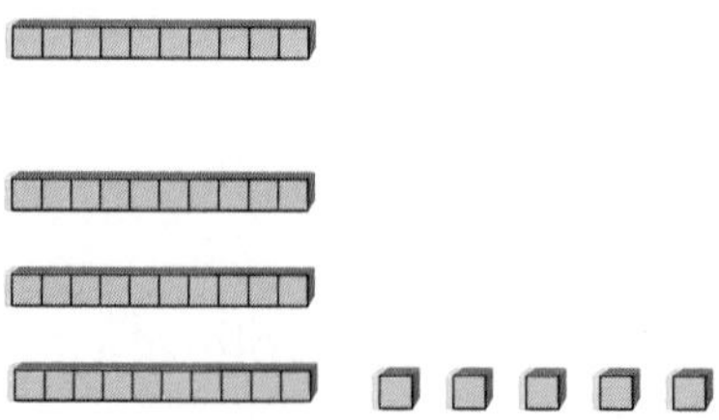

$$\begin{array}{r} {}^{1} \\ 15 \\ \times\ 3 \\ \hline 45 \end{array}$$

You send 45 videos each month.

Connecting Ideas

On page 448, you regrouped only ones when multiplying a two-digit number. Sometimes you can regroup tens when multiplying a two-digit number.

Find the product of 4×31.

Step 1
Think about
4 groups of 31.

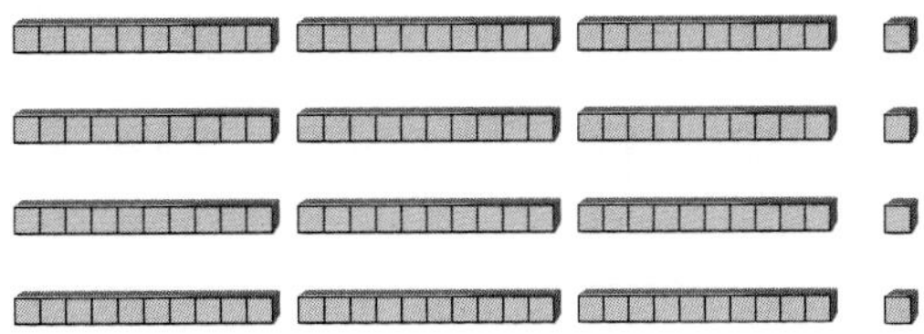

$$\begin{array}{r} 31 \\ \times\ 4 \\ \hline \end{array}$$

Step 2
Multiply ones.
4×1 one $= 4$ ones

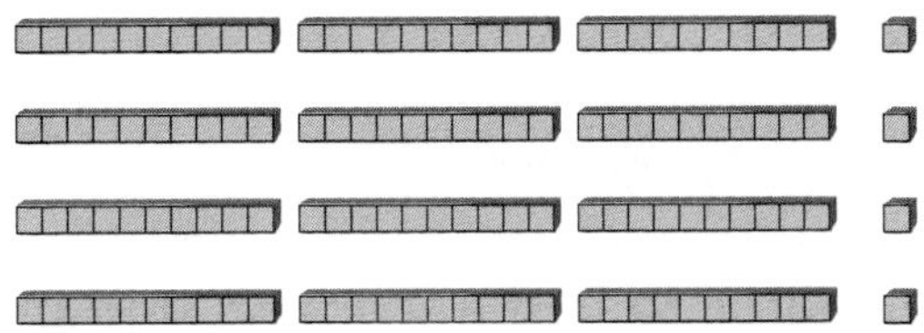

$$\begin{array}{r} 31 \\ \times\ 4 \\ \hline 4 \end{array}$$

Step 3
Multiply tens.
4×3 tens $= 12$ tens

Regroup 12 tens as
1 hundred 2 tens.

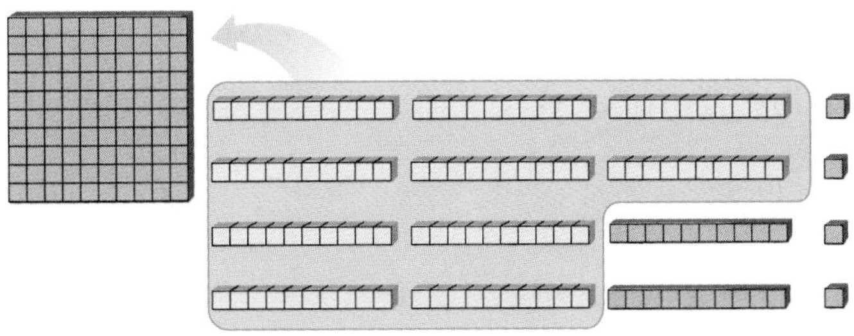

$$\begin{array}{r} 31 \\ \times\ 4 \\ \hline 124 \end{array}$$

12 tens

$4 \times 31 = 124$

Think and Discuss How do you know when you need to regroup ones or tens?

Try It Out

Find each product. Use base-ten blocks to help you.

1. $\begin{array}{r} 13 \\ \times\ 4 \\ \hline \end{array}$ **2.** $\begin{array}{r} 36 \\ \times\ 2 \\ \hline \end{array}$ **3.** $\begin{array}{r} 15 \\ \times\ 3 \\ \hline \end{array}$ **4.** $\begin{array}{r} 61 \\ \times\ 2 \\ \hline \end{array}$ **5.** $\begin{array}{r} 42 \\ \times\ 3 \\ \hline \end{array}$

6. 4×17 **7.** 1×28 **8.** 5×13 **9.** 2×64

Practice

Multiply.

10. $\begin{array}{r} 14 \\ \times\ 6 \\ \hline \end{array}$	**11.** $\begin{array}{r} 54 \\ \times\ 2 \\ \hline \end{array}$	**12.** $\begin{array}{r} 33 \\ \times\ 3 \\ \hline \end{array}$	**13.** $\begin{array}{r} 27 \\ \times\ 3 \\ \hline \end{array}$	**14.** $\begin{array}{r} 11 \\ \times\ 5 \\ \hline \end{array}$
15. $\begin{array}{r} 24 \\ \times\ 4 \\ \hline \end{array}$	**16.** $\begin{array}{r} 63 \\ \times\ 3 \\ \hline \end{array}$	**17.** $\begin{array}{r} 25 \\ \times\ 2 \\ \hline \end{array}$	**18.** $\begin{array}{r} 64 \\ \times\ 0 \\ \hline \end{array}$	**19.** $\begin{array}{r} 71 \\ \times\ 8 \\ \hline \end{array}$
20. $\begin{array}{r} 30 \\ \times\ 6 \\ \hline \end{array}$	**21.** $\begin{array}{r} 41 \\ \times\ 4 \\ \hline \end{array}$	**22.** $\begin{array}{r} 22 \\ \times\ 3 \\ \hline \end{array}$	**23.** $\begin{array}{r} 18 \\ \times\ 5 \\ \hline \end{array}$	**24.** $\begin{array}{r} 25 \\ \times\ 3 \\ \hline \end{array}$

25. 4×72	**26.** 2×26	**27.** 3×17	**28.** 1×92
29. 3×21	**30.** 5×14	**31.** 2×50	**32.** 4×52
33. 2×42	**34.** 3×72	**35.** 4×31	**36.** 5×40

Use a calculator to find each sum and product.

37. $56 + 56 + 56 + 56 + 56 + 56 = ■$
$6 \times 56 = ■$

38. $28 + 28 + 28 + 28 = ■$
$4 \times 28 = ■$

39. $92 + 92 + 92 = ■$
$3 \times 92 = ■$

40. $41 + 41 + 41 + 41 + 41 = ■$
$5 \times 41 = ■$

Problem Solving

41. A Space News reporter is taking a 3-D picture of 2 space soccer teams. Each team has 18 members. How many people will be in the picture?

42. After a soccer game, 8 players each gave a team photo to 30 different fans. How many photos did they give away?

43. It takes 8 seconds to send a news video to another space station. How long does it take to send 15 videos?

44. Carrie started watching a news video at 3:00 P.M. She stopped watching $1\frac{1}{2}$ hours later. What time was it when she stopped watching?

45. **Analyze** An ad on a Space News video says that space helmets are now on sale! Last week they cost $57 each. Now they are $46 each. How much money would you save by buying 4 helmets now instead of last week?

Project Link

Make a plan for your space station. Decide to have between 3 and 10 floors. Plan to have 5 to 15 apartments on each floor.

- How many apartments will you have?
- How many people can live in each one?

Review and Remember

Round each number to the underlined place.

46. $\underline{2}8$	**47.** $3\underline{4}9$	**48.** $\underline{6}85$	**49.** $\underline{3}12$	**50.** $\underline{8}91$	**51.** $\underline{7}2$
52. $\underline{8}1$	**53.** $\underline{2}92$	**54.** $\underline{7}15$	**55.** $\underline{6}24$	**56.** $\underline{1}02$	**57.** $\underline{4}3$

Time for Technology

Surf the Net

Explore Outer Space!

You can use the Internet to find information about space! Different **sites** can tell you how far away a star is or how many satellites are in space right now!

To find a site, you need to know its Internet address. Here are some site addresses to help you get started.

www.nasa.gov

www.stsci.edu

www.ncc.com/misc/hubble_sites.html

For Extra Practice, see Set B, page 480.

Space Garden

Sometimes you regroup ones and tens when you multiply.

Learning About It

A space-station gardener grows her flowers in boxes. She plants 23 flowers in each box. If she has 6 boxes, how many flowers does she have?

6 × 23 = ■

You can use base-ten blocks to find the product.

Step 1
Think about
6 groups of 23.

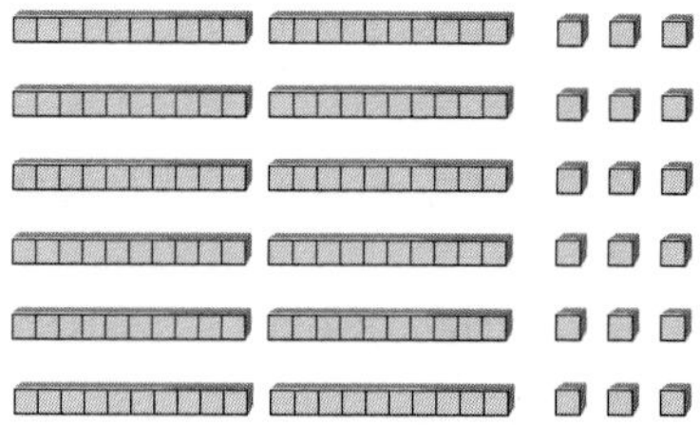

$$\begin{array}{r} 23 \\ \times\ 6 \\ \hline \end{array}$$

Step 2
Multiply ones.
6 × 3 ones = 18 ones

Regroup 18 ones as
1 ten 8 ones.

$$\begin{array}{r} {}^{1} \\ 23 \\ \times\ 6 \\ \hline 8 \end{array}$$

18 ones

Step 3
Multiply tens.
6 × 2 tens = 12 tens

Add the 1 regrouped ten.
12 tens + 1 ten = 13 tens

Regroup 13 tens as
1 hundred 3 tens.

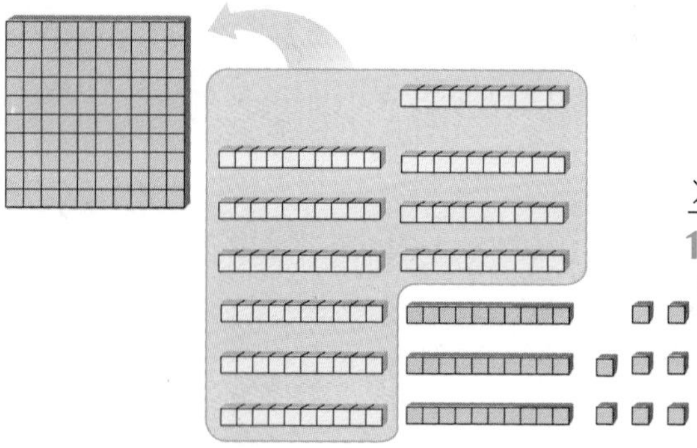

$$\begin{array}{r} {}^{1} \\ 23 \\ \times\ 6 \\ \hline 138 \end{array}$$

13 tens

She has 138 flowers.

Think and Discuss How would regrouping ones in 3×34 be different from regrouping ones in 3×37?

Try It Out

Find each product. Regroup when you need to.

1. 38×3	**2.** 25×5	**3.** 21×4	**4.** 46×2	**5.** 29×4

Practice

Find each product.

6. 22×7	**7.** 53×2	**8.** 99×1	**9.** 31×5	**10.** 28×4
11. 67×3	**12.** 45×4	**13.** 97×3	**14.** 80×2	**15.** 55×8

Problem Solving

Use the sign to solve Problems 16–19.

16. How much do 5 tulips and 8 roses cost?

17. Sira is going to buy 4 flowers. She wants at least one of each kind, but she wants to spend as little money as possible. What should she buy? How much will they cost?

18. Greg paid for a tulip with 4 twenty-dollar bills. What change should he get back?

19. **Create Your Own** Use the sign to write a problem that can be solved by multiplying.

Review and Remember

Find each product or quotient.

20. $54 \div 6$	**21.** 9×9	**22.** $40 \div 8$	**23.** $56 \div 7$	**24.** 4×7
25. $36 \div 9$	**26.** $72 \div 8$	**27.** 6×7	**28.** 3×9	**29.** $24 \div 6$

For Extra Practice, see Set C, page 480.

Two-Cube Cafe

Use what you know about multiplying to multiply greater numbers.

Learning About It

Mmmmm! At the Two-Cube Cafe, each meal is made up of just 2 small food cubes. On Monday the cafe served 137 meals. How many food cubes were served on Monday?

$2 \times 137 = \blacksquare$

You can use base-ten blocks to find the product.

Step 1
Multiply ones.
2×7 ones = 14 ones

Regroup 14 ones as 1 ten 4 ones.

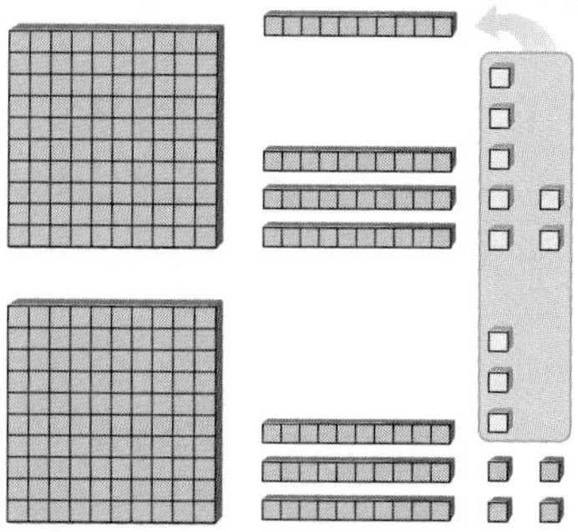

$$\begin{array}{r} {\scriptstyle 1} \\ 137 \\ \times \ \ 2 \\ \hline 4 \end{array}$$

14 ones

Step 2
Multiply tens.
2×3 tens = 6 tens

Add the 1 regrouped ten.
6 tens + 1 ten = 7 tens

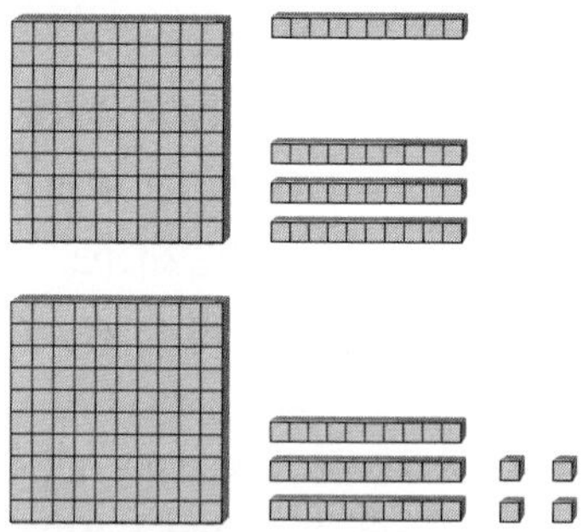

$$\begin{array}{r} {\scriptstyle 1} \\ 137 \\ \times \ \ 2 \\ \hline 74 \end{array}$$

Step 3
Multiply hundreds.
2×1 hundred = 2 hundreds

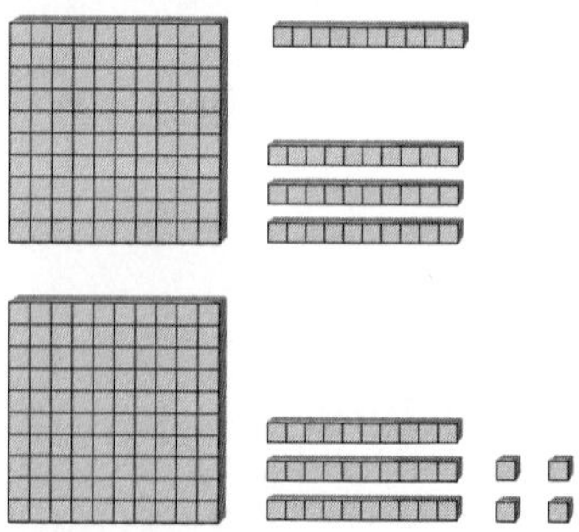

$$\begin{array}{r} {\scriptstyle 1} \\ 137 \\ \times \ \ 2 \\ \hline 274 \end{array}$$

The cafe served 274 food cubes on Monday.

Connecting Ideas

Now that you know how to multiply three-digit numbers, you can multiply money.

Look at how to find 6 × \$1.43.

Step 1

Multiply pennies.
6 × 3 pennies = 18 pennies

Trade 18 pennies for
1 dime 8 pennies.

$$\begin{array}{r} {\scriptstyle 1} \\ \$1.43 \\ \times \quad 6 \\ \hline 8 \end{array}$$

18 pennies

Step 2

Multiply dimes.
6 × 4 dimes = 24 dimes

Add the 1 dime.
24 dimes + 1 dime = 25 dimes

Trade 25 dimes for 2 dollars
5 dimes.

$$\begin{array}{r} {\scriptstyle 2\;\;1} \\ \$1.43 \\ \times \quad 6 \\ \hline 58 \end{array}$$

25 dimes

Step 3

Multiply dollars.
6 × 1 dollar = 6 dollars

Add the 2 traded dollars.
6 dollars + 2 dollars = 8 dollars

$$\begin{array}{r} {\scriptstyle 2\;\;1} \\ \$1.43 \\ \times \quad 6 \\ \hline \$8.58 \end{array}$$

6 × \$1.43 = \$8.58

Think and Discuss When you multiply money, how do you know where to place the decimal point in the product?

Try It Out

Multiply.

1. 134 × 3

2. 127 × 5

3. 154 × 6

4. 452 × 3

5. 759 × 2

6. \$1.26 × 4

7. \$2.41 × 3

8. \$7.53 × 6

9. \$4.81 × 7

10. \$6.50 × 4

Practice

Find each product.

11. 329 × 3

12. \$6.23 × 0

13. 111 × 4

14. 199 × 2

15. 147 × 5

16. \$2.77 × 3

17. 429 × 2

18. 231 × 4

19. 983 × 1

20. \$5.99 × 3

21. 3 × 292

22. 6 × 70

23. 9 × 800

24. 4 × \$2.63

25. 5 × 431

26. 2 × 748

27. 4 × 671

28. 9 × 302

29. 2 × \$384

30. 8 × 688

31. 0 × 949

32. 1 × 537

Problem Solving

33. On a space station an apple costs \$9.27. How much will it cost to buy 3 apples?

34. The menus on a space station are repeated every 60 days. Suppose chicken soup is served on the 60th day. How many days would you have been aboard to have had chicken soup served 4 times?

35. A space station stores 3 pounds of food each day for each person on board. How many pounds of food would be stored for 320 people for 1 day? for 3 days?

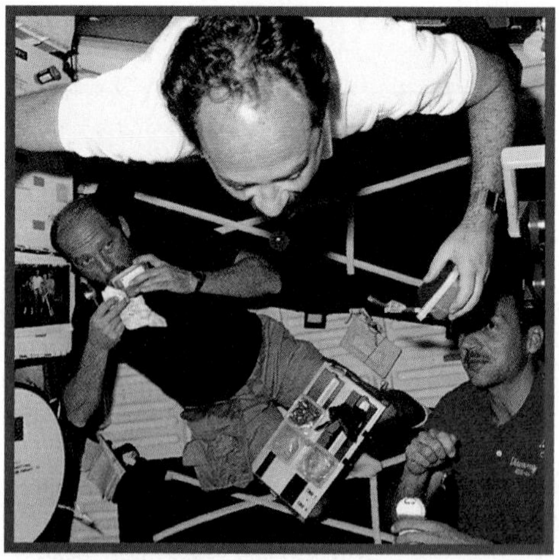

Science Connection This shuttle astronaut is "chasing" a juice bubble that escaped from the straw in his drink. His fork, spoon, and knife don't float around. They are magnetic, so they stick to the metal food tray.

36. **Using Estimation** A taco food cube costs $4.07. Would 2 taco food cubes cost more or less than $10? How do you know?

37. A can of Insta-Orange makes juice for 300 people. It takes 145 oranges to make 1 can of Insta-Orange. How many oranges are needed to make 3 cans?

Review and Remember

Add or subtract.

38. $84 + 27$

39. $96 - 49$

40. $328 - 117$

41. $951 + 280$

42. $1{,}120 + 2{,}341$

Critical Thinking Corner

Using Algebra **Logical Thinking**

Who Lives Where?

Amy, Bert, Cathy, and Dwayne have been visiting Earth. Now they are ready to go back to their home space stations. Use the clues below to match each person with his or her space station.

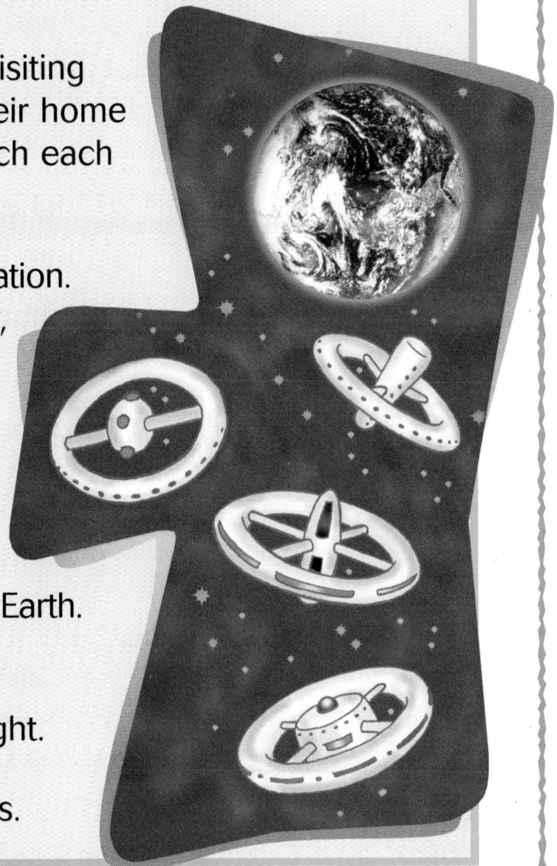

1. Each person lives on a different space station. The space stations are named Milky Way, Comet, Galaxy, and Starlight.

2. Cathy's space station is the farthest away from Earth. Her station is next to Starlight.

3. Bert lives on the space station closest to Earth. His station is next to Dwayne's station.

4. Galaxy is between Milky Way and Starlight.

5. Comet is not between any other stations.

High Jumpers

You can round to estimate products.

Learning About It

The nets are high, but teams love to play basketball at Moon Arena. That's because a player can jump 6 times as high there as on Earth. If you can jump 18 inches on Earth, about how high can you jump on the moon?

Since you want to know *about* how high, you do not need an exact answer. You can round to estimate the product.

Round to the nearest ten.

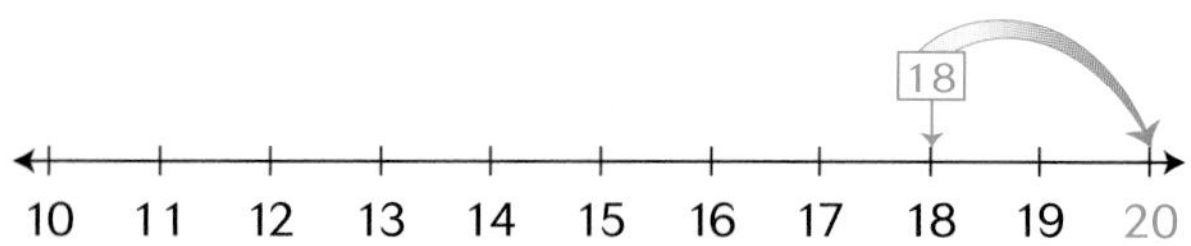

Multiply the rounded numbers.

$$\begin{array}{r} 18 \\ \times\ 6 \\ \hline \end{array} \quad \text{rounds to} \quad \begin{array}{r} 20 \\ \times\ 6 \\ \hline 120 \end{array}$$

You can jump *about* 120 inches high on the moon.

You can estimate the product of a three-digit factor the same way.

Estimate 5 × 314.

Round to the nearest hundred.

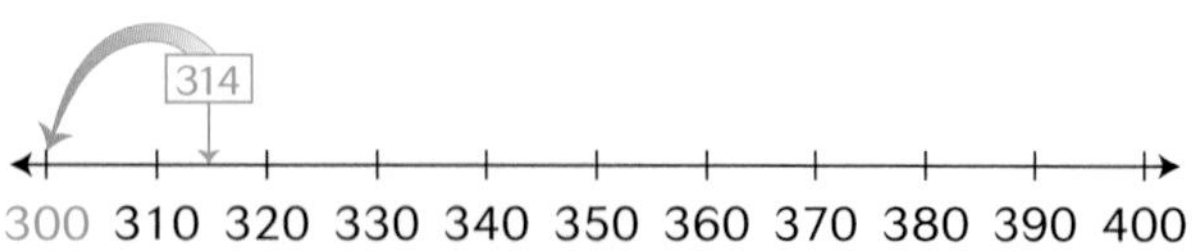

Multiply the rounded numbers.

$$\begin{array}{r} 314 \\ \times\ \ 5 \\ \hline \end{array} \quad \text{rounds to} \quad \begin{array}{r} 300 \\ \times\ \ 5 \\ \hline 1{,}500 \end{array}$$

5 × 314 is *about* 1,500.

Think and Discuss How would you estimate 2 × 53?

Try It Out

Round to the underlined place. Estimate each product.

1. $4 \times \underline{2}3$ **2.** $2 \times \underline{5}6$ **3.** $3 \times \underline{2}85$ **4.** $5 \times \underline{6}03$

Practice

Round each number to the underlined place. Then estimate each product.

5. $\underline{4}3 \times 6$ **6.** $\underline{3}7 \times 2$ **7.** $\underline{7}5 \times 8$ **8.** $\underline{8}9 \times 3$ **9.** $\underline{7}7 \times 5$

10. $\underline{2}51 \times 4$ **11.** $\underline{6}43 \times 5$ **12.** $\underline{4}29 \times 7$ **13.** $\underline{8}62 \times 5$ **14.** $\underline{8}1 \times 9$

Problem Solving

15. Three boxes of baseballs from Earth have just arrived on the moon. Each box holds 288 baseballs. About how many baseballs are there in all 3 boxes?

16. A ball can be thrown 6 times as high on the moon as on Earth. Suppose a ball that is thrown on Earth travels 70 inches. How high would the ball travel on the moon?

Review and Remember

www.sbgmath.com

Find each answer.

17. $72 \div 9$ **18.** 4×6 **19.** $124 + 236$ **20.** $485 - 24$ **21.** $40 \div 5$

Project Link

Draw a map for your space station.

- How many floors did you decide to have? How many apartments are on each floor?
- How many people can live in one apartment?
- How many people can live in the space station altogether?

Checkpoint

Multiplying by One-Digit Numbers

Use basic facts and patterns to help you multiply.
(pages 444–445)

1. $4 \times 2 = ■$
   $4 \times 20 = ■$
   $4 \times 200 = ■$
2. $3 \times 5 = ■$
   $3 \times 50 = ■$
   $3 \times 500 = ■$
3. $6 \times 7 = ■$
   $6 \times 70 = ■$
   $6 \times 700 = ■$
4. $5 \times 6 = ■$
   $5 \times 60 = ■$
   $5 \times 600 = ■$
5. $3 \times 7 = ■$
   $3 \times 70 = ■$
   $3 \times 700 = ■$
6. $6 \times 4 = ■$
   $6 \times 40 = ■$
   $6 \times 400 = ■$

Multiply. Regroup if you can. (pages 448–457)

7. 13×3
8. 24×3
9. 39×6
10. 27×2
11. 94×5
12. 62×7
13. $\$2.99 \times 5$
14. 651×4
15. 816×5
16. 213×4
17. 308×7
18. 914×5
19. 4×385
20. 6×294

Round each number to the underlined place.
Estimate the product. (pages 458–459)

21. $4 \times \underline{5}8$
22. $3 \times \underline{8}9$
23. $5 \times \underline{6}2$
24. $5 \times \underline{8}29$
25. $8 \times \underline{3}85$
26. $3 \times \underline{2}93$

Problem Solving

27. It's the grand opening of Futura Florists! Every day for 8 days they give away 50 roses. How many roses in all do they give away?

28. A Space News video showed how to make teriyaki chicken for 30 people. Mika made 9 times the amount shown. Will she have enough for 250 party guests? Explain.

29. A box of Space Crunchies costs \$7.20. Beth has \$21.36. How much more money does she need to buy 3 boxes?

30. **Using Estimation** At a golf course on the moon, golf balls sell for \$5.98 each. Will \$40 be enough to buy 8 golf balls? Explain how you know.

What do you think?
When you multiply a two-digit number by a one-digit number, what is the greatest number of tens you can have before you need to regroup? Explain.

Journal Idea Is the product of 3×43 more or less than 100? How do you know?

Critical Thinking Corner

Using Algebra **Visual Thinking**

Missing Patterns!

Part of each pattern below has been covered. Draw the part of each pattern that is missing.

1. 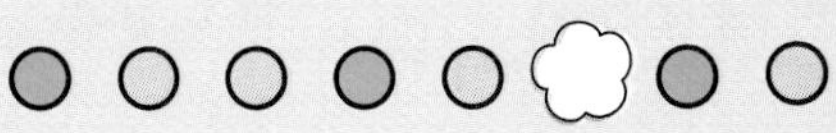

2. 

3. 

4. 

5. 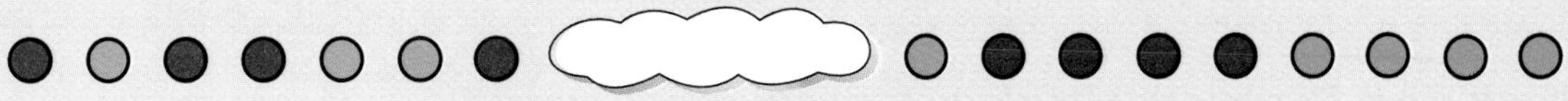

Left Out in Space

When a number can't be divided exactly, the quotient has a remainder.

Learning About It

Word Bank
remainder

The Ecology Club of Comet School uses 25 small spacecraft to pick up space litter. The club president wants the spacecraft to travel in groups of 7. How many groups of 7 will there be? Will any spacecraft be left over?

$25 \div 7 = ■$ or $7\overline{)25}$

There are 3 groups of 7.
There are 4 spacecraft left over.

▶ When dividing whole numbers, the number left over is the **remainder.**

$25 \div 7 = 3$ R4 ← This means there is a remainder of 4.

$$\begin{array}{r} 3 \text{ R4} \\ 7\overline{)25} \end{array}$$ ← remainder

Think and Discuss How many more spacecraft are needed to make 4 equal groups of 7?

Try It Out

Find each quotient.

1. $14 \div 3$ **2.** $53 \div 6$ **3.** $21 \div 4$ **4.** $30 \div 9$ **5.** $19 \div 2$

Practice

Find each quotient.

6. $3\overline{)10}$ **7.** $8\overline{)25}$ **8.** $2\overline{)14}$ **9.** $6\overline{)17}$ **10.** $5\overline{)35}$

11. $5\overline{)21}$ **12.** $1\overline{)8}$ **13.** $9\overline{)61}$ **14.** $4\overline{)12}$ **15.** $2\overline{)11}$

16. $16 \div 7$ **17.** $74 \div 8$ **18.** $50 \div 6$ **19.** $42 \div 7$ **20.** $50 \div 8$

Problem Solving

21. Students in the Ecology Club made 24 posters that said "Don't Litter in Space!" They displayed the posters in groups of 5. How many posters were left over?

22. Kenesha buys 3 spacecraft litter bags with a twenty-dollar bill. Each bag costs the same amount. If she gets $2 in change, how much does each bag cost?

23. **Analyze** Look back at Exercise 14. How does knowing your 4s facts help you know that the quotient will not have a remainder?

24. Use a calculator to find the quotient for each exercise below. What do you notice about how the quotients are displayed?

a. $16 \div 5$ **b.** $31 \div 5$ **c.** $36 \div 8$

Review and Remember

Find each answer.

25. 8×3 **26.** $46 + 32$ **27.** $15 \div 3$ **28.** $248 - 164$

29. $56 \div 7$ **30.** $47 - 36$ **31.** 8×8 **32.** $236 + 485$

For Extra Practice, see Set F, page 481.

Developing Skills for Problem Solving

First read for understanding and then focus on what to do with the remainder when you divide.

READ FOR UNDERSTANDING

The crew of Spaceship Vega is getting ready for a trip to the moon. There are 10 seats for passengers to ride in. Each seat can hold 3 people. There are 26 passengers going on the trip.

1. How many people can ride in each seat?
2. How many passengers are going on the trip?

THINK AND DISCUSS

MATH FOCUS

Interpreting Remainders When you divide, a remainder can sometimes affect the answer. Sometimes when you have a remainder, you need to round the quotient up to the next number. Sometimes you need to use the remainder itself. Sometimes you can just ignore the remainder.

Reread the paragraph at the top of the page.

3. Suppose there are only 2 passengers. How many seats would they need?
4. How many seats are needed for all 26 passengers?
5. Look back at your answer to Problem 4. What did you do with the remainder to solve the problem?

Show What You Learned

Answer each question. Give a reason for your choice.

Visitors who tour the moon need to carry flashlights. Each flashlight needs 5 batteries to work. If there are 47 batteries on Spaceship Vega, what is the greatest number of flashlights that will work?

1. Which of the following could you do to solve the problem?

   a. You could find $47 \div 5 = 8$ R7

   b. You could find $47 \times 5 = 235$

   c. You could find $47 \div 5 = 9$ R2

2. How should you use the remainder to solve the problem?

   a. Use it to round up the quotient, so the answer is 10 flashlights.

   b. Ignore the remainder, so the answer is 9 flashlights.

   c. Use the remainder, so the answer is 9 R2 flashlights.

Rob is packing snacks into boxes for a moon trip. He has 32 snacks. Each box holds 5 snacks. How many boxes does he need to pack all of the snacks?

3. Which should you do first to solve the problem?

   a. You should find $32 \div 5 = 6$ R2

   b. You should find $32 - 5 = 27$

   c. You should find $32 \div 5 = 5$ R7

4. How should you use the remainder to solve the problem?

   a. Use it to round up the quotient, so the answer is 7 boxes.

   b. Ignore the remainder, so the answer is 6 boxes.

   c. Use the remainder, so the answer is 6 R2 boxes.

5. **Explain** Would the number of boxes Rob needs change if he had 34 snacks? Why or why not?

A Great Divide

Using Algebra

Number patterns can help you see if a number can be divided by 2, 5, or 10.

Learning About It

Word Bank

divisible

When you divide a number by 2 and the remainder is 0, you can say that the number is **divisible** by 2.

Work with your partner to find numbers that are divisible by 2, 5, or 10.

What You Need

For each pair:
100 counters
three 1–100 charts
crayons

Step 1 Use a 1–100 chart. Circle all of the numbers on the chart that are divisible by 2. Use counters to help you decide.

- What patterns do you see?
- Do you think 102 is divisible by 2? Explain why or why not.

1	2	3	4	5	6	7	8	9	10
11	12	13	14	15	16	17	18	19	20
21	22	23	24	25	26	27	28	29	30
31	32	33	34	35	36	37	38	39	40
41	42	43	44	45	46	47	48	49	50
51	52	53	54	55	56	57	58	59	60
61	62	63	64	65	66	67	68	69	70
71	72	73	74	75	76	77	78	79	80
81	82	83	84	85	86	87	88	89	90
91	92	93	94	95	96	97	98	99	100

Step 2 Use a new 1–100 chart. This time circle the numbers that are divisible by 5.

- What patterns do you see?
- Do you think 104 is divisible by 5? Explain why or why not.

Step 3 Use a new 1–100 chart. This time circle the numbers that are divisible by 10.

- What patterns do you see?
- Do you think 120 is divisible by 10? Explain why or why not.

Think and Discuss Look back at your 1–100 charts. Which numbers are divisible by both 2 and 5? What do you notice about these numbers?

Practice

1. Behind the spacesuits there is a three-digit number. Each spacesuit is blocking a digit. You want to see if the number will have a remainder if it is divided by 5. Which spacesuit should you move?

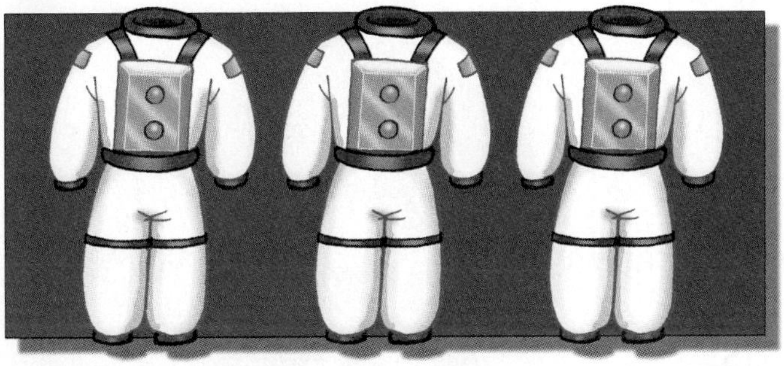

Tell whether or not each number can be divided by 2, by 5, or by 10 without a remainder.

2. 374 (2)	**3.** 965 (5)	**4.** 230 2, 5, 10	**5.** 732 (2)
6. 391 X	**7.** 305 (5)	**8.** 560 (5, 2, 10)	**9.** 281 X
10. 629 X	**11.** 860 2, 5, 10	**12.** 576 2	**13.** 475 5

Write *true* or *false* for the following sentences. Use your 1–100 charts to help you.

14. If a number is divisible by 10, it is also *always* divisible by 5.
    True
15. If a number is divisible by 10, it is also *always* divisible by 2.
    false
16. If a number is divisible by 2, it is also *always* divisible by 10.
    false

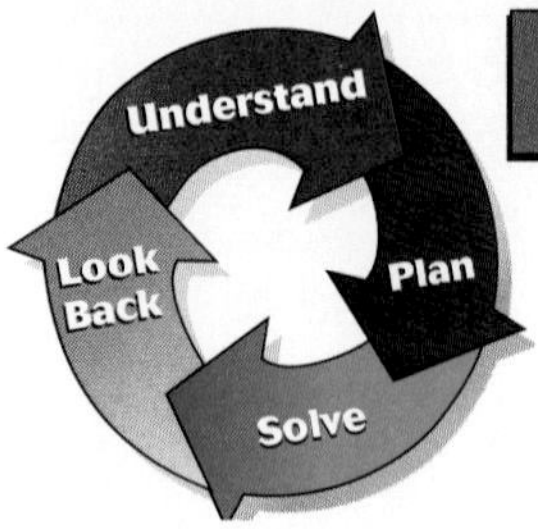

Problem Solving

Choose a Strategy

There is often more than one strategy that can help you solve a problem.

It's 2050 and your family is going on a 4-day trip to explore moon craters! You will explore 15 craters each day. How many craters will you explore on your trip?

UNDERSTAND

What do you need to find?

You need to find how many craters you will explore in 4 days.

PLAN

How can you solve the problem?

You can **write a number sentence** or you can **make a table**.

SOLVE

Write a Number Sentence

4 × 15 = ■

- 4 → number of days
- 15 → number of craters explored each day
- ■ → number of craters explored

4 × 15 = 60

Make a Table

Number of Days	Number of Craters Explored
1	15
2	30
3	45
4	60

You will explore 60 craters.

LOOK BACK

What addition sentence could you write to solve the problem?

Using Strategies

Solve these problems using these or other strategies you have learned.

- *Make a Graph*
- *Guess and Check*
- *Draw a Picture*
- *Find a Pattern*
- *Write a Number Sentence*
- *Use Logical Reasoning*

1. Together, Beth and Lee collect 31 moon rocks. Lee collects 3 fewer rocks than Beth. How many rocks do Beth and Lee each collect?

2. Joylin drives 100 miles each day on the moon's surface. How many days will it take her to go 2,000 miles?

3. **Science Connection** Neil Armstrong was the first person to set foot on the moon. That was in the year 1969. How many years ago was that?

Science Connection
Apollo 11 astronauts Neil Armstrong and Edwin Aldrin placed an American flag at their landing site on the moon.

4. The moon helps cause the ocean tides on Earth. Suppose low tide is at 11:30 A.M. and high tide is at 5:45 P.M. How much time is there between low tide and high tide?

5. Dan buys 2 items at the space museum gift shop. The items cost a total of $18. One item is twice the price of the other item. What are the prices of the items?

6. An object weighs about 6 times more on Earth than it does on the moon. Suppose an object weighs 11 pounds on the moon. How much would the object weigh on Earth?

7. To stay in shape on a space station, Nan does 20 sit-ups on Monday, 25 sit-ups on Tuesday, and 30 sit-ups on Wednesday. If she continues this pattern, how many sit-ups will she do on Friday?

8. At the Space Center, Ian trained 15 hours, Pam trained 6 hours, and Brad trained 32 hours. Bo and Dawn each trained 16 hours. Make a graph to show the number of hours each person trained.

On the Move

Knowing basic facts can help you divide larger numbers.

Learning About It

Whoosh! You zip through the travel tube of the space station. Three people can zip through the tube in 1 minute. How many minutes will it take 600 people to zip through the tube?

600 ÷ 3 = ■

Think: $\begin{array}{r}2\\3\overline{)6}\end{array}$

Think: $\begin{array}{r}20\\3\overline{)60}\end{array}$

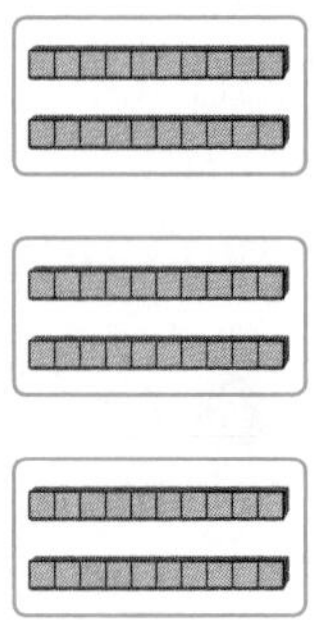

So, $\begin{array}{r}200\\3\overline{)600}\end{array}$

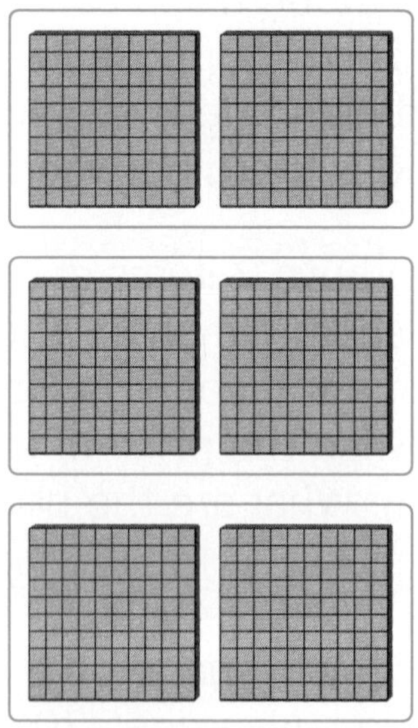

It will take 200 minutes for 600 people to zip through the tube.

Think and Discuss What fact can help you find 40 ÷ 2?

Try It Out

Use the basic fact to find each quotient.

1. $3\overline{)9}$	$3\overline{)90}$	$3\overline{)900}$	**2.** $2\overline{)8}$	$2\overline{)80}$	$2\overline{)800}$
3. $2\overline{)4}$	$2\overline{)40}$	$2\overline{)400}$	**4.** $7\overline{)35}$	$7\overline{)350}$	$7\overline{)3,500}$
5. $3\overline{)27}$	$3\overline{)270}$	$3\overline{)2,700}$	**6.** $8\overline{)32}$	$8\overline{)320}$	$8\overline{)3,200}$

Practice

Using Mental Math **Use a basic fact and mental math to find each quotient.**

7. $4\overline{)8}$	$4\overline{)80}$	$4\overline{)800}$	**8.** $3\overline{)3}$	$3\overline{)30}$	$3\overline{)300}$
9. $7\overline{)56}$	$7\overline{)560}$	$7\overline{)5,600}$	**10.** $4\overline{)24}$	$4\overline{)240}$	$4\overline{)2,400}$

11. $28 \div 7 = $ ■
$280 \div 7 = $ ■
$2,800 \div 7 = $ ■

12. $30 \div 6 = $ ■
$300 \div 6 = $ ■
$3,000 \div 6 = $ ■

13. $14 \div 7 = $ ■
$140 \div 7 = $ ■
$1,400 \div 7 = $ ■

Problem Solving

14. There are 240 students waiting to use the travel tube to go to school. The students are standing in groups of 8. How many groups of students are there?

15. It takes 120 seconds to make 4 trips by travel tube to the Galaxy Superstore. Each trip takes the same amount of time. How long does 1 trip take?

Review and Remember

Find each answer.

16. $12 - 7$	**17.** 40×2	**18.** $641 - 218$	**19.** $234 + 122$
20. 8×9	**21.** $74 \div 6$	**22.** $300 + 208$	**23.** $4,356 - 927$

For Extra Practice, see Set G, page 482.

Back in the Old Days

Basic division facts can help you to divide two-digit numbers.

Learning About It

Dawn has collected old toys and games for a sale at the Starlight School. She has 52 items divided equally among 4 boxes. How many items are in each box?

Base-ten blocks can help you find $4\overline{)52}$.

Step 1
Think about dividing 5 tens 2 ones into 4 equal groups.

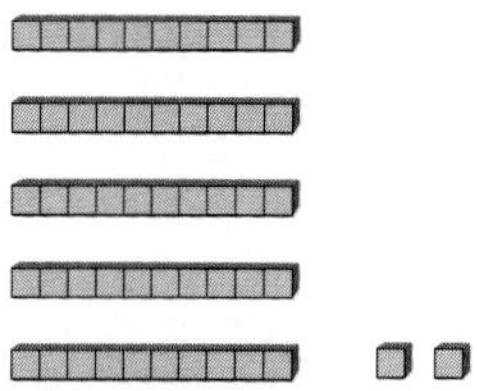

$4\overline{)52}$

Step 2
Divide 5 tens into 4 groups.
There is 1 ten in each group.
Write 1 over the tens place.
Then subtract 4 tens.

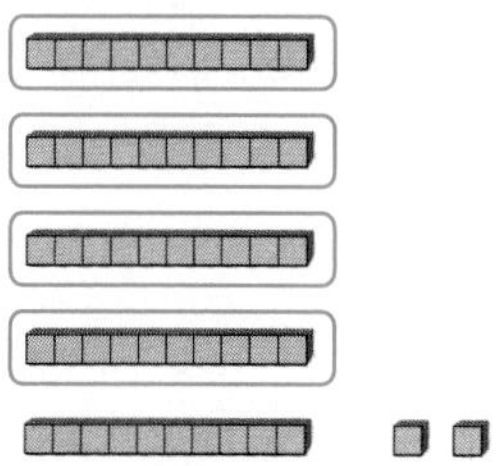

$$\begin{array}{r} 1 \\ 4\overline{)52} \\ -4 \\ \hline 1 \end{array}$$

1 ← 1 ten in each group
1 ← 1 ten left

Step 3
Regroup 1 ten 2 ones as 12 ones.

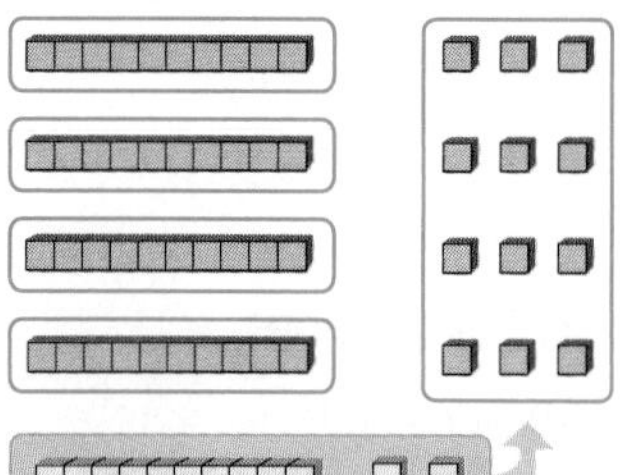

$$\begin{array}{r} 1 \\ 4\overline{)52} \\ -4\downarrow \\ \hline 12 \end{array}$$

Step 4
Divide 12 ones into the 4 groups.

There are 3 ones in each group.
Write 3 over the ones place.
Then subtract 12 ones.

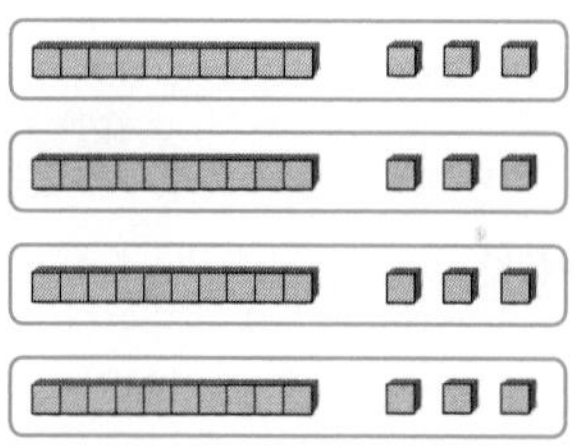

$$\begin{array}{r} 13 \\ 4\overline{)52} \\ -4 \\ \hline 12 \\ -12 \\ \hline 0 \end{array}$$

There are 13 items in each box.

Connecting Ideas

Sometimes when you divide a number, the remainder is greater than 0. When that happens, you need to write the remainder as part of the quotient.

Look at how to find 46 ÷ 3.

Step 1
Think about dividing 4 tens 6 ones into 3 equal groups.

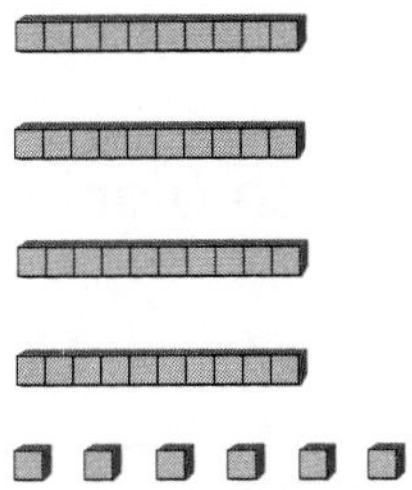

```
3)46
```

Step 2
Divide 4 tens into 3 groups.

There is 1 ten in each group.
Write 1 over the tens place.
Then subtract 3 tens.

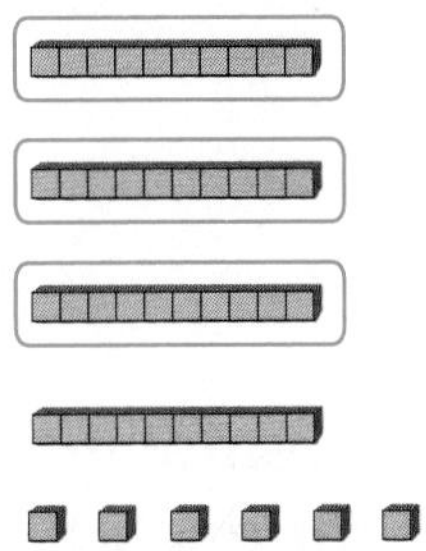

```
   1  ←1 ten in each group
3)46
 - 3
   1  ←1 ten left
```

Step 3
Regroup 1 ten 6 ones as 16 ones.

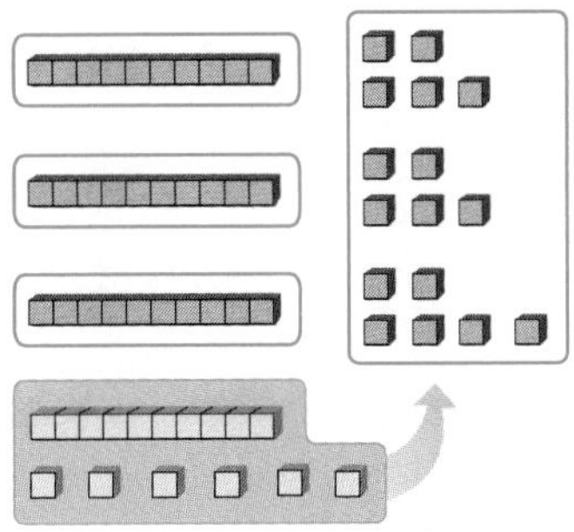

```
   1
3)46
 - 3↓
   16
```

Step 4
Divide 16 ones into the 3 groups.

There are 5 ones in each group.
Write 5 over the ones place.
Then subtract 15 ones.
There is one left.

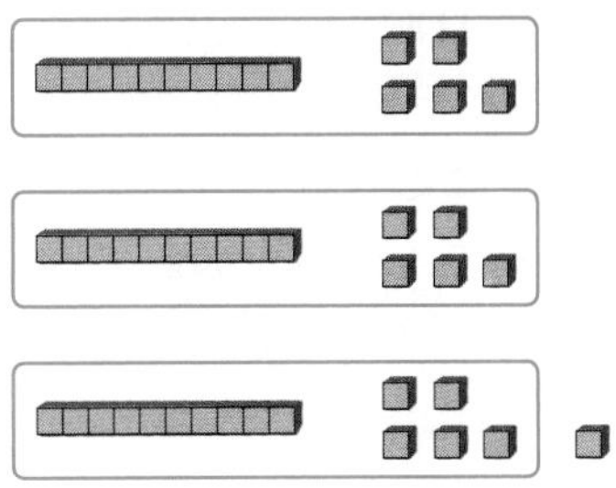

```
   15 R1
3)46
 - 3
   16
 - 15
    1
```

46 ÷ 3 = 15 R1

Think and Discuss Ty says that 45 ÷ 7 = 6 R8. How can you tell without dividing that the answer is incorrect?

Try It Out

Find each quotient. Use base-ten blocks to help you.

1. $3\overline{)71}$ **2.** $4\overline{)68}$ **3.** $2\overline{)36}$ **4.** $8\overline{)89}$ **5.** $6\overline{)75}$ **6.** $4\overline{)50}$

7. $5\overline{)78}$ **8.** $7\overline{)84}$ **9.** $1\overline{)94}$ **10.** $6\overline{)78}$ **11.** $8\overline{)96}$ **12.** $3\overline{)59}$

Practice

Find each quotient. Use base-ten blocks to help you.

13. $5\overline{)62}$ **14.** $2\overline{)27}$ **15.** $6\overline{)97}$ **16.** $3\overline{)36}$ **17.** $2\overline{)43}$ **18.** $1\overline{)22}$

19. $3\overline{)82}$ **20.** $5\overline{)94}$ **21.** $9\overline{)96}$ **22.** $8\overline{)89}$ **23.** $4\overline{)64}$ **24.** $6\overline{)72}$

25. $28 \div 2$ **26.** $89 \div 7$ **27.** $84 \div 5$ **28.** $47 \div 4$

29. $69 \div 4$ **30.** $65 \div 5$ **31.** $91 \div 6$ **32.** $98 \div 7$

Using Algebra **Using Mental Math Use mental math to compare. Use >, <, or = for each ●.**

33. $20 \div 2$ ● $20 \div 5$ **34.** $60 \div 3$ ● $60 \div 2$

35. $40 \div 2$ ● $400 \div 2$ **36.** $90 \div 9$ ● $70 \div 7$

37. $91 \div 7$ ● $77 \div 7$ **38.** $84 \div 6$ ● $96 \div 6$

Problem Solving

39. Leah phoned friends on other space stations to tell them about the toy sale. She spent $30 for a 5-minute phone call. If each minute cost the same amount, what was the cost for 1 minute? How much would it cost for 6 minutes?

40. All the items on one table at the toy sale were being sold for $200 each. There were 4 old computer games and 3 old toy robots on the table. How much would it cost to buy all the items?

41. Starlight School uses the money from the sale to buy 92 computers. They put the computers into 8 computer labs. Each lab gets the same number of computers. The rest are kept in the school library. How many computers are kept in the library?

Review and Remember

Find each answer.

42. 35 ÷ 7

43. 28 ÷ 4

44. 123 + 46

45. 14 + 18 + 75

46. 400 − 235

47. 8,194 + 32

48. 9 × 3 × 2

49. 7,204 − 685

50. 54 ÷ 8

51. 562 + 206

Project Link

Show these items on your map. How many will you need of each?

- one garden area for every 6 apartments
- one food store for every 120 people
- one swing set for every 18 apartments
- one school for every 75 apartments

www.sbgmath.com

Critical Thinking Corner

Number Sense

What's Wrong?

Mike makes and sells toy robots. He needs 4 computer chips to make each robot. He knows he has 23 computer chips left in his supply cabinet.

Suppose he gets an order for 6 toy robots. He estimates that 23 ÷ 4 is about 6, so he accepts the order. As he starts making the sixth robot, Mike realizes he will not have enough chips to finish the order. What did he do wrong?

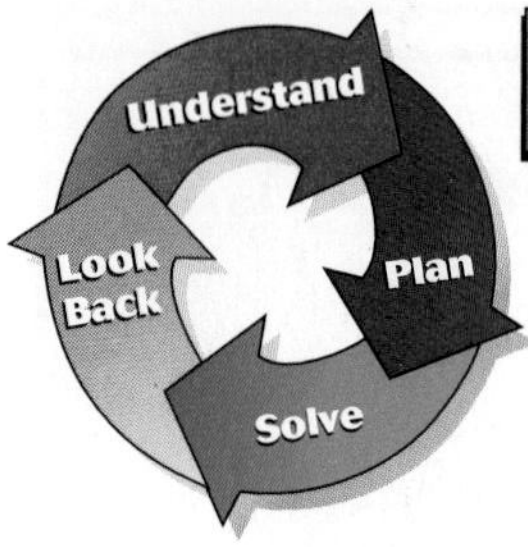

Problem Solving
Using Operations

Knowing how to add, subtract, multiply, and divide can help you solve problems.

You want to take some spaceship tours around Mars. There are 6 different tours of the planet. Each tour costs $725 and lasts 4 hours. You sign up for 12 hours of tours. How much money do you spend?

UNDERSTAND

What do you need to find?

First you need to find how many tours you will take. Then you need to find how much money you will spend on all the tours.

PLAN

How can you solve the problem?

Divide 12 by 4 to find the number of tours you will take. Then multiply that number by the cost of each tour.

SOLVE

Step 1

12 ÷ 4 = 3 tours

Step 2

$$\begin{array}{r} \$725 \\ \times \quad 3 \\ \hline \$2{,}175 \end{array}$$

You will spend $2,175.

LOOK BACK

How can you use addition to check your answer?

Show What You Learned

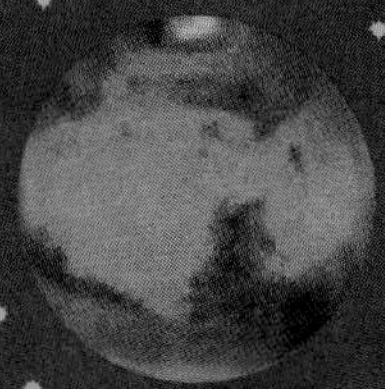

MARS IS OUR MISSION

OFFERING 6 EXCITING TOURS

- **View the Volcanoes**
- **See the Polar Caps**
- **Cruise Over Canyons**
- **Photograph Mars' Tiny Moon**
- **Fly Over Canals**
- **Track Giant Dust Storms**

Solve.

1. A group of 76 people are on a spaceship tour around Mars. Four people can view Mars through each window. How many windows will the group need to use?

2. **Science Connection** The moon is 240,000 miles from Earth. How far would a spacecraft travel if it made 2 trips to the moon and back?

3. A spacecraft leaves Earth with 45 people. It makes 2 stops. At the first stop, 95 people get on board. At the second stop, 15 people get on board. How many people are on board now?

4. One day a temperature of 430°C was recorded on the planet Mercury. Later the same day the temperature was 200°C. What was the difference between the two temperatures?

5. **Science Connection** A day on Mars is about 24 hours long. A day on Neptune is about 18 hours long. About how much longer is a day on Mars than a day on Neptune?

6. **Science Connection** Uranus was discovered in 1781. Neptune was discovered in 1846. How many years passed between the discovery of Uranus and the discovery of Neptune?

7. On a trip to the moon, a group of 5 people hire a guide for $80. Each person shares the cost equally. How much does each person pay?

8. **Create Your Own** Write a problem about living on a space station in the year 2050. Give it to a classmate to solve.

Checkpoint

Dividing by One-Digit Numbers

Find each quotient. (pages 462–463)

1. $5\overline{)23}$ **2.** $6\overline{)35}$ **3.** $2\overline{)19}$ **4.** $7\overline{)38}$ **5.** $4\overline{)28}$

6. $3\overline{)23}$ **7.** $8\overline{)66}$ **8.** $9\overline{)72}$ **9.** $6\overline{)56}$ **10.** $7\overline{)59}$

11. $15 \div 2$ **12.** $19 \div 3$ **13.** $28 \div 9$

14. $27 \div 4$ **15.** $74 \div 9$ **16.** $49 \div 6$

Using Mental Math Use a basic fact and mental math to find each quotient. (pages 470–471)

17. $4\overline{)8}$ $4\overline{)80}$ $4\overline{)800}$ **18.** $3\overline{)6}$ $3\overline{)60}$ $3\overline{)600}$

19. $4\overline{)12}$ $4\overline{)120}$ $4\overline{)1{,}200}$ **20.** $9\overline{)36}$ $9\overline{)360}$ $9\overline{)3{,}600}$

21. $5\overline{)45}$ $5\overline{)450}$ $5\overline{)4{,}500}$ **22.** $3\overline{)18}$ $3\overline{)180}$ $3\overline{)1{,}800}$

23. $7\overline{)14}$ $7\overline{)140}$ $7\overline{)1{,}400}$ **24.** $6\overline{)54}$ $6\overline{)540}$ $6\overline{)5{,}400}$

25. $32 \div 8 = ■$
$320 \div 8 = ■$
$3{,}200 \div 8 = ■$

26. $54 \div 9 = ■$
$540 \div 9 = ■$
$5{,}400 \div 9 = ■$

27. $18 \div 6 = ■$
$180 \div 6 = ■$
$1{,}800 \div 6 = ■$

28. $49 \div 7 = ■$
$490 \div 7 = ■$
$4{,}900 \div 7 = ■$

29. $30 \div 5 = ■$
$300 \div 5 = ■$
$3{,}000 \div 5 = ■$

30. $36 \div 4 = ■$
$360 \div 4 = ■$
$3{,}600 \div 4 = ■$

Divide. (pages 472-475)

31. $2\overline{)27}$ **32.** $4\overline{)44}$ **33.** $5\overline{)76}$ **34.** $4\overline{)72}$ **35.** $5\overline{)70}$

36. $5\overline{)65}$ **37.** $8\overline{)90}$ **38.** $6\overline{)79}$ **39.** $8\overline{)98}$ **40.** $6\overline{)69}$

41. $74 \div 3$ **42.** $69 \div 5$ **43.** $57 \div 4$

44. $65 \div 6$ **45.** $35 \div 2$ **46.** $86 \div 7$

Problem Solving

47. Two space stations are 84 miles apart. A shuttle that travels 7 miles a minute makes trips between the stations. How many minutes does one trip take?

48. **Analyze** David collects toys from Earth. He has 12 toy cars and 18 toy boats. He keeps all the toys in 6 boxes. Each box holds the same number of toys. How many toys are in each box?

49. The lunchroom of the Galaxy School has 96 tables. The tables are in 8 equal rows. How many tables are in each row?

50. **Using Mental Math** A car made for travel on the moon can go 300 miles in 6 hours. How far can it travel in 1 hour?

What do you think?

There are just enough chairs in the Galaxy School lunchroom to put the same number at each table. Suppose you divide the number of chairs by the number of tables. What would the remainder be? Explain how you know.

Journal Idea Explain how you could use base-ten blocks to find $93 \div 5$.

Project Wrap-Up

Life in Space

When your team has finished its space-station design, show it to the class.

- Tell how many apartments there are in the station. Tell how many people live there.
- Tell how the other things in the space station will help the people who live there.

Ask if anyone wants to live in your new space station!

Extra Practice

Set A (pages 444–445)

Use mental math to find each product.

1. 80×4

2. 70×7

3. 500×3

4. 600×8

5. 800×7

6. A robot can clean 30 windows in 1 hour. How many windows can the robot clean in 8 hours?

7. A space station sends 900 radio messages each day. How many messages does it send in a week?

Set B (pages 448–451)

Multiply.

1. 23×2

2. 73×3

3. 82×4

4. 14×5

5. 28×3

6. 3×23

7. 5×17

8. 4×32

9. 7×51

10. Wristwatch phones at the space station store sell for $49 each. How much will 2 phones cost?

11. Pocket computers sell for $62 each. Eric has $200. Does he have enough to buy 3 computers? How do you know?

Set C (pages 452–453)

Find each product.

1. 95×6

2. 48×7

3. 52×4

4. 86×5

5. 93×8

6. 2×42

7. 7×93

8. 4×24

9. 8×95

10. Tim can usually jump 16 inches high on Earth. On the moon he can jump 6 times that height. How high can he jump when he's on the moon?

11. Basketballs sell for $79. Suppose the Galaxy School basketball coach buys 9 basketballs. How much money will she spend?

Extra Practice

Set D (pages 454–457)

Multiply.

1. 422×5 2. 242×4 3. $\$2.23 \times 4$ 4. 875×8 5. $\$4.19 \times 7$

6. 4×326 7. 7×694 8. 8×132 9. $9 \times \$7.19$

10. In one month, the Satellite Deli served 495 meals to each of the 7 floors of a space station. How many meals were served in all?

11. Look back at Problem 10. What if each meal cost $8? How much would the meals for one floor of the space station cost?

Set E (pages 458–459)

Round each number to the underlined place. Then estimate each product.

1. $\underline{5}7 \times 4$ 2. $\underline{4}50 \times 6$ 3. $\underline{9}5 \times 6$ 4. $\underline{7}68 \times 9$ 5. $\underline{1}8 \times 8$

6. The Comet soccer team practices 3 hours at a time. There are 38 practices during the season. About how many hours does the team practice each season?

7. The Comet soccer team has 7 new uniforms. The cost for each new uniform is $810. About how much did the team spend on the new uniforms?

Set F (pages 462–463)

Find each quotient.

1. $4\overline{)15}$ 2. $2\overline{)9}$ 3. $7\overline{)22}$ 4. $5\overline{)19}$ 5. $3\overline{)17}$

6. $9\overline{)23}$ 7. $8\overline{)18}$ 8. $7\overline{)38}$ 9. $6\overline{)41}$ 10. $7\overline{)53}$

11. There are 20 people who want to go on a trip around Mars. Each spacecraft holds 6 people. How many spacecraft are needed for all 20 people?

12. The *Comet News* newspaper costs $5. Sergei has $34. How many copies of the newspaper can Sergei buy?

Extra Practice

Set G (pages 470–471)

Use a basic fact and mental math to find each quotient.

1. $5\overline{)250}$ **2.** $9\overline{)180}$ **3.** $2\overline{)120}$ **4.** $3\overline{)180}$ **5.** $7\overline{)420}$

6. $8\overline{)640}$ **7.** $4\overline{)160}$ **8.** $9\overline{)630}$ **9.** $2\overline{)1,000}$ **10.** $3\overline{)1,800}$

11. $4\overline{)2,800}$ **12.** $5\overline{)4,000}$ **13.** $8\overline{)4,800}$ **14.** $9\overline{)6,300}$ **15.** $6\overline{)4,200}$

16. $720 \div 9$ **17.** $540 \div 6$ **18.** $6,400 \div 8$ **19.** $4,900 \div 7$

20. $280 \div 4$ **21.** $560 \div 7$ **22.** $8,100 \div 9$ **23.** $3,500 \div 5$

24. Derek's mother is in charge of the space station robots. She earns $1,200 for 6 hours of work. How much does she earn each hour?

25. Each space station robot must have a checkup every 4 days. How many checkups will each robot get in 360 days?

Set H (pages 472–475)

Find each quotient.

1. $5\overline{)55}$ **2.** $4\overline{)43}$ **3.** $8\overline{)89}$ **4.** $7\overline{)71}$ **5.** $6\overline{)88}$

6. $5\overline{)67}$ **7.** $6\overline{)72}$ **8.** $8\overline{)96}$ **9.** $3\overline{)54}$ **10.** $2\overline{)35}$

11. $6\overline{)89}$ **12.** $9\overline{)95}$ **13.** $7\overline{)99}$ **14.** $4\overline{)65}$ **15.** $2\overline{)49}$

16. $83 \div 7$ **17.** $59 \div 3$ **18.** $91 \div 8$ **19.** $68 \div 4$ **20.** $75 \div 6$

21. $93 \div 5$ **22.** $48 \div 2$ **23.** $57 \div 4$ **24.** $79 \div 7$ **25.** $99 \div 9$

26. A toy maker can put together 1 toy robot every 6 minutes. How many toy robots can he put together in 60 minutes?

27. A used pocket video player costs $155. A new one sells for $255. How much would 2 new and 3 used pocket video players cost?

Chapter Test

**Round each number to the underlined place.
Then estimate each product.**

1. $\underline{8}2 \times 7$
2. $\underline{3}6 \times 6$
3. $\underline{7}82 \times 5$
4. $\underline{9}43 \times 8$

Multiply.

5. 90×8
6. 600×7
7. 80×6
8. 700×3
9. 71×5
10. 32×3
11. 56×4
12. 18×5
13. 8×43
14. 7×321
15. $6 \times \$3.29$

Divide.

16. $6\overline{)540}$
17. $9\overline{)2,700}$
18. $4\overline{)280}$
19. $6\overline{)3,600}$
20. $6\overline{)79}$
21. $5\overline{)47}$
22. $2\overline{)38}$
23. $9\overline{)93}$

Solve.

24. Tickets to see a movie at the space theater cost $35 each. Alex has $200. Does he have enough to buy tickets for himself and 5 friends? Explain.

25. Brad spent 3 months on the space station. The first month he gained 2 pounds. The second month he lost 3 pounds. The third month he gained 2 pounds. When he returned to Earth, he weighed 98 pounds. How much did he weigh before he left Earth?

Self-Check Look back at Exercises 1–4. Check to see that you rounded the numbers to the correct place.

Performance Assessment

Show What You Know About Multiplication and Division

1. Use the chart to answer Questions 1a–1c. Show your work in numbers, words, or pictures.

   a. Suppose you needed 6 of the same size note pads. Which size note pad would you pick? How much would you spend?

   b. You have $75 to spend on crayons. How many large boxes could you buy? How many medium boxes could you buy? How many small boxes could you buy?

   c. Suppose you need 60 crayons. Which is a better buy—3 boxes of 20 crayons or 2 boxes of 30 crayons? Explain your choice.

School Supplies in 2050	Price
Small note pad	$11
Medium note pad	$18
Large note pad	$24
Small box of crayons (12 crayons)	$25
Medium box of crayons (20 crayons)	$32
Large box of crayons (30 crayons)	$40

2. Kwon and his 7 friends share one of the bags of space rocks shown. They share all the rocks equally without having any left over.

   a. Which bag do they share? How many rocks does each person get?

   b. Kwon and his friends pick a second bag of rocks and try to share those rocks equally. They find that there are 4 rocks left over. Which bag did they pick?

Self-Check

For Questions 1a and 1b, did you remember to regroup ones whenever necessary?

For Question 2a, did you check that there were no rocks left over?

Extension

Thinking in Threes

When a number is divided by 3 and the remainder is 0, we say the number is **divisible** by 3.

Here's a fun way to tell if a number is divisible by 3. Follow the directions below. Be sure to follow the arrows!

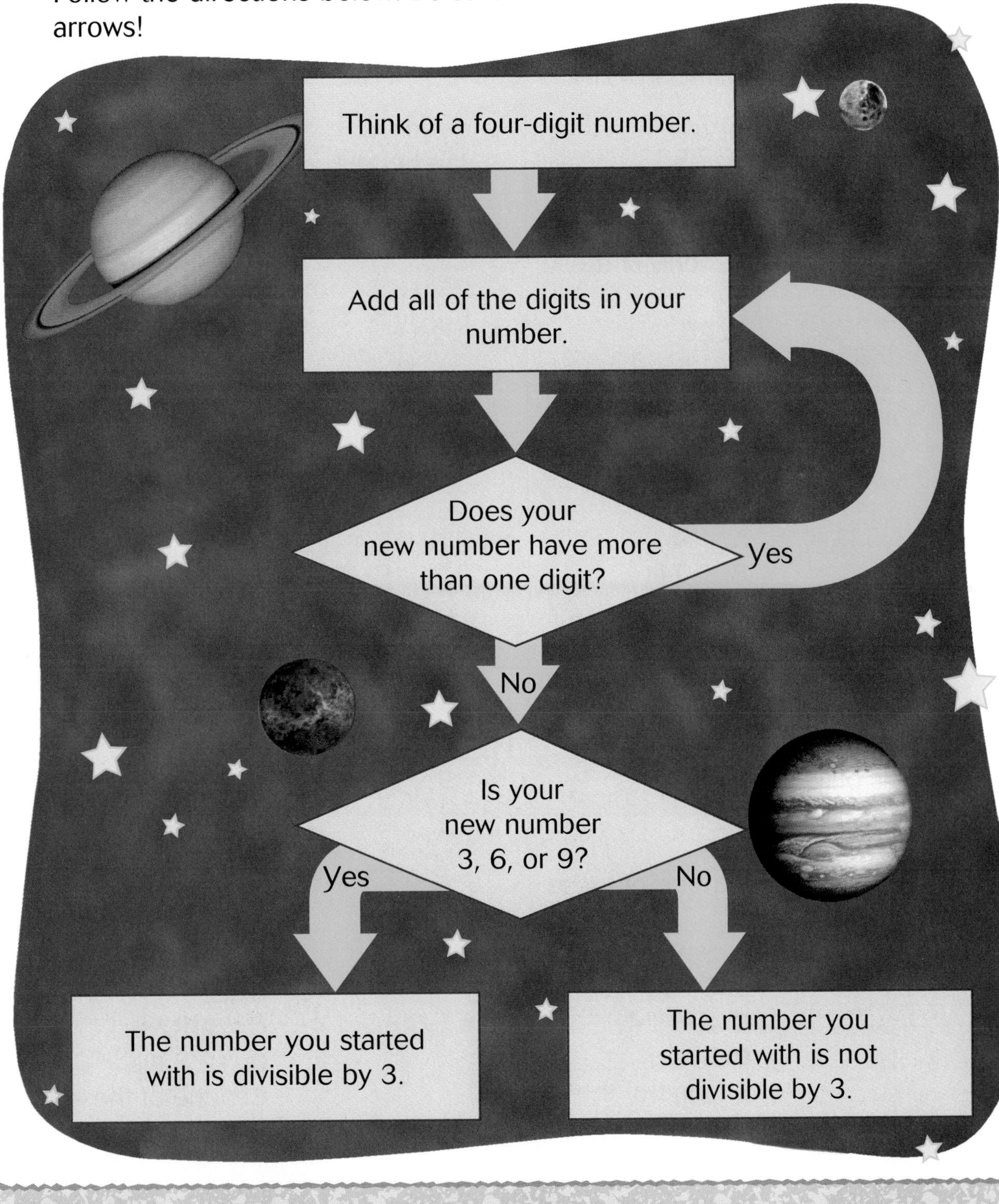

Cumulative Review

Preparing for Tests

Choose the letter for the correct answer.

1. $\begin{array}{r} \$62.49 \\ +\ 51.67 \\ \hline \end{array}$
   A. \$114.06
   B. \$114.16
   C. \$113.16
   D. \$143.06
   E. none of these

2. 4,215 + 3,128
   A. 7,343
   B. 7,333
   C. 1,078
   D. 1,087
   E. none of these

3. 4 × 7 = ■
   A. 28
   B. 11
   C. 24
   D. 21
   E. none of these

4. 700 − 341 = ■
   A. 495
   B. 1,041
   C. 459
   D. 359
   E. none of these

5. What digit is in the tens place? 7,438
   A. 3
   B. 4
   C. 7
   D. 8
   E. none of these

6. $\begin{array}{r} \$8.24 \\ \times\ \ 6 \\ \hline \end{array}$
   A. \$48.44
   B. \$8.30
   C. \$49.24
   D. \$8.03
   E. none of these

7. 28 × 3 = ■
   A. 31
   B. 25
   C. 84
   D. 94
   E. none of these

8. Which is the hottest temperature?
   A. 54°F
   B. 12°F
   C. 67°F
   D. 94°F
   E. none of these

9. $5\overline{)20}$
   A. 4
   B. 15
   C. 3
   D. 100
   E. none of these

10. 3.8 + 2.4 = ■
    A. 1.4
    B. 62
    C. 14
    D. 6.2
    E. none of these

11. 54 ÷ 9 = ■
    A. 7
    B. 4
    C. 6
    D. 42
    E. none of these

12. $4\overline{)86}$
    A. 21
    B. 22
    C. 21 R2
    D. 12 R2
    E. none of these

13. Jennifer buys 6 packages of clay. Each package has 5 clay pieces. Jennifer uses 12 pieces to make a bowl. How many pieces of clay are left?

A. 12
B. 18
C. 17
D. 42

14. What part of the circle is shaded green?

A. $\frac{3}{4}$
B. $\frac{3}{8}$
C. $\frac{5}{8}$
D. $\frac{3}{5}$

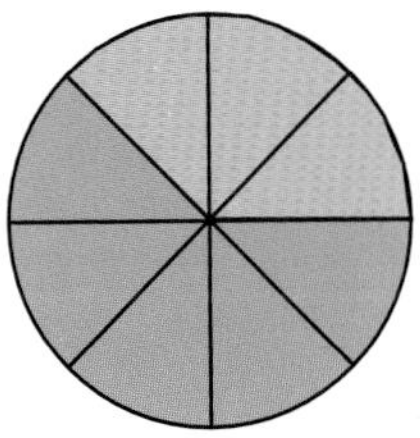

15. Tamara's mother put 8 peanut butter cookies, 6 oatmeal cookies, and 10 chocolate chip cookies on a plate. Tamara and her 7 friends shared the cookies equally. How many cookies did each person get?

A. 5
B. 4
C. 3
D. 2

16. Which figure shows a line of symmetry?

A. 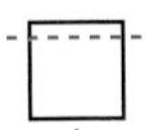
B. 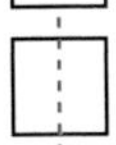
C. 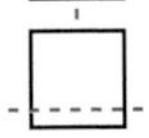
D. 

This graph shows the number of third-grade students who have different kinds of collections.

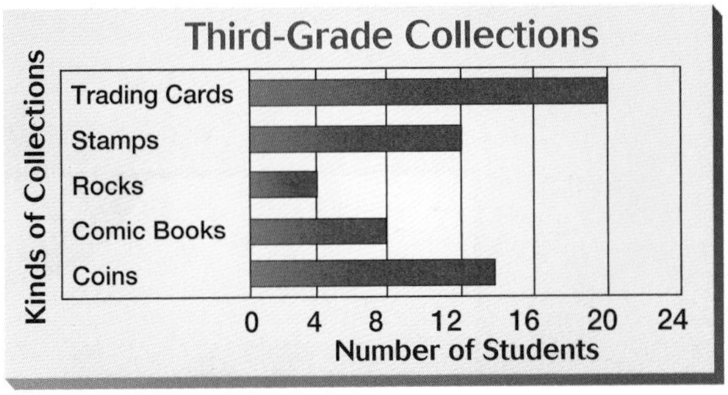

17. What kind of collection is kept by the greatest number of students have?

A. trading cards
B. stamps
C. comic books
D. coins

18. What kind of collection is kept by the least number of students?

A. trading cards
B. comic books
C. coins
D. rocks

19. How many students collect stamps?

A. 12
B. 13
C. 14
D. 10

20. How many more coin collections are there than rock collections?

A. 14
B. 12
C. 10

Test-Taking Handbook

Becoming a Better Test Taker

You've learned a lot of math skills this year! These skills will help you with your school work and with everyday activities outside of school. How can you show what you've learned in math? One way is by taking tests.

Did you know you could do better on tests just by knowing how to take a test? The test-taking strategies on these pages can help you become a better test taker. They might also help you think of test questions as a fun challenge! When you take a test, try to use these strategies to show all you know.

Multiple Choice Questions
Know Your ABCs!

For multiple choice questions, you are given several answer choices for a problem. Once you have solved the problem, you need to choose the right answer from the choices that are given.

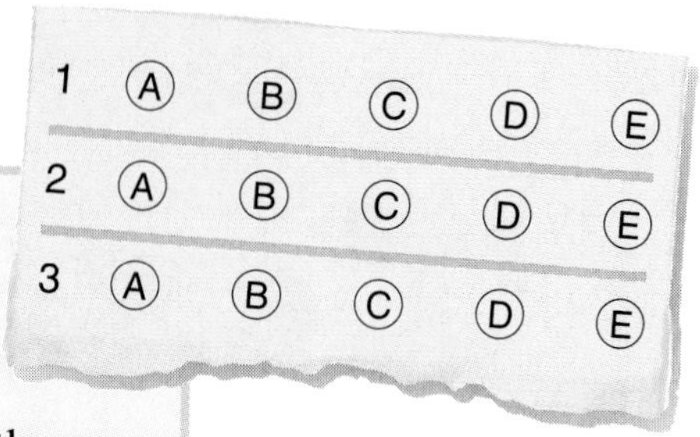

Example

5 × 3 = ■

A 8 **B** 15 **C** 2 **D** 20 **E** None of these

Think It Through

Read Did I read the problem carefully?
I need to multiply 5 times 3.

Identify Are there any answers that I know are wrong?
If there are five groups of 3, then 2 is too small, so I can ignore answer C.

Solve What is 5 × 3?
5 × 3 = 15

Check Is there a way that I can check my answer?
I can check using repeated addition.
3 + 3 + 3 + 3 + 3 = 15

Choose Which letter is next to my answer?
My answer is 15, and 15 is next to letter B.

Try It!

1. **6 + 10 = ■**

   A 16 **B** 4 **C** 60 **D** 7 **E** None of these

2. **24 − 8 = ■**

   A 14 **B** 32 **C** 6 **D** 16 **E** None of these

3. **6 × 3 = ■**

   A 18 **B** 9 **C** 20 **D** 12 **E** None of these

Testing Tips

- Estimate whenever you can before you solve a problem. You can use an estimate to check whether your answer is reasonable, or to identify answer choices that are not reasonable.
- Reread the question and check your work before choosing "None of these."
- Make sure you bubble in the letter on the answer sheet that matches your answer.

More Multiple Choice
One Step at a Time

Sometimes you need to do more than one step to answer a multiple choice question.

- Always look at all of the answer choices that are listed.
- Even if you find your answer among the choices, check your work. Answers that come from making common mistakes are usually included in the choices!
- If you are having trouble answering a question, go on to the next question and come back to the more difficult question later.

Example

Jen spent \$8 on rides and \$5 on food at the fair. Then she spent \$6 more on souvenirs. If Jen came to the fair with \$21, how much money does she have left?

A \$19 **B** \$2 **C** \$3 **D** \$40 **E** None of these

Think It Through

Read Did I read the problem carefully?
I need to find how much money Jen has left.

Identify Are there any answers I know are wrong?
Jen came with \$21 and spent money, so she can't have \$40 now. I can ignore answer D.

Solve How much money does Jen have now?
\$8 + \$5 + \$6 = \$19, so Jen spent \$19.
\$21 – \$19 = \$2, so Jen has \$2 left now.

Check Is there a way that I can check my answer?
I can check by adding all the amounts.
\$2 + \$8 + \$5 + \$6 = \$21

Choose Which letter is next to my answer?
My answer is \$2, and \$2 is next to letter B.

Try It!

1. **Lou is two years older than Gene. Gene is 3 years older than Deb. Deb is 5. How old is Lou?**

   A 6 **B** 9 **C** 10 **D** 31 **E** None of these

2. **Mary is coloring circles in this pattern: red, yellow, green, blue, red, yellow, green, blue. What color will the 14th circle be?**

   A Red **B** Yellow **C** Green
   D Blue **E** None of these

Grid Questions
Boxes and Circles

On some tests, you may be asked to put your answer in a grid. When you record answers in this way, it is important to write the answer properly in the boxes and circles.

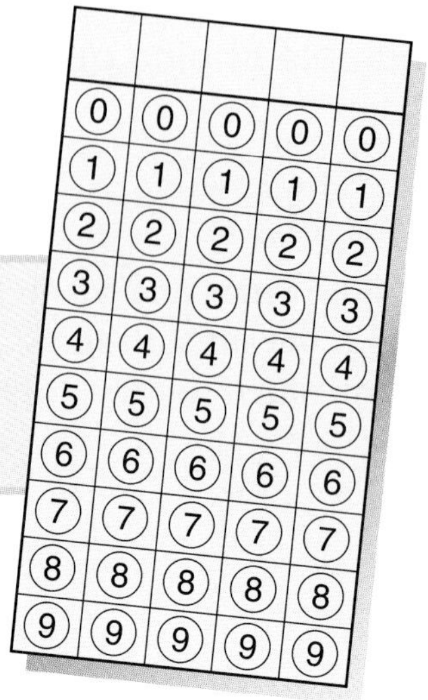

Example

43 + 27 = ■

Think It Through

Read Did I read the question carefully?
I need to add 43 and 27.

Solve What is the answer to the question?
43 + 27 = 70

Check Is there a way that I can check my answer?
I can estimate: 40 + 30 = 70.
My estimate is the same as my answer, so my answer is reasonable.

Grid How do I put my answer in the grid?
I need to write the answer in the boxes and fill in the correct circle under each box I use.

Step 1 Write your answer in the answer boxes at the top of the grid.

Step 2 Fill in the circle under each box for the number you wrote in the box.

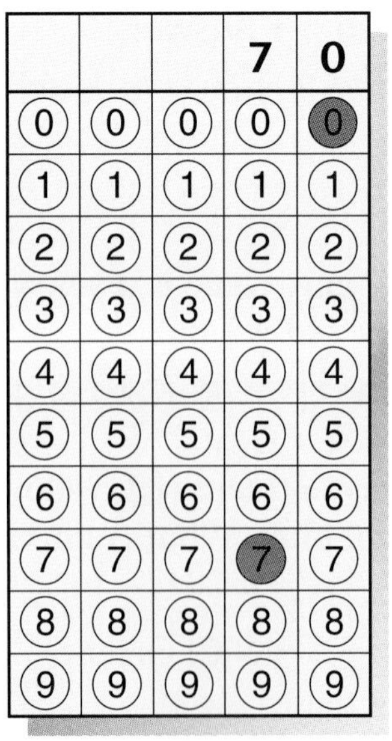

TESTING TIPS

- You can start your answer in any box in the grid, but don't leave *any* blank spaces between *any* part of your answer.
- Remember that 0 is a number! If you leave a blank space where a 0 should be, your answer will be wrong.
- When you fill in a circle, be sure to fill in the same number that you write in the box above. Try using your finger to help you stay in the correct column.

Try It!

Questions 1 and 2 have been answered in the grid. Can you tell which grid or grids have been filled in correctly?

1 3 × 6 = ▢

A

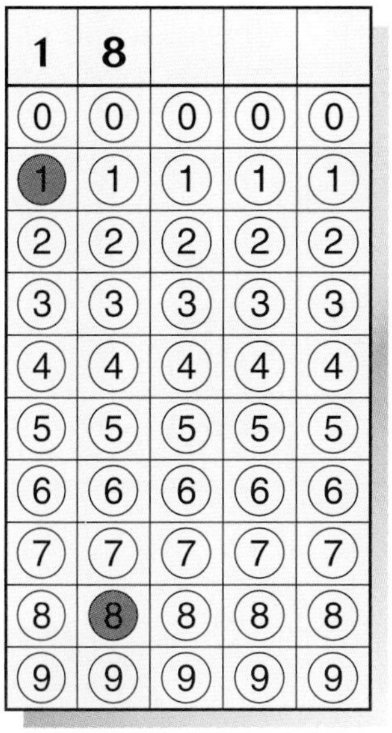

B

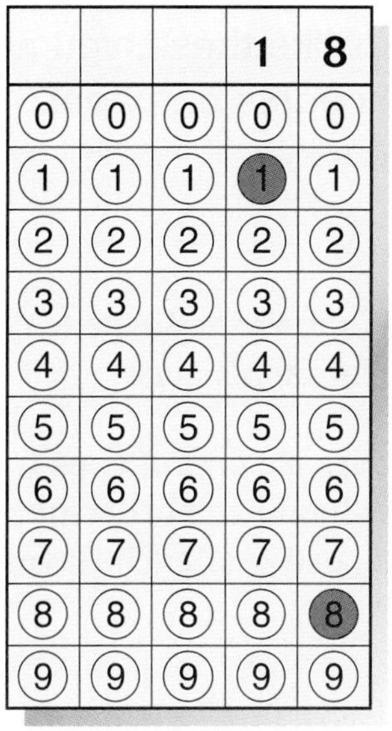

C

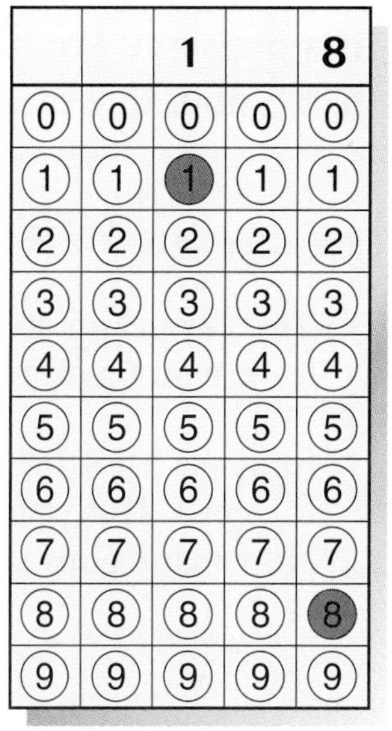

2 209 − 103 = ▢

A

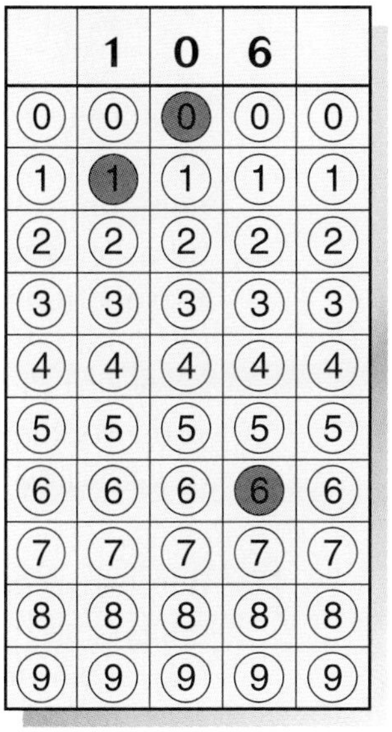

B

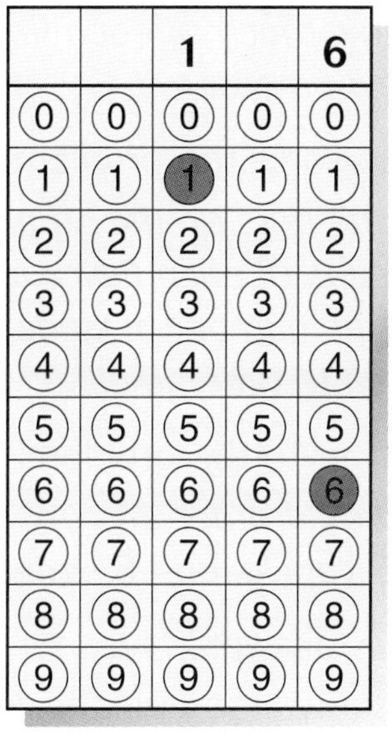

C

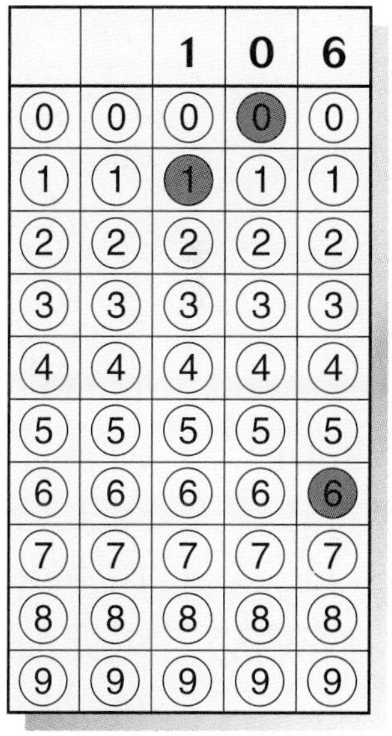

Now answer these questions on a separate sheet of grid-answer paper.

3 38 + 5 = ▢

4 264 + 138 = ▢

5 2 × 4 = ▢

6 6 ÷ 3 = ▢

7 Carie read 12 pages of her book on Monday and 14 pages on Tuesday. How many pages did she read in the two days?

Short Answer Questions
The Write Stuff

Sometimes a test question asks you not only to *solve* a problem but to show *how* you solved the problem. For questions like these, you need to be able to write your thoughts on paper.

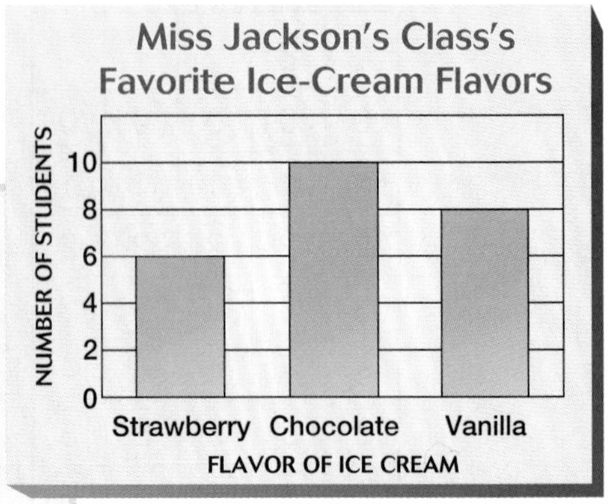

Example

The bar graph at the right shows the favorite ice-cream flavors of Miss Jackson's class.

Suppose Miss Jackson orders ice cream cups for the class. How many cups should she order in all? How many cups should she order of each flavor?

Think It Through

Read What am I being asked to write about?
I need to find how much of each flavor of ice cream should be ordered.

Plan What can I do to solve the problem?
I can compare the bars on the graph to find out how many cups of each flavor to order. Then I can add the number of students shown to find how much to order in all.

Solve What is the answer to the problem?
Miss Jackson should order 24 cups: 10 chocolate, 8 vanilla, and 6 strawberry.

Explain How did I get my answer?
The bar graph shows the number needed of each flavor, and that there are 24 students.

Try It!

Use the graph to answer Questions 1–2. Explain your answers.

1. **If you walked into the class, what flavor ice cream would you probably see the most students eating?**
2. **Three students who liked chocolate before like vanilla now. Does this change your answer for Question 1?**

TESTING TIPS

- Be sure to follow the directions carefully. Sometimes you will be asked to write an explanation in words. Other times you will be asked to show your work in numbers or with drawings.
- Be prepared to take more time to answer short answer questions than to answer multiple choice or grid questions.
- You can usually get partial credit for an answer. So, even if you can't solve the whole problem, write what you can!

Long Answer Questions
In Your Own Words

Long answer questions are like short answer questions, only they are longer and often have more than one step.

Example

Sean has 12 buttons. He wants to arrange them in equal rows. What are the different ways he can arrange them? Show your answer in numbers and with a drawing. Then explain your answer.

Think It Through

Read What am I being asked to write about?
I need to find all the ways Sean can arrange 12 buttons in equal rows.

Plan What can I do to solve the problem?
I can draw all the different arrangements.

Solve What is the answer to the problem?
Sean can arrange them in 2 rows of 6, 6 rows of 2, 3 rows of 4, 4 rows of 3, 12 rows of 1, or 1 row of 12.

Explain How did I get my answer?
I drew all the arrangements and then added to make sure that each one had 12 buttons.

Try It!

For Questions 1 and 2, use numbers and drawings to show your work. Be sure to explain how you got your answers.

1. **Jim is going on a trip. He takes 3 shirts: yellow, green, and red. He takes 2 pairs of pants: black and brown. Jim's trip is 8 days long. Will he be able to wear a different combination of shirt and pants each day?**
2. **Four friends are in line in order from youngest to oldest. Their ages are 7, 8, 9, and 12. Keesha is before Paul. Derek is after Paul. Ana is between two people, but she is not next to Derek. How much older is Paul than Keesha?**

- Remember to explain *how* you got your answer.
- When you're finished writing, read the question again to be sure you've answered it completely.
- Keep trying! If your first strategy doesn't work, try another one. You might get partial credit even if you can't find an answer.
- Long answer questions take longer to answer! Be patient, and take your time.

Tables

MEASURES

Customary

Length

1 foot (ft) = 12 inches (in.)
1 yard (yd) = 3 feet, or 36 inches
1 mile (m) = 1,760 yards, or 5,280 feet

Weight

1 pound (lb) = 16 ounces (oz)

Capacity

1 pint (pt) = 2 cups
1 quart (qt) = 2 pints
1 gallon (gal) = 4 quarts

Metric

Length

1 centimeter (cm) = 10 millimeters (mm)
1 meter (m) = 100 centimeters
1 kilometer (km) = 1,000 meters

Mass

1 kilogram (kg) = 1,000 grams (g)

Capacity

1 liter (L) = 1,000 milliliters (mL)

TIME

1 minute (min) = 60 seconds (s)
1 hour (h) = 60 minutes
1 day (d) = 24 hours
1 week (wk) = 7 days
1 month (mo) = 28 to 31 days, or about 4 weeks
1 year (yr) = 12 months, or 52 weeks, or 365 days

MONEY

1 penny = 1 cent (¢)
1 nickel = 5 cents
1 dime = 10 cents
1 quarter = 25 cents
1 half-dollar = 50 cents
1 dollar ($) = 100 cents

SYMBOLS

=	is equal to	10¢	ten cents
>	is greater than	$1.60	one dollar and sixty cents
<	is less than	6:45	six forty-five
. . .	and so on	°C	degree Celsius
		°F	degree Fahrenheit

Glossary

A

A.M. Used to show time between midnight and noon. (p.128)

addends The numbers that are added. (p. 48)

Example: 7 + 8 = 15
The addends are 7 and 8.

addition An operation on two or more numbers to find the sum. (p. 44)

Example: 4 + 2 + 3 = 9
The sum is 9.

angle Two rays with a common endpoint. (p. 366)

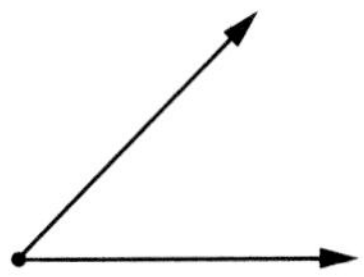

area The number of square units needed to cover a region. (p. 382)

array An arrangement of objects or numbers in rows and columns. (p. 178)

Example:

B

bar graph A graph with bars of different lengths to show information. (p. 256)

C

capacity The amount a container can hold. (p. 144)

centimeter (cm) A metric unit used to measure length. 100 centimeters equal 1 meter. (p. 152)

chance A possibility. (p. 274)

circle A closed plane figure. All the points of a circle are the same distance from the center. (p. 362)

cone A space figure with one circular flat surface and one curved surface that form a point. (p. 386)

Example:

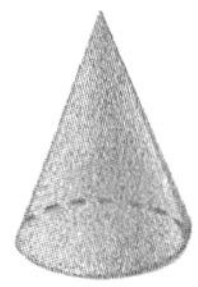

congruent Figures that have the same size and shape. (p. 370)

corner A point where two sides of a plane figure meet. Also, a point where more than two faces of a space figure meet. (p. 362)

Example:

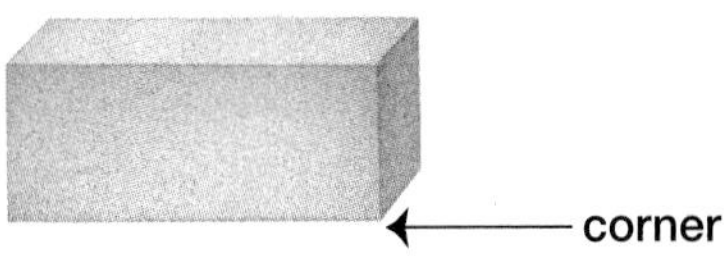

cube A space figure with six congruent square faces. (p. 386)

Example:

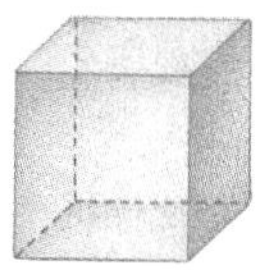

Glossary

cup (c) A customary unit used to measure capacity. 1 cup equals 8 ounces. (p. 144)

customary system A measurement system that measures length in inches, feet, yards, and miles; capacity in cups, pints, quarts, and gallons; weight in ounces, pounds, and tons; and temperature in degrees Fahrenheit. *See* Table of Measures. (p. 488)

cylinder A space figure with two faces that are congruent circles. (p. 386)

D

data Information that is gathered. (p. 252)

decimal A number with one or more places to the right of a decimal point. (p. 420)

Examples: 0.7, 1.8, 2.06

decimal point The dot used to separate dollars from cents and ones from tenths. (p. 420)

Examples: $1.54, 1.3

decimeter (dm) A metric unit used to measure length. 1 decimeter equals 10 centimeters. (p. 152)

degree Celsius (°C) A metric unit used to measure temperature. (p. 160)

degree Fahrenheit (°F) A customary unit used to measure temperature. (p. 148)

denominator The number below the fraction bar in a fraction. (p. 402)

Example: $\frac{2}{5}$ ← denominator

difference The answer in subtraction. (p. 62)

Example: $9 - 4 = 5$
The difference is 5.

digit Any of the symbols used to write numbers: 0, 1, 2, 3, 4, 5, 6, 7, 8, and 9. (p. 7)

divide To separate a number of items into groups of equal size. (p. 288)

dividend The number to be divided. (p. 292)

Example: $6\overline{)36}$ or $36 \div 6$
The dividend is 36.

divisible A number is divisible by another number if the remainder is 0 after dividing. (p. 466)

division An operation on two numbers that results in a quotient. (p. 288)

Example: $18 \div 2 = 9$

divisor The number by which another number is to be divided. (p. 292)

Example: $7\overline{)28}$ or $28 \div 7$
The divisor is 7.

E

edge The segment where two faces of a space figure meet. (p. 386)

Example:

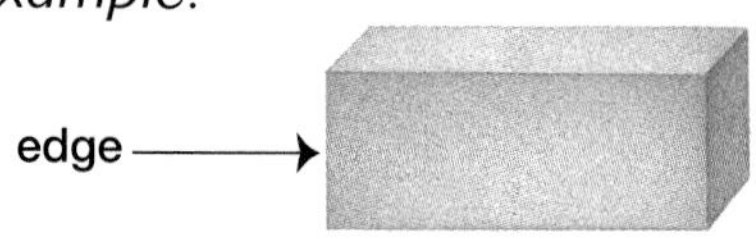

elapsed time The amount of time that has passed. (p. 132)

endpoint A point at the end of a line segment or ray. (p. 366)

equally likely Outcomes that have the same chance of occurring. (p. 272)

equivalent fractions Fractions that name the same number. (p. 404)

Examples: $\frac{1}{2}$ and $\frac{2}{4}$

estimate To give an approximate rather than an exact answer. (p. 82)

even A whole number that is divisible by 2. Even numbers have 0, 2, 4, 6, or 8 in the ones place. (p. 2)

expanded form A number written as the sum of the value of its digits. (p. 6)

Example: 1,000 + 200 + 30 + 4 is the expanded form of 1,234.

F

face A flat surface of a space figure. (p. 386)

Example:

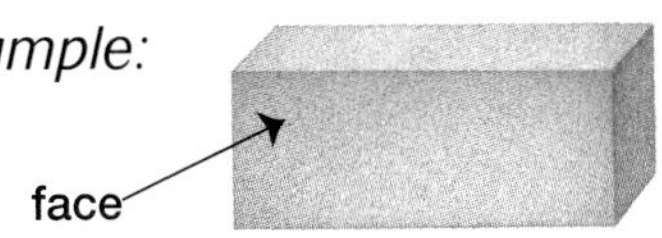

fact family Related facts using the same numbers. (p. 66)

Example:

$2 + 3 = 5$ $\quad$ $5 - 2 = 3$
$3 + 2 = 5$ $\quad$ $5 - 3 = 2$

or

$2 \times 5 = 10$ $\quad$ $10 \div 2 = 5$
$5 \times 2 = 10$ $\quad$ $10 \div 5 = 2$

factors The numbers that are multiplied to give a product. (p. 176)

Example: $3 \times 8 = 24$
The factors are 3 and 8.

foot (ft) A customary unit used to measure length. 1 foot equals 12 inches. Also an ancient Egyptian unit of measure equal to a human foot. (p. 140)

fraction A number that names part of a region or a part of a group. (p. 402)

Examples: $\frac{1}{2}$ and $\frac{6}{8}$ are fractions.

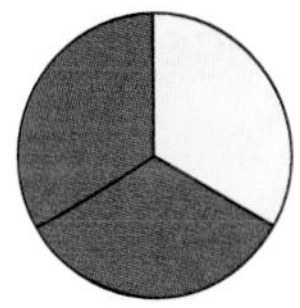

$\frac{2}{3}$ of the region is red.

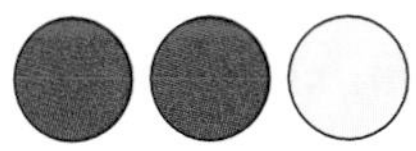

$\frac{2}{3}$ of the group is red.

front digit The digit in the place with the greatest value, used for front-end estimation. (p. 82)

front-end estimation A method using only the front-end digits to estimate sums, differences, products, and quotients. (p. 107)

G

gallon (gal) A customary unit used to measure capacity. 1 gallon equals 4 quarts. (p. 144)

gram (g) A metric unit used to measure how heavy an object is. 1,000 grams equal 1 kilogram. (p. 158)

Glossary

graph A drawing used to show information. (p. 256)

greater than (>) The symbol used to compare two numbers when the greater number is written on the left. (p. 22)

Examples: $7 > 4$, $9 > 6$

grouping property of addition The way in which addends are grouped does not change the sum. (p. 50)

Example: $2 + (4 + 5) = (2 + 4) + 5$

grouping property of multiplication The way in which factors are grouped does not change the product. (p. 234)

Example: $2 \times (3 \times 5) = (2 \times 3) \times 5$

H

hexagon A plane figure with six sides and six corners. (p. 362)

hour (h) A unit of time equal to 60 minutes. (p. 128)

hour hand The short hand on a clock. The hand on a clock that shows hours. (p. 128)

hundreds Groups of ten tens. (p. 86)

hundredths One or more of one hundred equal parts of a whole. (p. 424)

I

inch (in.) A customary unit used to measure length. 12 inches equal 1 foot. (p. 140)

K

kilogram (kg) A metric unit used to measure how heavy an object is. 1 kilogram equals 1,000 grams. (p. 158)

kilometer (km) A metric unit used to measure length. 1 kilometer equals 1,000 meters. (p. 152)

L

less likely Smaller chance that an event will happen. (p. 272)

less than (<) The symbol used to compare two numbers when the lesser number is written on the left. (p. 22)

Examples: $7 < 10$, $4 < 8$

line A collection of points along a straight path that goes on and on in opposite directions. A line has no endpoints. (p. 366)

line of symmetry A line on which a figure can be folded so that both sides match. (p. 374)

Example:

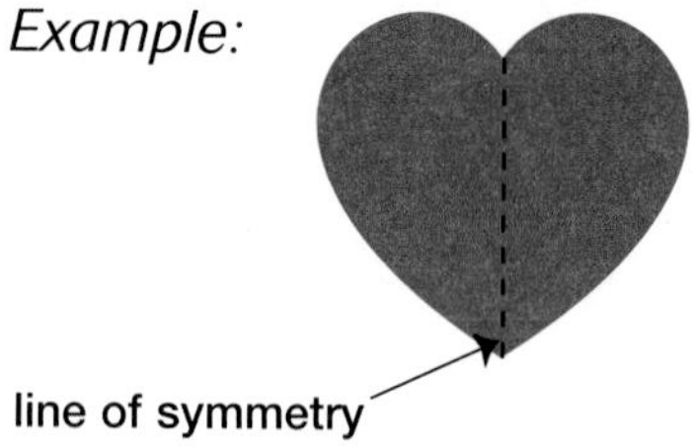

line segment A part of a line between two endpoints. (p. 366)

liter (L) A metric unit used to measure capacity. 1 liter equals 1,000 milliliters. (p. 156)

M

meter (m) A metric unit used to measure length. 1 meter equals 100 centimeters. (p. 152)

metric system A measurement system that measures length in millimeters, centimeters, meters, and kilometers; capacity in milliliters and liters; how heavy an object is in grams and kilograms; and temperature in degrees Celsius. *See* Table of Measures. (p. 488)

mile (mi) A customary unit used to measure length. 1 mile equals 5,280 feet. (p. 140)

milliliter (mL) A metric unit used to measure capacity. 1,000 milliliters equal 1 liter. (p. 156)

minute A unit of time equal to 60 seconds. (p. 128)

missing addend A number to be added to one or more other numbers to equal a given number. (p. 62)

Example: 5 + ■ = 8
The missing addend is 3.

mixed number A number written as a whole number and a fraction. (p. 414)

Example: $3\frac{1}{2}$

month One of the twelve parts into which the year is divided. (p. 136)

more likely Greater chance that an event will happen. (p. 272)

multiplication An operation on two or more numbers, called factors, to find a product. (p. 174)

Example: $4 \times 5 = 20$
The product is 20.

multiplication table A table that organizes multiplication facts. (p. 328)

multiply To find the total number of items in groups of equal size. (p. 174)

N

noon Twelve o'clock in the daytime. (p. 128)

number line A line that shows numbers in order. (p. 10)

Example:

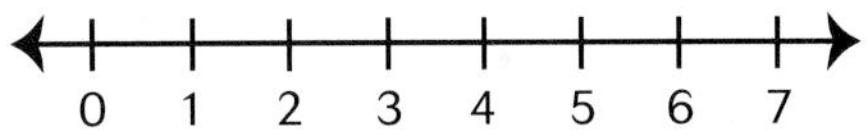

numerator The number above the fraction bar in a fraction. (p. 402)

Example: $\frac{2}{5}$ ← numerator

O

odd A whole number that is not divisible by 2. Odd numbers have 1, 3, 5, 7, or 9 in the ones place. (p. 2)

order property of addition The order in which addends are added does not change the sum. (p. 48)

Example: $9 + 3 = 3 + 9$

Glossary

order property of multiplication The order in which factors are multiplied does not change the product. (p. 179)

Example: $3 \times 2 = 2 \times 3$

ordered pair A pair of numbers that give the location of a point on a map or a graph. (p. 268)

ordinal numbers A number used to tell order or position. (p. 4)

Examples: first, fifth

ounce (oz) A customary unit used to measure weight. 16 ounces equal 1 pound. (p. 146)

outcome A result of a probability experiment. (p. 274)

P

P.M. Used to show time between noon and midnight. (p. 128)

palindrome A number, word, or sentence that reads the same backward or forward. (p. 123)

pentagon A plane figure with five sides and five corners. (p. 362)

perimeter The distance around a figure. (p. 380)

pictograph A graph that shows information by using pictures. (p. 260)

pint (pt) A customary unit used to measure capacity. 1 pint equals 2 cups. (p. 144)

place value The value determined by the position of a digit in a number. (p. 6)

Example: In 562, the digit 5 means 5 hundreds, the digit 6 means 6 tens, the digit 2 means 2 ones.

plane figure A geometric figure whose points are all in one plane. (p. 362)

Examples:

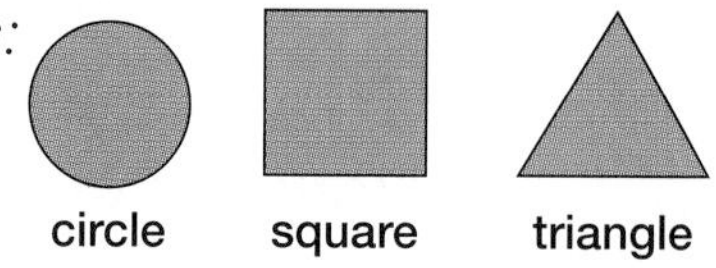

pound (lb) A customary unit used to measure weight. 1 pound equals 16 ounces. (p. 146)

probability The chance that an event will occur. (p. 272)

product The answer in multiplication. (p. 176)

Example: $4 \times 8 = 32$
The product is 32.

properties of 1 for division Any number divided by 1 is that number. Any number except 0 divided by itself is 1. (p. 310)

Examples: $6 \div 1 = 6$, $3 \div 3 = 1$

property of one for multiplication The product of any number and 1 is that number. (p. 196)

Examples: $6 \times 1 = 6$ and $1 \times 6 = 6$

pyramid A space figure whose base is a plane figure and whose faces are triangles with a common corner. (p. 386)

Example:

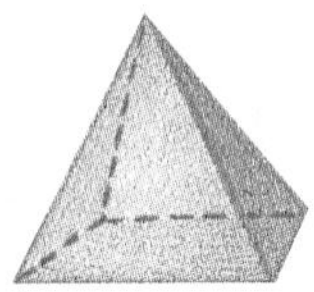

Q

quadrilateral A plane figure with four sides and four corners. (p. 363)

quart (qt) A customary unit used to measure capacity. 1 quart equals 4 cups. (p. 144)

quotient The answer in division. (p. 292)

Example: $24 \div 3 = 8$ or $\begin{array}{r}8\\3\overline{)24}\end{array}$
The quotient is 8.

R

ray A part of a line that has one endpoint and goes on and on in one direction. (p. 366)

rectangle A plane figure with four right angles and four sides. (p. 362)

Example:

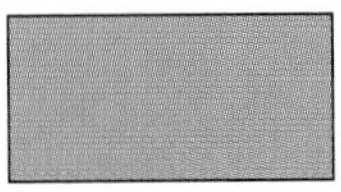

rectangular prism A space figure whose faces are all rectangles. (p. 386)

Example:

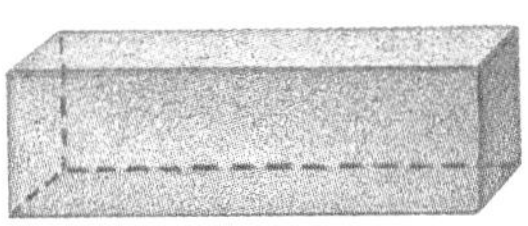

regroup To rename a number by exchanging base-ten materials of one value for base-ten materials that are equal to it. (p. 86)

Examples: 12 can be regrouped as 1 ten 2 ones. 253 can be regrouped as 2 hundreds 5 tens 3 ones.

remainder The number that is left after dividing. (p. 346)

Example: $42 \div 8 = 5$ R2
The remainder is 2.

right angle An angle that has the shape of a square corner. (p. 366)

Example:

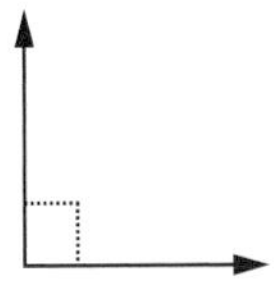

rounding Expressing a number to the nearest ten, hundred, thousand, and so on. (p. 10)

Example: 43 rounded to the nearest ten is 40.

S

side A line segment that is part of a plane figure. (p. 362)

similar Figures that have the same shape. They are not necessarily the same size. (p. 372)

space figure A geometric figure whose points are in more than one plane. (p. 386)

sphere A space figure shaped like a round ball. (p. 386)

square A rectangle with four equal sides and four right angles. (p. 362)

square number The product of two equal whole number factors. (p. 212)

Example: $5 \times 5 = 25$
25 is a square number.

Glossary

standard form A number written with commas separating groups of three digits. (p. 6)

subtraction An operation on two numbers to find the difference. (p. 56)

Example: 15 − 3 = 12
The difference is 12.

sum The answer in addition. (p. 48)

Example: 8 + 7 = 15
The sum is 15.

symmety A plane figure has symmetry if it can be folded along a line so that the two parts match exactly. (p. 374)

T

tally chart A chart used to record data. (p. 252)

tangram A Chinese puzzle that has seven geometric pieces. (p. 365)

tenths One or more of ten equal parts of a whole. (p. 422)

triangle A plane figure with three sides and three corners. (p. 362)

V

Venn Diagram A diagram that uses circles to show the relationships between groups of objects. (p. 263)

Example:

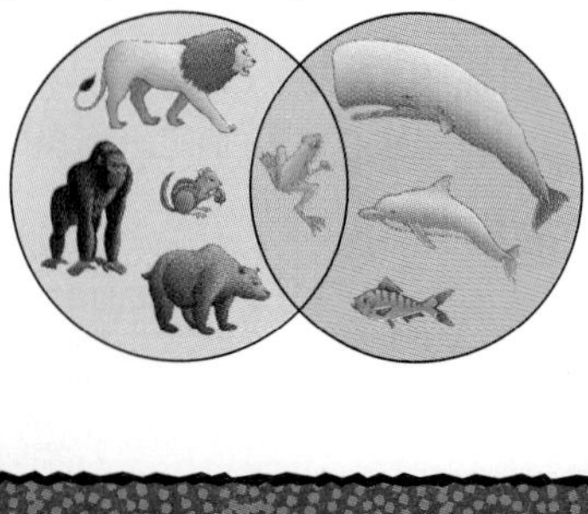

volume The number of cubic units needed to fill a space figure. (p. 390)

W

week A period of seven days. (p. 136)

Y

yard (yd) A customary unit used to measure length. 1 yard equals 3 feet. (p. 140)

year A period of 365 days divided into 12 months. (p. 136)

Z

zero property of addition The sum of any number and 0 is that number. (p. 48)

Example: 3 + 0 = 3

zero property of division 0 divided by any number except 0 is 0. You cannot divide a number by 0. (p. 310)

Example: 0 ÷ 12 = 0

zero property of multiplication The product of any number and 0 is 0. (p. 196)

Example: 5 × 0 = 0 and 0 × 5 = 0

zero properties of subtraction When 0 is subtracted from any number, the difference is that number. When a number is subtracted from itself, the difference is 0. (p. 110)

Examples: 7 − 0 = 7 and 12 − 12 = 0

Index

Index

Index

Index

Index

CREDITS

PHOTOGRAPHS

All photographs by Silver Burdett Ginn (SBG) unless otherwise noted.

Front cover: Silver Burdett Ginn.

v: Superstock. vi: Steve Skjold/PhotoEdit. x: Peter Cunningham/courtesy, Mendola, Ltd. 0–1: *bkgd.* Tom Stack for Silver Burdett Ginn. 1: *inset* Pat Clyne. 6: *l.* Ann Summa for Silver Burdett Ginn; *m.* Ann Summa for Silver Burdett Ginn; *r.* Ann Summa for Silver Burdett Ginn. 8: Ann Summa for Silver Burdett Ginn. 10: *b.* Robert Frerck/Odyssey Productions. 11: Jerry Jacka Photography. 13: Jerry Jacka Photography. 25: *t.* Boltin Picture Library. 29: Richard T. Nowitz Photography. 41: Painting by Maruice Bardin, 1936; Orinetal Institute, University of Chicago. 42: Edward McCain for Silver Burdett Ginn. 42–43: Edward McCain for Silver Burdett Ginn/courtesy, Arizona Sonora Desert Museum. 46: Superstock. 52: *t.* Ralph A. Reinhold/Animals Animals; *m.t.* John Colwell/Grant Heilman Photography; *m.b.* Robert Maier/Animals Animals; *b.* John Colwell/Grant Heilman Photography. 53: Robert Maier/Animals Animals. 56: Gerard Lacz/Animals Animals. 59: Kim Heacox/Ken Graham Agency. 63: Four By Five/Superstock. 64–65: Robert Fried/D. Donne Bryant Stock Photo. 68: Z. Leszczynski/Animals Animals. 69: *t.* Robert Maier/Animals Animals; *m.l.* Michael Fogden/Animals Animals; *m.r.* Irvin & Sue Hanley/Animals Animals; *b.* M. Austerman/Animals Animals. 78: *t.* Eric Burge/Flashback Photographics. 78–79: Eric Burge/Flashback Photographics. 83: Bern Pedit/Breck Kent. 85: Douglas Peebles Photography. 91: D. Donne Bryant Stock Photography. 93: Jeff Greenberg/PhotoEdit. 95: Jeff Schultz/Alaska Stock Images. 98: North Wind Picture Archives. 99: *t.* The Granger Collection, New York; *b.* Barry L. Runk/Grant Heilman Photography. 101: Breck P. Kent. 109: Superstock. 110: Kent & Donna Dannen. 111: *b.* Max Reid Imaging/Library of Congress. 113: *foreground* Abbe Boon for Silver Burdett Ginn; *inset* NASA. 126: *t.* 126–127: Valerie Santagto for Silver Burdett Ginn. 129: The Granger Collection, New York. 130: *t.* Jose Carrillo/PhotoEdit; *b.* Bill Bachman/Leo de Wys. 131: Superstock. 132: International Little League Baseball Public Relations. 134: David Stoecklein/The Stock Market. 135: David Stoecklein/The Stock Market. 148: *l.* Kathy Ferguson/PhotoEdit; *r.* Steve Skjold/PhotoEdit. 160: *l.* Tony Freeman/PhotoEdit; *r.* Frank Siteman/Stock Boston. 181: Superstock. 185: Richard T. Nowitz. 190: Merry Alpern for Silver Burdett Ginn. 192: Abbe Boon for Silver Burdett Ginn. 210: *t.* 210–211: Elliott Smith for Silver Burdett Ginn. 215: Murray & Associates/Picturesque Stock Photo. 229: Dallas & John Heaton/Stock Boston. 231: Michael Justice/The Image Works. 232: The Granger Collection, New York. 252: *t.* Art Wolfe/Tony Stone Images; *m.* Mike Andrews/Animals Animals; *b.* Michael Fogden/Animals Animals. 257: Steve Vidler/Leo de Wys. 260–261: Hamman/Heldring/Animals Animals. 263: *t.* Keren Su/Tony Stone Images; *m.* Penny Tweedie/Tony Stone Images; *b.* Henry Ausloos/Animals Animals. 270: Barbara A. Lewis. 286: *t.* Elliott Smith for Silver Burdett Ginn. 286–287: Elliott Smith for Silver Burdett Ginn. 294: *b.* Robert Houser for Silver Burdett Ginn. 299: *b.* Jacques Jangoux/Tony Stone Images. 302: *r.* Robert Houser for Silver Burdett Ginn. 322: *t.* Valerie Santagto for Silver Burdett Ginn. 322–323: Valerie Santagto for Silver Burdett Ginn. 327: Joe Viesti/Viesti Associates. 333: *l.* Elliott Smith for Silver Burdett Ginn; *r.* Elliott Smith for Silver Burdett Ginn. 341: Peter Cunningham/courtesy, Mendola, Ltd. 342: *t.* Popperfoto/Archive Photos; *b.* Jeff Lawrence/Stock Boston. 348: *t.* Jim Erickson/The Stock Market; *b.* Gabe Palmer/The Stock Market. 360: *t.* Merry Alpern. 360–361: Merry Alpern. 363: Silver Burdett Ginn/Courtesy, the Day Collection. 365: San Francisco Craft & Folk Art Museum. 366: Elliott Smith for Silver Burdett Ginn. 407: Dave Bartruff/Stock Boston. 411: Joe Viesti/Viesti Associates. 442: NASA. 442–443: NASA. 445: NASA/Tony Stone Images. 456: NASA. 457: NASA. 469: NASA. 476: *t., b.* NASA.

ILLUSTRATIONS

4–5: Andrew Shiff. 6: *l.* Keith LoBue; *r.* Carlyn Iverson. 12: Keith LoBue. 15: Stuart Zastrow. 18–19: Andrew Shiff. 20: *l.* Keith LoBue; *r.* Andrew Shiff. 21: Andrew Shiff . 22: Keith LoBue. 24: Keith LoBue. 27: Andrew Shiff. 28: Keith LoBue. 32–33: Stuart Zastrow. 40: Keith LoBue. 44–45: Skip Baker. 46: Gregg Valley. 47: Skip Baker. 48: Jeff Stock. 50–51: Skip Baker. 56: Lori Anzalone. 58: Lee Duggan. 60–61: Rose Mary Berlin. 62–63: Jeff Stock. 64: Angela Werneke. 66: Jody Jobe. 68: Bernard Adnet. 77: Linda Howard. 80–83: Jeff Stock. 81: Michael Sloan. 85: Jeff Stock. 88: Jeff Stock. 92: Jeff Stock. 93: Jim Frazer; Jeff Stock. 94–95: Jeff Stock. 100: Jeff Stock. 104: Jeff Stock. 106: Jeff Stock. 107: Michael Sloan. 108: Jeff Stock. 110: Jeff Stock. 112: Michael Sloan. 114–115: Jeff Stock. 122: Jeff Stock. 123: *t.* Jeff Stock; *b.* Jody Jobe. 128: *t.* Ken Bowser; *b.* Jody Jobe. 128–133: Peter Van Ryzin. 136–137: Ken Bowser. 138: Peter Van Ryzin. 139: Jody Jobe. 141: Ken Bowser. 145–146: Mitch Hyatt. 147: Ken Bowser. 148: Art Thompson. 150: John Berg. 152: Art Thompson. 152–154: Yemi. 156–157: Mitch Hyatt. 159: Mitch Hyatt. 160: Art Thompson. 161: Jody Jobe. 162: Ken Bowser. 168: Mitch Hyatt. 169: Peter Van Ryzin. 171: Jody Jobe. 175: Tim Mc Garvey. 176: Terry Boles. 177: Tim Mc Garvey. 178: Terry Boles. 179–180: Tim Mc Garvey. 182–183: Gregg Valley. 184: Terry Boles. 185: Tim Mc Garvey. 186: Terry Boles. 190–191: Terry Boles. 192–193: Tim Mc Garvey. 196–197: Terry Boles. 199–200: Terry Boles. 206: Terry Boles. 208–209: Gregg Valley. 212: Larry Jost. 217: Kieth LoBue. 218: Larry Jost. 220: Sarah Jane English. 222–223: Andrew Shiff. 226–228: Sarah Jane English. 230: Larry Jost. 236: Andrew Shiff. 238–239: Bernard Adnet. 245: Andrew Shiff. 253: Robert Roper. 255: Andrew Shiff. 257: *t.* Dan Clyne; *b.* Lisa Berrett. 258: Dan Clyne. 260: Bernard Adnet. 261: *t.* Bernard Adnet; *b.* Dan Clyne. 262: *t.* Dan Clyne; *b.* Bernard Adnet. 263: Robert Roper. 268–271: Bernard Adnet. 273: Art Thompson. 276–277: Gary Colby. 285: Dan Clyne. 290: Leslie Wolf. 292: Leslie Wolf. 296–297: Leslie Wolf. 301: Andrew Shiff. 303–304: Leslie Wolf. 306: Leslie Wolf. 308: Tim Harkins. 310: Kieth LoBue. 312: Tim Harkins. 319: Leslie Wolf. 324–327: Andrew Shiff. 330–332: Andrew Shiff. 334: Andrew Shiff. 338: Andrew Shiff. 341: Jim Frazer. 342: Tim Harkins. 343–344: Andrew Shiff. 357: Andrew Shiff. 364: Robert Roper. 380: Andrew Shiff. 386: Lorraine Dey. 388: Lorraine Dey. 405: Art Thompson. 406: Geo Systems. 408: Jenny Campbell. 409: Matt Zumbo. 411: Matt Zumbo. 412–413: Jenny Campbell. 414: Brad Black. 416: Jenny Campbell. 420: Jenny Campell. 424: Dave Allen. 426–427: Terry Boles. 428–429: Jenny Campbell. 431: *t.* Jenny Campbell; *b.* Stuart Zastrow. 433: Jenny Campbell. 437: Matt Zumbo 439: Bob Perry. 441: Deb Drummund. 444: Remy Simard. 448: Eddie Young. 450: Eddie Young. 452–453: Eddie Young. 454–455: Remy Simard. 457: *t.* Remy Simard; *b.* Eddie Young. 458: Remy Simard. 460: Eddie Young. 462: Remy Simard. 463: Eddie Young. 464–465: Remy Simard. 467: Eddie Young. 468: Remy Simard. 470–471: Remy Simard. 472: Eddie Young. 474–475: Remy Simard. 476–477: Eddie Young. 483: Remy Simard.485: Eddie Young.